AUTHOR

Alexandra Richards (*www.alexandrarichards.net*) grew up in the beautiful English county of Dorset, where she developed a love of rural life, the natural world and outdoor pursuits. She graduated from Durham University in 2000, where she read modern European languages. During her studies she spent a year teaching English in Réunion and took the opportunity to travel in the Mascarenes. Since that time she has been returning to the Mascarenes as often as possible and has updated the past five editions of this guidebook. Alex is a freelance travel writer with a passion for photography, natural history and adventure. She still divides her time between Dorset and Australia.

AUTHOR'S STORY

It was one of those decisions that changes your life immeasurably but the significance of which is not apparent at the time. As a modern European languages student, I was required to spend a year of my degree overseas, practising my French, Spanish and Italian. Having grown up a short ferry ride from Normandy, mainland France didn't seem exotic or adventurous enough so when I filled in my application to teach English in France I chose the overseas departments without knowing much about them at all. I could have ended up in French Guyana, Martinique or Guadeloupe but, as luck would have it, I was assigned to Réunion Island.

I really didn't know what to expect as I got off the plane in St-Denis in September 1998. There were new and memorable experiences around every corner: colourful markets, séga dancing, energetic hikes, geckos in the shower, even tales of black magic. I found the juxtaposition of European and African cultures fascinating. Few people outside France had heard of Réunion and that remained virtually unchanged until 2015 when the island made news headlines around the world after wreckage from missing Malaysia Airlines flight MH370 was found washed up on its shores.

It was while living on Réunion that I made my first trip to Mauritius. The things that struck me about the place then are the same things that have struck me about it on every visit since: the natural beauty; superb beaches; rich history; diverse cultures; and world-class hotels and service. The island's history is one of dashing colonialists, rugged pirates, slavery, sugar and spices, and the legacy of that past is visible in its buildings, landscape and population. While it may be tempting to hunker down in a luxury resort and make the most of the facilities, there is so much to be gained from venturing out and getting to know the island.

Visiting Rodrigues is almost like checking into a health retreat. Far less developed than Mauritius and with a very African feel, the island is blessed with untamed natural beauty, a stunning lagoon and wonderful, unspoilt beaches.

The Mascarene Islands inspired me to start writing about my travels, so I'm forever grateful to whichever official completely changed the course of my life in deciding to send me to Réunion Island back in 1998.

PUBLISHER'S FOREWORD   *Adrian Phillips, Managing Director*

If Mauritius were just a sun-sand destination, with nothing to tempt you outside the walls of its all-inclusive hotels, there wouldn't be a Bradt guide. And certainly not a Bradt guide moving into its ninth edition. The truth is that there's a great deal more to the Mascarene Islands, from a wild history of pirates and colonial rule to vibrant daily markets and *séga*, a dance originally performed by slaves. Alexandra Richards has made regular visits since first being assigned to Réunion as part of her university degree. She's the perfect person to take you outside the resorts to the real islands beyond.

Ninth edition published June 2016   First published 1988

Bradt Travel Guides Ltd
IDC House, The Vale, Chalfont St Peter, Bucks SL9 9RZ, England
www.bradtguides.com
Print edition published in the USA by The Globe Pequot Press Inc,
PO Box 480, Guilford, Connecticut 06437-0480

Text copyright © 2016 Bradt Travel Guides Ltd
Maps copyright © 2016 Bradt Travel Guides Ltd
Photographs copyright © 2016 Individual photographers (see below)
Project Manager: Katie Wilding
Cover research: Pepi Bluck, Perfect Picture

The author and publisher have made every effort to ensure the accuracy of the information in this book at the time of going to press. However, they cannot accept any responsibility for any loss, injury or inconvenience resulting from the use of information contained in this guide. All rights reserved. No part of this publication may be reproduced, stored in a retrieval system, or transmitted in any form or by any means, electronic, mechanical, photocopying, recording or otherwise without the prior consent of the publisher. Requests for permission should be addressed to Bradt Travel Guides Ltd in the UK (print and digital editions), or to The Globe Pequot Press Inc in North and South America (print edition only).

ISBN: 978 1 84162 924 7
e-ISBN: 978 1 78477 135 5 (e-pub)
e-ISBN: 978 1 78477 235 2 (mobi)

British Library Cataloguing in Publication Data
A catalogue record for this book is available from the British Library

Photographs Alamy: Hemis (H/A); Alexandra Richards (AR); Dreamstime: Bobbystrong (B/DT), Carolecastelli (C/DT), Dmitry Chulov (DC/DT), Fanglong (F/DT), Konstik (K/DT), Ravindran John Smith (RJS/DT), Vladvitek (V/DT), Youssouf Cader (YC/DT); FLPA: Biosphoto/Gregory Guida (B/GG/FLPA); l'Ile de La Réunion Tourisme: Corine Tellier (CT/IRT), Jerome Martino (JM/IRT); Mauritius Tourism Promotion Authority (MTPA); Neal Sullivan (NS); Shutterstock: Sebastien Burel (SB/S)
Front cover Sailing boats at Mahébourg (H/A)
Title page Cap Malheureux beach (C/DT), fairy tern (AR), Tamil temple at Sainte-Croix, Mauritius (MTPA)
Back cover Creole girl (AR), Cirque de Mafate (CT/IRT)

Maps David McCutcheon FBCart.S; colour map relief base by Nick Rowland FRGS; includes map data © OpenStreetMap contributors

Typeset by Wakewing, Chesham
Production managed by Jellyfish Print Solutions; printed in India
Digital conversion by www.dataworks.co.in

Acknowledgements

Researching and writing a new edition of this guidebook every three years is no small task and I am very grateful to those who help and support me.

I would like to acknowledge the Mauritius Tourism Promotion Authority, who helped organise my research trip. I am also very grateful to the Mauritian High Commission in Australia and the Australian High Commission in Mauritius for their support of this project.

A special thank you to Mila Ambroise and Christelle Bussac of White Sand Tours for the time and effort they devoted to organising my research trip. I am immensely impressed by their efficiency and professionalism. I am also grateful to the Mauritius Wildlife Foundation for their contribution to the sections on natural history and conservation.

The Rodrigues Tourism Office provided significant help and support. I would also like to thank Françoise Baptiste for her support of this guidebook, and express my admiration for the assistance and inspiration she provides to Rodriguan women looking to start their own businesses. For his help with the chapters on Rodrigues, I would like to thank Paul Draper. My best wishes go to everyone at CARE-Co – a truly inspirational team. Thank you also to Severine Clain for her advice on nightlife in Réunion.

I would like to take this opportunity to acknowledge Royston Ellis and Derek Schuurman, who were responsible for the first four editions of the guidebook, which began life as a guide to Mauritius only.

I would like to thank Alexandra Flanagan for her help in keeping my household running and looking after my many animals while I was totally occupied with this book.

My heartfelt thanks to the Rt Hon Baroness Sharples and to Alf Wallis for many years of unstinting support. I am also grateful to my good friend Julian, for his encouragement and faith in me.

A special thank you to my parents. To my late father, himself a writer who wrote wonderfully entertaining books and articles about his travels. And to my mother, for her support.

Finally, my thanks to Neal Sullivan for accompanying me on my last research trip, and for his assistance with the maps and photography.

Alexandra Richards

Contents

Introduction

It is easy to see why Dutch, French and English colonists spent hundreds of years tripping over themselves, and each other, to settle on the previously uninhabited Mascarene Islands. The Mascarenes, as Mauritius, Rodrigues and Réunion are known, are three very different islands but there is a lot to like about each one.

Plenty of holiday destinations offer stunning beaches, tropical warmth and fancy hotels but there are a few things that set Mauritius apart from its competitors. Firstly, and importantly during this era of increased threat to the global security environment, Mauritius is a comparatively safe destination. It is a relatively stable democracy with little serious crime and few health risks. Secondly, the service in the hospitality industry is exceptional; even mid-range hotels boast levels of service you would be lucky to find in a five-star hotel elsewhere. An immensely rich culture is another standout feature, the result of those eager European colonists bringing a cocktail of African and Indian people to the island, as well as Chinese migration. The blend of cultures is reflected in the fabulous cuisine, and memorable meals are to be had both in the island's world-class restaurants and at roadside food stalls selling cheap *samoussas* and curries.

While it may be tempting to stay within the confines of your luxury resort and make the most of the facilities, the real Mauritius lies right outside its gates and is easy to explore. Flamboyant temples and grand colonial mansions stand as monuments to the island's colourful past and present. A working tea plantation, sugar factories and rum distilleries are open to the public and make for fascinating, and tasty, excursions. Some of the large rural estates (or *domains*) have opened to the public and offer activities for the energetic, such as horseriding, canyoning and quad biking. Mauritius was the home of the dodo before it became extinct, and while I don't like your chances of spotting one of those in the wild, there is plenty of interest for nature lovers, such as tours of Ile aux Aigrettes nature reserve and hiking in the Black River Gorges National Park.

The island of Rodrigues, although part of Mauritius, is a place of simple charm. Whenever I visit, I am struck by the tremendous sense of community, and the laid-back way of life is certainly a lesson to us all. I am told that it resembles the Mauritius of 30 years ago and a visit to the island is a welcome escape from our fast-paced world, where high-tech time-saving devices, multi-tasking and real-time connectivity seem key to survival. Rodrigues has a far more African feel than Mauritius. While the majority of Mauritius's inhabitants are of Indian descent, the residents of Rodrigues are mostly descended from African slaves. The Port Mathurin markets are the highlight of the week for Rodriguans and for the tourist offer a fascinating insight into daily life.

Rodrigues is surrounded by a pristine lagoon and coral reef, perfect for snorkelling and diving. It also has some incredible beaches, which are almost

always empty, aside from the odd shepherd using the sand as a thoroughfare for moving his sheep. Off the coast lies the sand islet of Ile aux Cocos, a nature reserve and important seabird nesting site. I can honestly say it is one of the most beautiful places I have ever been – totally unspoilt and surrounded by a glorious, impossibly blue lagoon.

Tourism in Rodrigues isn't only in its infancy – it has barely left the maternity ward. Although development of the island's tourism potential has begun, with the expansion of the airport and creation of the island's first mid-range hotels, tourists are still a novelty here and receive an incredibly warm welcome. My advice is to get to Rodrigues as soon as possible, before it all changes.

Réunion is a fascinating place. Officially part of France, and therefore part of the European Union, it is inhabited by a cocktail of people of African, Indian, European and Chinese origin. The Creole culture is strong here and *séga* (a traditional dance with African roots), sorcery and occasional cockfights contrast with the ubiquitous croissants, Citroëns and boules tournaments.

I have been visiting Réunion for almost 20 years now and until 2015 almost no-one I spoke to knew of its existence, unless they were French. However, in July 2015, Réunion made the news around the world when wreckage belonging to missing Malaysia Airlines flight MH370 washed up on the east coast. Journalists flocked to the island and, having covered the wreckage story, began to write about the other issues affecting Réunion at the time: the erupting volcano and a frightening number of shark attacks. But Réunion is not nearly as dangerous as it may sound, in fact it is a very liveable place. Réunion was my home for almost a year and to my mind it is a kind of user-friendly, flat-packed paradise, where life is exotic yet easy and familiar. The atmosphere is tropical, yet the roads, doctors' surgeries and hospitals are of a reassuringly European quality.

While Réunion's beaches may not rival those of Mauritius, its natural beauty is world class. The rugged, mountainous interior attracts hikers, naturalists and adventure sports enthusiasts from around the globe. Having one of the world's most active volcanoes has also proven to be a tourism asset.

Each of the Mascarenes has its own trump card, as I am sure you will discover. However, in combination they are unrivalled. If you visit just one you'll love it, but if you can take in all three you'll be smitten.

Alexandra Richards

FOLLOW BRADT

For the latest news, special offers and competitions, subscribe to the Bradt newsletter via the website www.bradtguides.com and follow Bradt on:

 www.facebook.com/BradtTravelGuides
 @BradtGuides
 @bradtguides
 www.pinterest.com/bradtguides

QUICK REFERENCE GUIDE
Accommodation price codes and abbreviations for Mauritius and Rodrigues: page 64
Restaurant price codes for Mauritius and Rodrigues: page 66
Accommodation price codes for Réunion: page 273
Restaurant price codes for Réunion: page 275
Useful contacts in Réunion: pages 264–5

AUTHOR'S FAVOURITES Finding genuinely characterful accommodation or that unmissable off-the-beaten-track café can be difficult, so the author has chosen a few of her favourite places throughout the country to point you in the right direction. These 'author's favourites' are marked with a ✳.

MAPS
Keys and symbols Maps include alphabetical keys covering the locations of those places to stay, eat or drink that are featured in the book. Note that regional maps may not show all hotels and restaurants in the area: other establishments may be located in towns shown on the map.

Grids and grid references Several maps use gridlines to allow easy location of sites. Map grid references are listed in square brackets after the name of the place or sight of interest in the text, with page number followed by grid number, eg: [103 C3].

SEND US YOUR SNAPS!

We'd love to follow your adventures using our *Mauritius* guide – why not send us your photos and stories via Twitter (@BradtGuides) and Instagram (@bradtguides) using the hashtag #Mauritius. Alternatively, you can upload your photos directly to the gallery on the Mauritius destination page via our website (*www.bradtguides.com/mauritius*).

FEEDBACK REQUEST AND UPDATES WEBSITE

At Bradt Travel Guides we're aware that guidebooks start to go out of date on the day they're published – and that you, our readers, are out there in the field doing research of your own. You'll find out before us when a fine new family-run hotel opens or a favourite restaurant changes hands and goes downhill. So why not write and tell us about your experiences? Contact us on ☏ 01753 893444 or e info@bradtguides.com. We will forward emails to the author who may post updates on the Bradt website at www.bradtupdates. com/mauritius. Alternatively you can add a review of the book to www. bradtguides.com or Amazon.

Part One

MAURITIUS:
GENERAL INFORMATION

Country Mauritius is an independent state, consisting of the islands of Mauritius, Rodrigues and dependencies; it is known as Ile Maurice in French.

Location In the Indian Ocean, south of the Equator and just north of the Tropic of Capricorn. Latitude 20°S, longitude 57°E.

Size Mauritius 1,864km²; total area with dependencies 2,040km².

History Discovered by Arabs, then the Portuguese, Mauritius was first settled by the Dutch in 1598. It was claimed by the French in 1715 as Ile de France and captured by the British in 1810. It was a British colony until 1968 when it became an independent member of the Commonwealth. It became a republic in 1992.

Climate Hot summers (November to April) with average coastal temperatures of 27°C; warm winters (May to October), averaging 22°C. Interior temperatures are 3–5°C lower. Rainy season December to March, with the possibility of cyclones.

Nature Mountainous with plateaux; flowers, forests and crops; rare wildlife and nothing dangerous; 177km of coastline; fine beaches within coral reefs.

Visitors Tourists come all the year around; November to January are the most popular months; May and September–October the most pleasant.

Capital Port Louis

Government Parliamentary democracy based on the Westminster model of government. The president is the head of state but the prime minister and cabinet have constitutional power.

Population 1,324,851 (July 2015) of Indian, African, European and Chinese origin.

Economy Based on industrial and agricultural exports, tourism, financial services and information technology.

Language Official language English, but Creole most widely used. Most people speak (and read) French. Ancestral languages are also spoken by their respective communities, the main ones being Hindi, Urdu and Tamil.

Religion Hinduism, Christianity, Islam and Buddhism.

Currency Mauritian rupee (Rs), which is divided into 100 cents (cs).

Rate of exchange £1=Rs51; US$1=Rs35; €1=Rs40 (March 2016).

International telephone code +230

Time GMT+4

Electricity 220V AC

Weights and measures Metric system

Background Information

GEOGRAPHY

Its isolated location kept Mauritius from being settled until 1598 and even today many people don't know where it is. On a world map, it is a tiny dot in the vast expanse of ocean between southern Africa and Australia, overshadowed by its much larger neighbour, Madagascar, 880km to the west. Africa is the nearest continent and Mauritius is categorised as part of the Africa region.

Mauritius is part of the Mascarene Archipelago, together with its closest neighbour, the French island of Réunion (227km away), and its own territory, Rodrigues, which lies 622km to the east. The Cargados Carajos Archipelago, also known as the St Brandon Islands, 430km northeast of Mauritius, and the two Agaléga Islands, 1,122km to the north, are Mauritian dependencies.

Mauritius and the Seychelles claim ownership of Tromelin Island, a French possession, and in 2010, France and Mauritius agreed to jointly manage the tiny island. Ownership of the Chagos Archipelago, seven atolls comprising over 60 islands around 500km south of the Maldives, is disputed between the UK and Mauritius. The UK excised the archipelago from Mauritius in 1965, prior to independence, and it became part of the British Indian Ocean Territory (BIOT).

The island of Mauritius is 65km at its longest, and 45km across at its widest. It has 177km of coastline, almost entirely surrounded by coral reefs, while the centre is a great plateau punctuated by impressive mountains. The whole state, including its dependencies, has a land area of only 2,040km^2.

Around Mauritius itself there are more than 15 islets lying in their own lagoons, some of which can be visited. North of the island, uninhabited except for wildlife, are six small islands: Serpent, Round, Flat, Gabriel, Amber and Coin de Mire (pages 132–3). Round Island is an important conservation site, as is Ile aux Aigrettes, which lies to the southeast of Mauritius and is managed by the Mauritian Wildlife Foundation (MWF). Round Island is closed to visitors but guided tours of Ile aux Aigrettes are available (pages 163–4). Ile aux Aigrettes is within the Blue Bay Marine Park, one of Mauritius's Marine Protected Areas, the other major one being at Balaclava, off the northwest coast.The origins of the island of Mauritius date back some 13 million years, when masses of molten lava bubbled up beneath the ocean floor. It took over five million years to surface through the activity of two volcanic craters. The weathered crater rims of these once enormous peaks still remain as the mountain ranges of Black River, Grand Port and Moka.

Further volcanic activity followed four million years later, opening up the craters of Trou aux Cerfs, Bassin Blanc and Kanaka. The island's volcanoes have now been extinct for 200,000 years, although odd lava flows may have occurred up to 20,000 years ago.

The island's rugged profile is a constant reminder of these cataclysms. The jagged volcanic peaks tower over coastal plains smothered in sugarcane, leaves waving like long green ribbons in the wind. The broad plain of the north rises to an extensive, fertile plateau, itself broken by more volcanic steeples and gorges. This tableland (600m/1,970ft high) is bordered by mountains which roll down to the crags of the southern coastline. In some areas there are deep, and seldom explored, lava caves. The central highlands in the island's south, which have cooler temperatures and higher rainfall, are where tea is grown.

It is not the height of the mountains that is impressive, but the sheer oddity of their shape. The highest is Piton de la Petite Rivière Noire at 828m (2,717ft), which lies in the southwest of the island. Pieter Both, in the Moka mountain range, is next at 820m (2,690ft). Le Pouce, the thumb-shaped mountain looming behind Port Louis, is third highest at 811m (2,661ft).

Despite the mountains and a rainfall on the windward slopes of the central plateau that can amount to 5m (197in) a year, Mauritius is not an island of great rivers. There are some 60 small rivers and streams, many degenerating as they reach the coast into rubbish-clogged trickles through cement ditches and culverts. The Grande Rivière Sud-est is the largest at 39.4km long.

The island is divided into the same nine districts as it was when the British captured it in 1810. In a clockwise direction from the capital, these districts are Port Louis, Pamplemousses, Rivière du Rempart, Flacq, Grand Port, Savanne and Black River, with Plaines Wilhems and Moka in the centre.

The eccentric terrain of Mauritius means that the island is blessed with a diversity of scenery not usually found in such a small area, and as the roads are reasonably good, travel is not time-consuming.

The main harbour is at Port Louis, the capital, on the west coast. The airport is at the opposite side of the island, at Plaisance, not far from the old east coast harbour of Grand Port.

CLIMATE

Basically, there are two seasons: summer is hot and wet (November to April), winter is warm and dry (May to October).

On the coast average summer temperatures are around 27°C, and average winter temperatures are around 22°C. On the central plateau it is normally about three to five degrees cooler. The western and northern regions are slightly drier and warmer than the east and the south.

Winter brings the trade winds, which are predominantly southeasterly and are at their strongest in July and August. The south and east coasts can be unpleasantly windy at this time of year. The rainy season is roughly December to March, although rain is spasmodic. Rainfall tends to be lower in the west than elsewhere, and is highest in the centre of the island.

Mauritius, Rodrigues, Réunion and Madagascar are prone to tropical cyclones between December and March. A cyclone is a low-pressure system which produces gale-force winds of at least 120km/h. Gusts can reach over 360km/h. In the Southern Hemisphere the winds circulate in a clockwise direction, spiralling with force towards a centre, or eye. Around the centre of a cyclone, where most uplift occurs, there are torrential rains (up to 50cm per day). Cyclones usually form in the southwest Indian Ocean, north of Mauritius, embracing the island as they move southwards. The lifecycle of a cyclone is around nine days but its effect on the island lasts only a few days, according to its velocity. They typically move at 8–15km/h.

They can have a devastating effect on vegetation, insecure buildings and roads. Damage is caused by continuous winds and gusts, and flooding.

The cyclone season starts in November with the onset of summer. Meteorologists in Mauritius, Réunion and Madagascar track the storms and issue cyclone warnings. Around ten storms are tracked in each summer period and an average of five become cyclones. Each is given a name, beginning at 'A' then working through the alphabet.

Mauritius has a well-structured system of cyclone warnings and procedures. The warnings range from Class I, preliminary precautions (usually 36–48 hours before the cyclone strikes), to Class IV, when gusts of 120km/h or more have been recorded and are expected to continue. At Class III public transport will cease to operate and at Class IV you should stay inside until all warnings are cleared.

The Mauritius Meteorological Service has a website giving up-to-date weather information, which is particularly useful when a cyclone is approaching (*www. metservice.intnet.mu*).

NATURAL HISTORY

VOLCANIC ORIGINS OF FRAGILE ECOSYSTEMS Around eight million years ago, the lava that created Mauritius rose above sea level, throwing up the mountain ranges of Grand Port, Moka and Black River. Later, light grey rock, also of volcanic origin, was scattered across the island on a northeast–southwest axis, giving rise to Bassin Blanc, Trou aux Cerfs and the Kanaka Crater. Fragile ecosystems evolved gently in a predator-free haven.

First to appear on the lava formations were pioneer plants, like lichens, mosses and ferns. These were followed by other plants, seeds of which were brought by birds or washed on to the shores by the sea. In time, most of the island was swathed in lush rainforest. Where rainfall was lower, palm savannah replaced forest.

Some invertebrates, birds and bats found their way to Mauritius deliberately; others came accidentally due to gale-force winds. Reptiles (and more invertebrates) arrived by means of floating vegetation or driftwood. In time these evolved into a myriad species unique to Mauritius. When examining Mauritian fauna in terms of its links elsewhere, connections with the other Indian Ocean islands, Africa, Australasia and Asia are apparent.

Man's arrival in the Mascarenes signalled a wave of extinctions paralleled only by that which occurred in the Hawaiian Archipelago. Magnificent tropical hardwood forests were felled for construction, export and agriculture. It is not clear exactly how many endemic plant species were lost. Today, only token remnants of the original forests remain, mostly in the Black River Gorges National Park. But even there, fast-growing introduced plants have swamped the indigenous species.

With the original forests went a remarkable ensemble of animals, the most famed of which is the dodo (*dronte*). Also wiped out quickly – as in the other Mascarenes – were herds of giant tortoises and, offshore, the gentle, vulnerable dugong. Apart from the dodo, at least 20 species of endemic birds were exterminated.

The situation was worsened considerably by the introduction of man's invasive animal entourage: dogs, cats, rats, monkeys, rabbits, wild pigs, goats and deer all wreaked havoc on the island ecosystem, just as they have done on other islands around the globe. Further introductions were tenrecs (similar to hedgehogs) from Madagascar, mongooses and musk shrews, all of which have affected native fauna adversely. Snakes were also introduced, along with a host of birds, most of which now far outnumber the few remaining indigenous species.

By 1970, the situation for the remaining endemic Mauritian plants and animals looked bleak. Some conservation organisations abroad wrote the Mascarenes off as 'paradise lost'. In the mid 1970s, the Durrell Wildlife Conservation Trust (then the Jersey Wildlife Preservation Trust) and the Mauritian Government stepped in.

ENDEMIC AND INDIGENOUS FLORA with the Mauritian Wildlife Foundation

There are 671 species of indigenous flowering plant recorded in Mauritius, of which 311 are endemic (Mauritius has eight endemic plant genera), and 150 are endemic to the Mascarene Islands. Of the indigenous plant species, 77 are classified as extinct and 235 as threatened.

ISLAND COMMUNITIES Jonathan Hughes

Remote islands throughout the world house rather special communities of animals and plants. In order to colonise an isolated island a species must pass three great challenges. The first challenge is to arrange transportation, the second to establish a stable population upon arrival, and the third to adapt to the island's habitats. At each stage the chance of failure is high, but with luck, and a certain degree of 'evolutionary skill', some inevitably succeed.

Species arrive on remote islands either by 'active' means, such as swimming or flying, or by 'passive' means, such as floating with ocean and air currents or hitching a ride on or in another individual. This degree of mobility is not available to all animal and plant groups, hence on isolated archipelagos there is often a characteristic assemblage of flying animals such as birds, bats and insects, light animals such as spiders and micro-organisms, buoyant animals such as tortoises and snakes, and plants employing edible seeds such as fruit trees, airborne seeds such as grasses, or floating seeds such as the coconut palm. Large land mammals, amphibians and freshwater fish have obvious difficulties in colonising remote islands and are therefore often absent, unless introduced by humans.

Assuming the problem of transport is overcome, there is then the task of establishing a permanent population on the island. Pioneers with the highest chance of success are single pregnant females, or in the case of plants, individuals able to self-fertilise. Flying species may arrive en masse, while species carried by currents must chance successive landings on the same island.

As populations establish, the animal and plant community begins to exploit the island's resources, and some animals take on very unusual roles in the community, but one role that is left vacant is that of the large, fierce predator at the top of the food chain. Large predators need a lot of space and a lot of resources. Without an extensive range there simply isn't enough food to support a population of such animals. Hence, on all but the largest of islands, large predators are absent, leaving meat-eating to smaller, less demanding species.

The absence of large predators has a profound effect on species that are normally on their menu – their worries are over. Ground-foraging birds, with no need for a quick escape, tend to lose the ability to fly, marooning themselves in the process. The downfall of Mauritius's most famous former resident, the dodo, was a lack of fear, evidence of its worry-free lifestyle. Even where flightless birds are absent today, most remote islands have had them in the past. Island giants, such as the giant tortoises which used to wander through the Mauritius scrub, are also indications of a short food chain. Free from predators, but in stiff competition

Widespread habitat destruction has rendered many endemic plants extremely rare: some species are now down to just one or two specimens. Indigenous species, which are shared with Réunion and/or Rodrigues, have stood a better chance of survival. However, as on Réunion and Rodrigues, most of the flora you'll see on Mauritius is of introduced species.

To find examples of the impressive tropical hardwood trees that once covered much of Mauritius, go to the Black River Gorges National Park, where many are still represented. Only approximately 1.3% of Mauritius's virgin forest remains, and most of it is found in this national park.

Undoubtedly the island's best-known hardwood, the Mauritius ebony (*Diospyros tessellaria*) was in particularly high demand because it has the darkest wood of any

with each other, the bigger, stronger individuals tend to survive and the smaller, meeker ones don't, so that, over time, the population attains giant proportions.

Although a remote island offers unusual opportunities, it cannot carry an infinite number of animals and plants. As each new population arrives, the competition for food and space increases, and the community has to adjust. The pressure to adapt is intense and species change their characteristics dramatically in a short time. Less mobile species such as inland birds and plants, isolated from their mainland ancestors, soon spread throughout the various habitats found on the island and gradually adapt to each one; after a period of time the original founding species evolves into a string of new species. This explains why many of the animals and plants found on remote islands are endemics – types found nowhere else in the world.

Inevitably, at some point, after repeated immigrations, an island 'fills up' – the diversity of species reaches a maximum and there is literally 'no room at the inn'. Biologists have found that the number of species that any one island can support depends on several factors. The size of the island is the most influential of these. Larger islands, not surprisingly, can cater for more species, but the number of different habitats is also important. Islands that have forests, lagoons, lakes, scrub and cliffs, simply offer more opportunities than those covered in one type of vegetation, and consequently sustain more species. Nevertheless, at some point the island will be full, and from this moment on any new arrival will either perish from lack of food or be forced to usurp one of the residents – an act that leads to extinction. The rate at which species immigrate and cause such disruption is determined by the remoteness of the island. Islands distant from other lands experience few new arrivals and hence suffer extinctions less frequently. Islands near to a mainland have far more disruption, receiving new species and losing old ones at a daunting rate.

The remoteness of the Mascarenes protected the islands from excessive immigrations for millions of years, while the size of Mauritius and Réunion nurtured a diverse community. Then we arrived, in a wave similar to any other immigration. Like large predators, we needed space and resources too, but unlike the predators, we made sure that we got what we needed. We chopped down forests and introduced our favourite species, animals and plants that would never have been able to overcome the three challenges of island colonisation. Exposed to the new, advanced species from the mainland, the island community quickly lost many of its older residents in an event more profoundly disruptive than any witnessed by these islands since their abrupt beginnings.

tree. Its congener on Réunion (*D. borbonica*) is still quite plentiful but the Mauritian species was almost wiped out. Other impressive protected hardwoods found in Black River Gorges include various species of the genera *Mimusops* and *Sideroxylon*, as well as *Labourdonnaisia*. Quite a few of the rare, slow-growing hardwoods are shared with Réunion, such as the takamaka (*Calophyllum tacamahaca*), the 'rat' tree (*Tarenna borbonica*) and the bois blanc (*Hernandia mascarenensis*).

There are 89 species of orchid found in Mauritius. Of those, 94% are endemic to the Mascarenes/Madagascar region. Nine species are endemic to Mauritius only. Certain orchids, like *Oeniella polystachys* and *Angraecum eburneum*, have become rare, so attempts are being made to conserve them on Ile aux Aigrettes, where they can be seen in the wild. (For details of visits to Ile aux Aigrettes, see pages 163–4)

Seven species of palm are endemic to Mauritius. Most of these are in cultivation because in the wild they are all gravely threatened. Two palms – *Hyophorbe amaricaulis* and *Dyctosperma album* var. *conjugatum* – are down to a single wild individual each. The latter, which is sought-after for heart-of-palm salad, has been cultivated successfully by the Mauritian Wildlife Foundation (MWF) as part of a project to rescue all endangered flora. However, the species *Hyophorbe amaricaulis* appears to be doomed.

A problem facing botanists and conservationists currently is lack of information about the native flora. For instance, very little is known about pollinator agents. However, the MWF, in conjunction with several foreign universities, has been engaged in studies of Mauritian plant pollinators: bats, invertebrates like hawk moths, butterflies and beetles, passerine birds and reptiles like *Phelsuma* geckos. Where plants have been decimated, their pollinators suffer likewise, particularly those that are specifically associated with one or two plant species.

In terms of flowering plants, one of the most impressive endemics is the *bois bouquet banané* (*Ochna mauritania*). In summer (November to January), this small deciduous shrub can be seen covered in a display of white flowers, at Pétrin and in Black River Gorges National Park.

Of the various plants with medicinal properties, the best known is the *bois de ronde* (*Erythroxylon laurifolium*), the bark of which is used to treat kidney stones.

Finally, the national flower of Mauritius is the rare and beautiful *Trochetia boutoniana* (or *boucle d'oreille*, which means 'earring') of the Serculiaceae family. Forget about seeing this stunner in the wild, though – it is confined to a single mountaintop. But being the national flower, it is cultivated in various sites, for example at the Special Mobile Force Museum in Vacoas and in the grounds of the Forestry Service. The closely related (and just as beautiful) *Trochetia blackburniana* is a little more plentiful and can be seen along the road at Plaine Champagne. It also has lovely pinkish-crimson flowers.

FAUNA with the Mauritian Wildlife Foundation

The sole surviving endemic mammal is the striking Mauritius fruit bat (*Pteropus niger*), which still exists in fair numbers and is widespread throughout the island. Like its endangered cousin, the Rodrigues fruit bat (*P. rodericensis*), the much darker Mauritius fruit bat roosts in large trees by day and forages for fruit and flowers at night. These fruit bats belong to a predominantly Asian genus also present in Madagascar and the Comoros, where they reach their westernmost limit. A third Mascarene fruit bat, *Pteropus subniger*, is sadly extinct.

Birds

Birdwatchers visiting Mauritius are in for a treat. Although only nine endemic species still remain, they include some of the world's rarest birds.

By 1974, the fabulous pink pigeon (*Nesoenas mayeri*) was down to some 24 individuals. Following intensive captive-breeding efforts by the DWCT and MWF, this gorgeous pigeon (yes, it really is pink!) is now more plentiful, numbering some 400 birds. A substantial population is held in various captive-breeding centres and large numbers of captive-bred birds have been reintroduced into the wild. Successful predator-control programmes, carried out in woodland where wild pink pigeons nest, help tremendously. What was once the world's rarest pigeon can now be seen in its natural habitat at Black River Gorges National Park and Ile aux Aigrettes.

Another rarity which the DWCT and MWF have saved from certain extinction is the sole-surviving Mauritian raptor, the Mauritius kestrel (*Falco punctatus*). In 1973, when only four individuals could be found, it was declared the world's rarest bird. Causes for its dramatic decline included the extensive use of DDT, which was sprayed everywhere except for the Black River Gorges.

Captive breeding of the Mauritius kestrel started in very basic and primitive conditions in 1974 but was hampered by lack of knowledge about the bird. By 1978, the situation had become desperate and so little progress had been made that Carl Jones of the MWF was sent to close down the project. Fortunately his keen interest in hawks and his enthusiasm saw him revive the project and restart the captive breeding, which has led to such spectacular results. Hundreds of kestrels have been bred in captivity and released into the wild; today between 400 and 500 kestrels are estimated to be flying around Mauritius.

The phenomenal success which conservationists had with the pink pigeon and Mauritius kestrel meant they could turn their attention to yet another Mauritian endemic in dire straits – the echo parakeet (*Psittacula eques*). By the 1990s, about 15 birds remained, all in the upland forest of Macchabée ridge. It was regarded as the world's rarest wild breeding bird. In 2001/02, 21 hand-reared birds were released into the wild and management of wild nests allowed a further 21 birds to fledge naturally. The population now stands at around 600 birds.

For four of the five remaining endemic birds, all passerines (perching birds), things do not look too rosy at present. The Mauritius cuckoo-shrike (*Coracina typica*), Mauritius bulbul (*Hypsipetes olivaceous*), Mauritius olive white-eye (*Zosterops chloronothus*) and Mauritius fody (*Foudia rubra*) have all suffered heavy losses, caused by introduced predators (rats, mongooses, cats and monkeys) raiding their nests. All are classified as 'uncommon' in the definitive field guide

NARCOTIC INDULGENCES OF THE PINK PIGEON

The pink pigeon's continued existence has left some naturalists puzzled. It has been questioned why this bird survived the colonisers' presence on the island, when the similarly sized Mauritius blue pigeon, with which it shared its habitat, was exterminated.

The answer seems to lie in the pink pigeon's dietary preferences. Apparently, its favoured food was the fruit of a shrub known as *fangame* (*Stillingis lineata*), which has an intoxicating effect. It is said that when *fangame* berries were in season, the pink pigeons would gorge themselves and flop to the ground in a drug-induced daze. As such, they were an even easier target for hunters. However, the Dutch soon realised that every time they ate a pink pigeon pie, they felt quite dreadful. So the pink pigeons were left alone and are still around today, whilst the last Mauritius blue pigeon (*Alectroenas nitidissima*) was shot as long ago as 1826.

Birds of the Indian Ocean Islands (Olivier Langrand and Ian Sinclair, 1998) and are on the International Union for Conservation of Nature red list. At present there is particular concern for the striking Mauritius fody and olive white-eye, both of which have declined to fewer than 150 breeding pairs. In breeding plumage, the male fody is a living jewel, with a ruby-red head and upper breast and dark green underparts. The olive white-eye is equally spectacular, with its olive green back and spectacled eye ring. All of these threatened birds can be seen in the Black River Gorges National Park, their last stronghold. The MWF has released the Mauritius fody and olive white-eye on Ile aux Aigrettes and they have taken to their new home, with nearly 170 and 30 birds respectively now on the island.

Strangely enough, one endemic, the Mauritius grey white-eye (*Zosterops mauritanus*, locally known as *zozo maniok* or *pic pic*), has adapted very successfully to man's encroachment of its habitat. It is very common all over the island, entering hotel gardens freely, as its near relative on Réunion does there.

The Mascarene swiftlet (*Collocalia francica*) and Mascarene paradise flycatcher (*Terpsiphone bourbonnensis*) are shared with Réunion, where both are more plentiful than on Mauritius. Also shared with Réunion (and with Madagascar) is the larger Mascarene martin (*Phedina borbonica*).

Finally, of great interest to visiting birders is the Round Island petrel (*Pterodroma arminjoniana*). Amazingly, it is found only around Round Island (where it nests) and on the other side of the globe, around Trindade Island, Brazil. Some authorities previously considered it a full species (separate from the birds of Trindade). However, recent work has shown it is a hybrid of several gadfly petrels; research by the MWF is ongoing. It is endangered but, thanks to all the rehabilitation work that has been conducted on Round Island, its chances for survival have been improved significantly.

Reptiles The endemic birds – and to a lesser extent, plants – of Mauritius have received much international press coverage, but few people know that a fascinating ensemble of endangered reptiles exists there also, most significantly on a small chunk of volcanic rock called Round Island, 22km north of Mauritius.

Other offshore islets and the mainland itself support four endemic day geckos (genus *Phelsuma*), two more night geckos (genus *Nactus*) and two small skink species (genus *Gongylomorphus*).

Round Island is a tilted volcanic cone rising 278m above the sea. Its surface area covers 219ha. Surrounded by rough seas and often buffeted by strong winds, the island has remained uninhabited by man and rats, allowing reptiles, seabirds and plants that have perished elsewhere to survive. Five of Round Island's eight reptile species are now endemic to the island and endangered: the large Telfair's skink (*Leiolopisma telfairi*); the strangely nocturnal Round Island 'day' gecko (*Phelsuma guentheri*); the tiny nocturnal Durrell's night gecko (*Nactus durrelli*); and the remarkable keel-scaled boa (*Casarea dussumieri*). The fifth, the Round Island burrowing boa (*Bolyeria multocarinata*), was last seen in 1975 and is sadly presumed extinct. (For more information on Round Island, see pages 15–18 and 132.)

In recent years, a number of initiatives have been implemented to improve the long-term outlook for these species. As part of the Darwin Initiative Reptile Conservation Project, Telfair's skink was reintroduced to Ile aux Aigrettes and Coin de Mire. In January 2008, the MWF announced that the first of a new generation of Telfair's skinks had been discovered on Ile aux Aigrettes. This was the first time for 150 years that the skink had been known to reproduce naturally in the wild, outside of Round Island. Since 2008, the MWF has translocated 382 orange-tail skinks (*Gongylomorphus fontenayi* spp.) from Flat Island to Coin de Mire. Initial

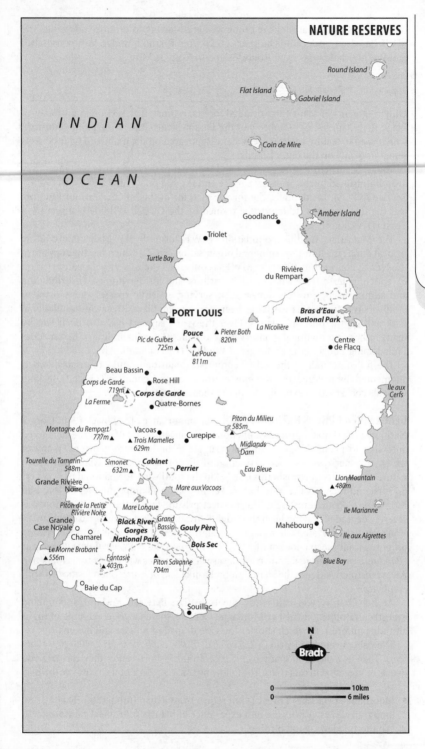

Round Island

Flat Island
Gabriel Island

INDIAN

Coin de Mire

OCEAN

Goodlands
Amber Island

Triolet

Turtle Bay

Rivière
du Rempart

■ **PORT LOUIS**

Pouce ▲ *Pieter Both
820m*

*Bras d'Eau
National Park*

*Pic de Guibes
725m* ▲
▲ *Le Pouce
811m*

La Nicolière

Centre
● de Flacq

Beau Bassin ●
● Rose Hill

*Corps de Garde
719m* ▲ ***Corps de Garde***

*Ile aux
Cerfs*

La Ferme ○
● Quatre-Bornes

*Montagne du Rempart
777m* ▲

Vacoas ●
▲ *Trois Mamelles
629m*

Curepipe ●

*Piton du Milieu
585m*

*Midlands
Dam*

*Tourelle du Tamarin
548m* ▲

*Simonet
632m* ▲ ***Cabinet***

Perrier

Eau Bleue

*Lion Mountain
480m* ▲

Grande Rivière ○
Noire

*Piton de la Petite
Rivière Noire* ▲

Mare Longue

Mare aux Vacoas

Ile Marianne

Grande
Case Noyale ○
● Chamarel ▲ ***Black River
Gorges
National Park***
*Grand
Bassin*

Gouly Père

Mahébourg ●

Ile aux Aigrettes

Le Morne Brabant
▲ *556m*

Fantasie
▲ *403m*

Bois Sec

*Piton Savanne
704m* ▲

Blue Bay

○ *Baie du Cap*

● Souillac

N

Bradt

0 —————— 10km
0 —————— 6 miles

observations show that they are doing well and starting to produce offspring. The MWF has also translocated Gunther's gecko from Round Island to Ile aux Aigrettes and Round Island boas from Round Island to Coin de Mire.

NATURE RESERVES AND CONSERVATION

Only fragments of Mauritius's original forests, estimated at 1.3%, remain today, at Black River Gorges, Bel Ombre and the Bassin Blanc Crater. The palm savannah, which used to feature in drier areas, has disappeared on the mainland with pockets remaining only on the outer islands.

Today, Mauritian nature reserves and national parks cover over 6,700ha. They are administered by the Forestry Service and the National Parks and Conservation Service (NPCS). Incidentally, the former director of the NPCS, Yousoof Mugroo, was the first overseas student to be trained by the Durrell Wildlife Conservation Trust (DWCT).

The Mauritian Wildlife Foundation (MWF, formerly the Mauritian Wildlife Appeal Fund) is a non-governmental organisation (NGO) which has the support of the NPCS. Founded in 1984, the MWF is concerned exclusively with conservation of endemic terrestrial wildlife in Mauritius and its territories, co-ordinating and administering projects aimed at preserving endemic species and ecosystem biodiversity. Much of its work has been done in the Black River Gorges National Park and on the offshore islands. Over the years, support has also been lent by many other international conservation organisations, including Chester Zoo, Philadelphia Zoo and the Endangered Wildlife Trust of South Africa.

The full-time staff of the MWF comprises Mauritians and expatriates, and is augmented by volunteers who come from various countries abroad, seeking valuable conservation experience after graduating at universities.

BLACK RIVER GORGES NATIONAL PARK The importance of the Black River Gorges National Park is that it protects a phenomenal concentration of gravely endangered animals and plants. Visitors will not struggle to find its rare denizens, many of which have narrowly escaped extinction. If there is one place in Mauritius which nature enthusiasts must visit, this is it. Set in the southwest, the national park covers 6,754ha and includes the Macchabée, Pétrin, Plaine Champagne, Bel Ombre and Montagne Cocotte forests. But don't expect pristine forest: the remaining forest is severely degraded, having been thoroughly invaded by fast-growing exotic plants.

At Pétrin and Plaine Champagne, you'll find heath-type vegetation flourishing on porous soil (keep a lookout for the lovely *Trochettia blackburniana*). Pandanus (*Pandanus microcarpus*), known locally as *vacoas*, thrives where terrain is marshier. A very distinctive tree is the weird, umbrella-like *bois de natte*, often festooned with epiphytes.

At Bel Ombre, you can study the transition between lowland and upland evergreen rainforest, whilst at Montagne Cocotte, there's a good example of high-altitude rainforest, in which shorter trees are draped in mosses and lichens.

The visitors' centre at Pétrin (☏ *258 0057;* ⊕ *07.00–17.00 Mon–Fri, 09.00–17.00 Sat–Sun*). There is a pleasant, shady picnic spot. In the visitors' centre they can give you details of suggested hiking trails. The following trails are some of the most worthwhile:

- **Macchabée (Macabe) Forest** 14km return from Pétrin (moderate). This loop trail allows visitors the best experience of Mauritian tropical rainforest. Wonderful views, good birding.

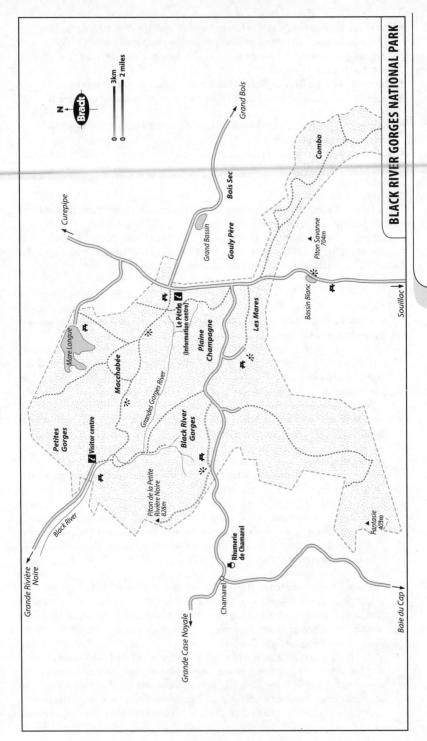

BLACK RIVER GORGES NATIONAL PARK

- **Parakeet** 8km one-way: Plaine Champagne to visitors' centre (tough). This is for adventurous, fit hikers, who will enjoy the steep trail joining Plaine Champagne with the gorges area. The really energetic can combine this with Macchabée for a 15km hike.
- **Piton de la Petite Rivière Noire** 6km return (moderate). This takes you to Mauritius's highest peak, at 828m. Fairly easy except for the last, steep stretch to the top.
- **Savanne** 6km return, from the end of Les Mares road (easy). Offers scenic views of southern Mauritius.
- **Bel Ombre** 18km return, Plaine Champagne to the reserve boundary (tough). Good birding in the tropical forest at lower elevations. Also, fruit bats and tropic birds.

There is also a second visitors' centre on the other side of the park inland from Grande Rivière Noire, on Les Gorges Road.

For more information about the reserve, contact the National Parks and Conservation Service of the Ministry of Agriculture and Natural Resources at Le Réduit (✆ *464 4016;* e *npcs@mail.gov.mu; www.npcs.govmu.org*).

DEAD AS A DODO

Most people have heard of the world's most famous extinct creature but few are aware that it was endemic to Mauritius.

The dodo (*Raphus cucullatus*) is believed to have been a flightless relative of the pigeon and a close relative of the Rodrigues solitaire (*Pezophaps solitaria*), which is also extinct. It would seem that the dodo lost its ability to fly due to the abundance of food close to the ground and the absence of mammalian predators.

With the arrival of Europeans in the late 16th century, the dodos' numbers started to decline and it is believed they were extinct by 1681. Dodos laid their eggs on the ground, making them easy targets for introduced predators, such as rats and pigs. The destruction of their habitat and these new predators were the principal causes of their demise, although the early settlers certainly ate their way through a good number of the hapless birds. Heyndrick Dircksz Jolinck led a Dutch exploration of Mauritius around 1598 and wrote:

> We also found large birds, with wings as large as of a pigeon, so that they could not fly and were named penguins by the Portuguese. These particular birds have a stomach so large that it could provide two men with a tasty meal and was actually the most delicious part of the bird.

The early settlers sketched the rather peculiar-looking birds but no physical evidence of their existence was found until the 19th century, leaving many to conclude in the interim that it was a mythical creature. This led to a fascination among the scientific community with finding dodo remains. In 1865, after 30 years of searching, George Clark, an English primary schoolteacher working in Mahébourg, found an assortment of dodo bones in marshy land known as Mare aux Songes, in the southeast of the island. At the time, indentured labourers were digging a railway line from Curepipe to Mahébourg and piling up the many assorted bones that they found. A young British civil engineer, Harry Higginson, took some of the bones to George Clark, who confirmed they were those of the

ROUND ISLAND *with the Mauritian Wildlife Foundation*

Round Island's troubles began in the 19th century, when goats and rabbits were introduced as a food source for fishermen, seabird-egg hunters and shipwreck victims. True to their form, these animals multiplied like flies, relentlessly munching away the hardwood forest on the upper slopes and the palm savannah on the lower slopes, which resembled that present in the drier areas of Mauritius, circa 1500.

Conservationists realised that urgent action had to be taken if Round Island's remaining plants and animals were to be saved. In 1976, the late Gerald Durrell and John Hartley made their first visit there. They were aghast at what they found: only two hurricane palms and eight Round Island bottle palms remained. The three species of skink and three species of gecko fed on a dwindling insect supply, and the two species of primitive boa on the diminishing lizard supply. Immediately, captive-breeding programmes were started at Jersey Zoo for the endemic reptiles. The Mauritius Government, under the Conservator of Forests and Wildlife Director A Wahab Owadally, rid the island of its goats by 1979. But the 3,000 undernourished rabbits still presented a major problem. So, the DWCT finally enlisted the assistance of the equally renowned New Zealand Department of Conservation. In 1986, the rabbits were completely eradicated.

dodo. Clark returned to the site to supervise further excavations; he sent hundreds of bones to the British Museum, for which he was paid a pound a piece, and those bones ended up in museums around the world.

In 1904, Louis Etienne Thirioux, a Port Louis hairdresser and amateur naturalist, found a complete dodo skeleton, which at the time was the only one in the world. The skeleton is now in the Natural History Museum in Port Louis.

In 2005, an international team of researchers excavated part of the Mare aux Songes and found fossilised dodo remains that had accumulated over centuries. Subsequent excavations suggested that dodos, along with other animals, became mired in Mare aux Songes trying to reach water during a long period of severe drought about 4,200 years ago.

In 2007, the discovery of 'Dodo Fred' added further to our knowledge of these birds. Fred and Debbie Stone were looking for cave cockroaches near Bois Chéri when they discovered bones that were later confirmed to be those of a dodo. These were the first dodo remains found in the highlands and proved that dodos inhabited that area. It is thought that Dodo Fred entered the cave to seek shelter from a violent cyclone, fell down a deep hole and could not climb out. Interestingly, during the excavation of the remains, the remains of another extinct bird, the Mauritian owl, were found. This discovery provided important DNA for determining the dodo's closest relatives. Test results showed the dodo was related to the Nicobar pigeon (*Caloenas nicobarica*) of the Malay Archipelago, the Solomon Islands and Palau, the tooth-billed pigeon (*Didunculus strigirostris*) of Samoa and the Victoria crowned pigeon (*Goura victoria*) of the New Guinea region. The dodo has to be one of the world's most famous birds and has become the reigning symbol of extinction. Its rather ridiculous appearance has contributed to its fame, and it is always depicted as a friendly and harmless creature as it was in Lewis Carroll's *Alice's Adventures in Wonderland*. In 2009, a previously unpublished 17th-century Dutch illustration of a dodo was sold at Christie's in London for £44,450, evidence that 300 years after its demise the dodo still fascinates us.

The poor Mascarene ecosystems! Not only have they been hammered by man and his animal followers, but they're riddled with invasive alien plants. Most of the animals and plants are species that have been introduced, and have subsequently run rampant to the detriment of indigenous flora and fauna.

Very prominent introductions include the *filao* (casuarina) tree (*Casuarina equisetifolia*), which often lines beaches and is useful as a windbreak. It originates in Malaysia. Great banyan trees (*Ficus benghalensis*) were brought from India, recognisable by their weird root systems dangling from their branches to the ground. Two distinctive Malagasy introductions are the flamboyant tree (*Delonix regia*) and the fan-shaped ravenala palm (*Ravenala madagascariensis*).

Privet and Chinese guava (*goyavier*) have spread at an alarming rate in the montane rainforests, often choking seedlings of slow-growing indigenous hardwoods. A horribly invasive bush is *Lantana camara*, the worst nightmare of conservationists. It is native to tropical America and has spread like wildfire in the Mascarenes.

Other tropical American invaders include sisal (*Furcraea foetida*), the morning glory creeper (*Ipomoea purpurea*), the prickly-pear cactus (*Opuntia vulgaris*) and the unmistakable poinsettia (*Euphorbia pulcherrima*).

In marshy areas, pampas grass (*Cortaderia selloana*), introduced from southeast Asia, is common. The originally Asian elephant ear (*Colocasea esculenta*) also frequents damp places. The staghorn fern (*Platycerium bifurcatum*), which one sees on so many rainforest trees, is actually Australian. Two of the most commonly used ornamentals, the bougainvillea (*Bougainvillea glabra*) and the frangipani (*Plumeria alba*), are tropical American species.

When the earlier settlers arrived in Mauritius, they introduced a selection of destructive animals, intentionally and by accident. A truly senseless introduction was the southeast Asian long-tailed macaque monkey (*Macaca fasicularis*), courtesy of the Dutch back in 1606. These primates are now abundant in Mauritius, where eradicating them is very difficult because Indo-Mauritians consider them sacred. They pose a very real threat to the endemic birds, reptiles, invertebrates and flora.

The results have been spectacular, to say the least. Almost immediately, most of the island's endemic and indigenous plants began sprouting scores of seedlings. The subsequent increase of fruit and insects has resulted in substantial increases in the reptile populations. The Forestry Department and an MWF botanist carried out an extensive programme to weed exotic plants and replant indigenous species. Today, the keel-scaled boa, Round Island day gecko and Telfair's skink are present in healthy, flourishing populations and new projects to fully restore the vegetation of the island and study the reptiles have been initiated by the MWF and its partners. Round Island represents one of the most spectacular examples of a DWCT-led conservation triumph and there are now plans to apply for World Heritage status for Round Island.

Bojer's skink (*Gongylomorphus bojeri*) is the island's most common reptile, also being present on several of the outlying islands, including Coin de Mire, Flat and Gabriel islands, and was probably exterminated on Mauritius by introduced rats, mongooses and Indian wolf snakes (*Lycodon aulica*).

Wild pigs (*Sus scrofra*), of Asian origin, abound too, but are very secretive and wary. No doubt they don't do terrestrial fauna much good, being the highly adaptable omnivores that they are, and are very destructive in native forests.

Brown rats and black rats arrived by means of ships and thoroughly invaded all the Mascarenes. Other introductions include the musk shrew, the black-naped hare (*Lepus nigricollis*) and the wild rabbit (*Oryctolagus cuniculus*), which was eradicated on Round Island after severely damaging the ecosystem there and has just about been eliminated elsewhere. The lesser Indian mongoose (*Herpestes javanicus*) is fairly often seen bolting across rural roads and was introduced in 1900 to reduce rats. It also munched its way through native bird populations.

Of the reptile introductions, the aggressive Indian wolf snake (*Lycodon aulicus*) is most often seen. We can only imagine what species this reptile wiped out while establishing itself in Mauritius, where it is now quite common.

Many birds have been introduced and those that established themselves are generally common and highly successful species. They are the birds you'll see in hotel gardens, parks and towns. Sadly, where they have an endemic relative, they far outnumber that species; like the red-whiskered bulbul, an Asian introduction, which is numerous, while the endemic Mauritius bulbul is uncommon.

The aggressive Indian mynah is to be seen in any urban centre, as are the house sparrow and house crow. Also regularly seen and heard is the zebra dove. The ring-neck parakeet (*Psittacula krameri*) can be confused with its endangered, endemic relative, the echo parakeet. However, their calls differ and both sexes of the ring-neck have red beaks, whilst only female echoes have black beaks.

Three small passerines (an order of birds characterised by the perching habit) from Africa are the spotted-backed weaver, the common waxbill and the yellow-eyed canary, all of which are now abundant. The bright red Madagascar fody has colonised all the Mascarenes. Seeing this little bird is guaranteed, but to stand the best chance of seeing its rare native congener, the Mauritius fody, you will need to go to Ile aux Aigrettes.

Some of the introduced birds have been far less invasive and are actually quite interesting. The common Indian francolin is present in grasslands and in sugarcane fields. More often seen is the Madagascar turtle dove.

Another skink found on Round Island is the pan-tropical Bouton's skink (*Cryptoblepharus boutonii*). Because of its long legs and claws, it is capable of staying on a rock while raging whitewater crashes over it. The ornate day gecko (*Phelsuma ornata*) remains common on Mauritius and Round Island. It forages by day for insects and nectar. The endemic Round Island day gecko, better known as Gunther's gecko (*P. guentheri*), is unusual among day geckos in that it is most active at night and is not brightly coloured like its relatives. Reaching a total length of nearly 300mm (1ft), it is the largest day gecko which still exists. They are often to be seen foraging in latan palms, for which they are important pollinators. Another gecko to be found on Round Island is the diminutive Durrell's night gecko (*Nactus durrelli*).

Round Island is best known among zoological circles for its two endemic snakes, which are so distinctive taxonomically that they have been accorded a family of their own: the Bolyeridae. Intriguingly, the only other animal families unique to the Mascarenes are also extinct: the Raphidae (the remarkable dodo and solitaires) and the

Mascarentous (Mascarene owl). The considerable regeneration of native vegetation on Round Island following the rabbit eradication means that the keel-scaled boa is now thriving and there may just be a very faint glimmer of hope for the Round Island burrowing boa. The keel-scaled boa is largely nocturnal, preying wholly on lizards. During the day, the boas tend to curl up in rock crevices or between fallen latan palm fronds. Sadly, no-one knows what the burrowing boa ate or how it lived.

The importance of Round Island as a refuge for a unique group of reptiles and plants cannot be overstated.

MARINE ENVIRONMENTAL AWARENESS   *with Tom Hooper*

By following a few simple guidelines you can enjoy the wonderful marine environment of the Mascarenes without damaging it.

BE CAREFUL WHERE YOU WALK There are many delicate organisms on the reef edge and shoreline which will break or be crushed if you walk on them. Corals are particularly vulnerable and are likely to die from being touched or smothered by silt. When you are diving and snorkelling be especially careful with your fins to make sure you don't break corals.

DON'T BUY SHELLS There are good reasons for not buying shells. The most beautiful and pristine shells are very rarely collected dead. They are taken live from the seabed and the animal inside is killed. While looking for and collecting shells there is also damage to the surrounding marine life. Lastly, even empty shells serve a useful purpose as homes for hermit crabs or a hard substrate for new growths of coral.

DON'T BUY CORALS, TURTLE SHELLS OR OTHER MARINE CURIOS Creating a market in these organisms leads to them being targeted for capture and the destruction of their surroundings during collection.

DISPOSE OF YOUR LITTER CAREFULLY A single piece of litter can destroy the illusion of wild remoteness and ruin a beach walk. With the introduction of cans and plastic bottles, wrappers and bags, even the coastlines of Rodrigues are beginning to suffer from the eyesore of scattered litter. Some of these items will take tens or hundreds of years to biodegrade.

SEAFOOD The demand for particular types of seafood can set a marine ecosystem off balance. In addition, some harvesting techniques are particularly damaging to the environment. Octopus populations are currently vulnerable in Rodrigues and the collection method damages the marine environment. Good fish to eat are the herbivorous fish which are caught in basket traps, such as unicorn and rabbit fish. These have a delicate taste and are excellent grilled.

AVOID EATING SHARK World populations of shark are in serious decline and as the top predators this has led to an imbalance in marine food chains. Areas of the Caribbean and Far East still use the lamentable practice of finning, which involves cutting fins from sharks for use in shark-fin soup, and then throwing them back alive.

ILE AUX AIGRETTES Ile aux Aigrettes is a 25ha reef-ringed coral islet about 1km off the southeast coast. It contains the last remaining traces of the lowland ebony forest that once dominated much of coastal Mauritius, as well as numerous other endemic animal and plant species threatened with extinction.

Since the MWF obtained the long-term lease of the islet in 1986, they've been engaged in extensive rehabilitation of the ecosystem there, which had been severely damaged over 400 years. The aim is that Ile aux Aigrettes should one day resemble its original state as closely as possible. To this end, the MWF has been weeding the islet and replanting with native plants, restoring the forest and reintroducing endemic birds and reptiles known to have once lived there. In recent years, the olive white-eye, Telfair's skink, Gunther's gecko and seabirds have been reintroduced. As the threat from highly invasive plants, such as giant acacia, is very real, general maintenance weeding will continue for years to come. Reintroductions of fauna will also continue.

Visitors can enjoy fascinating guided tours of the islet, see some very rare flora and fauna and witness conservation work in process. It is one of the best places to see the rare pink pigeon and the Mauritius fody, and the only place in the Mascarenes where giant Aldabra tortoises roam completely freely. Two tortoise species are known to have existed in Mauritius; both are now extinct, having been used as a source of protein by passing sailors. The giant Aldabra tortoises, which can weigh as much as 200kg, are native to the Seychelles but have been introduced to the island as the closest surviving relative of the lost species. Visitors are also likely to see colourful day geckos basking in the sun. Tours last around 2 hours and the guide will take the time to explain the geology and history of the island (for details, see pages 163–4).

OTHER PROTECTED AREAS North of Black River are two small mountain forest reserves, **Corps de Garde** and **Le Pouce**. The island's smallest reserve, **Perrier**, is only 1.5ha and is between Curepipe and the Mare aux Vacoas reservoir. It protects a small remnant parcel of transition forest between lowland and montane rainforest and harbours a large number of endemic plants. On the coast at Poste Lafayette is **Bras d'Eau National Park** (page 150).

Other nature reserves include Bois Sec, Cabinet, Combo, Flat Island, Gabriel Island, Coin de Mire, Gouly Père, Les Mares, Marianne Islet and Serpent Island.

MARINE LIFE The marine life of Mauritius has also suffered since man's arrival, although it is still an important attraction for visitors.

It is easy to visit coral gardens in depths of 7–20m through hotel diving centres (see pages 87–90). The range of fish to be seen, especially those engaging in antics like the boxfish with their curious sculling action and the trumpet fish with their darting movements, is fascinating.

The appeal of the reef is enhanced by the variety of the coral. Because of the sunlight that filters through sea of the right salinity and temperature, the coral thrives better in the waters of Mauritius than elsewhere. There are notable coral gardens at the southern corners of Mauritius, off Morne Brabant and Blue Bay.

Shell collecting has been rapacious since the 1960s and the Mauritius Scuba Diving Association now considers collecting unacceptable. To meet demand for souvenirs, shells are imported from overseas to be sold to tourists who want something pretty.

The rarest and most valuable shells in the world, such as the several varieties of conus, *Lambis violacea* and *Cypraea onyx-nymphal*, have been found off Mauritius.

Cone and cowrie shells, while delightful, can be deadly if of the *Conus aulieus*, *geographicus, marmoreus, rattus, textile* or *tulipa* species. Poison injected from their sharp ends can bring death within 150 minutes, with no known antidote. There have been 105 species recorded. Harp shells, four species with ribs resembling the strings of a harp, are attractive to collectors, especially the double harp (*Harpa costata*), which is not found outside Mauritian waters. There are 135 species of mitre shells (*Mitridae*), which are spindle- to oval-shaped and notched in front. Murex shells, such as *Murex tenuispina* with its elongated, jagged stem, are popular. The purple fluid secreted by them was used in ancient times as a dye.

Starfish are common and the presence of the crown of thorns (*Achantaster plancei*) is destructive to coral. An excellent specimen of the very rare *Acanthocidaris curvatispinis*, which is known only in Mauritius, is on display at the Natural History Museum in Port Louis. The collection of echinoderms there also contains a remarkable specimen of *Chondrocidaris gigantea*, exhibited in a special showcase as it is considered to be the most beautiful sea urchin in the world.

The Mauritian Marine Conservation Society (*www.mmcs-ngo.org*) is a non-government organisation which promotes marine environmental awareness and campaigns for protection measures. Coastal construction, marine pollution, over-fishing and cyclone damage threaten Mauritius's marine environment. In recent years the Mauritian Government has made increasing efforts to protect this important asset. The country's marine protected areas cover 7,216ha, with two of the main zones being the Blue Bay Marine Park in the southeast and the Balaclava Marine Park in the northwest. The Blue Bay Marine Park covers 353ha and with an average depth of just 5.5m and exceptionally clear waters, offers some of the best snorkelling in Mauritius.

At the same time as trying to protect the marine environment, the Mauritian Government is seeking to generate greater income from its oceans and is encouraging aquaculture (see page 33). The economic benefits will need to be carefully balanced against the effect on the marine environment.

HISTORY

For a small island which was uninhabited until the 1600s, Mauritius has a surprisingly rich history. The island was Dutch ... then French ... and finally British until the country's independence in 1968. Each of the colonial powers brought their own slaves or indentured labourers and voluntary migration boosted the population. The delightful blend of cultures visible in Mauritius today is the product of that eventful past.

DISCOVERY Mauritius is believed to have been discovered by Arab traders around AD975 as they travelled to the east coast of Africa. There is no evidence that they settled on the uninhabited island, which they referred to as Dina Arobi (Abandoned Island). Mauritius's neighbour, Madagascar, was inhabited but according to a 12th-century observer, Idrisi, its inhabitants had no boats capable of crossing the sea. Mauritius, Rodrigues and Réunion made their first known appearance on a map in 1502, indicated by their respective Arabic names: Dina Arobi, Dina Moraze and Dina Margabin.

THE ARRIVAL OF THE EUROPEANS In the wake of Vasco da Gama's penetration of the Indian Ocean via the Cape of Good Hope, came the Portuguese *conquistadores*. While they progressed along the African and Indian coasts, they never tried to

establish themselves properly in Madagascar and neighbouring islands. Pedro Mascarenhas (after whom the Mascarenes were named) is credited with the European discovery of Réunion in 1512 and Mauritius is said to have been discovered by navigator Diogo Fernandez Pereira in 1511.

The Portuguese stopped in at the islands to collect food and water but their visits would have been infrequent. On their way to and from India they preferred to use the Mozambique Channel, staying close to the African coast rather than risking the open sea. Mauritius became known on Portuguese maps as Ilha do Cirne, Island of the Swan, possibly after the 'land swan' which then inhabited the island: the dodo. A more prosaic theory is that the name was derived from that of a Portuguese vessel.

In 1528, Diego Rodriguez gave his name to the island still known as Rodrigues. Portuguese names have also survived on other neighbouring islands including Diego Garcia in the Chagos Archipelago, which was named after another Portuguese navigator.

The great bay on the southeast corner of Mauritius, now known as Grand Port, was a natural haven for ships. During the latter part of the 16th century, the island was probably used by pirates who preyed on the pilgrim route between India and Jeddah. Vessels from a Dutch fleet on its way from Amsterdam to Java sailed in during a violent storm in September 1598. Many of the crew were suffering from scurvy and the landfall was seen as a godsend. Admiral Wybrandt van Warwyck was in command of the fleet and he arrogantly named the bay Warwyck Haven, a name immediately forgotten. His choice of a name for the island, however, had a catchier ring to it – he claimed possession for the Stadtholder of the Netherlands, Prince Mauritius van Nassau.

The Dutch were fascinated by the island, especially by the trusting curiosity of the birds which had yet to learn fear and allowed themselves to be knocked down with a club. In Grant's *History of Mauritius*, published in London in 1801, the dodo is described as 'a feathered tortoise' whose sluggish movements made it an easy target for the laziest hunter. Although the Dutch called occasionally for shelter, food and fresh water they took little interest in developing the island.

The French and British, too, began to see possibilities for both trade and strategy in the Mascarenes and sent out expeditions in 1638. Their ships arrived too late. In May 1638, Cornelius Simonsz Gooyer had set up the first permanent Dutch settlement in Mauritius. He was sent by the Dutch East India Company and became the first governor, over a population of 25 colonists who planned to exploit the island's resources of ebony and ambergris, as well as rearing cattle and growing tobacco.

Over the next few years, 100 slaves were imported from Madagascar and convicts sent over from Batavia (now Jakarta). The convicts were Europeans, Indonesians and Indians and were employed in cutting ebony. The free colonists came from Baltic and North Sea ports, hardened men who were settlers out of desperation and coercion rather than through brave ideals. From its very first settlement, Mauritius had a mix of races that was to set a pattern for its future.

The settlers supported themselves by raising vegetables and livestock, which they sold to the company or, for more profit, to the crews of visiting French, English and pirate ships. Although the settlement grew to 500, it did not prosper.

The slaves from Madagascar escaped to the forest and began to exact revenge for Dutch cruelties by destroying their crops and slaughtering their cattle. Invasions by hungry rats added to the problems of the settlement. The lack of interest shown by the Dutch East India Company finally demoralised the colonists.

A few years after the Dutch founded a colony at the Cape of Good Hope in 1652, the island was abandoned completely, the European market for ebony being

glutted. Only the sugarcane that had been introduced from Batavia and the runaway Malagasy slaves in the forests remained.

The Dutch tried again in 1664, starting a settlement under the aegis of the Cape colony. They were more ambitious this time with attempts at agriculture on a commercial scale, including tobacco, sugarcane, indigo and maize. Deer, introduced from Java, thrived in the forests and were hunted for food and pelts. Forts were built on the eastern coast, forests cleared and domestic animals raised.

Legend has it that the Dutch were driven off for a second time in 1710 by the rats they had themselves accidentally introduced. Resentment at colonial bureaucracy also played its part, since the colony at the Cape received preferential treatment from the Dutch authorities. The settlers were ill-suited to be colonists – they suffered from the heat, were undisciplined, lazy and prone to drunkenness.

Meanwhile, a new state was forming in Madagascar. Called Libertalia, it was a pirate republic founded by a French adventurer and a defrocked Italian monk. There was no shortage of tough men, mostly pirates from every nation, who made Libertalia their home. From there they successfully plundered shipping throughout the Indian Ocean and their community thrived. These men were to contribute to the new colonisation of Mauritius.

FRENCH RULE The French East India Company had already occupied Bourbon (now Réunion) as a trading centre, and it had attracted as settlers a great number of pirates and their offspring by Malagasy women. The island had fertile soil but lacked harbours. The attraction of a vacant Mauritius with its well-protected bays was irresistible.

In September 1715, a preliminary expedition led by Guillaume Dufresne d'Arsel took possession of Mauritius in the name of King Louis XV of France, naming it Ile de France so its ownership would be in no doubt. D'Arsel placed the French flag near what is now Port Louis, drew up a document witnessed by his officers declaring the island French and, after three days, sailed away.

Nearly seven years passed before the French East India Company actually occupied the island. In 1721, a motley crew of company officials, settlers and slaves from Madagascar, Mozambique and West Africa landed. Swiss mercenaries made up the garrison; pirates and their women accompanied them. More women were rounded up on the waterfronts of St Malo and Bordeaux and shipped out to swell the island's population. It was hoped that a grant of land, a sum of money and the prospect of an imported wife would be enough to tempt men to settle.

For the first 14 years, the French colony followed the dismal experience of the Dutch. Only the most desperate and toughest of settlers survived, eking out a living from the pittance they earned from the company. Their appallingly treated slaves escaped to become *marrons* (runaway slaves), living in the forest and sabotaging the plantations.

A forlorn settlement of palm-thatched cabins sprang up near the west-coast harbour of Port Louis, where the French East India Company decided to build the capital. The company, however, maintained its headquarters in Bourbon, despairing of ever controlling its reluctant settlers or making a profit on the investment in Ile de France.

The solution was an inspired one. As the new Governor of Ile de France and Ile Bourbon, the French East India Company appointed an aristocratic sea captain, Bertrand François Mahé de Labourdonnais. He was 38 and full of ambition when he sailed into Port Louis harbour in 1735.

The wretched conditions of the settlers dismayed Labourdonnais. There were 190 whites on the island and 648 slaves, most of them African or Malagasy, and a few Indians.

Labourdonnais transformed the island from a colony of malcontents into 'the star and key of the Indian Ocean'. He was a born leader and as a naval man understood the lusty spirit of men with pirate blood flowing in their veins. He had an affinity with the struggling colonisers and he began by giving them self-respect and ambition.

He ordered that the seat of government of the two colonies be transferred from Bourbon, which was better established, to Ile de France and set up a council to administer the islands. He channelled the seafaring abilities of his settlers back to the sea, deliberately creating a navy of buccaneers.

The thatched hovels were demolished and in their place rose forts, barracks, warehouses, hospitals and houses, many of which survive in part of Port Louis today. Government House was built of coral blocks, roads were opened throughout the island and a shipbuilding industry commenced.

Although he had to import slaves, Labourdonnais made their lot easier by also importing ox-carts so slaves could be utilised for more skilled tasks. He turned many of them into artisans to make up for the lack of skilled men among the settlers. He also pushed through an agriculture programme that concentrated on feeding the islanders and on marketable produce. On his own estates he grew sugarcane, encouraging new settlers to start plantations of cotton, indigo, coffee and manioc. The first sugar factory was opened at Villebague in 1744, a salt pan was started and he even tried to rear silkworms.

Gradually a civilised life evolved in Port Louis, attracting colonisers from Bourbon, and even from good French families.

In 1746, with England and France at war, Labourdonnais led an expedition of nine ships from Ile de France to India. There they defeated a British squadron and captured Madras, the most important British outpost.

Labourdonnais's actions resulted in a conflict with Dupleix, his superior in India and caused his downfall. Dupleix wanted Madras razed to the ground but Labourdonnais refused because he knew the British would pay a ransom to get Madras back. He was accused of accepting a bribe to preserve Madras and was replaced as Governor of Ile de France. On his return to France he was thrown into the Bastille. Although in 1751 he was found innocent, he died a broken man two years later, aged 54. Labourdonnais is known as the father of the colony; his statue stands in Port Louis facing out across the harbour. The town of Mahébourg (started in 1805) is named after him. So, too, is Mahé, capital of the Seychelles.

In 1764, the French East India Company, brought to bankruptcy by the Seven Years War, made over its assets, including the Ile de France, to the French king. In 1767, the Royal Government was established on the island. At that time there was a population of 18,773 that included 3,163 Europeans and 587 free blacks. The rest (around 80% of the population) were slaves.

The appositely named Pierre Poivre (Peter Pepper) was picked as administrator. He introduced varieties of plants from South America, including pepper, and even offered tax incentives to planters to grow them. Under his influence, the colony developed as an agricultural and trading centre.

A French nobleman, Vicomte de Souillac, was made governor (1779–87), bringing an era of extravagance to the colony. Port Louis became renowned for its bright social life, duelling, gambling and hunting. Public affairs were neglected; fraud, corruption and dishonesty were commonplace and land speculation and scandals were rife.

In January 1790, a packet-boat arrived in Port Louis harbour from France, flying a new flag, the Tricolour. It brought news of the revolution. An elected assembly and municipal councils were set up and tribunals replaced courts of justice. A National Guard was formed, streets were renamed and revolutionary clubs started. Church property was confiscated and white, red and blue cockades were sported with delight. A guillotine was even erected in the Champ de Mars but its only victim was a dog (some historians say a goat), decapitated to try it out.

The colonists' enthusiasm for the revolutionary principles of liberty, equality and fraternity faltered when in 1796 two agents of the Directoire, wearing splendid orange cloaks, arrived from France and informed the startled colonists that slavery was abolished. The news was received with anger and the agents had to flee for their lives.

The last French governor of Ile de France was appointed by Napoleon Bonaparte in 1803 to bring the colony back to order after 13 years of autonomy. With such a task, it was inevitable that the governor, General Charles Decaen, would be unpopular. He dissolved all the elected councils and adopted a dictatorial attitude to administration.

BRITISH RULE Meanwhile, the British were expanding their influence in the Indian Ocean and in 1809, British forces from both the Cape and India occupied Rodrigues from where they prepared their attack on all the Mascarenes. Bourbon, which had been renamed Réunion during the revolutionary years, was taken. A major battle was fought between the French and British fleets off Grand Port in August 1810, and after prolonged fighting, the French won a victory that no-one expected.

In December 1810, 70 British vessels and 11,500 soldiers set sail from Rodrigues for the north of Ile de France. Their aim was not colonisation, but to neutralise the island so that it wouldn't be used as a base for French attacks on British vessels bound for India. British spies and reconnaissance had found a passage near Coin de Mire. Decaen was taken by surprise as he awaited the invasion in Port Louis. The British forces under General Abercrombie marched on the capital, meeting only token resistance.

Faced with the might of the British forces and the indifference of the settlers to remaining French, Decaen surrendered. Soldiers were allowed to leave the island and settlers who did not want to stay under a British administrator were permitted to return to France with all their possessions. These generous capitulation terms also included British pledges to preserve the island's laws, customs, language, religion and property.

The majority of settlers remained. Perhaps some expected the colony to be restored to France in peacetime. The Treaty of Paris did restore Réunion in 1814 but Mauritius was confirmed as a British possession.

A dashing, unorthodox personality in the Labourdonnais mould, Robert Farquhar became the first British governor in 1810. He soon revealed himself as remarkably independent of the British Government in London, taking advantage of the long time it took for despatches from London to reach Mauritius to act as he thought best.

Farquhar quickly won over the French settlers, particularly through his scrupulous interpretation of the capitulation terms. Since the settlers were allowed their customs, he permitted them to continue with the slave trade despite the British law of 1807, which prohibited trading in slaves in the British Empire.

Farquhar had to contend with many calamities during his administration, including an outbreak of smallpox in 1811 and of rabies in 1813. There was a disastrous fire in Port Louis in 1816 when 700 houses, mostly wooden, were destroyed, which resulted in new ones being built of stone. A cholera epidemic broke out in 1819, and there were fierce cyclones in 1818 and 1819.

Farquhar campaigned for reliance on sugarcane because it was the only money-making crop able to withstand cyclones, encouraging the planters to abandon coffee, cotton and their other crops. He also established Port Louis as a free port, open to ships of all nations, and stimulated food production and road building. He proved to the inhabitants that there were distinct economic advantages in being British rather than French.

He mixed with everyone and opened dialogue with non-white leaders. Although his stance on slavery seemed ambivalent, he believed in attacking the slave trade at its source (in this case Madagascar) and worked for its elimination there as a way of ending the trade to Mauritius. He set up an office for the registration of slaves and tried to improve their conditions in the face of hostility from their owners.

Yet, like Labourdonnais, Farquhar ran foul of his home government and was recalled to England in 1817. He returned to Mauritius, though, in 1820 as Sir Robert and governed for a further three years.

The attempts by the British Government to abolish slavery in Mauritius met with resistance from the planters who, having been persuaded to concentrate on sugar as an income-earning export crop, relied on slave labour to produce it. The arrival of Attorney General John Jeremy in 1832 to force through emancipation led to clashes and Jeremy was obliged to flee the island.

This time the planters' triumph was short-lived and slavery was abolished on 1 February 1835. The planters were paid over £2 million compensation, which they considered to be half the total value of their 68,613 registered slaves.

For the slaves the pleasure of emancipation was dulled by the imposition of a four-year period of apprenticeship during which they were supposed to work for their former masters in return for meagre wages. Not surprisingly, the scheme failed and slaves took up residence in unpopulated coastal areas where they suffered years of neglect. The wily planters turned to an alternative source of compliant labour: Indian migrants, known in Mauritius as 'the coolie trade'.

INDIAN MIGRATION Indian migrants had been in Mauritius since 1736 when Labourdonnais brought in 40 artisans from Pondicherry. In 1834, just prior to the abolition of slavery, Mauritius's sugarcane planters began to recruit workers from India to meet the demands of the rapidly expanding sugar industry. Following the abolition of slavery, the need for labour increased further. The indentured, or contracted, labour system was institutionalised in 1842 and, although most of the immigrants came from India, some also arrived from China, Madagascar and East Africa. Each of them was bound by a contract for a stipulated period but many settled permanently in Mauritius.

An immigration depot, Aapravasi Ghat, was built in Port Louis in 1849 to process the indentured labourers as they arrived. Today it is recognised as a UNESCO World Heritage Site and is open to the public (pages 108–9).

By 1923, when indentured immigration ceased, almost half a million people had arrived in Mauritius under the system. The impact of Indian immigration changed the course of the island's history and shaped its population. Now the majority, the Indians came to wield influence in all spheres, not only by their contribution of an efficient workforce that sustained the economy, but also by a vigorous intellectual force in politics.

In 1885, Mauritius gained a new constitution and elections were held for the first time in January 1886, marking the beginning of a parliamentary democracy. However, only those who were educated and owned property were eligible to vote, which translated to just 2% of the population.

In 1901, Mohandas Gandhi (later Mahatma Gandhi) visited Mauritius and was dismayed by the condition of the Indian population, in particular their lack of education and involvement in politics. In 1907, Gandhi sent Manillal Doctor, an Indian barrister and human rights activist, to Port Louis to campaign for the social, political and economic rights of indentured labourers. His motto made his aims clear: 'Liberty of individuals! Fraternity of man! Equality of races!'. In 1909, he put his suggestions for reform to a Royal Commission from Britain, which subsequently made wide-ranging recommendations for the reorganisation of agriculture, the civil service, education and the constitution.

THE 20TH CENTURY AND POLITICAL CHANGE World War I brought suffering to the island with drastic cuts in shipping causing food shortages and price rises. There was a local campaign after the war for Mauritius to be returned to France but the so-called 'retrocessionist' candidates were heavily defeated in the 1921 general election.

World War II brought infrastructural development. The British based a fleet at Port Louis and Grand Port, as well as building an airport at Plaisance and a seaplane base at Baie du Tombeau. A large telecommunications station was built at Vacoas, although the first underwater telephone cable, linking South Africa to Australia, had been laid to Mauritius in 1901.

After World War II, constitutional reform gathered pace as Britain began to relinquish control of the island and its other colonies. In 1948, a new constitution established a Legislative Council of 19 elected members, 12 appointed members and three ex officio members, and extended the right to vote to all adults who could write their name in one of the country's languages. Elections held later that year were won by the Mauritius Labour Party (MLP), and their success was repeated in 1953.

Another new constitution in 1958 expanded the vote to all adults over 21 years of age and divided the country into 40 single-member constituencies that elected representatives to the Legislative Council.

In the 1959 election (the first held following the introduction of universal adult suffrage), Hindu doctor (later Sir) Seewoosagur Ramgoolam, leader of the MLP, was victorious. He held the post of chief minister until 1968, when Mauritius became an independent country within the Commonwealth of Nations, with Queen Elizabeth II as head of state represented by a governor general. After independence, Ramgoolam became the country's first prime minister, a post he held until 1982. He went on to serve as governor general from 1983 to 1985, when he died in office. A giant of Mauritian politics, he is known as the 'father of the nation'.

In 1969, the Mouvement Militant Mauricien (MMM) was founded; it advocated socialism and quickly gathered support among the poor. In 1971, social and industrial unrest led by the MMM resulted in a state of emergency being declared, which lasted until 1976. The MMM's leaders, including Franco-Mauritian Paul Berenger, were jailed for a year.

In the 1982 election an alliance of the MMM and the Parti Socialiste Mauricien (PSM), led by Paul Berenger and a Hindu, British-trained lawyer, Anerood Jugnauth, captured all 60 directly elected seats. Anerood Jugnauth became prime minister with Berenger as his finance minister.

The alliance collapsed the following year, Berenger resigned with ten of his cabinet colleagues and Jugnauth dissolved parliament and called an election. Jugnauth formed a new party, the Mouvement Socialiste Militant (MSM), drawing on defectors from other parties and allying himself with Sir Seewoosagur's MLP and the Parti Mauricien Social Démocrate (PMSD). The new alliance won the election and Berenger became leader of the opposition. Jugnauth remained prime minister until 1995.

On 12 March 1992, Mauritius became a republic within the Commonwealth and the then governor, Sir Veerasamy Ringadoo, became the first president. In June 1992, Cassam Uteem, a Mauritian Muslim, was nominated as president, an office he held until February 2002, when he was forced to resign after refusing to give his assent to the proposed prevention of terrorism legislation following the 11 September 2001 terrorist attacks in New York.

At the general election held in December 1995, the opposition captured all 60 seats on Mauritius and allies took the two seats on Rodrigues. The victors were an opposition coalition and their leader, Dr Navin Chandra Ramgoolam, son of the much-revered Sir Seewoosagur Ramgoolam, became prime minister.

By the September 2000 elections, Navin Ramgoolam's popularity had fallen considerably. Many Mauritians felt he was out of touch with the island, having spent much of his life abroad, and allegations of corruption plagued his time in government. The elections saw Ramgoolam defeated by an alliance of the MSM and MMM. In an unusual step, it was agreed that Sir Anerood Jugnauth would be prime minister for the first three years of the parliamentary term, followed by Paul Berenger for the second three.

When he became prime minister in 2003, Paul Berenger was not only the first white but also the first non-Hindu prime minister since independence in 1968. Furthermore, he was the first Caucasian to lead an African country since the end of colonial rule. His time as prime minister came to an end in July 2005, when his party was defeated by the newly formed Socialist Alliance and Dr Navin Ramgoolam once more became prime minister. The result was not unexpected with rising unemployment in the sugar and textile industries, high-profile figures resigning from the government to join the opposition alliance and allegations of corruption all conspiring against the governing MSM–MMM coalition.

In 2010, a coalition comprising the MLP, MSM and PMSD was elected, with the MMM in opposition. Power was again in the hands of two men who have dominated Mauritian politics for decades: President Sir Anerood Jugnauth and Prime Minister Dr Navin Ramgoolam. In August 2011, the president's son, Pravind Jugnauth, pulled his party, the MSM, out of the alliance following allegations of corruption against some of his colleagues. The PMSD also left the coalition and the MLP continued to govern alone.

Sir Anerood Jugnauth resigned as president on 20 March 2012 at the age of 82, saying he could not support government policies. He was replaced by Kailash Purryag. A coalition known as the Alliance Lepep (Alliance of the People), comprising the MSM, PMSD and a new party, the Muvman Liberater (ML), won the October 2014 election, and Sir Anerood Jugnauth became prime minister. In June 2015, after Purryag resigned as president, Ameenah Gurib-Fakim, an eminent scientist, became the first female to be elected president of Mauritius.

GOVERNMENT AND POLITICS

Mauritius is a parliamentary democracy on the Westminster model, with 62 members of parliament elected to the National Assembly every five years on a first-past-the-post system. Mauritius is divided into 21 constituencies, each returning three members, apart from Rodrigues, which is a single constituency and returns two members. After a general election, the Electoral Supervisory Committee may nominate up to eight additional members. Known as the 'best loser' system, this allows for fair representation of ethnic and religious minorities in the National Assembly.

The president and vice-president are elected by the National Assembly for a five-year term. The presidential role, although important, is limited in powers to official and ceremonial procedures. Authority is delegated by him to the Council of Ministers, a body of ministers headed by the prime minister.

Government by coalition is a common feature of Mauritian politics. One of the main challenges facing any government of Mauritius is the constant effort that must be made to maintain harmony between the island's various ethnic groups. The growth of tourism has made this an even greater priority. Traditionally the Mauritian Labour Party (MLP) and the Mouvement Socialiste Militant (MSM) have attracted the Hindu vote, while the MMM has its base in the minorities, namely the Creoles, Muslims and non-Hindi-speaking Indians. It is no secret that many Mauritians of African descent feel disadvantaged and under-represented in politics. You only to have to visit the southwest of the island, the most Creole area, to see that this is one of the poorest parts of Mauritius. The social unrest that occurred following the death of the popular Creole singer, Kaya, in February 1999, is a reminder of how dangerous underlying discontent can be (see box, page 185).

MILITARY Mauritius has no military forces as such. Law enforcement, military and security functions are performed by units which fall under the Commissioner of Police. The only paramilitary units are the Special Mobile Force (SMF) and the National Coast Guard. Training is provided by British, French and Indian counterparts.

NATIONAL FLAG The flag of Mauritius consists of four equal-width horizontal stripes. In descending order these are red, blue, yellow and green, so when the flag is flying, red is at the top. The colours have been interpreted as red for freedom and independence; blue for the Indian Ocean; yellow representing the light of independence shining over the nation; and green standing for the agriculture of Mauritius and showing the country's colour throughout the 12 months of the year.

A second interpretation maintains that the colours stand for the island's different religious and ethnic groups. Red represents the Hindus, blue the Catholic population, yellow the Tamils and green the Muslims.

Crest The crest of Mauritius reflects its past, flanked by a dodo and a stag, both clutching shoots of sugarcane. The shield portrays a medieval ship, representing the island's discoverers, and three stylistic trees.

There is also a key and a shining star, depicting the country's motto that appears below it: STELLA CLAVISQUE MARIS INDICI (Star and key of the Indian Ocean).

ECONOMY

The influence on the economy of Sir Robert Farquhar, the first British governor, is enduring. Farquhar realised the value of an export-oriented economy but encouraged a reliance on one export only: sugar.

The reliance on a one-crop economy meant that the prosperity of Mauritius depended on the world demand for sugar and on climatic conditions. When both were favourable, Mauritius benefited. This is what happened in the early 1970s when economic growth averaged 9% per year. The standard of living improved visibly; new houses were built of concrete blocks and electricity served 90% of the island's dwellings. However, the pace of economic advance slowed as the sugar boom fizzled out. Mauritius responded to the challenge and diversified its economy, and it has

remained agile and responsive to change ever since. Textiles and tourism became mainstays of the economy, and in recent years the manufacturing sector has expanded to the production of diamonds, watches and jewellery. Mauritius has also successfully sought out new areas to drive economic growth, including offshore banking (pages 78–9), pharmaceuticals, communications and information technology.

The government created the Board of Investment (BOI) to encourage and facilitate investment in the country, and the BOI has successfully positioned the country as investment-friendly. For information on doing business in Mauritius, see pages 77–9.

Despite the recent global economic slowdown, Mauritius has consistently achieved growth rates of over 3% per annum. Mauritius is considered a relatively stable, peaceful democracy, has attracted considerable foreign investment and has one of the highest per-capita incomes in the African region. At the time of writing, Mauritius was the only African country ranked as a 'full democracy' in the Economist Intelligence Unit's Democracy Index, and the World Bank ranks it as the easiest country in Africa in which to do business. However, the World Bank also notes that inequality is growing in Mauritius and relative poverty increased from 8.5% in 2007 to 9.8% in 2012.

In 2015, Mauritius's gross domestic product (GDP) was US$20.9 billion (£13.5 billion), unemployment was 8.1% and inflation 3.5%.

INDUSTRY In 1970, Mauritius set up an Export Processing Zone (the EPZ) to promote the export of locally produced goods. A package of fiscal incentives, including exemption from certain taxes and duties, freedom to repatriate capital and profits, and a guarantee against state takeovers was offered. The scheme attracted investors from around the world. The EPZ drove the growth of the textile industry, which was largely a product of the island's Chinese population and investors from Hong Kong. Mauritius became one of the world's largest exporters of woollen knitwear. The textile industry was key to the island's economic growth, created new employment opportunities and strengthened the manufacturing base of the economy.

A range of factors, including competition from countries such as China, Bangladesh and Sri Lanka, began to threaten the textile industry in the 2000s. It became clear that the concentration on textiles could be as risky as the reliance on sugar had been. The industrial development strategy now aims for diversification and new target areas in manufacturing include electronics, jewellery, watches, medical devices and food processing. The industrialisation of sugar is also taking place with by-products such as molasses, rum, ethyl alcohol and acetic acid.

AGRICULTURE AND FISHING

Sugar When the sugarcane is fully grown, the roads of the flat lands in the north of Mauritius are like tunnels through the cane fields. With nothing to be seen except the blue sky above and the green ribbons of cane waving in the wind, it is easy to imagine that the whole of the island is one vast sugar plantation.

About 40% of Mauritius's surface is cultivated, of which 90% is under sugarcane. It is a perennial plant which relishes warm, humid tropical and subtropical climates. Sugarcane cuttings are planted and generally have a useful life of around seven years before yield is diminished and they need to be replaced. A single cane plant produces up to 20 litres of juice, from which around 2kg of sugar can be extracted. Around 500,000 tonnes of sugar are produced annually in Mauritius with most of it being exported to Europe. Of the total produced, around 35% comes from almost 30,000 small growers.

In the 1970s, sugar contributed around 25% of GDP but with the growth of other industries that figure has shrunk to around 3%. Thanks to an increasingly competitive international environment, for the past decade the industry has been facing one of its most challenging periods. It was hit particularly hard by the European Union's 2005 decision to reduce the price of sugar by 36%, and its directive in 2009 abolishing a sugar protocol which guaranteed the quantity and price of Mauritian exports.

The number of people employed in the industry has fallen and the proportion of land devoted to sugarcane is in decline. Some of the large sugar estates have diversified, in part through the establishment of so-called Integrated Resource Schemes (IRS) consisting of hotels, luxury villas and golf courses (see page 46). Bel Ombre in the south and Médine in the west are two such examples. Furthermore, estates have branched out into growing other crops, such as the wax-like anthurium flowers (*Anthurium andraeanum*) for export.

The number of sugar factories has also been in decline for some years, falling from 250 in the 19th century to just four today. Tall, crumbling chimney stacks are all that remain of many of them – monuments to the early days of the industry that made Mauritius.

The industry has had to be creative in order to remain viable by, for example, specialising in upmarket, unrefined sugar, producing rum, bio-ethanol for biofuel and carbon dioxide for the beverage industry.

Sugarcane was introduced from Batavia (Jakarta) by the Dutch in 1639. It was the French governor, Labourdonnais, who began sugar production in earnest. He set up the first sugar factory at Villebague in the centre of the island in 1744. By the time the British arrived in 1810 there were 10,000 acres under cultivation. The British governor, Farquhar, persuaded the settlers to expand their cane cultivation because of the crop's ability to withstand cyclones.

It was not until the abolition of duties on Mauritius-grown sugar in 1825, which allowed it to be imported into Britain on the same terms as sugar from the Caribbean, that the industry really began to thrive.

The early sugar mills relied on slaves and oxen to turn the rollers to crush the cane. The juice was extracted and collected in cauldrons where foreign matter was skimmed off. Then it was boiled, using the *bagasse* (crushed cane) as fuel, and the syrup was cooled until it crystallised into sugar.

Animal-driven mills were gradually replaced by machinery, with the last one closing in 1853. From 1864, railway lines opened to transport sugarcane. The main railway system operated until 1964, when it was closed down as it was thought to be uneconomic, since its use for profitable freight was confined to the crop season. One of the few remaining locomotives that was used to haul the sugarcane trolleys rests today on public display in the unusual setting of La Vanille Réserve des Mascareignes (page 166).

The island's volcanic beginnings caused the soil to be strewn with boulders and stones and every inch of the land used for cane growing has had to be cleared by hand. The gaunt piles of rock in the midst of the cane fields are a forceful reminder of the toil of the men and women who worked in the blisteringly hot sun to clean these patches in the volcanic blanket.

New cane is planted in cycles to be harvested after 14 to 18 months. The ratoons (shoots) appear from the second year onward. They are harvested every 12 months during the June to December cropping period. The stony nature of the soil still restricts mechanical harvesting, so in parts of the island you will see cane being cut by hand.

When cane is cut, it is transported as soon as possible to the nearest factory where it is bulk fed into mechanical crushers. A constant supply of cane is needed to maintain production, so the pace is frenetic. The factories are self-powered, as they were in the 19th century, only now it is more scientific. The waste cane, known as the *bagasse*, is used to produce electricity, not only for the factories but to augment the national supply.

The history of the sugar industry and the processes of sugar production are brilliantly explained at L'Aventure du Sucre, a museum housed in the former Beau Plan sugar factory near Pamplemousses (page 137).

Tea

The black tea you drink in Mauritius is grown on the island and comes in a variety of locally inspired flavours, such as vanilla and coconut.

The tea is produced predominantly for local consumption. Mauritius is unable to compete on the world market with countries such as Kenya, Sri Lanka and India because the teas with the best flavour are grown at heights greater than the altitude of the tea plantations on the island.

The central highlands south of Curepipe are the main tea-growing area. The cooler temperatures and the greater rainfall of the highland plateau suit tea. Being a plant that grows as a sturdy bush with deep roots and a long life, it can withstand winds of cyclonic force.

The crew-cut tops of the bushes have a pleasingly uniform appearance, thanks to the nimble fingers of tea pickers and an electric shearer. The picking is done with incredible dexterity early in the morning, mainly by women. Only the top two or three young leaves are removed from the branches. The green leaf is then bagged and transported to a factory where it is dried, fermented, chopped, sorted and prepared for packing.

Tea's roots in Mauritius go back to the 18th century, when it was grown by settlers for their own use. In the 19th century, Governor Robert Farquhar encouraged commercial cultivation. From the early 1960s, extensive planting was pursued and by the 1980s tea was the second-largest revenue earner in the agricultural sector. Since then the fortunes of the tea industry have fluctuated and by the mid 1990s, with tea prices dropping and sugar prices rising, tea bushes were being torn up to be replaced by sugar. Today Mauritius produces around 7,000 tonnes of tea per year.

It is worth taking the time to visit the working tea factory of Bois Chéri, near Curepipe, and see the production in progress (pages 167–8). The factory can also be visited as part of the Route du Thé (Tea Route, see page 168), which takes in Domaine des Aubineaux as well, a colonial house with a museum telling the story of tea, and the Domaine de St Aubin sugar estate and rum distillery.

Tobacco

Tobacco has been grown in Mauritius since 1639, when it was introduced by the Dutch. In the 19th century, Indian immigrants grew tobacco for their own consumption, and in 1810 the British attempted unsuccessfully to establish a tobacco industry. It was not until 1917 that tobacco was successfully produced on an industrial scale. In 1926, the British American Tobacco Company opened a cigarette factory on the outskirts of Port Louis. By the 1970s there were three factories on the island.

Although it is a major crop, tobacco is not exported and often falls short of local demand. Most of the tobacco is Virginia flue-cured, although Amarello air-cured is also produced. It is grown on small plantations by private planters under the supervision of the state-controlled Tobacco Board.

In recent years, tobacco production has declined and the volume of imported tobacco has increased. At the same time, smoking in Mauritius has been in decline.

Other produce As a small island with limited agricultural land, Mauritius relies on imports for around 70% of its food, which makes it vulnerable to global food price rises. Since the 2008 global food price crisis, the government has encouraged greater self-sufficiency through an expansion of agriculture. Farmers produce almost 100% of the vegetables consumed on the island, 60% of the potatoes and 33% of the onions. Manioc is a popular crop and is used to make biscuits (see pages 165–6). Markets showcase locally grown vegetables and fruit, such as the tiny, round Mauritian tomato known quaintly as *pomme d'amour* (love apple). Bananas, pineapples, papayas, mangoes, lychees, watermelons, coconuts and citrus thrive and are of commercial importance.

Spices are also grown locally. Vanilla is grown on the island and the complex process involved in its production is fascinating and explained at the Domaine de St Aubin (page 168).

Coffee is grown on a small scale because it is in flower during the risky cyclone season. It can be found in the Chamarel area of the south, growing in sheltered places by the ridges of the hillsides.

Enough poultry and eggs are produced for domestic needs. Only about 5% of the meat eaten on the island is grown there. Cattle-rearing has been developed on some sugar estates as part of the diversification policy but much of the island's beef is imported from Australia, and Mauritius produces only 2% of its milk. Goat meat is popular and is produced commercially. Pigs and sheep are also raised, but in small numbers. Venison and wild boar are reared and frequently feature on the menus of upmarket hotels and restaurants.

Fishing The romantic sight of a small rowing boat, bobbing peacefully in a sun-drenched lagoon while its crew pull up a net full of fish, is a glimpse of the tradition behind an expanding fishing industry. Mauritius has 1.9 million km² of marine surface area, known as its Exclusive Economic Zone (EEZ). The government has plans to make the most of that asset and fishing is being hailed as the next big thing in the Mauritian economy. Thankfully, the government has stated its commitment to developing the fishing industry in a sustainable way.

Since the first settlers came to Mauritius, fishing has been confined to the lagoon and offshore lagoon areas. Most fishermen, being Creoles of small means, do not have the equipment or the inclination for fishing far beyond the reefs. They use traditional methods, with wooden (or sometimes fibreglass) boats of 6–7m in length. The crew fish with handlines, basket traps, seines, gill nets and harpoons, and bring their catch ashore at fish landing stations. These artisanal fishing grounds, the only source of fresh fish supply, spread over an area of 1,020km² for Mauritius and 1,380km² for Rodrigues. Fish is an important source of protein in the local diet and all the fish caught by artisanal fishermen is consumed on the island.

Banks fishery is conducted by motherships using small dories with outboard motors. The mother vessel remains at sea for 30 to 60 days with the dories bringing in their catch for gutting and freezing twice a day. The mothership's load is landed at the fishing port of Trou Fanfaron in Port Louis as frozen fish, much of it *Lethrinus mahsena* (or *Sanguineus*), known locally as Dame Berri.

The areas fished are the St Brandon, Nazareth and Saya de Malha banks on the Mauritius/Seychelles ridge, and the Chagos Bank around the Chagos Archipelago submarine plateaux, which lie 20–25m below the surface.

Tuna fishing for mainly skipjack (*Katsuwonus pelamis*) and yellow-fin tuna (*Thunnus albacares*) is a major industrial activity. Tuna canning started in 1972 when most of the fish had to be imported from the Maldives.

International big-game fishing competitions are held frequently and are popular with tourists who pay high fees to participate. The catch is mainly marlin (*makaira*) and swordfish (*Xiphias gladius*). Smoked marlin is a delicious delicacy served in most upmarket hotels and restaurants.

In 2012, Mauritius entered into agreements with the European Commission to allow vessels from the UK, Spain, Portugal, Italy and France to fish in Mauritian waters. It made a similar agreement with Japan.

Fish farming is an old tradition, using *barachois*, or artificial sea ponds, to breed finfish, crabs, freshwater prawns and oysters. The local oyster (*Crassostrea cuculata*) lives, in brackish water on rocks and mangrove roots. Mauritius is currently exploring further aquaculture opportunities, such as salmon and lobster farming, and encouraging local farmers to join forces with big businesses. Mauritius has also begun processing fish waste for the extraction of omega-3-rich oil for use in the pharmaceutical industry.

Development of the EEZ is at present confined to the expansion of all sections of the fishing industry. For the future, however, studies have revealed a wealth of minerals on the ocean floor and there is also the possibility of ocean thermal energy conversion. It all seems a long way from the tranquil sight, beloved by tourists, of a fisherman casting his net in a picturesque lagoon.

TOURISM

Tourism is one of the island's biggest earners, contributing around 25% to the GDP and supporting around 25% of total employment. Since earnings from tourism circulate very quickly into the economy, the impact is considerable. However, tourism has also been a factor in the increase in imports, especially foodstuffs.

In 2014, Mauritius attracted just over a million tourists. Of these, 23% came from France, 14% from Réunion and 11% from the UK. China, Russia and India are becoming increasingly important markets for the Mauritian tourism industry. In 2014, visitor numbers from China were up 51.2% on the previous year's figures to 63,365.

The popularity of Mauritius with French tourists is not only because of the common language; with cheap flights from France to Réunion and a separate ticket on to Mauritius, the French can reach Mauritius at much less expense than their European neighbours flying direct. For them, too, the cost of living in Mauritius is remarkably low compared with that of France and Réunion. Many – whether affluent middle-aged or youthful backpackers – visit as independent travellers and keep the non-package hotels and guesthouses and self-catering units in business.

Studies have been made on the careful development of tourism in the future and the prospects are, with careful management, that tourism will continue to be an asset and not a blight on the island. Traditionally, government policy has been to preserve Mauritius as an upmarket destination. The emphasis throughout the industry has been on quality rather than quantity. However, in recent years the global economic slowdown has taken its toll on the tourism industry and forced a change in approach. A few charter flights were allowed to operate, there was a growth in all-inclusive hotels and resorts began to offer special deals to encourage Mauritians to stay with them. The years 2014 and 2015 have seen a recovery in visitor numbers. The island retains the numerous assets that set it apart from its competitors, including beautiful beaches, luxurious hotels, exceptional service, a fascinating blend of cultures and a reputation as a relatively safe destination. These assets, if well managed, will stand it in good stead for the future.

The Mauritius Tourism Promotion Authority is responsible for marketing the country as a tourist destination. As well as offices in Port Louis, the MTPA has representatives in many countries worldwide (see page 42).

INFORMATION TECHNOLOGY In an attempt to reduce its dependence on sugar and textiles, in 2001 the government launched an ambitious project to make Mauritius a 'cyber island'. A few kilometres south of Port Louis, the Ebène Cyber City, the island's information technology hub, stands on land formerly used for sugar production. It provides an internet data backup centre and servers for web-hosting, e-commerce and financial transactions. It is also being promoted as a bridge between Africa and Asia, acting as a landing point for a high-speed submarine communications cable linking Malaysia with South Africa.

There has been considerable investment in IT education to ensure the population can benefit from the jobs that are created. Mauritius is seen as relatively secure and stable, which encourages companies to take advantage of the cyber city's facilities.

PEOPLE

With a population of around 1.3 million and the highest population density in Africa, you would expect Mauritius to feel crowded, but it doesn't. Although the main towns are frequently teeming with pedestrians and the roads jammed with cars, deserted areas of beach and forest are easy to find.

The population is relatively young, with a median age of 33.9 years. In 2015, life expectancy at birth was 71.94 years for a man and 79.03 years for a woman, and the population was growing at 0.64%.

Mauritius was uninhabited when it was colonised, so the population you see today is descended from colonists, slaves, indentured labourers and traders. The result is a rich blend of people of European, African, Indian and Chinese descent. It is potentially an explosive mixture, although few tensions are apparent to the visitor. Mauritians generally embrace their ethnic identity but have an admirable respect for the beliefs and lifestyles of others.

The 1968 constitution recognised four separate groups: Hindus, Muslims, Sino-Mauritians and the general population (those of African and European descent). The ethnic groups have traditionally been fairly distinctive in appearance, religion and language, although the distinctions are becoming blurred with mixed marriages becoming more common in recent years.

Indo-Mauritians Indian immigrants arrived in numbers under the indentured labour system, although some came later from the Indian subcontinent. By 1861, the Indian population outnumbered the whites and Creoles by 192,634 to 117,416, forming the ethnic and cultural majority. They now make up 68% of the population.

There are two major groups by religious definition: Hindus (some of whom are actually Tamils) and Muslims. Many of the Muslims migrated independently from India and Pakistan as traders.

To confuse the situation, intermarriage has resulted in an Indo-Mauritian element being introduced into the Creole (Christian) population as well.

As well as forming the backbone of the labouring and agricultural communities, the Indo-Mauritians have developed through a history of industrial and political agitation to take vital roles in the economic and political life of the island.

Creoles Creoles are people of mixed African and European origin, and the majority are Roman Catholic. They are a diverse group, the result of intermarriage that cuts across class and ethnic considerations. They constitute around 27% of the total population and form a large working class. Creole Mauritians face the greatest hardships: poverty affects the Creole population far more than any other group, they are under-represented in politics, administration and business, and report widespread discrimination. Their language, Creole, is the lingua franca of the entire population, spoken by all races.

Sino-Mauritians Mauritians of Chinese origin are a small but ubiquitous ethnic community forming about 3% of the population; the majority are Hakka Chinese. While some Chinese were taken forcibly to Mauritius from Sumatra by the French in the 1740s, a greater number arrived voluntarily in the late 18th and 19th centuries, setting up shops and small businesses.

Today Chinese Mauritians own many of the island's retail outlets and restaurants, and they are reported to be the second-wealthiest ethnic group behind the Franco-Mauritians. The Chinese have made a notable contribution to the island's cuisine, and Chinese food can be found in private homes, restaurants and food stalls. Most Chinese Mauritians identify Creole as their primary language; fewer than 25% speak a Chinese language at home.

The island's Chinese influence is concentrated around Chinatown in Port Louis (page 102).

Franco-Mauritians The white population is descended from European, mostly French, settlers. Curiously, despite 158 years of British presence, only a handful of families think of themselves as Anglo-Mauritian. Franco-Mauritians make up only around 2% of the population but hold much of the island's private wealth and dominate the business world.

LANGUAGE

The official language of Mauritius is English, although most Mauritians are more comfortable speaking French. Both English and French are compulsory in the school system. The language of the people, however, is Mauritian Creole (Kreol Morisyen).

Although the Mauritians working in the tourism industry speak good English, the English-speaking visitor should not count on being understood everywhere on the island. English is the medium of teaching in schools and the working language of government and business, but beyond school and work it is rarely used.

French is spoken at home by about 4% of Mauritians. It is used in polite and formal circumstances, although not at government level. The daily newspapers are predominantly in French with occasional articles in English and Creole.

Creole is the lingua franca of Mauritius, understood and spoken by all Mauritians. It is the mother tongue of about 87% of the population but, amazingly, it was not until 2011, after much debate, that Creole was added as an optional subject to the primary school curriculum.

Creole is a French-based patois, and borrows most of its vocabulary from that tongue, although pronunciation is phonetic, unlike French. It also incorporates some English, African and Malagasy words, as well as a few from Chinese and Arabic languages. It evolved from the pidgin used by slaves to communicate with their French masters in the 18th century. Its popularity stems from the ease with which it can be learnt. Since the African population was disinclined to learn Indian

or Chinese languages, the new immigrants of the 19th century took to Creole as a simple means of communication.

Creole's lowly origins have caused the language to be treated with contempt in the past but its unifying value as the one language that all Mauritians speak and understand is clear. For many years there was no official written form of the language, but in 2011 and 2012 the government sought to standardise Creole by publishing a dictionary and grammar guide.

French-based Creole languages are spoken by around seven million people worldwide, mostly in the Caribbean and Indian Ocean, but each of the languages is slightly different. Even the Creole of neighbouring Réunion is not identical to that of Mauritius. Mauritian Creole is, however, closely related to Seychellois Creole, Rodriguan Creole and Chagossian Creole.

For the visitor wanting to speak Creole, there are several locally printed Creole phrasebooks on sale in Mauritius. It is an attractive, expressive language, often spoken by locals at high speed and with a good deal of emotion. (For useful phrases, see page 362.)

Mauritius has successfully preserved numerous ancestral languages. Hindi is spoken by many Indo-Mauritians; it is the medium for religious ceremonies and is looked on as a sign of education and prestige. The Indian equivalent of Creole is Bhojpuri, although its usage is in decline and it is now spoken by just 5% of the population. Other Indian languages spoken as mother tongues are Urdu, Telegu, Tamil and Marathi.

Less than 25% of the Chinese community speak Chinese languages, mostly Hakka and Cantonese.

RELIGION

There are nearly 90 different religious denominations represented in Mauritius. Since there is complete freedom of religion, new sects or groupings have emerged within the main religions of Hinduism, Christianity and Islam. Throughout Mauritius there are Gothic-style churches, high-domed temples, minareted mosques and ornate pagodas in the most unlikely places – the middle of a sugarcane field, by the racecourse or on the beach – testifying to the strong Mauritian belief in religion.

HINDUISM About 52% of Mauritians are followers of one of the many Hindu sects, the majority being Sanatanists, or orthodox Hindus.

Devout Hindus proclaim their faith with small shrines and red or white pennants fluttering outside their homes. Several villages have Hindu temples, the largest being at Triolet. Saints of other religions, especially the Roman Catholic Père Laval, whose shrine is at Sainte-Croix, are also worshipped by Mauritian Hindus.

Local Tamils have their own religion which has evolved since 1771, when the French granted permission for a Tamil temple in Port Louis. The reformist movement of Arya Samaj, in which worship is of the spirit Brahma and not of statues or idols, took hold from 1910, when the first 'Samaj' was opened in Port Louis. Tamils sometimes indulge in spectacular forms of worship in honour of different deities, such as fire-walking and piercing their flesh with enormous needles during Thaipoosam Cavadee (see pages 40 and 69). As with Christianity, there is a variety of sects including Kabir Panthis, a reformist group, Rabidass, and the Hare Rama Krishna sect.

CHRISTIANITY Christianity was the first religion in Mauritius and is now the religion both of the Creole and white population and of more than 80% of the Sino-Mauritians.

Roman Catholicism became the official religion of the Ile de France in 1721, spreading with the French conversion of their slaves and still permitted to flourish after the British arrived. There is a Roman Catholic cathedral, St Louis, in Port Louis.

Anglicans, Presbyterians and the evangelical Christian religions such as the Assembly of God and Adventists all play a part in society, as do at least a dozen other denominations including Jehovah's Witnesses and Methodists.

Christianity is the second-largest faith in the country, followed by around 28% of the population. In Rodrigues, 97% of the population is Roman Catholic.

ISLAM The Muslims of Mauritius form just over 17% of the total population. The majority are Sunni Muslims; the Shi'ite Muslims are very few and are subdivided into groups. One is the Cocknies from Cochin in the southwest of India, who came as boatbuilders to Mauritius. Since intermarrying with Creoles they have created a people known as Creole Lascars. In recent years a growing number of Creoles have converted to Islam. The best-known mosque in Mauritius is the Jummah (Friday) Mosque in Port Louis, which dates from 1850.

CHINESE RELIGIONS The Chinese religions are almost dying out since the majority of Sino-Mauritians have embraced Roman Catholicism. Buddhism is practised by just 0.4% of the population.

The first Chinese temple was opened in Port Louis in 1846. Other temples have since been opened by the Cantonese Nam Shun Fooye Koon society and the Hakka Heeh Foh society.

EDUCATION

The education system in Mauritius is based on the British model and is free up to university level. Education is compulsory up to the age of 16 and school transport is free. School attendance rates are high and the country's literacy rate is very respectable at almost 90%.

The majority of schools are state-run, but a significant number are controlled by the Roman Catholic Education Authority and the Hindu Education Authority.

Lessons are conducted mostly in English. French is compulsory and pupils also have the option to learn any of the languages spoken in Mauritius. In 2011, the government introduced Creole in primary schools. The School Certificate (O-level) and Higher School Certificate (A-level) examinations are prepared and marked by the University of Cambridge.

The University of Mauritius at Le Réduit was opened in 1965. Its original aim was to train civil servants in preparation for independence, but it has since expanded to offer faculties as diverse as ocean studies, agriculture, engineering and information technology. The University of Technology at Pointe aux Sables, founded in 2000, provides training in the areas considered to be of greatest importance to the island's economic development, such as technology, health sciences, business management and sustainable development and tourism. Many Mauritians strive to study at universities overseas, particularly in the UK, France and Australia.

CULTURE

Each of Mauritius's ethnic groups and religions brings its own unique qualities to the island's rich and varied culture. An exciting variety of cuisine, musical styles and languages are a part of everyday life.

MUSIC Mauritians grow up with music and dancing playing an important role in their lives: at family gatherings, festivals and celebrations.

Ubiquitous is the *séga* (pronounced 'say-ga'), which evolved from the spontaneous dances of African and Malagasy slaves. At night, after a day's toiling in the cane fields, slaves used improvised instruments to create a primitive music to which they could dance and forget their woes. At times, this meant defying their masters' prohibition of music and dancing, which aimed to sever the slaves from their African and Malagasy roots.

Songs were often about the slaves' plight and were highly critical of their masters. Girls danced to songs composed and sung by their admirers while the spectators encouraged them with hand clapping, foot stomping and chanting. The more impassioned the lyrics, the more heated the music and the more tempestuous the dancing.

On Mauritius's accession to independence, *séga* was adopted as the national dance and it has been flourishing and evolving ever since. Traditional *séga* is a courtship drama, beginning slowly with couples dancing apart from each other. As the beat intensifies, they shuffle closer together, hips swinging in time, but they never quite touch. The girl will sink to her knees at the cry of *en bas*, leaning back in the manner of a limbo dancer passing under a pole. What makes *séga* unique is the combination of musical influences it has absorbed over the centuries, until it has assumed its own immediately recognisable beat. Like the *ka-danse* or *zouk* music of the French West Indies, also sung in Creole patois, it has a similarity to Latin American music in its jaunty rhythms. *Séga* is as prolific on Rodrigues and Réunion as it is in Mauritius, but each of the islands has developed its own distinctive version.

Descendants of the primitive instruments used by the slaves can still be seen in *séga* bands today. Vital to *séga* is the distinctive drumbeat provided by the *ravane*, a goatskin tambourine. The *maravane* is a container (either wooden or fashioned from a gourd) filled with seeds or pebbles, which is shaken like the maracas. A triangle beaten with vigour adds a carillon voice echo.

Séga is a fantastic dance with a wonderful, joyful music that seizes spectators with an urge to join in, which they are encouraged to do at hotel performances. At hotel shows, the men will usually wear the traditional pedal pushers and a colourful shirt, while the women wear a billowing skirt.

Kaya, the popular Creole singer who was found dead in a police cell in February 1999, pioneered a new musical style in the late 1980s: *séggae*, a blend of reggae and *séga*. Kaya's work has been continued by his fellow Creole musicians and the mellow *séggae* is now popular throughout the western Indian Ocean islands (see box, page 185).

ARCHITECTURE Creole architecture can be appreciated both in small, simple dwellings, which are often painted in bright colours, and in grand colonial mansions, such as Eureka (page 200) and Château de Labourdonnais (page 137). A charming characteristic feature of such buildings is the carved wooden or metal fringes that decorate the roof, the *lambrequin*. Colonial-era buildings were designed to suit the tropical climate with high ceilings, window shutters and wide wrap-around verandas lined with ornate wrought-iron railings. Contemporary architecture in Mauritius mostly finds expression in new hotels since new houses tend to be standard, cyclone-proof concrete boxes. Many of the hotels are inspired by traditional architecture and plenty incorporate skilfully constructed thatched roofs.

2

Practical Information

WHEN TO VISIT

Mauritius's tropical climate means it offers warmth all year round; summer is hot and wet (November to April), winter is warm and dry (May to October).

The one time when it is not ideal to visit is January–March, when cyclones are most likely to occur. They don't happen every year but the cyclonic rains, which can last for several days, are an annual event and you could find yourself confined to the indoors for a portion of your stay. (See pages 4–5 for more information on cyclones.)

The high season for tourism, when holiday packages cost more, is November to early January. Hefty peak-season supplements are charged over Christmas and Easter. Flights should be less crowded outside European school holiday periods and hotels are noticeably so.

The weather is cooler from June to September with the temperature at sea level being about 22°C, and it can be windy at this time, more so on the east coast than the west. Package holiday prices are lower and hotels tend to host conference and incentive groups. September to October is perhaps one of the best times to travel as the weather is good but peak-season prices and crowds have not yet set in.

If climate is not the governing factor, choose when to visit according to your interests. For instance, the horse-racing season is from May to late November and the best deep-sea fishing and diving is from November to May. December is when local fruits are in abundance. You may like to time your visit to coincide with one or more of the island's many colourful festivals – pages 67–70.

There are many websites which offer useful tips and information to help you prepare for your visit. For details, see page 366.

HIGHLIGHTS

NATURAL HISTORY Natural history enthusiasts and hikers should head to the Black River Gorges National Park. There are hiking trails of varying difficulty, where glimpses of the rare pink pigeon and Mauritius kestrel are possible. Immensely worthwhile is a visit is Ile aux Aigrettes, a coral island off the south coast, which the Mauritian Wildlife Foundation is working hard to restore to its natural state.

HERITAGE One of the island's most impressive manmade attractions is **L'Aventure du Sucre** (Sugar World), a former sugar factory which has been transformed into a well-organised, modern museum telling the story of the industry on which the island was built. Its display on the island's history as a whole is one of the best in Mauritius. Equally fascinating are guided tours of the **Bois Chéri Tea Factory**, which are followed by a tasting. The tour can also be done as part of **La Route du Thé** (The Tea Route), which takes in three sites linked to the Bois Chéri Tea Estate.

Mauritius is home to two UNESCO World Heritage Sites: **Aapravasi Ghat**, the immigration depot built in 1849 to receive indentured labourers in Port Louis, and **Le Morne**, the distinctive mountain in the southwest of the island that is regarded as a symbol of resistance to slavery.

CULTURE Mauritius's delightful mixture of ethnicities provides a wealth of opportunities to experience local **culture**, and an abundance of cultures means an abundance of **festivals**. Most organised tours will include a stop at **Grand Bassin**, where visitors can learn about this sacred Hindu lake and watch the worshippers who flock to its shores. The lake really comes into its own during the Hindu festivals of **Ganesh Chaturthi** and **Maha Shivaratree**. The Tamil festivals are particularly colourful and fascinating – if you have a chance to watch **fire walking** or the **Thaipoosam Cavadee** pilgrimage, don't miss it. The island's wonderful **food** reflects the ethnic diversity of the population, and delicious meals showcasing local ingredients can be enjoyed equally in the fancy restaurants of upmarket hotels or at tiny, unassuming roadside stalls. Most hotels provide evening entertainment featuring local music and dance, in particular the fabulously energetic *séga*.

BEACHES I couldn't write about the highlights of Mauritius without mentioning the beaches – and, yes they really are as good as they look in the holiday brochures. Belle Mare, Trou aux Biches and Flic en Flac are considered to be among the island's finest.

Beyond the beaches all manner of **watersports** are on offer, from kayaking to kitesurfing. Non-motorised watersports may well be included in your accommodation package. Under the waves there are colourful coral reefs and a wealth of **diving and snorkelling sites**. For those who wish to explore the underwater world without getting wet, there are **submersible vessels** (classic submarines and ingenious underwater scooters) – a great option for children and non-divers.

Sailing, **deep-sea fishing** and **dolphin-watching** cruises are all popular with visitors.

SHOPPING A visit to one of the island's lively **markets** is fascinating – Port Louis's daily market is by far the largest but Mahébourg's Monday market also has plenty of variety. The hustle and bustle amidst the colourful displays of fruit, vegetables, spices and souvenirs represents an unforgettable snapshot of everyday life in the island's towns. For a shopping experience of a different kind, visit one of the upmarket **shopping centres** where tourists are tempted at every turn by diamonds, jewellery, clothing, model ships and duty-free prices (see pages 70–3).

RODRIGUES A trip to the island of Rodrigues is an ideal add-on to a stay in Mauritius. It is not a luxury holiday destination but an opportunity to stray well off the beaten track and retreat into a world where simplicity rules.

SUGGESTED ITINERARIES

Most people who visit Mauritius are seeking relaxation rather than adventure. However, there is plenty to see and around two weeks will allow you enough time to wind down and relax, as well as to explore some of the elements that make Mauritius distinctive. Mauritius is small enough that you can base yourself in one place and explore by taking day trips, either on organised tours, with a local driver, or in a hire car. For a memorable contrast, consider adding a few days in Rodrigues.

PORT LOUIS AND NORTHERN MAURITIUS A day will give you ample time to visit the island's invariably hectic capital, Port Louis, which is best explored on foot, making sure that you stop in at the bustling market, the waterfront, Aapravasi Ghat (where indentured labourers were processed) and your pick of the various museums.

You can combine a trip to Port Louis with contrastingly peaceful visits to the nearby Sir Seewoosagur Ramgoolam Botanic Gardens and the historic Château de Labourdonnais, a renovated Creole mansion. Also in the area is L'Aventure du Sucre, a fascinating museum that tells the story of the sugar industry. The north (at Mont Choisy) is where you can take a submarine or underwater scooter to view the coral reef at the edge of the lagoon (pages 89–90). Mont Choisy has a good beach, as does nearby Trou aux Biches, and while in the area, you can visit the tourist resort of Grand Baie. As you potter along the coast, stop in at Cap Malheureux to see the distinctive red church featured in so many postcards.

A catamaran cruise out to the islands off the north will take the best part of a day and provides some excellent snorkelling opportunities.

EASTERN MAURITIUS Less developed than the north, the east has some fabulous beaches, such as Belle Mare, and some of the island's finest golf courses. This coast is popular for sailing excursions, which typically take in the tourist trap of Ile aux Cerfs.

SOUTHERN MAURITIUS Wherever you are staying on the island, the south is worth a visit. It cleverly combines unspoilt scenery and diverse manmade attractions. Starting in the southeast, drop in to the historic town of Mahébourg, which hosts a lively Monday market. Nearby is the beautifully simple Rault Biscuit Factory, where manioc biscuits are made the old-fashioned way over fires fuelled by sugarcane.

Just south of Mahébourg you can snorkel in the impossibly turquoise waters within the protected marine reserve of Blue Bay and take a trip to Ile aux Aigrettes, a Mauritian Wildlife Foundation nature reserve. Back on the mainland is Vallée de Ferney, another nature reserve, which you can explore on foot or by 4x4.

Continuing along the south coast, La Vanille Réserve des Mascareignes is primarily a crocodile farm but is home to giant Aldabra tortoises, Rodrigues fruit bats and other wildlife from the region.

Nearby St Aubin, a colonial house built in 1819 is a good spot for lunch and you can take tours explaining the production of vanilla, sugar and rum.

Inland lie tea plantations and the unmissable Bois Chéri Tea Factory, which offers guided tours and tea tastings. From there it is a short drive to the sacred lake at Grand Bassin, a cultural highlight of the south.

WESTERN MAURITIUS In the southwest corner of the island is a flat-topped 556m rock crag known as Le Morne Brabant, which sits on a peninsula of the same name. It served as a refuge for runaway slaves in the 19th century and, as a result, has earned World Heritage Site status.

The west has excellent beaches, notably the ever-popular Flic en Flac, and is the best part of the island for deep-sea fishing. Casela World of Adventures has all manner of attractions, the best of which is Safari Adventures with its interactive big-cat experiences. You really need to set aside the bulk of a day for Casela, and there is a good restaurant there for lunch.

There are several places on the island where you can ride a horse along the beach and Haras du Morne offers that unforgettable experience in the west.

Heading inland towards Chamarel takes you through agricultural land, where sugarcane and pineapples cover the hillsides. The Rhumerie de Chamarel provides an insight into the rum-making process. From there it is a short drive to the Black River Gorges National Park and Grand Bassin.

CENTRAL MAURITIUS The island's largest nature reserve, the Black River Gorges National Park, is popular for hiking and is easily accessed from the south and the west of the island. Although the centre of the island is where most of the population lives, it holds the least interest for visitors. For most tourists, the only reason to venture to the traffic-heavy centre is to pick up a bargain at the market in Quatre Bornes.

TOURIST INFORMATION

The **Mauritius Tourism Promotion Authority (MTPA)** is the best source of information both prior to your trip and during it. It publishes information booklets on the island and has a website packed with useful information and links.

🖿 **MTPA Head Office** 4th Fl, Victoria Hse, Saint Louis St, Port Louis; ☎ 210 1545; e mtpa@intnet. mu; www.tourism-mauritius.mu. The MTPA has an information desk at the airport in Plaisance (☎ 637 3635).

For tourist information during your stay in Mauritius, you can call the tourism 24-hour information line (☎ *152*), which provides details of exchange rates, night-duty pharmacies, events, restaurants, etc in English and French. Unfortunately, the MTPA no longer operates tourist information centres on the island. However, your hotel or ground handler should be able to provide information on attractions and activities, and many of the resorts have tour operator desks on site, where you can book excursions.

A free tourist information magazine, *Islandinfo*, is published monthly and is found in most hotels, tourist attractions and at the airport. *Kozé* is a free publication listing what's on in terms of films, concerts, exhibitions, etc and is widely available.

TOUR OPERATORS

Below is a non-exhaustive list of tour operators that feature Mauritius:

UK
Aardvark Safaris RBL Hse, Ordnance Rd, Tidworth, Hampshire SP9 7QD; ☎ +44 1980 849160; e mail@aardvarksafaris.co.uk; www. aardvarksafaris.co.uk
Beachcomber Tours Direction Hse, 186 High St, Guildford, Surrey GU1 3HW; ☎ +44 1483 367494; www.beachcombertours.co.uk
Elegant Resorts Elegant Hse, Sandpiper Way, Chester Business Park, Chester CH4 9QE; ☎ +44 1244 897881; e enquiries@elegantresorts.co.uk; www.elegantresorts.co.uk
Rainbow Tours 2nd Fl, Layden Hse, 76–86 Turnmill St, London EC1M 5QU; ☎ +44 20 7666 1250; e info@rainbowtours.co.uk; www.rainbowtours. co.uk. Also runs tours to Rodrigues & Réunion.

Tribes Travel The Old Dairy, Wood Farm, Ipswich Rd, Otley, Suffolk IP6 9JW; ☎ +44 1473 890499; www.tribes.co.uk. Also runs tours to Rodrigues.

AUSTRALIA
Abercrombie & Kent Level 3, 290 Coventry St, South Melbourne, VIC 3205; ☎ +61 3 9536 1800; e contact@abercrombiekent.com.au; www. abercrombiekent.com.au
Above & Beyond 10/541 Church St, North Paramatta, NSW 2151; ☎ +61 1300 362166; e sales@aboveandbeyondholidays.com.au; www.aboveandbeyondholidays.com.au. Also runs tours to Rodrigues & Réunion.

Journeys Africa 9 Bramwell Ct, Cashmere, QLD 4500; ✆+61 1800 624268; e info@journeysafrica. com.au; www.journeysafrica.com.au. Also runs tours to Rodrigues & Réunion.

FRANCE
Exotismes 164 Rue Albert Einstein, Marseille 13013; ✆+33 8 26 96 50 00; e information@ exotismes.com; www.exotismes.fr. Also runs tours to Rodrigues & Réunion.
Havas Voyages Various offices; www.havas-voyages.fr
Kuoni Various offices; www.kuoni.fr. Also runs tours to Réunion.
Le Cercle des Vacances 4 Rue Gomboust, Paris 75001; ✆+ 33 1 40 15 15 01; www. cercledesvacancesluxury.com
Nouvelles Frontières Various offices; www. nouvelles-frontieres.fr. Also runs tours to Rodrigues & Réunion.
Passion des Iles Various offices; ✆+33 8 26 28 07 80; www.passiondesiles.com. Also runs tours to Rodrigues & Réunion.
Tropicalement vôtre 43 Rue Basfoi, Paris 75011; ✆+ 33 1 43 70 99 55; 96 Rue Pierre Corneille, Lyon 69003; ✆+33 4 72 32 26 89; www.tropicalement-votre.com. Also runs tours to Rodrigues & Réunion.

GERMANY
Dertour Various offices; ✆+49 69 153 22 55 33; e service@dertour.de; www.dertour.de. Also runs tours to Rodrigues & Réunion.

Escape Tours Hohenzollernstrasse 112, D-80796 Munich; ✆+49 89 8299 480; e info@escape-tours. de; www.escape-tours.de
Trauminsel Reisen Summerstrasse 8, D-82211, Herrsching; ✆+49 81 529 3190; e info@ trauminselreisen.de; www.trauminselreisen.de. Also runs tours to Rodrigues & Réunion.

ITALY
Best Tour Various offices; www.besttoursitalia.it. Also runs tours to Rodrigues & Réunion.
Idee Per Viaggiare Via Leonetto Capiello, 14 – 00125 Rome; ✆+39 6 520 981; e info@ ideeperviaggiare.it; www.ideeperviaggiare.it. Also runs tours to Rodrigues.

SOUTH AFRICA
Pentravel Various offices; www.pentravel.co.za. Also runs tours to Rodrigues.
True Blue Travel Adventures 30 Marine Dr, Paarden Eiland, Cape Town; ✆+27 21 510 0503; e info@truebluetravel.co.za; www.truebluetravel. co.za. Also runs tours to Rodrigues.

US
Aardvark Safaris 312 South Cedros Av, Suite 315, Solana Beach, CA 92075; ✆+1 858 523 9000; e info@aardvarksafaris.com; www.aardvarksafaris. com. Also runs tours to Rodrigues.
African Travel Inc 330 North Bd, Suite 950, Glendale CA 91230; ✆+1 800 421 8907; e info@ africantravelinc.com; www.africantravelinc.com

RED TAPE

ENTRY REQUIREMENTS To enter Mauritius, you will need a passport valid for the full duration of your stay, proof of a return or onward ticket and the address of confirmed accommodation on the island.

Tourists travelling on passports from the following countries are among those who do not require a visa: the UK, other European Union countries, the US, Canada, Australia, New Zealand, Israel, Botswana, South Africa, Zambia, Zimbabwe, Norway, Sweden, India, Russia and China. Holders of passports from certain other countries are granted stays of a limited duration on arrival; for instance, visitors from Comoros and Madagascar are granted two weeks, while visitors from many South American and African countries are granted 60 days. For those travelling on passports from some other countries, a visa is required prior to travel; for instance, Pakistan, Philippines, Indonesia, Mali, Somalia and Sri Lanka. For information on business visits, see pages 77–9. Entry requirements change, so please check the MTPA website (*www.tourism-mauritius.mu*) or the Passport and Immigration Office website (*http://passport.govmu.org*).

VISA ISSUE Visas can be obtained from Mauritian embassies and high commissions (see pages 46–7). Visa application forms are available online from the Passport and Immigration Office (*http://passport.govmu.org*). In addition to the form, you will need to send two recent passport-sized photographs and a photocopy of the data pages of your passport.

IMMIGRATION During your flight to Mauritius you should be given an international embarkation/disembarkation card and a health-related form. These need to be filled in before you join the immigration queue. Have them ready, together with your return air ticket and passport. The process may require some patience on your part.

You will be required to provide the address where you intend to stay or at least the name of your hotel. If you are hoping to camp bear in mind that there are no official campsites and camping is discouraged. You must have a return air ticket otherwise you may be asked to purchase one on the spot. You may also be asked to provide proof that you have sufficient funds to cover your stay. The amount of money that you have in your possession is not the sole criterion: your access to funds in an emergency is important too. According to the MTPA, you will be expected to have at least US$100 (around £64) per night.

The visitor who comes on a package holiday does not raise the same doubts that independent travellers do because the package tourist has prepaid accommodation and is under the auspices of the tour company. However, providing the independent traveller is a genuine tourist who will not engage in 'profit-making activities', which is forbidden, entry is usually granted after a few questions at the desk.

The second desk you come to is manned by a Ministry of Health and Quality of Life official. You will need to hand over the health form you filled in on the aircraft and you may be asked whether you are carrying any plant or animal material and whether you have visited a farm recently. This is part of the continual campaign to prevent malaria returning to Mauritius. If you have come from a malaria-infected country you could be asked to give a blood sample for precautionary analysis within a few days of your arrival.

CUSTOMS The red and green channel system operates in Mauritius but even if you opt for the green channel, you may be questioned before being allowed through. Up-to-date information on the regulations and allowances is available on the website of the Mauritius Revenue Authority (*www.mra.mu*).

Incoming visitors aged 16 and over are allowed to import free of duty:

Tobacco	up to 250g
Spirits	1 litre
Wine/beer	2 litres of wine, ale or beer
Perfume	10cl of perfume and 25cl of eau de toilette
Goods for personal use	up to the value of Rs15,000 (Mauritian passport holder), Rs7,500 (Mauritian passport holder under 12 years of age), Rs7,500 (foreign passport holder)

Restricted and prohibited goods A permit is required for the following goods: firearms and ammunition, weapons, plant material, animals and animal products. It is illegal to import or possess cigarette papers. Importation of obscene literature and pornography is prohibited.

Prescription drugs If you are carrying prescription drugs, they may be illegal for importing into Mauritius. You will need to keep them in the manufacturer's container with your prescription. You will need to have no more than three months' supply for prescription medication and no more than one month's supply for controlled drugs. Be prepared to present them for inspection to the customs officials.

Plants and animals All plants, plant material, seeds, soil, and animal material must be declared to customs and will be subject to inspection. This includes timber and handicrafts made from plant or animal material.

An import permit must be obtained in advance from the Ministry of Agro-Industry and Food Security for the importation of plants or plant parts. Applications for a permit are made using a form which can be downloaded from the ministry's website (*www.agriculture.govmu.org*) and there is a fee of Rs50 per permit. Permits are valid for four months.

To import a pet you will need to apply for a permit via the Veterinary Service of the Ministry of Agro-Industry and Food Security (✆ 454 1016; e *moa-dvs@govmu. org; www.agriculture.govmu.org*). Pets imported to Mauritius will be subject to quarantine; the period is dependent on the country of origin and the species. The cost of quarantine is met by the importer, along with import and veterinary fees.

Money Amounts of Rs500,000 (£9,000) or greater in any currency or in bearer negotiable instruments must be declared.

Drugs The penalties for trafficking drugs of any kind are severe. Don't risk it.

STAYING ON
Visa extensions Each application to stay longer than the period written by the immigration officer in a visitor's passport is treated according to the individual visitor's circumstances.

Applications are dealt with by the Passport and Immigration Office (*Sterling Hse, 9–11 Lislet Geoffrey St, Port Louis;* ✆ *210 9312;* e *piomain@mail.gov.mu; http:// passport.govmu.org;* ⊕ *09.00–14.30 Mon–Fri, 09.00–11.00 Sat*). A visa extension application form is available on the Passport and Immigration Office website. You will need supporting documentation for your application, including: a photocopy of the biographical data pages of your passport and the page containing the arrival stamp, a copy of an onward ticket, a bank statement, proof of a hotel booking or a letter from a local sponsor. If you are sponsored by a Mauritian, they will need to submit a letter of sponsorship containing their details and the nature of their relationship to you, their national identity card and a copy of a utility bill.

Work permits Foreigners are allowed to work in Mauritius only if they have a valid work permit, but the government has made every effort to simplify the process as it recognises the benefits of both foreign investment and foreign expertise. The main criteria are that the applicant for the work permit should possess the skills, qualifications and expertise for the role, should normally be aged between 20 and 60 years, and the employer should have made efforts to recruit suitably qualified staff locally. The applicant's passport needs to be valid for at least six months. Permits are usually granted for a maximum of four years.

The potential employer applies for the permit and pays the fee, which rises for each year of employment. Applications can be made online via the e-work permit system (*http://workpermit.mu*).

Residence permits If applying for a work permit (investor, professional or self-employed), you apply for a residence permit at the same time and receive what is called an 'occupation permit' to allow you to live and work in Mauritius.

There are several categories of people who are eligible for an occupation permit. Investor: a foreigner who invests a minimum of US$100,000 and is a shareholder and a director in a company incorporated in Mauritius. Professional: an expatriate employed by a company in Mauritius and earning a basic salary exceeding Rs60,000 per month (Rs30,000 for professionals in the ICT sector). Self-employed: a foreigner operating a one-person business and working exclusively for his/her own account is eligible upon an initial transfer of US$35,000 to Mauritius.

To be eligible for a residency permit as a retired non-citizen, you need to be at least 50 years of age and agree to transfer to your bank account in Mauritius a minimum of US$40,000 (£25,800) annually. To be considered a resident for tax purposes you need to spend at least 183 days per calendar year in Mauritius.

If you have had an occupation permit for three years or a retired non-citizen residency permit for three years, and you meet certain financial criteria, you can apply for a permanent residency permit. The permit is valid for ten years but it can be renewed provided you continue to meet the criteria. Foreigners who invest US$500,000 (£323,000) or more in a qualifying industry (such as agriculture, fisheries, banking or construction) are also eligible to apply for permanent residency. The application will be considered in conjunction with the proposed investment project.

Information on living, working, retiring and investing in Mauritius, and the various application forms, are available from the Board of Investment (*www. investmauritius.com*).

Integrated Resort Schemes/Real Estate Scheme
Since 2002, non-Mauritian individuals and companies have been allowed to purchase properties that are part of an Integrated Resort Scheme (IRS). An IRS must have certain characteristics, but broadly speaking, in return for purchasing a luxury villa, which is part of an IRS and costs a minimum of US$500,000, the individual is entitled to acquire Mauritian residence for the duration of the villa ownership. There is no restriction on the length of time that the villa can be rented out. IRS are not usually built on the beachfront but they are finished to a high standard and have extensive facilities. As well as luxury villas, they typically have restaurants, shops, swimming pools and a golf course. Maintenance, gardening and security are usually included. In 2007, the Government of Mauritius announced that the IRS concept would be extended to small landowners under a new scheme called the Real Estate Scheme (RES). This is essentially a slimmed-down version of the IRS with smaller land sizes (up to 10ha) and no minimum investment amount. Properties for sale are listed on www.lexpressproperty.com.

EMBASSIES, HIGH COMMISSIONS AND CONSULATES

Embassies, high commissions and consulates can provide information on Mauritius and deal with visa or work permit enquiries. (See also pages 77–9.) A full list of Mauritian embassies and high commissions around the world as well as embassies, high commissions and consulates in Mauritius, some of which are listed below, can be found at www.embassypages.com/mauritius.

IN MAURITIUS
Australia (High Commission) 2nd Fl, Rogers Hse, 5 President John F Kennedy St, Port Louis; 208 1700; e ahc.portlouis@dfat.gov.au; www.mauritius.embassy.gov.au

France (Embassy) 14 St Georges St, Port Louis; 202 0100; e ambafr@intnet.mu; www.ambafrance-mu.org

South Africa (High Commission) 1163 Pretorius St, Hatfield 0083, Pretoria; +27 12 342 1283; e mhcpta@mweb.co.za

US (Embassy) 4th Fl, Rogers Hse, 5 President John F Kennedy St, Port Louis; 202 4400; e usembass@intnet.mu

UK (High Commission) 7th Fl, Les Cascades Bldg, Edith Cavell St, Port Louis; 202 9400; e bhc@intnet.mu

GETTING THERE AND AWAY

A package including flights and hotel accommodation is one of the most cost-efficient and popular ways of visiting Mauritius. Many tour operators offer visits to Mauritius in combination with another destination; it is an ideal spot for a week's relaxation after a safari in Africa. Booking your flights and accommodation as a package need not restrict your freedom to explore the island.

BY AIR

From Europe It takes around 12 hours to fly to Mauritius direct from Europe. The fact that it is a long way and that there are no cheap charter flights has helped Mauritius preserve the qualities that make it attractive.

UK Air Mauritius and British Airways each offer non-stop flights from London. Air Mauritius operates daily flights for much of the year and several flights per week during low season. British Airways operates several flights per week. Emirates offers daily flights via Dubai, where you can choose to stop over. It is also possible to fly via Paris with Air France.

France Air Mauritius and Air France operate frequent flights from Paris Charles de Gaulle. Alternatively, you can fly via Réunion with Air France or Air Austral.

Germany Air Mauritius offers frequent flights from Frankfurt, Düsseldorf and Munich via Paris Charles de Gaulle. Condor operates direct flights from Frankfurt.

Italy Meridiana offers flights between Mauritius and Milan. Air Mauritius offers flights to many European cities via Paris Charles de Gaulle using codeshare arrangements with various airlines.

From Africa The closest mainland gateways are those in Africa. It takes around 4 hours to fly from Nairobi, Durban or Johannesburg to Mauritius and around 5 hours from Cape Town. From **Johannesburg**, **Durban** and **Cape Town** there are flights by Air Mauritius and South African Airways. British Airways also flies from Cape Town to Mauritius via Johannesburg. Air Mauritius operates flights from **Nairobi**. Regular Air Mauritius and Air Madagascar flights link **Madagascar** and Mauritius; flight time to Antananarivo is just under 2 hours.

From other Indian Ocean islands Air Mauritius offers several flights a day between **Réunion** (Roland Garros and Pierrefonds) and Mauritius; flight time is around 45 minutes from Roland Garros and 55 minutes from Pierrefonds. Air Austral also operates regular flights on the Mauritius–Réunion route. Air Mauritius flies several times a day between Mauritius and **Rodrigues** (flight time around 1 hour 30 minutes).

From the US/Canada There are no direct flights between North America and Mauritius. The best option is usually to fly via London or Paris.

From Australia Air Mauritius operates direct flights from **Perth** with a flight time of around 8 hours 30 minutes, but the return flight is usually at least an hour shorter. You can connect to other Australian cities on local carriers under codeshare arrangements. Emirates via Dubai is another option but takes considerably longer.

From the Middle East Air Mauritius operates direct flights in a codeshare arrangement from **Dubai** with Emirates. Flight time is around 6 hours 30 minutes.

From Asia Air Mauritius operates flights from **Mumbai**, **Delhi**, **Bangalore** and **Chennai**. Flight times from Mumbai, Bangalore and Chennai are around 6 hours, and from Delhi around 7 hours 30 minutes. Air Mauritius flies between Mauritius and **Beijing**, **Hong Kong** and **Shanghai**. Flight time is around 10 hours. Air Mauritius flies to/from **Kuala Lumpur** (7 hours) and onwards to **Singapore**.

Whichever way you fly to Mauritius, it is essential that you have a confirmed return, or onward, ticket in your possession when you arrive. There is more on the immigration requirements on pages 43–4.

Air Mauritius: the nation's airline
When Air Mauritius began in 1967, it was an airline without an aircraft. It started operating flights in 1972 but didn't buy its own aircraft until 1975. It has remained small ever since although it is known in international aviation circles for doing big things. In 1987, it became the first airline in the world to order higher gross weight 767/200 Extended Range jetliners from Boeing which entered service in 1988.

By 2015, Air Mauritius was serving 21 destinations on four continents with a fleet of 12 aircraft. It services other destinations through codeshare arrangements with other airlines, in particular with Air France, using Paris Charles de Gaulle Airport as a hub.

As a rule, the cabin crew are professional and friendly. As airline food goes, the quality is good in all classes, but don't forget to make the airline aware of any special dietary requirements at the time of booking. The Airbuses have a satisfactory seat pitch of 81cm (32in) in economy class, personal video screens and in-seat telephones in all classes, whilst business-class passengers enjoy 'lie-flat seats' with a 180cm (60in) pitch. Air Mauritius no longer offers a first-class category, but some flights to Europe offer premium economy as well as economy and business. All flights are non-smoking.

For most Air Mauritius international flights the baggage allowance is 23kg (50.6lb) of checked baggage in economy class 30kg (66lb) in business class. The baggage allowance is only 15kg (33lb) on flights between Mauritius and Rodrigues. On international flights infants under two years of age are allowed 10kg (22lb) plus a pram and one piece of hand baggage. A small extra allowance is provided for sports equipment. If you are carrying a wedding dress, you can ask that it be stored in the business-class coat compartments, otherwise it can be stowed in the overhead lockers or boxed and checked in as hold baggage.

The airline's head office is located in President John F Kennedy Street in Port Louis and has an efficient ticketing office on the ground floor. Tickets can also be purchased via the company's website (*www.airmauritius.com*) or by contacting their call centre.

If you do choose to fly Air Mauritius, the in-flight magazine *Islander* is worth a read as it frequently contains articles on culture, activities, tourist attractions, shopping, etc.

The Air Mauritius website (*www.airmauritius.com*) is very informative and includes timetables, descriptions of the packages they offer and the hotels used, and a comprehensive list of their airline offices around the world.

Sir Seewoosagur Ramgoolam International Airport The airport at Plaisance, in the southeast of the island, is small but modern with good facilities. In 2013, an impressive new terminal building opened, doubling the airport's capacity and creating a separate area for flights to Rodrigues.

There are a few duty-free shops both on arrival and on departure. In the departure area are a café and shops selling local goods, from handicrafts to smoked marlin, although these are considerably more expensive than in many other outlets on the island. Money can be changed at the bank counters in the main hall, which are open during all international arrivals. The airport has free Wi-Fi. The public are not allowed to enter the check-in departure area and baggage security screening is done at the entrance to the building. For more information about the airport, visit http://aml.mru.aero.

'Yu Lounge' (✆ *603 6666;* e *resa@yulounge.com; www.yulounge.com*) is a VIP terminal for passengers travelling by private or commercial jet, with dedicated concierge, customs, immigration, dining and bar, plus luxury transfer service. If you feel compelled to keep working there is a fully equipped meeting room, secretarial services and free Wi-Fi.

Luggage Delivery of luggage is usually prompt unless there are several aircraft arriving at the same time and there are usually plenty of trolleys available. If you use the services of the porters, who wait outside the arrivals lobby, you may want to give a small tip.

Getting to your hotel If you have booked your holiday as part of a package, transfers to your hotel will probably be included. Even budget hotels booked independently can usually arrange transfers for a fee.

All the major car-hire companies have desks at the airport.

If you need a taxi it helps to know the current fare to your destination and the tourist information counter at the airport should be able to tell you. At night you could well be charged double. It is best to agree the price before starting your journey.

During the day there are public bus services from the airport to Mahébourg and Curepipe, from where buses serve other parts of the island. The information counter can provide details on bus services from the airport.

See pages 58–62, for further information on car hire, bus services and driving.

BY SEA Cruise liners occasionally call at Mauritius, either on round-the-world voyages or on cruises from southern and eastern Africa. A Costa Croisières (*www.costacroisieres.fr*) ship is based in Port Louis from December to March and operates cruises in the region, taking in Réunion, Madagascar, the Seychelles and east Africa. The Mauritian Government is currently having a push to improve port facilities and encourage more cruise ships to the island.

Cargo ships come frequently but few of them carry paying passengers and those that do only carry about a dozen.

There are regular passenger sailings between Mauritius and Rodrigues (see page 223), and a couple of services a year between Mauritius and Agaléga (page 201).

For detailed information, contact the Mauritius Shipping Corporation (*Nova Bldg, 1 Military Rd, Port Louis;* 217 2284; e *info@mscl.mu; www.mauritiusshipping.net*).

Réunion The Mauritius Shipping Corporation used to operate a passenger service between Mauritius and Réunion. At the time of writing the service had ceased and there were no plans to resume it.

Rodrigues See page 223.

HEALTH *with Dr Felicity Nicholson*

The only proof of vaccination required is against **yellow fever** for those over one year of age arriving from areas at risk of yellow fever transmission. This includes most of sub-Saharan Africa and parts of South America. The decision whether to take the vaccination will depend on whether you are at risk of disease from the country you are coming from and whether you are able to receive the vaccine. If you are arriving into Mauritius from an endemic zone then seek specialist advice as to whether you need the vaccine or can take an exemption certificate.

The traveller to any tropical country will benefit from the following vaccinations: tetanus, diphtheria and polio and hepatitis A. For longer trips, ie: four weeks or more hepatitis B vaccine should also be considered and for shorter trips if you are working in hospitals or with children. You are advised to visit your doctor well in advance of your trip to plan the vaccine schedule.

According to the Mauritian authorities, there is no **malaria** risk in Mauritius or Rodrigues. Visitors generally do not take anti-malaria medication.

To combat the annoyance of mosquitoes during the night, most hotels supply an electric mosquito repellent vaporiser. You should use a DEET-containing repellent (50–55%) for the body, particularly in the evenings. Remember though that there may also be day-biting mosquitoes that can carry dengue fever (see below) or chikungunya (see box, page 51) so keep your repellent to hand at all times.

Although the water in Mauritius is officially safe to drink in most places, water, and ice, can be the cause of minor upsets. A sensible precaution is to drink only bottled water (obtainable everywhere), to clean your teeth with bottled water and to do without ice in your drinks. Bottled soft drinks, mixers and soda water are usually served cold. Do not drink tap water during or after a cyclone or heavy rains as bacteria and viruses can be washed into the water supply and treatment problems may occur.

Mauritius is considered to have no **rabies** in terrestrial animals but does potentially have rabies in bats. Exposure to bat saliva or brain tissue should be considered a potential risk and medical help should be sought as soon as possible. On the whole the risk for travellers is very low.

Stonefish and **lionfish** stings do occur and can be dangerous. If you are stung, seek medical attention immediately.

For those who are looking for it, romance is easy to find in Mauritius. However, AIDS is present on the island and visitors should be aware of the dangers.

DENGUE FEVER This acute febrile illness is caused by the dengue virus and is transmitted by day-biting mosquitoes. The incubation period of the disease is from three to 14 days and classically starts with pain behind the eyes, followed by fever, rash and joint pain, among other symptoms. The illness is often self-limiting though unpleasant and treatment is supportive and symptomatic. There are no vaccines or

tablets to prevent dengue fever. There are four serotypes; second infections with a different serotype can lead to more serious and potentially fatal disease. It is wise to use insect repellents on exposed skin during daylight hours.

AFRICAN TICK BITE FEVER African tick bite fever is caused by the bacteria *Rickettsia africae* and is spread by the bite of ticks that feed on cattle and game. The disease is usually mild and rarely has serious consequences. Symptoms include the abrupt onset of fever, headache, muscle pain, enlarged lymph nodes, and mouth ulcers. About 25% of cases develop a maculopapular or blistering rash. Treatment is with doxycycline 100mg twice a day for one to two weeks.

It is sensible to check yourself for ticks after walking in scrubby areas and remove the ticks carefully as described below.

Ticks should ideally be removed as soon as possible, as leaving ticks on the body increases the chance of infection. They should be removed with special tick tweezers that can be bought in good travel shops. Failing that, you can use your finger nails by grasping the tick as close to your body as possible and pulling steadily and firmly away at right angles to your skin. The tick will then come away complete as long as you do not jerk or twist. If possible, douse the wound with alcohol (any spirit will do) or iodine. Irritants (eg: Olbas oil) or lit cigarettes are to be discouraged since they can cause the ticks to regurgitate and therefore increase the risk of disease. It is best to get a travelling companion to check you for ticks and if you are travelling with small children remember to check their heads, and particularly behind the ears. An area of spreading redness around the bite site, or a rash or fever coming on a few days or more after the bite, should stimulate a trip to the doctor.

TRAVEL CLINICS AND HEALTH INFORMATION A full list of current travel clinic websites worldwide is available on www.istm.org. For other journey preparation

CHIKUNGUNYA VIRUS INFECTION

Chikungunya is a viral disease that is transmitted by mosquitoes. It is endemic to large parts of Africa, the Middle East, India and southeast Asia, and has some similarities to dengue fever, which is widespread in most tropical regions.

During 2006 there were increased numbers of cases of chikungunya reported in Réunion, Mauritius and the Seychelles, with over 1,100 cases reported in Mauritius by March 2006. The main preventive measure taken by the authorities is to spray against mosquitoes and to reduce their breeding grounds. Cases continue to occur though in smaller numbers in more recent years but it is still wise to take precautions as described on page 50.

Symptoms appear between four and seven days after a bite by the infected mosquito. A high fever and headache occur, with significant pains in the joints (eg: ankles and wrists). Most patients recover fully over a period of a few weeks, although 5–10% of patients will experience joint symptoms that can persist for a year or more. The virus is rarely fatal.

There is no vaccine available to protect against chikungunya. Travellers are advised to take precautions against insect bites (ie: use insect repellent on areas of exposed skin), particularly during daylight hours when these mosquitoes are active. Pregnant women and those with chronic illnesses should seek specific expert advice before travelling.

information, consult http://travelhealthpro.org.uk (UK) or http://wwwnc.cdc. gov/travel/ (US). Information about various medications may be found on www. netdoctor.co.uk/travel. All advice found online should be used in conjunction with expert advice received prior to or during travel.

Medical services in Mauritius Wherever you are staying, the management will recommend the nearest doctor or dentist for an emergency. The larger hotels have a nurse and small dispensary on their premises, and a roster of doctors on call.

Medical facilities in Mauritius are reasonable. Private clinics and ambulances tend to be better equipped than their public counterparts, although they can be costly so travel insurance is advisable. More complicated cases may need to be evacuated to South Africa or Réunion. Medical services in Rodrigues are limited and many patients are sent to Mauritius for treatment (see page 224).

LONG-HAUL FLIGHTS, CLOTS AND DVT   *Dr Felicity Nicholson*

Any prolonged immobility, including travel by land or air, can result in deep-vein thrombosis (DVT) with the risk of embolus to the lungs. Certain factors can increase the risk and these include:

* Previous clot or a close relative with a history
* Being over 40, with increased risk over 80 years old
* Recent major operation or varicose-veins surgery
* Cancer
* Stroke
* Heart disease
* Obesity
* Pregnancy
* Hormone therapy
* Heavy smoking
* Severe varicose veins
* Being very tall (over 6ft/1.8m) or short (under 5ft/1.5m)

A deep-vein thrombosis causes painful swelling and redness of the calf or sometimes the thigh. It is only dangerous if a clot travels to the lungs (pulmonary embolus). Symptoms of a pulmonary embolus (PE) – which commonly start three to ten days after a long flight – include chest pain, shortness of breath, and sometimes coughing up small amounts of blood. Anyone who thinks that they might have a DVT needs to see a doctor immediately.

PREVENTION OF DVT
* Keep mobile before and during the flight; move around every couple of hours
* Drink plenty of fluids during the flight
* Avoid taking sleeping pills and excessive tea, coffee and alcohol
* Consider wearing flight socks or support stockings (see *www.legshealth. com*)

If you think you are at increased risk of a clot, ask your doctor if it is safe to travel.

Public hospitals

✚ **Dr Jeetoo Hospital** Volcy Pougnet St, Port Louis; ✆ 212 3201
✚ **Ear Nose & Throat Hospital** Vacoas; ✆ 286 2061
✚ **Flacq Hospital** ✆ 413 2532
✚ **J Nehru Hospital** Rose-Belle; ✆ 267 4951
✚ **Mahébourg Hospital** Cent Gaulettes St, Mahébourg; ✆ 631 9556
✚ **Princess Margaret Orthopaedic Hospital** Candos, Quatre Bornes; ✆ 425 3031
✚ **S Bharati Eye Hospital** Moka; ✆ 433 4015
✚ **Sir Seewoosagur Ramgoolam National Hospital** Pamplemousses; ✆ 243 3661
✚ **Souillac Hospital** Souillac; ✆ 625 5532

Private clinics

✚ **Apollo Bramwell** Royal Rd, Moka; ✆ 605 1000; www.apollobramwell.com
✚ **City Clinic** 102–6 Sir Edgar Laurent St, Port Louis; ✆ 242 0486

✚ **Clinique de Grand Baie** Sottise Rd, Grand Baie; ✆ 263 1212
✚ **Clinique de l'Occident** Coastal Rd, Flic en Flac; ✆ 453 5858
✚ **Clinique de Lorette** Higginson Av, Curepipe; ✆ 670 2911
✚ **Clinique du Nord** 81 Coastal Rd, Baie du Tombeau; ✆ 247 2532; e cdnord@intnet.mu
✚ **Clinique Ferrière** College Lane, Curepipe; ✆ 676 3332
✚ **Clinique Mauricienne** Le Réduit; ✆ 763 0439
✚ **Fortis Clinique Darné** Georges Guibert St, Floréal; ✆ 729 0967
✚ **Nouvelle Clinique du Bon Pasteur** Thomy Pitot St, Rose Hill; ✆ 464 2640

Vaccination centres and pharmacies

✚ **International Vaccination Centre** Mutual Aid Bldg, Victoria Sq, Port Louis; ✆ 212 4464

Pharmacies Pharmacies are well stocked with European/US proprietary medicines, are open in the evenings in most towns, and there are dispensaries and health centres in most villages.

MEDICAL TOURISM

Medical tourism, particularly cosmetic surgery and dentistry, is on the rise with a growing number of clinics offering treatment and recovery in Mauritius for procedures such as hair transplants, breast augmentation and cosmetic dentistry. Special packages are available, including flights, accommodation and treatment. Facilities are generally modern and treatment in Mauritius may be cheaper than in your home country but, as with all medical tourism, it pays to do your research. Many of the doctors seem to be trained in France, so it is worth checking whether English is spoken at your preferred clinic.

One of the larger clinics is Centre de Chirurgie Esthétique de l'Océan Indien in Trou aux Biches (✆ 265 5050; e contact@estetic.info; www.esthetiqueoceanindien.com), which offers hair transplants, cosmetic dentistry and cosmetic surgery, including breast augmentation, lipo-sculpture, rhinoplasty and face lifts.

SAFETY

As with all travel, it is worth checking your own government's advice for Mauritius before deciding whether to travel and what precautions to take while travelling. The UK Foreign and Commonwealth Office provides useful advice for travellers (www.fco.gov.uk), as do the US Department of State (www.travel.state.gov) and the Australian Department of Foreign Affairs and Trade (www.smartraveller.gov.au).

Although Mauritius enjoys a relatively low crime rate, petty crime is on the increase. Many attribute this to an increase in drug taking. Pickpockets are reported to target tourists in busy areas such as Port Louis market and Grand Baie, whilst

self-caterers should be aware of the increase in reports of housebreaking. Visitors should take sensible precautions, including avoiding walking alone at night, not leaving valuables visible in cars and taking care of bags and valuables when walking in towns and tourist areas.

Mid-range, upmarket and luxury hotels typically have robust security arrangements but, as in any country, you should secure any valuables in your hotel safe and always make sure your room is locked. In January 2011, an Irish tourist was murdered in her room in a resort in the north of the island. This was an extremely unusual occurrence and a huge shock to the tourism industry in Mauritius; as such it received a good deal of publicity around the world but is not indicative of an increased threat to tourists from violent crime.

In 2003, the Police du Tourisme (Tourism Police) was set up to patrol tourist areas and assist local police in the investigation of crimes against tourists. The Tourism Police can often be seen patrolling the beaches in specially marked 4x4 vehicles and they have a hotline number – ☏ 213 2818 – for the reporting of incidents.

The Tourism Police publishes a leaflet entitled 'Spend a safe holiday in Mauritius'. Its advice includes: secure your valuables in the hotel safe, avoid carrying your passport unless needed, do not leave valuables in your car, park your car in well-lit areas, avoid showing large sums of cash in public, do not walk alone at night and ensure service providers hold a valid licence. The leaflet specifies that tourists should check that any provider of boating excursions or watersports holds a pleasure craft licence. The craft should display a registration number preceded by PC for commercial activities, and not PPC (private pleasure craft). A small coastguard service operates in Mauritius and hotel watersports centres are generally well run.

Hawkers operate on many of the island's beaches and in some towns. You will have no recourse if any items you buy from them are faulty, and please do not buy items made from shells as this contributes to the destruction of the marine environment.

A vast army of dogs wanders the streets and beaches of Mauritius: some are strays but others simply have careless owners. There is always the possibility of confrontation, particularly as they often go around in packs. I was told by a friend living locally that the best defence while walking alone is an umbrella. If a dog with dubious intentions approaches, simply erect the umbrella in its direction and its shield-like appearance should be enough to deter the beast. Take care whilst driving as the roads are not well lit and dogs tend to appear from nowhere.

An increasingly common menace, which my mother and I experienced first hand, is the terrifying 'mugger monkey'. Over the years, the island's monkeys have come to associate people with food, and in some areas bold monkeys try to intimidate passers-by into handing over an edible bounty by rushing at them, teeth and gums bared. You don't need to be carrying food to be subjected to this kind of attack. I almost lost my camera bag to a monkey who assumed the bag contained a hidden stash of bananas. Areas where you need to be particularly vigilant to 'mugger monkeys' include the Alexandra Falls lookout and Grand Bassin sacred lake.

On one of my visits to Mauritius I met a charming British couple who specifically asked me to write about the dangers of slippery tiles in bathrooms. I met them in a Mauritian hospital – the husband had fallen on wet tiles in the bathroom of an upmarket hotel and broken his leg. As a result, they discovered that there are no regulations requiring non-slip tiles in bathrooms in Mauritius, and, in fact, there are almost no non-slip bathrooms on the island. While many of the hotel bathrooms look spectacular, they are pretty slippery. So, tread carefully.

A relatively new danger is that presented by speedboats and jet skis, which roar along the coasts in front of hotels. Swimmers have been seriously injured and even killed, so be vigilant or stick to marked bathing areas.

If you are considering sailing your own vessel around the Mascarene Islands, it is worth noting that piracy emanating from Somalia is a significant threat in the northwest Indian Ocean and the Gulf of Aden, and incidents have occurred close to the Mauritian Exclusive Economic Zone. There is an international effort to combat piracy in the region, and in 2011 and 2012, Mauritius signed agreements with the European Union and the UK for suspected pirates to be tried and detained in Mauritius.

WOMEN TRAVELLERS

Lone women travellers receive a fair amount of attention from males. It is usually well-meaning curiosity but don't take chances that you would not take in your home country. For instance, don't accept a lift from a lone male or group of men. Don't walk alone at night and try to avoid dimly lit areas, such as beaches. Even during the day, make sure that you are not too isolated on a beach.

Dress standards in Mauritius are conservative. While swimwear is perfectly appropriate on the beach and around the pool, it is not appropriate elsewhere. There are no nudist beaches.

Women who are expecting to visit a temple or sacred site should dress appropriately or carry a shawl to cover their shoulders and/or head, if required.

TRAVELLERS WITH A DISABILITY

While most modern buildings in Mauritius conform to international standards for disabled access, there is no requirement for hotels to construct rooms equipped for the disabled. Even large modern hotels built in the last few years lack specially designed rooms.

However, most hotels claim that they can accommodate disabled guests by giving them a room on the ground floor. This is all very well but many hotels have numerous steps linking their facilities and lifts are not always on hand. Contact the hotel direct in order to gather as much information as possible.

Hotels which have rooms equipped for the disabled include Hilton Mauritius Resort and Spa, Preskil Beach Resort, One&Only Le St Géran and Sugar Beach Resort.

Although pavements are present in large towns, such as Port Louis and Curepipe, they are often poorly maintained. The coastal resorts tend to be quite spread out and frequently lack pavements, making wheelchair access difficult. Public transport does not offer wheelchair access but local ground handlers, such as White Sand Tours (page 58), can assist by providing wheelchair-friendly transport.

TRAVELLING WITH KIDS

Mauritius is a very child-friendly destination. While some of the island's hotels are geared towards couples rather than families, most cater very well for children. You can expect mid-range, upmarket and luxury hotels to have well-equipped kids' clubs; some also have teenagers' clubs and a baby-sitting service. The programme of activities at these clubs is impressive and means parents can have plenty of child-free time should they need it. For those who fear their holiday may be ruined by

other people's screaming children, there are adults-only hotels (such as Paradise Cove) and many hotels (such as Sugar Beach Resort) endeavour to keep one end of the hotel child-free.

GAY/LESBIAN TRAVELLERS

Mauritians are generally friendly and welcoming to all travellers. However, traditional values are tightly held and homosexuality is not accepted by everyone. There are no gay clubs or bars on the island but gay parties are sometimes organised at one of the clubs or privately. The Mauritian gay community has a strong online presence and websites such as www.gaystaymauritius.com can provide further information on travelling to the island. Travellers should avoid public displays of affection and note that, while the law does not criminalise homosexuality in itself, the act of sodomy is illegal regardless of sexual orientation.

WHAT TO TAKE

The glib answer is plenty of money as there are endless opportunities to spend it in Mauritius. Credit cards are widely accepted and all the main towns have ATMs.

Apart from specific personal items like prescription medicines, you should be able to get everything you need but some items may be more expensive than in your home country. Suncream, insect repellent, camera equipment and other such essentials are very expensive locally. It is worth packing medication for minor stomach upsets, and seasickness tablets if you plan to head out deep-sea fishing.

For clothes, casual elegance is a good guideline. On the coast at any time of the year, you will need lightweight, preferably cotton clothing. Something warmer will be necessary in the evenings, for women a cardigan or shawl should suffice. Most hotels require men to wear trousers and shirts in the restaurant in the evenings. If you plan to do some hiking, sturdy trainers are sufficient for the trails in Mauritius. Hotel boutiques and shopping centres have a range of clothing appropriate for the climate. Some areas of the coast have sea urchins so you may like to take reef shoes for swimming and snorkelling.

Three-pin and continental two-pin sockets are both used, so take the appropriate adaptors if you need them. Modern buildings and hotels tend to have three-pin UK-style plugs, whilst budget hotels and self-catering accommodation often have two-pin plugs. Occasional power failures do occur so it is prudent to carry a pocket torch.

Of course, don't forget adequate travel insurance.

From 2016 plastic bags will be banned in Mauritius, so it is best to leave them at home.

MAPS There are several small maps of Mauritius and Rodrigues available as part of the tourist office literature, which will be sufficient for most visitors. Ground handlers and car-hire companies also provide good maps of the island. The Globetrotter travel map has useful detail and includes maps of Port Louis, Curepipe and Grand Baie. For hikers, a map of the Black River Gorges National Park is available from the visitor centre at Le Pétrin (page 195).

MONEY

The legal unit of currency is the Mauritian rupee (Rs), which is divided into 100 cents. There are banks with ATMs in most towns around the island, including several

in Grand Baie and Flic en Flac. Banking hours are generally 09.00–15.00 Monday–Friday; some are open on Saturday mornings. Banks are closed on Sundays and public holidays. Foreign-exchange counters in tourist areas often have longer opening hours.

The Bank of Mauritius, the Central Bank (*www.bom.mu*), oversees the proper functioning of the banking system and implements the financial and monetary policies of the government. It used to administer exchange control but since 1983 the rupee has been linked to a basket of currencies relevant to foreign trade. The exchange rate fluctuates daily and is determined by the Central Bank.

You can change foreign currency at banks and exchange bureaux; you will usually need to have your passport with you. Some mid-range and all upmarket and luxury hotels offer foreign-exchange services, although the commission may be higher than at banks.

Credit cards, such as Visa and MasterCard, are widely accepted in Mauritius. Most upmarket and luxury hotels will also accept American Express.

Currency exchange rates in March 2016 were as follows: £1=51; US$1=Rs35; €1=Rs40.

BUDGETING

The thrifty, independent traveller staying in cheap, basic accommodation and eating in budget restaurants, travelling by bus, and enjoying free outdoor pursuits could live on £60 per day. Since there is bound to be a time during your stay when you will want to do or buy something you haven't anticipated, or treat yourself to a nice hotel or meal, allow extra. Excursions and activities can be pricey.

If you are on a half-board (dinner, bed and breakfast) package holiday at an upmarket beach resort, you will have to buy lunch, which can be expensive in hotels. However, there is always the opportunity to eat outside the resorts and you can get a decent lunch in a reasonable local restaurant for Rs400. Alternatively, you can pick up ten *samoussas* or similar snacks from roadside stalls for around Rs20. Drinks are expensive in hotels; even bottled water with your dinner can cost over Rs200. A number of resorts offer all-inclusive packages, which may be an economical option if you plan to spend a lot of time in your hotel.

If you're staying in self-catering accommodation you should find the cost of household items and food averaging out at less than at home, particularly if you buy your food at local markets. For beer drinkers, you can keep the cost of drinks down by buying local Phoenix beer, rather than imported beers (see pages 66–7).

Taxis have meters but drivers will only use them if you insist. It is often better to negotiate the fare before the journey. Taxi drivers know their value, especially as resort hotels are isolated and a taxi is usually the only way to reach or leave them, so allow extra cash for unexpected taxi journeys, particularly since the island-wide bus service stops running early in the evening.

There is a 15% government tax on hotel accommodation but this is usually included in the room rate. There is also a tax of 15% on meals in restaurants and this may or may not be included in the prices on the menu. A footnote will explain if it is.

TIPPING Tipping in restaurants is usually left to your discretion, although you should check that a service charge is not going to be added to the bill before you dish out tips. In restaurants where no service charge is added, you could leave 5–10% of the bill, according to your satisfaction with the service. In basic eateries tipping is not expected.

Many hotels ask that you do not tip individual staff, but instead place any tips in the tipping box at reception to be divided among all staff. For airport porters Rs100 is usually sufficient. Taxi drivers don't expect tips but they are gratefully received.

GETTING AROUND

INBOUND TOUR OPERATORS If you are happy to forego your independence for a while, the easiest way to get around and see the sights of Mauritius is by taking one of the tours run by a tour operator. They provide an instant introduction to the island, enabling the visitor to discover places that they can return to later and explore independently. Inbound tour operators (ground handlers) meet arrivals at the airport on behalf of the hotels and overseas tour operators. They provide leaflets about their services to incoming guests and many have desks at hotels.

The larger tour operators, listed below, can organise almost anything, including car hire, private driver/guide and all manner of activities and excursions. They can also provide guides fluent in a range of languages. Group excursions last either a half or full day and most include lunch and entrance fees to the attractions visited.

White Sand Tours was established in 1974 and is one of the most successful and innovative destination management companies in Mauritius. The company employs 180 highly competent staff and has its own fleet of well-maintained vehicles. In 1996, it was the first destination management company in the Indian Ocean to obtain the ISO9002 certificate, an internationally recognised quality assurance standard. In 2008, it was the first to launch a Sustainable Development Charter, which encompasses employee welfare, environmental awareness, socially responsible tourism, corporate responsibility for the wider community and a collective movement for sustainable development. As well as the usual tours, either chauffeur-driven or in groups, the company can arrange activities such as deep-sea fishing, sailing, helicopter flights, horseriding, mountain climbing and trekking. They also specialise in organising weddings.

Smaller tour operators usually specialise in a few organised group tours and most are to be found around Grand Baie and Trou d'Eau Douce. Their prices may not include entrance fees.

GBTT (Grand Baie Travel & Tours) Royal Rd, Grand Baie; ✆263 8771; e resa.gbtt@intnet.mu; www. gbtt.com

Mauritours S Venkatesananda St, Rose Hill; ✆467 9700; e mauritours@mauritours.net; www. mauritours.net

Mautourco 84 Gustave Colin St, Forest Side; ✆670 4301; e info@mautourco.com; www. mautourco.com

SummerTimes 5 Av Bernardin de St Pierre, Quatre Bornes; ✆427 1111; e summer@ summertimes.intnet.mu; www.summer-times. com

White Sand Tours 10 Robert Edward Hart St, Curepipe; ✆605 1500; e contact@whitesand.mu; www.whitesandtours.com

DRIVING There are around 2,000km of decent, tarred roads throughout Mauritius. A well-maintained motorway crosses the island diagonally from the airport in the southeast corner, travelling through Port Louis and north to Grand Baie.

Little-used country roads are not in such good condition.

Driving is on the left. Although the standard of driving is generally fairly good (higher than in neighbouring Réunion), drivers are not courteous. Do not expect other drivers to give way or to stop at pedestrian crossings, or to wait for a safe moment to overtake. Outside the towns, there are stretches of open road without

traffic, which make driving pleasant. However, roads are not well lit at night so watch out for pedestrians and stray dogs. You are likely to see some unusual sights on the roads, such as tiny motorbikes piled high with sugarcane, bags full of

GETTING MARRIED

The same romantic qualities that make Mauritius an appealing honeymoon destination have made it a popular place for visitors to marry. Wedding packages feature in the brochures of most overseas tour operators, whose local representatives handle the arrangements.

Most wedding packages mean that many of the administrative formalities are carried out for you. The tour operator will usually arrange a special licence to allow you to be married from three working days after your arrival in Mauritius. You will need to visit the Civil Status Office in Port Louis before your wedding day to obtain special dispensation under Mauritian law and to have all your documents verified. Divorced ladies must allow a minimum 300-day gap between the divorce and new wedding date, or a pregnancy test taken locally must be negative.

It is possible to arrange a wedding independently but allow plenty of time to gather the required paperwork. If your hotel is not organising your wedding, local ground handlers can assist. You will need to take to Mauritius originals of all documents plus copies certified by a solicitor. For any documents not in English, you will need a certified translation. Vital is a certificate issued under the authority of the prime minister to the effect that the couple are not citizens or residents of Mauritius. You will need to apply for the certificate at least one month before the date of the proposed wedding to the Registrar of Civil Status (*7th Fl, Emmanuel Anquetil Bldg, Port Louis;* \ *201 1727;* e *civstat@mail. gov.au*). You will also need to supply a series of documents: two photocopies of each birth certificate and two photocopies of the pages showing the issuing authority and personal details of each passport, and any other documents, for instance, to prove divorce or the demise of a former spouse.

A couple can choose to be married at the Civil Status Office, on a beach or in their hotel, in which case the ceremony is performed by the Civil Status Officer of the locality where the couple are staying. There are more unusual options too, like Ile des Deux Cocos, a small island off the coast, or on board a catamaran or even the Blue Safari submarine off the north coast.

Religious weddings are also possible but can only take place on weekdays. As well as birth certificates and passports, you will need to provide christening certificates and documents from both your churches at home confirming that you are free to marry. For Roman Catholic weddings, you need to contact the Episcopate of Port Louis (\ *208 3068*). Information should also be obtained from the diocese in which you normally reside.

If you are carrying a wedding dress on your flight, you can ask the airline to store it in the business-class coat compartments, otherwise it can be stowed in the overhead lockers or boxed and marked as fragile and checked in as hold baggage.

Information on getting married in Mauritius is available at www.tourism-mauritius.mu and http://csd.pmo.govmu.org. The requirements do change from time to time, so it is important to check unless a local ground handler is making the arrangements for you.

2

groceries or family members. Watch out for hand signals as some drivers use them to indicate they are about to turn or to beckon cars behind to overtake.

Take care to observe the speed limit of 110km/h on the motorway, 80km/h on open roads and 40km/h in built-up areas. Fixed and mobile speed cameras are relatively new to Mauritius but they are used with much enthusiasm. There is a far greater police presence on the roads than there was in the past, and it is not uncommon for them to stop cars simply to check drivers' licences. If you are fined for speeding, you will need to go to court to pay. In December 2008 it became compulsory for cars registered in Mauritius to be fitted with rear seatbelts and the driver is held responsible if they are not worn.

Negotiating Port Louis by car requires patience as traffic builds up to horrendous proportions during the day. Most of the streets are one-way, which adds to the confusion for the uninitiated. If you only want to hire a taxi for one day, let it be the day you go to Port Louis. Similar traffic congestion occurs in the residential areas of the centre, such as Quatre Bornes and Curepipe.

Parking in most parts of Mauritius is free. Parking zones, applicable if you are parking on the street, exist in Port Louis, Rose Hill, Quatre Bornes and Curepipe between 09.00 and 16.30. Parking tickets must be purchased in advance from a filling station and displayed inside the windscreen. In Port Louis, there are car parks at the Caudan Waterfront, such as the Granary, where you can simply buy a ticket on arrival.

Both petrol and diesel are readily available at filling stations throughout the country, but it is worth keeping your tank at least half full, especially for distance driving at night as there are very few petrol stations open at night.

Car and motorbike hire The minimum age for hiring a self-drive car varies from 20 to 25 years, according to the hire company. All companies require that the driver has been in possession of a valid driver's licence for at least one year. The car-hire company will need to view your licence. The rental must be paid in advance. Payment of a daily premium reduces the insurance excess and a daily driver and passenger personal accident insurance is available. Cars can usually be delivered and recovered anywhere on the island and there are car-hire desks at the airport.

Europcar operates one of the largest fleets of rental cars in Mauritius, with cars ranging from Hyundai Atos to BMW X3s or convertible Mini Coopers. They have desks at many hotels around the island and their staff are efficient and helpful. As an example of daily rates, Europcar charges around Rs2,000 per day (one to six days) for a small, three-door car with unlimited mileage (fuel is not included).

If you don't want to drive yourself, the car-hire companies will provide a driver. Not only does this save you having to cope with local driving conditions but there is also the bonus of having a private guide too. A chauffeur-driven service provided by the main companies will add around Rs750 per 8-hour day to your bill. Overtime, Sundays and public holidays may be extra.

There are few places offering **mopeds** and fewer still offering **motorbikes**, and it is risky to hire from an unofficial provider. Mopeds are available from around Rs800 a day, including helmet. Crash helmets are compulsory when driving or riding a motorbike or moped. Please avoid riding at night.

Car-hire companies

ABC Car Rental Albion Docks Bldg, Trou Fanfaron, Port Louis; 216 8889; e abccar@intnet. mu; www.abc-carrental.com

Avis DML Bldg, M1 Motorway, Port Louis; 116 Av Sir Guy Forget, Quatre Bornes; 427 6312; e sales@avismauritius.com; www.avismauritius.com

Budget Rent a Car S Venkatesananda St, Rose Hill; ✆ 697 2014; e budget@mauritours.net; www.budget.com.mu

Dodo Touring & Co Ltd St Jean Rd, Quatre Bornes; ✆ 425 6810; e dtc@intnet.mu

Europcar Av Michael Leal, Les Pailles; ✆ 286 0140; e europcar@intnet.mu; www. europcar.com. See ad, page 94.

GBTT (Grand Baie Travel & Tours) Royal Rd, Grand Baie; ✆ 263 8771; e resa.gbtt@intnet.mu; www.gbtt.com

Hertz Gustave Colin St, Forest Side; ✆ 670 4301; e hertz@mautourco.com; www.hertz.mu

Mango Beach Tours Royal Rd, Triolet; ✆ 708 2878; e info@mauritius-carhire.com; www. drive-mauritius.com

Ola Mauritius SSR International Airport, Plaine Magnien; ✆ 5790 0575; e info@ olamauritius.com; www.olamauritius.com

Pingouin Car SSR International Airport, Plaine Magnien; ✆ 5916 8667; e customerservice@ pingouin-carhire.com; www.carrental-mauritius. com

Sixt Rent a Car 5 Av Bernardin de St Pierre, Quatre Bornes; ✆ 250 9999; e sixt@intnet.mu; www.sixt.mu

Wind Surf Tours Royal Rd, La Preneuse; ✆ 255 7779; e resa@carhiremauritius.com; www. carhiremauritius.com

Motorbike- and moped-hire companies

Ola Mauritius SSR International Airport, Plaine Magnien; ✆ 5790 0575; e info@ olamauritius.com; www.olamauritius.com

Pingouin Car SSR International Airport, Plaine Magnien; ✆ 5916 8667; e customerservice@pingouin-carhire.com; www. carrental-mauritius.com

Wind Surf Tours Royal Rd, La Preneuse; ✆ 255 7779; e resa@carhiremauritius.com; www. carhiremauritius.com

Bicycle hire While short rides along the coast can be very pleasant, the towns are not generally cyclist-friendly and in areas of heavy traffic there are no cycle lanes into which one can escape. All bikes used on the road need to be registered at a police station for a small fee but if you hire a bike, this will already have been done.

Bicycles can be hired from hotels by the hour, half day and day. Some offer this service for free, but others charge around Rs350 per day. Some hotels also organise group bicycle tours. Some agencies in Grand Baie and most inbound tour operators can arrange bicycle hire. A list of cycling shops offering bike hire is available at www.cycle.mu, which also has information on cycling events.

For information on mountain biking, see pages 92–3 and 286.

TAXIS One thing Mauritius is not short of is taxi drivers. Wherever you go, taxi drivers will wave animatedly at you, shout out to you and do their best to persuade you that you need their services. Although most taxis now sport nifty modern meters, they are rarely used. It is as well to negotiate a fare before you start your journey but be prepared to bargain.

Most taxi drivers will be only too happy for you to rent their taxi for several hours or a whole day and will act as a de facto tour guide. You can expect a day tour of the island in a taxi to cost around Rs2,500–3,500. Bear in mind that taxi drivers are paid a commission by certain shops and attractions to take tourists there, so if you have a fair idea where you want to go you may have to be fairly insistent to ensure you don't spend too much time deviating to the taxi driver's preferred haunts.

Most hotels have a taxi stand and display the fares agreed with the drivers at reception. However, if you take a taxi from a stand not linked to a hotel and negotiate a price, you will often find it is even cheaper than hotel taxi prices.

In most towns taxis are to be found close to the bus station but tend to be available only at conventional times (06.00–20.00). They can also be telephoned

(there are two dozen companies listed in the phone directory) and there are 24-hour and night services. Many drivers have mobile phones with numbers also listed in the directory. There are a number of private cars operating as illegal taxis (*taxi marron*).

Taxi trains tout for custom among passengers queuing for buses or follow regular routes, picking up passengers on the way and charging little more than the bus fare for a seat in a shared car. These taxis are usually old boneshakers but they do offer a cheap alternative and will operate late into the night on popular routes.

Below is a selection of taxi companies offering services targeting the tourism sector, including airport transfers:

🚕 **Taxicab Mauritius** 📞 212 5478; e info@taxicabmauritius.com; www.taxicabmauritius.com

🚕 **Taxi Service Mauritius** 📞 5728 1471; e contact@taxiservicemauritius.com; www.taxiservicemauritius.com

🚕 **Taxis Mauritius** 📞 5794 5443; e bookings@taxismauritius.com; www.taxismauritius.com

HELICOPTER HIRE

The Air Mauritius Bell Jet Ranger helicopter, with seats for four passengers, is available for hire with pilot for sightseeing and for transfers from/to the airport.

In 2015, the cost of transfer from the airport to a hotel was Rs22,000 for two people plus Rs5,000 for each additional passenger. Sightseeing helicopter flights start at Rs13,000 for two people for 15 minutes, rising to Rs34,000 for 1 hour.

Bookings should be possible through your hotel or tour operator. Alternatively, contact Air Mauritius directly (📞 603 3754; e helicopter@airmauritius.com; www.airmauritius.com).

BUSES

Mauritius is blessed with a decent bus service, a boon to the independent traveller. Since so many people live outside the towns where they work, they depend on the bus service for transportation and their patronage keeps it flourishing.

The bus service is run on a co-operative basis by different operators. The buses can be pretty ancient and many of the bus drivers seem to think the size of their vehicle is enough to intimidate other road users to get out of their way. Catching the bus can be a fun experience – for a start, the buses usually proudly sport amusing names painted on their sides and are individually decorated by their drivers, particularly in the lead-up to festivals.

Express buses are not non-stop but take a shorter route between points and stop less frequently, although they charge the same fare as the slower buses. The fares are low, with a trip across the island from Port Louis to Mahébourg (which involves a change) costing Rs150 or so, and from Grand Baie to Port Louis around Rs40. It is important when getting on a bus to ask the conductor where it is going since the town on the front is not necessarily its destination. You can buy your ticket from a conductor on the bus. As the usual flow of passenger traffic is to Port Louis in the morning and out of Port Louis in the evening, making a connection in country districts sometimes takes ages.

Buses operate from 05.30 to 20.00 in urban areas and from 06.30 to 18.30 in rural areas. There is a late-night service until 23.00 between Port Louis and Curepipe via Rose Hill, Quatre Bornes and Vacoas. During the day, services tend to operate as the bus fills up, rather than to a strict timetable.

Bus timetables are available on the National Transport Authority website (*http://nta.govmu.org*), or you can call them on 📞 202 2800.

HITCHHIKING Hitchhiking is seldom practised by Mauritians. With the bus service reaching the depths of nearly every village, Mauritians are knowledgeable about how to get around their island easily and inexpensively. Some foreigners do hitchhike, although as with hitchhiking in any country, you should be wary, particularly at night, and women should definitely not hitchhike alone.

ACCOMMODATION

Mauritius provides a huge range of accommodation, from budget guesthouses to some of the world's most luxurious hotels; camping, however, is discouraged and there are no official campsites.

Service throughout Mauritius is superb, a fact which owes much to the Hotel School of Mauritius. The school offers courses for all hospitality and tourism personnel, from chefs to airline cabin staff.

Until 2012 there was no official rating or classification system for hotels in Mauritius, rather hotels which used a star rating would award it themselves. In April 2012, the MTPA launched an official hotel classification system based on international standards. Where star ratings are listed for hotels in this guidebook, they are the rating awarded by the MTPA. For the purposes of this guide, we have divided accommodation into five categories, determined principally by the hotel's star rating and its public rates. The categories, which are defined below, are luxury, upmarket, mid range, budget and shoestring.

Almost all hotels in Mauritius publish their rates in euros only as most of their guests are Europeans and the euro is considered more stable than the Mauritian rupee. Therefore, we have provided rates in euros below.

LUXURY These hotels and resorts regard themselves as six-star properties. Rooms will be spacious and superbly finished with all the facilities that you would expect – a large en-suite bathroom, air conditioning, satellite television, DVD, international direct-dial (IDD) telephone, minibar and safe. Many will include 24-hour private butler service. Luxury villas and presidential suites with rooms for staff are often a feature of these resorts. There will be a choice of restaurants and bars offering world-class cuisine and at least one of the restaurants is likely to be endorsed by a renowned chef. Facilities will be extensive, usually including numerous free watersports, a dive centre, several pools, tennis, a gym and a kids' club. Many of these resorts will have their own golf course or offer access to one nearby. No luxury hotel would be complete without a spa, offering a variety of massages and treatments, as well as saunas, steam rooms, jacuzzis and relaxation areas.

UPMARKET Equates roughly to four- and five-star international standards. Rooms will be en suite and equipped with air conditioning, television (including satellite channels), IDD telephone, minibar and safe. There will be excellent resort-style facilities, usually including free, non-motorised watersports, such as snorkelling, glass-bottom boat trips, pedaloes and kayaks. Many hotels also offer free waterskiing but this is sometimes limited to a certain number of hours. These hotels typically feature a spa, several pools, a dive centre, a gym, tennis courts and a kids' club. Some of these resorts will have their own golf course or offer access to one nearby. There will be regular evening entertainment and activities are often organised during the day. At such hotels there is typically a choice of restaurants and bars, and the standard of cuisine is high.

MID RANGE A wide selection of acceptable hotels offering comfortable accommodation, roughly equivalent to three-star international standards. Many of the large hotels in this category, particularly those owned by the main hotel groups, such as Beachcomber, have extensive facilities. Rooms will be en suite and typically have air conditioning, television, IDD telephone and safe. Most will have a minibar or mini fridge. Hotels by the coast will usually offer some free non-motorised watersports, such as pedaloes, kayaks and snorkelling. Other watersports may have to be paid for. Some will have a kids' club and there may be entertainment one or two nights a week.

BUDGET No frills accommodation, ranging from boarding houses to self-catering accommodation to medium-sized hotels offering basic facilities.

SHOESTRING Basic accommodation aimed at those on a very limited budget, likely to be self-catering.

PRICES AND TERMS Price brackets have been supplied as a guide only – rates do change regularly, according to season and demand. It is therefore better to judge a hotel by its description than by the price. In any case, if the hotel is booked as part of a package holiday including flights, the public rate is never what you, the guest, actually pay. Even for those who make their own hotel bookings direct, there could be significant discounts on the public rates at luxury, upmarket and mid-range properties. The majority of hotels offer considerable discounts for children and infants are often accommodated free of charge. It is worth visiting the websites of hotels as many, particularly the larger ones, publish special offers on the internet. If you are resident in Mauritius, the website www.marideal.mu offers special deals for accommodation, as well as activities and spa treatments. The price brackets are based on the hotels' public rates for a standard double room, per room per

ACCOMMODATION PRICE CODES: MAURITIUS & RODRIGUES

Double room per night on HB:

Luxury	$$$$$	Rs24,750+
Upmarket	$$$$	Rs11,000–24,750
Mid range	$$$	Rs5,500–11,000
Budget	$$	Rs2,750–5,500
Shoestring	$	up to Rs2,750

AI means all-inclusive: breakfast, lunch, dinner, snacks and drinks are included in the room rate. Usually available only as part of a package at a resort hotel.

FB means full board: breakfast, lunch and dinner (meals are often buffets or table d'hôte menus) are included in the room rate.

HB means half board: breakfast and dinner are included in the room rate. Few hotels allow you to change to breakfast and lunch. Usually a buffet dinner; speciality à la carte restaurants may be available for a supplement.

BB means bed and breakfast is included in the room rate.

RO means room only: no meals are included in the room rate.

night during high season on half board (dinner, bed and breakfast), two people sharing. However, budget and shoestring properties are likely to be sold on a bed and breakfast or self-catering (room only) basis, rather than half board.

EATING AND DRINKING

FOOD Just thinking about the food I've eaten in Mauritius makes my mouth water, from the delicious French-style crêpes served with local vanilla tea for breakfast to the delight of *salade de palmiste* (heart of palm salad) and the beguiling taste of *fish vindaye* (fish curry) for lunch, then a dinner of *samoussas* and *gâteaux piments* (chilli bites) from a street stall.

Many of the island's top hotels have superb fine-dining restaurants and attract world-class chefs. Most hotels make an effort to showcase local cuisine and will have Creole and Indian nights at least once a week.

The true adventure of eating in Mauritius is for the streetwise since so many delicious – and cheap – dishes are available from roadside stalls or small restaurants that specialise in Creole food or European dishes with a local zest.

The influences of Creole cuisine are African and Indian, with a dash of French. The recipes of slaves and indentured labourers have been blended with French ingenuity to produce an array of irresistible dishes, most of which are mildly spiced. The Chinese influence has been confined to particular areas, such as *mine* (noodles) and the ever-popular fried rice.

A favourite local dish, available from street vendors, is *dholl purées*: thin pancakes, made from wheat flour dough and ground split peas and cooked on a griddle. They are served plain, or rolled around a spoonful of *rougaille* or *brèdes*, and wrapped in paper. The Indian-originating *purée*, with its African/French filling, is an example of the successful blend of culinary traditions. *Rougaille* is a spicy condiment often made with *pommes d'amour*, the tiny cherry tomatoes that are grown and eaten all over the island. *Brèdes* are part of the daily diet of Mauritian country dwellers, cooked either plain or with meat or fish. They are green leaves – such as watercress, spinach, the leaves of tuber plants and Chinese cabbage – tossed with onions, garlic and red chillies in hot oil until the water has evaporated.

More substantial meals are also available from street sellers, such as *poisson vindaye*, seasoned fried fish coated with a *masala* of mustard seeds, green chillies, garlic and turmeric, often eaten cold with bread. *Achards légumes*, pickled vegetables mixed with spicy paste and vinegar, are also sometimes eaten with bread.

The sweet tooth is catered for with many Tamil specialities, such as *gâteau patate*, a wafer-like pastry of sweet potato and coconut. There is an abundance of tropical fruit too, especially the small pineapples dexterously peeled into spirals, with the stem remaining as a handle.

All street eating costs little since office and shop workers on small salaries are the main customers. Some workers carry their lunch with them in plaited reed baskets, dainty square boxes suspended from a string handle with a cover concealing the contents. These containers, called *tentes*, are made from pandanus leaves. They are sold in the markets and make good souvenirs.

Mauritians do not only eat in the street. There are inexpensive eateries in all the towns, where the typical dishes will be meat, chicken or fish served either as *carri* (curry), *daube* (stewed with potatoes and peas) or *kalya* (cooked with saffron and ginger/garlic). Snacks, called *gadjacks*, are served in bars on small saucers, like Spanish *tapas*, to accompany drinks. The range is generous, from *rougaille ourite* (octopus in tomato) to *croquettes volaille* (chicken bites).

Snoeck rougaille (salted fish in tomato) is a frequent standby if fresh fish is not available, and shrimps or lobster are also sometimes served in *rougaille*. *Camarons* (prawns) served with watercress salad are a favourite with Franco-Mauritians. Wild boar, hare and venison are widely available in restaurants, even out of the hunting season. Goat (*cabri*) is sold in the meat markets in the way that mutton is sold in Europe and is served in curry. The exotic *palmiste* (for which miniature palm trees are especially cultivated to yield their hearts) is sometimes served boiled instead of in a salad, with a Creole sauce.

Most restaurant menus do not contain many options for vegetarians. However, the majority of establishments will proudly create a dish especially for you, usually *carri de légumes* (vegetable curry). If you eat fish you'll be spoilt for choice, with delicious red snapper, dorado (mahi mahi), tuna and swordfish on offer. One of the highlights is, of course, *marlin fumé* (smoked marlin), served as an expensive but superb starter.

Restaurant prices may not include 15% tax, so be prepared for it to be added to your final bill.

DRINKS A popular Mauritian drink is *alooda*, sold on the streets and in markets by energetic salesmen praising their own product. It consists of dissolved, boiled china grass (*agar agar*) and sugar, which has been strained and allowed to set and then grated, to which is added water, milk, rose syrup and soaked *tookmaria* (falooda) seeds.

As you would expect, beer, wine and spirits are far more expensive in hotels than they are in local shops.

Beer At the beginning of the 1960s, Pierre Hugnin listened to the suggestion of a friend from Tahiti that he should start a brewery. At the time, 18,000 hectolitres of beer were imported into Mauritius annually. While going into the figures for the project, Hugnin had the well water at his proposed site in Phoenix analysed and found it ideal.

The first Mauritian beer, Phoenix, was brewed by Mauritius Breweries Limited in August 1963. With beer seen as an acceptable drink in multi-religious Mauritius, MBL launched a second beer, Stella, two years later and began to distribute Guinness, which has been brewed under licence since 1975. Phoenix (5% vol) has become synonymous with beer for Mauritians and is the company's bestseller. In 2003, MBL merged with another beverage firm to form the Phoenix Beverages Group (*Phoenix Hse, Pont Fer, Phoenix;* \601 2000; e *pbl@pbg.mu; www.phoenixbeverages. mu*). The company now produces non-alcoholic beverages as well as an expanded range of alcoholic drinks, including Blue Marlin, a stronger beer (6% vol), Phoenix Special Brew (6.5% vol), Stella Pils (a lager) and Phoenix cider.

RESTAURANT PRICE CODES: MAURITIUS & RODRIGUES

To assist you in choosing a restaurant, we have provided a rough indication of the price using codes to represent the average price of a main course:

Expensive	$$$$$	Rs1,635+
Above average	$$$$	Rs1,090–1,635
Mid range	$$$	Rs544–1,090
Cheap & cheerful	$$	Rs272–544
Rock bottom	$	up to Rs272

Phoenix beer has won many international awards for its quality. Mauritius sugar is used in the production of beer (where other breweries might use maize or rice) since it produces a beer that is more digestible. Top-quality hops come from Australia and Europe. The beer has a clean and refreshing taste with lots of flavour.

Spirits Around 200 years ago, a commentator on Mauritius complained: 'The facility with which spirits, especially arrack of inferior quality, are to be procured is more fatal to the soldiers than exposure to the sun, or any other effect of the climate.'

Rum-making on the island dates back to 1639, following the introduction of sugarcane by the Dutch, when it was made from cane juice even before people knew how to extract the crystals. Alcohol is now the most successful by-product of sugar, obtained by turning molasses into fine spirit.

There are many rums produced in Mauritius, including the romantic-sounding Green Island Rum. Most households and bars keep a variety of *rhum arrangé*, made by adding their own choice of fruit and/or spices to a large bottle of rum and leaving it to mature for a few months. The story of rum-making on the island is told at the Rhumerie de Chamarel (page 187), as well as at L'Aventure du Sucre (page 137) and Le Saint Aubin (page 168).

Wine Mauritius does not have the climate for growing grapes, so most of the wine served on the island is imported. South African, Australian and French wines are all widely available and most of the upmarket hotels have a sommelier on hand to help you match your wine to your meal. Be aware that the mark-up on wines served in hotel restaurants is often significant, so it is worth checking the price before you commit to a bottle.

Edward Clark Oxenham, a descendant of British colonials, was a pioneer who tried to grow grapes on his farm in Rodrigues. He failed, but with help from the Pasteur Institute of Paris started to produce wine from dried grapes and local fruits in 1931. He moved to Mauritius and in 1932 founded the company that now bears his name. Today Oxenham (*St Jean Rd, Phoenix;* ✆ *696 7950;* e *eureka@intnet.mu; www.oxenham.mu*) produces wine locally from imported grape concentrate and local fruit, such as lychee wine, and has also branched out into producing brandy, rum and other spirits.

In 2014, Phoenix Beverages (page 66), best known for its beers, began bottling its own range of wines in Mauritius, known as Gr8 Cape. The wine is produced in South Africa and is available in red, white and rosé. Unsurprisingly, wines produced in Mauritius are considerably cheaper than imported ones.

PUBLIC HOLIDAYS AND FESTIVALS

PUBLIC HOLIDAYS Public holidays for religious and state occasions threatened to overwhelm working life in Mauritius, multiplying until there were 28 official days off work a year, in addition to weekends. Now the number of statutory public holidays has been reduced to 15. These are as follows:

New Year's Day	1 January
New Year	2 January
Chinese Spring Festival	variable (January/February)
Thaipoosam Cavadee	variable (January/February)
Abolition of Slavery	1 February

Maha Shivaratree	variable (February/March)
National Day	12 March
Ougadi	variable (March/April)
Labour Day	1 May
Assumption	15 August
Ganesh Chaturthi	variable (August/September)
Divali	variable (October/November)
Arrival of Indentured Labourers	2 November
Eid El Fitr	variable (November/December)
Christmas Day	25 December

Employees are also permitted to have two additional days' leave a year to celebrate religious festivals that are no longer official public holidays. Leave is granted at the employee's request even if the employee doesn't belong to the religion celebrating the festival. Some of these festivals are so popular with everyone, regardless of their religion, that they become like public holidays, with shops and businesses closed.

Since many of these festivals depend on different religious calendars, the days on which they are held vary each year and will not always be in the months shown below.

FESTIVALS

Sankranti	January
Holi	March
Mehraj Shariff (Muslim)	March
Varusha Pirappu (Tamil New Year)	April
Shabbe Baraat (Muslim)	April
Good Friday	March/April
Easter Monday	March/April
Seemadree Appana Parsa (Telegu)	May
Sittarai Cavadee (Tamil)	May
Corpus Christi	May/June
Eid al-Adha (Muslim)	August–September
Raksha Bandhan (Hindu)	August
Anniversary of Père Laval's Death	9 September
Mid-Autumn Festival (Chinese)	October
All Saints' Day	1 November
Yaum Un Nabi	November
Ganga Asnan	November
Boxing Day	26 December

Sankranti The first of the year's religious festivals, it is celebrated in the beginning of the Tamil month Thai, and is also known as Thai Pongal. It is an occasion of thanksgiving for the harvest which is represented by the ceremonial boiling of *pongal* (rice, sugar, milk and dhal). It is customary to wear new clothes at this time.

Chinese Spring Festival This is New Year's Day and spring-cleaning combined. The festival begins on the eve of the Chinese New Year with an explosion of firecrackers to chase away evil spirits. It takes place in January or February and does not fall on the same day every year because of the irregularity of the lunar month.

During the week before New Year's Day there is a thorough spring-cleaning of the home. Traditionalists visit pagodas on New Year's Eve with offerings and prayers of thanksgiving. Neither scissors nor knives are used on the day and the colour red, symbolic of happiness, is favoured. Food is displayed in an honoured place in the home in the hope of abundance in the coming year. Cakes made of rice flour and honey, called wax cakes because of their texture, are shared with relatives and friends.

Thaipoosam Cavadee This Tamil ritual is named after the wooden yoke – the *cavadee* – decorated with flowers and palm leaves and with a pot of milk suspended from each end, which a devotee fulfilling a vow carries across his/her shoulders in procession to their temple. There it is placed before the deity when, despite the long, hot ordeal, the milk should not be curdled.

The *cavadee* procession, while colourful and spectacular, is awe-inspiring because of the penance undergone by the participants who walk with their bodies pierced with needles, hooks hanging from their flesh and skewers threaded through their tongues and cheeks. If you are in Mauritius during this festival, it is certainly worth watching the processions through the streets.

Maha Shivaratree This Hindu festival honouring the god Shiva takes place over three days. It begins with a night-long vigil and the following day devotees dressed in pure white carry the *kanwar*, a wooden arch decorated with flowers, paper and tiny mirrors, in procession to the sacred lake, Grand Bassin. Most of the island's Hindus make the pilgrimage to the lake, some taking two days to walk there. Worshippers believe the lights they launch on the lake on banana leaves and their offerings of flowers and fruit will float to the Ganges. They carry water from Grand Bassin home to their temple. *Poojas* (worship with food) are celebrated that night in the temples dotting the banks of the lake, the air heavy with the sweet smell of burning incense sticks and reverberating with prayers broadcast from loudspeakers.

This is reputed to be the largest Hindu festival celebrated outside India and is reminiscent of the great rituals on the banks of the holy Ganges.

Holi A happy time for Hindus when greetings are exchanged and revelry erupts with the squirting of coloured water and the spraying of coloured powder on one another, and on everyone else the revellers come across. Holi is a noisy and cheerful festival, which represents the victory of divine power over demonic strength. On the eve of Holi, bonfires symbolise the destruction of the demon Holika.

Ougadi Telegu New Year.

Eid El Fitr The annual month of fasting (Ramadan) by Muslims, during which they neither eat nor drink between sunrise and sunset, comes to an end with this festival. Prayers are offered at mosques during the day.

Ganesh Chaturthi Celebrated on the fourth day of the lunar month of August/September by Hindus of Marathi faith as the birthday of Ganesh, the god of wisdom and remover of all obstacles. Processions are held with devotees escorting pink, elephant-nosed effigies to the sea and dusting onlookers with scarlet powder.

Corpus Christi Devout Roman Catholics join in a procession through the streets of Port Louis in May or June on the occasion of Corpus Christi.

Eid al-Adha Sheep and goats are sacrificed in ceremonial slaughter for this Muslim festival and the meat is shared with family and friends. The day commemorates Abraham's willingness to sacrifice his son for God, and the events symbolise the Muslim ideal of sacrifice and dedication.

Père Laval Pilgrims of all faiths gather at the tomb of Father Jacques Desiré Laval throughout September, but particularly on 9 September, the anniversary of his death. Many come in hope of a miracle cure. For more information, see page 111.

Divali Clay oil lamps and paper lanterns with candles in them are placed in front of every Hindu and Tamil home on this Festival of Lights. Hills and valleys sparkle in the night as lights burn to celebrate the victory of Rama over Ravana, and Krishna's destruction of the demon Narakasuran, the victory of good over evil.

All Saints' Day The day on which cemetery cleaning takes place and flowers are placed by Roman Catholics on the graves of the dead.

Yaum Un Nabi The birth and death anniversaries of the Prophet Muhammad are commemorated on the Prophet's Day, following 12 days during which the faithful gather in mosques throughout the island, devoting themselves to religious study.

Ganga Asnan For Hindus this is the time of ceremonial bathing in the sea for purification, since they believe the holy water of the Ganges will be able to purify them. At the beaches special lifeguard units are set up to ensure the safety of bathers.

Muharram An important Muslim festival known in Mauritius as Yamsey, featuring figures and towers called *ghoons*, carried in procession through the streets in commemoration of the death of the grandson of the Prophet.

Fire-walking At the Tamil temple in Terre Rouge and at other temples in predominantly Tamil areas, *teemeedee* (fire-walking) takes place between October and March. Worshippers walk over beds of red-hot embers which represent the outstretched sari of Draupadee. They prepare for the ordeal by fasting, ritual bathing and a blessing before walking unscathed on the glowing embers to the accompaniment of chants from supporters.

SHOPPING

The government has done all it can to promote Mauritius as a 'shopping paradise'. In 2005, it announced plans to become one of the world's few duty-free islands by abolishing, over the following four years, its 80% tax on 1,850 different types of goods, including clothing, electronics and jewellery. It also offered incentives for investors to build large retail centres and shopping malls.

Certainly, a lot of money could be spent buying intricately carved model ships, diamonds, jewellery and designer clothing. Shops targeting tourists are found throughout Mauritius, but are concentrated around the Caudan Waterfront in Port Louis (page 107), Grand Baie and Ruisseau Creole in the island's west. In recent years a series of new, large, modern shopping malls has sprung up across the island, such as Les Halles in Phoenix, Bagatelle in Moka, Cascavelle in Flic en Flac and La Croisette in Grand Baie. They are designed to appeal to the local market as well as visitors, but thanks to the unstable economic climate, they are

struggling to fill the shops in some of these malls and it remains to be seen how they will fare in the future.

Clothing made in Mauritius can be bought in Floréal (page 193), but much of the 'designer' clothing on sale on the island these days is fake.

Shops in Port Louis sell everything from the latest electronic goods to coconut husks for polishing wooden floors. Near the harbour, the large and modern **Caudan Waterfront** (↖ *211 9500*; e *caudan@intnet.mu; www.caudan.com*) offers something for everyone with duty-free jewellery, clothing boutiques, bookshops, model ship shops and a craft market, where local artisans can be seen at work.

Shops in Port Louis are open 09.00–17.00 on weekdays. On Saturday they close at midday and only a few shops open on Sunday mornings. Shops in Curepipe and Quatre Bornes are open 10.00–17.30 daily except Thursday and Sunday, when they close at midday.

Discounts on marked prices may be available and it is always worth trying to negotiate, although Mauritians are usually more successful. Bargaining on unmarked prices, particularly in markets, is expected but requires patience.

Markets Markets are good places to shop, as prices tend to be lower than in shops, and you can pick up vanilla and other spices to take home. Self-caterers will find a good range of fresh fruit and vegetables. They are held in the following towns:

Port Louis	Monday to Saturday
Grand Baie	Monday to Saturday
Goodlands	Tuesday and Friday
Curepipe	Wednesday
Quatre Bornes	Thursday and Sunday
Vacoas	Tuesday and Friday
Mahébourg	Monday
Centre de Flacq	Wednesday and Sunday
Plaine Verte	Tuesday and Saturday

Duty-free goods The duty-free shops primarily sell jewellery, watches and electronic goods. Particularly popular are the duty-free diamonds, which can range from 0.1 to 10 carats and from £50 to £300,000. The shops involved in the scheme display a tax refund logo. For duty-free purchases, buyers need to show a foreign passport and air ticket in the same name, so remember to take both when you go shopping. Payment must be made with foreign currency, travellers' cheques or credit card, and at least 48 hours before the purchaser's intended departure. You can claim back 15% VAT at the airport, provided you have the paperwork for your purchase. Information on duty-free shopping is available at www.taxfreeshopping.mu.

Jewellery The production of jewellery for export has become a thriving industry, and some jewellers even have boutiques in the upmarket hotels. For handmade work – even to your own design – try the award-winning **Ravior** (*88 St Jean Rd, Quatre Bornes*; ↖ *454 3229*; e *ravior@intnet.mu; www.ravior.com*). Ravior also has shops at Ruisseau Creole shopping centre in Rivière Noire (↖ *483 6585*) and at the airport.

Family-run business **Adamas** has been selling diamonds and jewellery in Mauritius since 1987. Adamas has a diamond showroom in Mangalkhan, Floréal (↖ *686 5246*; e *adamas@intnet.mu; www.adamasltd.com*), where visitors can learn about diamond cutting and polishing, or even watch their commissions being made. It also has outlets at the Caudan Waterfront in Port Louis (↖ *210 1462*), Richmond

Hill complex in Grand Baie (✆ 269 1609) and Cascavelle shopping centre in Flic en Flac (✆ 450 9018).

Another well-known name in the local jewellery industry is **Poncini**, which has its headquarters in one of the handsomest buildings in Port Louis – a wooden, colonial Creole house built in 1850 (*Place du Théâtre, 2 Jules Koenig St;* ✆ 212 0818; e contact@poncini.com; www.poncini.com). It also has shops at the Caudan Waterfront in Port Louis (✆ 211 6921), on Royal Road in Curepipe (✆ 674 7044) and Sunset Boulevard in Grand Baie (✆ 263 8607).

The newly converted Citadel in Port Louis contains a series of shops targeting the tourist market, including **Trésor**, a diamond and jewellery shop (✆ 217 4040; e info@tresordiamonds.com). Trésor also has a shop in Grand Baie, on Sunset Boulevard (✆ 263 2518).

Model ships The model shipbuilding industry started small in the 1960s but has become a proud Mauritian tradition. There are now several workshops on the island.

The intricate detail in the models is incredible: some of take them up to 450 hours to make. The 250 or so different models available include replicas of famous ships such as the *Golden Hind*, HMS *Victory*, HMS *Bounty*, *Mayflower*, USS *Constitution* and *Cutty Sark*. Each is made by hand exactly to scale, using camphor or teak: camphor for the keel, hard *bois de natte* for the masts, yards and pulley blocks, soft lilac for the helm and capstan. Prices range from Rs1,000 to over Rs30,000. Model ships can be sent worldwide, or packed for taking in the hold, as checked baggage, on the plane home (a surcharge may apply). Many of the workshops also produce fine furniture.

One of the best-known manufacturers is **Historic Marine** in Goodlands (✆ 283 9404; e info@hismar.mu; www.historic-marine.com), which has been producing model ships since 1982. The company now makes around 2,000 models per year. Visitors can visit the model ship workshop and buy the finished articles on site (page 135). They can even make a model of your own boat. Not all of the model ships on sale in Mauritius are made in Mauritius but Historic Marine prides itself on being ethical and on providing employment to Mauritians, so its models are produced in Mauritius.

You will find model ship shops around the island and in some hotels but most are concentrated around Curepipe. **Comajora** at La Brasserie Road, Forest Side (✆ 675 1644; www.knegroup.com), has a shop just outside Curepipe. **Bobato** has a showroom at 53A Sir John Pope Hennessy Street, Curepipe (✆ 675 2899; e info@bobatoshipmodels.com; www.bobatoshipmodels.com). **First Fleet Reproductions** is at 74–76 Royal Road, Phoenix (✆ 698 0161; e contact@first-fleet-reproductions.com; www.first-fleet-reproductions.com). **Qetsia Boutique** at the Citadel in Port Louis (✆ 233 2800) also sells model ships.

Mauritius Glass Gallery The aim of the Mauritius Glass Gallery is to produce handmade glass objects from recycled glass and promote environmental awareness. The workshop at Pont Fer, Phoenix, is open to the public and there are regular glass-blowing demonstrations (for details, see page 199). The products can be bought at Pont Fer (✆ 696 3360; e mgg@pbg.mu), in the craft market at the Caudan Waterfront (✆ 210 1181), at the Super U Commercial Centre in Grand Baie (✆ 269 0376) and at the airport.

Textiles Textile manufacture remains an important industry, although it is less central to the economy than it was owing to diversification. While most of the

finished goods are exported to Europe, once the manufacturers have completed their quotas, the remainder can be sold at home.

The island has made a name for itself in the knitwear field and shops can be found all across Mauritius. In the Floréal Square, there are a number of shops that sell good-quality clothes. Using wool spun at Ferney Spinning Mills, Floréal Knitwear (*www.floreal-knitwear.com*) makes clothes for a number of well-known international brands, including Marks and Spencer, John Lewis and Pringle, but you can pick up the garments in Mauritius at a fraction of the price, often before the brand label has been sewn in. Floréal Knitwear now has factories in Madagascar and Bangladesh, as well as Mauritius.

Visitors to Mauritius used to flock to the innumerable 'designer' stores on the island believing that they were getting fabulous discounts on famous brands, Ralph Lauren in particular. It wasn't until 2004 that it was confirmed that some of these shops stocked fake designer clothing made on the island and the government ordered them to be shut down. Canny shoppers will be quick to spot that fakes (often Dolce and Gabbana, Chanel, Armani, etc) are still sold in some shops.

If you want custom-made clothing, dressmakers and tailors can run up garments in a few days. Short-term visitors should commission the work on arrival to ensure that it is ready in time for departure.

Souvenirs Those looking for a reminder of Mauritius to take home with them are spoilt for choice. If your home country allows the importation of plant material, the wax-like anthuriums grown in Mauritius are sold packed in cardboard boxes for travelling. They should keep for a few weeks when you get them home.

Local delicacies such as smoked marlin, tea, sugar, rum and vanilla make lovely gifts and can be bought at the airport just before departure if you have left your shopping until the last minute. Spices are easy to transport and are inexpensive in markets. Many of the handicrafts on sale in Mauritius are imported, mostly from Madagascar. If items are made in Mauritius, they will usually be labelled accordingly. The Made in Moris Association was created in 2013 to bring together companies which manufacture goods in Mauritius. A list of its members is available online (*www.madeinmoris.com*). For more information on tracking down products made in Mauritius, see page 107.

ARTS AND ENTERTAINMENT

The arts flourish in Mauritius despite a lack of appreciation and encouragement from the outside world. The Ministry of Arts and Culture promotes the Mauritian arts scene and its website (*htttp://culture.gov.mu.org*) provides a list of events and cultural organisations. The free magazine *Kozé* provides information on events, exhibitions, etc.

Alliance-Française (*1 Victor Hugo St, Bell Village, Port Louis;* \ *212 2949;* e *afim. web.mas@gmail.com; www.afmaurice.org*) is very active in its encouragement of the arts and the French language. Opened in 1884, the Mauritian Alliance Française was the first created outside France and aimed to keep the French language alive under British rule. It is balanced out by the **British Council** (*Royal Rd, Rose Hill;* \ *403 0200;* e *general.enquiries@mu.britishcouncil.org; www.britishcouncil.mu*), which teaches English language, offers opportunities to study in the UK and promotes British artists, in particular the music scene.

LITERATURE Several slim volumes of verse, belles-lettres and travelogues by local authors are to be found hidden away in Mauritian bookshops. Robert Edward Hart,

who died in 1954, was Mauritius's most renowned poet, and was awarded the OBE and the French *Légion d'honneur*. His house at Souillac is now a museum (page 166).

Mauritian writer and painter Malcolm de Chazal (1902–81) is best known for his *Sens Plastique*, a compilation of several thousand aphorisms and pensées. Born in Vacoas of a French family, de Chazal wrote in French. His surrealist work was highly praised by French literary figures.

Much of Mauritian literature is written in French, some in English and very little in Creole. Playwright Dev Virahsawmy, a retired politician, is an advocate of the Creole language and writes works only in that language.

Each June, Le Prince Maurice Hotel hosts Le Prince Maurice Prize for literature with a theme of love. The prize alternates between English and French writers each year and the winner receives a two-week stay at the hotel.

Shelf-loads of books, mostly in French, have been written about Mauritius, many with slavery as their theme. The island has been the setting for novels, too, the most famous being the pastoral French novel *Paul et Virginie* by Bernadin de Saint Pierre, which was first published in 1773. Its sentimental tale of love and heartbreak, based on the wrecking of the *St-Géran* in 1744, is remarkable for the accuracy of its nature notes and description of an idyllic Mauritius when it resembled a garden of Eden.

Bookshops For its population and high literacy rate, Mauritius is poorly served for bookshops (*librairies* in French). While there are a number of them on the island, most of these combine stationery supplies with a stock of books for students and a few general volumes in French and some in English. The best bookshops are in Curepipe and Port Louis.

THEATRE, DANCE AND ART There are some local folklore and dramatic societies that occasionally perform cultural shows and plays. The old opera house in Port Louis (*Municipal Theatre;* \ *212 1090*), built in 1822, has been lovingly restored and is a fine setting for local drama with performances usually in the evenings. The Plaza Theatre (*Royal Rd, Rose Hill;* \ *424 1145*) is part of the Beau Bassin/Rose Hill town hall complex, a Baroque 1920s creation by Coultrac Mazérieux which has become a prestigious venue for Mauritian and foreign cultural activities. **Opera Mauritius** (\ *466 9988;* e *info@operamauritius.com; www.operamauritius.com*) is a non-profit organisation which puts on operas, musicals and ballets. It also runs training programmes for young professionals and underprivileged children. The first Mauritius Theatre Festival was held at the Mahatma Gandhi Institute in Moka in May 2015 and there are plans for it to be an annual event.

For tickets to concerts and plays, contact the island's ticket office, Otayo (\ *466 9999;* e *info@otayo.com; www.otayo.com*).

The island's largest art gallery is Raphael in Pointe aux Canonniers (\ *263 6470;* ⊕ *09.30–19.00 Mon–Sat*), which was established by Mauritian artist Chayetan Seebaluck, and exhibits works by local and international artists. An art gallery at the Beau Bassin/Rose Hill town hall complex is named after the Mauritian artist Max Boullé (\ *454 9500*), and often features exhibitions by local artists. Commercial art galleries are found in Quatre Bornes, Grand Baie, Pointe aux Cannoniers, Rivière Noire and Port Louis (page 108). There is a greater concentration of galleries around the touristy areas. Galerie du Moulin Cassé in Pereybère (\ *727 0672;* ⊕ *10.00–18.00 Fri*) is in a converted 19th-century sugar mill and has permanent exhibitions by Diane Henry, natural world photographer, and Malcolm de Chazal (1902–82), Mauritian artist.

NIGHTLIFE For most tourists, nightlife will centre on their hotel since the hotels tend to be isolated on the coast and, with the exception of those in Grand Baie and Flic en Flac, they are far from local nightspots. Hotel evening entertainment is of a good standard, with live bands, dancing and theme nights. Most hotels feature weekly *séga* shows, which are certainly worth seeing.

In recent years, a few hotels have established upmarket clubs open to the public. Shanti Maurice in the south of the island has the Fish and Rhum Shack, a barefoot restaurant rustic beach bar (page 160). C Beach Club at Heritage Le Telfair is a similar concept with a beachside bar, restaurant and regular live entertainment (page 161). Entry for the day will cost around Rs600 and includes use of the pools, watersports facilities and access to the bar and restaurant.

For nightlife outside the hotels, the focal points are the tourist areas of Grand Baie and Flic en Flac. Grand Baie used to be the place to go but Flic en Flac is becoming increasingly popular. Many nightclubs open on Wednesday, as well as Friday and Saturday evenings. Entry is often free, especially for women, but can cost around Rs300. For additional information, see the chapter on the relevant geographical area.

Casinos Mauritians love to gamble. Most casinos offer fruit machines as well as a variety of tables (roulette, blackjack, etc). Dress standards call for more than beachwear. The casinos are generally open from early evening for playing the slot machines, but only from 21.00 for gambling at the tables. On Sundays, they open at about 15.00.

☆ **Casino de Maurice** Teste de Bush St, Curepipe; ✆ 602 1300

☆ **Flic en Flac Casino** Pasadena Village, Flic en Flac; ✆ 453 8022

☆ **L'Ámicale Casino** 6 Chausée St, Port Louis; ✆ 210 9713

☆ **Le Casino du Caudan** Port Louis Waterfront; ✆ 210 4203

☆ **Senator Club** Rue la Source, Centre de Flacq; ✆ 413 3000

☆ **Senator Club** Royal Rd, Grand Baie; ✆ 263 2030

☆ **Senator Club** Labourdonnais St, Mahébourg; ✆ 631 2990

☆ **Senator Club** Edith Cavell St, Port Louis; ✆ 208 8800

☆ **Senator Club** Royal Rd, Triolet; ✆ 261 5903

☆ **Ti Vegas** Royal Rd, Quatre Bornes; ✆ 454 8800

☆ **Ti Vegas** Super U, Grand Baie; ✆ 269 1448

PHOTOGRAPHY

Mauritius offers some wonderful opportunities for the photographer. It is advisable to bring all your equipment, including spares, with you as the cost of photography paraphernalia is likely to be higher than in your home country. Digital photography equipment and printing are available in outlets around the main tourist resorts. Printing and downloading of photos onto disk are available at the larger internet cafés.

Most Mauritians are quite happy to have their photos taken but you should ask permission first. Permits are not required for photography but you are not allowed to take photographs of the harbour and the airport.

MEDIA AND COMMUNICATIONS

MEDIA Newspapers in Mauritius enjoy a reputation for lively debate and freedom of expression, with the independent press curbed only by self-censorship. The first

newspaper was published in 1773 and there have been more than 600 titles since then, including *Le Cernéen*, started in 1832 as the first newspaper that did not have to be submitted to the government for approval.

The most popular daily papers are *Le Matinal* (*www.lematinal.com*), *Le Mauricien* (*www.lemauricien.com*) and *L'Express* (*www.lexpress.mu*), which are published in French, with occasional articles and advertisements in English. *L'Express* also publishes a version in Rodrigues. Larger hotels often sell English and other foreign newspapers, and provide daily news summaries in several languages. The *Mauritius News* (*Ashleigh Court, 29 Loates Ln, Watford WD17 2PJ;* \ +44 7912 483036; e *editor@mauritiusnews.co.uk; www.mauritiusnews.co.uk*) is a UK-based, English-language news resource.

The Mauritius Broadcasting Corporation (MBC) (*Louis Pasteur St, Forest Side;* \674 0475; *http://mbc.intnet.mu*) is the national broadcaster. It operates 17 television channels in Mauritius and four in Rodrigues, as well as seven radio stations. It broadcasts in 12 languages, although the Creole channel was not launched until 2013. The BBC World Service can be received on kHz1575.

Television broadcasting began in Mauritius in 1964 but was not introduced to Rodrigues until 1987. Most hotels in the mid-range, upmarket and luxury categories have satellite channels, including BBC World and CNN.

POST In 1815, it took 17 weeks for news of Napoleon's defeat to reach Port Louis. Today Mauritius Post (*www.mauritiuspost.mu*) provides a quick and reliable service. Mail to/from Europe takes about a week, and approximately ten days to/from the US.

Most towns and villages (and the airport) have a post office. The general post office in Port Louis is a squat Victorian granite-block building in Quay Street on the waterfront. Adjacent to it is the Mauritius Postal Museum (page 110).

Interactive kiosks have been installed in many of the island's post offices. These offer local and international phone calls, internet access (Rs10 for 15 minutes), email and printing (Rs1.50 per page). Many also offer Wi-Fi.

Post offices are open 08.15–16.00 Monday–Friday and 08.15–11.45 Saturday.

TELEPHONE The island's telecommunications infrastructure is run by Mauritius Telecom, whose corporate office is at Telecom Tower, Edith Cavell Street, Port Louis (\ *203 7000; www.mauritiustelecom.com*).

You should be able to use your international roaming mobile phone in Mauritius as coverage is very good in most areas, although not as good in Rodrigues. The principal mobile network providers are Orange, Cellplus (code CELLPLUS-MRU or CELL+) and Emtel (code Emtel or MRU10). Prepaid SIMs are available locally and offer cheaper call rates than your roaming mobile. Some people bring a second mobile phone (SIM unlocked) and buy a starter pack from a local provider.

If you see some impossibly tall and straight palm trees on the island, they are in fact mobile-phone cell towers in disguise.

The International Direct Dialling code to contact Mauritius or Rodrigues from overseas is 230, followed by a seven-digit number. Mobile numbers are eight digits and begin with 5.

To call overseas from Mauritius, dial 020 followed by the country code, area code and local number. Hotels tend to add a considerable mark-up to the basic cost of an international call, so it is worth checking rates before making a call. A number of companies have launched prepaid phonecards, offering attractive call rates to major destinations from land lines and mobiles. Some of the most popular are Yello and

EasyCall, which are widely available in local shops. Just dial the number listed on the card, enter your PIN and then the number you wish to call. It is worth noting these cards cannot always be used on public payphones or hotel phones.

Mauritius Telecom sells Smart Cards, which can be used in the island's nearly 650 phone booths to make local and international calls.

Useful telephone numbers are:

National directory enquiries ☏150	**International call assistance** ☏192
International directory enquiries ☏190	**Tourist information** ☏152

INTERNET ACCESS/EMAIL Most mid-range, upmarket and luxury hotels offer internet access (sometimes at a fee), either in your room or in the hotel business centre. Most hotels now offer wireless internet, available either in your room or in a given area of the hotel. Most offer this as a free service, but some charge around Rs250 per hour. Many restaurants and cafés offer Wi-Fi, but internet cafés have all but died out in the last few years. Wi-Fi is available at the Sir Seewoosagur Ramgoolam International Airport.

Mauritius Post offers internet access at its post offices (see page 76).

BUSINESS

Over the past four decades Mauritius has successfully followed an economic strategy of diversification and industrialisation. One element of this was to attract direct foreign investment, with the result that Mauritius has developed good facilities for business. There are direct scheduled flights from Europe, Africa, the Far East and Australasia, a reliable infrastructure and sophisticated communication links. The local workforce is an added advantage with Mauritius enjoying the highest adult literacy rate in Africa and most individuals being fluent in English and French. The success which Mauritius has experienced has been recognised by a number of international organisations. In the World Bank's *Doing Business Survey 2016*, Mauritius was ranked 32 out of 189 countries and first in the sub-Saharan African region. The full country report is available at www.doingbusiness.org.

BUSINESS ASSISTANCE There are a number of organisations that exist both to develop and promote Mauritius as a centre for business and investment, and also to provide support to existing companies.

Mauritius Chamber of Commerce (MCCI)
3 Royal St, Port Louis; ☏208 3301; e mcci@intnet. mu; www.mcci.org. Founded in 1850, the MCCI now has 400 members representing a wide spectrum of economic sectors from commerce & industry to banking, insurance, transport & tourism. Affiliated to the MCCI are the Chinese Chamber of Commerce, the Indian Traders' Association & the Mauritius Chamber of Merchants. The MCCI's activities include constant dialogue with government, trade fair & mission organisation, providing commercial information & defending the economic interests of Mauritius through contact with the European Union. There is a consultancy service for small businesses & computer & system analysis courses are held. Every year the MCCI issues an annual report, essential reading for anyone interested in doing business in Mauritius.

Board of Investment (BOI) 10th Fl, 1 Cathedral Sq Bldg, 16 Jules Koenig St, Port Louis; ☏203 3800; e contact@investmauritius.com; www. investmauritius.com. The BOI was established in 2001 as the body responsible for promoting Mauritius as an international investment & business centre. It is also charged with considering investment proposals & issuing investment certificates. In recent years, the BOI has opened offices in Paris & New Delhi. Its website contains useful information on working & living in

Mauritius, investment opportunities & legislation relevant to doing business.

International Management (Mauritius) Ltd (IMM) Les Cascades Bldg, Edith Cavell St, Port Louis; 212 9800; e ds@cimglobalbusiness.com; www.cimglobalbusiness.com. IMM is a member of the CIM Financial Group, which is a wholly owned subsidiary of the Rogers Group, one of the largest & best-known companies in Mauritius, with representation in the UK, Australia, South Africa & Singapore. IMM helps clients to set up, manage & administer offshore entities including companies, trusts & funds & to liaise with the FSC (see right). IMM carries a stock of ready-formed shelf companies & can obtain name approval for new companies within 2 working days. IMM also provides consultancy services to clients wishing to be onshore rather than offshore & provides advice on obtaining residency permits. Provides support such as directorship, secretarial accounting and tax.

Financial Services Commission (FSC) FSC Hse, 54, Cybercity, Ebene; 403 7000; e fscmauritius@intnet.mu; www.fscmauritius.org. The FSC was established in 2001 under the Financial Services Development Act & is the independent regulator of non-bank financial services. The FSC licenses, regulates & supervises the non-banking offshore sector, while co-ordinating government agencies & private organisations dealing with the sector.

OFFSHORE BUSINESS CENTRE As part of its continuing diversification strategy and in order to sustain economic growth, the government initiated offshore business in Mauritius in 1992. Offshore activities include banking, insurance, fund management, trusteeship of offshore trusts, operational headquarters, international consultancy services, shipping and ship management, and aircraft financing and leasing.

Offshore banks operating in Mauritius include Bank of Baroda, Banque Internationale des Mascareignes, Barclays, Deutsche Bank, HSBC and Investec.

There are considerable incentives for offshore business activities in Mauritius. Personal and corporate tax rates are only 15% and dividends are tax-free. Furthermore, Mauritius has double taxation agreements with 43 countries and several more currently under negotiation. Those already completed include China, France, Germany, India, Italy, Pakistan, South Africa, Sweden, Singapore and the UK. Offshore companies can take advantage of those treaties and may obtain a certificate of fiscal residence from the Mauritian tax authorities stating that a company is resident in Mauritius for the purpose of tax.

Other financial institutions which support the development of Mauritius as a financial centre include the Development Bank of Mauritius (*www.dbm.mu*), State Investment Corporation (*www.stateinvestment.com*) and Stock Exchange of Mauritius.

The **Stock Exchange** (*4th Fl, 1 Cathedral Sq Bldg, 16 Jules Koenig St, Port Louis;* 212 9541; e *stockex@sem.intnet.mu; www.stockexchangeofmauritius.com*) was launched in 1989 and is playing an important role in mobilising funds on behalf of companies listed on the Stock Exchange. Similarly, the offshore banking sector is authorised to provide loans in foreign exchange to the EPZ sector at competitive rates. The Mauritius Leasing Company provides financial leases up to 100% of the value of production equipment for a period of three to seven years.

Mauritius is also a freeport which was established in 1992 under the control of the Mauritius Freeport Authority (*10th Fl, 1 Cathedral Sq Bldg, 16 Jules Koenig St, Port Louis;* 203 3800; e *contact@investmauritius.com; www.efreeport.com*). The freeport is a regional warehousing, distribution and marketing centre and has seen significant infrastructure development in recent years by private developers. Companies import goods mainly from China, India and Thailand and then re-export to Madagascar, Hong Kong, Singapore and African countries. The principal products re-exported are frozen fish, textiles, machinery and electronic equipment, chemicals, foodstuffs and pharmaceuticals.

However, Mauritius should not be thought of as a tax haven manipulated by 'brass plate' operators. A proven presence locally must be established (for which accountants and company formation firms can be hired) to obtain a tax residence certificate. This enables offshore companies to have an optional zero tax rate and exemption from profit tax, stamp duties and capital gains tax.

BUSINESS ACCOMMODATION Most luxury, upmarket and some upper mid-range hotels cater extremely well for business guests. Business and conference centres provide all the facilities you may need, including secretarial services and assistance with local contacts. Such hotels regularly host conferences and incentive groups. For business accommodation in Port Louis, the **Labourdonnais Waterfront Hotel** (page 103) and **Le Suffren Hotel & Marina** (page 103), both near the Caudan Waterfront Complex, are the best options.

BUSINESS VISA As with tourist visas, business visitors from certain countries do not require a visa (see page 44). For stays longer than 90 days per calendar year, a work permit is required. Applications are made through the Board of Investment – further information is on its website (*www.boimauritius.com*). For more information, see page 45.

WORKING HOURS For the public sector, working hours are 09.00–16.00 Monday–Friday and 09.00–12.00 Saturday. The number of staff is reduced on Saturdays, so for the sake of your sanity it is advisable to carry out administrative formalities on weekdays.

Private enterprises are usually open 08.30–16.15 Monday–Friday and 09.00–12.00 Saturday.

CULTURAL ETIQUETTE

Reproduced here (translated from the French by the MTPA) is the Code of Ethics for Tourists, since it shows how great is the concern of Mauritians for the right approach to visitors to their country:

You are already most welcome in Mauritius. You'll be even more so if you will readily appreciate that our island …

- considers its most important asset is its people. They are well worth meeting and enjoying a friendly chat with;
- possesses a rich capital of cultures, needs and values which it cherishes more than anything else;
- is ready to give you value for money, but is not prepared to sell its soul for it;
- has wealth of its own, which deserves to be preserved;
- treats all its visitors like VIPs, but does not take kindly to those who overact the part;
- is not all lagoon and languor, and boasts a host of many-splendoured sights;
- considers, without being prudish, that nudity when flaunted can be provocative and offensive;
- is not a faraway paradise of unlimited licence;
- takes pride in serving you with a smile and would be grateful for a smile in return;
- and will bare its soul willingly if you will handle it with care.

Beachwear is acceptable in tourist resorts but is less so in local towns and villages. Tourists should dress appropriately when visiting religious buildings (no shorts,

miniskirts, etc). It is a good idea for women to carry a light cardigan or shirt and sarong for this purpose. Shoes should be removed when entering temples and mosques, and you may also be asked to remove leather items at some Hindu temples. At mosques you may be required to cover your head. Nudism is not allowed anywhere on the island. Although some female tourists sunbathe topless, it is not encouraged.

Mauritians are generally traditional and conservative – public displays of affection are best avoided, particularly away from the resorts. Pointing at people is considered to be impolite – a general wave in the right direction is more appropriate. When Mauritians walk into a shop or restaurant they greet those present and they appreciate it when visitors do likewise. As you explore Mauritius, be prepared for lots of questions. Mauritians are curious and their motivation is usually simply a desire to learn about your country and practise their language skills.

In recent years there has been an increase in the number of people begging, including children, particularly around the main commercial centres, markets and tourist attractions. Beggars are not usually aggressive and a gentle refusal to a demand for money, accompanied by a smile, is normally accepted immediately.

Although it should not affect travellers, many Mauritian women are the victims of sexual abuse and domestic violence. There is a hotline for reporting incidents of domestic violence (\ *211 0725*).

TRAVELLING POSITIVELY

I am sure that you will thoroughly enjoy visiting Mauritius and Rodrigues. You may feel that you wish to repay the hospitality you experience by helping the local community in some way. Below is a selection of particularly worthwhile projects and details of how you can lend support.

CARE-CO (RODRIGUES) CARE-Co (Rodrigues), formerly known as Craft Aid Rodrigues, is a wonderful project, giving people with disabilities a vastly improved life and a place in society. I am fortunate enough to have visited the CARE-Co workshop in Rodrigues several times and can assure you that donations are put to excellent use, including hearing aids, family support, educational tools, and equipment for the Gonzague Pierre-Louis Special Learning Centre. For further information, see box, page 242.

How you can help
- Buy CARE-Co products. You can also buy the jewellery online at www. beaucoco.co.uk. For UK partners, write to: CARE-Co, Camp du Roi, Rodrigues, Mauritius.
- For coconut jewellery (*bijoux coco*), you can order a full-colour catalogue. The catalogue costs £3 to produce so any contributions are very welcome. The cost of the catalogue will be reimbursed on your first order.
- Cheques or donations can be sent in any major currency. Donate to CARE-Co (Rodrigues), Mauritius Commercial Bank, Port Mathurin; account number 360000940.
- Those who donate any amount exceeding £15 receive direct reports from the Gonzague Pierre-Louis Special Learning Centre.

MAURITIAN WILDLIFE FOUNDATION (MWF) The Mauritian Wildlife Foundation conserves Mauritius's remaining plants and animals.

How you can help

- Book an excursion to Ile aux Aigrettes, which contains the last remnants of native coastal forest and is the probable site of the dodo's extinction. Excursions are offered in most Mauritius hotels and a portion of the tour fees supports wildlife conservation.
- On Rodrigues, book a guided hike along Sentier Pasner, a visit to the Grande Montagne Nature Reserve or the Solitude endemic nursery. Contact the MWF directly (*Forestry quarters, Solitude, Rodrigues;* ✆ *+230 831 4558;* e *mwfrod@ mauritian-wildlife.org; www.mauritian-wildlife.org*).
- Donations are vital to the continuation of the MWF's work. You can donate via the MWF website, or contact the MWF directly (*The Fundraising Manager, Mauritian Wildlife Foundation, Grannum Rd, Vacoas;* ✆ *697 6097;* e *jgardenne@ mauritian-wildlife.org; www.mauritian-wildlife.org*).
- The MWF is staffed by Mauritians and expatriates, as well as overseas volunteers. To apply for a volunteer placement with the MWF, please consult the website and contact the secretary (e *executive@mauritian-wildlife.org*).

SHOALS RODRIGUES Shoals Rodrigues is a non-governmental organisation (NGO) that studies and monitors the marine ecology of Rodrigues and, through various programmes, promotes marine environmental awareness amongst Rodriguans of all ages, thus working towards a sustainable development of the lagoon.

The organisation accepts volunteers from around the world on placements. If this interests you, or you would like to make a donation to the organisation, please contact Jovani Raffin at Shoals Rodrigues, Pointe Monier, Rodrigues (✆ *831 1225;* e *admin@shoalsrodrigues.intnet.mu; www.shoals-rodrigues.net*).

See box *Shoals Rodrigues*, page 218.

SMALL & MEDIUM ENTERPRISE AUTHORITY (SMEDA) SMEDA (*www.smeda.mu*) supports and facilitates the development of entrepreneurship in Mauritius and Rodrigues. It promotes the manufacture and sale of handicrafts and by buying goods from SMEDA outlets you ensure part of your payment goes to the Mauritian and Rodriguan artisans who made them. Handicrafts sold in other outlets, including the markets, are often imported. SMEDA craft shops can be found at:

Craft Market Caudan Waterfront, Port Louis; ✆ 210 0139

Plaine Corail Airport Rodrigues; ✆ 832 7653

SSR International Airport Plaine Magnien; ✆ 637 4828

Village Artisanal Mahébourg Museum Compound, Mahébourg; ✆ 631 3879

FONDATION ESPOIR ET DEVELOPPEMENT (FED) Created and financed by Beachcomber Hotels, this organisation helps provide training and work to school leavers and runs the 'Local Hands' project. **Local Hands** is a group of around 60 artisans from underprivileged backgrounds who make handicrafts for sale to the tourist market. Their products are sold in Beachcomber hotels and at their two small shops in Trou aux Biches (page 118).

3

Activities

For many visitors, turning over to tan the other side will be the extent of their physical exertion whilst in Mauritius. However, there is plenty to keep the more energetic amused. Activities, watersports in particular, are generally run by the large resort hotels.

If you are resident in Mauritius, the website www.marideal.mu offers special deals for accommodation, activities and spa treatments.

SPA TREATMENTS

While most of the luxury, upmarket and mid-range hotels on the island have their own spa (some of which are open to non-hotel residents), those who are staying in smaller establishments without such facilities can take advantage of the growing number of spas opening outside the hotels.

The island's spas are typically operated by well-trained staff and offer a range of massages and treatments. Some even offer comprehensive wellness programmes lasting several days. You can expect to pay around Rs1,500 for a 45-minute facial, Rs1,000 for a 45-minute body massage.

The following is a selection of spas which operate outside the hotels or are hotel spas open to the public:

Emeraude Spa Emeraude Beach Attitude, Royal Rd, Belle Mare; ☏401 1400; www. emeraudebeach-hotel-mauritius.com. A small spa with 2 massage rooms, offering a complete range of massages, body care & facials.
Genna Wellness Lounge Be Cosy Apart'Hotel, Coastal Rd, Trou aux Biches; ☏265 7206. A small, modern wellness lounge offering massage & beauty therapy. Professionally run by an Australian expat with lots of experience.
Grand Baie Gym & Hydrospa X Club Rd, Grand Baie; ☏263 9290; e grandbaiegym@live.com; www.grandbaiegym.com; ⏰ 06.00–21.00 Mon–Fri, 07.30–19.30 Sat, 09.00–13.00 Sun & public holidays (spa closed Sun). Offers a gym, pool, spa, beauty treatments, weight-loss programmes, hairdresser & a range of group classes, such as martial arts, dance & aerobics. There is a café selling healthy treats. Temporary

membership of the gym is from Rs1,398 per week, Rs690 per day.
Mont Choisy Spa Coastal Rd, Mont Choisy; ☏265 6789; e spamontchoisy@orange.net; www. spamontchoisy.com; ⏰ 10.00–19.30 Tue–Sun
Om Spa Royal Rd, Beegun Complex, Flic en Flac; ☏5769 2676; e omspa-mu@yahoo.com; www. omspamauritius.com; ⏰ 09.15–17.30 Tue–Sat, 09.15–13.00 Sun & public holidays. Offers traditional & Ayurvedic massage, plus beauty treatments.
Rituals Bois Rouge/Fond du Sac; ☏266 9595; e rituals@spaconcept.mu; www.rituals.mu; ⏰ 09.00–19.00 Mon–Sat including public holidays. Has 5 treatment rooms & a spacious spa suite for couples with outdoor bath. The spa also includes a hammam, vichy shower & a power plate studio for slimming programmes & muscle toning.
Rituals Level 1, Tower C, Nexteracom Bldg, Ebène; ☏468 1800; e ritualsebene@spaconcept.mu;

www.rituals.mu; ⏱ 09.00–19.00 Mon–Thu, 09.00–20.00 Fri–Sat. Ayurvedic & traditional treatments.
Rituals La Balise Marina, Rivière Noire; ☏ 406 9200; e rituals@spaconcept.mu; www.rituals.mu; ⏱ 09.00–19.00 Mon–Sat. Ayurvedic traditional treatments.
Spa Viva 102 St Jean Rd, Quatre Bornes; ☏ 467 8907.

Surya Coastal Rd, Pereybère; ☏ 263 1637; e info@spasurya.com; www.mauriweb.com/surya; ⏱ 09.00–20.00 daily. This Ayurvedic spa between Grand Baie & Pereybère offers a range of relaxing massages & treatments. As well as one-off treatments, programmes lasting from 3 days to 3 weeks are available. Yoga classes are available.
Trou aux Biches Beach Spa Coastal Rd, Trou aux Biches; ☏ 256 2012

GOLF

Mauritius has eight 18-hole golf courses; all but one are attached to a hotel. Several of the courses were designed by famous golfers, including Bernhard Langer and Ernie Els. Some hotels offer packages which include golf. Most hotel courses are open to non-residents on payment of a green fee. Expect to pay around Rs4,000–7,000 for 18 holes at the top courses; children pay approximately half price. Clubs, trolleys and other equipment can usually be hired. The price of club hire varies enormously, but expect to pay Rs500–1,600 for a full set, and around Rs275 for a trolley. A golf cart will cost around Rs1,750 for 18 holes, a caddy around Rs350. Lessons with a golf pro will cost in the region of Rs3,000 per hour. It is advisable, and often a requirement, to book tee-off times.

18-HOLE COURSES

Constance Belle Mare Plage Belle Mare; ☏ 402 2600; e headpro@bellemareplagehotel.com; www.bellemareplagehotel.com. 2 impressive courses designed with both professional & amateur golfers in mind. The Legend is an 18-hole, par-72 course designed by Rodney Wright & British player/commentator Peter Alliss, 3-time winner of the PGA Championship. Built on a former hunting reserve, accuracy on the tree-lined fairways is one of the main challenges, along with the ponds where deer drink in the mornings. The Links is an 18-hole, par-71 championship course, also designed by Rodney Wright & Peter Alliss. Only the Links course is open to non-residents of the hotel.
Heritage Golf Club Coastal Rd, Bel Ombre; ☏ 623 5600; e info@heritagegolfclub.mu; www.heritagegolfclub.mu; ⏱ 07.00–16.00 daily. An 18-hole, par-72 championship course designed by South African architect Peter Matkovich plus a 9-hole 'pitch & putt' par-3 course. In a stunning setting on 100 acres sandwiched between hills covered with sugarcane & the ocean, the course was designed to be accessible to a wide range of golfers yet be able to host a championship; it therefore offers 5 tee options. Residents of Heritage Le Telfair & Heritage Awali hotels will have green fees included in their package.

Ile aux Cerfs Golf Club Ile aux Cerfs; ☏ 402 7720; e info@iacgolf.mu; www.ileauxcerfsgolfclub.com; ⏱ 06.30–18.30 daily, last tee-off time for 18 holes is 14.00. An 18-hole, par-72 championship course endorsed by Bernhard Langer & voted tenth in the World's Top One Hundred Courses by *Golf World* magazine. An incredible course on the small offshore island of Ile aux Cerfs – all 18 holes have views of the sea. The 9 lakes & the obvious space limitations of playing on an island make this a challenging course. There is a superb clubhouse, which includes an impressive restaurant & bar with views of the course.
Mauritius Gymkhana Club Suffolk Rd, Vacoas; ☏ 696 1404; e mgymclub@intnet.mu; www.mgc.intnet.mu. An 18-hole, par-68 course, the oldest on the island & the only private club. Golf was played here as early as 1844. To play here you must be a member of the club or a guest of a member. Tee-off times must be booked in advance.
Paradis Hotel Le Morne Peninsula; ☏ 401 5050; e paradis@bchot.com; www.paradis-hotel.com. An 18-hole, par-72 championship course set against the stunning backdrop of Le Morne & on the water's edge, designed by Peter Matkovich.
Tamarina Golf Estate Tamarin Bay; ☏ 401 3006; e info@tamarinagolf.mu; www.tamarinagolf.mu. Another stunning 18-hole par-72 course, with

views of Mt Rempart & the waters of Rempart River featuring on many of the holes. Being on the west, it gets beautiful sunsets. The course was designed by Rodney Wright & undulates over 206ha. There are 5 tee options. Many of the hotels on the west coast can arrange for guests to play at this course. The clubhouse restaurant has stunning views of the mountains & serves excellent light meals.
The Anahita Golf Course Beau Champ; 402 3125; e teetime.anahita@fourseasons.com; www. anahita.mu. An 18-hole, par-72 championship course designed by Ernie Els. It is on the water's edge & claims one of the most stunning 18th holes in the world, with its fantastic ocean backdrop.

Green fees, including buggy, GPS & practice balls are Rs7,500.

9-HOLE COURSES
Le Saint Geran Poste de Flacq; 401 1888; f 401 1888; e reservations@ oneandonlylesaintgeran.com; www.lesaintgeran. oneandonlyresorts.com. A 9-hole, par 33-course, complete with clubhouse & the One&Only Golf Academy.
Le Shandrani Blue Bay; 603 4343; e shandrani@bchot.com; www.shandrani-hotel. com. A 9-hole, par-29 'pitch & putt' course. Only open to residents of Le Shandrani Hotel & Mauritian residents.

HORSE RACING

Horse racing takes place at the **Champ de Mars** racecourse in Port Louis every Saturday during the season from May until the end of November/early December. The highlight is the **Maiden Plate**, which is usually run in September. The sport is very popular amongst Mauritians, primarily because they love to gamble, and the centre of the racecourse fills with stalls, snack bars and bookmakers on race days.

Tour operators can arrange a day out at the races, which usually includes access to a VIP area. A cheaper option, and one which allows you to soak up the atmosphere, is to buy basic entry to the stands, which costs around Rs150–175, depending on the races being held. Entry to the rest of the course is usually free. For more information contact the **Mauritius Turf Club**, Eugene Laurent St, Port Louis (211 2147; e shanip@mauritiusturfclub.com; www.mauritiusturfclub.com).

HORSERIDING

Most hotels can arrange horseriding, although it is often cheaper to arrange it directly with the stables. The standards of horses and safety vary and, if you are not offered a riding hat, you should ask for one (you may have to insist). Do check that all the equipment is safe before setting off. Jodhpurs and riding boots are not usually available, so suitable clothing (long trousers and sensible, enclosed shoes) must be worn.

Some hotels offer horseriding along the beach, something many people dream of doing, but don't overlook the inland estates which offer riding – it is a great way to explore the island's interior.

One-hour treks typically cost Rs1,000–1,500, a half-day ride with lunch around Rs2,500.

Centre Equestre de la Louisa Belle Vue, Pamplemousses; 5440 8887; e ecurie@intnet.mu. A riding school, rather than a trail riding business. Excellent facilities, including well-maintained outdoor schools, & French instructors specialising in dressage & showjumping, plus a vaulting instructor from Poland. Frequented by expats.

Centre Equestre de Riambel Coastal Rd, Riambel; 5729 4572; www. centreequestrederiambel.com. Offers rides along the usually deserted, 2.5km-long beach at Riambel.
Domaine de l'Etoile Royal Rd, Moka; 5729 1050; e info@terrocean.mu; www.terrocean.mu. Offers guided rides through the 1,200ha estate.

Forbach Stables Esperance Trebuchet; 264 9044; e info@horseridingmauritius.com; www. horseridingmauritius.com; ⊕ Tue–Sun. A well-run stables with outdoor school about 15mins from Grand Baie. Caters for all levels of experience (min age 3 years), offering riding lessons & hacking, including beach rides. It is approved by the Mauritius Turf Club as a home for retired racehorses. Also offers livery.

Haras du Morne Le Morne Peninsula; 450 4142; e info@harasdumorne.com; www. harasdumorne.com. Opened in 2008 & run by people with an extensive equestrian background. The facilities are good & in an amazing setting at the foot of Le Morne. Beach rides are available.

Horse Riding Delights Mont Choisy Sugar Estate, Grand Baie; 265 6159/421 1166 (after hours); e horseriding@montchoisy.com. A highly professional stables run by former jockey Sylvain. Rides are through the estate's private deer park, a fantastic, historic setting, featuring a charming traditional home as the centrepiece. The remains of the sugar factory & lime kilns add to the atmosphere & even the horses enjoy stabling in imposing, old, stone buildings. Riding hats must be worn & can be borrowed on site. There are 9 horses & rides are limited to groups of 7. Rides take place at 08.30 & 15.00 Mon–Fri, 08.30 Sat.

La Vieille Cheminée Route Principale, Chamarel; 483 5249; e caroline@lavieillecheminee.com; www.lavieillecheminee.com; ⊕ Mon–Sat. Riding is on the 250ha working farm, through sugarcane, pineapple fields & forest. These have to be the best cared-for horses on the island – owner Caroline adores them. There are 5 horses, most of which are Boerpeds, well suited to the terrain. Rides are tailor-made to suit clients' riding ability. Refreshingly, they will not lump you in with a group of other riders of varying ability but will instead take you out in your own small group. No experience necessary.

Maritim Hotel Turtle Bay, Balaclava; 204 1000; e info.mau@maritim.de; www.maritim. com. Offers riding to hotel residents only, along the beach & through the countryside around the hotel.

3

FOOTBALL

Football is Mauritius's national sport and is played by amateur teams throughout the island. All the main towns have a stadium for local league matches, although unofficial games are played with passion wherever there is a space large enough.

Mauritians are devoted fans of English football and the shirts of English clubs are everywhere. Liverpool and Manchester United receive the most support, but residents of the village of Arsenal tend to support, unsurprisingly, Arsenal. The addiction is perpetuated by the fact that there is more English football on television in Mauritius than in England itself!

The Mauritius Professional Football League runs the local competition (233 2500; www.mpfl.mu).

DEEP-SEA FISHING

Mauritius has some of the best deep-sea fishing waters you can find and people come from all over the world just for that reason. World-record catches off Mauritius include the mako shark, blue shark, skipjack tuna and the renowned blue marlin. Although the west coast is regarded as the best area for deep-sea fishing, the northern and eastern coasts can offer rewarding trips.

If the primary purpose of your visit to Mauritius is fishing, you may want to take account of the following seasons:

Wahoo/hammerhead shark	September–December
Blue marlin/sailfish	November–March
Mako shark	November–April
Yellow fin tuna	March–May
Black marlin, skipjack tuna, barracuda	all year

Most of the deep-sea fishing companies operate modern, well-equipped boats that can reach deep waters in no time at all. The boats usually have three 'fighting' chairs in the stern and outriggers so that three baits can be trolled at a time. Any fish that is caught remains the property of the boat owner, although 'catch and release' is now being practised in Mauritius.

Almost all hotels and tour operators will be able to arrange deep-sea fishing trips.

In most cases, the crew of deep-sea fishing boats are incredibly poorly paid, particularly when you consider the amount of skill involved. If you feel that they have looked after you well, a tip will make a lot of difference to them.

The price will vary between boats, but a half-day trip (usually 6 hours) costs from around Rs15,000 per boat (usually six people) and a full day (usually 9 hours) Rs20,000. This will include all the equipment, snacks and drinks.

DEEP-SEA FISHING OPERATORS

Northern Mauritius

Organisation de Pêche du Nord (also known as Corsaire Club) Mont Choisy; ☎ 265 5209;
Sportfisher Sunset Bd Complex, Grand Baie; ☎ 263 8358; ☎ 263 6309; e sportfisher@orange. mu; www.sportfisher.com

Eastern Mauritius

Royal Big Game Fishing Trou d'Eau Douce; ☎ 5775 2279; e info@royalbiggamefishing.com; www.royalbiggamefishing.com

Southern Mauritius

Domaine du Pêcheur Vieux Grand Port; ☎ 634 5097; e dchasseur@intnet.mu
Lifestyle Boating Mauritius Place du Moulin, Bel Ombre; ☎ 622 2567; e bookings@ lifetyleboating.com; www.lifestyleboating.com

Western Mauritius

✴ **JP Henry Charters Ltd** La Balise Marina, Rivière Noire; ☎ 729 0901; e resa@jph.mu; www. jph.mu. Widely acknowledged as the island's best deep-sea fishing operator, this long-established, family-run firm has a superb range of modern boats & knowledgeable crew. They can arrange a trip to suit all levels of experience & ability. Also offers jigging.
La Pirogue Big Game Fishing Flic en Flac; ☎ 453 8054; e info@lapiroguebiggame.com; www.lapiroguebiggame.com
Morne Anglers Club Rivière Noire; ☎ 483 5060; e lmaclub@intnet.mu; www.morneanglers. com. A members' club which organises various competitions.

While all deep-sea boats are equipped for anglers, the enthusiast who wants to buy equipment can do so from:

Quay Stores 3 President John F Kennedy St, Port Louis; ☎ 212 1043

Rods & Reels La Preneuse; ☎ 483 5060; e jphenry@intnet.mu

SCUBA DIVING AND SNORKELLING

The reefs off Mauritius offer excellent conditions for scuba diving and snorkelling: warm, crystal-clear water, calm seas and varied marine life. Although pollution, overfishing, poaching in protected waters and the stealing of shells have taken their toll in some areas, there are still numerous excellent dive sites around. Many experts rate them as better than those to be found around the main Seychelles islands or off Sri Lanka.

Although diving can be done throughout the year, June–July is considered by experienced divers to be the least suitable time, on account of the weather and reduced visibility. Summer is considered the best time as the warm waters attract an abundance of marine life.

Most hotels offer snorkelling equipment and trips, either free of charge or for a small fee. Masks, snorkels and flippers can be bought quite cheaply in tourist areas. The lagoons of the northeast and west coasts are good snorkelling areas, as are the waters around Trou aux Biches and Blue Bay.

There are plenty of scuba-diving centres on the island. Instructors should have Professional Association of Diving Instructors (PADI) or Confédération des Activités Subaquatiques (CMAS) qualifications, which ensure that they have undergone professional training and rigorous safety tuition. Many of the dive centres belong to the Mauritian Scuba Diving Association, based in Beau Bassin (🕻 454 0011; e msda@intnet.mu; www.msda.mu).

Prices start at around Rs1,000 for a single dive including all equipment. For a course of five dives, expect to pay about Rs6,000–9,000 with equipment, and about Rs16,500–17,500 for ten dives. For beginners, many dive centres offer a resort course, which consists of a lesson in a pool followed by a sea dive and these cost around Rs1,650–2,000. Rates do not usually include insurance, so if your travel insurance does not cover diving, you would be advised to pay the additional amount, usually about Rs150–250, for medical insurance. Many dive centres also offer PADI courses and will be able to provide more information and prices.

Divers should not touch any seashells underwater and should remember that it is illegal to remove shells from the sea.

DIVING CENTRES The following list is a selection of dive centres from around the island.

Northern Mauritius

Atlantis Diving Centre Trou aux Biches; 🕻265 7172; e vb@atlantisdiving.info; www. atlantisdiving.info
Blue Water Diving Le Corsaire, Trou aux Biches; 🕻265 7186; www.bluewaterdivingcenter.com
Diving World Le Canonnier, Le Victoria & Le Mauricia hotels; 🕻263 1225; e info@diving-mauritius.com; www.diving-mauritius.com
Orca Dive Club Merville Beach Hotel; 🕻5940 2016; e info@orca-diveclub-mauritius.com; www. orca-diveclub-mauritius.com

Eastern Mauritius

Dive Passion Mauritius Tropical Attitude, Trou d'Eau Douce & The Residence, Belle Mare; 🕻5856 5527; e info@divepassionmauritius.com; www. divepassionmauritius.com
Dive Time Belle Mare; 🕻5256 7737; e info@divetimemauritius.com; www.divetimemauritius.com

Southern Mauritius

Coral Dive Centre Blue Bay; 🕻6604 1084; e contact@coraldiving.com; www.coraldiving.com
Diving World Le Shandrani Hotel; 🕻263 1225; e info@diving-mauritius.com; www.diving-mauritius.com
Mauritius Dive Adventures Bel Ombre; 🕻5253 2338; e diving@mauritiusdiveadventures.com; www.mauritiusdiveadventures.com

Western Mauritius

Exploration Sous-marine Villas Caroline, Flic en Flac; 🕻453 8450; e szalay@intnet.mu; www. pierre-szalay.com
Nemo Dive Centre Sofitel Imperial Hotel, Wolmar; 🕻453 8976; e nemodivingcentre@hotmail.fr; www.nemodivingcentre.net
Sun Divers La Pirogue Hotel, Wolmar; 🕻403 3900; e sundiver@intnet.mu; www.sundiversmauritius.com

DIVE SITES The Mascarenes are volcanic isles, so much of the terrain you see whilst diving consists of rock formations like overhangs, walls and caverns. Abundant and diverse corals colonise such formations – some 200 species are said to be present.

The best dive spots include Le Morne in the southwest, the west coast off Flic en Flac and north to Trou aux Biches and Grand Baie. In the southeast, diving is

good off Vieux Grand Port. Some of the very best diving, however, is around the northern offshore islets, like Coin de Mire.

The southwest coast Most of the sites in this area are about 30 minutes by boat from the shore and they are all on the seaward side of the barrier reef, where marine life is abundant. You can explore sites like **Needle Hole**, **Jim's Place** and **Anthony**, all of which are shallow dives (12–18m). Highlights include magnificent corals and swarms of fish like sergeant-majors, goldies and surgeonfish, and all boast excellent visibility with exceptional conditions for underwater photography. A deeper dive is **Michel's Place**, at 38m, which features flat corals, lots of clownfish, and triggerfish. Apparently green and hawksbill turtles are also common.

Another deep one is the drop-off called **Cliff** (average depth 22m) opposite Le Paradis Hotel. Conditions can be quite badly affected by a strong tidal surge. Moray eels are seen on most dives.

One of the most beautiful and popular sites in the area is known as the **Japanese Gardens**. At 14–28m, they are so named because of the diversity of corals in the coral garden there. There is very little current and visibility is good. Abundant fish include parrotfish, pipefish and ghost morays.

A flat, horseshoe-shaped reef well known to divers is **Casiers** (average depth 26m), where shoals of barracuda, kingfish and surgeonfish are usually encountered. Tidal influence is a little more pronounced and visibility can be adversely affected by suspensions in the water.

The west coast Ideal for beginners is **Aquarium**, a rocky reef area that harbours the likes of angelfish, clownfish and butterflyfish plus lots of wire coral. The dive starts at 7m and descends to 18m. Visibility is usually good but watch out for poisonous stonefish. This is the site where night dives are conducted for experienced folk.

For some cave diving, try the **Cathedral** (18–27m). The dive takes place on the drop-off, enters a chamber and then a huge underwater cave, in which lionfish, squirrelfish, kingfish and crayfish are often seen. Light filters into the cave through a crack in the ceiling creating the impression of being in a cathedral. Experienced divers rate the site highly.

Also for experienced divers is **Manioc**, a deep dive on rock faces, which begins at 32m and descends to 45m. Game fish, including kingfish, tuna and barracuda, often make an appearance. Impressive emperor angelfish abound and white-tipped reef sharks are occasionally seen. Divers are almost guaranteed sharks, rays, tuna and barracuda at **Rempart L'Herbe**, also known as **Shark Place**. The sharks are typically grey reef sharks, although hammerheads occasionally visit the area. It's a deep dive (42–54m) on a pinnacle with steep slopes covered in pink and black coral.

Off the coast opposite the Villas Caroline is the ***Kei Sei 113***, a barge which was deliberately sunk in 1988 to form an artificial reef at a depth of 40m. It is partly covered with corals and residents typically include giant moray eels, red snappers and hawkfish.

The north coast The Trou aux Biches area is some 300m from a large reef. This is great for snorkelling, as there's little in the way of surf. From the north, you could visit about ten different sites, of which **Coin de Mire** and **Flat Island** are among the best. It takes about 90 minutes to reach Coin de Mire, where the rock walls drop to about 100m. The sites around the island are suitable only for experienced divers because of the tides and currents. Average depth is 10–20m and the dives are usually drift dives. Barracuda, dogtooth tunny, large parrotfish, wahoo and

white-tipped shark are common and there are lots of oyster clams, cowries and hermit crabs. To the north of Coin de Mire is Flat Island, but because of strong currents and rough seas this is dived only during the summer and only by highly experienced divers. To the north of Flat Island, beneath Pigeon Rock, is the famous **Shark Pit**, where divers can watch sharks swirling around the pit for oxygen from the waves crashing above.

There are also a number of sites off Grand Baie. One of the best is **Tortoise** (13m), which lies just 1.5km offshore. The flat reefs are home to a variety of colourful tropical fish, moray eels, octopus, stonefish and lionfish. **Coral Gardens** (average depth 15m), halfway between Grand Baie and Coin de Mire, consists of coral banks between which are sand gullies. The coral and the visibility are generally good, and the site is popular for night dives. Commonly seen are squirrelfish, trumpetfish and goldies. **Night dives** off **Grand Baie** are said to be incredible. At night, colours on the reefs are far brighter than by day and a mass of marine animals emerge from their daytime hideouts.

A good option for novices is the **Pereybère** site, at only 12m, where tropical reef fish abound. Divers may see octopus, moray eels and stonefish.

In 1987, the **Stella Maru**, a Japanese trawler, was deliberately sunk 1.5km west of Trou aux Biches by the Mauritius Marine Conservation Society. The ship lay on its side until 1992 when a cyclone forced it upright, where it remains. Stonefish, spotted morays and green morays are often seen. This dive, which reaches a depth of 26m, is highly recommended by experienced divers.

The east coast A bit wilder and rather less affected by mass tourism than the other regions, the east coast offers some excellent diving. Drift dives are typical in the area. At **The Pass** (8–25m) you can drift-dive through the 'pass' in the barrier reef, admiring the psychedelic tapestries of coral and reef fishes. Turtles and sharks are often seen.

Lobster Canyon (25m), approximately 1.6km offshore, takes divers through a short cave full of crayfish, along a wall and into a canyon, where sharks and eagle-rays may be seen. At times visibility is limited to 10m owing to high levels of plankton.

OTHER UNDERSEA EXPERIENCES

There are plenty of alternatives to diving and snorkelling for those who want a glimpse of underwater life. Most hotels offer trips in **glass-bottom boats**, which sail over the reef. This is a good way for children to see and learn about marine life.

UNDERSEA WALKS Undersea walks involve plodding along the seabed wearing a lead belt, whilst air is pumped into your helmet from the boat above. It is advertised as being suitable for children over seven years of age. Sadly, this activity is damaging the marine environment and thousands of pairs of feet per year gradually destroy what lies beneath them. If you are still interested, walks usually last 20–25 minutes and cost around Rs1,200 per person. The main operator is **Captain Nemo's Undersea Walk** (*Coastal Rd, Grand Baie;* 263 7819; e undersea@intnet.mu; *www. underseawalk.8k.com*).

SUBMERSIBLES Submersibles are another option suitable for children and adults alike (although not claustrophobics!).

Blue Safari Submarine Coastal Rd, Grand Baie; 265 7272; e reservation.online@blue- safari.com; www.blue-safari.com. A 15min boat trip takes you to the holding ship, from where

you board the submarine for the 40min dive. The submarine can hold 10 people & reaches a depth of 35m. There you can see the coral reef, a shipwreck & tropical fish. The submarine departs every hour 08.30–16.30 in summer & 08.30–15.30 in winter. You need to allow about 2hrs for the whole experience, including time to complete the paperwork, etc. Adult/child Rs4,400/2,700. Reservation essential. You can book exclusive use of a 5-person submarine for a special meal or even a wedding (Rs25,000). Blue Safari Submarine also offers 30min rides on 2-seater, James Bond-style, **submersible scooters**. You can pilot the scooter yourself & it is simple to operate. There are lots of advantages to this, especially if diving

& snorkelling are not your cup of tea. The driver & passenger can talk to each other during the dive, you don't have to be a diver or even strong swimmer & your head doesn't get wet. You dive in a group of 5 scooters, accompanied by 2 divers for safety. You must be over 16 years of age to drive a scooter & over 12 years to be a passenger. As with the submarine, the experience takes around 2hrs, departing every hour 09.00–16.00 in summer & 09.00–1500 in winter. Double scooter Rs5,800 (2 people), Rs4,400 (1 person).
Scubadoo Trou aux Biches; 265 6365; www. scubadoo.summerfuntour.org. Another submarine scooter experience. A 35min dive costs Rs2,500 pp. Min age 8 years.

SAILING

Conditions for sailing are usually excellent. Many of the beach hotels have small sailing dinghies which guests can use within the waters of the lagoon, usually without charge.

Catamaran cruises are popular and full-day trips usually include snorkelling and lunch. Most companies also offer a 2-hour sunset cruise, and some offer overnight cruises. A full-day trip usually costs around Rs1,500–2,500. Sadly, some crews, particularly in the touristy north of the island, are unaware of the destruction that their actions cause to the marine environment. Many drop their anchors on the coral in the same area each day and it has become such a big business that as many as half a dozen catamarans will be anchored in the same place at the same time for snorkelling. Thankfully in some areas buoys have been placed to prevent destruction of the coral. A cruise from the west coast is likely to be more relaxing and less crowded than one from the north and JP Henry Charters are one of the best, most environmentally aware operators on the island. A more expensive but more pleasurable experience is to charter a yacht.

Grand Baie Yacht Club (263 8568) has a temporary membership scheme for visitors.

In recent years, several companies have started offering catamaran cruises to the **St Brandon Archipelago** (pages 201–3), primarily targeting fishing and diving fans. These include Saint Brandon Cruises (5728 3030; e info@saintbrandon. com; www.saintbrandon.com) and Mauritius Catamaran (269 1000; e info@ mauritiuscatamaran.com; www.mauritiuscatamaran.com). It takes around 30 hours to reach the islands by catamaran and the cruises typically last around ten days.

YACHT/CATAMARAN CHARTER AND CRUISES

Catamaran Cruises Mauritius Pointe d'Esny, Mahébourg; 5728 3030; e contact@catamaran-cruises.com; www.catamarancruisesmauritius.com

Croisières Australes Sunset Bd, Grand Baie; 210 0884; e cruise@c-australes.com; www. croisieres-australes.com

Croisières Turquoise Coastal Rd, Mahébourg; 631 1640; www.croisieres-turqoise.com

✳ **JP Henry Charters Ltd** Rivière Noire; 729 0901; e resa@jph.mu; www.jph.mu

Lifestyle Boating Mauritius Place du Moulin, Bel Ombre; 622 2567; e bookings@ lifetyleboatingmauritius.com; www. lifestyleboatingmauritius.com

Mauritius Catamaran Grand Baie Business Park, Grand Baie; 269 1000;

e info@mauritiuscatamaran.com; www.
mauritiuscatamaran.com

Oceane Coastal Rd, Trou d'Eau Douce; ☎480
2767; www.oceane.mu

DOLPHIN- AND WHALE-WATCHING AND SWIMMING WITH DOLPHINS
Dolphin-watching cruises depart early in the morning (around 07.00) and usually last a couple of hours. The west coast is the best for dolphins, which tend to spend several hours each morning in Tamarin Bay. Most hotels and tour operators can organise these excursions. Both bottlenose and spinner dolphins live in the waters of Mauritius. Many of the operators encourage you to jump into the water and snorkel near the dolphins once you have found them, allowing you to watch these graceful creatures underwater. It can get a little frantic and crowded if several operators find the same pod of dolphins, and remember the smaller the boat you go on, the fewer people there will be. Your boat operator should not chase the dolphins or try to prevent them leaving the bay; it is reassuring to know the dolphins are free to go if the mood takes them. The dolphins have not been tamed in any way and there is no guarantee you will find them on a particular outing, although JP Henry Charters does offer to take you out again another day if you don't see dolphins on their trip. A dolphin-watching cruise typically costs around Rs1,500–1,750.

Humpback whales can be seen off Mauritius between July and November, on their migration to warmer waters. Sperm whales are seen almost all year round. A 4-hour whale-watching trip should cost around Rs2,000 per person. You need to go beyond the lagoon to see whales, so the sea can be rough.

Dolswim Rivière Noire; m 5422 9281;
e dolswim@intnet.mu; www.dolswim.com. Offers
dolphin- & whale–watching trips.
JP Henry Charters Ltd Rivière Noire; ☎729
0901; e resa@jph.mu; www.jph.mu. Will take a
max of only 6 people, which is good for both the
dolphins & the people.

Lifestyle Boating Mauritius Place du
Moulin, Bel Ombre; ☎622 2567; e bookings@
lifetyleboatingmauritius.com; www.
lifestyleboatingmauritius.com

WINDSURFING

The popularity of windsurfing and the ideal conditions for it have resulted in many competitions, including World Championships, being held in Mauritius. The majority of hotels in the luxury, upmarket and mid-range categories will have windsurfers available for their guests and many will also offer instruction (usually payable). **Club Mistral** (*Anse la Raie;* m 5474 2107; e *anselaraie@club-mistral.com*) also offers equipment hire and tuition. Sailing or reef shoes should be worn to prevent coral cuts.

KITESURFING

One of the increasingly common sights to be seen in the waters off Mauritius is kitesurfers, who skim along the water on a small board while attached to a large kite and float into the air intermittently, performing a variety of impressive mid-air acrobatics. It is advisable not to attempt kitesurfing unless you are a good swimmer, and have some experience of surfing, windsurfing, paragliding and kiting. The conditions for kitesurfing are excellent, particularly during winter when there are reliable trade winds of 15–30 knots. The best spots for kitesurfing are Le Morne and La Prairie (good for beginners) in the southwest, Bel Ombre in the south,

Belle Mare and Pointe d'Esny in the east, Cap Malheureux and Grand Gaube in the north. Kitesurfing schools are found at many hotels, including Kuxville at Cap Malheureux (page 131), Le Shandrani Hotel in Blue Bay (page 155) and Heritage Le Telfair (page 161). Kitesurfing is also available at Otentic luxury tented camp (page 148).

Club Mistral Anse la Raie; m 5474 2107; e anselaraie@club-mistral.com
KiteGlobing Bel Ombre; ☎605 5334; e info@kiteglobing.com; www.kiteglobing.com
Kitesurf Paradise Ltd Trou d'Éau Douce; ☎743 4298; e mauritius.kitesurf@gmail.com; www.mauritius-kitesurf.com

Le Morne Kite School Morne Brabant; m 5731 9767; www.lemorne-kiteschool.com
Otentic Deux Frères; m 5941 4888; e info@otentic.mu; www.otentic.mu
Wind & Water Blue Bay; m 5719 8894; www.windandwatermauritius.com. Also offers wakeboarding & stand-up paddle.

WATERSKIING

With its calm lagoons, Mauritius is an ideal location for waterskiing, particularly for beginners. At luxury, upmarket and some of the better mid-range hotels, waterskiing is free, although it may be limited. Other mid-range hotels may offer waterskiing at a fee. If your hotel does not offer waterskiing, it can be arranged through an independent watersports company.

Lifestyle Boating Mauritius Place du Moulin, Bel Ombre; ☎622 2567; e bookings@lifetyleboating.com; www.lifestyleboating.com. Offers a range of watersports, including waterskiing, snorkelling & dolphin cruises.

HIKING AND ADVENTURE SPORTS

While you can arrange hiking excursions independently, it is probably better to do so through a reputable local tour operator or one of the companies that specialise in hiking. The Black River Gorges National Park is the pick of the hiking venues. (For information on hiking in the Black River Gorges National Park, see pages 195–7.) A challenging hike is the one ascending Le Morne Brabant, but you are rewarded with spectacular views (see box, page 176).

A growing number of the island's private estates or *domaines* are opening up to the public and typically offer **guided nature walks** and **hiking**, as well as **quad biking** and **4x4 tours** (see pages 198–9).

As you would for hiking anywhere, be sure to take appropriate footwear, water, rain gear, suncream and protective wear for the tropical sun. The Mauritian mountains really don't require any special skills and you need only an average level of fitness to attempt them. However, to avoid the risk of getting lost, it's advisable to contact your tour operator about arranging a local guide for you.

There are some impressive **caves** in Mauritius, many of which were used as shelters by runaway slaves or by pirates in days gone by, but these should never be explored alone. Again, speak to a local tour operator if you wish to visit any of them. They should be able to arrange transport, entry permission and an experienced local guide.

Adventure sports companies

Adventure sports, like canyoning, climbing, ziplining (flying-fox), mountain biking & off-road driving, are not as big in Mauritius as they are in Réunion. Nevertheless, there are a number of companies that offer these types of activities, usually within the private estates:

Incentive Partners Ltd Domaine de Chazal Chamouny; 422 3117; e reservation@ incentivepartnersltd.com; www.chazalecotourism. com. Offers a range of land- & water-based activities including ziplining, canyoning, hiking & 4x4 tours.

Kart Loisir La Joliette, Petite Rivière; 233 2223; e kartloisir@intnet.mu; from 09.00 daily. Offers go-karting & quad biking.

Otelair Eau Coulée; m 5251 6680; e info@ otelair.com; www.otelair.com. Offers hiking, canyoning, rock climbing, mountain biking & kayaking. Team-building days can be arranged.

Otentic Deux Frères; m 5941 4888; e info@ otentic.mu; www.otentic.mu. Offers kayaking & snorkelling excursions from their tented camp on Grande Rivière Sud-est.

Trekking Ile Maurice Rivière Noire; m 5428 1909; e yan@trekkingmauritius.com; www. trekkingmauritius.com. Offering birdwatching, guided hikes & trail running around the southwest of the island, including hikes of Le Morne Brabant (page 176).

Vertical World PO Box 289, Curepipe; 251 1107; e vertical@verticalworldltd.com; www. verticalworldltd.com. Specialises in hiking, canyoning, rock climbing & mountain biking. Canyoning is done at Tamarind Falls with half- & full-day trips available. Canyoning & mountain biking combined activities also available.

Yemaya m 5752 0046; e adventure@ yemayaadventures.com; www.yemayaadventures. com. Specialises in hiking, mountain biking & sea kayaking.

Private estates

The following private estates offer activities such as hiking, mountain biking, quad biking & 4x4 tours. For more information, see the *What to do* & *What to see* sections of the relevant chapter.

Southern Mauritius

Frederica Nature Reserve Bel Ombre; 623 5522; e info@domainedebelombre.mu; www. domainedebelombre.mu

Vallée de Ferney Forest & Wildlife Reserve Ferney; 729 1080; e lavalleedeferney@intnet.mu; www.valleedeferney.com. Has more of a conservation focus than other estates. Hikes with or without a guide; guided tours (on reservation) depart at 10.00 & 14.00. 4x4 tours are available by reservation. You may spot tropic birds, olive-white eyes, Mauritius fodies, Mauritius kestrels & pink pigeons. Every day at 12.00 the staff feed a kestrel family so visitors can see them close up. A former hunting lodge has been converted into a rustic restaurant serving Creole cuisine & specialising in game.

Vallée des Couleurs Mare Anguilles, Chamouny; m 5471 8666; e info@lavalleedescouleurs.com; www.lavalleedescouleurs.com; 08.30–17.30 daily; adult/child Rs300/150. About 10km north of Souillac, this activity centre has been created around a multi-coloured exposed area of earth, similar to the 7 coloured earths of Chamarel. Hiking, quad biking (Rs2,300 for 1hr) & ziplining (Rs1,975 for 4 lines) are available. There is a café & a restaurant & a good play area for children.

Western Mauritius

Casela World of Adventures Royal Rd, Cascavelle; 452 2828; e casela@intnet.mu; www.caselapark.com. A safari-park-style area, with resident zebra, ostrich, deer, wild pigs & giant tortoises, can be explored in a safari bus, on a Segway or on a quad bike. Casela also offers ziplining, canyoning & an adventure trail (Via Ferrata circuit). It involves climbing, trekking & ziplining in either a half-day or a full-day circuit.

Central Mauritius

Domaine de l'Etoile Royal Rd, Moka; m 5729 1050; e info@terrocean.mu; www.terrocean.mu

BEACHCOMBER 'SPORT AND NATURE' Beachcomber's Le Shandrani Hotel (603 4540) runs a daily programme of sports and nature activities which cater for all levels of fitness and are open to non-residents. The programmes, which last either a full day or half day, are an ideal way to see beautiful parts of the island, whilst doing some exercise. Some of the programmes are suitable for children.

SKYDIVING

Skydive Austral Rivière du Rempart; 499 5551; e info@skydivemauritius.com; www. skydivemauritius.com. Offers tandem skydiving from 10,000ft. Prices from Rs13,000.

Mauritius.
What better place to cruise around in a convertible.

Europcar   Call us now on **(230) 286 0140**

Part Two

MAURITIUS AND
ITS DEPENDENCIES

4

Port Louis

You may notice that the pronunciation of Mauritius's capital varies. The French pronunciation is *Por' Louie*, the English is *Port Loo-iss*, but many locals compromise and use *Port Loo-ee*. While its correct pronunciation may be debatable, its importance to Mauritius is not. Port Louis is Mauritius's seat of government, its main port and, with some 150,000 inhabitants, its most populous town.

Port Louis is a chaotic but charming city, which combines new buildings with old. It is wedged between the sea and a mountain range, whose oddly shaped peaks contrast with the uniformity of the city. In the centre of the mountain range is Le Pouce (The Thumb), poking 811m into the sky in a hopeful hitchhiker's gesture. On its left, distinguished by the boulder balanced precariously on its tip, is Pieter Both, named after the first governor-general of the Dutch East Indies, who drowned in the bay. To the right the city's boundary extends along a switchback of daunting crags: Snail Rock, Goat Rock, Spear Grass Peak and Quoin Bluff. The sheer sides of Signal Mountain (323m) dominate the western flank of the town.

Solid Victorian warehouses and modern concrete towers crowd the flat expanse of the city. Houses claim the land right up to the foothills of Pouce Valley, leaving open spaces only on the plain of the Champ de Mars racecourse and the isolated 86m-high hill in the middle of the city, on which perches the fort known as the Citadel.

HISTORY

The city was first settled by the Dutch but was named Port Louis in 1722 by the French. The name was probably chosen to honour the then young King Louis XV (1715–74), or perhaps to link the settlement with Port Louis in Brittany from where, at that time, French seamen sailed for India. When Mahé de Labourdonnais arrived here in 1735, dense vegetation covered the area, except for land cleared between where the theatre now stands and the Chien de Plomb at the bayside, which was the ships' watering point. There were 60 mud huts thatched with palm leaf in this clearing, the homes of the French East India Company staff. Soldiers lived in makeshift shelters of straw. The stream running down from Pouce Mountain formed a swampy gully dividing the plain in two. The right side, as viewed from the sea, became the residential area while the left was given over to commerce. A statue of Mahé de Labourdonnais, erected in 1859, stands overlooking the harbour he created. Nearby, a stone set into the lawn at the foot of the palm trees commemorates the 250th anniversary of his founding of Port Louis.

AROUND TOWN – AN OVERVIEW

THE CITADEL [99 H4] Viewed from the Citadel hill, the layout of the city is uncomplicated: rectangular street blocks as far as the eye can see. A French post existed

here in the 18th century but the fort was begun in 1834 and named Fort Adelaide after Queen Adelaide, wife of William IV. It was built by the British who were worried that the French settlers would revolt against the abolition of slavery, as they had in 1832. Its solid, dark grey, volcanic stone walls and two-tiered rooms, built around a central barrack square, are a formidable, albeit depressing sight. It was completed in 1840 and was garrisoned by a detachment of over 200 Royal Irish Fusiliers. Slavery was abolished in 1835 without too much ado so, even before it was completed in 1840, the Citadel's raison d'être had faded. Fear of war with France led to it being further fortified but it never saw the action for which it had been prepared. It was abandoned for over a century but has been brought back to life in recent years with a major renovation. It now houses shops aimed at tourists and is a great viewpoint from which to see the city. The Champ de Mars racecourse is clearly visible and on race days you will find crowds of Mauritians watching the action from the Citadel. The large green shed you can see by the harbour stores the island's sugar before it is transferred to ships for export.

THE WATERFRONT For those arriving by car, the waterfront is the best area to park (pages 102–3) and a good starting point for exploring the city. The wide esplanade makes for pleasant wandering around the harbour.

The very smart **Caudan Waterfront** [104 C1] (*www.caudan.com*) is quite a contrast to the older parts of the city further inland. This modern complex includes apartments, offices, a cinema, bank, museum, casino, craft market, shops and restaurants. A marina, Bassin des Chaloupes, provides boat moorings with easy access to the city.

While the waterfront all seems rather modern, elements of the city's history remain tucked away here. On the harbour side of the complex, the building known as the **Observatory** was built in 1832 on the site of an old French powder magazine, and was the first meteorological observatory in the Indian Ocean. Between the Astrolabe Centre and the Granary Car Park is a restored **18th-century windmill** [104 E1]. It was built in 1736 to grind wheat but was converted to a signal tower after the British took possession of the island in 1810. Restored in 1998, it now contains a small museum (⊕ *10.00–12.00 & 13.00–15.00 Mon–Fri; admission free*) displaying historic photographs of the harbour and the history of wheat. From upstairs in the windmill you get a good view of the working harbour and the attractive, restored Creole building, with wooden shingle roof, which houses the **National Coast Guard**. Nearby, in a building completed in 1868, is the **Postal Museum** [104 F2] (page 110).

At the northern end of Port Louis's waterfront, beyond the postal museum and the Granary Car Park, is **Aapravasi Ghat** [104 G2]. This glum-looking immigration depot was built in 1849 to process labourers as they arrived and is now a UNESCO World Heritage Site (pages 108–9).

THE CITY On the other side of the main road from the harbour is the city. Tall royal palms form an avenue of greenery leading from the waterfront up the centre of **Place S Bissoondoyal** [104 E3–4] (formerly Place d'Armes) to **Government House** [104 E4]. The name was officially changed from Place d'Armes to honour a Mauritian politician and independence leader but many locals still refer to it by its old name. The roads at each side of the lawns are Duke of Edinburgh Avenue (on the left, facing Government House) and Queen Elizabeth Avenue (on the right). The old thoroughfares of Royal Street and Chaussée Street meet in front of Government House. The Chaussée, originally a causeway of rough stones constructed over a swamp, was rebuilt in 1779 by a French engineer. The trickle that remains of Pouce Stream runs down a concrete gully under the small **Chaussée Bridge** [104 E4].

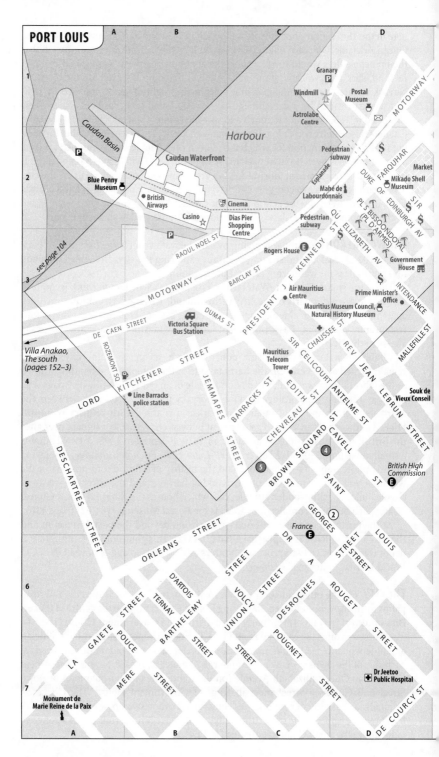

PORT LOUIS

Harbour

Caudan Basin

Caudan Waterfront

Blue Penny Museum

British Airways

Casino

Cinema

Dias Pier Shopping Centre

see page 104

Granary

Windmill

Postal Museum

Astrolabe Centre

Pedestrian subway

MOTORWAY

Market

Esplanade

Mahé de Labourdonnais

Mikado Shell Museum

DUKE OF FARQUHAR

RAOUL NOEL ST

Pedestrian subway

Rogers House

MOTORWAY

BARCLAY ST

PL S BISSOONDOYAL (PL D'ARMES)

DUKE OF EDINBURGH AV

SIR SEEWOOSAGUR RAMGOOLAM ST

QUEEN ELIZABETH AV

Government House

Air Mauritius Centre

Prime Minister's Office

INTENDANCE

J F KENNEDY

Mauritius Museum Council, Natural History Museum

DE CAEN STREET

DUMAS ST

Victoria Square Bus Station

PRESIDENT

CHAUSSEE ST

REV

JEAN

MALLEFILLE ST

Villa Anakao, The south (pages 152–3)

ROZEMONT SQ

KITCHENER

STREET

Mauritius Telecom Tower

SIR CELICOURT ANTELME ST

LEBRUN STREET

Souk de Vieux Conseil

LORD

Line Barracks police station

JEMMAPES

BARRACKS ST

EDITH ST

CHEVREAU ST

BROWN SEQUARD ST

CAVELL

4

5

SAINT

British High Commission

DESCHARTRES STREET

STREET

GEORGES

France

2

ST

LOUIS STREET

ORLEANS STREET

STREET

DR

A

STREET

D'ARTOIS STREET

TERNAY STREET

BARTHELEMY STREET

UNION STREET

VOLCY STREET

DESROCHES

POUGNET STREET

ROUGET STREET

GAIETE STREET

POUCE

MERE STREET

STREET

STREET

Dr Jeetoo Public Hospital

LA

Monument de Marie Reine de la Paix

DE COURCY ST

98

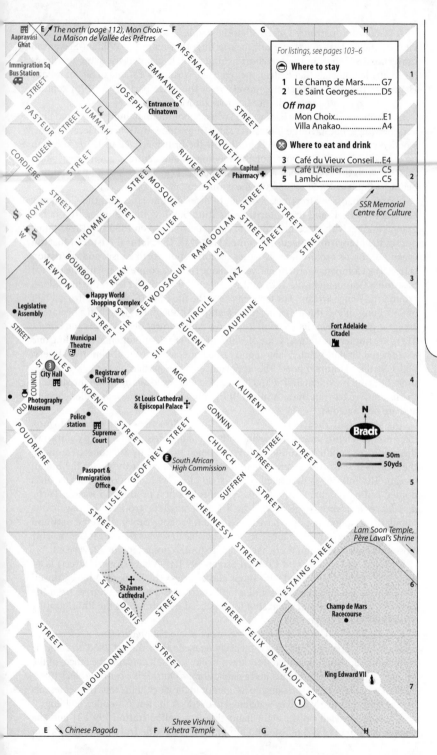

E↗ The north (page 112), Mon Choix –
La Maison de Vallée des Prêtres

Aapravási Ghāt

Immigration Sq Bus Station

ARSENAL STREET

EMMANUEL STREET

JOSEPH STREET

JUMMAH STREET

PASTEUR STREET

QUEEN STREET

CORDIERE STREET

Entrance to Chinatown

ANQUETIL STREET

RIVIERE STREET

Capital Pharmacy ✚

ROYAL STREET

NEWTON STREET

L'HOMME STREET

MOSQUE STREET

OLLIER STREET

BOURBON STREET

REMY ST

DR SIR SEEWOOSAGUR RAMGOOLAM STREET

NAZ ST

STREET

STREET

STREET

SSR Memorial
Centre for Culture

For listings, see pages 103–6

🏠 **Where to stay**
1 Le Champ de Mars........ G7
2 Le Saint Georges............. D5

Off map
  Mon Choix.......................... E1
  Villa Anakao...................... A4

🍽 **Where to eat and drink**
3 Café du Vieux Conseil.... E4
4 Café L'Atelier.................... C5
5 Lambic............................... C5

Legislative Assembly

Happy World
Shopping Complex

EUGENE

VIRGILE

DAUPHINE

Fort Adelaide
Citadel

Municipal
Theatre

SIR

MGR

LAURENT STREET

STREET

N

Bradt

0   50m
0   50yds

JULES ST

City Hall

COUNCIL ST

Registrar of
Civil Status

KOENIG STREET

St Louis Cathedral
& Episcopal Palace ✝

GONNIN STREET

Photography
Museum

OLD

Police
station

Supreme
Court

POUDRIERE

LISLET GEOFFREY STREET

Passport &
Immigration
Office

CHURCH STREET

🅴 South African
High Commission

POPE HENNESSY STREET

SUFFREN STREET

STREET

Lam Soon Temple,
Père Laval's Shrine

ST DENIS STREET

St James
Cathedral

FRERE FELIX DE VALOIS ST

D'ESTAING STREET

Champ de Mars
Racecourse

LABOURDONNAIS STREET

STREET

King Edward VII

①

E ↘ Chinese Pagoda

F Shree Vishnu
Kchetra Temple

G

H

A statue of a matronly Queen Victoria stands at the entrance to Government House [104 E4] with a statue of a nearly forgotten man, Sir William Stevenson (governor 1857–63), in the forecourt behind her. He claimed the same privileges for Mauritian officials that British ones enjoyed. Nearby is a statue of Sir John Pope Hennessy, the most outstanding governor of the latter part of the 19th century (1883–89), sympathetic to calls of Mauritius for Mauritians.

Government House dates back to 1738 when Labourdonnais built the ground floor and the wings that form the forecourt's sides from stone. In General Decaen's time, wooden upper storeys were added, just before the British arrived in 1810. Although no longer the home of the governor, the building is at the centre of government since, together with the office block adjoining it and the **Legislative Assembly Chamber** behind it (built in 1965), it is part of the parliamentary complex.

Nearby Chaussée Street has shops and offices on one side, and the **Company Gardens** [104 C4] and the **Mauritius Institute** building on the other. The rather grand building with graceful arches was constructed between 1880 and 1884; it now houses the **Mauritius Museums Council** [104 D4]. The **Natural History Museum** (page 110) on its ground floor is rather eccentric, but worth a visit, and admission is free. The Company Gardens derives its name from its connection with the French East India Company in the 18th century, when it was created from the marshland around the Pouce Stream. For ten years after the fire of 1816, which destroyed half of Port Louis, it was the site of the town market. Although it is less than a hectare in area, the garden seems larger, with its narrow paths, flower beds, shrubs and ponds. There are numerous statues, some of which are national monuments, including one of Adrien d'Epinay, planter, lawyer and campaigner against the abolition of slavery, and Léoville l'Homme, poet. The importance of the garden as the city becomes more built-up is evident and at lunchtimes you will see locals enjoying the shade of the impressive banyan trees. At night, the gardens attract a rather seedier element and are best avoided.

The **Municipal Theatre** [99 E4] on Jules Koenig Street has been restored to look like another Victorian warehouse but with its colonnaded front a sharp contrast to the mediocre buildings around it. It was opened in 1822 by Sir Robert Farquhar, the island's first British governor, and is said to be the oldest theatre in the Indian Ocean. The interior is decorated in the style of a classic London theatre, with a domed ceiling painted with cherubs. The theatre's first production was *La Partie de Chasse de Henri IV* performed by a Creole amateur troupe. The days of its popularity as an opera house have passed and for many years it was left empty and unused. It is now only by chance that you'll be able to see inside since it is invariably closed and shuttered, and there have been no productions here for a few years.

Opposite the theatre, **Old Council Street** [99 E4] (Vieux Conseil Street) is an attractive cobbled lane lined with shops and eateries. The **Souk du Vieux Conseil** [99 D4] has modern boutiques and a food court; it is a welcome retreat from the hectic city centre and not a bad spot for lunch. At its entrance is the **Photography Museum** [99 E4] (page 110).

City Hall [99 E4], built in 1965 on the site of a colonial predecessor, is a few yards away on Jules Koenig Street. It was officially opened on 25 August 1966, to coincide with Port Louis being upgraded from town to city status. It contains the offices of the Municipal Council of Port Louis, and a public library. Outside is a concrete block tower without walls, with steps spiralling up its interior to the clock at the top. This represents the fire towers formerly used by watchmen to overlook the town's wooden buildings.

Beyond City Hall on the right-hand side is a **police station** [99 E4] and the **Supreme Court** [99 E4] (a listed building), with the **Cathedral Square** [99 F4] on

the left. Now a garden, the square contains the remains of a fountain dating to 1788, an obelisk, and what appears to be a statue of medieval King Louis IX of France, also known as St Louis, erected in 1896.

The Roman Catholic **St Louis Cathedral** [99 F4] is the third church on this site. Built in 1932 in awesome twin-towered imitation Gothic, it replaced the previous one, demolished in 1925. An earlier church on the site dating from 1756 was destroyed by a cyclone. Within is the tomb of the wife of Mahé de Labourdonnais.

The **Episcopal Palace** [99 F4], a 19th-century mansion with airy verandas more suited in style to the tropics than the cathedral, stands behind it.

The Anglican **St James Cathedral** [99 F6] has its entrance on Poudrière Street. It is by no means grand; it looks rather like a small New England mission church with its single, cream-plastered spire. It was built in 1828, incorporating the 2m-wide walls of the original building, a French powder magazine. Its stoutness made it a useful cyclone shelter in the last century. Even on a hot day it is cool inside, it has a vaulted wooden ceiling and wood-panelled walls. Displays inside the cathedral tell the story of Anglicanism on the island.

There are some small wooden mansions from the French period in the block between Poudrière Street and St Georges Street. There are also a large number of embassies and high commissions in the area. (For details, see pages 46–7.)

At the end of Pope Hennessy Street is the **Champ de Mars Racecourse** [99 H6]. People still promenade here as they did in the 19th century, although joggers and children have taken the place of crinolined ladies and their beaux. There is a **statue of King Edward VII** [99 H7] in the centre and the tomb of Malartic (governor 1792–1800) at the far end. This is a striking setting for racing with a backdrop of gaunt mountains acting as a natural amphitheatre for the drama played out on the plain. (See also pages 84 and 108.)

The Champ de Mars has been a racecourse since the Mauritius Turf Club was founded by an English army officer, Colonel Edward Draper, in 1812, making it the oldest racecourse in the southern hemisphere and one of the oldest in the world. Draper oversaw the building of the track on what was then the army parade ground. At first, only horses belonging to the English garrison were ridden by young army officers, until the French settlers showed interest and entered their own horses. By 1837, horse racing was firmly established. Today the Mauritians' love of gambling ensures that races are always well attended.

On the north side of the Champ de Mars, at the corner of Dr Eugene Laurent and Corneille streets, is the **Lam Soon Temple** [99 H6] ($\oplus$ *06.00–14.00 daily*), which is actually two temples. The newer one, built in the 19th century, is in the foreground, a curious adaptation of British colonial architecture to Buddhist needs, the columns of the veranda painted red and gold and the interior devoted to worship. The centre altar is extravagantly carved while the interior walls are simple.

The **Shree Vishnu Kchetra Temple** [99 G7] is in a tranquil location in St Denis Street, parallel to the Champ de Mars, one block away. It serves Hindus and Tamils. The older Hindu temple is simply laid out with bright paintings and statues and places for offerings of coconuts and incense. Worshippers toll the bell to wake the gods.

In the same compound is a new Tamil temple and an ancient, sacred peepul tree (*Ficus religiosa*, known as a 'bo-tree' in Sri Lanka). The temple is closed for five minutes at midnight when it is considered a dangerous time to disturb the gods.

The **Jummah Mosque** [104 G4], with its 'wedding cake' architecture, is, unsurprisingly, on Jummah Mosque Street. The mosque extends an entire block, its white towers and friezes imposing grace on the clutter of lock-up shops beneath its balconies. Its huge teak doors are priceless, ornately carved and inlaid with ivory.

The muezzin's call from the minaret before dawn is the signal not only for prayer but for the cacophony of the city to erupt. This mosque, built in the 1850s and extended over the years, is the island's most impressive and opened when Muslims formed an exclusive merchant group in the neighbourhood. A group of Muslim merchants banded together and bought two properties and built the mosque on the site. Visitors can enter the inner courtyard outside prayer times. In the courtyard is an old badamier tree, older than the mosque itself.

Near the mosque in Royal Street is **Chinatown** [99 F1], a clutter of stores, warehouses and restaurants, its shops bright with the plastic and chrome knick-knacks much in demand by modern-day Mauritians. The location of Chinatown so near to the mosque has caused some tension between the two communities, which at its height resulted in the burning down of the Chinese-run Amicale Casino.

Between Farquhar and Queen streets is Port Louis **market ✳** [104 F3], selling fruit and vegetables, meat, fish, clothing and handicrafts. The wrought-iron work above the entrance has the initials VR (Victoria Regina) intertwined in it. In 2004, the market buildings were completely renovated. As a result, the market lost some of its grubby charm and a greater proportion of it (mostly the first floor) was taken over by souvenir stalls. It may not feel as 'authentic' as it once did but it is still an exciting, bustling place, which offers an insight into the everyday lives of Mauritians and is one of the main attractions of the city for visitors. (See also page 107.)

At the southern end of the city, along Jemmapes Street from the Victoria Square bus station are the **Line Barracks** [104 A3], whose foundations go back to the early days of the French occupation, when they housed 6,000 men, as well as rebel colonists after the French Revolution. A police station, the police headquarters and the traffic branch are there now.

Signal Mountain between Plaine Lauzon and the city marks the western end of the mountain range around Port Louis. A beacon used to be kept alight on its summit at night, and flags hoisted there during the day as a guide for approaching vessels. At the foot of the mountain is the **Marie Reine de la Paix monument** [98 A7] and its pleasant gardens, where the first Mauritian bishop was consecrated in 1989. The Edward VII Boulevard provides a spectacular view of the city and harbour.

Sainte-Croix, a suburb of Port Louis nestling below Long Mountain, is famous for its church, a modern-style replacement of the original, with its shrine containing the body of **Père Laval** (page 111).

GETTING THERE AND AWAY

BY BUS The **Immigration Square bus station** [104 G3] is at the end of Pasteur Street, still known by city denizens as Hospital Street, because of the hospital that was in the square. It is difficult to know which bus queue to join since there are limited signs but other passengers are helpful. Buses from here serve the north of the island and include an express service to Grand Baie, which takes around 30 minutes.

The **Victoria Square bus station** [104 B2] is off Dumas Street. Buses leave throughout the day bound for central towns, such as Curepipe, from where you can get buses to the south (including the airport) and west. The long, dilapidated, two-storey building used to be the main railway station and offices.

BY CAR The motorway from the south leads into Port Louis, and continues straight along the waterfront. Although traffic congestion has improved since the opening of a new motorway by-passing Port Louis, the road into the city is invariably slow going with a rush hour that seems to last half of the morning and most of the afternoon.

Parking zones exist in Port Louis, for which you have to purchase tickets in advance from a petrol station (page 60) if you intend to park on the street. The most convenient car park for the centre, market and waterfront is **The Granary** [104 F1], on the harbour side of the highway. The Granary allows you to buy a ticket on the spot and avoid the hassle of the parking zone system. In 2015, the rates were Rs25 for the first 2 hours, and Rs25 for every additional hour or part thereof. The Granary is a short walk from the Astrolabe Centre and Port Louis Waterfront (the esplanade), and from there a pedestrian subway leads to the city. You can also park at the Caudan Waterfront, near the Blue Penny Museum, for around Rs30 per hour.

BY TAXI Taxis are more expensive in Port Louis than elsewhere and the attitude of the drivers is predatory. Be sure to negotiate a reasonable fare. There is a taxi stand at Place S Bissoondoyal (Place d'Armes) and one at the Victoria Square bus station.

TOURIST INFORMATION

There is no longer a tourist information centre in Port Louis, but you will find brochures on the attractions at the Caudan Waterfront. For embassies and high commissions, see pages 46–7.

WHERE TO STAY

UPMARKET

Labourdonnais Waterfront Hotel [104 C1] (105 rooms) Caudan Waterfront; ☎ 202 4000; e info@indigohotels.com; www. labourdonnais.com. By far the most elegant accommodation in the city, overlooking the harbour. This 5-star hotel caters largely for business guests. En-suite rooms have AC, TV, phone, internet connection, minibar & safe. Facilities include 2 restaurants, a pool, gym & elaborate conference facilities. There is a small spa & guests can use the more extensive spa facilities at Le Suffren Hotel, as well as the restaurant there. **$$$$**

Le Suffren Hotel & Marina [104 A1] (102 rooms) Caudan Waterfront; ☎ 202 4900; e info@indigohotels.com; www.lesuffrenhotel. com. The 4-star sister hotel of the Labourdonnais, this also targets business travellers & overlooks the harbour at Caudan Waterfront. Rooms have either harbour or mountain views & are equipped with AC, TV, phone, safe, minibar & tea/coffee facilities. There is a manmade beach area, pool, spa, restaurant & bar, & guests can use the restaurants at the Labourdonnais. Catamaran cruises available (payable). Adjacent to the hotel are executive self-catering apartments with use of hotel facilities. **$$$$**

MID RANGE

Le Champ de Mars [99 G7] (40 rooms) 22 Frère Félix de Valois St, Champ de Mars; ☎ 212 7373; e resa.hcdm@intnet.mu; www. lechampdemarshotel.com. Overlooks the racecourse. Simple but comfortable en-suite rooms with AC, TV, phone & safe. Free Wi-Fi. **$$$**

Le Saint Georges [98 D5] (82 rooms) 19 St Georges St; ☎ 211 2581; e reservation@ saintgeorgeshotel-mu.com; www. saintgeorgeshotel-mu.com. Centrally located 3-star hotel offering simple en-suite rooms with AC, TV, phone, safe & minibar. There is a restaurant & a pool. **$$$**

Mon Choix [99 E1] Vallée des Prêtres (4 rooms) Senneville; ☎ 217 0505; e dodoisland@ intnet.mu; www.ecomauritius.com. Friendly guesthouse in a quiet location in the hills above Port Louis. You will need a car to reach this one but there is a lot to be said for its peaceful setting with views of the valley towards the capital. The 4 rooms (2 en suite) are nicely furnished & have minibar & tea/coffee facilities. There is a kitchen, pleasant dining & sitting rooms, a pool & large garden. Breakfast is provided & dinner is available on request. The owners make a real effort to run an eco-friendly guesthouse. Not suitable for children. **$$$**

4

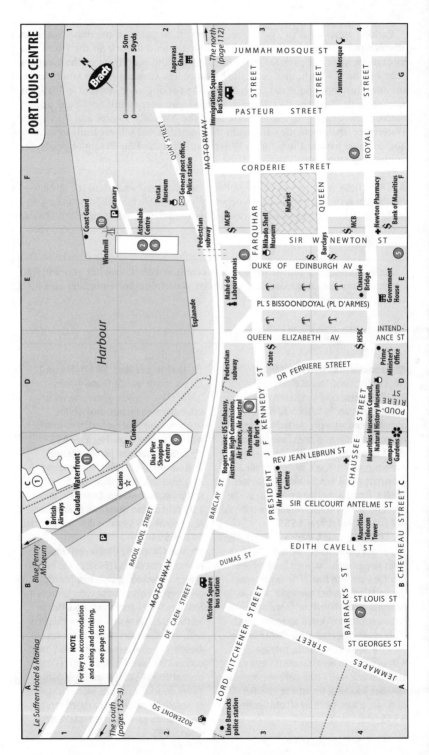

PORT LOUIS CENTRE

N

Bradt

0   50m
0   50yds

Harbour

Le Suffren Hotel & Marina

Blue Penny Museum

The south
(pages 152–3)

NOTE
For key to accommodation
and eating and drinking,
see page 105

British Airways

Caudan Waterfront

Casino

Cinema

Dias Pier Shopping Centre

Coast Guard

Windmill

Granary

Astrolabe Centre

Postal Museum

General post office,
Police station

Pedestrian subway

The north
(page 112)

Aapravasi Ghat

Immigration Square Bus Station

JUMMAH MOSQUE ST

PASTEUR   STREET

CORDERIE   STREET

Market

Mikado Shell Museum

MCBP

Mahé de Labourdonnais

FARQUHAR

Barclays

MCB

Newton Pharmacy

Bank of Mauritius

SIR W NEWTON ST

QUEEN

ROYAL

Jummah Mosque

STREET

STREET

STREET

G

F

E

DUKE OF EDINBURGH AV

Chaussée Bridge

PL S BISSOONDOYAL (PL D'ARMES)

Government House

QUEEN   ELIZABETH   AV

HSBC

State

INTEND-
ANCE ST

Pedestrian subway

Prime Minister's Office

DR FERRIERE STREET

POUD-
RIERE
ST

Rogers House: US Embassy,
Australian High Commission,
Air France, Air Austral

Pharmacie
du Port

Air Mauritius Centre

REV JEAN LEBRUN ST

Mauritius Museums Council,
Natural History Museum

Company Gardens

CHAUSSEE   STREET

BARCLAY ST

PRESIDENT   J F KENNEDY   ST

SIR CELICOURT ANTELME ST

Mauritius Telecom Tower

EDITH CAVELL ST

CHEVREAU STREET

DUMAS ST

Victoria Square bus station

BARRACKS   ST

ST LOUIS ST

ST GEORGES ST

LORD KITCHENER STREET

DE CAEN STREET

MOTORWAY

RAOUL NOEL STREET

Esplanade

QUAY STREET

MOTORWAY

ROZEMONT SQ

Line Barracks police station

JEMMAPES   STREET

104

BUDGET

 Villa Anakao [98 A4] (10 rooms) 154 Royal Rd, Pointe aux Sables; 234 2035; e reservation. mauritius@villa-anakao.com; www.villa-anakao. com. A pleasant guesthouse around 10mins south of Port Louis, on the seafront. Carefully decorated en-suite rooms with AC & terrace. There is a restaurant & bar. **$$**

✗ WHERE TO EAT

Cheap eateries abound: snack bars, *samoussas* sellers and even fast-food outlets. There are restaurants scattered throughout the Port Louis Waterfront area and a food court in the Caudan Waterfront with numerous outlets serving snacks, ice creams and fast food.

✗ **Café du Vieux Conseil** [99 E4] Old Council St; 211 0393; ⊕ for lunch Mon–Fri. Cuisine: French, Creole. In a quiet, restored cobbled lane, opposite the theatre. Alfresco dining & an almost Mediterranean atmosphere. Excellent food & service. The menu lists only a few dishes & is changed frequently, but there is sufficient variety, including vegetarian specialities & Australian beef. **$$$$**

✗ **Lambic** [98 C5] 4 St Georges St; 212 6011; ⊕ 08.00–late Mon–Sat. Cuisine: European. In a 19th-century colonial house is this gastro-pub & beer house with a fabulous atmosphere. It has around 70 beers on offer, as well as dishes featuring beer, such as beer battered fish & chips, & wild boar roasted in beer. **$$$$**

✗ **Le Courtyard** [104 B4] Cnr St Louis & Chevreau sts; 210 0810; ⊕ for lunch Mon–Sat, for dinner Thu/Fri. Cuisine: European. As the name

suggests, tables are arranged in an attractive courtyard, providing a welcome retreat from the city streets. A sophisticated restaurant & very popular. Reservation recommended. **$$$$**

✗ **Yuzu** [104 C1] Labourdonnais Waterfront Hotel, Caudan Waterfront; 202 4000; ⊕ for lunch & dinner Mon–Fri, dinner Sat. Cuisine: Asian. An upmarket restaurant within the hotel serving Asian fusion dishes, combining Thai, Vietnamese, Chinese & Japanese cuisine. **$$$$**

✗ **Café L'Atelier** [99 C5] 12 St Louis St; 208 4915; ⊕ 09.00–17.00 Mon–Fri. Cuisine: European. This café in an old warehouse building has an industrial/art gallery feel & is a good spot for lunch. Upstairs is a bookshop with a good supply of Mauritian literature & books about the island. **$$$**

✗ **Carri Poulé** [104 E3] 3 Duke of Edinburgh Av; 212 4883; ⊕ for lunch Mon–Sat, for dinner Fri/Sat. Cuisine: Indian, Creole. Serves well-prepared Indian dishes with a Mauritian touch, not the stereotyped offerings of European 'Indian' restaurants. **$$$**

✗ **La Bonne Marmite** [104 E4] 18 Sir William Newton St; 212 2403; ⊕ for lunch Mon–Fri. Cuisine: Creole, French, Indian, Chinese. Established in 1973, this is a café, pub & restaurant in one. The café is on the ground floor & serves a buffet lunch. Behind it is the Rocking Boat Pub (page 106). The restaurant is upstairs in a grand room with table d'hôte & à la carte menus. Reservation recommended. **$$$**

✗ **Le Capitaine** [104 C1] Caudan Waterfront; 213 0038; ⊕ for lunch & dinner daily. Cuisine: seafood, Creole, Indian. In a good location, overlooking the harbour. Excellent seafood & good service. Reservation recommended. **$$$**

✗ **Namasté** [104 C1] Caudan Waterfront; 211 6710; ⊕ for lunch & dinner Mon–Sat, for dinner Sun. Cuisine: north Indian. Fine cuisine in

the historic setting of the old observatory building. The décor is fascinating, with the original walls of the observatory adding atmosphere. The food is authentic & delicious, carefully prepared with spices imported from India. Live Indian music on Fri, Sat & Sun evenings. Reservation recommended. $$$

✗ **The Deck** [104 C1] Caudan Waterfront; m 5759 2344; ⊕ for lunch & dinner Mon–Sat. Cuisine: European, seafood. The location is great: floating on a pontoon in the harbour, a good vantage point for watching goings-on on the water & on the shore. They specialise in seafood & serve generous portions. $$$

✗ **Beer & Spice** [104 E2] Astrolabe Centre; ✎211 4087; ⊕ 09.00–01.00 daily. Cuisine: Italian, Creole. At the city end of the Astrolabe Centre. Informal dining on a terrace overlooking the harbour. Friendly service & excellent pizzas, plenty of options for vegetarians. The owner is happy to prepare dishes not on the menu for those with special dietary requirements. The large portions make this good value for Port Louis. $$

✗ **First Restaurant** [104 F4] Cnr Royal & Corderie sts; ✎212 0685; ⊕ for lunch & dinner Tue–Sun. Cuisine: Chinese. The entrance is on Corderie St & the restaurant is upstairs. Tasty, reasonably priced dishes. Regarded as one of the best Chinese restaurants on the island; Sun lunch yum-cha is popular. Try the roast duck. $$

✗ **Le Bistrot du Port** [104 E2] Astrolabe Centre, Caudan Waterfront; ✎210 6586; ⊕ 08.30–late

Mon–Sat. Cuisine: French, Creole. Casual dining on the waterfront; has an extensive menu. $$

✗ **Le Life** [104 D3] Rogers Hse, President John F Kennedy St; ✎212 6565; ⊕ 09.00–17.00 Mon–Sat. Cuisine: Creole, European. Has the same owner as Le Patio at Caudan Waterfront. A modern café/bar serving light meals. A popular lunch spot for local office workers. $$

✗ **Le Patio** [104 C2] Dias Pier, Caudan Waterfront; ✎213 5353; ⊕ 09.00–17.00 Mon–Sat. Cuisine: Creole, European, ice cream. A modern, clean, informal café within the Dias Pier shopping centre. Serves good light meals, such as salads, sandwiches & crêpes, at reasonable prices. $$

✗ **Mammamia Che Gelato** [104 C1] Caudan Waterfront; ✎263 8441; ⊕ daily. Cuisine: ice cream. For ice cream head to this clean & modern shop opposite the casino. Good-quality ice cream & sorbets & a decent range of flavours. $$

✷ ✗ **Saveurs des Iles** [104 F1] Place du Moulin, Caudan Waterfront; ✎213 5853; ⊕ 11.00–22.00 daily. Cuisine: Creole, French, Chinese. A delightful restaurant away from the hustle & bustle of the city, just in front of the windmill on the waterfront. Seating is in a sturdy, volcanic stone building or outside on a terrace overlooking the working harbour & restored Creole building which houses the National Coastguard office. The menu is extensive & reasonably priced, with dishes starting from as little as Rs100. The Mauritian curries are excellent. $$

NIGHTLIFE AND ENTERTAINMENT

In 1722, there were 125 drinking shops known to the police in Port Louis. The French governor, Ternay, found this excessive and closed all but 30, eventually reducing that number to four. Since then, they have seen a resurgence and there is now a plentiful supply.

The Caudan Waterfront is the place to go of an evening, with its restaurants, bars, cinema and casino. **The Post Box Lounge Bar** at the Labourdonnais Waterfront Hotel [104 C1] has plenty of old-fashioned charm with its vintage décor, and serves impressive cocktails. Its sister hotel, Le Suffren Hotel & Marina, has two good bars open daily: **Spinnakers**, where sports matches are played on large plasma screens, and **On the Rocks**, a trendy lounge bar. **Watchout Nightclub** [104 C1] opened in 2015 upstairs at the Caudan Waterfront, overlooking the harbour. The **Rocking Boat Pub** at La Bonne Marmite Restaurant on Sir William Newton Street (reservation essential) has been designed to project the ambience of a traditional English pub with low lighting and dark décor. **Lambic** (*4 St Georges St;* ✎*212 6011*) is a beer-lover's delight with around 70 beers, and the restaurant serves dishes featuring beer should you get peckish (page 105).

The **Caudan Waterfront Casino** [104 C2] (✎ *210 2191*) is open daily except Monday. The slot machines are open 10.00–02.00 and the tables 20.00–04.00.

CINEMA **Star cinema** [104 C2] (☏ *211 5361*) in the Caudan Waterfront Complex has three screens showing international films.

SHOPPING

Shops in Port Louis are typically open 09.30–17.00 Monday–Friday and 09.00–12.00 Saturday. A few open on Sunday morning.

The **market** [104 F3] between Queen and Farquhar streets is open 06.00–18.00 Monday–Saturday and 06.00–12.00 Sunday. There is a fantastically colourful fruit and vegetable market, which contains two intriguing *tisane* (herbal remedy) stalls. Both have been there for generations and claim to offer a cure for every imaginable ailment, from rheumatism to cellulite, with their unassuming bundles of twigs and leaves. Their cures have become so well known that they now take orders from overseas via email. **Tisane Mootoosamy** (☏ *424 3140*) is run by the fourth generation of the family, Jay, who told me the plants are all picked on the 'black moon' to ensure their potency is at its strongest. They are then dried and blended to make remedies using recipes created by his great-great grandfather in 1896. In 2013, Jay represented Mauritius at a UNESCO conference on herbal medicine. Above the fruit and vegetable market, on the first floor, is the place for souvenirs, although you may have to look hard to find items made in Mauritius. The colourful bags, wooden objects and spices are largely imported from Madagascar or Africa. While many stallholders will tell you their vanilla is grown in Mauritius, most of the vanilla in the market comes from Madagascar. If you want to be sure you are buying Mauritian vanilla, it is best to purchase it directly from the grower, such as St Aubin in the south of the island (page 168). Pickpockets are said to operate around the market and, although the atmosphere isn't threatening, the tenacious sales techniques can be rather tiresome. You are expected to barter. On the opposite side of Farquhar Street is the meat and fish market. The **Caudan Waterfront** [104 C1] (☏ *211 6560*) contains a vast range of shops: jewellery, fashion, carpets, crafts and souvenirs, some of which are duty free. Opening hours are 09.30–17.30 Monday–Saturday, 09.30–12.30 Sunday, and there is an information kiosk in the Barkly Wharf building. It's relatively hassle-free shopping with no real hard sell, although prices may be a little elevated. On the ground floor of Barkly Wharf, **Bookcourt** (☏ *211 9146*) is a well-stocked bookshop which has English-language titles on the Mascarene Islands, including this one. There is a **craft market** within the Caudan Waterfront, not far from the casino, where you can see artisans at work. The **Mauritius Glass Gallery** has an outlet here (☏ *210 1181*). The **Small and Medium Enterprise Development Authority (SMEDA)** also has a shop here, where you can be sure of buying locally made products (see also pages 70–3). Opposite it is Presqu'ile, which also sells products made on the island, such as sugar, handmade soap and tea.

On weekend evenings there is an open-air market at the Caudan Waterfront, called **Le Souk**.

OTHER PRACTICALITIES

MONEY AND BANKING Branches of the major **banks**, including HSBC [104 D4] (*Pl d'Armes;* ☏ *203 8333*) and State Bank of Mauritius [104 D3] (*1 Queen Elizabeth Av;* ☏ *202 1111*). Mauritius Commercial Bank [104 E4] (*9–15 Sir William Newton St;* ☏ *202 5000*) and Barclays [104 E4] (*Sir William Newton St;* ☏ *207 1800*) can be found a short distance from the harbour. They have ATMs.

COMMUNICATIONS The **General Post Office** [104 F2] (📞 *208 2851;* ⊕ *08.15–11.15 & 12.00–16.00 Mon–Fri, 08.00–11.45 Sat*) and the Postal Museum are near the harbour at the end of Sir William Newton Street. **Internet access** is available at the post office.

Payphones can be found around the Caudan Waterfront.

MEDICAL CARE The **Dr Jeetoo Public Hospital** [98 D7] (📞 *212 3201*) is on Volcy Pougnet Street. There are several pharmacies, including the well-stocked **Newton Pharmacy** [104 E4] (*10 Sir William Newton St;* 📞 *208 7048*), **Capital Pharmacy** [99 G2] (*57 Sir Seewoosagur Ramgoolam St;* 📞 *216 9000*) and **Pharmacie du Port** [104 D3] (*9 Rue President J F Kennedy;* 📞 *208 1037*).

WHAT TO SEE AND DO

HORSE RACING At the historic Champ de Mars racecourse [99 H6]. The season lasts from May until the end of November/early December, with race days usually every Saturday. A memorable day out but expect lively crowds as Mauritians love their racing. For more information, see page 84.

ART There are several commercial art galleries in Port Louis, including **Didus** (📞 *210 7438*) in the Caudan Waterfront [104 C1], which has a permanent exhibition, sells works by local artists and can arrange shipment.

HIKING The mountains around Port Louis provide superb views of the city and surrounding countryside. Hiking **Le Pouce** (811m) takes around 3 hours (return) and the path is well signed. It is relatively easy but steep in parts, particularly towards the summit of the thumb from which it takes its name. You can tackle the walk either from near Moka or from Port Louis. Coming from Port Louis along the M2, take the second exit marked Moka and the first left marked Eureka. Around 100m before Eureka turn right and you will see a track marked 'Le Pouce'. Alternatively buses from Port Louis's Victoria Square bus station to Nouvelle Découverte will drop you off at the start of the track.

Scaling **Pieter Both** (820m) is rather more strenuous and requires a guide; the summit demands climbing gear and if you reach the top you will need to rappel down.

Local adventure sports companies, such as **Otelair** (📞 *696 6750; www.otelair.com*) and **Vertical World** (📞 *697 5430; www.verticalworldltd.com*) offer guided hikes of Le Pouce and Pieter Both, and will supply climbing gear for the latter. **Yemaya** (📞 *752 0046; www.yemayaadventures.com*) offers guided hikes of Le Pouce.

AAPRAVASI GHAT ✳ [104 G2] (*1 Quay St;* 📞 *217 7770; www.aapravasighat.org;* ⊕ *09.00–16.00 Mon–Fri, 09.00–12.00 Sat; admission free*) You can wander or take a guided tour around the buildings of the immigration depot built in 1849 to receive indentured labourers, now a UNESCO World Heritage Site. A well laid-out, modern visitor centre explains the history of indentured labour in Mauritius and provides an insight into the origins of the island's population.

Between 1834 and 1923 almost 500,000 indentured labourers arrived in Mauritius to replace the labour lost following the abolition of slavery in 1835. While many worked in the island's sugar plantations, others were transported from Mauritius to other British colonies. The majority came from India but some also arrived from southeast Asia, Madagascar and East Africa.

The depot originally consisted of a gatekeeper's office, hospital block, kitchens, immigration office, other staff offices, sheds, stables and privies. Today only parts of it remain, including the gatekeeper's office, hospital block, wharf steps and immigrants' sheds. You can walk up the steps, as those early immigrants did when they disembarked their ships, and then wander around the remaining stone buildings.

PHILATELISTS' HEAVEN

Mauritius holds a special place in the affections of stamp collectors since the first stamps issued there are now among the greatest rarities in the philatelic world. In 1993, at an auction in Zurich, a buyer paid the equivalent of US$3.3 million for 'the crown jewel of philately', an envelope – 'the Bordeaux cover' – with two stamps on it, sent from Mauritius to a Bordeaux wine importer in 1847. This is the only cover known with the two values (one penny and twopence) of the Mauritius 'Post Office' series.

Mauritius was the first British colony to use adhesive postage stamps, and was only the fifth country in the world to issue stamps, in 1847. The first 1,000 postage stamps (500 at a penny value and 500 at twopence) were produced by Joseph Barnard, a watchmaker and jeweller of Port Louis, who engraved the dies on a copper plate and laboriously printed the stamps one at a time, direct from the engraving. Despite his skills as a craftsman, the results were very primitive compared with the famous penny blacks of Britain. They also contained an error. Instead of the words POST PAID he engraved POST OFFICE in the left-hand margin. The stamps were released on 21 September 1847. On the same day, Lady Gomm, the governor's wife, used a considerable number of the orange-red one-penny value on invitations to a ball at Le Réduit. Only 15 one-penny stamps and 12 of the blue twopenny value are believed still to exist.

Barnard was instructed to produce further stamps in 1848. To facilitate printing, he engraved each stamp 12 times on the plate. The result was that no two stamps were identical, although they had the correct words POST PAID on them. These stamps, which were in use until 1859, are also highly prized among collectors.

Another fascinating rarity turned up in a philatelist's collection in 1994. Two twopenny blue stamps postmarked 9 November 1859 revealed spelling errors. One shows 'Maurituis', the other 'Mauritus'. The issue appears to have been withdrawn from circulation the same day. Being unique, the stamps are priceless.

After 1859, mass-produced stamps, printed in Britain, were issued. However, stocks of frequently used stamps were often exhausted before fresh supplies arrived from London. Consequently, the lower-value stamps were surcharged, creating more stamps of interest to collectors.

The first pillar boxes were erected in Port Louis in the early 1860s. Special date stamps for mail collected from them were used from 1885 to 1926 in Port Louis, Beau Bassin, Curepipe, Mahébourg and Rose Hill. Examples of such cancellations are rare.

Other historical events have also given Mauritius stamps special value. Airmail services were launched to Réunion in 1933 and to Rodrigues in 1972. The first use of aerogrammes in Mauritius was on 27 December 1944.

Today, used postage stamps and first-day covers are sold in shops selling tourist souvenirs in Port Louis and Curepipe, and stamps can be bought in the General Post Office and at the Postal Museum in Port Louis.

4

NATURAL HISTORY MUSEUM [104 D4] (*Mauritius Institute Bldg, Chaussée St;* ✆ *212 0639;* e *mimuse@intnet.mu; www.mauritiusmuseums.com;* ⊕ *09.00–16.00 Mon/Tue & Thu/Fri, 09.00–12.00 Sat; admission free*) The natural history museum was established in 1826 and moved to this attractive building in 1885. It is small and certainly not modern or high-tech, but with free entry it is worth a visit and should take no more than 30 minutes to wander around. Its most famous display is a goose-down-clad dodo replica; there are also skeletons of dodos found on the island and a Rodrigues solitare. Many of the exhibits are old and there are rather a lot of bizarre taxidermy and models of the region's animals, birds and marine life, which gives it a quirky feel.

PHOTOGRAPHY MUSEUM [99 E4] (*Old Council St;* ✆ *211 1705;* e *photomuseemaurice@ yahoo.com;* ⊕ *10.00–15.00 Mon–Fri; admission adult/child Rs300/150*) In a restored street on the opposite side of Jules Koenig Street to the theatre. An intriguing little private museum containing old cameras and prints of Port Louis in colonial days, many showing horse-drawn taxis. One photograph, dated 1956, shows the last passenger train leaving Curepipe for Port Louis. A highlight is the daguerreotype, the first commercially successful photographic apparatus, developed in 1839 by Jacques Daguerre. It created an image of a silver-surfaced copper plate but the process was superseded by other technologies and had almost completely died out by the 1860s. Mauritius received its first daguerreotype in 1840, just six months after France bought the licence from Daguerre.

BLUE PENNY MUSEUM [104 B1] (*Le Musée, Caudan Waterfront;* ✆ *210 8176;* e *bluepennymuseum@intnet.mu; www.bluepennymuseum.com;* ⊕ *10.00–17.00 Mon–Sat, last entry is at 16.30; admission adult/child Rs245/120*) The stamp collection includes the famous 'Post Office' stamps issued in 1847 (see box, page 109). Paintings, photos, documents and nautical charts from the island's colonial days are also on display, and the museum provides a good history of Port Louis. The shop sells books on the Mascarene Islands and souvenirs.

POSTAL MUSEUM [104 F2] (*Quay St;* ✆ *213 4812;* e *postalmuseum@mauritiuspost. mu; www.mauritiuspost.mu;* ⊕ *09.00–16.30 Mon–Fri, 10.00–15.30 Sat; admission adult/child Rs150/90*) An interesting, neatly laid-out museum within a stern Victorian granite-block building on the waterfront. It displays the postal history of Mauritius from the issuing of the first stamp on the island in 1847 and the establishment of a coach service. On display is some of the equipment used in post offices over the years, as well as cancelling machines, letter boxes and vending machines. The collection of stamps is impressive, and includes an original penny black. It arrived in Mauritius because when the engraver began work on Mauritius's first stamp, he copied from the penny black. Souvenir packs of stamps, letter openers, paperweights and other objects with a postal theme are on sale.

MIKADO SHELL MUSEUM [104 E3] (*6 Sir William Newton St;* ✆ *208 1900;* e *Mikado@ intnet.mu;* ⊕ *09.00–17.00 Mon–Fri, 09.00–13.00 Sat; admission free*) Above the jewellery shop, this is one of the most significant shell collections in the Indian Ocean – some 3,000 shells from around the world.

SSR MEMORIAL CENTRE FOR CULTURE [99 H2] (*87 Sir Seewoosagur Ramgoolam St, Plaine Verte;* ✆ *242 0053; www.mauritiusmuseums.mu;* ⊕ *09.00–16.00 Mon, Tue, Thu, Fri, 09.00–12.00 Sat; admission free*) This house, where Sir Seewoosagur

Ramgoolam lived from 1935 to 1968, contains exhibits on the life of this much-loved former Mauritian leader. The centrepiece is a photographic exhibition showing significant events in his life.

PERE LAVAL'S SHRINE [99 H6] (*Ste-Croix;* ℡ 242 2129) Father Jacques Desiré Laval (known locally as Père Laval) was born in France in 1803 and brought up in a strict religious atmosphere, qualifying as a medical doctor before becoming a priest. In 1841, he arrived in Mauritius as a missionary and converted thousands of recently freed slaves to Catholicism, becoming known as the Apostle of the Blacks. He died on 9 September 1864. He was beatified in 1979, following Pope John Paul II's visit to Mauritius, and is regarded as the island's 'national saint'. He is venerated by followers of all faiths who attribute miraculous healing powers to his name. Throughout September, and particularly on the anniversary of his death, people from around the world flock to his tomb in Ste-Croix, many in hope of a miracle healing. The tomb can be visited at any time of year. A rather gaudily coloured plaster effigy covers it. Ste-Croix is a suburb of Port Louis and is easily reached by bus from the Immigration Square bus station.

4

RUNNING RACES IN MAURITIUS

Since 2006 Mauritius has hosted a trail-running race, known as Royal Raid, which now attracts runners from around the world. Three races are held simultaneously (15km, 35km and 80km) in the south and southwest of the island and take you through the Yemen Nature Reserve, the Black River Gorges National Park and the sugarcane fields of the Domaine de Bel Ombre. The race is usually held in May. For details, visit www.royalraid.com.

The Mauritius Marathon takes place in July in the southwest and follows the coast, providing beautiful views. There are three distances to choose from: 10km, 21km and 42km. For details, visit www.mauritiusmarathon.com.

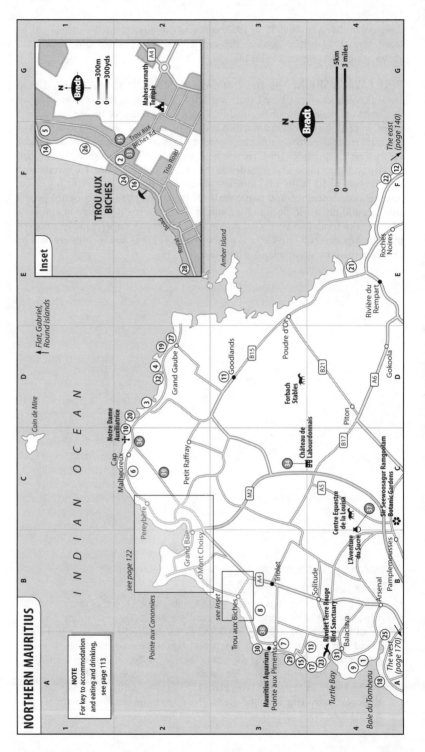

NORTHERN MAURITIUS

NOTE
For key to accommodation and eating and drinking, see page 113

INDIAN OCEAN

Coin de Mire

Flat, Gabriel, Round islands

Amber Island

Pointe aux Canonniers

see page 122

Pereybère

Grand Baie

Mont Choisy

Trou aux Biches

see inset

Mauritius Aquarium, Pointe aux Piments

Turtle Bay

Baie du Tombeau

Cap Malheureux

Notre Dame Auxiliatrice

Petit Raffray

Grand Gaube

Goodlands

Poudre d'Or

Roches Noires

Rivière du Rempart

Forbach Stables

Château de Labourdonnais

Piton

Gokoola

Triolet

Solitude

Rivulet Terre Rouge Bird Sanctuary

BalaClava

Arsenal

Pamplemousses

Centre Equestre de la Louisa

L'Aventure du Sucre

Sir Seewoosagur Ramgoolam Botanic Gardens

The west (page 170)

The east (page 140)

Inset

TROU AUX BICHES

Maheswarnath Temple

Trou aux Biches Rd

Trio Road

Royal Road

0   300m
0   300yds

0   5km
0   3 miles

5

Northern Mauritius

Northern Mauritius is divided into two districts: Pamplemousses in the west and Rivière du Rempart in the east.

The coast of Pamplemousses is largely given over to tourism and includes a string of resorts around Turtle Bay and, further north, the island's main tourist hot spot, Grand Baie. Just inland are three of Mauritius's main tourist attractions: Aventure du Sucre, Château de Labourdonnais and the Sir Seewoosagur Ramgoolam Botanic Gardens. The district's boundary is the mountain range encircling Port Louis, with Crève Coeur, behind Pieter Both, as its southernmost village.

Rivière du Rempart is a compact district with a less developed coast than that of the northwest, which is largely made up of rugged beaches and the odd fishing village. Inland, is the industrial/agricultural area of Goodlands, where Historic Marine produces its intricate model ships. The town of Rivière du Rempart is in the east of the district, originally named Rampart River for its steep banks.

Sugarcane is very much a feature of life and the landscape in the north, as it has been for centuries. The importance of sugar in the area gave rise to the construction

NORTHERN MAURITIUS
For listings, see pages 115–18, 119–21, 130–2 & 133 unless otherwise stated

Where to stay

Where to eat and drink

of the island's first railway line in 1864. The Northern Line, which connected Port Louis to Pamplemousses and Flacq, was used to transport sugar to Port Louis. It stopped carrying passengers in 1956 and was closed down completely in 1964.

BAIE DU TOMBEAU TO POINTE AUX PIMENTS

The elbow of land just north of Port Louis is named **Baie du Tombeau** (Tomb Bay), in memory of George Weldon, an English merchant who was drowned there in 1697. He was not alone in his fate and treasure hunters are convinced that treasure lies in this bay, a legacy of the many ships wrecked in its waters. If ferreting for treasure doesn't interest you, then there is little to keep you in the village of Baie du Tombeau; while there is a public beach here, it doesn't rival the others in the area.

Back on the main road from Port Louis to the north, you pass through the village of **Arsenal**. Although locals are quick to point out the link with the English football team of the same name, the name actually comes from the munitions stores which the French had here.

Inland from Arsenal is the small village of **Pamplemousses**, which is home to the **Sir Seewoosagur Ramgoolam Botanic Gardens** [112 C4], one of Mauritius's best-known tourist attractions (see pages 135–6).

The **Church of St François** in the village of Pamplemousses was built in 1743 and is one of the oldest on the island. Its cemetery contains the tomb of Abbé Buonavita (1752–1833), who was Napoleon's almoner (distributor of alms) on St Helena. He settled in Mauritius after Napoleon's death in 1821. Villebague, Governor of Mauritius from 1756 to 1759, is also buried here. Behind the primary school in Pamplemousses is the **Bassin des Esclaves** (Slave Pond), where it is said slaves were washed before being sold.

Not far from Pamplemousses are two sites that evoke the area's agricultural history: **L'Aventure du Sucre** [112 C4] tells the story of the island's sugar industry (page 137), while the restored 19th-century **Château de Labourdonnais** [112 C4] gives an insight into the life of a wealthy sugar-estate owner.

Southeast of Pamplemousses village is **La Nicolière Reservoir**. The road to this large body of water is lined with sugarcane and pineapples and leads over the dam wall. A viewpoint on the other side of the dam provides views of the forested hills around the reservoir and, in the distance, the east coast. It is a popular spot with locals, for picnics, walks and fishing, but sadly the area is often thick with litter. The road continues steeply uphill through woodland and then farmland, where the island's only commercial cows' milk producer is based, before it joins the road back towards the coast.

Back on the coast near **Balaclava**, **Turtle Bay** [112 A4] is a marine park which offers good snorkelling. The coast here is naturally largely rocky, although the hotels lining the coast have each created their own beaches. From the coast you can see ships queuing to enter Port Louis harbour. The ruins of an 18th-century **French arsenal** are here and, further north, at **Pointe aux Piments**, lie the remnants of the **Batterie des Grenadiers**. Some of the most impressive ruins are within the grounds of the Maritim Hotel. Non-residents can obtain permission to visit them at the security hut by the entrance.

🏠 **WHERE TO STAY** Many of the hotels that line this area of coast, particularly the luxury and upmarket ones, are fairly isolated, wedged between cane fields and the sea. Most have excellent facilities and are within walking distance of other hotels but there is no popping out to local shops and bars on foot. Bear in mind that from

most beaches along this stretch of coast you can see cargo ships heading into Port Louis; while this appeals to some people it puts others off staying in the area. On the plus side, being in the west, you will see some wonderful sunsets.

Luxury

⌂ **Angsana Balaclava** [112 A4] (51 rooms, 1 villa) Balaclava; 204 1888; e balaclava@angsana.com; www.angsana.com. An intimate hotel with high standards of accommodation & service. The suites are spacious & all, apart from the 18 garden suites, have a small private pool. The beach is small but pleasant & has been extended around the saltwater pool. Being at the end of a line of hotels, the sea here tends to have less watersports traffic than at other hotels in the area. The rooms are in 3-storey thatched buildings around a central pool & restaurant/bar area. The rooms are spacious, feel luxurious, have all the facilities of a 5-star hotel & feature large, impressive bathrooms. The beachfront pool suites have an enticing stone bathtub. As well as the saltwater pool, there is a freshwater one. The spa facilities are good, each treatment room being designed for couples & having its own changing room. There are 2 very good restaurants & guests can request a romantic dinner for 2 served in any part of the resort by their own private chef & waiter. Non-motorised watersports are included in the room rate. The hotel is popular with guests from Asia, & is decorated with an Asian theme. **$$$$$**

⌂ **The Oberoi** [112 A4] (48 rooms, 28 villas) Turtle Bay, Balaclava; 204 3600; e reservations@oberoi-mauritius.com; www.oberoihotels.com. This hotel, which is a member of 'Leading Small Hotels of the World', prides itself on excellent service & guest privacy. Thoughtful architecture uses natural materials to recreate the charm of a village set in 20 acres of tropical gardens. The luxurious accommodation includes 18 sumptuous villas with private pool. Interior design is natural elegance with memorable touches like the woven sugarcane headboards, sunken marble bath & small private tropical garden with outdoor shower. It'll leave you planning to redecorate when you get home! Rooms are equipped with everything you could possibly need. There are stunning swimming pools, tennis courts, a watersports centre (even waterskiing is free) & a dive centre. The spa offers all sorts of pampering, including free yoga & t'ai chi classes. The food is, of course, excellent. It's a romantic, relaxation-focused retreat rather than a family hotel. **$$$$$**

Upmarket

⌂ **Intercontinental Mauritius** [112 A4] (210 rooms) Balaclava; 261 1200; e sales@icmauritius.com; www.intercontinental.com. A new hotel typical of this large international chain. The hotel has good conference facilities & is well set up for children with family rooms & a kids' club. Rooms are on the small side but have all the features you would expect of an Intercontinental. There are 5 restaurants & a small spa. In some ways it lacks soul – it could be a large international hotel anywhere. It is very popular with guests from India & China. **$$$$**

⌂ **Le Victoria Hotel** [112 A4] (254 rooms) Pointe aux Piments; 204 2000; e victoria@bchot.com; www.levictoria-hotel.com. A Beachcomber property whose rooms are some of the most spacious on the island (standard rooms are 60m²). It also has suites & family apartments. All are equipped with AC, TV, phone, minibar, safe, tea/coffee facilities & balcony/terrace. There are 3 restaurants, including 1 Italian. There are the usual free watersports, a dive centre, spa, tennis courts, 1 large swimming pool & a kids' club. Guests can use the golf course at Trou aux Biches Resort & Spa. The beach here is good, but it is wise to wear reef shoes for swimming because of the urchins & coral. It is a large, lively hotel with constant entertainment; the facilities & room sizes make it appealing for families. The all-inclusive package is popular. **$$$$**

⌂ **Maritim Resort & Spa** [112 A4] (215 rooms) Turtle Bay, Balaclava; 204 1000; e info.mau@maritim.de; www.maritim.com. This large hotel stands in 25ha of tropical gardens containing 18th-century French ruins. The rooms & suites are equipped with AC, TV, phone, minibar, safe & balcony/terrace. Bathrooms in the standard rooms are rather small. The 17 suites are a significant step up from the rooms & there is a 2-bedroom luxury villa. There are 5 restaurants & 3 bars, plus a spa, 9-hole golf course, watersports, dive centre, tennis & horseriding. Decent standards without too many frills. Many guests find the

AI option good value for money. The clientele is predominantly German & it is popular for weddings. **$$$$**

⌂ **Westin Turtle Bay Resort & Spa** [112 A4] (190 rooms & suites) Turtle Bay, Balaclava; ☎204 1400; e westin.mauritius@westin.com; www. westinturtlebaymauritius.com. Formerly The Grand Mauritian, this is a large property with beautifully decorated & particularly spacious rooms with balcony/terrace. It is on a very attractive stretch of beach. There is a spa, 2 pools, 4 restaurants, tennis, watersports, a dive centre & a kids' club. **$$$$**

Mid range

⌂ **Le Meridien** [112 A3] (265 rooms) Village Hall Lane, Pointe aux Piments; ☎204 3333; e resa@lemeridien.mu; www.lemeridien.com/ mauritius. A large hotel, popular with families & as a conference venue. The rooms & suites are in 3 blocks of 3 storeys on either side of an impressive lobby area. The buildings aren't particularly pretty but rooms are spacious, with room for children. There are 5 restaurants & bars, 2 pools, tennis courts, a gym & spa, as well as the usual free watersports. Children are well catered for with a kids' club & babysitting service. It is looking a little tired & I have heard reports of poor service. **$$$**

⌂ **Le Récif** [112 A3] (70 rooms) Coastal Rd, Pointe aux Piments; ☎261 0444; e resa@recif-hotel.com; www.lerecif.com. The 3-star hotel is located on a good stretch of beach (although a little rocky), & guests can step straight from the pool onto the sand. Rooms are en suite & equipped with AC, TV & phone. They are on the small side but have a clean, modern feel. Facilities include a restaurant, a bar, pool, watersports, a small spa & kids' club. **$$$**

⌂ **Ravenala Hotel** [112 A4] (272 rooms) Turtle Bay, Balaclava; ☎204 3000; www.theravenala-hotel-mauritius.com. Formerly La Plantation, this hotel has been completely renovated. It offers 4-star accommodation set in 8 acres at the centre of the bay. The rooms are spacious & have AC, TV, phone, safe & balcony/terrace. It is family-friendly, with 102 family suites. There is a broad selection of restaurants, including some which are for adults only. Facilities include 2 pools, spa, watersports, a dive centre, tennis courts, fitness centre & a kids' club. **$$$**

⌂ **The Address Boutique Hotel** [112 A4] (42 rooms) Port Chambly Village, Terre Rouge;

☎405 3000; e reservations@ addressboutiquehotel.com; www. addressboutqiuehotel.com. Small 4-star hotel within a Mediterranean-village-style complex of private apartments & a few shops. Set on an estuary with views out to sea, around 15mins' drive from Port Louis; there is no beach. Rooms are modern & have all you need but don't aim to be luxurious. They are en suite (shower, no bath) with AC, TV, phone, safe & Wi-Fi. The superior rooms are considerably larger than the standard rooms but only the 2 executive suites have a balcony. The pool area is very pleasant, although rather overlooked by the rooms, & there are 2 restaurants, a gym & small spa. **$$$**

⌂ **Veranda Pointe aux Biches Hotel** [112 E2] (115 rooms) Royal Rd, Pointe aux Piments; ☎265 5901; e resa@veranda-resorts.com; www. veranda-resorts.com. An informal family-friendly hotel on the beach. The architecture is rustic but modern. 'Barefoot bliss' is the theme of the hotel, which features sand floors, including in the reception & beach bar. Rooms have en suite, AC, TV, safe, minibar & balcony/terrace. The 44 family rooms have a separate children's bedroom area. There is also a wing for couples, with its own pool, beach restaurant & bar. There is a small spa & kids' club. They offer limited watersports as motor boats are banned in front of the hotel, but that makes for peaceful swimming. Wi-Fi is free. The hotel operates a free shuttle to Grand Baie 3 times a week. **$$$**

⌂ **Villas Mon Plaisir** [112 A3] (41 rooms) Coastal Rd, Pointe aux Piments; ☎261 7471; e villasmp@intnet.mu; www.villasmonplaisir.com. A well-maintained, small, 3-star hotel popular with independent travellers on a budget. In a quiet cul-de-sac with easy access to the beach, the hotel has cosy en-suite rooms in 2-storey buildings around a small central garden & pool area. The rooms have AC, TV, phone, safe & balcony/terrace overlooking the pool. There are 3 family rooms. The bar & restaurant are pleasant & have a sea view, being situated between the rooms & the sea. Kayak, pedalo, snorkelling & glass-bottom boat trips are free & there is a dive centre next door. Free Wi-Fi. **$$$**

⌂ **Voile Bleue** [112 A3] (22 studios) Pointe aux Piments; ☎265 6800; e hello@voilebleue. mu; www.voilebleue.mu. A good option for those wanting to self-cater but also looking for some

hotel services. Self-catering AC studios in a modern complex of 2-storey buildings around a pool. The studios have well-equipped kitchenettes, TV, safe & free Wi-Fi, & a daily maid service. The beach here isn't good for swimming, being rather rocky, but the accommodation is close to the beautiful beach at Trou aux Biches. A continental breakfast is included, served in the restaurant overlooking the sea. **$$$**

Budget

⌂ **La Margarita** [112 A4] (19 rooms) Coastal Rd, Pointe aux Piments; ☎ 261 3969; e margarita@intnet.mu; www.lamargaritahotel. com. A small hotel opened by the owners of Villas Mon Plaisir in 2007, which aims to be equivalent to 2-star. It is about 200m inland from Villas Mon Plaisir & the beach, on the coastal road. Set behind high walls, it doesn't look like much from the outside. However, behind the austere exterior hides clean, modern, but simple accommodation

in a 3-storey building around a small pool. Rooms are en suite & have AC, TV, safe & balcony/terrace. There is a restaurant & guests can use the facilities at Villas Mon Plaisir. There are some unsecured parking places by the road. **$$**

⌂ **Les Cocotiers** [112 A4] (48 rooms) Le Goulet, Baie du Tombeau; ☎ 206 8600; e info@ cocotiers-hotel-mauritius.com; www.cocotiers-hotel-mauritius.com. A 2-star hotel 15mins from Port Louis. 2-storey buildings are gathered around a small pool. All rooms are en suite with AC, TV, phone, safe, & balcony/terrace. Tea/coffee facilities & stocking of the minibar are at additional cost. The rooms are simple but nicely decorated & there is a restaurant & bar. There are relatively few activities/facilities included in the price, & the immediate surrounds have little to offer in the way of entertainment, so if you stay here you will probably want to have access to a car or take some excursions. Wi-Fi is free in public areas. An AI package is available. **$$**

✗ **WHERE TO EAT** There is a small supermarket in Pointe aux Piments and numerous snack vendors. Most of the hotels in this area have restaurants which are open to non-residents.

✳ ✗ **Oryza Angsana Balaclava** [112 A4] Balaclava; ☎ 204 1888; ⏱ for dinner daily. Cuisine: European, Creole. An intimate, upmarket restaurant serving creative dishes & with an impressive wine cellar. Excellent service. Reservation essential. **$$$$**

✗ **Chez Tante Athalie** Royal Rd, Mon Goût, Pamplemousses; ☎ 243 9266; ⏱ for lunch Mon–Sat. Cuisine: Creole. On the road from the botanical gardens to Centre de Flacq. A quirky table d'hôte restaurant serving tasty traditional meals. Dining is in an open-sided shed overlooking a garden crammed with a collection of vintage cars. At the time of writing, they were offering an Rs550 table d'hôte menu. Reservation recommended. **$$$**

✗ **La Table du Château** [112 C3] Château de Labourdonnais, Mapou; ☎ 266 9533; ⏱ 09.00–17.00, Sat dinner. Cuisine: Creole, French. A clean, modern restaurant & tea room in the grounds of the mansion, with views of the impressive chateau built in 1859 (page 137). Nicely presented dishes, many of which use fruit from the orchard. **$$$**

✳ ✗ **Le Fangourin** [112 C4] L'Aventure du Sucre, Beau Plan; ☎ 243 7900; ⏱ 09.00–17.00 daily. Cuisine: Creole, French. Set in the grounds of

the old Beau Plan sugar factory, which now houses the Aventure du Sucre sugar museum. Dining is indoors or outdoors, overlooking attractive gardens &, in the distance, Pieter Both mountain. The menu is diverse & sophisticated with seafood, meat & vegetarian dishes as well as light snacks. Meals are beautifully presented, as well as in any fine-dining restaurant, & the service is excellent. The fabulous desserts are made with special, unrefined sugar from the estate. The dark chocolate fondant gateau with vanilla ice cream is incredible. Dishes featuring Aventure du Sucre's own New Grove rum are also a hit. **$$$**

✗ **Café Mon Plaisir** Royal Rd, Pamplemousses; ☎ 243 9347; ⏱ for lunch daily. Cuisine: Creole, Indian, European, Chinese. In a handy location, opposite the car park for the botanical gardens. **$$**

✗ **Café Valse de Vienne** Powder Mill Rd, Pamplemousses; ☎ 243 8465; ⏱ 09.00–17.00 daily. Cuisine: Austrian, European. Opposite the Church of St François. Has a pleasant atmosphere & serves a range of light meals, crêpes & excellent pastries. **$$**

✗ **Le Langouste Grillé** [112 B3] Coastal Rd, Pointe aux Piments; m 5779 1852; ⏱ for lunch &

dinner daily. Cuisine: Creole, seafood. Next to the aquarium (see pages 137–8). There is no shortage of rustic charm – tables are on a covered terrace with a floor of waste coral, lampshades made from woven pandanus hats & a bar made from old oil drums. The owner works with local fishermen to get the best seafood. Grilled lobster is a speciality & the crispy calamari is very tasty. Wi-Fi is free. $$
✗ **Le Pêcheur** Royal Rd, Pamplemousses; m 5931 5967; ⏲ for lunch & dinner daily. Cuisine:

Creole, seafood. Simple seafood dishes & tasty curries with an array of accompaniments. The owner has a couple of fishing boats, so the seafood here is fresh. Good value. $$
✗ **Villas Mon Plaisir** Coastal Rd, Pointe aux Piments; ✆ 261 7471; ⏲ for lunch & dinner daily. Cuisine: Creole, Chinese. Open-sided restaurant with views of the ocean & plenty of choice on the menu. $$

TROU AUX BICHES TO POINTE AUX CANONNIERS

From Pointe aux Piments the coast road runs parallel to the main road, through the village of **Trou aux Biches** (Hole of the Does), so named because there is supposed to have been a small watering hole here frequented by female deer. In contrast, Trou aux Cerfs (Hole of the Stags) at Curepipe was said to be used by the males of the species.

Despite extensive tourism development and a very large resort hotel in its centre, Trou aux Biches retains the feel of a village lived in by Mauritians. A far quieter alternative to Grand Baie, it features a beautiful, long beach, wide lagoon with excellent snorkelling and a range of accommodation and restaurants. The hotels along this stretch of coast are broken up by private houses, and in the early morning you will see a steady stream of locals exercising on the sand and swimming in the numerous fenced areas designed to protect swimmers from boat traffic.

At the main road junction in the centre of Trou aux Biches are the **police station**, the entrance to the public beach and a development of shops aimed at tourists. These include two small shops stocking products made in Mauritius by a group called **Local Hands**. A co-operative of around 60 artisans from underprivileged backgrounds creates jewellery, pottery and intricate handicrafts using wood, recycled material and coconuts. On the other side of the road is the large, modern self-catering complex, known as **Be Cosy** (page 120), which contains a mini supermarket and small day spa (page 134).

The northern end of Trou aux Biches seems to almost blend into **Mont Choisy**, which has one of the best beaches in the area. The beach curves around a large bay lined with casuarina trees, stretching to **Pointe aux Canonniers**. There are no hotels along this stretch, which means on weekdays the beach is virtually empty. However, on weekends the beach is crowded with Mauritians; buses bring them down from the large population areas around Port Louis and in the central plateau. Families set themselves up under the casuarina trees, makeshift shops selling inflatable creatures and other beach paraphernalia spring up and by the afternoon there is usually singing and dancing. Between Mont Choisy and Pointe aux Canonniers the road is lined with flame trees and when they are flowering the road becomes covered with a red carpet of petals. At Pointe aux Canonniers are some impressive private beach houses and several trendy restaurants and bars catering largely for expats.

Inland from Trou aux Biches is **Triolet**, which boasts the largest **Hindu temple** [112 G2] in Mauritius. It is an amalgamation of seven temples added to the original Maheswarnath Temple, built in 1857. As soon as you arrive, an elderly gentleman will probably appear out of nowhere to give you a guided tour. A donation to the temple is usually all that is required in exchange. He may seem eccentric but he appears to know his stuff. The main street through Triolet is busy and prone to

traffic jams but, for those stuck in their cars, refreshments are close at hand with many stalls selling fruit, vegetables and snacks along the road.

WHERE TO STAY

Upmarket

Le Cardinal [112 F1] (13 rooms) Coastal Rd, Trou aux Biches; 204 5200; e info@lecardinalresort.intnet.mu; www.lecardinalresort.com. A boutique hotel finished to a very high standard. The hotel is on a small stretch of beach & all rooms face the sea. Rooms are spacious with modern fixtures & fittings. There are 2 penthouses, one of which has its own pool. The hotel markets itself as a couples' retreat but there is a duplex suitable for families. Room facilities include AC, TV, minibar, safe & Wi-Fi. There is an à la carte restaurant, bar, pool & a massage room. Guests can use the gym, tennis courts & spa at Casuarina Hotel. **$$$$**

Trou aux Biches Resort & Spa [112 F1] (333 rooms, including 27 villas) Trou aux Biches; 204 6800; e trouauxbiches@bchot.com; www.trouauxbiches-resort.com. Stretching along one of the island's best beaches, this is a large resort but the rooms are arranged in crescents, each with a swimming pool in the centre, to ensure an intimate feel. The rooms are exceptionally modern & spacious, especially in the beachfront suites. All accommodation, apart from junior suites, has an outdoor shower. The upstairs beachfront suites have a decent-sized plunge pool, while those downstairs have a tiny pool, more like an outdoor bath. They are also visible from the beach. Free Wi-Fi throughout the resort. There are 6 restaurants offering a variety of cuisine, watersports facilities, a large spa, gym, kids' & teens' clubs. The hotel was built with eco-friendly aims; for example, used water is collected & stored under the 6 tennis courts. **$$$$**

Mid range

Casuarina Hotel [112 F1] (95 rooms) Trou aux Biches; 204 5000; e casuarina@intnet.mu; www.hotel-casuarina.com. Across the road from the beach, the hotel is a mass of white, thatched cottages, round like toadstools. The rooms are comfortable but not outstanding with AC, TV, safe, minibar & balcony/terrace. The 15 family bungalows have 2 bedrooms, a living/dining area, kitchenette & bathroom. They sleep up to 2 adults & 4 children (1 room with 2 sets of bunk beds), although 6 may be a bit of a squeeze. Kitchens

are well equipped. The 13 sea-view rooms were renovated in 2012 & have free Wi-Fi. There are 2 restaurants, a bar, 2 pools, spa, gym, tennis court, kids' club & plenty of watersports. **$$$**

Coral Azur Beach Resort [122 A3] (88 rooms) Mont Choisy; 265 6070; e mont_choisy@intnet.mu; www.coralazur.com. The beach immediately in front of the hotel is pretty but small, although the fabulous beaches of Mont Choisy & Trou aux Biches are nearby. Close to amenities – shops, bank, taxis & restaurants. The rooms are in 2-storey units; they are fairly small & unfussy but they are en suite with AC, TV, phone, minibar, safe & balcony/terrace. There is a choice of restaurants, a pool, small spa, tennis court & free kayak & pedalo. A lively hotel on a lively little stretch of beach – the constant whining of speedboats being the inevitable downside. **$$$**

Hotel des 2 Mondes [112 A3] (16 rooms) Coastal Rd, Mont Choisy; 265 7777; e contact@hoteldes2mondes.com; www.hoteldes2mondes.com. Around 100m from the beach, across the road. Rooms are simply furnished but comfortable, with en suite, AC, flatscreen TV with DVD player, phone, safe, balcony/terrace & Wi-Fi. There is also a 2-bedroom apartment. There is a restaurant, a tiny pool & a very small, basic spa area. Accommodation & facilities are on a par with some in the budget category but the prices are mid range. **$$$**

Hotel Le Canonnier [122 A1] (284 rooms) Pointe aux Canonniers; 209 7000; e canonnier@bchot.com; www.lecannonier-hotel.com. This is a large, 4-star, family-focused hotel, set on a peninsula surrounded by sea & beaches on 3 sides. The rooms have sleek, modern décor, AC, TV, minibar, safe & balcony/terrace. The 2-bedroom apartments are designed for families. There are some interesting ruins in the 17 acres of tropical gardens: a 19th-century lighthouse (now housing the kids' club), cannons & an old fortress. The wellness centre's 6 massage cabins are built around an ancient banyan tree. Extensive facilities, lots of free activities & watersports, always something going on & very child friendly. The AI is popular. **$$$**

Hotel le Palmiste [112 B3] (81 rooms) Morcellement les Mascareignes, Impasse le Palmiste, Trou aux Biches; 265 6815; e info@

hotel-lepalmiste.mu; www.hotel-lepalmiste. mu. A 3-star equivalent, 200m from the beach. Accommodation is in 3-storey buildings around a pool area. Rooms are unremarkable, equipped with en suite, AC, TV, phone, safe, minibar, Wi-Fi & balcony/terrace; there are 12 family rooms. There is a restaurant, a bar, a nightclub, 2 pools, watersports (payable) & a small spa. It is a fair walk to the beach, & there are better options in the same price bracket. **$$$**

⌂ **Le Sakoa** [112 F2] (16 apts) Coastal Rd, Trou aux Biches; ☏ 483 4970; e info@sakoa-management.com; www.lesakoa.com. A small, homely hotel, which has a good reputation among independent travellers. Accommodation is in 2-storey thatched buildings, located in a well-maintained tropical garden on a gorgeous stretch of beach. Rooms are en suite, with kitchenette, AC, TV, phone, safe & balcony/terrace. They are spacious & clean. The kitchenettes are simple but are a useful addition for those wanting to self-cater part of the time; surprisingly, tea & coffee is not supplied in the room. Garden rooms are cheaper than sea-view rooms but some of them suffer from road noise. Room 14, one of the upstairs rooms closest to the sea, has the best view of the coast. There is a good restaurant, small pool, daily maid service & regular evening entertainment. Pedaloes & kayaks are available free of charge. Wi-Fi is free & there is a computer at reception for guest use. **$$$**

Budget

⌂ **Be Cosy Apart' Hotel** [112 F2] (127 apts) Coastal Rd, Trou aux Biches; ☏ 204 5454; e info@beapart.com; www.beapart.com. An outstanding self-catering option. A thoroughly modern complex of fully equipped studios & apartments 100m from the beach. The apartments are arranged around a very pleasant garden/pool area. They are spacious & have AC, TV, safe & up-to-date bathrooms. There are welcome hotel touches, like luggage porters, daily maid service & breakfast can be included at the restaurant on site. There is secure parking, plenty of restaurants within walking distance, & a small day spa within the complex. Very good value for money. **$$**

⌂ **Bois d'Oiseaux** [122 A3] (10 apts) Coastal Rd, Trou aux Biches; ☏ 265 5341; e hitie@boisdoiseaux.com; www.boisdoiseaux.com. Simple self-catering accommodation on the seafront. The 2 villas have 3 or 4 bedrooms & private pool, & the 8 duplexes have 2 or 3 bedrooms. The accommodation is well equipped, Wi-Fi is available & daily maid service is included. There is a pool overlooking the ocean, & a dive centre nearby. **$$**

⌂ **Grand Baie Travel & Tours Holiday Rentals** Coastal Rd, Grand Baie; ☏ 454 4038; e resagbtt@intnet.mu; www.gbtt.com. Offers self-catering accommodation at several complexes around Mont Choisy. They are well maintained, have a pool & prices include linen & daily maid service but no meals. Bookings can be made at the GBTT address above. They also organise airport transfers & excursions. **$$**

⌂ **Le Grand Bleu Hotel** [122 A4] (62 rooms) Coastal Rd, Trou aux Biches; ☏ 265 5812; e contact@legrandbleuhotel.com; www.legrandbleuhotel.com. A small budget hotel across the road from the beach at the far northern end of Trou aux Biches. Accommodation is in smallish, basic rooms with en suite, AC, TV, phone, safe, fridge & balcony/terrace. Family rooms are available. The rooms furthest from the road are quieter. There is a restaurant & 2 pools. **$$**

⌂ **Residence C'est Ici** [112 F2] (5 villas/apts) Coastal Rd, Trou aux Biches; ☏ 265 5231; e reservation@cestici.com; www.cest-ici.com. A complex within an attractive beachfront garden offering a variety of accommodation from a 1-bedroom studio to a 3-bedroom villa. They are well equipped, have AC, daily maid service & free Wi-Fi. **$$**

⌂ **Sous le Badamier** [122 B2] (12 rooms) Coastal Rd, Pointe aux Canonniers; ☏ 263 4391; e info@souslebadamier.com; www.souslebadamier. com. A charming little guesthouse around a courtyard with a badamier tree in the centre. The en-suite rooms are bright & fresh with AC, TV, safe & minibar. The open-air restaurant serves Creole cuisine. Free internet access on the ground floor. The hotel is not on a beach but offers a shuttle service (payable) to Mont Choisy Beach, & there is a tiny pool. Diving & accommodation packages are available. **$$**

✕ **WHERE TO EAT** For self-caterers there's the **Choisy Royal supermarket**, in a colourful building at the southern end of the main road through Mont Choisy (Coastal Road); also **Chez Popo** at the Pointe aux Piments end of Trou aux Biches.

�Ҳ **Hangar** [122 A2] Hidden Reef Garden, Coastal Rd, Pointe Aux Canonniers; ☏ 263 7285; ☺ 11.00–late Tue–Sun. Cuisine: European, bar/pub. A pub/sports bar popular with expats & tourists. It can become crowded at times, especially when big sporting matches are being shown on the big screen. $$$

✗ **La Bay des Pirates** [122 A4] Coastal Rd, Mont Choisy; ☏ 265 5104; ☺ 10.00–late daily. Cuisine: pizza, pasta, bar. An open-air bar/restaurant in the centre of Mont Choisy. $$$

✗ **Le Off** [122 B2] Coastal Rd, Pointe aux Canonniers; ☏ 263 6357; www.le-off.mu; ☺ 11.00–late Tue–Sat, 11.00–18.00 Sun. Cuisine: European, Asian. Opened in 2013, this trendy bar/restaurant is hidden behind a high wall, where comfy chairs & beanbags are arranged around a pool. Children are welcome & there is a children's play area. The menu is modern & carefully prepared using fresh, high-quality ingredients. They are known for their burgers & their prawns with vanilla. Food is served all day, & a musician accompanies brunch on Sun. Popular with French expats. $$$

✗ **Le Pescatore** [122 A3] Coastal Rd, Mont Choisy; ☏ 265 6337; ☺ for lunch & dinner Mon–Sat. Cuisine: Creole, European, seafood. A good upmarket option right on the seafront with lovely views & superb seafood. $$$

✗ **Le Sakoa** [112 F2] Coastal Rd, Trou aux Biches; ☏ 483 4970; www.lesakoa.com; ☺ lunch & dinner daily. Cuisine: Creole, European. An intimate, peaceful restaurant with a view of the hotel pool & the ocean beyond. Dishes are nicely presented & cater for a wide range of tastes. At the time of writing, they were offering 3-course dinners for Rs1,000. The location invites you to take a post-meal walk along the beach. $$$

✗ **Café de la Paix** [122 A4] Coastal Rd, Mont Choisy; ☏ 265 5335; ☺ 09.00–15.00 & 18.00–22.30 daily. Cuisine: Creole, Chinese, seafood. A great little restaurant serving good food at reasonable prices. The décor is simple, with tables on a covered terrace or small indoor area. There is a good selection of vegetarian dishes on offer. The shrimps in garlic butter & the sweet & sour chicken are particularly good. They also serve some decent cocktails, including a very good planter's punch. $$

✗ **Ippocampo** [112 F2] Coastal Rd, Trou aux Biches; ▥ 5828 0601; ☺ 11.30–15.00 & 18.00–late Mon–Sat. Cuisine: Creole, seafood. Located around 100m from the public beach, on the opposite side of the road from the police station. This small restaurant/bar punches above its weight, serving excellent dishes at reasonable prices. It attracts locals & tourists alike, & hosts regular theme nights. $$

✗ **L'ananas** [112 E2] Morc Jhubboo, Trou aux Biches; ▥ 5767 2716; ☺ Mon–Sat for lunch & dinner, dinner only in winter. Cuisine: Creole, European. Around 100m inland from the police station, on the left. All seating is upstairs. An informal option with good quality, reasonably priced food. $$

✳ ✗ **Le Fournil** [122 A2] Coastal Rd, Pointe aux Canonniers; ☏ 263 3030; ☺ 06.30–19.00 Mon–Sat, 06.30–16.00 Sun. Cuisine: French, bakery. This great little spot wouldn't look out of place on a Paris street. Modern, chic & clean, it carefully replicates a traditional French boulangerie & pâtisserie, including classics such as éclairs au café (coffee eclairs), brioche & baguettes. There are a few tables inside, or you can take your goodies away and picnic. $

OTHER PRACTICALITIES

Money and banking There is a branch of MCB and an ATM near the public beach in the centre of Trou aux Biches. The new **police station** is opposite the bank.

Communications There are payphones and a **post office** at Trou aux Biches public beach. **Internet access** is available at the post office.

GRAND BAIE

Grand Baie gapes inland beyond **Pointe aux Canonniers**, providing a deep and sheltered bay, often as calm as a lake. It is the place for watersports, shopping, nightlife, self-catering accommodation, and a selection of hotels and restaurants that are among both the worst and best on the island.

Northern Mauritius GRAND BAIE

5

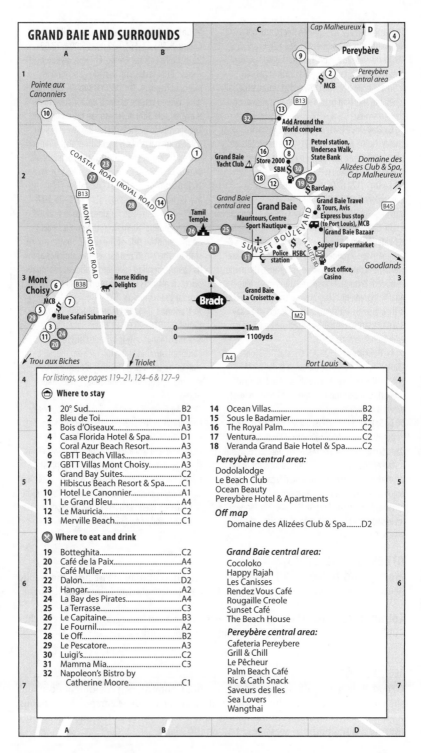

GRAND BAIE AND SURROUNDS

There is plenty to do in Grand Baie. All manner of excursions and watersports can be arranged by one of the many activity operators with offices here, and the bars and restaurants which line the bay make it a great place for an evening out. Grand Baie is the safety valve of Mauritius – the place where ordinary tourists, and locals, can go to let off steam without having to pretend to be wealthy jetsetters. Unfortunately, over the years this has resulted in a lowering of the usual excellent standards of the hospitality industry in Mauritius. While Grand Baie has developed into a fun place to stay if you like a lively after-beach life, courtesy, warmth and style have been sacrificed to some degree. Petty crime is also a by-product of the development, so visitors are advised to be vigilant.

The beach in Grand Baie is small and right next to the busy road and shops. If you walk around the coast in the direction of Pereybère, you will come to **La Cuvette Public Beach** [122 C2], which is also small but more peaceful on weekdays than the one in the centre of Grand Baie and benefits from having a small park between it and the road. However, on the weekends, La Cuvette is bustling with Mauritians and the many snack bars in the park do a roaring trade.

Grand Baie is well served for centres of worship. At the western end of Grand Baie is the very colourful **Surya Oudaya Sangam Tamil Temple** [122 B3]. As is the tradition for Tamil temples, the roof and walls are crammed with statues of gods. It is open to visitors (you will need to remove your shoes), and local tour guides will often offer to take you there. You are likely to be asked for a donation of Rs100 if you wish to take photos. In the centre of Grand Baie, right on the seafront is a Roman Catholic **church** [122 C3], SS Anges Gardiens. The architecture is simple and understated, allowing the ocean backdrop to shine. Across the road is a **mosque** [122 C3]. The church and the mosque have come to a mutually beneficial arrangement. The church is packed on Sundays and the mosque is packed on Fridays, so on Sundays the church uses the mosque parking and on Fridays the mosque uses the church parking.

The street which heads inland from the centre of Grand Baie beside La Jonque Restaurant (Racket Road), is lined with small shops aimed at tourists. While many of the shops sell imported souvenirs, the one known as Presqu'ile sells products made in Mauritius. Around 150m along Racket Road on the right is **Grand Baie Bazaar** [122 D3] (⏰ *09.00–18.00 Mon–Sat, 09.00–12.00 Sun & public holidays*), a collection of around 120 stalls, where eager sellers tout touristy souvenirs and imitation designer clothes. The rather gaudy statues of gods add a quirky atmosphere. As you walk down Racket Road, you will notice the very simple dwellings visible down the side roads are a far cry from the glamorous areas of Grand Baie a few hundred metres away.

If you take the road to the Super U supermarket and continue on past the Super U complex you will come to a roundabout which joins the motorway. Near the roundabout is the new **La Croisette** [122 C3] shopping mall with clothing shops, a Food Lovers supermarket, a cinema and a food court.

GETTING THERE AND AWAY The **bus stop** [122 D2] in Grand Baie is on the coastal road, just outside La Jonque Restaurant. Buses operate regularly between here and the Immigration Square bus station in Port Louis, including an express service which departs every hour. At the time of writing a one-way trip to Port Louis cost Rs38. Non-express buses also link Grand Baie to the other coastal villages of the north and east, including Pereybère, Cap Malheureux, Mont Choisy and Trou aux Biches.

TOURIST INFORMATION There is no tourist office as such but there are countless travel agencies who arrange excursions and who can give advice. Everyone in

Grand Baie is very keen to share their wisdom on hotels, boat trips and tours but remember that they are wise to tourists and that a relative or friend almost certainly owns the hotel, boat or tour company which they recommend. The warning to be vigilant about purchasing tours from unlicensed operators is more pertinent in Grand Baie than any other part of the island.

WHERE TO STAY
There is certainly no shortage of accommodation in Grand Baie; as well as hotels, there are copious apartments and houses to rent. Much of the accommodation is cheap and cheerful.

Luxury

The Royal Palm Hotel [122 C2] (69 suites) Coastal Rd, Grand Baie; 209 8300; e royalpalm@ bchot.com; www.royalpalm-hotel.com. Located at Grand Sable, adjoining Grand Baie, this is the flagship of the Beachcomber Group & a member of 'Leading Hotels of the World'. The luxurious suites are on 3 storeys & face the sea. They're thoughtfully decorated with colonial-style furnishings & have all the features that you would expect from a world-class hotel, including personal butler service. The beach is sheltered & pristine with fine white sand. There are 3 pools, a superb spa, excellent sports facilities & most watersports are free. Service is first-class & no wonder – the hotel claims that staff outnumber guests by 3 to 1. The atmosphere is peaceful with an air of self-satisfied superiority – the hotel widely claims to be the best in Mauritius. **$$$$$**

Upmarket

20° Sud [122 B2] (36 rooms) Coastal Rd, Pointe Malartic, Grand Baie; 263 5000; e info@20degressud.com; www.20degressud. com. A 4-star boutique hotel full of charm. The rooms are decorated individually, with a homely, elegant, colonial style. All rooms have a stylish en suite, AC, TV, phone, Wi-Fi, minibar, safe & balcony/terrace. The 6 suites have an outdoor jacuzzi or plunge pool. The beach is small & it's a windy spot but there are good beaches nearby. There is a restaurant, a bar, 2 pools, small spa & some watersports. Guests can dine on the hotel's restored 1929 motorboat or sail to Flat Island, where the hotel can provide lunch at a little restaurant within a 19th-century ruin. Popular with French & Belgian travellers. Children under 5 years are not permitted at the hotel. The hotel also offers 4 luxury villas nearby. **$$$$**

Le Mauricia [122 C2] (237 rooms) Coastal Rd, Grand Baie; 209 1100; e mauricia@bchot.

com; www.lemauricia-hotel.com. A lively, centrally located 4-star hotel on a decent beach. It is family-friendly & has apartments with 2 bedrooms & 2 bathrooms. More upmarket accommodation is available in suites with a private pool. Extensive facilities include a shopping centre, 2 pools, a gym, spa, tennis, a kids' club & a nightclub open 4 nights a week. The usual watersports are on offer & there's a dive centre. The building isn't pretty but this is a popular, mass-market hotel with lots going on. The AI package is popular & guests can use the facilities at Le Canonnier Hotel. **$$$$**

Mid range

Merville Beach Hotel [122 C1] (169 rooms) Coastal Rd, Grand Baie; 698 9800; e reservation@luxresorts.com; www. mervillebeach.com. A 3-star resort between Grand Baie & Pereybère. Colourful en-suite rooms, either in an uninspiring 3-storey block or thatched cottages (deluxe & family rooms). All face the sea & have AC, TV, phone, minibar, safe & balcony/terrace. Facilities include 2 restaurants, pool, spa, tennis, gym, golf, watersports & a dive centre. There is a nice wide beach & the nightlife of Grand Baie is close by, but not too close. Entertainment every evening. **$$$**

Veranda Grand Baie Hotel & Spa [122 C2] (94 rooms & apts) Coastal Rd, Grand Baie; 209 8000; e resa@veranda-resorts.com; www.veranda-resorts.com. Located on the side of the bay between the centre of Grand Baie & La Cuvette Public Beach, this hotel is rated 3 stars. The beach immediately in front of the hotel is very small but you can walk around the shore to La Cuvette Public Beach. In the other direction, it is a short walk into the centre of Grand Baie, so the hotel is popular with those who enjoy the local nightlife. The hotel puts on entertainment every night & on a Tue this involves a ritual where guests are invited to write their problems on a

piece of paper, so that they can be burned in a bonfire on the beach. The idea is that the cathartic effect will help you to enjoy your holiday. Rooms are comfortably furnished & have AC, TV, phone, minibar, safe, tea/coffee facilities & balcony/terrace. Family apartments have a kitchenette. Facilities include 2 restaurants, 2 small pools, tennis court, gym, small spa & a kids' club. Prices include limited non-motorised watersports (kayak & pedalo). Guests on AI have access to facilities at other Veranda Group hotels. **$$$**

Budget

🏠 **Grand Bay Suites** [122 C2] (26 apts) Coastal Rd, Grand Baie; m 5772 9303; www.grandbaysuites.com. Self-catering accommodation within walking distance of the centre of Grand Baie. The apartments are around a small pool. They are spacious & adequately equipped, but are not as luxurious as the advertising would suggest. There is little space to relax around the pool & the nearest beach is the one in Grand Baie. There is a nightclub & supermarket next door to the complex but it doesn't seem to suffer too much from noise. There are a few parking spaces & although they are not behind locked gates, there is CCTV. **$$**

🏠 **Ocean Villas** [122 B2] (31 rooms & apts) Coastal Rd, Grand Baie; ✆ 263 1000; e stay@ ocean-villas.com; www.ocean-villas.com. A Mediterranean-style complex on a pleasant beach offering a range of accommodation, including 3- & 4-bedroom self-catering apartments, studios & double rooms. All have en suite, AC, TV, phone & free Wi-Fi. The villas have a good kitchen, complete with proper cooker & oven. 2- & 3-storey villas accommodate up to 9 people but prices are according to the number of guests, so you don't pay for 6 when there are only 2 of you. The accommodation is in 2 sections: Ocean Villas & Ocean Beach. The rooms in the Ocean Beach section are more upmarket & in a quieter part of the hotel with its own pool. There are 3 pools altogether, a restaurant, small spa, some free watersports & maid service. **$$**

🏠 **Ventura Hotel** [122 C2] (28 rooms) Coastal Rd, Grand Baie; ✆ 263 6030; e info@hotelventura. net; www.hotelventura.com. Behind a row of shops, with the main road, private bungalows & large gardens between it & the beach. The rooms, studios & 2-bedroom family units are in small 2-storey blocks grouped around a pool. All come with en suite, AC, TV & phone, & most have a balcony/terrace. There is a decent restaurant here. **$$**

🍴 **WHERE TO EAT** Diners are spoilt for choice in Grand Baie, with restaurants and snack bars offering a variety of cuisine to suit all budgets.

For self-caterers there is a **Store 2000 supermarket** [122 C2] (⊕ *07.30–19.30 Mon–Sat, 07.30–12.00 Sun & public holidays*) on the coastal road at the Pereybère end of town. A little further into Grand Baie is the **L'Epicerie** (✆ *269 1123;* ⊕ *07.30–19.00 Mon–Thu, 07.30–20.00 Fri/Sat, 07.30–12.30 Sun*), which sells a range of fine food and treats. There is also a large and well-stocked **Super U supermarket** [122 D3] (⊕ *09.00–20.30 Mon–Thu, 09.00–21.00 Fri/Sat, 09.00–13.00 Sun & public holidays*), which is clearly signposted and just inland from the centre of Grand Baie. Beyond the Super U, at La Croisette shopping mall is a **Food Lovers Supermarket** (⊕ *09.00–21.00 Mon–Thu, 09.00–22.00 Fri/Sat, 09.00–17.00 Sun*), an upmarket, deli-style supermarket.

Here is a selection of Grand Baie's restaurants:

🍴 **Le Capitaine** [122 B3] Coastal Rd; ✆ 263 6867; ⊕ for lunch & dinner daily. Cuisine: seafood. Well-regarded restaurant in a romantic setting overlooking the bay. Superb seafood platter. Reservation recommended. **$$$$**

🍴 **Botteghita** [122 C2] Coastal Rd; ✆ 263 1635; ⊕ for dinner Mon–Sat. Cuisine: Italian. A pleasant Italian across the road from the beach in the heart of Grand Baie. Tue is truffle night, Thu fish night & on

weekends there is often low-key live Mediterranean music. Serves a wide range of Italian wines. **$$$**

🍴 **Cocoloko** [122 C3] Coastal Rd; ✆ 263 1241; ⊕ 09.00–late daily. Cuisine: European, light lunches. An inviting bar/restaurant across the road from the bay. A good spot for pizza & other light lunches. Free Wi-Fi. **$$$**

🍴 **Happy Rajah** [122 C3] Super U shopping complex; ✆ 263 2241; ⊕ for lunch & dinner Mon–

Sat. Cuisine: Indian. Popular with locals & tourists alike for its authentic Indian dishes. $$$

✗ **La Terrasse** [122 C3] Coastal Rd; ☎263 6391; ⊕ 10.00–14.00 & 17.30–22.00 Wed–Mon, closed Sun lunch. Cuisine: Creole, French, Chinese, seafood. A relaxed restaurant with good service, around 1km south of the centre of Grand Baie, near the national coast guard office. The 1st-floor dining area is above a fairly busy road but does have sea views. Consistently good, unpretentious dishes at reasonable prices. $$$

✱ ✗ **Les Canisses** [122 C3] Coastal Rd; ☎263 5231; ⊕ daily, Jun–Oct closed Tue. Cuisine: European, seafood, Italian. In a stunning location overlooking the bay. While waiting for your meal to arrive you can walk down onto the small, peaceful beach, a pleasant retreat from the centre of town. The menu is sophisticated & the dishes beautifully presented, yet the prices are very reasonable. They use the highest-quality ingredients, including meat from Australia. The lamb shank is excellent, as are the giant prawns. If you are on a tight budget, the pizzas are very affordable. There is a cocktail bar & live music every evening. $$$

✗ **Luigi's** [122 C2] Coastal Rd; ☎269 1125; ⊕ for dinner Tue–Sun, lunch Sat. Cuisine: Italian. Just north of town, next to L'Epicerie. This very popular restaurant offers plenty of choice, from homemade pizza & pasta to sumptuous seafood dishes with a Mediterranean twist. Wi-Fi available. $$$

✗ **Mamma Mia** [122 C3] Coastal Rd; m 5422 4556; ⊕ for dinner Wed–Mon, lunch Sat/Sun. Cuisine: Italian. Across the road from the bay but with good sea views. A popular pasta & pizza joint, which also does take-away. $$$

✗ **Napoleon's Bistro by Catherine Moore** [122 C1] ☎263 3251; ⊕ for breakfast, lunch & dinner Mon–Sat. Cuisine: European. Within the Around the World complex between Pereybère & Grand Baie. Nestled in a peaceful, shady walled garden, this has a very pleasant atmosphere. A

fantastic choice of salads on the menu, as well as pasta dishes. Good value for money. Le Square Beauté in the same complex offers massage & beauty treatments if you wish to kill 2 birds in 1 visit. $$$

✗ **Rendez Vous Café** [122 C3] Coastal Rd; m 5712 9538; ⊕ 07.30–late daily. Cuisine: Creole, French. Friendly & relaxed. A varied menu from pizza to curry. There is a lounge, bar & Wi-Fi. $$$

✗ **Rougaille Creole** [122 C3] Coastal Rd; ☎263 8449; ⊕ 12.00–22.00 Tue–Sun. Cuisine: Creole, seafood. A great little restaurant, close to Sunset Bd. Simple but first-class, traditional cuisine. Excellent value for money. $$$

✗ **The Beach House** [122 C3] Coastal Rd; ☎263 2599; ⊕ 11.00–midnight daily. Cuisine: European. A popular restaurant/bar on the beach with views across the bay & regular live music. Burgers & steaks are the speciality. At the top of mid-range price-wise. $$$

✗ **Café Müller** [122 C3] Coastal Rd; ☎263 5230; ⊕ 08.00–17.00 Mon–Fri, 08.00–17.00 Sat. Cuisine: European, light meals. Tucked away off the main coastal road just past the Tamil temple as you enter Grand Baie from Pointe aux Canonniers, on the opposite side of the road. This little gem serves homemade light meals, specialising in salads (you can choose your own ingredients) & crèpes. In summer a buffet brunch runs on Sat. The garden setting is refreshingly quiet for Grand Baie. $$

✗ **Dalon** [122 D2] Racket Rd (Chemin Bazaar) St; m 5706 4073; ⊕ 10.00–18.00 Mon–Fri, 10.00–22.00 Sat/Sun. Cuisine: European, light meals, Creole. A vintage-style open-air café on the road to the Grand Bazaar; unfortunately it gets quite a bit of traffic noise. Very laidback atmosphere. Salads & pizzas are the staples here, & are done very well. $$

✗ **Sunset Café** [122 C3] Sunset Bd; ☎263 9602; ⊕ 08.00–23.00 daily. Cuisine: European snacks & light lunches. European atmosphere, right on the seafront with beautiful views of the bay. $$

NIGHTLIFE Most hotels in the mid-range and upmarket categories organise evening entertainment in the form of live bands, *séga* nights or themed evenings. Some even have their own nightclubs. However, for nightlife outside of the hotels, Grand Baie is the place to go in the north. Most nights of the week you will find something going on, although Sundays are a little quieter. The nights for clubbing in Grand Baie are typically Wednesday, Friday and Saturday. Entry to nightclubs is typically free, especially for females, or around Rs100–150.

Bars, like **Banana Beach Club** (✎ *263 8540*), with loud music and sand on the floor, are open all day until late, closing only when they feel like it. Banana Beach

Club has been around for years and soon becomes a favourite for most visitors to Grand Baie. **Cocoloko** (✆ *263 1241*) restaurant/bar draws a good crowd. The décor is very pleasant, there are big screens for sports fans and free Wi-Fi. **Azallé** (✆ *263 8800;* ⏰ *10.00–late daily*) across the road from the ocean has a restaurant, bar, comfy chairs dotted around a courtyard with a coral floor and a dance floor. There is live music Friday and Saturday nights. **B52** (✆ *263 0214*) is on the corner of La Salette Road (the turning to Super U) and the coastal road; it is a cocktail bar with regular live music. **Beach House Bar** (✆ *263 2599*) is a trendy restaurant/bar on the beach with regular live music and big screens showing sporting matches. Expats and tourists flock to **Hangar** [122 D2] (formerly Patch n'Parrot) in the Hidden Reef complex at Pointe aux Canonniers (✆ *263 7285; www.projecthangar. club;* ⏰ *11.00–late Tue–Sun*) for the tropical pub atmosphere, dancing and a variety of sports on the big screen. Around 5% of its turnover goes to community projects. Nearby, **Le Off** (✆ *263 6357; www.le-off.mu;* ⏰ *12.00–late Tue–Sat, 11.00–18.00 Sun*) has a fantastic atmosphere: hidden behind high walls is a relaxing oasis with comfy chairs and beanbags around a pool, individual lounge areas under cabanas and a bar and a restaurant.

Popular nightclubs are **Les Enfants Terribles** (✆ *263 8117*) on the road to Pointe aux Canonniers, which has several bars and attracts a slightly older crowd than some of the other nightspots. **Zanzibar** (✆ *263 3265;* ⏰ *23.00–late Mon–Sat*), adjoining Banana Beach Club is an old favourite for many but is now known as **Kamikaze**. **Godfather Club** (✆ *263 3000*) on the beach near the Royal Palm has several rooms each with different types of music, and is popular with locals and tourists. **Insomnia** (📱 *5258 5859*), on the coastal road in the centre of town is Chinese-run and targets the Chinese market. To the north of the town centre is **Buddha Bar** (✆ *263 7664*). **Stardance** (📱 *5709 7886*) is on the road towards Pereybère and plays mainly R n' B and Ragga, nearby is **OMG** (📱 *5929 4537*), another very popular club, which hosts regular events. **Vintage Lounge & Bar** (📱 *5770 2952*) has regular karaoke, as well as DJs.

OTHER PRACTICALITIES
Money and banking Perhaps because there are so many opportunities to spend money in Grand Baie, there are plenty of banks and ATMs, mostly along the coastal road.

Communications The **post office** [122 D3] (⏰ *08.30–16.00 Mon–Fri, 08.30–11.30 Sat*) is in the Richmond Hill Complex next to the Super U supermarket on La Salette Road. There are **payphones** in Grand Baie. The post office has **internet access** and many of the bars and cafés offer Wi-Fi.

PEREYBÈRE

The coastal road from Grand Baie to Cap Malheureux passes through **Pereybère**, which offers a pleasant, sheltered bay and beach, popular with local families at weekends. It is quieter, less touristy and more authentically Mauritian than Grand Baie but is growing rapidly and with just 2km separating the two it probably won't be long before they meet in the middle.

WHERE TO STAY Most of the accommodation in the area is aimed at budget travellers. There is a particularly healthy population of self-catering apartments on offer.

Mid range

⌂ **Dodolalodge** [122 D1] (18 rooms) Coastal Rd, Pereybère; ℡ 263 8140; e dodolalodge@ yahoo.com; www.dodolalodge.com. Clean, modern accommodation across the road from the beach, in the centre of the village. 12 rooms have kitchenettes, all have en suite, AC, safe, balcony/ terrace & daily maid service. There is a communal kitchen & a restaurant. **$$$**

⌂ **Domaine des Alizées Club & Spa** [122 D2] (80 apts) Chemin Vingt Pieds, Pereybère; ℡ 263 2198; www.evaco-alizees.com. A large, modern 4-storey apartment complex built as an RES scheme for foreign investors. It lies inland from Grand Baie & Pereybère & offers 4-star 1-, 2- & 3-bedroom apartments. They are finished to a high standard & have everything you need. There is a restaurant on site serving breakfast, lunch & dinner with tables arranged under thatched cabanas over water. The grounds are pleasant, there is a pool & a spa, but you will need a car to reach local restaurants & the beach. The Evaco group has built & runs several other RES complexes in the area. **$$$**

⌂ **Hibiscus Beach Resort & Spa** [122 C1] (50 rooms) Coastal Rd, Pereybère; ℡ 263 8554; e resa@hibiscus.intnet.mu; www.hibiscushotel. com. In a pretty garden on the seafront. The rooms are spacious & newly refurbished, with AC, TV, phone, minibar & balcony/terrace, although not all have a sea view. There is a restaurant on the water's edge, & there is a private manmade beach with sunloungers to make up for the lack of natural beach. The public beach is within easy reach. There is a good pool, watersports, a dive centre, small spa & kids' play area. The HB option is reasonable value for money. **$$$**

⌂ **Oasis Villas** (18 villas) Route du Vieux Moulin, Pereybère; m 5791 6225; e resa@ oasisvillasmauritius.com; www.oasisvillasmauritius. com. Spacious, modern, upmarket villas run by the Evaco group. Villas have 1, 2 or 3 bedrooms, AC, fully equipped kitchen, impressive outdoor living area with plunge pool & free Wi-Fi. **$$$**

⌂ **Ocean Beauty** [122 D1] (9 rooms) Pointe d'Azur Lane, Pereybère; ℡ 263 3039; e info@ocean. mu; www.ocean-beauty.com. A boutique hotel on the beach at Pereybère. The en-suite rooms & suites are modern, tastefully furnished & equipped with AC, TV, safe, minibar, tea/coffee facilities, Wi-Fi & balcony/terrace. The double rooms have a microwave. Some suites have a 2nd bedroom,

& some have a kitchenette. There is a pool with sea view & some watersports are free. There is no restaurant (breakfast is served in your room) although for independent travellers this offers the opportunity to sample local eateries. The hotel can arrange dinner on the beach for special occasions. **$$$**

Budget

⌂ **Bleu de Toi** [122 D1] (8 rooms, 1 apt) Coastal Rd, Pereybère; ℡ 269 1761; e info@ bleudetoi.mu; www.bleudetoi.mu. Charming guesthouse accommodation in a large villa, at the entrance to Pereybère coming from Grand Baie. Rooms are individually decorated in shabby-chic style, equipped with en suite, AC, TV, safe, minibar & Wi-Fi. Some rooms have a terrace. In the garden, there is a delightful, new self-catering studio, which sleeps 2 adults & 2 children. Every effort is made to make guests feel at home; for instance, you can help yourself to tea & coffee in the guest lounge at any time. Rooms are sold on B&B only but many local restaurants provide a free shuttle service & the guesthouse cooks a seafood barbecue once a week. It is not on the seafront but the beach is about 5mins' walk away & there is a decent pool. While there may not be many facilities or activities at the guesthouse, it is close to touristy spots where all manner of entertainment can be arranged; there is a bus stop nearby & bike hire is available. A great budget option if you don't mind a walk to the beach. **$$**

⌂ **Casa Florida Hotel & Spa** [122 D1] (80 rooms & apts) Mont Oreb Lane, Pereybère; ℡ 263 7371; e florida@intnet.mu; www.casaflorida.net. Basic accommodation set back down a lane 5mins' walk from the beach & the centre of Pereybère. The Mediterranean-style buildings are rather dated but set in attractive gardens. The rooms, self-catering studios & 2-bedroom apartments are equipped with AC, TV, fan, safe, fridge, tea/coffee facilities & balcony/terrace. Most have an en suite. There is a restaurant, a pool, small spa & tennis courts (racquets & balls aren't supplied). They keep the prices pretty low. **$$**

⌂ **Le Beach Club** [122 D1] (16 apts) Coastal Rd, Pereybère; ℡ 263 5104; e beachclub@intnet. mu; www.le-beachclub.com. Clean, comfortable studios & apartments on the seafront, by a small beach but close to the Pereybère Public Beach. The accommodation is en suite & has AC. Rooms

are cleaned daily & all linen is provided. There is a bar/restaurant, pool table & table tennis. There is no pool but the sea here is suitable for swimming/snorkelling. Breakfast is available. Well located for self-caters, a short walk from the village centre. **$$**

🏠 **Pereybère Hotel & Apartments**
[122 D1] (21 rooms & apts) Coastal Rd, Pereybère; ☎ 263 8165; e pereyberehotel@intnet.mu;

www.pereyberehotel.com. A range of AC accommodation across the road from the beach: en-suite hotel rooms & self-catering studios & 2-bedroom apartments. The block is around a small pool, which feels a little closed in with the building towering over it & there is no garden. On the plus side, it is not far to the beach & local restaurants. The restaurant on site specialises in seafood. Free Wi-Fi. **$$**

✖ WHERE TO EAT

✖ **Sea Lovers** [122 D1] Coastal Rd; ☎ 263 6299; ⊕ for breakfast, lunch & dinner daily. Cuisine: French, seafood, Creole. In a converted seafront home at the northern end of the public beach. Indoor & outdoor dining – the tables on the huge terrace have great sea views, & there is a relaxing bar. Hosts events regularly, particularly jazz. **$$$$**

✖ **Grill & Chill** [122 D1] Coastal Rd; m 5250 7640; ⊕ for dinner Mon–Sat. Cuisine: Creole, seafood. A relaxed restaurant/bar specialising in grilled seafood & meat, & with an impressive cocktail menu. **$$$**

✖ **Palm Beach Café** [122 D1] Public Beach; ☎ 263 5821; ⊕ 08.30–22.00 daily, closes at 18.00 Thu & Sun, closed in winter. Cuisine: Creole, European, seafood. A small restaurant in a stunning location at the Grand Baie end of Pereybère Beach, overlooking the water. Grilled fish & meat are the speciality, along with an impressive array of salads. **$$$**

✖ **Wangthai** [122 D1] Beach Hse, Coastal Rd; ☎ 263 4050; ⊕ for lunch Tue–Sat, for dinner daily. Cuisine: Thai. Tasty, authentic Thai cuisine. **$$$**

✖ **Cafeteria Pereybère** [122 D1] Coastal Rd; ☎ 263 8539; ⊕ 10.00–22.00 daily. Cuisine: Chinese, Creole. Casual restaurant/bar among the casuarinas near the beach. Nothing special but is in a good location. Also does take-away. **$$**

✳ ✖ **Le Pêcheur** [122 D1] Coastal Rd; m 5931 5967; ⊕ for lunch & dinner daily. Cuisine: Creole, seafood. Across the road from the beach in the centre of Pereybère. This unassuming restaurant specialises in seafood, which is as fresh as it comes because the owner, Suraj, also owns a couple of fishing boats. The dishes are beautifully presented & Creole dishes are accompanied by an impressive variety of side dishes. On Fri nights in summer they do a Creole buffet & séga night for Rs750 (reservation essential), which includes 3 courses & a homemade rum. They also offer free transport for customers in the Grand Baie to Cap Malheureux area. **$$**

✖ **Saveurs des Iles** [122 D1] Coastal Rd; ☎ 262 8286; ⊕ for lunch & dinner daily. Cuisine: Creole, European, seafood. An informal restaurant across the road from the beach. It has an extensive, reasonably priced menu & serves generous portions. **$$**

✖ **Ric & Cath Snack** [122 D1] Coastal Rd; m 5741 4374; ⊕ 07.00–22.00 Mon–Sat, 07.00–12.00 Sun. Cuisine: Creole, seafood. A tiny, narrow café across the road from the beach. Serves delicious Creole dishes, salads & ice cream. Very popular with locals, which is always a good sign. **$**

NIGHTLIFE Pereybère is less lively than Grand Baie by night but it does have one claim to fame – a karaoke bar. **Julie Bar** on the coast road (☎ 269 0320) caters not only for frustrated sopranos but also for sports fans with a large television screen. On Saturday evenings there's a *séga* show. The Redcat Beach Lounge is at the heart of the area's bar scene.

CAP MALHEUREUX TO GRAND GAUBE

Cap Malheureux is the most northerly point of Mauritius, 22km from Port Louis, and it was here that the British landed in 1810. From Cap Malheureux, the view of **Coin de Mire** (Gunner's Quoin) shows the wedge shape that gave the island its name (the quoin was the wedge used to steady a cannon). There is a picturesque,

much–photographed, red-roofed Roman Catholic church close to the beach, **Notre Dame Auxiliatrice**✴ [112 C2]. The red roof of the church, the pink and orange bougainvillea growing near it and the turquoise ocean with Coin de Mire on the horizon combine to create a stunning scene. There is a small parking area next to the church, but it is on a sharp corner and gets pretty crowded so do take care. As it is a popular stop for tourists, hawkers operate in and around the church. Services are held at the church on Saturdays at 18.00 and Sundays at 09.00. During the week from about 13.00, cheerful fishermen gather round a set of scales near the church, weighing, sorting and selling their catch of colourful fish.

Heading east from Cap Malheureux, the coastal road turns inland through stone-encrusted patches of cane, touching the coast again briefly at **St François** before reaching **Grand Gaube**. *Gaube* or *goab* is the local word for an inlet or bay. This small village is still very much a fishing community and groups of fishermen can be seen relaxing in the evenings with a game of *boules* or dominoes by the beach. The bay is crammed with colourful fishing boats. Although there are a few hotels on the edge of the village, it is largely untainted by tourism and there is an atmosphere of the 'real Mauritius'.

Grand Gaube is somewhat isolated, but the industrial town of **Goodlands** [112 D3] is not far inland. As you travel around Mauritius you will notice each village has a 'village of' motto and in the case of Goodlands, it is the 'village of discipline', perhaps because people here work particularly hard. Perhaps 'village of concrete' would have been just as appropriate, because there is certainly plenty of it – it is not an attractive town. **Historic Marine**, makers of wooden ship models, is on the St Antoine Industrial Estate. Visitors can watch the models being made in the workshop (weekdays only), which is fascinating, and buy the finished products on site (page 135).

WHERE TO STAY
Upmarket

🏠 **Blumarine Attitude Hotel** [112 D2] (182 rooms) Anse La Raie, Cap Malheureux; 📞 204 3820; e info@blumarine-hotel.com; www.blumarine-hotel-mauritius.com. Essentially this is 2 4-star hotels in one: a lively family hotel & a quieter section for adults only with 41 rooms, known as Blumarine Boutique. Facilities include a small spa, tennis courts, a kitesurfing school, kids' club & reef conservation education centre known as Nauticaz. Guests in the adults-only section can use the facilities at the family hotel, but not vice-versa. The family section has 2 restaurants, a snack bar & pool, all of which can get pretty chaotic & noisy. Walking from the main hotel to the boutique section, you pass the property's small beach, shared by both sections. The boutique hotel has 2 pools, a bar & restaurant. The rooms here are of a higher standard, & it is all just a bit calmer than next door, although it feels a little cramped. The outdoor bath in the junior suites looks rather uncomfortable & tricky to get into, plus there is the fear people on the 1st floor will look down from

above. Couples searching for a romantic retreat in the area would be better off staying at Paradise Cove (below), just across the bay & owned by the same group – it has better facilities & beaches. **$$$$**

🏠 **Lux* Grand Gaube** [112 D2] (198 rooms) Grand Gaube; 📞 204 9191; e reservation@luxresorts.com; www.luxresorts.com. A good-quality hotel in a quiet location, within easy reach of the north's attractions & with beautiful views across the ocean to Coin de Mire. There are 6 room categories, meaning everyone should find something to suit their needs. Rooms & suites are well equipped, with AC, TV, phone, Wi-Fi, safe, minibar, tea/coffee facilities & balcony/terrace with sea view. There is a 2-bedroom villa with private pool & beach area. There are 5 restaurants, 3 pools, a spa, watersports, dive centre, tennis courts, golf driving range, gym, cinema & kids' & teenagers' clubs. Certainly no shortage of entertainment for the family, & there is a good beach. **$$$$**

✴ 🏠 **Paradise Cove Boutique Hotel** [112 D2] (67 rooms) Anse La Raie, Cap

Malheureux; 204 4000; e info@pcove.mu; www.paradisecovehotel.com. The outdoor space & public areas are what makes this romantic, adults-only hotel. It enjoys an enviable position on a peninsula, which means the beaches are essentially private. The hotel has created lots of romantic little sun-lounging cabanas for couples around the peninsula, & comfy double beanbag loungers are liberally sprinkled throughout. An exquisite infinity pool on the tip of the peninsula has views of Coin de Mire across the ocean. Accommodation is in 2- & 3-storey complexes around a small cove with a spotlessly clean beach. The rooms, refurbished in 2013, are not large but are pleasantly furnished & equipped with AC, TV, phone, Wi-Fi, safe, minibar & balcony/terrace. There are tennis courts, a small spa, gym & watersports. Plenty of little luxuries without going overboard. Being small it has an intimate feel, & no ugly scrums for the buffet as in some of the larger resorts. **$$$$**

🏠 **Zilwa Attitude Hotel** [112 D2] (214 rooms) Grand Gaube; 204 3800; e info@zilwa-hotel.com; www.zilwa-hotel-mauritius.com. A new hotel with good facilities on a beautiful stretch of coast. The natural materials in the rooms, such as rustic wooden headboards, conjure a relaxed feeling. Family rooms with 2 bedrooms available. There are 6 restaurants, which makes for plenty of variety. Lots to do, including 4 pools, spa, watersports, tennis, open-air cinema & kids' club. A good number of watersports are free, including stand-up paddle. There is a dive centre & kitesurfing school. Free Wi-Fi. The AI package is popular. **$$$$**

Mid range

🏠 **Calodyne sur Mer** [112 D2] (82 rooms) Mirabelle Av, Calodyne; 288 2590; e info@hotelcalodynesurmer.com; www.hotelcalodynesurmer.com. At the end of a residential street on a quiet part of the coast near Grand Gaube with views of Coin de Mire. Rooms are simply but comfortably furnished, with AC, TV, phone, safe & balcony/terrace. Family apartments have 2 or 3 bedrooms & a kitchenette. There are 2 restaurants, regular evening entertainment, a pool, massage rooms & a kids' club. Kayaks, lasers & pedaloes are available free of charge. There aren't many hotels or attractions nearby & you would need a bike or car to explore the area. **$$$**

🏠 **Coin de Mire Attitude** [112 C2] (102 rooms) Coastal Rd, Bain Boeuf, Cap Malheureux; 204 9900; e info@coindemire-hotel.com; www.coindemire-hotel.com. A 3-star hotel across the road from a small beach & a pretty lagoon. Rooms have been thoughtfully renovated & have AC, phone, TV, safe & balcony/terrace. Children can be accommodated in all 3 categories of room, making this hotel popular with families. There are 2 pools, limited free watersports, tennis court, bicycles, a restaurant, small spa & small kids' club. Wi-Fi zone available. The pool area suffers from some road noise & can feel crowded. AI package available. **$$$**

🏠 **La Demeure Saint Antoine** [112 E3] (4 rooms) Royal Rd, St Antoine, Goodlands; 282 1823; e info@lademeuresaintantoine.com. While Goodlands may not be an obvious area to stay, this guesthouse has its appeal, being in a grand Creole home constructed in 1830. The en-suite rooms are full of character & breakfast is served on the delightful veranda overlooking the gardens. **$$$**

🏠 **Veranda Paul & Virginie Hotel & Spa** [112 D2] (81 rooms) Coastal Rd, Grand Gaube; 288 0215; e resa@veranda-resorts.com; www.veranda-resorts.com. A well laid-out, adult-only hotel in this quiet fishing village. Thatched blocks of 2- & 3-storey houses with clean, comfortable en-suite rooms. All rooms have AC, TV, phone, minibar, safe & balcony/terrace. There are 2 restaurants, 1 of which is at the end of a jetty, 2 pools & a small spa. A good range of non-motorised watersports are free & bikes can be hired. Wi-Fi is free in public areas. Being child-free & in a quiet location, the emphasis is on tranquillity & relaxation. Priced at the top end of mid-range. **$$$**

Budget

🏠 **Kuxville Beach Cottages** [112 C2] (25 apts/villas) Coastal Rd, Cap Malheureux; 262 7913; e info@kuxville.com; www.kuxville.com. Good-quality self-catering accommodation with 1 or 3 bedrooms. In addition to the original beachside accommodation, there are 4 eco lodges in a garden with pool across the road from the beach. The eco lodges are cheaper than the other accommodation. There is no restaurant but staff can prepare meals for you. B&B & HB packages are available, except for the eco lodges, which are self-catering only. There is a daily maid service. There is a dive centre & kitesurfing school on site. Run by a German family with a conspicuously German atmosphere. **$$**

✕ WHERE TO EAT

✕ **La Demeure Saint Antoine** [112 D3] Royal Rd, St Antoine, Goodlands; ☏ 282 1823; ⏰ lunch & dinner Tue–Sat. Cuisine: Creole. This table d'hôte within a grand home built in 1830 has plenty of atmosphere. The food is excellent & the setting transports you to the 19th century. The veranda is a very pleasant spot to sit. Reservation recommended. $$$

✕ **Restaurant Amigo** [112 C2] Royal Rd, Cap Malheureux; ☏ 262 6248; ⏰ for lunch & dinner Mon–Sat. Cuisine: Creole, European, seafood. On the B45 road which heads inland from Cap Malheureux towards Port Louis. The seafood dishes are particularly good. Sooner or later the owner is bound to boast to you that Jacques Chirac has been there, so I'll spoil the surprise & tell you now. $$$

✕ **Di Sab** Coastal Rd, Grand Gaube; ☏ 288 1146; ⏰ 10.00–22.00 daily. Cuisine: Creole, European. A great little restaurant on the main road through the village. Nice, modern décor & serves authentic Creole meals. Grand Gaube is a fishing village, so what better place to choose a fish dish? $$

✕ **Le Coin de Mire** [112 C2] Cap Malheureux; ☏ 262 8070; ⏰ 10.30–22.00 daily. Cuisine: Creole, seafood. In a lovely position opposite the red church, on the 1st floor. The fish is as fresh as it gets – bought directly from the fishermen who come ashore next to the church. $$

NORTHERN OFFSHORE ISLANDS

COIN DE MIRE One of the most memorable and photographed sights in the north is this distinctively shaped island on the horizon. It is a nature reserve, 4km from Cap Malheureux, and the waters around it offer excellent snorkelling. Tours of the islands of the north don't usually visit Coin de Mire because it is very difficult to land here, but many include it as a snorkelling stop (see page 86). Graceful white *paille en queues* (tropic-birds) can be seen soaring around the black cliffs.

FLAT, GABRIEL, ROUND, SERPENT AND AMBER ISLANDS Off the northern coast beyond Coin de Mire are Flat, Gabriel, Round, Serpent and Amber islands, which are all uninhabited.

The most visited of these are **Flat Island** (L'île Plate) and **Gabriel Island** (L'îlot Gabriel). Gabriel Island in particular can get very busy with boatloads of people arriving, playing loud music. Flat Island has a lighthouse built in 1855, which is still operating, and there is good snorkelling around both islands. During the 19th century the British sent people suffering from malaria and other diseases to Flat Island to prevent them infecting others, and there is a graveyard from the period on the island. Near Flat Island is the famous, ominously named dive spot known as The Shark Pit (page 89). (For further details of excursions, see page 86.)

Round Island (L'île Ronde) cannot be visited without a permit, since it is a nature reserve. The island, which is kidney-shaped, not round, and about 1.5km² in area, is some 22km from Mauritius. Its flora and fauna are fascinating as much of it is rare, having evolved in isolation without the attentions of the early colonists (see also page 10).

Neighbouring **Serpent Island** (L'île aux Serpents), a large barren rock with no serpents or snakes, is a sanctuary for birds, and so not open to the public.

Amber Island (L'île d'Ambre) is so called because of the ambergris which used to be found there. It is largely surrounded by mangroves. The ill-fated *St Géran* was wrecked on the Amber Island reefs in 1744 with heavy loss of life. The tragedy inspired the Mauritian love story of *Paul et Virginie*, written by Bernadin de St Pierre. A monument commemorating the disaster was erected at Poudre d'Or in 1944 and artefacts recovered from the ship can be seen at the National History Museum in Mahébourg (page 110). Amber Island is a popular picnic spot for

Mauritians on weekends, and can be visited by tourists on excursions arranged locally (see below).

POUDRE D'OR TO RIVIERE DU REMPART Poudre d'Or is an authentic fishing village with a sturdy building built in 1864 as a chest hospital. The name could have derived from gold found in the region or, more likely, from the golden powder sands found here. Virginie, the fictional heroine of St Pierre's novel *Paul et Virginie*, is supposed to have been washed ashore on this coast, prompting Mark Twain to observe wryly that it was 'the only one prominent event in the history of the island, and that didn't happen'. Nevertheless, there is a monument to Paul and Virginie in the village.

The road winds down the unspoilt northeast coast towards the largely residential town of **Rivière du Rempart**.

WHERE TO STAY

Upmarket

🏠 **Radisson Blu Azuri Resort & Spa** [112 E4] (160 rooms) Haute Rive; ✆ 402 3700; e info.azuri@ radissonblu.com; www.radissonblu.com. In an isolated spot on the northeast coast within the new Azuri development near Rivière du Rempart. Most of the rooms are designed with families in mind & can sleep 2 adults & 2 children; the 19 superior beachfront rooms are aimed at couples. Adjacent to the hotel are 60 suites, townhouses & penthouses for self-caterers. There are 3 restaurants, including an à la carte seafood option if you tire of buffets. Facilities include 2 pools, spa, gym, tennis & watersports. **$$$$**

WHAT TO DO IN NORTHERN MAURITIUS

Most hotels offer or can arrange excursions, activities and watersports, as do the numerous travel agents in Grand Baie. Cruises to the nearby islands and deep-sea fishing are particularly popular. For more information on the activities listed below, see pages 85–90.

ISLANDS OF THE NORTH Tour operators and many hotels can organise boat trips to the islands of the north; they typically depart from Grand Baie, Cap Malheureux and the hotels. Flat Island and Gabriel Island are the most visited. They are just 200m apart and sit in the same lagoon, but Flat Island tends to be quieter as it is harder for boats to get in close to the shore. The crossing from the mainland should only be done in fair weather; in rough seas it can be dangerous. At 10km, the crossing from Cap Malheureux is the shortest and takes 1–2 hours, whereas from Grand Baie it takes 3–4 hours. Catamaran cruises typically allow you around 4–5 hours on the island, snorkelling and sunbathing, and a barbecue lunch is provided.

White Sand Tours (m 605 1500; *www.whitesandtours.com*) offers a full-day catamaran cruise visiting **Gabriel Island**, with snorkelling and a barbecue lunch. For the more energetic, **Yemaya Adventures** (✆ 752 0046) offers half-day and full-day sea kayak excursions to **Amber Island**, where you can explore the mangroves.

SPORTS

Scuba diving The reefs off the northern coast and the islands off Cap Malheureux offer some of the best diving in Mauritius. There are many scuba-diving operators in the north of the island catering for all levels and experience. For more information, see pages 86–9.

Snorkelling The best snorkelling in northern Mauritius is in the lagoons at Turtle Bay, Trou aux Biches, Pereybère, Grand Baie and around Flat and Gabriel

islands. There are numerous half- and full-day cruises around the north and east that include snorkelling, such as the White Sand Tours full-day catamaran cruise to Gabriel Island. For more information, see page 133.

Other undersea experiences Those who don't want to dive can experience underwater life on an undersea walk or in a submersible, such as the Blue Safari Submarine or a submersible scooter. For more information, see pages 89–90. The north is where these activities take place.

Deep-sea fishing Although the west coast is reputed to be the best for deep-sea fishing, several companies offer trips from the northern coast. For more information, see pages 85–6.

Watersports The north of the island, Grand Baie in particular, has the island's greatest range of watersports. These activities are based around the hotels, but local tour operators can also organise watersports.

Golf There is a nine-hole course at **Trou aux Biches Resort and Spa** [112 F1]. For more information, see pages 83–4.

Horseriding Most hotels and tour operators can arrange horseriding. There are some good riding stables in the north, including **Horse Riding Delights** at the Mont Choisy Sugar Estate (✆ 265 6159; www.horseridingdelights.com), **Forbach Stables** [112 D3] near Grand Baie (✆ 264 9044; www.horseridingmauritius.com) and **Centre Equestre de la Louisa** [112 C4] near Pamplemousses (m 5440 8887). For more information, see pages 84–5.

Hiking and adventure sports Yemaya Adventures (*Grand Gaube*; m 5752 0046) offers hiking, mountain biking and sea kayaking. For more information, see pages 92–4.

SPA TREATMENTS

Genna Wellness Lounge Be Cosy Apart'Hotel, Coastal Rd, Trou aux Biches; ✆ 265 7206. A small, modern wellness lounge offering massage & beauty therapy. Run by an Australian expat with lots of experience.

Grand Baie Gym & Hydrospa X Club Rd, Grand Baie; ✆ 263 9290; ⊕ 06.00–21.00 Mon–Fri, 07.30–19.30 Sat, 09.00–13.00 Sun & public holidays; spa closed Sun. Offers a gym, pool, spa, beauty treatments, weight-loss programmes, hairdresser & a range of group classes, such as martial arts, dance & aerobics. Decent café on site. Temporary membership of the gym is available.

Surya Coastal Rd, Pereybère; ✆ 263 1637; e info@spasurya.com; www.mauriweb.com/surya; ⊕ 09.00–20.00 daily. This Ayurvedic spa between Grand Baie & Pereybère offers a range of relaxing massages & treatments. As well as one-off treatments, programmes lasting from 3 days to 3 weeks are available. Yoga classes are also available.

Trou aux Biches Beach Spa [112 B3] Coastal Rd, Trou aux Biches; ✆ 256 2012.

CASINO There is a **Ti Vegas** casino [122 D3] at the Super U complex in Grand Baie (✆ 269 1448).

SHOPPING Grand Baie has shopping opportunities for all budgets, from the market stalls of Grand Baie Bazaar [122 D3] to the upmarket boutiques of Sunset Boulevard. For jewellery and diamonds there is an Adamas at the Richmond Hill Complex near the Super U supermarket. La Croisette is a new shopping centre on

the edge of Grand Baie, which hasn't attracted the crowds they expected. It has an upmarket supermarket and a range of shops aimed at tourists and locals. Most overseas visitors are underwhelmed because it is akin to any large shopping centre in their home country.

Historic Marine ✳ in Goodlands (✆ *283 9404*; e *info@hismar.mu; www.historic-marine.com;* ⊕ *09.00–17.00 Mon–Fri, 09.00–12.00 Sat/Sun*) is certainly worth a visit. You can tour the model ship workshop and watch the incredibly skilled and patient staff perform their intricate tasks. The resulting models are exquisitely detailed and are on sale in the shop. You can even commission a model of your own boat. By buying here you can be sure the model you purchase is made in Mauritius; there are, sadly, many imported models for sale on the island. Prices range from €50 to several thousand euros.

The **Saga World** complex (⊕ *09.00–18.00 Mon–Sat, 09.00–15.00 Sun*) opposite the botanical gardens at Pamplemousses has a number of upmarket shops selling rugs, clothing and jewellery.

There are several commercial art galleries in the north, including **Galerie du Moulin Cassé** in Pereybère (✆ *727 0672*; ⊕ *10.00–18.00 Fri*), in a converted 19th-century sugar mill. It has permanent exhibitions by Diane Henry, natural world photographer, and Malcolm de Chazal (1902–82), Mauritian artist. Seebaluck Art Gallery in Pointe aux Canonniers (✆ *263 6470*; ⊕ *09.30–19.00 Mon–Sat*) has local and international art.

WHAT TO SEE IN NORTHERN MAURITIUS

SIR SEEWOOSAGUR RAMGOOLAM BOTANIC GARDENS ✳ [112 C4] (*Pamplemousses;* ✆ *243 9401; gardens* ⊕ *08.30–17.30 daily; admission Rs200; golf cart with driver adult/child Rs250/100*) Formerly known as the Royal Botanic Garden, this is one of the island's most popular tourist attractions, located 11km northeast of Port Louis. Most hotels and travel agents offer tours to the gardens and they are easily accessible from Port Louis by bus from the Immigration Square bus station or from Grand Baie (bus route 216). There are also buses from the coastal towns of the north. Buses stop on the main road and the garden is a five-minute walk away. There is a large car park at one entrance, which is where most people will enter, although the main entrance, which has no parking, is on the other side with impressive gates scrolled in wrought iron and which won first prize in the International Exhibition at London's Crystal Palace in 1862. The gate was a gift from François Liénard, a Frenchman, born in India in 1783, who lived in Mauritius. There is a memorial obelisk to him in the garden.

The garden covers 60 acres so a guide or good map is essential to get the most out of it. Official guides (with a badge) are available (*Rs50 pp, Rs40 pp for groups of 5 or more*) by the main gate and the entrance from the car park. It is by no means obligatory to have a guide and their sales pitch can sometimes be rather pushy. The ticket booths sell comprehensive guidebooks on the gardens but the leaflets, which have a good map, are sufficient to find your way around.

The gardens' origins go back to 1729 when a French colonist acquired about half the present site, then called Mon Plaisir. Mahé de Labourdonnais bought it in 1735 and created a vegetable garden (to the left of the present main entrance) beside his own residence, Château de Mon Plaisir, to supply vegetables to his household, the town and visiting ships. The garden was also used as a nursery for plants imported from Europe, Asia and South America. Mulberry bushes were planted in the hope of starting a silkworm industry but were replaced by *bois*

noir (*Albizia lebbeck*), to be turned into charcoal for use in the manufacture of gunpowder for the island's defence.

When, in 1770, the garden became the private property of Pierre Poivre, administrator of the island, Pamplemousses flourished. He cultivated spices such as nutmeg and cloves, as well as ornamental trees. In 1810, the garden reverted to government ownership and was neglected by the British until James Duncan was appointed director in 1849. He introduced many of the palms including the royal palms (*Roystonea regia* and *Roystonea oleracea*), which add a majestic splendour to the main avenue. Thousands of eucalyptus trees were planted in the garden after the malaria epidemic of 1866, for transplanting in swamps to dry them out and reduce mosquito-breeding grounds. Since 1913 the garden has been under the control of the Ministry of Agriculture.

Today the garden boasts 500 species of plant, of which 80 are palms and 25 are indigenous to the Mascarene Islands. The numerous highlights include the impressive giant water lilies (*Victoria amazonica*), which float like giant baking tins in a rectangular pond. Their flowers open for two days only, from the late afternoon to the following morning. On the first day they are cream-coloured with a heady fragrance, on the second they are pink, and on the third day as they are dying they are purple. Another pond contains the white and yellow flowers of the lotus (*Nelumbo nucifera*), which is venerated by Hindus. The betel nut palm (*Areca cathecu*) grows nearby. Its orange fruit contains the betel nut which is sliced, mixed with lime paste, wrapped in the leaf of the vine (*Piper betel*) and chewed. It's a cancer-causing stimulant which depresses the appetite and stains the gums and lips an alarming red. The talipot palms (*Corypha umbraculifera*) are said to flower once every 40 to 60 years with over 50 million tiny blooms, reaching a height of 6m above the tree. After waiting so long to flower just once, the tree dies.

The **Château de Mon Plaisir** looks impressive but lightweight, perhaps because it is not the original home of Labourdonnais but an English-built office mansion, now used for administration and exhibitions. In front of the château are trees planted by visiting royal and political dignitaries, such as Nelson Mandela. The nearby **sugar mill** is a reconstruction built in 1953, showing how an oxen-driven mill would have worked. Nearby are two memorials to former prime minister and governor general Sir Seewoosagur Ramgoolam: one is on the spot where he was cremated on 17 December 1985. His ashes were scattered on the Ganges, in India.

The **tortoise pen** houses Aldabra tortoises, first brought to the gardens in 1875 from Aldabra Island to protect them from being wiped out by seabirds (when young) or being eaten by humans (when older). The **stag park** contains the *Cervus timorensis russa* deer, first introduced in 1639 from Batavia.

Animals to be seen at liberty include the indigenous fruit bat (*Pteropus niger*), two species of rat (the brown Norway rat and the black arboreal Asiatic rat), and the Madagascar tenrec (*Tenrec ecaudatus*). The large, black butterfly with blue windows on its wings is the *Papilio manlius*.

Indigenous birds include the moorhen (*Gallinula chloropus pyrrhorrhoa*), with its red bill, and the green-backed heron (*Butorides striatus rutenbergi*). The small greyish bird in groups with a 'tip-tip-tip' call is *l'oiseau Manioc* (*Malacirops borbonicus mauritianus*). Species of the *Phelsuma* lizard may be seen on palm trees.

There are several **monuments** in the garden including a stone slab which the sentimental believe marks the grave of the fictitious lovers Paul and Virginie. Their creator, Bernadin de St Pierre, is remembered with a bust.

You could spend several hours wandering through the gardens, so a picnic is not a bad idea. Stalls in the car park sell refreshments.

L'AVENTURE DU SUCRE ✱ [112 C4] (*Beau Plan, Pamplemousses;* ✆ *243 7900;* e *aventure.sucre@intnet.mu; www.aventuredusucre.com;* ⊕ *09.00–17.00 daily; admission adult/child/under 6 Rs380/190/free*) In 1999, the Beau Plan sugar factory, which had been operating since 1895, closed down. In October 2002, it was converted into a fascinating high-tech museum covering the history of sugar, the history of Mauritius and the process of sugar production. It is undoubtedly one of the top attractions on the island. The museum provides one of the most comprehensive and digestible histories of Mauritius available on the island. It has been designed with both adults and children in mind, with plenty of interactive exhibits for younger visitors and over 30 short films. The exhibits on slavery and the treatment of slaves and runaways are particularly thought-provoking. The visit culminates in a tasting of export-quality sugars and Aventure du Sucre's own New Grove rum, which includes three rums made with special sugars. A good selection of sugar products, rum and other souvenirs are on sale at the shop. On Wednesday mornings, visitors can take part in cane-cutting with a local cane-cutter, who demonstrates how to get the job done with a machete. Later, you crush the cane you cut and use the juice to create your own cocktail. Quad biking is also available around the sugarcane fields (*Rs1,000 pp, Rs1,500 per couple*). There is a lot to see, so allow approximately 2 hours for self-guided tours, including tasting. There is an excellent restaurant, Le Fangourin, which serves delicious meals and special sugar desserts, as well as dishes featuring their own New Grove rum (page 117).

CHATEAU DE LABOURDONNAIS ✱ [112 C4] (*Mapou;* ✆ *266 9533; www. chateaulabourdonnais.com;* ⊕ *09.00–17.00 daily; admission adult/child Rs375/200*) A Creole mansion built in 1859 for Christian Wiehe at the heart of his agricultural estate. His descendants still own the estate and lived in the house until 2006, when the restoration of the building, which had fallen into disrepair, began. The restoration took four years, and the house opened to visitors in 2010. Although some French experts were called in, much of the restoration work was done by local artisans, including the wonderful metal railings along the veranda. A video tells the fascinating story of the restoration and audio in the various rooms reflecting family life (currently only in French) brings the place alive. The house has a wonderfully romantic, doll's-house exterior. Built largely of teak, it features a colonnaded veranda on both the ground and first floors, and aubergine-coloured shutters. The wallpaper in the dining room, which depicts countryside scenes of deer and birds in a forest, is the original, painstakingly restored. There is no disabled access but disabled guests can view a virtual tour on a screen on the ground floor. You cannot wear high-heeled shoes or take photographs in the chateau. After visiting the house you can explore the 150-year-old orchards and at the end of the tour you can taste fruit juice, rum and fruit jelly made on the estate. In the garden, an area surrounded by an original wrought-iron fence and once used to keep horses is now home to tortoises. There is a modern restaurant in the grounds (page 117) and a well-stocked shop.

MAURITIUS AQUARIUM [112 A3] (*Coastal Rd, Pointe aux Piments;* ✆ *261 4561;* e *bookings@mauritiusaquarium.com; www.mauritiusaquarium.com;* ⊕ *09.30–17.00 Mon–Sat, 10.00–16.00 Sun & public holidays; admission adult/child Rs300/150*) Opened in 2004, the aquarium has filled an important gap in the island's attractions. It is small but thoughtfully designed and offers a good opportunity to see some of the creatures you'll observe while snorkelling or diving off Mauritius, except in the aquarium they have handy labels. Favourites include the Picasso triggerfish

(*Rhinecanthus aculeatus*), Moorish idol (*Zanclus cornutus*), domino fish (*Dascyllus aranus*), white tip reef sharks (*Triaenodon obesus*) and green sea turtles (*Chelonia mydas*). There are freshwater fish too, such as the carp caught locally by the manager. Children will enjoy the touch pool. There is a small souvenir shop and snack bar. The fish are fed daily at 11.00 and 15.00, and a marine biologist provides a guided tour at these times.

RIVULET TERRE ROUGE BIRD SANCTUARY [112 A4] (*Terre Rouge;* \ *217 2886; www.npcs.govmu.org;* ⊕ *Oct–Apr 07.00–15.00 Sat–Sun; free admission*) Each year around 1,200 migratory birds escape the northern hemisphere winter by coming to this 26ha wetland reserve, which is open to the public from October to April on weekends. There is a visitor centre and viewing platform with telescope, but it is all very low key and rather underwhelming.

MAURITIUS ONLINE

For additional online content, articles, photos and more on Mauritius, why not visit www.bradtguides.com/mauritius.

6

Eastern Mauritius

The district of Flacq occupies most of the east of the island, which for our purposes extends from Roches Noires in the northeast down to Bois des Amourettes in the southeast.

Much of eastern Mauritius was covered with ebony forest when the Dutch settled here in the 17th century, but it didn't take them long to start felling the trees to make a road northwards from their settlement at Grand Port. The French continued attacking the forests, using the timber to build ships and houses. Today the land is primarily devoted to sugarcane.

The beaches around Belle Mare are glorious, if a little windy in winter, and have attracted a string of upmarket hotels. However, there is still mid-range and budget accommodation to be found. The area is popular with golfers, who come to take advantage of the two Constance Belle Mare Plage courses (page 83).

The uninhabited sand island of Ile aux Cerfs, off Trou d'Eau Douce, is one of the best-known tourist attractions of the east, with its miles of beaches, copious watersports facilities and championship golf course belonging to Le Touessrok Hotel.

The area south of Trou d'Eau Douce is largely undeveloped owing to the lack of beaches. Driving along this coast is a real pleasure, with the road sandwiched between the sea and unspoilt fishing villages.

ROCHES NOIRES TO BELLE MARE

South of Rivière du Rempart is the bulge of **Roches Noires**, with weekend houses – *campements* – facing the turquoise sea. The term *campement* originally referred to a weekend house made of *ravenala* and straw. Nowadays the word is applied to the ever-multiplying concrete villas.

In summer, this coast is pleasant, but it suffers from strong southeast winds in winter. Hawkers on motorbikes, loaded with goods of every description, travel the roads selling their wares to women working in the fields who can't go to town to shop.

From Roches Noires the road trickles peacefully down the east coast, passing through **Poste Lafayette** and along the edge of the **Bras d'Eau National Park** (page 150). The coast is lined with casuarinas, bent by the winter winds. Eucalypts are also common here, sharing their unmistakable scent, while bougainvillea provides colour. The area is sparsely populated and the coast road provides memorable views across unspoilt bays. There are some beaches but the sea is rougher than in other areas and they don't compare to those further south; that said, you may sometimes have a beach to yourself here. The town of **Poste de Flacq** is little more than a road junction, although there is a petrol station.

The heart of the Flacq district is **Centre de Flacq**, a town of about 16,000 inhabitants. It's a busy place with confusing roads and lots of traffic. Nearby

St Julien village has a sizeable church and, opposite it, a cemetery containing numerous historic graves from the colonial period, many of them constructed from sombre black volcanic rock. These include the grave of Louis Gaud Comte de Ravenel (1747–1824), a prominent French naval figure whose various appointments included captain of Port Louis. He remained in Mauritius after the British took over in 1810, earning a living growing cloves and nutmeg, until his death in 1824.

Belle Mare, **Palmar** and the surrounding area offer some of the island's best beaches. Belle Mare Beach is true postcard material, with a long white-sand beach, shallow turquoise waters and a border of casuarina trees. The old **lime kiln** among the trees is one of many along this coast, where coral was burnt over casuarina wood fires to extract the lime. Among the trees, mobile eateries sell *samoussas* and

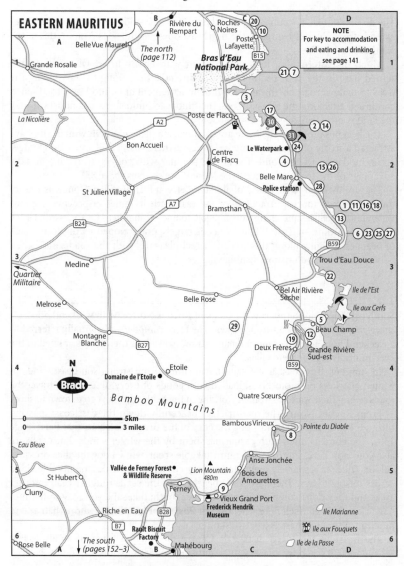

EASTERN MAURITIUS

NOTE
For key to accommodation and eating and drinking, see page 141

other light bites, while hopeful pineapple sellers on mopeds chug up and down the beach looking for customers.

The eastern beaches are not easily reached by bus, but a taxi is inexpensive from anywhere on the east coast. The village of Belle Mare is small but has a couple of small supermarkets, a few clothing shops, a pharmacy, car hire and excursions companies and a **police station**. At the northern end of Belle Mare, opposite Belle Mare Plage Hotel, are a few modern shops aimed at tourists, an ATM and MCB currency exchange counter.

Sadly, the large upmarket hotels which have come to dominate this area of coast have brought with them jet skis, banana boats and waterskiing tourists. At times, you strain to hear the gentle lapping of the ocean over the wailing of outboard motors.

One of the best things about the area is that whilst there are hotels on the beach side of the road, the opposite side is still the domain of small farmers, who seem to tend their modest crops at all hours of the day. Vegetables such as onions, chillies and aubergines are the main crops, grown for sale at local markets. You will often see teams of local ladies harvesting the vegetables, wearing their wide pandanus leaf hats, long skirts and wellington boots.

WHERE TO STAY

Luxury

Constance Le Prince Maurice [140 C1] (89 suites) Poste de Flacq; ✆ 402 3636; e info@ princemaurice.com; www.princemaurice.com. A luxurious member of the Leading Hotels of the World in a quiet location on a pretty bay. 64 junior suites, 12 family suites, 12 villas & 1 'princely suite', some of which are on stilts over the water. All are very private & superbly appointed with large en suite, balcony/terrace & free Wi-Fi. 9 of the villas have a private pool; the other 3 are on stilts. The main pool is brilliantly designed & when viewed from the hotel foyer seems to flow into the sea. There are 3 restaurants, including Le Barachois, a small floating seafood restaurant. The wine cellar, complete with tasting area, stores an incredible 25,000 bottles. There is a very impressive spa & a wide range of free watersports, including waterskiing. Other amenities include a gym, tennis, kids' club & free access to the golf courses of Constance Belle Mare Plage Golf (page 83). The service is discreet & you really do feel pampered. **$$$$$**

One&Only Le Saint Géran [140 C1] (163 rooms) Poste de Flacq; ✆ 401 1688; e info@ oneandonlylesaintgeran.mu; www.lesaintgeran. oneandonlyresorts.com. A well-known, world-

class hotel in a superb location on a peninsula rimmed with white sand. The junior suites have a view of either the sea or lagoon & come with butler service, as well as everything else you'd expect from a first-class hotel. 1 junior suite is suitable for disabled guests. There is also a sumptuous 2-bedroom villa. There are 3 lavish restaurants, including an extremely upmarket Indian on the water's edge. Facilities include a casino, a Gary Player-designed 9-hole golf course & an elegant spa, which offers all manner of indulgent treatments. Free watersports include waterskiing & small-game fishing. There are 5 tennis courts, a gym offering personal training & a dive centre. As well as a kids' club, there is 1 for teenagers. The hotel prides itself on its service & even provides a beach concierge service. **$$$$$**

Upmarket

⌂ **Ambre Hotel** [140 D2] (297 rooms) Coastal Rd, Belle Mare; ✆ 401 8188; e info@ambre.mu; www. ambremauritius.com. A 4-star AI hotel on a lovely beach. Rooms have contemporary décor, AC, TV, phone, minibar, safe, balcony/terrace & Wi-Fi. The 17 family units have 2 bedrooms. There are 3 restaurants, 2 bars, a nightclub, pool, spa, gym, extensive watersports, tennis courts, kids' club & teenagers' club. **$$$$**

⌂ **Constance Belle Mare Plage** [140 D2] (256 rooms) Belle Mare; ✆ 402 2600; e info@bellemareplagehotel.com; www. bellemareplagehotel.com. This sprawling resort stretches along a pristine beach. Although this is a big hotel, there is plenty of space so it doesn't tend to feel too crowded. As well as 235 rooms & suites, there are 20 luxurious 2- & 3-bedroom villas & a huge presidential villa on the beach. There are 2 rooms with disabled facilities. The accommodation is stylish & comfortable, with the usual upmarket amenities. The villas are impressive, each with private pool & butler service. There are 7 restaurants, including the first-class Blue Penny Café (page 144) & those at the golf courses. A popular hotel with golfers, who take advantage of the 2 18-hole championship courses (page 83). Also available are a choice of 4 pools, a fitness centre, spa, tennis, watersports & a kids' club. Good value for money. **$$$$**

✳ ⌂ **La Maison d'Eté** [140 F4] (16 rooms) Coastal Rd, Poste Lafayette; ✆ 410 5039; e info@ lamaisondete.com; www.lamaisondete.com. A

great find for those wanting a peaceful stay in Mauritius in intimate surroundings. The French owner, Brigitte Baranès, has brought a Parisienne's sense of style to the hotel, which is beautifully decorated throughout with great attention to detail. Her aim was to create somewhere people felt at home, & she has certainly achieved that. The rooms are all sea-facing & individually decorated. They have a luxurious yet homely feel, & many have a fabulous over-sized bathtub. One, known as La Vigie, is built on stilts & has a large wrap-around balcony jutting out over the beach, making it feel like you are on the bows of a ship. The Hemmingway Bar is a delightful, relaxing space where you feel like a guest in a friend's beach house. There is space to dine in your room or on the terrace, & there is also a superb restaurant & outdoor lounge bar on site (page 144). There are 2 pools & an inviting private beach area with loungers, plus there is the option of the adjacent public beach. The sea can be wild here & you shouldn't swim beyond the reef due to currents. There are no motorised watersports, which contributes to the serenity, but kayaks & snorkelling equipment are available free of charge. The service is excellent & the absence of buffets (except for Sun lunch) makes meal times very civilised. Very good value for money. **$$$$**

⌂ **La Palmeraie** [140 D2] (60 rooms) Coastal Rd, Belle Mare; ✆ 401 8500; e resa@palmeraie-hotel.com; www.hotel-palmeraie.com. A boutique hotel with a Moroccan theme, on a nice stretch of beach. The abundance of concrete means it is rather less attractive than its thatched competitors. The en-suite rooms have AC, TV, phone, minibar, safe & balcony/terrace. There is a choice of restaurants, a spa, watersports (a few are included) & kids' club. At the bottom end of the upmarket range in terms of price but the facilities are closer to mid range or 3-star. **$$$$**

⌂ **Long Beach** [140 D2] (255 rooms) Belle Mare; ✆ 401 1919; e info@longbeach.mu; www. longbeachmauritius.com. A new concept from Sun Resorts featuring ultra-modern, urban architecture. It is on the site of the old Coco Beach Hotel & care was taken to protect the environment during the knock-down-rebuild process – 1.5 million plants were removed & replanted & the new hotel was designed to use green energy, in particular solar. The 5 restaurants, bars & a nightclub sit around a central plaza, giving a

village feel. The disadvantage is that when the hotel is full, the village feels very crowded. The dining options are excellent & include Chinese, a superb Japanese & Italian. The sports facilities are extensive & include a pool, tennis courts, watersports (non-motorised are free), pitch & putt & a climbing wall. **$$$$**

🏠 **Lux* Belle Mare** [140 D2] (174 suites, 12 villas) Belle Mare; 📞 402 2000; e reservations@luxislandresorts.com; www.luxislandresorts.com. Located on a super stretch of beach is this large resort hotel, whose suites are in 3-storey buildings with thatched roofs. Rooms are spacious, well equipped & have light, fresh, modern décor. The luxury villas are delightful & have kitchenette, dining room, butler service, sumptuous bathroom, private garden & plunge pool. The hotel has a spa, a vast pool with palm trees seemingly growing in it, tennis courts, a gym, kids' club & teens' club. The many free watersports include waterskiing. Aside from the main restaurant, there is a beach restaurant, an Indian/seafood one & a very nice Asian one (page 144). **$$$$**

🏠 **Maritim Crystals Beach Hotel** [140 D2] (181 rooms) Belle Mare; 📞 402 7800; e reservation.mac@maritim.de; www.maritim.com. A 4-star member of the large German hotel chain, on the beach at the southern (Palmar) end of Belle Mare. The rooms face the sea, are a reasonable size, have a modern, almost urban décor & all the essential inclusions, including Wi-Fi. There are 4 restaurants, a large pool, watersports, dive centre, tennis, gym, wellness centre offering beauty treatments & massage, & a kids' club. **$$$$**

🏠 **Radisson Blu Poste Lafayette Resort & Spa** [140 F4] (100 rooms) Poste Lafayette; 📞 402 6200; e info.pl@radissonblu.com; www.radissonblu.com. Adults-only hotel in an isolated spot on an unsheltered portion of the rugged northeast coast. Modern, minimalist décor is a feature of the rooms, which are typical of a big, international brand. The rooms are on the small side. There are 3 restaurants, including an Asian one by the pool, & a spa. It is advisable to wear reef shoes in the sea here. **$$$$**

🏠 **Sankhara Villa** [140 C1] (1 villa) Poste Lafayette 📞 243 7335; e reservations@iliad.mu; www.sankhara-villas.com. A luxurious 5-bedroom, Balinese-inspired villa on a secluded beach. It sleeps up to 14 & has a hammam, pool, gym kayaks, pedaloes, bicycles & maid service. Chef

& butler available at extra cost. Weddings can be arranged at the villa; the garden & beach area can accommodate up to 150 guests. There is little in the area so it would be advisable to hire a car. **$$$$**

🏠 **Solana Beach** [140 C2] (117 rooms) Belle Mare; 📞 402 7200; e info@solanabeach.mu; www.solanabeach.mu. A 4-star hotel at the northern end of Belle Mare. The rooms are all sea-facing; they are a reasonable size, are family friendly & have AC, minibar, safe, phone & Wi-Fi. The deluxe rooms & junior suites are decorated in neutral tones & have 4-poster bed, while the superior rooms are smaller & more colourful. The 3 restaurants include 1 for adults only, serving Asian cuisine. There is a pool, small spa, tennis, gym, watersports & kids' club. **$$$$**

✴ 🏠 **The Residence** [140 D2] (163 rooms) Belle Mare; 📞 401 8888; e info-mauritius@theresidence.com; www.theresidence.com. The entrance is suitably grand for a hotel which is impressive in every way. The style is that of a colonial palace. The rooms & suites are spacious & beautifully decorated, equipped with everything you need, including butler service. The bathrooms deserve special mention – they are superb. Surprisingly for a modern luxury hotel, not all the rooms face the sea but those with a view of the garden are cheaper. There are 3 restaurants, including the unforgettable La Plantation (page 144) right on the beach. Facilities include an excellent kids' club, tennis courts, many free watersports (including waterskiing) & a fabulous spa. Reasonable value for money. **$$$$**

Mid range

🏠 **Emeraude Hotel** [140 C2] (61 rooms) Coastal Rd, Belle Mare; 📞 401 1400; e info@hotelemeraude-mauritius.com; www.emeraudebeach-hotel-mauritius.com. A 3-star hotel across the road from the northern end of the beach, where 2-storey white cottages with thatched roofs are scattered in a garden. All rooms are en suite but with shower only, no bath. They are small, clean & simply furnished with AC, TV & phone. The hotel provides a bar on a traditional cart on the beach so its guests don't have to run back across the road for drinks. Guests can also get a boat to Ile aux Cerfs from sister hotel, Le Tropical at Trou d'Eau Douce. There are 2 small pools, a tiny spa offering massage & beauty therapies, a restaurant & a bar

with sand floor, plus a kids' club. Diving & kitesurfing are available. Glass-bottom boat & snorkelling are included. The AI package is good value. **$$$**

🏠 **Jalsa Hotel & Spa** [140 C1] (66 rooms) Poste Lafayette; ✆ 410 5282; e info@jalsabeach. com; www.jalsabeach.com. A 4-star hotel on an isolated piece of coast. The rooms are comfortable & have what you need but are not particularly fancy. There is little in the area, but on site are a restaurant, bar, spa, gym, watersports & shops. Wi-Fi is available in the lobby but not the rooms. **$$**

🏠 **Le Surcouf Hotel & Spa** [140 D2] (55 rooms) Coastal Rd, Palmar; ✆ 415 1800; e surcouf@intnet.mu; www.lesurcouf.mu. A reasonable-quality hotel in an excellent location. The rooms are adequate, with en suite, AC, TV, balcony/ terrace & room for children. Snorkelling & kayaking are free but other watersports are payable. There is a pleasant pool area, restaurant & small spa. Wi-Fi in public areas but not in rooms. **$$$**

🏠 **Veranda Palmar** [140 D2] (76 rooms) Coastal Rd, Belle Mare; ✆ 402 3500; e resa@veranda-resorts. com; www.veranda-resorts.com. A relaxed 3-star,

AI hotel on a superb stretch of beach. The nicely decorated en-suite rooms are equipped with AC, TV, phone, minibar, safe & balcony/terrace. There are 2 restaurants (1 on the beach), 2 bars, a pool, small spa, kids' club & a good choice of free watersports. Bike hire is available & AI guests have use of the facilities at other Veranda hotels. There is plenty of evening entertainment. As with all Veranda hotels, efforts are made to introduce guests to Mauritian traditions & culture through optional activities such as visits to local villages & cooking classes. **$$$**

Budget

🏠 **Orchid Villas** [140 D2] (6 villas) Coastal Rd, Belle Mare; ✆ 415 1350; www.orchidvillas.mu. Self-catering accommodation in 6 modern villas about 250m from the beach. You can rent the whole villa or a room within a villa, which means you can choose an en-suite or shared bathroom. Each villa has a decent kitchen, pool, garden, AC, TV, safe & daily maid service. Wi-Fi is free. Seasons Restaurant is on site (see below). A car is advisable as there are no shops nearby. **$$**

✖ WHERE TO EAT

✖ **Blue Penny Café** [140 D2] Constance Belle Mare Plage; ✆ 402 2600; ⏱ 19.30–22.00 Mon–Sat. Cuisine: European. Far from being a café – this is an exclusive restaurant which is likely to offer you one of the finest dining experiences of your life. It is worth ordering tea at the end of your meal just to see the elaborate preparation, where the leaves are meticulously weighed at your table in hand-held scales. Reservation recommended. **$$$$$**

✖ **Deer Hunter** [140 C2] The Legend Golf Course, Belle Mare; ✆ 402 2600; ⏱ for breakfast, lunch & dinner daily. Cuisine: Creole, European. If you've seen enough of the beach, this may be the restaurant for you, with its sweeping views of the golf course. You may even spot a deer drinking at one of the lakes. Traditional Creole dishes are given a creative twist. Both the food & service are excellent, making it very popular so you will need to book well in advance. A continental breakfast is available for early golfers 06.30–09.30. **$$$$**

✖ **East** [140 D2] Lux* Belle Mare, Belle Mare; ✆ 402 2000; ⏱ for dinner daily. Cuisine: Indochinese. An upmarket restaurant within the hotel, with sea views. Carefully crafted, beautifully presented dishes. If you struggle to choose a wine

from the wide selection, the highly qualified sommelier can provide invaluable advice. **$$$$**

✴ ✖ **La Maison d'Eté** [140 C1] Coastal Rd, Poste Lafayette; ✆ 410 5039; ⏱ for lunch & dinner daily. Cuisine: European, seafood, Creole. A delightful restaurant & lounge bar in this boutique hotel with an upmarket feel. Sliding glass doors mean diners are protected from the easterly winds but can still enjoy a view of the gardens & sea. The menu is sophisticated with particularly fine seafood dishes, & the presentation is exquisite. The service is as good as any 5-star hotel. Reservation recommended. **$$$$**

✖ **La Plantation** [140 D2] The Residence Hotel, Belle Mare; ✆ 401 8888; ⏱ for lunch & dinner daily. Cuisine: Creole, seafood. Built in the style of a planter's house, perched on the beach away from the main body of the hotel. A great place to treat yourself. The food is as fantastic as the setting & the service is both friendly & slick. Reservation recommended. **$$$$**

✖ **Seasons Restaurant** [140 D2] Coastal Rd, Belle Mare; ✆ 415 1350; ⏱ for lunch & dinner Mon–Sat, lunch Sun. Cuisine: Creole, European, Indian, Chinese. Opposite farmland south of Belle Mare, in the Orchid Villas complex. It doesn't have

a view, but uses fresh ingredients to prepare tasty food showcasing Asian flavours. $$$

✗ Symon's Tropical Restaurant [140 C2] Coastal Rd, Belle Mare; \ 415 1135; ⏲ 11.00–midnight daily. Cuisine: Creole, Chinese, Indian, seafood. An old favourite around these parts. Also does take-away & there's a lively bar. $$$

✗ Chez Manuel St Julien Village; \ 418 3599; ⏲ for lunch & dinner Mon–Sat. Cuisine: Chinese, Creole. Inland, just off the A7 between Centre de Flacq & Quartier Militaire. Has been operating for over 30 years, specialising in Chinese food. Offers plenty of choice & has a good reputation among locals. $$

✗ Empereur Coastal Rd, Belle Mare; \ 415 1254; ⏲ for lunch & dinner daily. Cuisine: Chinese, Creole. It doesn't look like much but this restaurant has a reputation for good Chinese fare. $$

✗ Vicky's Restaurant Coastal Rd, Belle Mare; m 5773 1035; ⏲ 09.30–21.30 daily. Cuisine: Creole, seafood, Chinese. Modest restaurant in the centre of the village serving authentic local food with friendly service. $$

TROU D'EAU DOUCE

The fishing village of **Trou d'Eau Douce** is an early Dutch settlement. The **Puits des Hollandais**, meaning 'Wells of the Dutch', is an extinct crater well used for fresh water and Trou d'Eau Douce refers to this freshwater spring although, since it is often pronounced *Tro do-doo*, some historians have assumed it is named after the dodo, which lived in this region.

In the centre of Trou d'Eau Douce is a large black **church** of volcanic rock, Notre Dame des Bon Secours. The black rock, combined with the church's blue windows, gives it an unusual, rather gloomy atmosphere.

Opposite the tourist information office in Trou d'Eau Douce are the remains of a **lime kiln** on the waterfront. You can climb it for views over the bay but take care as there is no hand rail and the stone steps are uneven.

Off Trou d'Eau Douce lies **Ile aux Cerfs**, an uninhabited island which has been transformed into a tourist attraction, with miles of beaches, numerous watersports and a handful of restaurants. It is marketed as a 'paradise island' and is a popular excursion but many travellers find it too touristy and overpriced. The island has a total area of 300ha, much of which has been transformed into the superb Le Touessrok Golf Course (see below). Local operators selling trips to Ile aux Cerfs line the road through the village, clamouring for the attention of tourists. This can be rather off-putting, but almost all hotels can organise the excursion.

If you walk far enough around from the boat landing area, you should be able to find a quiet spot on the beach. Once you've settled down, it probably won't be long before a passing gentleman offers you a pineapple or coconut. It's almost worth the Rs100 just to watch him expertly hack the pineapple into the classic ice-cream-cone shape.

TOURIST INFORMATION There is no tourist information office in Trou d'Eau Douce, but tour operators will leap out and try to sell you excursions.

🏠 WHERE TO STAY

Luxury

 **Shangri-La Le Touessrok Resort & Spa**

[140 D3] (203 rooms) Trou d'Eau Douce; \ 402 7400; e sltr@shangri-la.com; www.shangri-la.com. This hotel has long been one of the most luxurious on the island. After being taken over by the Shangri-La Group, it was extensively renovated & re-opened in 2015. The rooms are spacious & have all the features you would expect of a luxury hotel. They are beautifully decorated with a fresh, beach-house feel & all have sea views. The 4 restaurants provide plenty of dining choices. As well as a world-class golf course (see above), there are 2 pools, a spa, tennis courts, fitness centre & kids' club. $$$$$

Mid range

🏠 **Friday Attitude** [140 D3] (51 rooms) Coastal Rd, Trou d'Eau Douce; ✆ 204 3800; e info@hotels-attitude.com; www.friday-hotel-mauritius.com. Formerly the Bougainville Hotel, this property was completely renovated in 2014. It now offers good-quality 3-star family-friendly accommodation on a very pleasant beach. Rooms have AC, TV, safe, phone but tea/coffee facilities are at extra cost. The 16 family units have separate children's bedrooms. There is a restaurant, bar, pool, a massage kiosk & limited free watersports. **$$$**

🏠 **Silver Beach** [140 D3] (60 rooms) Coastal Rd, Trou d'Eau Douce; ✆ 480 2600; e silverbeach@intnet.mu; www.silverbeach.mu. A fairly unattractive building but this 3-star is on a beautiful stretch of beach. 30 comfortable sea-facing rooms & 30 garden-view bungalow rooms with AC, TV, phone, safe & balcony/terrace. The bungalows are cheaper & sleep 2 adults & 2 children. Facilities include a restaurant, pool, regular evening entertainment & some free non-motorised watersports. **$$$**

🏠 **Tropical Attitude** [140 D3] (58 rooms) La Pelouse, Trou d'Eau Douce; ✆ 480 1300; e info@ hotels-attitude.com; www.tropical-hotel-mauritius.com. A friendly 3-star, adults-only hotel in a great location, close to Ile aux Cerfs. The rooms have sea view, are pleasantly decorated & equipped with AC, TV, phone, minibar, safe & balcony/terrace. The restaurant, like the rest of the hotel, has wonderful sea views & there is a pool & 2 treatment rooms for massage. Non-motorised watersports are free & there is a dive centre. The hotel operates free boat trips to Ile aux Cerfs twice daily. **$$$**

Budget

🏠 **Stylia Villas** [140 D3] (6 villas) Coastal Rd, Trou d'Eau Douce; m 5258 2871; www.myvillasmauritius.com. The same owners as Villa Pareo. A modern complex (built in 2012) comprising 2 beachfront villas with 4 garden villas behind. Each has 3 en-suite bedrooms, fully equipped kitchen, private pool & Wi-Fi. There is a manager on site, who can help organise excursions, daily maid service & for a supplement a chef can prepare your meals. The garden villas are considerably cheaper than the beachfront, but are exactly the same layout & only a short walk to the beach. Min stay is 5 nights. **$$**

🏠 **Villa Pareo** [140 C4] (1 villa) Coastal Rd, Trou d'Eau Douce; m 5258 2871; www.myvillasmauritius.com. A modern villa on the coastal road, around 50m from the beach. The villa was built in 2008 & has 3 bedrooms, each with its own bathroom; it can sleep up to 10 people. It is spacious, modern & equipped with everything you could need – a real home away from home. There is a shared garden, private terrace & pool. Excursions can be arranged. Good value for money, especially for large families or groups. **$$**

✖ WHERE TO EAT

✖ **Le Café des Arts** Victoria Rd, Trou d'Eau Douce; ✆ 480 0220; www.maniglier.com; ⊕ for lunch & dinner Mon–Sat. Cuisine: Creole, European, seafood. Down narrow roads (signed from the church), a former sugar mill built around 1840 has been carefully restored to house an art collection & restaurant. The yellow shutters are a cheerful contrast to the dark volcanic rock from which the mill was built & there is a pool in the garden. Inside the brick walls are decorated with a collection of paintings by French artist Yvette Maniglier, the last student of Matisse. Amidst the collection are the restaurant tables, where you can enjoy a creative menu. Reservation essential. **$$$$**

✖ **Chez Gilda** Coastal Rd, Trou d'Eau Douce; ✆ 480 1253; ⊕ 08.30–22.30 Mon, Wed–Sat, 14.00–22.30 Sun. Cuisine: Creole, European, seafood. Charming restaurant & bar in an old, stone building & with a terrace out the back overlooking the bay. Gilda had a good apprenticeship, growing up as the daughter of Tino of Chez Tino fame. Serves croissants & patisserie for breakfast, as well as pizzas, panini & full main courses later in the day. Pizza from Rs200, main courses from Rs300. Free Wi-Fi. Good value. **$$**

✖ **Green Island Beach Restaurant** Coastal Rd, Trou d'Eau Douce; m 515 0240; ⊕ for lunch & dinner Tue–Sun. Cuisine: Creole, European, Chinese, seafood. Across the road from the ocean. Is not cheap but offers plenty of variety. **$$**

✖ **Chez Tino** Coastal Rd, Trou d'Eau Douce; ✆ 480 2769; ⊕ 09.30–14.30 & 19.00–21.30 Mon–Sat, 09.30–14.30 Sun. Cuisine: Creole, Chinese, seafood. This one has been around for a long time & has a reputation for unfussy, traditional food at reasonable prices. Plenty of choice on the menu. On the first floor, with sea views. **$**

✕ Les Hollandais Coastal Rd, Trou d'Eau Douce; m 5491 5678; ⊕ for breakfast, lunch & dinner Mon–Sat. Cuisine: snacks, pizza, Creole. Near the church. Homemade patisserie makes this a good breakfast/morning tea stop. Snacks & pizza on offer at lunch, Creole dishes also available. **$**

OTHER PRACTICALITIES There is a **post office** in the centre of Trou d'Eau Douce, which offers **internet access**; **Chez Gilda** (see page 146) has Wi-Fi.

In the village centre are a **pharmacy** (⊕ *08.00–20.00 Mon–Sat, 07.00–13.00 Sun*) and **supermarket** (⊕ *08.00–20.00 Mon–Sat, 07.00–13.00 Sun*).

SOUTH OF TROU D'EAU DOUCE TO BOIS DES AMOURETTES

Travelling south from Trou d'Eau Douce, the road heads inland and passes through the village of **Bel Air Rivière Sèche** before turning back towards the coast and crossing over the **Grande Rivière Sud-est**.

At the mouth of the river is a fishing village. There is a small waterfall where the river dives into the sea, which is often visited during tourist boat trips. It can also be reached on foot. Follow the signs marked GRSE to the parking area and it's about a 15-minute walk. The hype about the waterfall is rather overblown; it isn't particularly impressive and the area is usually covered in litter.

Across the river is the village of **Deux Frères** (Two Brothers), with another village, called **Quatre Sœurs** (Four Sisters), a little further on. The story goes that the land was inherited by the siblings and distributed as the village names indicate. The scenery along this road is beautiful, with sugarcane clinging to the impossibly steep slopes of the **Bamboo Mountains** on one side and fishing boats huddling together in turquoise water on the other. Villagers grow neat rows of vegetables between the road and the sea, using every inch of land.

The mountain range descends to the sea at the headland of **Pointe du Diable** (Devil's Point), where the ruins of French batteries are listed as a national monument. Cannons here date from 1750 to 1780 and were used to guard two wide gaps (North and Danish passages) in the reef. The devil of this point was said to be responsible for upsetting the magnetic compasses of ships passing the headland.

The road follows the coast around the edge of the peninsula, from where **Ile aux Fouquets** and **Ile de la Passe** are visible. An unmanned lighthouse on Ile aux Fouquets marks the rocks at the southern entrance through the reef into Grand Port. During the battle for Grand Port, Ile de la Passe was captured by the British, who kept the French flag flying to lure in French vessels. Ruined fortifications remain on the island.

At **Anse Jonchée** is a bright orange kiosk outside a modest home on a sharp bend opposite the sea, where Laurianne Ghansseeram (\ *634 5557*) sells **essential oils** and candles. The oils include ylang ylang, frangipani, eucalyptus, peppermint and cinnamon. The garden where she grows the plants is on the opposite side of the road and Laurianne will be happy to show you around. When I last visited in 2015, Laurianne had acquired her own simple but effective wood-fired still – she had previously been using the still of a nearby estate. With over ten years' experience in oil distillation, Laurianne is very knowledgeable on their various medicinal uses. Prices start at Rs500 for 10ml.

Legend says that French soldiers used to duel over the girls they met at **Bois des Amourettes** (Young Lovers' Wood). Swords have been found in the vicinity of the cave and rock known as **Salle d'Armes** down on the sea's edge. There is a wooden pier in the village with a plaque commemorating Sarah Outen who was the first woman to row solo from Australia to Mauritius. The journey took the 24-year-old

124 days and she landed at this spot on 3 August 2009. On the southern side of the village is **Senteur des Iles** (m *5772 6291*), which produces essential oils, in particular ylang ylang and geranium, and sells handicrafts and souvenirs.

⌂ WHERE TO STAY
Luxury
⌂ Four Seasons Resort Mauritius at Anahita [140 D4] (136 suites & villas) Beau Champ; ☏ 402 3100; e reservations.mas@fourseasons.com; www.fourseasons.com. The hotel opened in Oct 2008 as part of a village-style Integrated Resort Scheme (IRS), which includes residential villas & a range of facilities. The marketing emphasises its lush, tropical surrounds rather than being a traditional beach resort, as this area of coast is known for its mangroves & lack of sandy beaches. There are, however, 3 manmade beaches. Hotel accommodation is divided between the resort's private island & the mainland; you can also rent a villa with 2–5 bedrooms. Bicycles are available to help you get around the resort. Rooms are beautifully decorated & come complete with private garden, plunge pool & outdoor shower. There are 4 restaurants, 4 pools, tennis, a spa & kids' club. One of the hotel's main draw cards is a stunning 18-hole golf course, designed by Ernie Els (see page 84). **$$$$$**

Mid range
⌂ Laguna Beach [140 D4] (64 rooms) Grande Rivière Sud-est; ☏ 417 5888; e info@ lagunabeachhotel.mu; www.lagunabeachhotel.mu. A collection of whitewashed thatched buildings at the mouth of Grande Rivière Sud-est. The hotel has created a small beach but it is a windy spot. Rooms face the sea & have AC, TV, phone, safe, minibar, tea/coffee facilities & balcony/terrace. The standard rooms are rather small. Facilities include pools, small spa, gym, kids' club, some free watersports & Wi-Fi in public areas. **$$$**

✳ **⌂ Otentic** [140 C4] (12 tents, 1 chalet) Deux Frères; m 5941 4888; e info@otentic.mu; www. otentic.mu. Refreshingly different. Julien, creator of this luxury safari tent retreat, looked long & hard for the perfect location & the setting on the edge of the Grande Rivière Sud-est, close to where it enters the sea, is ideal. It is beautifully peaceful & wooden platforms overlooking the river invite you to sit & relax, but there are also plenty of activities. You can use the mountain bikes, stand-up paddles & kayaks at any time. It is an easy paddle up the river to the Grande Rivière Sud-est waterfall & you are likely to see monkeys & fruit bats on the way. There are some fabulous excursions/activities available, including kitesurfing, kayaking around Ile aux Cerfs, snorkelling in nearby Eau Bleue, where the water really is exceptionally blue, & hiking the surrounding mountains. A free boat shuttle takes guests to Ile aux Cerfs daily. Great care is paid to environmental impact: the furniture is largely made from recycled materials & the place is run on solar power. The tents have a double bed & 2 or 3 singles, with bases made from palettes. The en-suite bathrooms are rustic & open air. Superb Creole meals are prepared & served outside, near the pool (see below). Otentic has a lovely, friendly, relaxed feel & is great for children. The longer the stay, the cheaper the per-night price. **$$$**

Budget
⌂ La Case du Pêcheur [140 C5] (16 rooms) Anse Bambous; ☏ 634 5675; e cindyduval15@ gmail.com; www.sheercat.com. Rustic accommodation near Pointe du Diable. En-suite rooms in thatched buildings on the water with AC & a small terrace. The coast here is far from the idyllic beaches for which Mauritius is known; instead mangroves grow at the water's edge & there is no lagoon. This in itself has its attractions: tranquillity & natural beauty. Shellfish are farmed here, some of which are served in the restaurant (see below). There is also a small pool. Nature trails through the mangrove forest start here. **$$**

✕ WHERE TO EAT
✕ **La Case du Pêcheur** [140 C5] Anse Bambous; ☏ 634 5675; ⊕ for lunch daily. Cuisine: Creole, seafood. Specialises in crabs, oysters & lobsters, which are farmed on site. They also do a good venison curry. You can walk off your lunch on the nature trail. **$$$**

✳ ✕ **Otentic** [140 C4] Deux Frères; m 5941 4888; ⊕ for lunch & dinner on reservation. Cuisine: Creole. The kitchen made from palettes & odds & ends may not look like much but the staff produce some excellent, authentic Creole food using fresh ingredients. The crab soup is superb.

You can either sit at a communal table & share stories with other guests, or at individual tables on a deck overlooking the river. It is worth noting it is a steep walk down to the open-air restaurant from the car park. If you are not staying at Otentic, a reservation is essential for meals. Great value. $$

WHAT TO DO IN EASTERN MAURITIUS

MARKETS There is a large market in **Centre de Flacq** on Wednesdays and Sundays, and there is a large supermarket in the town too.

ILE AUX CERFS For those whose accommodation doesn't provide trips to Ile aux Cerfs, there are other ways of getting there. Almost every second person you pass in Trou d'Eau Douce will offer to take you there but be wary as their service may not be reliable, particularly when it comes to bringing you back again. Operators with reasonable reputations include **Vicky Tours** (m *5773 1331; www.vvvickyboattours. com*) and **Falcon Boats** (\ *480 2681; www.falconboats.mu*), both of which have sales representatives in Trou d'Eau Douce. Expect to pay around Rs300 per person return by ordinary boat, which takes around 15 minutes, or around Rs450 by speedboat, which only takes around five minutes. Boats leave at regular intervals, usually every 30 minutes between 09.00 and 16.30 but you should confirm with your particular operator the time of the last trip back to the mainland. The departure point is clearly marked in Trou d'Eau Douce and you can buy tickets on the spot.

A number of operators, such as **White Sand Tours** (\ *208 5424*), Falcon Boats and Vicky Tours, offer full-day group excursions to Ile aux Cerfs, which usually include a barbecue and a visit by boat to the small waterfall at Grande Rivière Sud-est. Such excursions cost around Rs1,000 per person. A visit to the waterfall and Ile aux Cerfs without lunch costs around Rs700.

BUY ESSENTIAL OILS The east of the island is the place to buy essential oils. **Laurianne Ghansseeram** ✳ (\ *634 5557*) sells oils and candles from her small kiosk in Anse Jonchée (page 147). **Senteur des Iles** at Bois des Amourettes (m *5772 6291*) specialises in ylang ylang and geranium.

LE WATERPARK AND LEISURE VILLAGE [140 C2] (*Coastal Rd, Belle Mare;* \ *415 2626; www.maurinet.com/waterpark;* ☉ *10.00–17.30 daily; admission adult/child Rs350/185*) An amusement park with numerous waterslides and fairground rides, located amidst the agricultural land opposite the public beach.

YACHTING/CATAMARAN CRUISES Catamaran cruises and sailing trips frequently depart from Trou d'Eau Douce, usually stopping off at Ile aux Cerfs. For more information, see above.

DEEP-SEA FISHING While the east coast is not as highly regarded for deep-sea fishing as the west coast, fishing trips are available. For more information on deep-sea fishing companies and tour operators, see pages 85–6.

GOLF Some of the island's best golf courses are on the east coast. For more information, see pages 83–4.

KAYAKING Otentic (*Deux Frères;* m *5941 4888;* e *info@otentic.mu; www.otentic. mu*) offers kayaking excursions from their tented camp on Grande Rivière Sud-est. For more information, see page 148.

KITESURFING The east coast is more windy than other parts of the island, particularly from April to October, and offers some good kitesurfing. For more information, see pages 91–2.

WHAT TO SEE IN EASTERN MAURITIUS

BRAS D'EAU NATIONAL PARK [140 C1] (*Poste Lafayette*) This coastal national park covers around 500ha and contains the ruins of an old sugar factory, lime kiln, 200-year-old well & railway. An old house contains a visitor centre with displays on local flora and fauna. Nearby is the start of a marked 4km walking trail over mostly flat terrain, which leads to the beach. The park contains mainly exotic plant species but plenty of indigenous birds.

DOMAINE DE L'ETOILE [140 B1] (*Royal Rd, Moka;* 729 1050; e *resa.cieletnature@drbc-group.com; www.cieletnature.com;* 09.30–16.30 *daily*) Although covered in the chapter on the centre of the island, Domaine de l'Etoile is easily reached from the east and offers a variety of activities. For details, see page 199.

FOLLOW BRADT

For the latest news, special offers and competitions, subscribe to the Bradt newsletter via the website www.bradtguides.com and follow Bradt on:

f www.facebook.com/BradtTravelGuides
🐦 @BradtGuides
📷 @bradtguides
📌 www.pinterest.com/bradtguides

above **Le Morne Brabant in the southwest of Mauritius is regarded as a symbol of resistance to slavers** (YC/DT) pages 172–3

right **Now a UNESCO World Heritage Site, Aapravasi Ghat was built in 1849 to receive indentured labourers** (AR) pages 108–9

below **The colonial house of the administrator in Port Mathurin, Rodrigues, was built in 1873** (NS) page 229

above   There are seven species of sea turtle left in the world and five are found around Réunion. Pictured, a green sea turtle (AR) page 344

left   The brightly coloured ornate day gecko is often spotted on trees in Mauritius (NS) page 10

below   Dolphin watching is a popular activity in the waters surrounding the Mascarene Islands (F/DT) pages 91 & 291

above left In 1973 the Mauritius kestrel was named the rarest bird in the world, but now there are estimated to be between 400 and 500 on the island (B/GG/FLPA) page 9

above right The rare pink pigeon is thriving on Ile aux Aigrettes (NS) page 9

right Fairy terns are one of several bird species which nest on Ile aux Cocos Nature Reserve off Rodrigues (AR) pages 244–5

below left The giant Aldabra tortoises at François Leguat Giant Tortoise and Cave Reserve in Rodrigues are related to the species that once roamed the Mascarenes (NS) page 244

below right The Mauritius fody can be seen on Ile aux Aigrettes (B/DT) page 9

above Ziplining in Rodrigues overlooking the fabulous lagoon is a memorable experience (NS) pages 239–40

left Like many of Mauritius's rural estates, Domaine de l'Etoile can be explored on a quadbike tour (AR) page 199

below Horseriding along Flic en Flac Beach, western Mauritius (AR) page 184

above   The warm, clear waters off Mauritius are rich in marine life and offer excellent snorkelling (AR) pages 86–9

below left   Réunion's innumerable waterfalls and spectacular gorges are ideal for canyoning (NS) page 286

below right   Réunion's cirques offer world-class hiking. Pictured here, Cirque de Cilaos (AR) page 355

above Tea has been grown on Mauritius since the 18th century (K/DT) page 31

left Efforts have been made to preserve Réunion's delightful *'ti cases*, the humble dwellings of ordinary families (AR) page 260

below The salt pans at Tamarin, western Mauritius, have been producing salt for over 175 years (AR) page 173

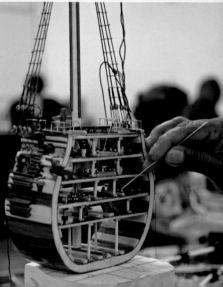

above   Colourful handicrafts are a feature of the weekly market in St-Pierre, Réunion (AR) page 321

right   *Rhum arrangé* is made by adding fruit and spices to white rum and allowing it to ferment for several months (JM/IRT) page 67

below left   The Rault Factory, near Mahébourg, has used the same methods to make its manioc biscuits since 1870 (AR) pages 165–6

below right   Model ship making is a proud tradition on Mauritius. Pictured here, the workshop of Historic Marine in Goodlands, which can be visited (AR) page 72

above Hindu temple at Anse La Raie on the north coast of Mauritius
(AR) pages 129–30

left In April 1977 when Piton-de-la-Fournaise erupted, the lava flowed down the east coast destroying everything in its path but miraculously separated and travelled around this church, now known as Notre Dame des Laves (Our Lady of the Lava)
(NS) page 309

below The much-photographed Notre Dame Auxiliatrice at Cap Malheureux
(AR) page 130

7

Southern Mauritius

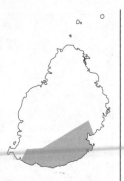

The south extends from historic Vieux Grand Port in the southeast to Baie du Cap River, on the border between the districts of Savanne and Black River, in the southwest.

Saved by a lack of beaches, for many years the south of Mauritius avoided the tourist development that had taken place elsewhere. Over the past decade some large hotels and integrated resort schemes have sprung up and become a feature of the south, but this coast still remains less developed than other parts of the island.

The southeast is most visitors' first experience of the island, having arrived at the international airport at Plaisance. Many simply pass through the area, returning only to catch another flight, but there is plenty to see here.

The ruins and monuments around Vieux Grand Port attest to its dramatic past: the first landings of the Dutch in 1598 and the naval battle between the English and French in 1810. Nearby is the south's main town, Mahébourg, a fishing community crammed with colourful old houses and known for its lively Monday market.

There are a few accommodation options around Pointe d'Esny and Blue Bay, not far from the airport. The sea here is a marine park and offers excellent snorkelling. Just off the coast is the coral island known as Ile aux Aigrettes, which is a nature reserve run by the Mauritian Wildlife Foundation and well worth a visit.

Savanne is the southernmost district of Mauritius, stretching westwards from the sugar-growing village of Savannah along a coast that is the island's most rugged. Cane fields interspersed with fishing villages dominate the coast, while the interior around Grand Bois is tea-growing country. Close to the tea plantations is Grand Bassin, a lake sacred to Hindus.

In 2004, the Bel Ombre Sugar Estate, prompted by the downturn in the sugar industry, allowed three upmarket hotels to be constructed on some of its coastal land. Thankfully the hotels were built in such a way as to minimise any negative impact on the local area and the community. The building of several other hotels in the area followed. For visitors looking for tranquillity, the area around Bel Ombre now offers a peaceful alternative to the north, east and west coasts.

VIEUX GRAND PORT AND MAHEBOURG

Vieux Grand Port was named Warwyck Bay in 1598 by the Dutch, who made two attempts to establish a colony here before they left in 1710. The French named the bay Port Bourbon and planned to have the headquarters of the French East India Company there, although after a feasibility study they chose Port Louis instead.

Port Bourbon then became Port Sud-est and slipped into decline. Governor Decaen visited the harbour in 1804 and sensed its vulnerability. He abandoned the

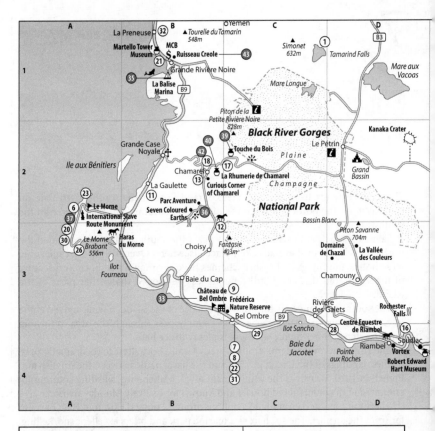

SOUTHERN MAURITIUS

For listings, see pages 155–6, 158–9 & 160–2 unless otherwise stated

🛏 Where to stay

1	7 Cascades Lodges (p196)	C1
2	Astroea Beach	H2
3	Auberge de St Aubin	E3
4	Blue Lagoon Beach	H2
5	Chill Pill Guesthouse	G2
6	Dinarobin Hotel Golf & Spa (p173)	A2
7	Heritage Awali Golf & Spa Resort	C4
8	Heritage Le Telfair Golf & Spa Resort	C4
9	Heritage The Villas	C3
10	La Hacienda	H1
11	La Reine Creole (p175)	B2
12	La Vieille Cheminée (p178)	B3
13	Lakaz Chamarel (p178)	B2
14	Le Jardin de Beau Vallon	H2
15	Le Preskil Beach Resort	G2
16	Le Rochester	D4
17	Les Chalets en Champagne (p178)	C2
18	Les Palmiers (p178)	B2
19	Lodges Andrea	E4
20	Lux* Le Morne (p174)	A3
21	Marlin Creek Residence (p175)	B1
22	Outrigger Mauritius Beach Resort	C4
23	Paradis Hotel & Golf Club (p173–4)	A2
24	Paradise Beach	H2
25	Pingouin Villas	H2
26	Riu Hotels (p174)	A3
27	Shandrani Resort & Spa	G2
28	Shanti Maurice	D4
29	So Sofitel	C4
30	St Regis (p174)	A3
31	Tamassa	C4
32	The Bay (p175)	B1

✴ Where to eat and drink

	7 Cascades (p197)	(see 1)
33	Château de Bel Ombre	B3
34	Chez M	E2
35	Coral Tree (p175)	B1
36	Domaine du Cachet (p179)	B2
37	Embafilao (p177)	A2
38	La Belle Creole	H2
39	La Varangue sur Morne (p178)	C2
40	L'Alchemiste (p179)	B2
41	Le Bois Chéri	E2
42	Le Chamarel (p179)	B2
	Gin'ja	(see 8)
	Le Jardin de Beau Vallon	(see 14)
	Le St Aubin	(see 3)
	Plantation Club	(see 22)
	Rochester	(see 16)
43	The Toaster (p177)	B1

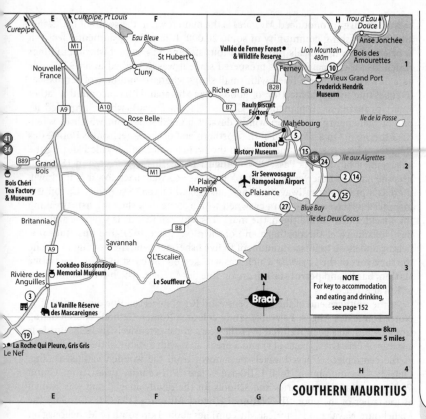

E   Curepipe, Pt Louis   F   G   H   Trou d'Eau
Curepipe   Douce
                           Eau Bleue   Anse Jonchée
                    [M1]   Vallée de Ferney Forest ● Lion Mountain
                           St Hubert○ & Wildlife Reserve   480m   Bois des
Nouvelle   Cluny   Ferney   [10]   Amourettes   1
France   ○Vieux Grand Port
                                 Riche en Eau   [B28]   Frederick Hendrik
        [A9]   [A10]   [B7]   Museum
               Rose Belle   Rault Biscuit
                                     Factory   Ile de la Passe
41   Mahébourg○
34   [5]
[B89] Grand   National   [15]   Ile aux Aigrettes
       Bois   History Museum   38 24   2
Bois Chéri   [M1]   Plaine   ②⑭
Tea Factory   Magnien Sir Seewoosagur
& Museum   ○Plaisance Ramgoolam Airport
                                                 ④⑤
Britannia○   [B8]   ②⑦   Blue Bay
                                                 Ile des Deux Cocos
        [A9]   Savannah○   3
Rivière des   Sookdeo Bissoondoyal ○L'Escalier
Anguilles   ○ Memorial Museum
③   Le Souffleur ○
          La Vanille Réserve   N
          des Mascareignes   **Bradt**
19   NOTE
○●La Roche Qui Pleure, Gris Gris   For key to accommodation
Le Nef   and eating and drinking,
                                                        see page 152

                                  0   8km
                                  0   5 miles

E   F   G   H   4

                              SOUTHERN MAURITIUS

manning of the old Dutch posts and built a new town on the opposite side of the bay. Mahébourg, after Mahé de Labourdonnais, was his original name for this new town but he soon changed it for reasons of diplomacy to Port Imperial. He renamed Port Louis at the same time, as Port Napoleon.

When the British tried to take Grand Port in August 1810 they were soundly beaten. Both sides used subterfuge but the French were more successful. They moved the buoys marking the passage through the reef, causing British vessels to run aground. The victory of the French is recorded at the Arc de Triomphe in Paris. Four months later, however, the island capitulated and Port Imperial became Mahébourg again.

The crouching lion of **Lion Mountain** (480m) guards the bay around **Vieux Grand Port**, the site of the first Dutch settlement. Some of the oldest buildings in Mauritius, with foundations dating back to the 17th century, are to be found in this town. The ruins of the Dutch **Fort Frederick Hendrik** are located in a park at the northern end of the town. The park also contains the **Frederick Hendrik Museum** [153 H1], which tells the story of the Dutch on the island (see page 165).

About 3km from Vieux Grand Port, on the coastal side of the road at **Ferney**, is an obelisk, erected on 20 September 1948, to commemorate the landing of the Dutch 350 years before to the day. Bodies of the Dutch settlers are buried at the foot of Lion Mountain. Nearby is **Vallée de Ferney Forest & Wildlife Reserve** [153 G1], where passionate conservationists are endeavouring to restore and protect native vegetation (see page 164).

Mahébourg (pronounced *My bore*) is the main town in the south of the island, a laid-back fishing community of some 20,000. It has a very authentic feel – it is oriented towards locals rather than tourists, and has some historic buildings which give it character. It has prospered since it was described in a 1973 guide as 'a down-at-heel town lined with small shops where friendliness of service has to substitute for sophistication of goods'. Rue Shivananda has acquired a rather smart **promenade** (Esplanade Sir Charles Gaëtan Duval), which, provided it's one of Mahébourg's rare non-windy days, is a good spot from which to watch the fishermen. On a headland at the northern end of the waterfront is **Pointe des Régates**, where there is a memorial to the French and English killed 'during the engagement off Ile de la Passe 20–28 August 1810'. This was erected in 1899 and lists the names of the vessels that took part. As you walk back towards the town, there is a preserved railway building constructed in 1865. At Pointe Canon is a memorial to slavery, a column crowned with a stone disk showing fists breaking the shackles that bound them. The **market** is between Rue de la Colonie and Rue des Hollandais, at the northern end of town (see page 162). The **bus station** is nearby and close to it is a monument to five fishermen who died trying to rescue the survivors of the *Crysolite* which was wrecked off the coast in 1874. The **police station**, **banks** and **petrol station** are on Rue des Créoles, which is a continuation of Royal Road.

At the southern end of the town centre, off Royal Road (on Rue du Souffleur), is **Notre Dame des Anges**, a sizeable sandy-coloured Roman Catholic church dating from 1849. It has been restored over the years, most extensively in 1938. Inside is a statue of Père Laval (page 111) and a pretty altar with a statue of the Virgin Mary as the centrepiece. Carved angels peer down from the wooden vaulted ceiling. Outside, is a monument to F J Thiersé, a late 19th-century priest from Grand Port who created sanctuaries and schools for the disadvantaged and was known as the father of the poor. The **National History Museum** [153 G2] (formerly the Mahébourg Naval and Historical Museum) lies about 1km south of Mahébourg on the main road (A10) (see page 111). About 1km north of Mahébourg is the Rault Biscuit Factory, which has been producing manioc biscuits since 1870. The short guided tour is fascinating (see page 165).

To the south of Mahébourg lies **Ile aux Aigrettes** [153 H2], an island nature reserve managed by the Mauritian Wildlife Foundation. Many of the plants found there grow nowhere else and there is a good chance of seeing pink pigeons, one of the rarest birds in the world (see pages 163–4).

Further south, **Blue Bay** [153 G2] offers a good beach, fabulous turquoise lagoon and a range of accommodation. An area off the coast was declared a protected marine park in 1997; the water is clear and the snorkelling excellent. Just off the coast, opposite the Shandrani Hotel, is Ile des Deux Cocos, which is run by Lux Resorts but can be visited (pages 162–3).

The only disadvantage to the hotels here is that they can suffer from aircraft noise. The **Sir Seewoosagur Ramgoolam International Airport** [153 G2] lies just inland, at **Plaisance** (see page 49).

GETTING THERE AND AWAY The **bus station** in Mahébourg is at the northern end of Rue Shivananda and there is a **taxi stand** nearby. Buses operate regularly between Mahébourg and Curepipe, via the airport and Rose Belle. Passengers can change in Curepipe for onward journeys to Port Louis and the north coast. Direct buses between Mahébourg and Port Louis are less frequent. There are also buses from Mahébourg to Centre de Flacq, Blue Bay, Souillac and Le Val.

TOURIST INFORMATION There is no tourist office in either Vieux Grand Port or Mahébourg but the people are very friendly and helpful. If you are staying in the area, your hotel should be able to offer advice and arrange excursions.

WHERE TO STAY

Upmarket

Shandrani Resort & Spa [152 D4] (327 rooms) Blue Bay; 603 4343; e shandrani@ bchot.com; www.beachcomber-hotels.com. The road to the hotel follows the airport runway then twists & turns through sugarcane fields. The rooms, which include 36 family apartments, are spread through spacious grounds. They all face the sea & are well equipped, including AC, TV, phone, safe, minibar, tea/coffee facilities & Wi-Fi. Family apartments are thoughtfully designed, with a separate en-suite bedroom with TV for up to 3 children under 12. Those with restricted mobility should note that there are 2 steps in superior rooms. There are 5 restaurants, a pitch & putt golf course, 2 pools, tennis, watersports, bike hire, gym, kids' club & an impressive spa. More recent additions are a dive centre, sailing school & kitesurfing school. Interestingly, there are 3 types of beach: bay, lagoon & ocean. Lots of facilities & endless activities, but you do get some aircraft noise. The hotel's AI package 'serenity plus' has been well received by travellers – included in the price are all meals & drinks, watersports (including unlimited waterskiing), & unlimited golf on the hotel's 9-hole pitch & putt. **$$$$**

Mid range

Astroea Beach [153 H2] (16 rooms) Pointe d'Esny, Blue Bay; 631 4282; e info@ astroeabeach.com; www.astroeabeach.com. A cosy adults-only hotel on a small beach within walking distance of Pointe d'Esny Beach. The rooms are simply furnished with AC, TV, safe, tea/coffee facilities, balcony/terrace & Wi-Fi. For groups there are 2-bedroom bungalows. There is a restaurant, 2 massage rooms & some free non-motorised watersports. There isn't much in the way of entertainment but if you are after somewhere quiet & low key, this could suit. **$$$**

Blue Lagoon Beach Hotel [153 H2] (72 rooms) Pointe d'Esny, Blue Bay; 631 9046; e blbhotel@intnet.mu; www. bluelagoonbeachhotel.com. In pleasant gardens overlooking the lagoon, just 10km from the airport. Rather plain en-suite rooms with AC, TV &

phone; some have balcony/terrace. A fridge in your room will cost Rs50 per day. Only superior rooms have a safe. There are 2 restaurants, a pool & some free non-motorised watersports. Gets some noise from the airport. Seems rather overpriced. **$$$**

Le Preskil Beach Resort [153 G2] (156 rooms) Pointe Jérome, Mahébourg; 604 1000; e info@preskilbeachresort.mu; www. preskilbeachresort.mu. The location of this 4-star hotel is stunning & very private – on a peninsula with views to Ile aux Aigrettes across a shallow, protected turquoise lagoon. Rooms have sea views & are en suite with AC, TV, phone, Wi-Fi, minibar, safe & tea/coffee facilities. There is 1 room with disabled facilities. The standard rooms are smallish but well decorated. The cottages are lovely but try to get 1 with direct beach access if you can. There are 2 pools, 3 restaurants, tennis, a gym, a spa offering massage & a kids' club. The selection of free watersports is impressive & includes waterskiing. The hotel is popular as a base for windsurfing & kitesurfing, & as a departure point for trips to Ile aux Aigrettes. Aircraft noise does not seem to be such an issue here – aircraft can be seen in the skies above the area but are usually too high to be heard at the hotel. **$$$**

Lodges Andrea [153 E4] (10 lodges) Rivière des Anguilles; m 5772 9303; e info@andrea-lodge. com; www.andrea-lodge.com. The lodges are set on a clifftop among the cane fields of the Union Sugar Estate east of Souillac. They each accommodate 2 people, are modern, private & have sea view, fan, safe & tea/coffee facilities. They aren't luxurious but they are nicely done. There is a restaurant serving breakfast & dinner (lunch on request) & a pool. Hiking & guided tours can be arranged. **$$$**

Paradise Beach [153 H2] (12 apts) Pointe d'Esny; 403 5308; e reservations@paradisebeach. mu; www.paradisebeach.mu. Upmarket, modern, well-maintained self-catering apartments in a 3-storey building on a beautiful part of the coast. The 8 3-bedroom apartments & 2 4-bedroom penthouses are equipped with everything you need, including a modern kitchen, espresso machine, TV, DVD player, Wi-Fi & iPod docking station. The grounds are beautifully maintained, with a pool & inviting sun lounges. Bike, kayak & car hire can be

arranged. Watersports & shuttle to nearby shops on request. Maid service 6 days a week &, for a fee, a local chef will come & cook for you in your apartment. Entry to the complex is controlled by a security guard, which is reassuring. Ground-floor apartments cost a little more than those on the first floor. A superb self-catering option. **$$$**

Budget

⌂ **Chill Pill Guesthouse** [153 G2] (8 rooms) 6 Rue Shivananda, Mahébourg; m 5715 7744; e aquarellaamu@email.com; www.chillpillmaurice. com. Simple but spotless accommodation around a courtyard on the seafront (no beach). The rooms have sea view, en-suite shower, AC, TV, mini fridge, tea/coffee facilities, balcony & Wi-Fi. The thatched bungalow is particularly cute – the one that's almost dipping its toes in the water. Breakfast is served in the dining room overlooking the bay, & there is a pool. There is no restaurant but there are several nearby. **$$**

⌂ **La Hacienda** [153 H1] (4 villas) Vieux Grand Port; ☎ 263 0914; e lahacienda@orange.mu; www.lahaciendamauritius.com. Rustic but modern villas in attractive grounds on a hillside beneath Lion Mountain, overlooking the coast. There are 3

1-bedroom villas & 1 with 2 bedrooms. Each has AC, TV, safe, Wi-Fi & fully equipped kitchen. There is a pool & breakfast is provided. 24hr security. The nearest good beach is Blue Bay, around 11km away. The estate offers pleasant walks, including to Lion Mountain, bike hire & excursions can be arranged. Vallée de Ferney Nature Reserve is nearby, & Ile aux Aigrettes is within easy reach **$$**

⌂ **Le Jardin de Beau Vallon** [153 H2] (4 rooms) Beau Vallon; ☎ 631 2850; e beauvallon. fvl@intnet.mu; www.lejardindebeauvallon.com. Charming guesthouse accommodation & table d'hôte in an 18th-century house within a pretty garden. The rooms are thoughtfully decorated in a colonial style, with en suite, AC, safe, minibar & Wi-Fi. The pavilion is most spacious & private, & has a TV. The guesthouse is away from the coast but buses stop around 100m from the entrance, & there is a pool on site. **$$**

⌂ **Pingouin Villas** [153 H2] (5 apts, 2 studios) 94A Daurades Rd, Blue Bay; ☎ 637 3051; e resa@ pingouinvillas.com; www.pingouinvillas.com. Around 200m from the beach & beautiful Blue Bay. Basic but clean self-catering accommodation with TV, phone, Wi-Fi, safe, fan (no AC) & balcony/ terrace. Apartments sleep up to 6 people & are cleaned twice a week. **$$**

✖ **WHERE TO EAT** There are dozens of snack vendors around the bus station in Mahébourg and in front of the nearby market, which has all the fresh fruit and vegetables you could need. For self-caterers, there is a London Way **supermarket** at the southern end of town, on the coastal road to Pointe d'Esny (⊕ *Mon/Tue & Thu–Sat, mornings only Sun*).

✖ **La Belle Creole** [153 H2] Coastal Rd, Pointe Jérôme; m 5255 1701; ⊕ 10.00–20.00 (22.00 in summer) daily. Cuisine: Creole. On the banks of an inlet, just south of Mahébourg heading towards Pointe d'Esny. The thatched roof & rustic décor complement the authentic Creole cuisine. Try a tasty wild boar dish & some of the rather unusual rums, such as chilli or garlic flavour. In summer there is a *séga* show on Fri evenings. Reservation recommended. **$$$**

✖ **Le Jardin de Beau Vallon** [153 H2] Beau Vallon; ☎ 631 2850; ⊕ 09.00–22.00 daily. Cuisine: Creole, European. A table d'hôte restaurant in a refurbished colonial house set in pleasant, peaceful gardens between the SSR International Airport &

Mahébourg. A good spot to enjoy a meal *en route* to the airport. The meals & service are of a good standard. Reservation recommended. **$$$**

✖ **Les Copains d'abord** Rue Shivananda, Mahébourg; ☎ 631 9728; ⊕ for lunch & dinner daily. Cuisine: European, Creole, seafood. Near the junction with Rue Suffren, opposite the promenade, with views of the bay. The menu is extensive & varied, & includes pasta, venison dishes & traditional curries. **$$$**

✖ **Le Phare** Rue des Hollandais, Mahébourg; ☎ 631 2698; ⊕ 09.00–22.00 daily. Cuisine: Creole, seafood, Chinese. A bright, modern restaurant/bar not far from the market. **$$**

OTHER PRACTICALITIES

Communications The **post office** is on Rue des Créoles and offers **internet access**.

Heading southwest towards Souillac from the busy area around the airport, you step back into a far more traditional, rural Mauritius of cane fields and small village communities.

The village of **L'Escalier** takes its name from Baron Daniel l'Escalier, a French officer. There is a road here, which winds through sugarcane fields to **Le Souffleur**, a blowhole formed in the rocks of the coast (see page 166).

Rivière des Anguilles (Eel River) has some wonderful old wooden buildings on the main street where hard-working, skilled people follow their chosen trade – an old-fashioned barber, a tailor, a bicycle repairer, and more. Incidentally, the barber, Mr Samoon of New Look Coiffeur, does an excellent men's haircut. Now in his 60s, he has been a hairdresser since he was 13 years old and wields a cut-throat razor with alarming skill. The town has all the essentials: petrol station and ATMs, plus plenty of fruit and vegetable stalls and pavement vendors. Just south of the Rivière des Anguilles is **La Vanille Réserve des Mascareignes** [153 E3], formerly known as the La Vanille Crocodile and Tortoise Park (see page 166).

North of the town is the immaculately maintained **Britannia Sugar Estate**. The odour of warm sugar pervades the air and workers swathed in protective clothing tend the sugar crop. Just north of here is a turning to the village of Camp Diable and the **Tookay Temple**, an impressive colourful Tamil temple in the midst of the cane fields (you will need to remove your shoes to visit).

Further north on the main road (A9) is the turning to **Grand Bois**, which is surrounded by fields of tidy tea bushes belonging to the **Bois Chéri Tea Estate** [153 E2]. One can only marvel at the women who work in the fields plucking the tea leaves with mechanical precision and dropping them into wicker baskets hanging from their heads. Their speed and dexterity is even more amazing when you consider how meagre the rewards are. They work from 06.00 to midday and are paid about Rs5 per kilogram picked; on a good day they can pick around 60–80kg. The leaves they pick are transported to the nearby Bois Chéri Tea Factory, which has produced tea since 1892. It is worth taking a guided tour of the factory and museum, followed by a tea tasting (see pages 167–8).

Off the road to Souillac, 2km south of Rivière des Anguilles, is **Le Saint Aubin**, an attractive colonial house built in 1819. The house has been transformed into a restaurant (page 159), and the estate provides tours explaining vanilla, sugar and rum production. The anthuriums cultivated here are of the *andreanium* type and have been grown in the region for around 200 years. The wax-like leaf (actually the flower spathe) is normally pink although some varieties are blood red and others white. The plants, which bloom all year, are grown in humid, warm conditions under vast awnings of netting. (For details, see page 168.)

The fishing town of **Souillac** lies midway between the east and west corners of the island. It is named after Vicomte de Souillac, Governor of Mauritius from 1779 to 1787, who encouraged settlers to develop the south of the island. He created a port here, which was used to transport sugar from Souillac to Port Louis. There is a ponderous, black stone Roman Catholic church dedicated to St Jacques, built between 1853 and 1856, and restored in 1997. The **post office** is housed within a Victorian red-brick building, formerly a railway station.

On the coast in the town are the **Telfair Gardens**. Charles Telfair was a British planter who arrived with Governor Farquhar in 1810 and took over the sugar factory at Bel Ombre. He published pamphlets on his enlightened treatment of slaves which only won him censure from abolitionists. He was a keen amateur botanist. The

garden bearing his name is mostly lawn, badamier (Indian almond) and banyan (*Ficus benghalensis*) trees, and drops steeply down to the sea. It is a popular picnic spot for locals, but bathing in the sea below is dangerous because of currents.

Across the road from the ocean, the building that houses the **police station** was used in the 18th century to accommodate slaves working on the sugar plantations, who every morning would walk down to the wharf at Port Souillac. After the opening in 1878 of the Rose Belle/Souillac branch of the Port Louis to Mahébourg railway line, the building was used for train passengers. The railway closed in 1954.

A little further along the coast is the site of the house where **Robert Edward Hart**, half-French, half-Irish Mauritian poet and writer, spent his last years. In 1967, the house was turned into an evocative free **museum** [152 D4]. In 2002, the Mauritius Museums Council was forced to rebuild the house because of its poor condition, but it has been kept as close to the original as possible. (See page 166.)

Hart is buried in the **cemetery** on the point across the bay. He shares it with a number of British and French soldiers and drowned seamen whose tombs have been defaced by the fierceness of the elements. Bones were scattered around the graveyard by the cyclone of 1962.

Inland from Souillac are **Rochester Falls** [152 D3]. The falls are signed from the main road just west of Souillac and reached via rough tracks through cane fields. You can drive to within about 250m of the falls. Many of the signs to the falls are messily handwritten, some with spelling errors. That is because they were erected by some entrepreneurial locals who earn their living from Rochester Falls, either by selling coconuts and pineapples at a makeshift stall or by guiding tourists the last few hundred metres of the walk. Fed by water flowing down from the Savanne Mountains, they are not high but reveal ancient vertical columns created in the rocks by the constant pounding of the falling water.

Also inland from Souillac, about 10km north of the town, is **La Vallée des Couleurs** [152 D3], an exposed area of the stratum under the earth's crust, similar to the Seven Coloured Earths at Chamarel, which has expanded to offer outdoor activities and a small geological museum (see page 169).

On the coast just beyond Le Nef is **Gris Gris** [153 E4], a viewpoint where black cliffs drop away sharply. There is a beach where swimming is dangerous, despite the apparent shallow lagoon formed by the reef that runs close to the shore. The name *Gris Gris* is associated with local witchcraft. There are deep chasms in the cliffs surrounding the beach which lead to a distinctive headland known as **La Roche Qui Pleure** [153 E4] (The Crying Rock), so called because one of the rocks here is said to resemble a crying man. You can walk out on the headland to look for the face but take care, as the path is steep and the rocks uneven. The rock that you're looking for is on the furthest point, facing out to sea. When the waves roll in water drenches his face and he is then crying.

 WHERE TO STAY

Budget

🏠 **Auberge de Saint Aubin** [153 E3] (3 rooms) Royal Rd, St Aubin, Rivière des Anguilles; ✆625 1513; e sales@saintaubin.mu; www.saintaubin. mu. Peaceful guesthouse accommodation in a 1908 Creole cottage in the grounds of the St Aubin estate, a few kilometres north of Souillac. The rooms are beautifully furnished, in keeping with the historic surrounds. The table d'hôte meals are a good opportunity to compare experiences & exchange

recommendations with other guests. There is a pool; bikes are available but it would also be handy to have a car if staying here. Priced at the top end of the budget category. **$$**

Shoestring

🏠 **Le Rochester** [152 D4] (3 rooms) Coastal Rd, Souillac; ✆625 4180; e lerochester@hotmail.com. Above the restaurant (page 159), basic en-suite rooms, 2 of which have AC. **$**

✘ WHERE TO EAT

✳ ✘ **Le Saint Aubin** [153 E3] Rivière des Anguilles; ☎ 625 1513; ⏱ 09.00–17.00 Mon–Sat. Cuisine: Creole, seafood. In the historic St Aubin planter's mansion. The table d'hôte menu uses homegrown ingredients to create delicious local dishes, such as heart of palm salad, freshwater prawns with watercress, chicken with vanilla & pineapple mousse. A good selection of wines is available too. The Route du Thé includes lunch here (see page 168). $$$$

✘ **Le Batelage** Village des Touristes, Coastal Rd, Souillac; ☎ 625 6083; ⏱ 12.00–17.00 & 18.00–21.30 daily. Cuisine: European, Creole, seafood. A long-established open-air restaurant overlooking the water. Good traditional & seafood dishes made with local fresh ingredients. Dinner on reservation only. $$$

✘ **Le Bois Chéri** [153 E2] Grand Bois; ☎ 507 0216; ⏱ for lunch daily. Cuisine: Creole, European. In a lovely setting within the Bois Chéri Tea Estate, on a hill with views to the coast. Serves excellent Creole dishes & some tea-flavoured specialities.

You may be asked to pay a Rs100 entry fee to the grounds if you have not been for a tour of the tea factory, but this can be redeemed against the cost of your meal. If you eat here, you can walk around the lake surrounded with tea bushes, take a kayak or pedalo out on the water, or fish in the lake. $$$

✘ **Rochester Restaurant** [152 D4] Coastal Rd, Souillac; ☎ 625 4180; ⏱ 11.00–15.00 & 18.00–21.30, closed Tue dinner. Cuisine: Creole, Indian, European, seafood. The sort of restaurant every traveller hopes to find. In Dec 2004, Mr & Mrs Appadu converted the front room of their home into a tiny restaurant (6 tables), which has been so successful it has now expanded significantly. It is clean, nicely decorated, has a well-stocked bar & serves a wide range of delicious traditional food. The old stone building adds interest. $$$

✘ **Chez M** [153 E2] Bois Cheri Rd, Grand Bassin; ☎ 617 9872; ⏱ 10.00–15.00 daily. Cuisine: Creole, seafood. Next to the Bois Chéri tea factory, this is a casual restaurant without much atmosphere. $$

RIAMBEL TO BAIE DU CAP

The village of **Riambel** marks the beginning of a long rugged beach that stretches up to **Pointe aux Roches**. Swimming here is dangerous because of currents and rocks – the signs on the beach leave you in no doubt, 'if you bathe here, you may be drowned'.

Riambel has an unusual claim to fame: it is the home of an energy **vortex**, one of only 14 in the world. The site opened to the public in 2007 and is visited by those wanting to replenish their energy stores (see page 169).

Just off Pointe aux Roches, in **Baie du Jacotet**, is **Ilot Sancho**. During the preliminary forages of the British in 1810, the French battery on this coral islet was captured and a French colonist taken hostage in exchange for supplies. Rumours of treasure buried on the island have never been proved. It is now covered in scrub.

As you continue along the coast, you enter the domain of the **Bel Ombre Sugar Estate**. The Bel Ombre factory has now closed, although sugarcane is still grown here and transported to other factories for processing. In 2004, a few luxury hotels were built on some of the estate's coastal land, along with a championship **golf course** (pages 83–4). The development of this area has included a new road, making this part of the island more accessible. The **Château de Bel Ombre** [152 B3], a colonial house across the road from the coast, has been converted into an excellent restaurant (page 162). It is a robust building of volcanic rock with a wide veranda overlooking attractive gardens and a fountain; you can visit the building without eating here. Although there was some objection from local communities to the tourism development of the area, this appears to have been controlled by a government policy of compensation and a requirement for the hotels to recruit at least 40% of their staff from the area. A reserve has also been created here, the **Frédérica Nature Reserve** [152 C3], which offers guided tours and outdoor

activities (see page 164). Opposite Heritage Le Telfair Hotel is **Place du Moulin** (⏱ *07.30–17.00 Mon–Fri, 08.30–13.00 Sat/Sun*), a small complex of shops in converted sugar factory buildings. There is an upmarket grocery shop here, which is handy if you are self-catering at Heritage Le Villas (see below), and an ATM.

The road continues along the coast, passing through yet more cane fields and fishing villages. The area is refreshingly devoid of development. Opposite the **St Martin Cemetery** is a monument recalling the landing of survivors from the wreck of the British steamer *Travessa*, which foundered in 1923 on its journey from Australia. After 25 days at sea in an open lifeboat, having travelled 1,610 nautical miles and battling scorching heat, storms, hunger and thirst, 16 survivors were washed ashore at Bel Ombre on 29 June. Two days earlier, another lifeboat of survivors had come ashore on Rodrigues Island. The cigarette-tin lid, which was the measure for the daily water ration for the survivors in the Bel Ombre lifeboat during their ordeal at sea, is an exhibit at the National History Museum (see page 165).

Baie du Cap is a quiet beachside village, whose inhabitants work in the cane fields or as fishermen. Just west of the village, overlooking the sea, is a monument to Matthew Flinders, who left the UK in 1801 on a scientific voyage of discovery to New Holland (Australia). On the way back to the UK in 1803 he stopped at Baie du Cap and was detained by the French governor, Decaen. He was released in 1810 and his book *A Voyage to Terra Australis* (which gave Australia its name) was published in 1814, the day before he died.

On the road to **Choisy**, a village in the hills behind Baie du Cap, there are good views of the sea; look back before you get to **Chamarel**.

⌂ WHERE TO STAY

Luxury

✳ ⌂ **Heritage the Villas** [152 C3] Bel Ombre; ☎ 605 5000; e info@heritageresorts. mu; www.heritageresorts.mu. Luxury 2, 3- & 4-bedroom villas on the Domaine de Bel Ombre, on a hillside overlooking the coast & the manicured golf course. These high-end villas are exceptionally well appointed & maintained. They are very private, have fully equipped, modern kitchens & everything else you may need, including daily maid service & free Wi-Fi. Each villa has its own infinity pool. Guests have access to the facilities of the 2 Heritage 5-star hotels (Heritage Le Telfair & Heritage Awali, plus C Beach Club adjacent to Heritage Le Telfair; see page 161). This means a choice of 12 restaurants, 2 spas & useful services like the kids' club. A golf cart is allocated to every villa so you can get around the estate & down to the beach in front of the hotels. Guests receive one green fee per day at the Heritage Golf Club. For a fee you can have meals & spa treatments in your villa. Villas can either be purchased as part of an IRS scheme, or rented short term. **$$$$$**

⌂ **Shanti Maurice** [152 D4] (61 rooms) Rivière des Galets, Chemin Grenier; ☎ 603 7200;

e reservation@shantimaurice.com; www. shantimaurice.com. Relaxation is made easy here with superb service, a fabulous spa, fitness centre & yoga. The setting is peaceful – no noisy motorised watersports here, although they can be arranged nearby. The suites are large & beautifully decorated, & there are 17 sumptuous beachfront 1- & 2- bedroom villas with private pool. There are 3 excellent restaurants, which pride themselves on using local, seasonal produce. In 2014, the hotel opened a rustic-style, traditional 'rum shed', where you can choose from 180 types of rum from around the world. It is family friendly & there is a kids' club. Staff can prepare a picnic for you to enjoy within the 36 acres of grounds. **$$$$$**

Upmarket

⌂ **Heritage Awali Golf & Spa Resort** [152 C4] (160 rooms) Coastal Rd, Bel Ombre; ☎ 601 1500; e info@heritageresorts.mu; www. heritageresorts.mu. The African-inspired design is used to great effect throughout, from the bedrooms to the spa. There are 154 rooms, 5 suites & 1 villa with private pool. 1 room has disabled facilities & wheelchair access around the resort is

generally good. The standard rooms are spacious & well equipped, with a large balcony/terrace. The 4 restaurants include a new adult-only Indian; there is also a *boma* where African theme nights are held around the bonfire. The facilities are extensive & include 3 pools, tennis, gym, watersports, Segway, a hairdresser & a kids' club. A total of 12 restaurants are available at the Domaine de Bel Ombre, including those at Heritage Le Telfair & Château de Bel Ombre. The spa is huge & offers all manner of pampering – massage, relaxation areas, pools, steam rooms & a sauna. For golfers, the stunning Heritage Golf Club opposite the hotel will be hard to resist. A premium AI package is available, which includes wine & spirits, 1 spa treatment per day, an excursion to Frédérica Nature Reserve (page 164) & entry to the Seven Coloured Earths at Chamarel. Guests also have access to C Beach Club, adjacent to Heritage Le Telfair (see below). If you plan to indulge yourself while in Mauritius, the AI package could be a very economical way of doing so. The hotel has a relaxed atmosphere for a 5-star property, more so than neighbouring Le Telfair, & there is plenty to do. **$$$$**

✳ 🏠 Heritage Le Telfair Golf & Spa Resort
[152 C4] (158 rooms) Coastal Rd, Bel Ombre; ☎601 5500; e info@heritageresorts.mu; www. heritageresorts.mu. The hotel is part of the Domaine de Bel Ombre (the Bel Ombre Sugar Estate). Although both are 5-star, it has a more upmarket & exclusive feel than its sister hotel, Awali. Everything about Le Telfair evokes colonial times, giving the impression you are a guest at the vast home of a wealthy, 19th-century sugar baron. The hotel, built on either side of the Citronniers River & spread over 15ha, is a member of Small Luxury Hotels of the World. The rooms are housed in 2-storey villas of 6 or 8 rooms, which means the hotel is unlikely to feel crowded. All the rooms are enormous & unusually light & airy; they feature AC, TV, DVD, phone, safe, minibar, balcony/terrace & free Wi-Fi. Butler service is available in all suites. There are 3 impressive restaurants on site, including the excellent Gin'Ja (page 162). Diners also have access to all restaurants within Domaine de Bel Ombre (including those at Heritage Awali & Château de Bel Ombre), making a total of 12 restaurants. Don't miss the sophisticated Cavendish Bar, complete with pianist, cigar lounge & reading area. The facilities are first class: tennis, gym, extensive watersports, kitesurfing & kids' club.

The spa is beautiful, with a gorgeous, bright-blue vitality pool at its centre. Rates include green fees for the Heritage Golf Club (page 83). Opposite the hotel is the Frédérica Nature Reserve, with hiking, 4x4 & quad biking available (page 164). The neighbouring C Beach Club is a trendy, modern restaurant, bar & pool on the beach. **$$$$**

✳ 🏠 Outrigger Mauritius Beach Resort
[152 C4] (181 rooms) Allée des Cocotiers, Bel Ombre; ☎623 5000; e resa.mauritius@outrigger-mu-com; www.outrigger.com. On a quiet, unspoilt stretch of beach; there are no neighbouring hotels to the east of this one & you are likely to have the beach to yourself if you head in that direction. The resort has an atmosphere of grandeur with Arabian-inspired architecture in parts, including in the extravagant spa. The rooms & suites all face the sea, are decorated in relaxing, neutral tones & have all the facilities you would expect in a 5-star, including gorgeous oversized baths & free Wi-Fi. It has a romantic feel & is ideal for a wedding or honeymoon, but the hotel is also family friendly – there are family rooms & a kids' club. One of my favourite features of the resort is the solarium at the spa; a rooftop circular pool sits within a circular rock wall which frames the sky above. There are 3 restaurants; Willie's Rum & Crab Shack on the beach pairs crab dishes with rums. The extensive facilities include 4 pools, tennis courts, plenty of free watersports, dive centre & gym. The Plantation Club is a VIP area with its own restaurant (page 162), bar & pool. During the day it is reserved for guests staying in club rooms, suites & villas; it is open to all for dinner. The service throughout the resort is exceptional. It is well designed & spread out, so it is unlikely to feel crowded even if it is full. Interestingly, it is the only 5-star on the island not to have a dress code in the restaurants, because the emphasis is on relaxation. **$$$$**

🏠 So Sofitel [152 C4] (92 rooms) Coastal Rd, Bel Ombre; ☎605 5800; e h6707@sofitel.com; www. sofitel-so-mauritius.com. The 84 suites & 8 villas are within an Integrated Resort Scheme, where foreigners can buy luxury villas. The hotel opened in 2011; it has a completely modern, urban décor. Rooms look like the London flat of a 20-something banker, rather than evoking tropical Mauritius. One drawback of the rooms is that the only bath in the suites is outside – lovely in good weather but this part of the coast tends to be rather windy. On the plus side, the beds are exceptionally comfortable.

There are 2 restaurants, 2 bars, an attractive pool, small spa, gym & kids' club. $$$$

⌂ **Tamassa** [152 C4] (214 rooms) Coastal Rd, Bel Ombre; ☏ 603 7300; e reservation@luxislandresorts.com; www.tamassaresort.com. A hotel designed to appeal to a young clientele, with a trendy, modern feel, an emphasis on sport & a party atmosphere. The architecture is not to everyone's taste, being dominated by fairly charmless red-roofed buildings reminiscent of a Spanish resort village. Rooms face the sea & are equipped with AC, TV, phone, Wi-Fi, minibar, safe & balcony/terrace. There are 2 restaurants, 3 pools, a spa, watersports, a dive centre, tennis, a nightclub, kids' club & teenagers' club. Golf is available at the nearby Heritage Golf Club. $$$$

✕ WHERE TO EAT

⁕ ✕ **Château de Bel Ombre** [152 B3] Bel Ombre; ☏ 623 5620; www.domainedebelombre. mu; ⏱ for dinner Mon–Sat. Cuisine: European, Creole. Creative cuisine in the refined setting of the beautifully restored chateau, which dates from the early 1800s & overlooks attractive gardens & the golf course. Tables are on the veranda or inside. The menu is extensive & uses produce, in particular game, from the estate. The service is exceptional. Perfect for a special occasion. Reservation recommended. $$$$$

⁕ ✕ **Gin'ja** [152 C4] Le Telfair Hotel, Bel Ombre; ☏ 601 5500; ⏱ for lunch & dinner daily. Cuisine: Asian, seafood. A stylish, modern restaurant overlooking the ocean. Sophisticated, exotic cuisine showcasing Asian flavours. Superb sashimi & duck dishes. The presentation is beautiful & the service is very attentive. Reservation recommended. $$$$$

⁕ ✕ **Plantation Club** [152 C4] Outrigger Mauritius Beach Resort, Bel Ombre; ☏ 623 5000; ⏱ for dinner daily. Cuisine: Creole, European. A plantation-style building houses this fine-dining restaurant & bar around a central courtyard with pool. The chef takes traditional Mauritian dishes & gives them an incredible twist, for instance *dhal puri* with *foie gras*, quail biryani & local venison with chocolate sauce. The desserts are equally imaginative, such as the 'hot & cold' where traditional hot *rasgulla* is served within a ball of ice. The sommelier has a diverse selection of wines from which to recommend a choice, including many from Australia & New Zealand. The wall of the tea library is filled with shelves of exotic tea. $$$$$

✕ **Mo Filaos** Coastal Rd, Baie du Cap; ☏ 796 6160; ⏱ 11.00–22.00 Tue–Sun. Cuisine: Chinese, seafood. A neat little restaurant in this tiny village, overlooking the park & ocean. $$

WHAT TO DO IN SOUTHERN MAURITIUS

MARKET Mahébourg ⁕ has a market every morning from 06.00, but the big one is the 'foire de Mahébourg', which takes place every Monday morning. It's near the bus station, between Rue de la Colonie and Rue de Labourdonnais. Outside under shade sails are row upon row of stalls selling household goods, clothing and flawless fresh fruit and vegetables. Inside is more of the same, plus spices and a few handicrafts. Chillies, aubergines and tomatoes provide pops of colour, while the smell of salted fish competes with the smell of incense. Stallholders shout excitedly to attract the attention of local buyers, who come here to stock up on the essentials. While portions of Port Louis market are shamelessly aimed at tourists, the Mahébourg market is more of an authentic locals' market, which also makes it ideal for self-caterers.

ILE DES DEUX COCOS This small sand island off the coast at Blue Bay is run by Lux Island Resorts but is open to residents and non-residents of the company's hotels. A very pleasant day can be spent on the island, lounging on the sand, snorkelling in the bay, taking a glass-bottom boat trip and indulging at the restaurant and bar. If it weren't for the fabulously attentive service, excellent food and luxurious lounge chairs, it would feel as if you were on a desert island. There is a Moroccan-style villa on Ile des Deux Cocos, built in 1920 for the then British governor, who used it for lavish parties. Most visitors opt for a day excursion to the island but you can rent

the two-bedroom villa overnight and have the whole island to yourself. It is also a popular spot for weddings. Thankfully there is a limit to the number of people allowed on the island at any one time, so it doesn't tend to feel crowded. Visits to Ile des Deux Cocos can be booked at Lux Island hotels or through tour operators. A full day (10.00–16.00) on an all-inclusive basis (including boat transfer) costs around Rs2,700 per person. For details, visit www.iledesdeuxcocos.com.

SPORTS

Golf The **Golf du Château** at Bel Ombre is one of the best courses on the island For more information, see page 83.

Horseriding Centre Equestre de Riambel [152 D4] (m *5729 4572; www. centreequestrederiambel.com*) offers rides on the typically deserted beach at Riambel For more information, see pages 84–5.

Scuba diving Several hotels around Blue Bay offer diving. For more information, see pages 86–7.

Sailing/catamaran cruises For details of companies offering cruises and yacht charter in the area, see pages 90–1.

Deep-sea fishing The south is less well known for deep-sea fishing than other areas. For more information, see pages 85–6.

Kitesurfing The wild south coast is popular with kitesurfers. Several of the hotels in the area have kitesurfing schools catering for all levels of experience and ability. For more information, see pages 91–2.

Ziplining, canyoning and other outdoor activities Domaine de Chazal [152 D3] (*Chamouny;* \ *422 3117;* e *reservation@incentivepartnersltd.com; www. chazalecotourismmauritius.com*) has a circuit of ziplines over Rivière des Galets, ranging from 60m to 250m in length. You can stop for a swim at the base of a waterfall during the circuit and have a Creole meal at the end. Canyoning, 4x4 tours and hiking are also available. There is a restaurant on site serving food prepared using ingredients produced on the property. For more information, see pages 92–3.

NATURE RESERVES

Ile aux Aigrettes ✳ [153 H2] (*Excursions arranged directly with the Mauritian Wildlife Foundation, via tour operators or your hotel;* \ *631 2396 or* e *reservation@ mauritian-wildlife.org (reservations); www.mauritian-wildlife.org; admission adult/ child Rs800/400*) This coral islet is a nature reserve managed by the Mauritian Wildlife Foundation (MWF). Conservationists are working to restore it to its original state, by clearing exotic species of plants and replacing them with native ones. Endangered endemic birds and reptiles have been re-introduced to the island which is a safe haven for them away from introduced species such as rats, cats and monkeys which prey upon their young. Visitors have a good chance of spotting rare pink pigeons, olive white-eyes, Mauritius fodies, Gunther's geckos and Telfair's skinks as well as discovering fascinating plants, giant Aldabra tortoises roaming free in the wild and cannons left by the British after World War II.

The tour starts with a short boat trip to the island, leaving from Pointe Jérome, about 500m south of Le Preskil Hotel at Blue Bay. One of the MWF rangers will

7

take you on a guided tour of the island and talk you through the flora, fauna and history. Being a coral island, it is very hot so remember to take a hat, water and mosquito repellent with you. There is a small exhibition on the extinct fauna of the Mascarenes, to highlight what has been lost already from the islands and the importance of the MWF conservation work (for more information, see pages 80–1).

Tours start at 09.30, 10.00, 10.30 and 13.30, 14.00 and 14.30 (mornings only on Sundays) and last about 2 hours. It is money well spent as not only is the tour a fascinating insight into what the coastal forests of Mauritius would have looked like around 400 years ago, but part of the tour fee goes directly towards the continuation of MWF's work. There is also a small shop on the island, where the money you spend benefits MWF's conservation projects.

Vallée de Ferney Forest & Wildlife Reserve [153 G1] (*Ferney;* ✆ *729 1080;* e *lavalleedeferney@intnet.mu; www.valleedeferney.com;* ⊕ *09.00–16.00 daily; hiking (3km) adult/child non-guided Rs345/207, guided Rs750/375; 4x4 (1 hr) adult/child Rs1,280/640, with lunch Rs1,900/950*) A 200ha reserve with conservation at the heart of everything it does. It is an initiative of the government and a not-for-profit organisation, so by visiting you are doing your bit to contribute to the conservation efforts. The team is working to restore native forest and eradicate invasive species, such as traveller's palm and goyavier. The visitor's centre has informative exhibits on the flora and fauna of the area. This is part of the reserve's important educational role, teaching Mauritian youngsters about the importance of protecting the local environment.

Visitors can hike around the reserve with or without a guide; guided tours (on reservation) depart at 10.00 and 14.00. The guides are knowledgeable and really enhance the experience as they explain the plant and animal life, including the detrimental effects of the various invasive plant species. 4x4 tours are on reservation. Keen-eyed visitors have a chance of seeing tropic birds, olive-white eyes, Mauritius fodies, Mauritius kestrels and pink pigeons. Every day at 12.00 the staff feed a kestrel family so visitors can see them close up. A former hunting lodge has been converted into a rustic restaurant serving Creole cuisine and specialising in game. You can also taste coffee grown on site, and there is a small exhibition on the history of coffee on the island. There is also a restaurant on the coast, La Falaise Rouge. Bring sturdy shoes and mosquito repellent.

Frédérica Nature Reserve [152 C3] (*Bel Ombre;* ✆ *623 5615;* e *frederica@ domainedebelombre.mu; www.domainedebelombre.mu*) A nature reserve (and deer farm) of 1,300ha bordering the Black River Gorges National Park, and which offers attractive scenery and the opportunity to see deer, fruit bats, monkeys and native plants. The approach is via the estate's sugarcane fields before you climb up into the reserve, which is largely grassland with the odd wooded area and waterfall. The area is managed in conjunction with the Mauritian Wildlife Foundation (MWF) and guided tours with MWF staff can be arranged. The MWF has installed nest boxes for native birds and is attempting to regenerate the vegetation within specific areas by planting endemic and indigenous species. If you are particularly lucky you may see a Mauritius kestrel or echo parakeet. Visitors can explore the area via guided hiking, quad biking, 4x4 buggy, Segway and 4x4 tours; commentary on the flora and fauna is provided. Photo safaris are a new addition to the programme. The reserve is also used for hunting, principally deer, but pheasants have been introduced recently.

Bookings for all activities can be made through most tour operators, preferably two–three days in advance. Long trousers are recommended for quad biking, and

proper shoes. The following minimum age requirements apply: 18 years for a double quad bike, 16 years for a single quad bike, 12 years for a quad-bike passenger.

WHAT TO SEE IN SOUTHERN MAURITIUS

FREDERICK HENDRIK MUSEUM [153 H1] (*Vieux Grand Port;* ☎ *634 4319;* ⊕ *09.00–16.00 Mon, Tue, Thu, Fri, Sat, 09.00–12.00 Sun, closed public holidays; admission free*) This small museum on the site of the first Dutch settlement charts the history of the Dutch on the island. Finds from archaeological digs in the area illustrate the story. In the grounds are the remains of the first Dutch settlement, Mauritius's earliest colonial structures, and French buildings constructed on top of the original Dutch ones. The ruined buildings you see today were the bakery (closest to the sea) and a store/prison (near the road). Just south of the museum is a tower known as the Tour des Hollandais, the Tower of the Dutch, used as a vantage point to monitor the coast.

THE NATIONAL HISTORY MUSEUM [153 G2] (*Royal Rd, Mahébourg;* ☎ *631 9329;* ⊕ *09.00–16.00 Mon, Wed–Sat, 09.00–12.00 Sun & public holidays; admission free*) On the main road just south of Mahébourg is the French colonial mansion built in 1722, which houses the museum formerly known as the Mahébourg Naval and Historical Museum. It is here that, in 1810, wounded British and French naval commanders, Willoughby and Duperré, were brought for medical treatment. The battle is described in the museum, which contains relics from numerous ships that have been wrecked off Mauritius over the years, including *Le Saint Géran*. The tragedy was the inspiration for the love story *Paul et Virginie*, by Bernardin de St Pierre. Paul attempts to save his beloved but, for the sake of modesty, she refuses to remove her heavy clothing and is drowned. Accounts of the shipwreck tell of other women making the same terminal decision. As well as naval history, the museum has exhibitions on the island's history in general, including some evocative pictures from the Dutch, French and British periods and portraits of the island's key historical figures, such as Prince Mauritius of Nassau and Mahé de Labourdonnais. The displays on the British period are upstairs and include the abolition of slavery.

In the grounds of the museum are the wooden huts of the **Village Artisanal**. The idea is that local artisans can be seen at work but sadly the huts are often empty; a range of handicrafts is on sale.

BISCUTERIE H RAULT (BISCUIT FACTORY) ✳ [153 G1] (*Mahébourg;* ☎ *631 9559;* e *biscuit.manioc@orange.mu; www.biscuitmanioc.com;* ⊕ *09.00–15.00 Mon–Fri; admission adult/child Rs200/140 with tasting*) Quaint, quirky and well worth a visit. Since 1870, this small, family-run business has been producing biscuits made from manioc (a root vegetable, which looks rather like a sweet potato). The business is now in the hands of the fourth generation of the family. A fascinating guided tour explains the process from raw vegetable to finished biscuit. The 11 staff still do everything by hand, wearing delightfully old-fashioned, apricot-coloured bonnets and aprons. The manioc is ground down to a powder, and weighed on a fabulous set of scales made in Liverpool, UK, in 1869. The biscuits are cooked over burning sugarcane leaves, as they have been for well over a century. The tour culminates in a tasting of the biscuits in various flavours – chocolate, coconut, custard, star anise and cinnamon. They are gluten-free and while they may seem quite dry compared with your average biscuit, it is easy to get a taste for them served with a cup of vanilla tea. If you want to stock up, they are very reasonable and start from Rs65 per pack. The factory is about 1km north of Mahébourg: after the Cavendish Bridge

follow the brown tourist attraction signs depicting a factory (don't be put off by the narrow residential streets lined with corrugated iron).

LE SOUFFLEUR [153 F3] (⊕ *06.00–18.00 Mon–Fri, 07.00–12.00 Sat; admission free*) Le Souffleur is about 15km south of Mahébourg near the village of L'Escalier. The sea used to spout spectacularly from this blowhole at high tide. Erosion has deprived it of the power it had 150 years ago when a writer remarked that 'it roared furiously to a height of fully sixty feet', though it still roars a little when the tide is high, and more so when the seas are rough. It is signed from L'Escalier, and takes you along a rough road through the sugarcane fields of the Omnicane estate best suited to a 4x4.

LA VANILLE RESERVE DES MASCAREIGNES [153 E3] (*Senneville, Rivière des Anguilles;* \ *626 2503;* e *crocpark@intnet.mu; www.lavanille-reserve.com;* ⊕ *09.30–17.00 daily; admission adult/child Rs395/225 weekdays, Rs225/100 weekends & public holidays*) Located just south of the town of Rivière des Anguilles, the park was created in 1985 by an Australian zoologist as a crocodile farm. Nile crocodiles are still bred here for their skins (there are some 2,000 of them) but the park has grown into a mini zoo with macaques (*Macaca fascicularis*), iguanas, deer, wild boar and freshwater fish. A favourite with visitors are the giant Aldabra tortoises (*Geochelone gigantea*), which roam in a large open space where visitors can walk freely amongst them. Visitors can also walk through the Rodrigues fruit bat (*Pteropus rodericensis*) enclosure. In the insectarium over 23,000 species of butterflies and beetles are displayed. The cool, shady walkways through the lush forest make this an ideal excursion on a hot day. Because spraying would upset the ecology, there are mosquitoes too, but repellent can be bought at the shop, which also sells crocodile-skin goods. There is a licensed restaurant, where crocodile meat is the main feature of the menu. The meat comes from the tail of three-year-old crocodiles and is part of the commercial side of the park.

Feeding time (see the crocs leap out of the water for chicken carcasses) is on Wednesday and Saturday at 11.30. Guided tours are on the hour, every hour and included in the entry fee. Some of the park is wheelchair-accessible, including the tortoise area. As indicated above, admission is cheaper on weekends but it tends to be busier then.

SOOKDEO BISSOONDOYAL MEMORIAL MUSEUM [153 E3] (*Royal Rd, Tyack, Rivière des Anguilles;* \ *626 3732; www.mauritiusmuseumscouncil.com;* ⊕ *09.00–16.00 Mon, Tue, Thu, Fri; admission free*) Sookdeo Bissoondoyal was a prominent figure in Mauritian politics until his death in 1977 and was a key figure during the transition to independence in 1968. The house where he was born has been made into a small museum telling the story of his life.

ROBERT EDWARD HART MEMORIAL MUSEUM [152 D4] (*Autard St, Souillac;* \ *625 6101;* ⊕ *09.00–16.00 Mon & Wed–Fri, 09.00–12.00 Sat; admission free*) This museum on the site of Hart's home offers the visitor a very personal insight into the life and work of this well-known Mauritian poet. In 2002, the original house was destroyed for safety reasons and a replica built in its place. The interior has been left, as far as possible, as it was when Hart died. Quotes from Hart's work are displayed, as are personal belongings such as photographs, a pith helmet, his OBE (1949) and his *Légion d'honneur* (1950). The museum is next to Telfair Gardens; follow the signs and don't be put off by the route through narrow residential streets.

BOIS CHERI TEA FACTORY ✳ [153 E2] (*Bois Chéri, Grand Bois;* ☎ *507 0216;* ⏰ *08.30–16.30 Mon–Fri, 08.30–14.30 Sat; factory tour, museum plus tea tasting adult/child Rs500/250; museum & tea tasting Rs250/125; tea tasting only Rs200/ Rs100*) This working tea factory turns 40 tonnes of tea leaves into ten tonnes of tea per day. Guided tours (which start at 09.30) take you through the whole process, from the drying of the leaves when they are first received through to the flavouring of the tea and finally the packaging. Much of the machinery is wonderfully basic and old fashioned but still does the job. It is certainly worth doing the factory tour when it is operating, but be warned that the machinery is noisy. Tours take place every 30 minutes in the mornings and in winter the factory usually operates only on a Wednesday, due to the reduced harvest. The main harvest season is October to March, and 80% of the picking is done by hand because only the young leaves are suitable.

7

MEHENDI (HENNA TATTOOING)

The art of *mehendi*, or henna tattooing, has been practised for thousands of years and is very much a part of Hindu and Muslim tradition, particularly in marriage ceremonies. Immigrants to Mauritius brought their tradition and skills with them, and visitors to the island are likely to see young Mauritian women with their hands and feet beautifully decorated. There is now a growing number of skilled henna artists offering *mehendi* to tourists wanting to follow the trend set by numerous celebrities, such as Madonna and Naomi Campbell.

The origins of *mehendi* are unclear, although it is believed to have originated in Mesopotamia before being introduced to India in the 12th century. The leaves of the henna bush (*Lawsonia inermis*) are harvested, then dried and crushed to make a fine powder. It is then mixed with rosewater or essential oils, cloves and water to make a paste. The henna paste seen in Mauritius uses plants grown on the island. The henna artist applies the paste to the skin in intricate patterns. After a few hours the paste crumbles away, leaving the skin temporarily stained in a shade between orange and brown. The tattoo gradually fades and usually disappears completely between one and three weeks later. The trick to prolonging the life of the tattoo is to ensure the paste remains moist while on the skin. This is done by spraying it with water or a mixture of lemon juice and sugar.

Mehendi is typically applied to the hands and feet and almost any design can be drawn by a skilled henna artist. Indian and Pakistani designs are often very ornate, giving the appearance of a lace glove or stocking. They traditionally reflect nature and include leaves, flowers and birds. Middle Eastern designs are mostly made up of floral patterns, while north African *mehendi* is typified by geometric shapes. Today these styles are often mixed, and some artists now use Chinese and Celtic symbols.

For weddings, it is traditional for the female friends and family of the bride-to-be to spend several hours, or even days, preparing her *mehendi* and discussing the forthcoming marriage. The *mehendi* is intended to charm and seduce the bridegroom, and in Hindu tradition his initials may be hidden among the designs for him to find on the wedding night.

Mehendi can be organised via many hotels, and there are often artists at markets and shopping centres. Prices range from Rs300 to Rs5,000 depending on the size and intricacy of the design.

To the right of reception is a museum which charts the history of tea and exhibits various machines which have become obsolete over the 115 years that the factory has been in production. A short drive brings you to a wooden building overlooking a lake and tea bushes, where you can taste a number of the teas produced in the factory, such as vanilla (my favourite), coconut and mint flavours. There is also a good restaurant here with views to the coast (page 159). Packets of tea are on sale in the shop and make a good souvenir or gift.

Tour buses seem to arrive around 11.00 and it can get busy at this time. The factory is closed on Sundays and public holidays but the restaurant, museum and tea tasting are open daily. It may be wise to phone ahead.

LE SAINT AUBIN ✳ (*Rivière des Anguilles;* \ *625 1513;* e *lesaintaubin@intnet. mu;* ⊕ *09.00–17.00 Mon–Sat; admission adult/child Rs500/250; admission & lunch Rs1,300/650*) At the heart of a sugar estate is a picturesque colonial house, built in 1819 using wood taken from ships. Visitors can learn about some of the island's main agricultural and horticultural activities here: vanilla, sugar, rum and anthurium production.

The production of vanilla is immensely complicated and the short video and exhibits on the processes involved are fascinating – in total it takes around 18 months to produce the vanilla pods we see in our supermarkets, which perhaps explains why it is so expensive. The method of pollination by hand was discovered by a slave on neighbouring Réunion Island and allowed the vanilla orchid, which is native to Mexico, to be grown outside that country.

A sugar factory was built here in 2011, around the remains of the old sugar factory of 1819; an original square chimney survives and has been incorporated into the new factory. The sugar is used to produce rum, which you can taste and buy on site. Tours of the factory and the distillery explain the production of sugar and rum.

Children are catered for with a playground and a 'mini farm', which is home to chickens, deer, peacocks and monkeys.

The shop sells souvenirs, including vanilla, sugar, rum and tea. Upstairs in the main house is a small museum containing old photographs of the house and pictures of historic ships. It is here that you can see how ships' timbers were used to construct the house in 1819; the centre of the spiral staircase was the mast of a wrecked vessel and the beams also came from ships. The house was moved to its present site in 1970, further away from the factory. The restaurant here is excellent (page 159) and accommodation is available in a cottage on the estate (page 158).

LA ROUTE DU THE (THE TEA ROUTE) \ *626 1513;* e *lesaintaubin@ intnet.mu; www.larouteduthe.mu; adult/child Rs2,000/1,000, including lunch*) A combined tour, allowing you to visit three sites linked to the Bois Chéri Tea Estate. Unless you are on an organised tour, transport is not provided between the three points and you must make your own way. The route begins at Domaine des Aubineaux near Curepipe, a colonial mansion built in 1872 as the home of the estate's owner. The interior contains furniture and photographs from the period. The second stop is Bois Chéri Tea Factory for a guided tour and tasting (page 167). Finally, you visit Le Saint Aubin, where lunch is provided (see above). All three are interesting sites and the obvious advantage of the combined tour is that it works out cheaper than visiting the three separately.

LA VALLEE DES COULEURS [152 D3] (*Mare Anguilles, Chamouny;* m *5471 8666;* e *info@lavalleedescouleurs.com; www.lavalleedescouleurs.com;* ⊕ *08.30–17.30*

daily; adult/child rs300/150) About 10km north of Souillac, this activity centre has been created around a multi-coloured exposed area of earth, similar to the Seven Coloured Earths of Chamarel. It is less visited than Chamarel and claims to have 23 colours of earth as opposed to seven. It was discovered in 1998 when the landowners were ripping up their tea bushes to plant sugarcane. It lies within a 450 acres, part of which is forested, and which has good views of the coast. A walking circuit takes you past areas of endemic plants, a few animals (deer, ducks, tortoises, etc) and waterfalls, as well as the coloured earth. Two of the six waterfalls are suitable for swimming. A small geology museum explains the volcanic origins of Mauritius, and of the coloured earth, which was essentially caused by deposits of volcanic ash. Quad biking (*Rs2,300 for 1hr*) and ziplining (*Rs1,975 for 4 lines*) are available for the energetic. There is a café and a restaurant on site, and a good play area for children.

SPIRITUAL CENTRE OF RIAMBEL – THE VORTEX [152 D4] (*Coastal Rd, Riambel;*
m *5736 9038;* e *infos@lumieresdelaudela.com; www.lumieresdelaudela.com;* ⏀ *09.00–17.00; admission free*) The vortex is signed from the main road. It is reputed to be one of 14 energy centres on earth which have healing powers for body and spirit. The vortex is marked by a ring of stones and around it are areas set aside for each of the body's chakras. People come here to meditate and restore their inner balance. It is recommended that you spend around 20 minutes in the centre of the circle, followed by 20–30 minutes in whichever of the little coloured cabins correspond to the chakras you feel need attention. There is usually a volunteer on hand to show you what to do, and a sign explains it too. It gets particularly busy on weekends.

I know people living on Mauritius who swear by the vortex, and it certainly does seem to have a special quality. Whatever your beliefs, devoting time to being still and meditating has to have its benefits.

FOLLOW BRADT

For the latest news, special offers and competitions, subscribe to the Bradt newsletter via the website www.bradtguides.com and follow Bradt on:

f www.facebook.com/BradtTravelGuides
🐦 @BradtGuides
📷 @bradtguides
📌 www.pinterest.com/bradtguides

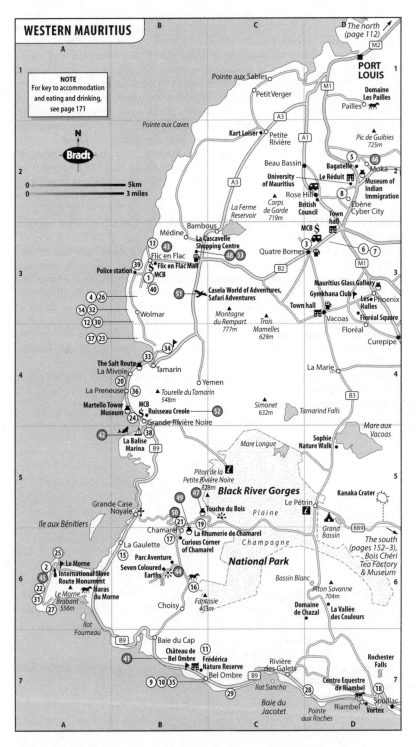

WESTERN MAURITIUS

D *The north* (page 112)

PORT LOUIS

NOTE
For key to accommodation and eating and drinking, see page 171

N

Bradt

0 _____ 5km
0 _____ 3 miles

Pointe aux Sables

Petit Verger

Pointe aux Caves

Kart Loisir • Petite Rivière

Domaine Les Pailles

Pailles

Pic de Guibies 725m

Beau Bassin

Bagatelle

Moka

La Ferme Reservoir

Corps de Garde 719m

University of Mauritius

Rose Hill

Le Réduit

Museum of Indian Immigration

Médine

Bambous

British Council

Ebène Cyber City

La Cascavelle Shopping Centre

Town hall

Flic en Flac

(13) **(43)**

Flic en Flac Mall

(48) **(53)**

Quatre Bornes

MCB $

(3)

(6) **(7)**

Police station **(39)**

(1)

MCB

(40)

(4) **(26)**

(51)

Casela World of Adventures, Safari Adventures

Mauritius Glass Gallery

Gymkhana Club

Les Halles

Phoenix

(14) **(32)**

Wolmar

Montagne du Rempart 777m

Trois Mamelles 629m

Town hall

Floréal Square

(12) **(30)**

Vacoas

Floréal

(37) **(23)**

Curepipe

(33) **(34)**

The Salt Route

La Mivoie

Tamarin

Yemen

La Marie

(20)

La Preneuse **(36)**

Tourelle du Tamarin 548m

Simonet 632m

Tamarind Falls

Martello Tower Museum

MCB $ **(24)**

Ruisseau Creole **(52)**

Mare aux Vacoas

Grande Rivière Noire

(38)

(42)

La Balise Marina

Mare Longue

Sophie Nature Walk

Piton de la Petite Rivière Noire 828m

Black River Gorges

Kanaka Crater

Grande Case Noyale

(49) **(47)**

Ile aux Bénitiers

(50)

Touche du Bois

Plaine

Le Pétrin

Chamarel

(21) **(19)**

La Rhumerie de Chamarel

Grand Bassin

(17)

Curious Corner of Chamarel

Champagne

The south (pages 152–3), Bois Chéri Tea Factory & Museum

La Gaulette

(15)

Parc Aventure

National Park

(25)

Le Morne

Seven Coloured Earths

(44)

(2)

(45)

International Slave Route Monument

Haras du Morne

(16)

Bassin Blanc

Piton Savanne 704m

(22)

Le Morne Brabant 556m

Choisy

Fantasie 403m

Domaine de Chazal

La Vallée des Couleurs

(31)

(27)

Ilot Fourneau

Baie du Cap

Château de Bel Ombre

(11)

Frédérica Nature Reserve

Rivière des Galets

Rochester Falls

(41)

Bel Ombre

(9) **(10)** **(35)**

(29)

Ilot Sancho

(28)

Centre Equestre de Riambel

(18)

Baie du Jacotet

Pointe aux Roches

Riambel

Souillac

Vortex

8

Western Mauritius

The district of Black River covers the west coast of Mauritius, extending from the southwest, by Baie du Cap, northwards to the boundary of Port Louis. It was called Zwarte River by the Dutch and Rivière Noire by the French, who created the district in 1768. The river itself is not black, so the name probably refers to the black rocks of its bed and banks.

The southwest has traditionally been the most 'African' part of the island. Creole lifestyle dominates, with Catholic churches rather than Hindu temples providing the focal point for communities. In the far southwest corner of the island is Le Morne Brabant, a striking, black, rocky mountain towering over the peninsula on which it sits. Runaway slaves took refuge on the mountain and its connections to slavery have led to it being afforded UNESCO World Heritage status.

In recent years, the west of the island has attracted a large number of expats, mostly from South Africa, who live in new developments along the coast. Amidst all the development around Tamarin are some surviving salt pans, which are still operational.

WESTERN MAURITIUS
For listings, see pages 173–7, 178–9 & 179–82 unless otherwise stated

🛏 Where to stay
1 Aanari Hotel & Spa..........B3
2 Dinarobin Hotel
Golf & Spa.....................A6
3 El Monaco (p191)..............D3
4 Escale Vacances...............A3
5 Eureka (p197)...................D2
6 Gold Crest (p191)..............D3
7 Gold Nest (p191)...............D3
8 Hennessy Park (p190)......D2
9 Heritage Awali Golf &
Spa Resort (p160)..............B7
10 Heritage Le Telfair Golf
& Spa Resort (p161)......B7
11 Heritage the Villas
(p160).............................B7
12 Hilton Mauritius
Resort & Spa...................A3
13 Klondike..........................B3
14 La Pirogue.....................A3
15 La Reine Creole............B6
16 La Vieille Cheminée....B6
17 Lakaz Chamarel...........B6
18 Le Rochester (p158).....D7
19 Les Chalets en
Champagne..................B5
20 Les Lataniers Bleus.....B4
21 Les Palmiers..................B5
22 Lux* Le Morne.............A6
23 Maradiva......................A4
24 Marlin Creek
Residence....................B4
25 Paradis Hotel &
Golf Club......................A6
26 Pearle Beach
Resort & Spa.............A3
27 Riu Hotels.....................A6
28 Shanti Maurice (p160).....D7
29 So Sofitel (p161–2)...........C7
30 Sofitel L'Imperial
Resort & Spa..................A3
31 St Regis...........................A6
32 Sugar Beach
Resort & Spa...................A3
33 Tamarin..........................B4
34 Tamarina Golf
Estate & Hotel................B4
35 Tamassa (p162)................B7
36 The Bay...........................B4
37 The Sands Resort...........A4
38 Vanilla House..................B5
39 Villas Caroline................B3
40 West Palm Bed &
Breakfast Inn.................B3

🍴 Where to eat and drink
41 Château de
Bel Ombre (p162)............B7
Citronella Café........(see 32)
Club House at Tamarina
Golf Estate.............(see 34)
42 Coral Tree.....................A5
43 Domaine Anna..............B3
44 Domaine du Cachet.......B6
45 Embafilao......................A6
46 Escale Creole (p197).....D2
Ginger Thai..........(see 4)
47 La Varangue sur
Morne..........................B5
48 Lakaz Cascavelle........B3
49 L'Alchemiste.................B5
50 Le Chamarel................B5
51 Le Mirador.....................B3
Les Coquillages......(see 12)
Les Palmiers............(see 21)
Paul et Virginie.....(see 14)
The Cilantro.............(see 23)
52 The Toaster....................C4
Vanilla Bean............(see 38)
53 Walnut & Thyme.............C3

Western Mauritius

8

171

Tamarin Bay is also known for the dolphins which visit almost every morning, and it is here that the island's dolphin-watching excursions focus their searches.

The west is the driest and sunniest of the island's coasts and it boasts dramatic sunsets and superb beaches, making it a popular weekend escape for Mauritians and holiday destination for foreigners. There is accommodation to suit all budgets, particularly around the growing coastal resort of Flic en Flac. The hotels at Le Morne are predominantly upmarket and it is a beautiful area in which to stay.

The west is the best coast for deep-sea fishing. This is particularly so around the area of Grande Rivière Noire, where the ocean floor drops away to a great depth, attracting large predators to feed on smaller fish.

The Black River Gorges National Park is by far the island's largest nature reserve. For walkers and nature lovers, the park offers spectacular scenery and wildlife. For further details, see pages 195–7.

MORNE BRABANT TO TAMARIN

The sheer cliff of the square-shaped **Morne Brabant** (556m) rises dramatically out of the southern peninsula, dominating the west coast of the island with its looming presence. Runaway slaves fled to Le Morne during the 18th and early 19th centuries, taking refuge in its caves. On 1 February 1835, fearing that the police party sent to tell them slavery was abolished had come to capture them, the slaves threw themselves off the summit to their deaths. A sadness haunts the mountain still. A community for freed slaves was set up at the southern foot of Le Morne but was later moved to the present location of Le Morne village. Their descendants still live there today and regard Le Morne, which came to symbolise the suffering of the island's slaves, as sacred. In 2008 Le Morne was declared a UNESCO World Heritage Site and the following year UNESCO unveiled a memorial at the foot of Le Morne, as part of its Slave Route Project. The **International Slave Route Monument** [170 A6] (⊕ 09.30–16.00 Tue–Sat, 09.30–12.30 Sun) lies just beyond the Dinarobin Hotel, across the road from the public beach. At its centre is a black granite block engraved with the image of a slave, around which are a series of stones and sculptures symbolising the countries from which the slaves came. In front of the memorial is inscribed in Creole, French and English, a verse of the poem 'Le Morne. Territoire Marron!' by Sedley Assone:

> There were hundreds of them, but my people the maroons chose the kiss of death over the chains of slavery. Never must we forget their noble deed, written in the pages of history for the sake of humanity.

Large hotels and some upmarket homes now lie at the foot of Le Morne; it is a breathtaking setting between the austere cliff and the gentle beaches. Between the hotels, there is access to the pleasant public beach and a large, shallow lagoon. On weekends families of Mauritians come here to picnic and it is popular with kitesurfers. There is a small complex of upmarket shops and an ATM opposite Paradis Hotel.

The foothills of the island's highest mountain, **Piton de la Petite Rivière Noire** (Little Black River Mountain – 828m), reach down to the road near **La Gaulette**. The village has undergone a complete change of image in recent years, from shabby and run-down to super-trendy kitesurfing haunt. Kitesurfing shops and new bars seemed to pop up almost overnight. By the coastal road at Petite Rivière Noire is an adorable, tiny, thatched chapel with outdoor pews, **Notre Dame de Fatima**.

A French soldier called Noyale retired to the area on the coast now known as **Case Noyale**. He was renowned for his hospitality and built a resthouse at **Petite Case Noyale**, but was murdered by runaway slaves. Today, it is a poor area of the island and humble corrugated iron and concrete dwellings are crammed in between the road and the sea, a stark contrast to the large, wealthy expat communities further north on this coast. There is a turning next to the church at **Grande Case Noyale** [170 B5] that leads to **Chamarel** and into the **Black River Gorges National Park** [170 C5/6] (pages 195–7). Staying on the coast road, mountains are the main feature of the landscape on the drive towards Port Louis. Beyond the Black River mountain range is **Simonet** (632m), in the Vacoas mountain range, overlooking the plain between Montagne du Rempart and Yemen to the sea at Tamarin. By the coast is **Tourelle du Tamarin** (548m), but it is the profiles of the upturned, udder-like **Trois Mamelles** (629m) and the mini Matterhorn, **Montagne du Rempart** (777m), that really catch the eye.

Grande Rivière Noire is the departure point for catamaran cruises, dolphin-watching trips and deep-sea fishing. Some of the operators now depart from the newly constructed **La Balise Marina** (*www.labalisemarina.com*), a luxurious development of waterfront apartments and offices with their own moorings.

Between Grande Rivière Noire and Tamarin is the **Ruisseau Creole** shopping centre, with over 50 shops and numerous restaurants (page 183). The modern shopping centres and housing developments in the area are indicative of the recent influx of foreigners, particularly South Africans.

The road to **Tamarin** runs beside salt pans, where seawater flows through a series of pools and, via evaporation, produces salt. Salt pans were introduced to Mauritius during French rule (1715–1810) and the ones you see here have been producing salt for over 175 years. In the early morning, ladies can be seen shovelling the salt and carrying it on their heads to the salt stores. If you think they look too heavily dressed for the weather, in their wellington boots and long skirts, the clothing is necessary to protect their skin from the salt. Guided tours explaining salt production are available at **The Salt Route** (see page 184).

Dolphins are regular visitors to the deep bay at Tamarin, usually in the mornings when they spend several hours playing here. The waters here are popular with **surfers** too as the beach is one of few on the island to have decent waves. The sand is not the perfect shade that it is elsewhere on the island: it is a rather grubby grey-brown, but it is a very popular beach with locals nonetheless.

 WHERE TO STAY

Luxury

☀ 🏠 **Dinarobin Hotel Golf & Spa** [170 A6] (175 rooms) Le Morne Peninsula; ☎ 401 4900; e dinarobin@bchot.com; www.dinarobin-hotel. com. A brilliantly designed all-suite Beachcomber hotel in a stunning setting at the foot of Le Morne & on a good, long stretch of beach. The suites are arranged in crescents of 2-storey thatched buildings, each with a pool at the centre, which means you can always find a peaceful spot in which to sunbathe or swim. There is also an adult-only crescent. For families & groups there are 3 villas with 4 bedrooms. The emphasis is on relaxation & luxury. The junior suites have a light, airy bedroom & sitting area, plus a huge bathroom. The senior suites have a separate

sitting room with dining area. All suites have a large covered veranda looking out to sea. Rooms have everything you'd expect from a top hotel, including Wi-Fi. There are 4 excellent restaurants, tennis & a fitness centre. There is a superb Clarins spa, which also offers Ayurvedic treatments. If the calm here becomes too much you can head next door to the livelier Paradis & use the facilities or eat at one of the restaurants; there is a regular shuttle service. Watersports take place here & at Paradis. Guests have access (payable) to the Paradis Golf Academy, Heritage Golf Club & the course at Tamarina Golf Estate. **$$$$$**

🏠 **Paradis Hotel & Golf Club** [170 A6] (285 rooms, 26 villas) Le Morne Peninsula;

401 5050; e paradis@bchot.com; www.paradis-hotel.com. This huge Beachcomber resort boasts an 18-hole golf course, deep-sea fishing, dive centre & 4 restaurants. The hotel is fronted by a beautiful beach & lagoon, & uses lots of traditional materials, like wood & thatch. Rooms have the usual upmarket facilities & are particularly spacious; there are also 13 luxury villas. Sports are free, except golf, scuba diving, deep-sea fishing & mountain biking. Golf is big here: it has its own golf academy. The tennis facilities are exceptional – 6 floodlit courts. There are 4 restaurants, a spa & kids' club. Guests can use many of the facilities, including the restaurants, at the Dinarobin Hotel. Great for families & sports enthusiasts. **$$$$$**

🏠 **St Regis** [170 A6] (172 rooms) Le Morne Peninsula; ☎ 403 9000; e stregismauritius@stregis.com; www.stregismauritius.com. A relatively new luxury hotel designed to evoke a bygone, colonial era. Beautifully decorated, incredibly spacious, sea-facing suites & villas with all the bells & whistles, including 24hr butler service. There are 6 upmarket restaurants, a spa, pool, gym, tennis, watersports, including kitesurfing, & everything else you would expect from a luxury hotel. The hotel prides itself on its exceptional service. **$$$$$**

Upmarket

🏠 **Lux* Le Morne** [170 A6] (149 rooms) Le Morne Peninsula; ☎ 401 4000; e reservation@luxislandresorts.com; www.luxislandresorts.com. Popular hotel on a beautiful stretch of beach. Rooms & suites are in 2-storey colonial-style villas. They are nicely decorated with AC, TV, minibar, safe, free Wi-Fi & sea-facing balcony/terrace. There are 3 restaurants, 3 bars, 4 pools, a spa, numerous free watersports, a dive centre, gym & tennis courts. There are both kids' & teenagers' clubs. Plenty of entertainment & activities. **$$$$**

🏠 **Riu Hotels: Coral** [170 A6] (166 rooms), **Creole** (147 rooms), **Le Morne** (218 rooms); ☎ 650 4200; www.riu.com. Riu has 3 4-star all-inclusive hotels on the peninsula & guests at each hotel can use the facilities at the other Riu properties. Creole & Le Morne are on the same site. Creole is a lively, family-friendly hotel with regular evening entertainment, a nightclub & karaoke. Le Morne is an adult-only hotel designed to be a quieter alternative. Nearby Coral is also family friendly. The rooms in each are generally plain, equipped with AC, TV, phone, safe & minibar. Only Le Morne has

free Wi-Fi in the rooms; at the others it is payable. Between the 3 hotels there is a choice of restaurants, although I have heard plenty of reports of the food being rather hit & miss. Facilities on site include pools, spa, watersports & a dive centre. The hotels are in a very windy spot popular for kitesurfing & windsurfing, so the majority of guests come for those activities. The gardens are frequently littered with their equipment. When occupancy is low the hotels target Mauritians for weekend breaks, which means they can get crowded & chaotic. If windsurfing & kitesurfing are not the focus of your holiday, there are better options in less windy spots. **$$$$**

Mid range

🏠 **Les Lataniers Bleus** [170 B4] (3 villas, 2 rooms) La Mivoie, Rivière Noire; ☎ 483 6541; e latableu@intnet.mu; www.leslataniersbleus.com. A good budget-style option but priced at the bottom end of mid-range. The clean, simple villas, each with 2 to 5 bedrooms, are set in pretty gardens. You can either rent the whole villa for self-catering, or just 1 en-suite bedroom. It is on a pretty beach & there are shops within walking distance. Villas have a living room, kitchen, dining area, AC, TV & phone. The 2 Frangipanes rooms have en suite, minibar & kettle but no kitchenette. There is a pool, Wi-Fi access & a good table d'hôte restaurant. **$$$**

🏠 **Tamarina Golf Estate & Hotel** [170 B4] (50 rooms) Tamarin Bay; ☎ 401 8500; e resa@tamarinahotel.com; www.tamarinahotel.com. A small 4-star hotel on the beach at Tamarin Bay & within the Tamarina Golf Estate. The beach is popular with locals & dolphins are often seen in the bay, which is where most of the island's dolphin-watching excursions occur (page 91). Rooms are nicely furnished with AC, TV, safe, balcony/terrace & en suite (shower but no bath). The hotel is not designed to accommodate young children – there are no communicating rooms, no extra bed in the rooms & no kids' club. As well as the 18-hole championship golf course, there are 2 restaurants, 4 pools & massage is available in the small spa. The hotel's AI package includes 1 green fee or spa treatment per day, & entrance to Casela each day. **$$$**

🏠 **Tamarin Hotel** [170 B4] (71 rooms) Tamarin; ☎ 483 6927; e resaweb@hoteltamarin.com; www.hoteltamarin.com. Located across

the road from Tamarin Public Beach & in the village. The hotel seems to have been around since the 1970s & still sports décor from that area, so prepare to be amazed by colours you never knew existed. Accommodation is in unattractive, colourful concrete boxes. Rooms have en-suite facilities, AC, phone, safe & balcony/terrace. Wi-Fi is free. There is a restaurant, a pool & a kids' club, but a lack of secure parking. The hotel is known for its surfing & other watersports are available nearby (payable). When visited in 2015 the hotel was in need of extensive refurbishment, but new management had just taken over & we were told refurbishment was planned. **$$$**

🏠 **The Bay Hotel** [170 B4] (16 rooms) Cocotiers Av, La Preneuse; 483 7042; e thebayhotel@intnet.mu; www.thebay.mu. A lovely little hotel featuring traditional thatched buildings, on the beach at La Preneuse. Rooms are modern, clean, nicely decorated & have AC, TV, phone, safe, Wi-Fi (free) & minibar. Superior rooms & suites face the sea & have tea/coffee facilities & balcony/terrace. The public areas have a fresh, beachy feel; there is an open-air restaurant overlooking the pool & the sea. Massages & natural therapies are available. There are a few watersports available at a fee. **$$$**

Budget

🏠 **La Reine Creole** [170 B6] (4 rooms) 103 Rue des Manguiers, La Gaulette; 451 5558; e info@mauritius-lrc.com; www.mauritius-lrc.com. A small, family-run B&B off the coastal road between Le Morne & La Gaulette. There is 1 double room, 1 twin & 2 studios with kitchenette & balcony. The studios are more appealing than the rooms & have AC. It is by no means flash but is comfortable enough &

reasonably priced. They can prepare lunch & dinner for an additional Rs400/600 pp respectively. **$$**

🏠 **Marlin Creek Residence** [170 B4] (15 rooms) 10 Colonel Dean Av, Rivière Noire; m 5491 9727; e speleca@yahoo.fr; www.marlin-creek.com. Rooms are in a thatched 3-storey building facing the pool & colourful garden. They have a modern feel & are equipped with trendy en suite, AC, TV, safe & minibar. A 3-bedroom self-catering bungalow is also available. Breakfast is served near the pool; there are 2 bars but no restaurant, although there are plenty nearby. Wi-Fi available. Not on the beach but near the marina from where catamaran & deep-sea fishing excursions leave. It would be wise to have a car if staying here so you can get to the beach at Flic en Flac & try the local eateries. Popular with kitesurfers. **$$**

🏠 **Vanilla House** [170 B5] (9 rooms) Coastal Rd, Grand Rivière Noire; 483 6778; www.mauritius-guest-house.com. A well-run guesthouse in a leafy garden on the edge of Grande Rivière Noire. The rooms are very comfortable & furnished in shabby-chic style, with en suite, AC, TV, fridge, microwave, kettle, toaster & free Wi-Fi. Communicating rooms are available for families. There are 2 sitting rooms & a good selection of books; a pool & bicycles are available free of charge. There is a good restaurant serving lunch (page 177), dinner is available on request & is usually cooked on a barbecue by the pool. Breakfast is served on the veranda of your room. It is not on the beach but there are some good beaches within a few km. It is not in the centre of a village either & the emphasis is on peace & quiet rather than entertainment, so it would be handy to have a car if staying here. **$$**

✕ WHERE TO EAT

✕ **Big Willy's** Route du Barachois, Tamarin; 483 7400; ⏱ 14.00–02.00 Tue–Fri, 09.00–02.00 Sat, 11.00–21.00 Sun. Cuisine: Creole, European. A hugely popular pub in a garden setting with a lively nightlife. **$$$$**

✕ **Coral Tree Restaurant** [170 A5] La Balise Marina, Grande Rivière Noire; 483 1111; ⏱ 08.00–23.00 daily. Cuisine: European, international. A trendy, modern restaurant within the La Balise Marina. It overlooks the water & has views of the mountains. There is a pool, well-stocked bar & a big screen for sports fans. **$$$$**

✕ **Al Dente** Ruisseau Creole, Rivière Noire; 483 7919; ⏱ for lunch & dinner daily. Cuisine: Italian, seafood. A good range of dishes, including homemade pasta, & a take-away kiosk for pizza. **$$$**

✳ ✕ **Club House at Tamarina Golf Estate** [170 B4] Tamarin Bay; 401 3006; ⏱ for breakfast & lunch daily. Cuisine: European. The restaurant & bar at Tamarina Golf Club are open to the public & have spectacular views of the surrounding mountains. It's a very peaceful spot. They serve excellent light meals, such as burgers & pizzas. The

seafood pizza with smoked marlin is very tasty. Good value for money. $$$

✗ **Enso Village Walk** La Gaulette; ☎ 451 5907. Cuisine: Creole, European. The kitesurfing crowd

has certainly changed La Gaulette & this trendy restaurant/lounge bar with a young vibe is front & centre of that change. There are pool tables, a simple menu, regular live music & free Wi-Fi. $$$

HIKING LE MORNE BRABANT

Katharine Fahrland

Hiking to the top of the monolithic basalt rock face, so spectacularly positioned on Le Morne Peninsula in the southwest of the island, was the highlight of our visit to Mauritius. While the majority of holidaymakers confine themselves to the luxury resorts and beaches that line the peninsula around the base of the rock, we chose an early-morning start and a dose of sweat to reach the top (556m above sea level). We were rewarded with stunning views of the surrounding ocean, lagoon, coral reef, smaller islands and verdant hills. We are regular runners and hikers, but still found the hike challenging and indeed a bit scary at points – you will find yourself on the edge of a few precipices!

Because the mountain was declared a World Heritage Site by UNESCO on 6 July 2008, and is situated on private property, it is not permitted to hike it independently; we had to engage the services of one of two authorised guide companies (see below). The downside of this is that it will set you back about Rs1,500 per person; the upside is that the knowledgeable local guides will educate you on local flora and fauna (including the rare endemic species *Trochetia boutoniania*, the national flower of Mauritius), island history and local folklore.

As you huff and puff up the steep mountain, the storyteller guides – who effortlessly bound up the rocks like goats – will recount the history of how the peninsula served as a refuge for runaway slaves (known as 'marrons') during the 19th century. According to legend, after slavery was abolished on 1 February 1835, the police sent an expedition to inform the marrons living on Le Morne. The escaped slaves, thinking they would be caught and returned to slavery, committed suicide by jumping off the cliff.

In 2003, archaeologists, anthropologists and historians undertook field work to establish if this legend is true. Three caves were identified, with evidence of human habitation. However, the lack of any source of fresh water on the mountain makes sustained human habitation on the summit unlikely. But the historical literature and oral testimonies do attest to slaves having settled on the plateau of Le Morne Peninsula, where they cultivated crops and raised goats.

The hike is rigorous, so come prepared with hiking boots or trainers, plenty of water, and a small pack in order to keep your hands free – in several parts you scramble over rocks, and in other steep sections your ascent is assisted with a rope. The entire hike takes 3½ to 4 hours, in groups of seven to ten people, departing at 07.00 in the winter (April–October) and 06.00 in the summer (November–March), so you are best off eating a light breakfast beforehand. The pick-up point is at the Paradis Hotel & Golf Club.

Advance bookings are required, and payment can be made in cash during the hike.

Local Spirit Allan Ramalingum; e info@localspirit.mu
Yanature ☎ 5428 1909; e henri@yanature.com; www.trekkingilemaurice.com

✕ Frenchie Café Rivière Noire; ✆ 483 6125; ⊕ for lunch & dinner Tue–Sat. Cuisine: European. Set back from the coastal road but well signed. A large outdoor covered area is furnished with European style. The Sun brunch (11.00–16.00) is popular & costs around Rs600. I have heard mixed reports about the food, however. $$$

✕ La Bonne Chute La Preneuse; ✆ 483 6552; ⊕ for lunch & dinner Mon–Sat. Cuisine: European, Creole, seafood, game. It may not look like much from the outside but this restaurant has a reputation for good food, in particular game & seafood. $$$

✕ Sirokan Coastal Rd, La Gaulette; ✆ 451 5115; ⊕ for lunch & dinner daily. Cuisine: European, seafood, Creole. On the coastal road at the northern end of the village. Unpretentious restaurant serving good-quality, nicely presented food. $$$

✕ Vanilla Bean [170 B5] Vanilla Hse, Coastal Rd, Grande Rivière Noire; ✆ 483 5292; ⊕ 08.30–16.00 Mon–Fri, 08.30–12.00 Sat. Cuisine: European, light meals. A relaxed, modern coffee shop run by a mother & daughter team.

They serve delicious homemade cakes & light lunches, & there are plenty of healthy options, including sugar free & paleo. $$$

✕ Embafilao [170 A6] Le Morne Peninsula; ✆ 401 4085; ⊕ 08.00–15.30 daily. Cuisine: Creole, Chinese, seafood. On the public beach near Dinarobin Hotel. Casual outdoor dining at reasonable prices. Expect to pay around Rs150 for a grilled fish skewer. Take-away available. $$

✕ Mam Gouz Coastal Rd, Tamarin; m 5732 8440; ⊕ 11.30–15.00 & 18.00–22.00 Tue–Fri, 11.30–23.00 Sat, 11.30–15.00 Sun. Cuisine: crêperie. A touch of France. Serves tasty traditional crêpes & light meals. $$

✕ L' Epicerie Barachois Rd, Cap Tamarin; ✆ 483 8735; ⊕ 08.30–18.30 Mon–Sat. Cuisine: European. An upmarket delicatessen selling a good range of tasty treats, many of which originate from France. Meat, seafood, cheese, chocolates & pâtisserie are on offer. $

✕ The Toaster [170 C4] Ruisseau Creole; m 5496 2301; ⊕ for lunch Mon–Sat. A kiosk within the shopping centre selling lovingly made wraps & snacks. $

NIGHTLIFE Most hotels in the mid-range and upmarket categories organise evening entertainment in the form of live bands, *séga* nights or themed evenings. **Big Willy's** (*Route du Barachois, Tamarin;* ✆ *483 7400;* ⊕ *14.00–02.00 Tue–Fri, 09.00–02.00 Sat, 11.00–21.00 Sun*) is at the heart of the nightlife scene outside the hotels. This pub/restaurant with a dance floor is in a garden setting and is the haunt of the growing South African expat community in the area. Also popular with expats **Frenchie Café** (see above), which is a cocktail bar as well as a restaurant and has DJs on a Saturday.

CHAMAREL AND SURROUNDS

At Grande Case Noyale is the turning inland towards **Chamarel**. It is not signed but there is a sign for the restaurant, Le Chamarel. It is a steep, winding road with spectacular views of the coast, Le Morne Brabant, **Ile aux Bénitiers** and the countless colours of the lagoon. The first layby is not the best one to pull over and admire the view; there is a better and safer viewpoint further up. About 6km from the coast is the village of Chamarel, which lies amidst fields of pineapples and sugarcane. There are several tourist attractions nearby and in recent years the village has grown considerably with new restaurants popping up every few yards. There is also accommodation in the area if you fancy some time away from the beach.

On a private estate just south of Chamarel village are the **Seven Coloured Earths of Chamarel** [170 B6], which have formed via the decomposition of volcanic rock into clay. The colours are predominantly red, brown, yellow and purple, with some violet, green and blue, and are best seen with the sun on them. Since the 1960s a great deal of fuss has been made about the Seven Coloured Earths and for many years, when the island didn't have as many tourist attractions as it does now, it

was considered one of the top excursions. However, for many visitors the coloured earths are an anticlimax, perhaps because they have heard so much hype.

Also on the estate, and perhaps more interesting, is a **waterfall**, which plunges 100m down a sheer cliff face (page 186). Chamarel is known for its **coffee**, although buying a sample is not as easy as you may think as most is sold to hotels or Curepipe supermarkets. There is a shop at Le Chamarel restaurant which sells it, as does the souvenir shop at the Seven Coloured Earths.

On the main road through Chamarel, 3km from the village in the direction of Grand Bassin, is **Rhumerie de Chamarel** [170 B6], which explains the process of producing rum from sugarcane (see page 187).

The Chamarel road continues up to the forest plateau of **Plaine Champagne**, at 737m above sea level. Off this road is a viewpoint overlooking the Black River Gorges National Park (page 195) and a second viewpoint with views of **Alexandra Falls** and the coast. Each is a short walk from their respective car park. The area is part of the nature reserve and glimpses of deer, monkeys and mongoose are likely.

🏠 WHERE TO STAY

Mid range

✳ 🏠 **Lakaz Chamarel** [170 B6] (20 villas) Pinot Canot, Chamarel; ☎ 483 5240; e lakazchamarel@intnet.mu; www.lakazchamarel. com. Elegant boutique accommodation in 20 villas for 2 or 3 people, set in a stunning tropical garden. The rooms have an air of luxury & encourage relaxation with thoughtful inclusions like handmade toiletries & an outdoor shower. There are several villas with private pool & garden, & even those that don't have a private pool share a pool with only a handful of other villas. Refreshingly, there is no TV in the villas, but there is a comfortable TV room & guest lounge. A small spa can provide massages. There is a restaurant serving breakfast, lunch & dinner. A wonderful, private & tranquil retreat with the kind of service you would find in a 5-star resort. **$$$**

Budget

🏠 **La Vieille Cheminée** [170 B6] (3 villas) Chamarel; ☎ 483 4249; e caroline@ lavieillecheminee.com; www.lavieillecheminee. com. Delightfully rustic self-catering accommodation on a working farm, which grows pineapples, sugarcane & palm trees. There is a 3-bedroom house & 2 cottages with 1 bedroom

each. The 1-bedroom cottages have AC, while the 3-bedroom house has fans. The large house & 1 of the cottages have a fireplace on the terrace for cool winter evenings; each has a garden area. There are no TVs & no internet; just a wonderful opportunity for total relaxation. The décor is rustic but very nicely done in traditional Creole style. The farm is on a hill with views of the surrounding countryside. Guests can wander the farm on foot or on a guided horseride from the well-run stables. There is a small pool with a little bar on a hill in the middle of the property; a very peaceful spot. This is one of few Mauritian properties which takes recycling seriously & does what it can to limit its impact on the environment. **$$**

🏠 **Les Chalets en Champagne** [170 B5] (3 villas) 110 Route Plaine Champagne, Chamarel; m 5988 7418; e lcc@jadegroup.mu; www. leschaletsenchampagne.mu. Pretty wooden mountain lodges with 2 or 3 AC bedrooms, living/ dining area, fireplace, TV & kitchenette. Guided hikes of the surrounding forests are available. A pleasant mountain escape. **$$**

🏠 **Les Palmiers** [170 B5] (5 rooms) Chamarel; ☎ 483 4364. Simple accommodation in the centre of Chamarel, above the excellent restaurant of the same name (page 179). **$$**

✗ WHERE TO EAT

✗ **La Varangue sur Morne** [170 B5] Coeur Bois; ☎ 483 5710; ⊕ for lunch daily, dinner by arrangement. Cuisine: Creole, European, game, seafood. If you can get a table on the open side of the restaurant or outside there are wonderful views

of the surrounding mountains & down to the coast. You do need to book for lunch. It is a popular stop for organised tours, which tend to arrive at about 13.30. (usually only weekdays). Next to the restaurant is a small wood museum (page 187). **$$$$**

✘ **L'Alchemiste** [170 B5] Royal Rd, Chamarel;
483 4980; www.rhumeriedechamarel.com;
⏱ for lunch Mon–Sat. Cuisine: European, Creole. A
gourmet restaurant at the rum distillery, specialising
in local produce, including game. The wooden tables
& views of the countryside give it a chic, rustic,
hunting lodge feel. There are, of course, dishes
& cocktails featuring rum. The food & service are
excellent. $$$$

✘ **Le Chamarel** [170 B5] Chamarel; 483 4421;
www.lechamarelrestaurant.com; ⏱ for lunch
daily. Cuisine: Creole, European, game, seafood.
You feel perched on the edge of the world as you
sit on the veranda overlooking forest, plain & sea.
The menu is extensive & the food is of a good
standard. It's advisable to book for lunch, & tour

groups stop here from about 13.00 on Wed & Sat.
There is a small souvenir shop. $$$$

✘ **Domaine du Cachet** [170 B6] Chamarel;
m 5934 6197; ⏱ for lunch Mon–Sat. Cuisine:
Creole, seafood. A relatively smart little place on the
road to the Seven Coloured Earths.The menu has
plenty of choice & the food is nicely presented. $$$

✻ ✘ **Les Palmiers** [170 B5] Chamarel; 483
8364; ⏱ 10.00–17.00 daily. Cuisine: Creole. This
is the place for delicious home-cooked meals. Mrs
Beehary has turned part of her home in the village
of Chamarel into a cosy restaurant. Traditional
Creole food, made using homegrown ingredients,
including organic vegetables grown by Mr Beehary,
is served on banana leaves. Great value for money
& friendly service. $$

WOLMAR AND FLIC EN FLAC TO PORT LOUIS

A few kilometres off the main road to Port Louis (A3), Wolmar and Flic en Flac have
seen considerable development over recent years with hotels and holiday houses
multiplying at an alarming rate. The village of **Wolmar** has largely disappeared and
luxury hotels now dominate this stretch of coast, giving it an air of exclusivity. **Flic
en Flac** has a broader range of accommodation and all the trappings of a tourist
resort: restaurants, travel agents and souvenir shops.

Despite the rows of Spanish Costa-style holiday homes opposite, the Flic en Flac
public beach remains relatively unspoilt. Mauritians flock here on weekends and
picnic among the casuarina trees around the old lime kiln, and the snack bars do
a swift trade.

The name 'Flic en Flac' is thought to come from Old Dutch, an onomatopoeic
word for the sound of hands slapping goatskin drums. Say it quickly.

TOURIST INFORMATION The outlets you see in Flic en Flac advertising tourist
information are not MTPA tourist information offices; rather they are private
companies. While they can provide information on excursions, bear in mind they
will be trying to sell their own products.

🏠 WHERE TO STAY

Luxury

✻ 🏠 **Maradiva Hotel** [170 A4] (65 villas)
Wolmar; 403 1500; e reservation@maradiva.
com; www.maradiva.com. The epitome of luxury.
Believe it or not, the most basic accommodation
here is a 163m² villa with private pool, outdoor
dining area, open-air garden shower, plasma
TV, DVD/CD, internet, minibar, safe & 24hr butler
service. There are 2 restaurants, including 1
specialising in pan-Asian where you can marvel at
the skills of the tepanyaki chef. The spa is superb &
offers a range of treatments, including Ayurvedic
therapies. There is a lovely outdoor heated pool

& the treatment rooms have a sauna & shower
attached. The usual watersports, beautiful pools,
tennis, free use of bikes & a kids' club are available.
The icing on the cake is a gorgeous beach. A hotel
designed for romantic relaxation rather than family
fun. Ideal for a honeymoon. $$$$$

Upmarket

🏠 **Hilton Mauritius Resort & Spa** [170 A3]
(193 rooms) Wolmar; 403 1000; e info_
mauritius@hilton.com; www.hilton.com. Forget all
images that you have of Hilton hotels as concrete
monstrosities in smoggy city centres. This is an

architecturally striking hotel with grand gardens & public areas. It is particularly beautiful at night when flaming torches are lit around the grounds with great ceremony at 19.00 by members of staff who may normally go unseen, such as boat-house, gardening & kitchen staff. The sea-facing rooms & suites include 2 rooms with disabled facilities. Rooms have all that you'd expect from a first-class hotel & are decorated in warm colours. There are lots of activities during the day & entertainment several evenings per week. The 3 restaurants include an excellent Thai (page 181). The spa offers all manner of pampering & there are plenty of land & watersports available, many of which are included. There is a kids' club & gorgeous pools. A popular hotel for conferences, which are most common between May & Sep, should you wish to avoid them. **$$$$**

🏠 **La Pirogue** [170 A3] (248 rooms) Wolmar; 📞 403 3900; e info@lapirogue.mu; www. lapirogue.com. This large 4-star hotel first opened in 1976 but renovations have kept it up to date. The rooms are in thatched bungalows spread over a large area dotted with palm trees, & there is a beautiful beach. All rooms are ground floor & have AC, TV, minibar, phone, safe & terrace. Superior rooms are closer to the ocean. There is a room equipped for the disabled. There is a choice of bars & restaurants, including the romantic Paul et Virginie seafood restaurant (page 182), & plenty of entertainment. A huge, winding pool is the centrepiece of the hotel. The sports facilities are impressive & include tennis courts, a gym with martial arts area, a wide range of watersports & a dive centre. Kids' & teenagers' clubs are on offer. Guests can use some of the facilities at neighbouring Sugar Beach, such as the spa. **$$$$**

🏠 **Sofitel L'Imperial Resort & Spa** [170 A3] (191 rooms) Wolmar; 📞 453 8700; e h1144@ sofitel.com; www.sofitel.com. The architecture & décor of this large hotel give it an Asian flavour & it is particularly popular with guests from that part of the world. The rooms & suites have all the facilities of an upmarket hotel; the beds here are Sofitel's 'my bed' & are particularly comfortable. There are 4 restaurants (1 contains both Chinese & Japanese sections), gym, tennis, watersports, a dive centre & spa. Surprisingly for a large resort, there is only 1 main pool but the hotel is on a long stretch of beach & the small pool in the spa is free & surrounded by relaxation cabins if you want

some quiet time. The hotel is popular with families & there is a kids' club. It is worth noting the family suites overlook the garden & not the sea. **$$$$**

✳ 🏠 **Sugar Beach Resort & Spa** [170 A3] (258 rooms) Wolmar; 📞 403 3300; e info@ sugarbeachresort.mu; www.sugarbeachresort. com. Colonial-style architecture & manicured lawns create the desired impression of an elegant sugar estate. The rooms, suites & beach villas are beautifully furnished & well equipped, with en suite, AC, TV, phone, minibar, safe, free Wi-Fi & balcony/terrace. The interconnecting rooms are ideal for families. The 3 restaurants, including 1 Italian, offer an excellent variety of cuisine. There are 2 pools, a gym, watersports, 6 floodlit tennis courts, kids' club & teenagers' club. One of the pools is designated as 'quiet' which means you shouldn't be bothered by other people's children. The spa is impressive – the large hammam is wonderful & can be booked for 30mins free usage. There is even a martial arts area. The hotel is spread along 500m of beautiful beach & there is a wonderful feeling of space, so however full the hotel may be, it is unlikely to feel crowded. The sunsets are fabulous. Guests can use some of the facilities at neighbouring La Pirogue. Great value for money & the service is excellent. **$$$$**

🏠 **The Sands Resort** [170 A4] (91 rooms) Wolmar; 📞 403 1200; e info@sands.mu; www. sands.mu. This 4-star is less luxurious than many of its exclusive neighbours, but very comfortable & welcoming. The rooms are modern & particularly large, with huge en-suite bathrooms (with bath & shower), AC, TV, phone, minibar, safe & Wi-Fi. All rooms face the sea. The pool is fairly small but there is a good stretch of beach. The spa facilities include free sauna & hammam. The hotel targets couples & there is no kids' club. There are 3 restaurants, a bar, tennis, dive centre & many watersports, including waterskiing, are included. Unusually for a hotel of this type, the Sands welcomes outsiders, including locals, to their entertainment evenings. Fri night dinner, entertainment & dancing are particularly popular with locals, who mingle with the hotel guests. **$$$$**

Mid range
🏠 **Aanari Hotel & Spa** [170 B3] (50 rooms) Pasadena Village, Coastal Rd, Flic en Flac; 📞 453 9000; e reservations@aanari.com; www.aanari.

com. Across the road from the beach in the Pasadena shopping complex, which houses the Spar supermarket, bars, restaurants & nightclubs. The location isn't very appealing but the rooms are modern with en suite, AC, TV, phone, safe & minibar. There is a Chinese restaurant & a very small spa area with 2 massage cabins but only guests in club rooms can use the jacuzzi & sauna free of charge. Not for those seeking a relaxing retreat. **$$$**

🏠 **Pearle Beach Resort & Spa** [170 A3] (74 rooms) Coastal Rd, Wolmar; 📞 401 6300; e info@ pearle-beach.com; www.hotelpearlebeach.com. All but 10 of the rooms face the pool/sea, so try to get 1 that does. The rooms are nicely decorated with en suite, AC, flat-screen TV, phone, safe, minibar & tea/coffee facilities. The hotel has only 1 restaurant but in a place of this size that isn't really an issue & plenty of restaurants are nearby. There is a pool, small spa, watersports & evening entertainments; no kids' club but babysitting can be provided (payable).Considering the location, this is reasonable value for money. **$$$**

Budget

🏠 **Escale Vacances** [170 A3] (6 apts) Coastal Rd, Flic en Flac; 📞 453 9389; e ffagency@intnet. mu; www.fftourist.com. Across the road from the beach in the centre of Flic en Flac. Simple self-catering duplexes with 1 bedroom, shower, living room with sofa-bed & equipped kitchenette (microwave, fridge, etc), AC, TV & balcony/terrace. Facilities include a good pool, private parking, daily maid service & free Wi-Fi. **$$**

🏠 **Klondike Hotel** [170 B3] (31 rooms) Coastal Rd, Flic en Flac; 📞 453 8333; e info@klondikehotel. com; www.klondikehotel.com. At the northern end of Flic en Flac. Cottages house 20 rooms with AC, TV, safe, phone & minibar. There are also 11 bungalows with kitchenette (4–8 people). There is a good pool & a newly created beach, as well as a restaurant & bar. Regular live entertainment including a *séga* show on Sat. Some free watersports, a dive centre & tennis court. Popular with German guests. **$$**

🏠 **Villas Caroline** [170 B3] (74 rooms) Coastal Rd, Flic en Flac; 📞 453 8411; e caroline@intnet. mu; www.villa-caroline-hotel-mauritius.mu. Has expanded over the years to rooms plus self-catering bungalows for either 2 or 4 people. Rooms are nicely furnished & have AC, TV, phone, safe, minibar & balcony/terrace. Standard rooms have a kitchenette; superior rooms are smarter but have no kitchenette. Bungalows also have a well-equipped kitchen. Public areas are very pleasant, with a pool, small spa, open-air international restaurant, bar & shop. There is a fantastic beach that is separated from the main strip of beach. Live music daily except Sun & a barbecue & *séga* show on Sat. Some free non-motorised watersports & there is a dive centre, where English & German are spoken. **$$**

🏠 **West Palm Bed & Breakfast Inn** [170 B3] (20 rooms) Sea Breeze Lane, Flic en Flac; 📞 453 9728; e resa@westpalm-mauritius.com; www. westpalm-mauritius.com. A comfortable, large guesthouse in the village of Flic en Flac, a 5min walk from the beach. Rooms are simple but clean & comfortable with AC, minibar & Wi-Fi. There is a restaurant & a small pool in the garden. **$$**

✕ **WHERE TO EAT**   For self-caterers there is a **Spar supermarket** in the Pasadena Village Complex near Flic en Flac Beach (🕒 *08.00–20.00 Mon–Sat, 08.00–17.00 Sun*) and a new, larger and smarter supermarket within La Cascavelle shopping centre on the road into Flic en Flac. There is also a small supermarket on the coast road and another in the group of shops beyond the Flic en Flac Mall, on the way out of town.

✕ **Ginger Thai** [170 A3] Hilton Resort; 📞 403 1000; 🕒 for dinner Tue–Sun. Cuisine: Thai. The Thai chef here conjures up excellent dishes. Elegant setting with tables indoor & out. Very plush with prices to match. Reservation necessary. **$$$$$**

✕ **The Cilantro** [170 A4] Maradiva Hotel, Wolmar; 📞 403 1500; 🕒 for dinner Mon–Sat. Cuisine: Pan-Asian. A fine-dining restaurant offering plenty of variety, with Indian, Thai & Japanese on the menu. Dinner at the tepanyaki counter, watching the skilled chefs perform, is entertaining. **$$$$$**

✕ **Beach Shack** Coastal Rd, Flic en Flac; 📞 453 9080; 🕒 for lunch & dinner daily. Cuisine: European, Creole, seafood. Modern restaurant across the road from the beach. Specialises in grilled seafood & meat, including good-quality Waygu & Black Angus from Australia. Main courses range from Rs600 to Rs2,500. The bar here is popular in the evenings. Free Wi-Fi. **$$$$**

✗ Citronella Café [170 A3] Sugar Beach Resort, Wolmar; ☎ 453 9090; ⊕ for lunch Tue–Sun, for dinner Mon–Sat. Cuisine: Italian. Upmarket Italian restaurant on the beachfront. Diners can watch the chefs prepare delicious pizza in the wood-fired oven. The service here is excellent. There are inexpensive options on the menu, with main courses priced from Rs350. $$$$

✗ Domaine Anna [170 B3] Flic en Flac; ☎ 453 9650; www.domaineanna.net; ⊕ for lunch & dinner Tue–Sun. Cuisine: European, Chinese, seafood. Turn right from the road into Flic en Flac coming from the main Port Louis–Tamarin road (A3). You will need a car or taxi to reach it from Flic en Flac. Elegant dining in a colonial-style building surrounded by forest & lakes; you can also eat in thatched pavillons on the edge of the lakes. Seafood is prepared in a variety of ways, including with a choice of Chinese sauces. Lobster is the chef's speciality. Reservation necessary. $$$$

✗ Lakaz Cascavelle [170 B3] Cascavelle Shopping Centre; ☎ 452 9200; ⊕ for lunch & dinner Mon–Sat. Cuisine: Creole. This large restaurant/bar at the shopping centre serves a buffet lunch (*Rs300*) & dinner (*Rs450*) of Creole dishes. There is a popular bar here with regular live music & a nightclub at weekends. $$$

✗ Le Mirador [170 B3] Casela World of Adventures, Royal Rd, Cascavelle; ☎ 452 0845; ⊕ 10.30–16.00 daily. Cuisine: Creole, French. It takes the best part of a day to wander around Casela, & it is worth stopping here for lunch. The restaurant is on a hill & has wonderful views of the west coast. Serves tasty Creole dishes & reasonably priced light lunches, such as salads & pizza. $$$

✗ Les Coquillages [170 A3] Hilton Resort; ☎ 403 1000; ⊕ 12.00–17.00 Mon–Sat. Cuisine: European, Creole, seafood. Informal but upmarket restaurant

right on the beach, with tables on the sand. Excellent food, service & views. $$$$

✗ Paul et Virginie Restaurant [170 A3] La Pirogue Hotel; ☎ 403 3900; ⊕ for lunch daily, for dinner Mon–Sat. Cuisine: seafood. Upmarket open-air dining on the beach, with seafood the focus. Lunch is relatively casual, dinner more sophisticated & the thatched pavilions create a romantic setting. $$$$

✗ Twin's Garden Coastal Rd, Flic en Flac; ☎ 453 5250; ⊕ for lunch & dinner Wed–Sat, lunch Tue. Cuisine: European, Creole. Across the road from the beach. Modern, attractive restaurant & lounge bar. Unfortunately, the food & service are a bit hit & miss. On Fri night there is a buffet & *séga* show. $$$

✗ Walnut & Thyme [170 C3] Cascavelle Shopping Centre, Flic en Flac; ☎ 452 9022; ⊕ 09.30–18.00 Mon–Sat, 09.30–15.00 Sun & public holidays. Cuisine: European. The nicest place for a coffee at the shopping centre. If you are in Mauritius for an extended period & missing English food, there is a tempting deli section with lots of imported treats, like long-life Devonshire clotted cream. They even do an all-day English breakfast. They have a good gluten-free & organic ranges. Open for dinner some evenings during summer – call for details. $$$

✗ Chez Leslie Coastal Rd, Flic en Flac; ☎ 453 8172; ⊕ for lunch & dinner Tue–Sun. Cuisine: Creole, Chinese. Unassuming, inexpensive, friendly restaurant at the northern end of Flic en Flac. $$

✗ Banane Créole Royal Rd, Flic en Flac; ☎ 453 9826; ⊕ lunch & dinner Mon–Sat. Cuisine: Creole, Chinese, pizza, snacks. Also take-away. On the road into Flic en Flac, on the left. There is something for everyone on the very varied menu. Plenty of cheap options available & its popularity with locals is a good sign. $

NIGHTLIFE Although not yet on the scale of Grand Baie, Flic en Flac's nightlife has grown rapidly in recent years and there are now plenty of options outside the hotels. There is a **casino** and several bars across the road from the beach, around the Pasadena Village shopping complex. Many of the bars are open from mid-morning until late. French-owned **Kenzi Bar** (☎ *494 4133*; ⊕ *Mon–Sat*) near West Palm Bed and Breakfast, behind the Pasadena Village, has regular live music and gets a good crowd on the dance floor. There is sand on the floor and rum behind the bar, giving it a truly tropical flavour, which is perhaps what makes it so popular with expats and tourists. **Shotz** (☎ *453 5626*), opposite the public beach, has comfy chairs on a wooden deck, plus indoor and outdoor dance floors. Next door is **Shine** (m *5748 1582*), a champagne bar, which also serves light meals, like pizza. **Twin's Garden**

(page 182), opposite the beach, is a lounge bar, as well as a restaurant. **Teasers** (m *5721 2729*) opposite the police station is popular with locals.

SHOPPING Flic en Flac has lots of touristy shops, selling cheap clothing and souvenirs. There are two shopping malls: the Flic en Flac Mall at the northern end of town and the Pasadena Village opposite the police station near Flic en Flac Beach. The abundance of tourists in the area means that shopkeepers tend to try it on when it comes to price. A few words of Creole usually do the trick.

Ruisseau Creole [170 B4] (✆ *483 8000;* e *contact@ruisseaucreole.com; www. ruisseaucreole.com; shops* ⊕ *09.30–18.30 Mon–Sat*) is a large shopping centre at Rivière Noire, which targets the tourist market and well-heeled Mauritians. It opened in June 2005 and has around 50 shops selling jewellery, clothing, handicrafts and art, as well as restaurants and bars. There is also a bank with ATM and free parking. A free shuttle is available from most hotels on the west coast.

Another large shopping centre, **La Cascavelle** [170 C3], was recently built on the road into Flic en Flac. The complex includes clothing boutiques, a golf shop, bookshop, supermarket, pharmacy, banks and food court. There is even a go-kart track.

OTHER PRACTICALITIES There is a **petrol station** [170 B3] on the road into Flic en Flac, as well as a **pharmacy**. Pharmacies are also in the Pasadena Village and La Cascavelle Shopping Centre. The **police station** is on the main road into Flic en Flac, opposite the Pasadena Village.

Money and banking On the road into Flic en Flac is a Barclays Bank and at the Cascavelle Shopping Centre and HSBC. There is also an ATM at the Pasadena Village.

Communications The **post office** is across the road from the Pasadena Village, behind the police station; **internet access** is available.

WHAT TO DO IN WESTERN MAURITIUS

SPORTS

Deep-sea fishing The island's first deep-sea fishing clubs were set up around the area of Grande Rivière Noire as the deep waters here provide ideal conditions. There is now a good choice of operators based in the southwest of the island. This is where you will find Le Morne Anglers' Club (*www.morneanglers.com*), which hosts some big competitions. For more information, see pages 85–6.

Scuba diving The southwest and west coasts have excellent diving sites for all levels of experience, including a number of shipwrecks. Many of the hotels have dive centres, and there is a good choice of dive operators to choose from around Flic en Flac and Le Morne. For more information, see pages 86–9.

Kitesurfing Parts of the southwest coast have ideal conditions for kitesurfing, which is booming around Le Morne Peninsula and Grande Rivière. Kitesurfing shops and clubs have sprung up in recent years, and many of the hotels in the area offering kitesurfing for a fee. For more information, see pages 91–2.

SeaKarting SeaKarts are a cross between a jet-ski and a go-kart. The departure point for this adrenalin-packed activity is at Grande Rivière Noire (m *5499 4929;*

e *contact@fun-adventure.mu; www.fun-adventure.mu*). After a safety briefing, where they tell you confidently that it is impossible to capsize a SeaKart, you head out into the open water, accompanied by a speedboat. The SeaKarts take up to two adults and a child, and no more than six SeaKarts go out at a time. They are easy to operate and go surprisingly fast as you zip up and down the coast. Prices are 1 hour Rs5,300, 2 hours plus breakfast or afternoon tea Rs9,500, full day with lunch Rs19,000 (prices are per SeaKart; each one takes up to two adults and one child). The minimum age to drive is 16 years.

Golf The 18-hole course at Paradis Hotel is open to non-residents. Many of the hotels on the west coast can also arrange for guests to play at the 18-hole course at the Tamarina Golf Estate on the Médine Sugar Estate. For more information, see pages 83–4.

Go-karting Speedomax Mauritius (m *5448 1070; www.speedomaxmauritius. com*) at the Cascavelle Shopping Centre is large and modern and even has a restaurant on site. An 8-minute session costs Rs650.

Horseriding Available at **La Vieille Cheminée** at Chamarel, **Haras du Morne** [170 A6] at Le Morne Peninsula and **Le Ranch** near Rivière Noire. For more information, see pages 84–5.

SPA TREATMENTS Outside the hotels there are a few small spas in the Flic en Flac area, such as **Om Spa** (*Complex Beegun, Royal Rd, Flic en Flac*; m *5769 2676; www. omspamauritius.com;* ⊕ *09.15–17.30 Tue–Sat, 09.15–13.00 Sun & public holidays*), which offers traditional and Ayurvedic massage, plus beauty treatments.

WHAT TO SEE IN WESTERN MAURITIUS

THE SALT ROUTE (LA ROUTE DU SEL) [170 B4] (*Mont Calme, Royal Rd, Tamarin;* ✆ *483 8764;* e *montcalme@intnet.mu;* ⊕ *08.30–17.00 Mon–Sat; admission adult/ child Rs200/100*) The salt pans at Tamarin have been producing salt for over 175 years. Today the pans yield around 1,300–1,400 tons of salt per year. Guided tours of around 15 minutes explain the process of salt production. Seawater is pumped into the pools, of which there are 1,586, and then flows through a series of pools at different temperatures. Between five and ten days later it reaches the last pool, the water evaporates and it crystallises into salt. The hardworking ladies of the salt pans collect the salt and carry it in tubs or baskets on their heads to one of nine salt stores, where it is dried. Each tub of salt weighs around 20kg and sometimes you can see women carrying two or even three tubs on their heads. If you want to see the ladies in action you will need to be there before 09.30 as they typically work in the early morning to avoid the heat. Culinary and cosmetic products made from the salt are on sale in the small shop.

MARTELLO TOWER MUSEUM [170 B4] (*La Preneuse Rd, Grande Rivière Noire;* ✆ *471 0178;* e *foemau@intnet.mu;* ⊕ *09.30–16.30 Tue–Sat, 09.30–13.30 Sun; admission adult/ child Rs80/50, adult Rs60 on weekends*) In the 1830s, the British built five Martello Towers, with sturdy walls and cannon, to protect the island. They were in the process of negotiating the abolition of slavery, a proposition which faced hefty resistance from the French sugarcane planters, who relied on slave labour. The British feared a rebellion by the planters might be followed by a French invasion and so built the

towers, which have come to symbolise the abolition of slavery. The tower at Grande Rivière Noire has opened as a museum, where a short video is followed by a guided tour. On display are cannon, coins and military paraphernalia from the period.

CASELA WORLD OF ADVENTURES ✳ [170 C3] (*Royal Rd, Cascavelle;* ☏ *401 6500;* e *caselaresa@medine.com; www.caselapark.com;* ⊕ *May–Sep 09.00–17.00 daily; Oct–Apr 09.00–18.00 daily; admission adult/child Rs740/475*) Casela has expanded greatly in recent years, cementing its position as one of the island's top attractions. Access is off the Black River road between Tamarin and the turning to Flic en Flac. Allow a full day to explore the park, particularly if you are doing any of the interactive experiences or activities. Casela began life as a bird park and birds still feature heavily, including in a walk-through aviary. Look out for the endemic species, like the Mauritius pink

KAYA

In the early hours of the morning of Sunday 21 February 1999, Joseph Reginald Topize, better known as Kaya, was found dead in a high-security police cell.

His death brought Mauritius to a standstill but, more importantly, it revealed how important it is for the government to address potential racial tension.

Kaya was a popular Rastafarian singer, an important Creole figure known throughout the Indian Ocean islands and beyond. His group, Racinetatane, was responsible for launching *séggae*, a blend of reggae and *séga*, in the late 1980s.

In early 1999, the Mouvement Républicain (MR) began a campaign for the decriminalisation of cannabis smoking. On 16 February, a concert was held in support of the campaign and Kaya was asked to perform.

The following day, he and eight others were arrested for smoking cannabis in public. All but Kaya denied the charge and were released. Kaya admitted it and was sent to a high-security cell at Line Barracks, known locally as Alcatraz.

He was granted bail of Rs10,000 but his family could not raise the money. Surprisingly, the MR did not attempt to pay the bail, although Kaya had performed for free at their concert.

When his body was found in the cell, it was clear that he had died of head injuries and an autopsy later confirmed this. News of Kaya's death, apparently a result of police brutality, swept through the island. Groups of protesters gathered, and by the afternoon there were widespread riots. Severe rioting continued for three days. Police stations were attacked and buildings set alight all over Mauritius. Hundreds of police officers and rioters were injured during the unrest, many by gunshot wounds. Several people were killed.

News of Kaya's death spread to Réunion too, where I was living at the time, and I vividly remember the anger amongst the Creole population there.

The unrest in Mauritius began to take on a political and racial tone. Creoles vented their frustration at what they considered to be their disadvantaged position in society and rebelled against the Indo-Mauritian-dominated authorities.

Something positive did come out of Kaya's death – it forced politicians to acknowledge the discontent of the Creole community and a government department was set up to address their concerns. The events were a reminder that Mauritius's ethnic cocktail, which is an asset in so many ways, can also be an explosive mixture. It seems that politicians have learnt their lesson and realise that constant efforts must be made to listen to and involve all communities.

pigeon. Lemurs, pygmy hippos, tortoises and giraffes are among the animals dotted around the spacious site, which is well laid out with plenty of shaded walks. For an additional fee you can feed the giraffes (*Rs100*) or interact with the pygmy hippos (*Rs250*) or rhino (*Rs2,000*). Within a large safari park area are African and other animals, including zebra, ostrich, oryx, impala, tortoises and rhino. A drive through the park in a safari vehicle is included in the entry fee, or you can pay an additional fee to explore on a guided Segway (*Rs1,500 for 1hr*), quadbike (*Rs2,620 for 1hr*), 4x4 buggy (*Rs2,620 for 1hr*) or horseback (*Rs2,500 for 1hr*) tour. Also included in the entry is viewing the big cats (lions, tigers, cheetahs, servals, and caracals) at the Safari Adventures end of the park, but interaction with the big cats is payable (see below). Various adventure activities can be booked, including ziplining (flying-fox) over the ravines surrounding the sugarcane fields, canyoning, canyon swing and a high ropes course. Giant slides, a petting farm and tilapia fishing are popular with children, and if the weather turns there is a 4D cinema. It is an incredible cinema experience with moving seats and all sorts of other effects, but I won't spoil the surprise. There is a lovely restaurant with views of the coast (page 182).

SAFARI ADVENTURES ✳ [170 C3] (*Casela World of Adventures, Cascavelle;* ☏ 4525546; e *safari-adventures@intnet.mu; www.safari-adventures-mauritius.com;* ⊕ *09.00–16.00 Mon–Sat*) Located at Casela World of Adventures, Safari Adventures was established in 2006 by renowned wildlife experts Graeme and Julie Bristow from Zimbabwe, who are now assisted in the management of the park by their son, Ben. They and their staff are highly knowledgeable, experienced and committed to animal welfare. Safari Adventures offers the rare opportunity to interact with a range of big cats, including lions, cheetahs, tigers and, more recently, the park's new servals and caracals. All of the interactions are wonderful, memorable experiences, and enhanced by the presence of a knowledgeable keeper. If you don't fancy getting too close you can simply observe the big cats from a platform or take a safari-style drive through parks containing adult lions and tigers. The pick of the options has to be 'walking with lions'. In a small group and accompanied by guides you take the lions for a walk around the reserve (no leads, they're free, but far more obedient than my dogs). It is an unforgettable experience and I'd recommend it to any animal lover. You'll need comfortable walking shoes and ideally long trousers and mosquito repellent. Photographs and video are taken during the walk, which you can buy on DVD as a souvenir. Reservation essential. There is a minimum height requirement of 1.5m for all interactions and walks, and a minimum age of 15. Approximate prices are 15-minute interaction Rs750, drive-through Rs320, walking with lions Rs3,750 per person. You will also need to pay the Casela entrance fee.

THE SEVEN COLOURED EARTHS [170 B6] (*Mare Anguilles, Chamarel;* ☏ 622 6177; ⊕ *08.30–17.00 daily; admission adult/child Rs200/100*) Signed from the village of Chamarel, a track through the private estate leads first to a waterfall then on to the coloured earths. Both attractions involve parking the car for a short walk. The track is lined with the Arabica coffee plants for which the area is known and 'heart of palm salad trees'. The Chamarel Waterfall is the island's highest and tumbles 100m down a sheer cliff face. A viewing platform allows you to see the denuded coloured earth from above. The colours are at their best early in the morning. For many people, it doesn't live up to the hype and there is little else to see or do on site, aside from an enclosure of giant tortoises. The waterfall is pretty but still doesn't justify the entry fee. Specimens of the coloured earths in glass tubes are on sale in the small shop. There is also a snack bar.

LA RHUMERIE DE CHAMAREL [170 B6] (*Royal Rd, Chamarel;* \ *483 4980;* e *info@ rhumeriedechamarel.com; www.rhumeriedechamarel.com;* ⊕ *10.00–17.00 Mon– Sat; admission & guided tour adult/child Rs370/200*) On the main road through Chamarel, 3km from the village in the direction of Grand Bassin. The *rhumerie* was purpose-built as an attraction in 2008 and is modern and well laid out. It has become one of the island's top attractions. Admission includes a 30-minute guided tour explaining the process of producing rum from sugarcane, followed by a rum-tasting of several varieties from white rum to aged rum. The tour is more interesting during sugarcane harvest season (July–December), when the machinery is operating. There is a shop selling rum and souvenirs, and an excellent upmarket restaurant serving local produce (open for lunch, see page 179). If you have lunch here the tour is included, which is a good option.

CURIOUS CORNER OF CHAMAREL [170 B6] (*Mare Anguilles, Chamarel;* \ *483 4200;* e *info@curiouscornerofchamarel.com; www.curiouscornerofchamarel.com;* ⊕ *09.30–17.00 daily; admission adult/child Rs275/150*) A bizarre new addition to the tourist scene in more ways than one: surprising that it should exist in a small village in Mauritius, and bizarre because of its puzzling contents. It consists of a series of illusions, including a mirror maze and an upside-down room.

TOUCHE DU BOIS [170 B5] (*Coeur Bois;* \ *483 5710;* e *varangue@intnet.mu;* www. varanguesurmorne.com; ⊕ *11.00–15.00 daily; admission Rs100*) This small but fascinating museum is on the site of the Varangue sur Morne restaurant and was created by the owner, a keen woodworker. It has been nicely put together and shows the various uses of wood, past and present, including in religion, sport, music and medicine.

SEND US YOUR SNAPS!

We'd love to follow your adventures using our *Mauritius* guide – why not send us your photos and stories via Twitter (@BradtGuides) and Instagram (@bradtguides) using the hashtag #Mauritius. Alternatively, you can upload your photos directly to the gallery on the Mauritius destination page via our website (*www.bradtguides.com*).

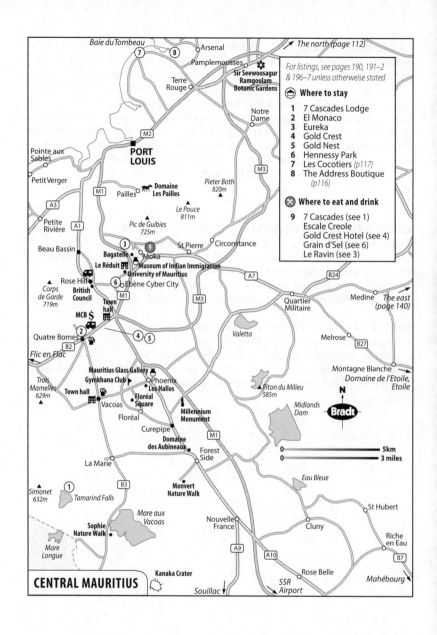

CENTRAL MAURITIUS

Baie du Tombeau

7 8 Arsenal

The north (page 112)

Pamplemousses

Sir Seewoosagur
Ramgoolam
Botanic Gardens

Terre
Rouge

Notre
Dame

For listings, see pages 190, 191–2
& 196–7 unless otherweise stated

Where to stay

1 7 Cascades Lodge
2 El Monaco
3 Eureka
4 Gold Crest
5 Gold Nest
6 Hennessy Park
7 Les Cocotiers *(p117)*
8 The Address Boutique
    (p116)

Where to eat and drink

9 7 Cascades (see 1)
    Escale Creole
    Gold Crest Hotel (see 4)
    Grain d'Sel (see 6)
    Le Ravin (see 3)

M2

PORT
LOUIS

Pointe aux
Sables

Petit Verger

Pieter Both
820m

M1 Pailles Domaine
Les Pailles

Le Pouce
811m

M3

Petite
Rivière A1

Pic de Guibies
725m

Beau Bassin

Bagatelle Moka 9 St Pierre Circonstance

Le Réduit Museum of Indian Immigration
University of Mauritius

Rose Hill Ebène Cyber City

A7

B24

Corps
de Garde
719m

British
Council

Town
hall

M1

Medine The east
(page 140)

Quartier
Militaire

Melrose B27

MCB $

Quatre Bornes B2

Flic en Flac

2

4 5

Valetta

Montagne Blanche
Domaine de l'Etoile,
Etoile

Trois
Mamelles
629m

Mauritius Glass Gallery
Gymkhana Club

Town hall Phoenix
Les Halles

Floréal
Square

Vacoas

Floréal

Piton du Milieu
585m

Midlands
Dam

N

Bradt

Millennium
Monument

Curepipe Domaine
des Aubineaux

M1

La Marie

Forest
Side

0   5km
0   3 miles

Simonet
632m 1

B3

Monvert
Nature Walk

Eau Bleue

Tamarind Falls

Mare aux
Vacoas

St Hubert

Sophie
Nature Walk

Nouvelle
France

Cluny

Riche
en Eau

Mare
Longue

A9

A10

B7

Kanaka Crater

Rose Belle

Mahébourg

CENTRAL MAURITIUS

Souillac

SSR
Airport

UPDATES WEBSITE

You can post your comments and recommendations, and read the latest
feedback and updates from other readers online at www.bradtupdates.com/
mauritius.

9

Central Mauritius

At around 600m above sea level, the centre of the island is noticeably cooler and wetter than the coast; temperatures are generally 3–5°C lower. Two districts make up the area: Plaines Wilhems to the south and west of centre and Moka to the north and east.

The central plateau is characterised by extinct volcanic craters, lakes, rivers and waterfalls. Some of the island's most spectacular scenery lies within the Black River Gorges National Park, which protects Mauritius's remaining forests and offers good opportunities for hiking. The centre of the island is densely populated, particularly around Quatre Bornes and Curepipe, and traffic congestion is a perpetual problem. A motorway runs from the airport in the southeast to Port Louis via the residential towns that stretch along it.

PLAINES WILHEMS

Although Plaines Wilhems has had settlers since 1690, officially it only became an inhabited district in 1877. Since then it has burgeoned into the island's most densely populated region, with at least 30% of Mauritius's population living in the plateau towns of Beau Bassin, Rose Hill, Quatre Bornes, Phoenix, Vacoas, Floréal and Curepipe.

The district begins as a thin wedge between the Port Louis and Black River districts. It follows the motorway southwards, widening gradually around the plateau towns. In the south, beyond Curepipe, it borders the districts of Grand Port and Savanne. The northern part of Plaines Wilhems is largely residential, while the south is characterised by tea plantations, forests and reservoirs.

Plaines Wilhems was sparsely populated until 1861, when a cholera epidemic caused the first exodus from Port Louis of people seeking a healthier climate and swelled the population to 28,020. The malaria epidemic of 1866–68 accelerated the drift. This migration resulted in ghettos. Whereas Port Louis had been a cosmopolitan mixture, the races here divided to form new towns. Those of French origin settled in Curepipe, whilst the upper class of the Indian and Creole population chose Rose Hill. The division between social/ethnic groups was emphasised by the trains, which had three separate classes, and were used by the plateau town dwellers to commute every day to Port Louis. Now the settlements from Beau Bassin to Curepipe have merged into a single, built-up area, but the divisions remain by tradition.

BEAU BASSIN AND ROSE HILL Beau Bassin and **Rose Hill** (pronounced *row-zil*) are intertwined, largely residential, sister towns that hold little interest for the average tourist. They are essentially part of the commuter belt of Port Louis. Although Beau Bassin/Rose Hill was declared a town in 1896, it was not until 1927 that it was decided

to build its **town hall**. This resulted in the series of linked, two-tiered pavilions that lie off the main road just outside the centre of Rose Hill. As well as the town hall, the complex includes the **Plaza Theatre**, with an extravagant rococo interior of gold leaf and maroon plush. It was originally built as a cinema (1929–32) but on 12 June 1934 the Mauritius Dramatic Club performed an inaugural play, *The Last of Mrs Cheney*.

Beau Bassin has a small municipal park, **Balfour Gardens**, overlooking the **Plaines Wilhems Gorge**, where there is a waterfall. Across this valley is Le Réduit (see page 198). **La Tour Blanche**, a white manor house built in 1834, lies to the south of the garden. This is where Charles Darwin stayed during his visit in 1836. At the other side of the town are the island prisons, the police training school and the college of education.

In Rose Hill a number of solid Victorian buildings have been preserved amidst the lock-up shops and concrete apartment blocks of this bustling town. Some say its name comes from the rosy glow of sunset on Corps de Garde Mountain behind it, whilst others claim the town, being on a hill, was named after Rose, the mistress of the landowner. **Corps de Garde** mountain (719m) won its name because a French military post was established on it to control the bands of runaway slaves in the region. On Royal Road is the busy **market** (⊕ *06.00–18.00 daily*), selling fruit, vegetables, clothing, handicrafts and more. Nearby **Arab Town** (⊕ *Fri–Wed*) is a bazaar with a higgledy-piggledy collection of stalls and the atmosphere of a souk. Further north on Royal Road is the **Church of Notre-Dame de Lourdes**, a hefty, black, volcanic stone building. The **British Council** is also on Royal Road (❀ *403 0200;* e *general.enquiries@mu.britishcouncil.org; www.britishcouncil.mu*).

Close to Rose Hill is **Ebène**, the home of Cyber City, Mauritius's information technology hub. Modern, multi-storey buildings line the motorway. Construction began here in 2001 as part of the government's plan to make information technology one of the pillars of the economy, and it has boomed.

Getting there and away The **bus station** in Rose Hill is at Place Margéot. There are regular buses from Victoria Square in Port Louis to Rose Hill, and some continue via the other plateau towns to Curepipe. There are also buses linking Rose Hill and Centre de Flacq.

 Where to stay *Map, page 188* If you really need to stay in the Beau Bassin/Rose Hill area and don't have friends or relatives who can put you up, you may struggle for options. However, Ebène has hotels aimed at business travellers.

Upmarket

🏠 **Hennessy Park Hotel** (108 rooms) 65 Ebène Cyber City; ❀ 403 7200; e reservations@hennessyhotel.com; www.hennessyhotel.com. A modern, 4-star business hotel. The en-suite rooms are nicely decorated with AC, TV, phone, minibar, safe, tea/coffee facilities & high-speed internet connection. There are also 4 spacious suites. As well as the main restaurant, there is a sushi bar & a pizza bar. The conference facilities are high-tech, & there is a pool, spa & gym. A shuttle service operates to Port Louis, where guests can use the facilities at the Labourdonnais & Suffren hotels (page 103). **$$$$**

✖ **Where to eat**

✖ **Grain d'Sel** [map, page 188] Hennessy Park Hotel, 65 Ebène Cyber City; ❀ 403 7200; ⊕ for breakfast, lunch & dinner daily. Cuisine: European, international. A modern restaurant within the hotel with a creative menu & good standards of food & service. **$$$**

✖ **Le Pékinois** 4 Ambrose St, Rose Hill; ❀ 454 7229; ⊕ for lunch & dinner Tue–Sun. Cuisine: Chinese, grills. **$$**

Other practicalities Royal Road is the main street, on which you'll find **banks, ATMs, shopping malls** and **payphones**.

QUATRE BORNES The main road from Rose Hill (Royal Road) takes you to the St Jean's Church roundabout, where you can either continue to Phoenix and Curepipe or turn right to Quatre Bornes. The town was so named as four former sugar estates (Bassin, La Louise, Palma and Beau Séjour) shared a common four-point boundary.

With a population of over 80,000, Quatre Bornes has developed on either side of the main road as the centre of five residential communities. The emergence of a large middle class in the area is apparent from the presence of modern shops, supermarkets and good-quality restaurants and snack bars.

The **market** is centrally located on St Jean Road, the main road through the town. The markets on Thursday and Sunday are reputed to be the island's best for clothing, handicrafts and household items; on Wednesday and Saturday there are fruit and vegetable markets. There are plenty of discount clothing shops on the same road, especially in the **Orchard Centre**, which is just west of the market. The shopping centre is relatively modern and has a food court, where Wi-Fi is available. A little further on is the **police station**, near the Total **petrol station**.

Getting there and away The **bus station** is roughly in the middle of St Jean Road, near the junction with Victoria Avenue. There are regular buses to and from Port Louis via Rose Hill and Beau Bassin. Buses also depart from Quatre Bornes for Curepipe, Baie du Cap and Wolmar (via Flic en Flac).

 Where to stay *Map, page 188*

Budget

⌂ **El Monaco** (93 rooms) 17 St Jean Rd; 425 2608; e elmo@intnet.mu; www.el-monaco.com. Set back from the main road in attractive gardens, the hotel is a warren of en-suite rooms of different vintages (the hotel was begun in 1971), with fan (no AC), TV & phone. It has a restaurant, pool & conference room. A basic hotel catering largely for tour groups from Réunion. **$$**

⌂ **Gold Crest Hotel** (50 rooms) Georgetown Bldg, St Jean Rd; 454 5945; e resa@goldgroup. mu; www.goldgrouphotels.com. In the centre of town above a shopping complex. The unfussy en-suite rooms have AC, TV, safe, phone & Wi-Fi, & overlook the central plaza. It has a restaurant (see below), small spa & a conference room. **$$**

⌂ **Gold Nest Hotel** (33 rooms) Cnr St Jean Rd & Orchidées Av; 454 5945; e resa@ goldgroup.mu; www.goldgrouphotels.com. Clean, comfortable en-suite rooms with AC, TV, phone & safe. There is a restaurant specialising in Indian cuisine, a gym & a conference room. **$$**

✕ **Where to eat** For self-caterers there is a supermarket within the Orchard Centre.

✕ **Gold Crest Hotel** [map, page 188] St Jean Rd; 454 5945; ⊕ for lunch & dinner daily. Cuisine: Indian, Chinese, Creole, European. Pleasant AC restaurant serving a wide range of dishes. **$$**

✕ **Namaste** St Jean Rd; 427 4654; ⊕ 10.30– 22.30 daily. Cuisine: Indian. The sister restaurant of Namaste in Port Louis. Serves good-quality, authentic Indian cuisine & attracts a good local crowd. On Sat evening there is a popular buffet for Rs450. **$$**

✳ ✕ **Quartier Gourmet** Ylang Ylang Av, Sodnac; m 5440 1740; www.quartiergourmet.

com; ⊕ 10.00–18.00 Mon–Fri, 09.00–14.00 Sat. Cuisine: European; gluten-free. A great find, tucked away on residential streets in the suburb of Sodnac, near Quatre Bornes. This deli is crammed with delicious healthy food, including gluten-free & sugar-free options, & treats from Europe, like Swiss-style chocolate made in Mauritius, South African cheese & wine. They even stock sugar-free chocolate. Bread is baked on site using flour from France & Germany; this is the only gluten-free bakery on the island. They also sell good-quality homewares & gifts. Upstairs is a small restaurant

(⏰ 11.00–16.00 Mon–Fri, 11.00–14.00 Sat) decorated with African artwork. The restaurant focuses on gluten-free & sugar-free dishes. The menu is not extensive but there are some great, creative choices. If you are living locally, it's a good place to meet friends for coffee. $$

Other practicalities There is an internet café in the library at the **town hall** on St Jean Road (✆ *454 8054*) and internet access is available at the **post office**. The food court in the Orchard Centre has Wi-Fi.

Money and banking The banks are mostly on St Jean Road, including a branch of Mauritius Commercial Bank with an **ATM**, opposite the market. There is also a branch of HSBC on the corner of Avenue des Rosiers and Avenue des Palmiers, near the market. The Barclays is near the Shell petrol station.

VACOAS-PHOENIX Southeast of Quatre Bornes lies another residential area, **Vacoas-Phoenix**, created by the merging of two towns in 1963. 'Les Vacoas' was so named in the 18th century after the pandanus trees (known locally as vacoas – pronounced 'vak-wa') that grew in the region.

Residential and agricultural, it produces mainly vegetables and has some light industry. The heart of the town is a crossroads with a **taxi stand**, a **public toilet**, a **petrol station** and the **municipality building**.

The British presence in Mauritius lingered on at Vacoas with a land-based communications station on St Paul Avenue, and with British instructors training the men of the Special Mobile Force, which has its headquarters in Vacoas-Phoenix. The frightfully British **Gymkhana Club** (*www.mgc.mu*) on Suffolk Road originally opened in 1849 as a polo club for officers. It now has an 18-hole golf course (page 83), tennis courts, swimming pool, squash courts, gym, snooker table and a modern clubhouse with a view of the golf course. It also has a restaurant with a stage, a lounge bar and library. The atmosphere is of a well-run establishment with dedicated, long-serving staff. Temporary membership is available to visitors on a daily or monthly basis.

Phoenix is an industrial area, with Mauritius Breweries producing their Phoenix and Stella beers at **Pont Fer**. Pont Fer also has a **Mauritius Glass Gallery** workshop, where bottles, lamps and ornaments are made from recycled glass (see page 199). One of the island's largest shopping centres, **Les Halles**, lies just outside Phoenix. It is slick and modern and has shops selling clothing, cosmetics, home wares and electronics; there is a decent food court with free Wi-Fi.

In the **Phoenix Cemetery** on Closel Road (⏰ *06.00–18.00 daily*) are eight Commonwealth war graves from World War I and 17 from World War II. A memorial commemorates Commonwealth casualties of World War I and II, who are buried elsewhere in Mauritius and whose graves could not be maintained. In 2015, Australian frigate HMAS *Anzac* visited Mauritius and a service was held at the cemetery to commemorate around 40 Australian-Mauritians who fought in World War I. The service also honoured navy bandsman Arnold Partington from Tasmania, who died of illness during World War II aboard HMAS *Canberra* while it was off Mauritius and was laid to rest in Phoenix Cemetery. He is the only Australian serviceman buried on the island.

✗ Where to eat On the road to Floréal from Phoenix there is a **Continent supermarket**.

✗ Mandarin Restaurant St Paul Rd, Vacoas; ✆ 696 4551; ⏰ for lunch & dinner daily. Cuisine: Chinese. Popular restaurant with tables around a dance floor. $$$

FLOREAL Floréal lies on the outskirts of Curepipe. Members of the diplomatic community live here, in country houses set in large gardens on leafy lanes. Floréal is a comparatively new community, having been begun by Governor Hesketh Bell during his tenure (1916–24).

Export-quality knitwear is produced at the **Floréal Knitwear Factory**, which has a boutique in Mangalkhan.

Floréal Square on John Kennedy Street (⊕ *09.00–17.00 Mon–Fri, 09.00–16.00 Sat*) contains a few shops (mostly clothing, but also jewellery, art and carpets) and a café (see below). It is a pleasant shopping experience and the sales techniques are far less pushy than those in the touristy clothing shops in towns on the coast and in Curepipe.

More expensive, but just as popular, are the area's duty-free diamond shops, such as Adamas in Mangalkhan (see also pages 71–2).

✗ Where to eat

✗ **Floréal Café** Floréal Sq, 1 John Kennedy St, Floréal; ☎ 698 8040; ⊕ 09.30–17.30 Mon–Fri, 09.30–16.00 Sat. Cuisine: European. Homemade meals, light snacks & pastries. $$$

✗ **La Clef des Champs** Queen Mary Av, Floréal; ☎ 686 3458; ⊕ lunch & dinner Mon–Sat. Cuisine: European. Upmarket restaurant in a converted house, run by well-known French chef Jacqueline

Dalai. It caters for Floréal's diplomatic residents & well-heeled gourmets. Beautifully presented dishes. Reservation recommended. $$$

✗ **L'Epicerie** Royal Rd, Floréal; ☎ 697 5429; ⊕ 08.30–18.30 Mon–Sat. Cuisine: European. A branch of the upmarket chain of delicatessens, which sells a good range of tasty treats, most of which originate from France. $

CUREPIPE Many writers have seen Curepipe as a dismal place. Mark Twain described it as 'the nastiest spot on earth'. Michael Malim, writing in the 1950s book *Island of the Swan*, which caused a stir in Mauritius when it was published, said, 'it seems drowned in some immemorial woe … stricken and inconsolable'. Mauritians themselves say there are two seasons in Curepipe: 'the rainy season and the season of rains'. In fact, its annual rainfall matches London's. It can be humid ('God – the dankness of it all,' wrote Malim) and temperatures as low as 7°C have been known.

Perhaps its off-putting publicity is a campaign by the 85,000 or so residents to keep visitors away. They like their privacy. The avenues of the residential areas are lined with tall bamboo hedges, hiding the old, French-style, verandaed villas, wooden cottages and concrete, cyclone-proof houses. Streets have no names displayed, nor numbers on the houses, so only those familiar with the town will find their way around. It is not a welcoming place, with its grim market building of upturned culverts. The town seems to have no heart, either geographically or spiritually.

Its origins go back to the 18th century when it was a halt for travellers from one side of the island to the other. The usual story is that travellers stopped to smoke there, after which they would clean (cure) their pipes. However, its name is more likely to have come from a village in France.

One of Curepipe's most attractive buildings, the **town hall**, wasn't originally in Curepipe at all. The whole structure was moved from Moka in 1903. The **town hall** overlooks a large compound of open square and gardens with the **Carnegie Library** and the former railway station close to it. Nearby is the towering, Gothic-style Roman Catholic **Ste Thérèse Church** built in 1872. The formal **gardens**, with lawns, flowerbeds and pathways, soften the administrative square and provide relief from the chaos of the open-air market nearby. The gardens include a memorial to Abbé de la Caille, the 18th-century surveyor of the island, and a romantic statue of Paul and Virginie, which is a bronze replica of Mauritian sculptor Prosper d'Epinay's original. There are other listed national monuments in Curepipe, notably

the grim stone building of **Royal College**, the island's most prestigious school, and the **war memorial** in front of it.

It is tempting to wonder if the **market** building will ever be declared a national monument; it is certainly a unique feature of Curepipe's skyline, with its ugly concrete pipes pointing upwards. The **public toilets** are closed for cleaning every day, 06.00–06.30, 10.30–10.45, 15.00–15.15 and 17.15–17.30. Be warned.

Curepipe is another popular town for shopping. As well as the usual imitation designer clothing and duty-free jewellery shops, there are numerous handicraft outlets, including several model ship shops.

Curepipe has its own small **botanical gardens** (⊕ *08.30–17.00 daily; free admission*) to the southwest of the centre; there are entrances on Botanical Gardens Street and on Robinson Street. The gardens opened in 1870 and cover almost 27 acres. They are less impressive and less formal than the Sir Seewoosagur Ramgoolam Botanic Gardens (page 135), but pleasant nonetheless and free to wander around. The last remaining specimen of the rarest palm tree in the world (*Hyophorbe amaricaulis*) is found here, protected by fencing.

If you have hired a driver to tour the island they will almost certainly include a visit to the extinct volcanic crater of **Trou aux Cerfs**. If you are driving yourself, you can reach Trou aux Cerfs from the centre of Curepipe: follow Sir John Pope Hennessy Street for about 800m, then turn right into Edgar Hughes Street. It is a short climb to the parking area and you can then walk around the crater, which is around 350m in diameter, 80m deep and lies at 650m above sea level. The inside of the crater is heavily wooded. If you've been to Réunion you won't be overly impressed by the crater, but the views are far-reaching and it is the most vivid reminder of the island's volcanic origins. The panoramic view takes in the plateau towns and the mountains to the north and northwest, including the three cones of **Trois Mamelles** (629m). The parking area overlooks the unsightly spread of Curepipe, with the Church of St Thérèse standing out on the horizon amidst all the concrete.

On the road from Curepipe to the motorway is the **Millennium Monument**, an 18m-high tower made of no fewer than 3,500 dark blue basalt stones, some six or seven million years old. It was erected by the Ministry of Arts and Culture to 'celebrate the passage of the Republic of Mauritius into the third millennium'.

Getting there and away The north and south **bus stations**, are on Sir J H Jerningham Street, near the market and on either side of Châteauneuf Street. Buses from Port Louis to Curepipe leave from the Victoria Square bus station. There are regular buses to Mahébourg, via Rose Belle and the airport. Buses also depart from Curepipe for Centre de Flacq, Souillac, Grand Bassin (via Bois Chéri) and Wolmar (via Flic en Flac). The best place to find a **taxi** is on Châteauneuf Street. If you are in your own **car**, be aware that Curepipe is one of the towns where street parking coupons (bought at petrol stations) are required.

 ## Where to stay

Budget

🏠 **Auberge Madelon** (25 rooms) Sir John Pope Hennessy St; \676 1520; e madelon@intnet. mu; www.auberge-madelon.com. Just north of the town centre. Simple, slightly tired en-suite rooms with fan, TV & phone. There is a restaurant, small pool & Wi-Fi. **$$**

Shoestring

🏠 **Harry Inn Guesthouse** (18 rooms) Sir J H Jerningham St; \670 6667; www.harryinn.com. Simple en-suite rooms with TV, minibar & safe. Free Wi-Fi at reception. Breakfast is provided & there is a kitchen on the 1st floor. **$**

✕ Where to eat The **Prisunic supermarket** near the town hall stocks all the essentials. For cheap snacks, try the stalls around the market.

✕ Ginger Garden Village Shopping Centre, Botanical Gardens St; ☎ 676 0250. Cuisine: European, Creole. An attractive, modern restaurant serving good-quality dishes. $$$
✕ La Potinière Hillcrest Bldg, 18 Sir Winston Churchill St, Curepipe; ☎ 670 2648; ⊕ for lunch

Mon–Sat, for dinner Tue–Sat. Cuisine: French, crêpes, Creole, snacks. Claims to be the oldest restaurant in Mauritius. Has a sophisticated summery atmosphere. Reservation recommended. $$$

Other practicalities

Communications The **post office** is near the market and offers internet access.

Money and banking Banks, including branches of Barclays, HSBC and Mauritius Commercial Bank, are found on Royal Road, in the centre of town.

BLACK RIVER GORGES NATIONAL PARK AND AROUND ✳

Access to the Black River Gorges National Park from Curepipe and Vacoas is via **La Marie**. There is a memorial here to the hapless English adventurer Matthew Flinders who, having helped explore and map Australia, stopped off in Mauritius in 1803, unaware that the British and French were at war. He was arrested by the French and imprisoned on Mauritius for six years.

About 3km southeast of Curepipe, off the A10, is the **Monvert Nature Walk**, which has an arboretum of endemic trees, a fernery and trails through the forest. It is a protected area managed by the National Forestry Service and there is a visitor centre. The walks are not difficult, but remember to use mosquito repellent.

Along the road (B3) to the national park are two important bodies of water. The reservoir of **Mare aux Vacoas** is the largest in Mauritius, a mountain lake at 600m above sea level, surrounded by pine forest. Unlike many of the reservoirs it can be visited by road and is a popular spot for local fishermen. Southwest of the lake is a visitor centre with information on the local flora and walks in the area. This is the starting point of the **Sophie Nature Walk**, which is an easy 45-minute walk through a wooded area to the shores of the lake.

Further on through the forest, where deer abound, is a motorable track leading to **Mare Longue**, another reservoir. The track passes through the shorn terrain of tea plantations and through woods where monkeys leap excitedly out of the way of the occasional car. It is possible to hike from the main road on forest trails to reach the waterfalls of Sept Cascades, also known as **Tamarind Falls**. You can see the falls from a viewpoint near the village of Henrietta, and you can walk from there to the falls. It is wise to go with a guide and allow 4 hours to visit the seven main waterfalls. From Henrietta you can drive to Tamarind Falls Reservoir, which is surrounded by traveller's palm. There is accommodation and a restaurant here (pages 196–7).

The main road continues southwards, passing into the Black River Gorges National Park, and reaches a crossroad at **Le Pétrin**. This is on the eastern edge of the park and there is a new visitors' information centre (☎ *258 0057*; ⊕ *07.00–17.00 Mon–Fri, 09.00–17.00 Sat/Sun*) with good, shaded picnic facilities. At the visitor centre are maps of the various hiking trails around the national park and staff are on hand to assist. Nearby is a fenced bird release area, where birds are kept prior to their release into the national park.

Black River Gorges is the largest national park in Mauritius (6,574ha) and protects the remaining native forests on the island. It is home to many of the rare

endemic plants and birdlife, and offers spectacular natural scenery and excellent walks. However, some areas where conservation projects are in progress are off-limits to visitors. These areas are clearly marked. (For detailed information, including a map of the national park, see pages 12–14.)

At Le Pétrin, the turning to the east leads to **Grand Bassin**, a natural lake in the crater of an extinct volcano at 702m above sea level, regarded as sacred by Hindus. It is also known as **Ganga Talao** (Lake of the Ganges) because Hindus believe it is linked to the Ganges by an underground stream. The road to the lake is extra wide to allow for pilgrims to walk alongside it and two towering 33m-high statues stand sentinel on either side of the approach. On the right is the god Shiva and on the left is the goddess Durga. Hindus come here regularly to pray in the temples and in front of the ornate statues of gods which stand in the water. They leave offerings of fruit and incense on small pedestals on the lake's edge. Japanese macaque monkeys and birds watch carefully from a distance, before raiding the fruit left for the gods, while fish and eels in the lake gorge themselves on the dropped offerings. When you visit, keep an eye out for eels – locals believe seeing them brings luck.

Grand Bassin features on the itineraries of all tour operators and coaches of tourists tend to arrive from late morning and throughout the afternoon. Scores of tourists line up for a Hindu blessing, each returning to the coach proudly sporting a token *tika* (red dot) on their forehead. Early morning and late afternoon are the best times to visit. Shoes should be removed before entering any of the temples. During the festival of **Maha Shivaratree** (page 69), in honour of the god Shiva, is when Grand Bassin really comes to life. For several days during February/March hundreds of thousands of Hindus make the journey to the lake, where they leave offerings for Shiva and take holy water from the lake to purify their bodies. Traditionalists make the pilgrimage following an all-night vigil, dressed in white and carrying the *kanwar*, a highly decorated wooden structure which they make themselves. Nowadays it is not unusual to see families making the journey by car but the number of pilgrims on foot lining the roads is still an incredible sight.

During **Ganesh Chaturthi** (page 69), Hindus gather at the lake to pray and to place statues of the elephant-headed god Ganesh in the water. It is a joyful festival: the music and chanting is almost hypnotic, and the worshippers' colourful clothing is contrasted against the often grey skies and water.

The **Kanaka Crater** lies off the road that goes beyond Grand Bassin towards **Bois Chéri**. Along with nearby Bassin Blanc, Trou aux Cerfs and Grand Bassin, it is thought to have been one of four volcanoes on the island active during the past 700,000 years. It is overgrown but you can clamber up the sides of the extinct volcano and look into it. Along this road is the entrance to tea-growing country, with hills up to 500m above sea level covered with the close-cropped bushes. This area is covered in *Chapter 7*.

 ## Where to stay *Map, page 188*

Budget

⌂ **7 Cascades Lodges** (5 lodges, 1 house) Pitois Rd, Henrietta; m 5290 7380; e info@7cascades.com; www.7cascades.com. Don't be too put off by the approach, down narrow, rough roads past the Tamarind Falls Reservoir. The lodges & restaurant were built in 2014 to a good standard, in a quiet setting overlooking the reservoir & with views of the mountains around Port Louis. Each has a double bedroom, en suite, minibar & a small sitting area where a child could sleep. A 4-bedroom house (the villa) is also available & has its own small pool. There is a restaurant on site, which is just as well as it is a fair drive to the nearest one. Activities are available, including quad biking & mountain biking (included for lodge guests) & canyoning at Tamarind Falls can be arranged. A good base for walks to Tamarind Falls. **$$**

Where to eat *Map, page 188*

✗ 7 Cascades Pitois Rd, Henrietta; m 5290 7380; ⊕ for lunch daily, dinner on reservation. Cuisine: Creole, European, Indian. An open-fronted restaurant with views of Tamarind Falls Reservoir & the surrounding countryside. The menu offers plenty of choice & the setting is relaxing. They cater for lunches & weddings, so it is worth telephoning in advance to check they are open. $$$

MOKA

This district is part of a plateau of scrub, sugarcane and, in the midlands area, tea. It caters for the educational and academic overspill of Port Louis, with the University of Mauritius and the Mahatma Gandhi Institute, and also the Mauritius Broadcasting Corporation. Nearby is the president's official residence at Le Réduit.

Coffee was planted here when it was introduced from Al Makha in Yemen, hence the name 'Moka'. Its boundary runs along the mountains ringing the south of Port Louis to Pieter Both, then skirts below La Nicolière Reservoir, across Nouvelle Découverte Plateau – embracing the agricultural centre of the island – to the outskirts of Curepipe and Rose Hill.

The approach to Moka is by the two-lane motorway that links Port Louis with the residential plateau towns. After crossing the St Louis Stream, the road passes through **Pailles**, a suburban community with a church, temple and mosque overshadowed by **Pailles Hill** (225m) and the peaks of the **Moka mountain range**.

Southwest of Le Réduit is **Bagatelle**, a relatively new, large and very modern shopping centre with 130 shops and a food court.

There is little of interest to tourists in the Moka area, aside from **Eureka**, a colonial house open to the public and where accommodation is available. The lane leading to it lies off to the right, just after the road to Moka crosses the rubbish-clogged Moka River. Although it has a French colonial appearance with its 109 doors and windows and encircling veranda, it was built by an Englishman, with the help of a French carpenter, at the beginning of English colonisation. It gained its name when Eugène Leclézio, a wealthy lawyer and planter, cried 'Eureka' as his bid to buy the house at auction in 1856 was accepted. See also page 200 and below.

WHERE TO STAY *Map, page 188*
Mid range

 Eureka (3 rooms) Moka; ☏ 433 8477; e eurekamr@intnet.mu; www.maisoneureka.com. Accommodation is available in 3 cosy wooden guesthouses in the grounds of Eureka, a colonial house built in 1830 (page 200). They are simply furnished, equipped with double bedroom, bathroom & kitchenette. They sleep 2 adults & a baby. If you want to escape the heat of the coast for a few days, then this is an option. Priced at the bottom end of mid range. $$$

✗ WHERE TO EAT *Map, page 188*

✗ Le Ravin Eureka, Moka; ☏ 433 4501; e eurekamr@intnet.mu; www.maisoneureka.com; ⊕ for lunch daily. Cuisine: Creole, French. This restaurant comes with plenty of atmosphere: dining is on the veranda of the colonial house, overlooking the grounds. You can wander through the house & admire its 19th-century furniture while waiting for your meal. The Creole dishes are excellent & there are some more upmarket European dishes on offer too. It is easily reached from Port Louis so is popular for business lunches. $$$

✗ Escale Creole Moka; m 5422 2332; www.escalecreole.net; ⊕ for lunch Mon–Fri on reservation. Cuisine: Creole. This delightful table d'hôte, run by mother & daughter, lies to the east of Moka on the B46. Tables are arranged on a homely veranda in a shady garden. Delicious traditional menus are prepared using only fresh ingredients & with great attention to detail.

Meals must be booked a day in advance & it is worth trying to book when the tour groups are not visiting. Friendly service & authentic Creole dishes make this memorable. $$

AROUND LE REDUIT

AROUND LE REDUIT Although many Mauritians aspire to studying at an overseas university, they do have an option locally. The **University of Mauritius** at Le Réduit was created in 1965 with the help of a £3 million grant from the British Government. The **Mahatma Gandhi Institute**, for the study of Indian and African cultures, is within walking distance of the Le Réduit campus. The institute contains the **Museum of Indian Immigration** (page 200).

In 1748, the French governor built a small wooden fort, surrounded by a ditch and stone walls, on a 290m-high bluff between two rivers. It was to serve as a redoubt (*réduit*) for women, children and valuables of the French East India Company if ever the island was invaded. It became the official residence of the French, and then the British, governors of the island and was extended several times to create a rather grand house. The gardens are equally impressive, filled with a mixture of native and exotic plants.

Today, Le Réduit is the president's official residence and is therefore only open to the public two days a year. Apparently the president is not keen on tourists strolling around his backyard, scrutinising his flowerbeds.

The eastern part of the Moka district is sparsely populated, with **Quartier Militaire** on the main road (A7) the only settlement of any size. It was once a military post offering protection to travellers against attacks by runaway slaves. After passing through Quartier Militaire the road continues to Centre de Flacq and the east coast.

WHAT TO DO IN CENTRAL MAURITIUS

HIKING The Black River Gorges National Park provides the island's best opportunities for hiking and seeing wildlife. For more information, see pages 12–14, and pages 92–3. Alternatively, try the hike to Tamarind Falls (page 195).

HORSERIDING **Domaine de l'Etoile** at Moka offers horseriding. For more information, see opposite.

OTHER SPORTS The **Mauritius Gymkhana Club** (*Suffolk Rd, Vacoas;* \ *696 1404;* e *recep.mgp@intnet.mu; www.mgc.intnet.mu*) has an 18-hole golf course (page 83), tennis courts, pool, squash courts, gym, snooker table and a modern clubhouse with a view of the golf course. It also has a restaurant, bar and library. Temporary membership is available to visitors on a daily or monthly basis.

QUAD BIKING Available at Domaine de l'Etoile (opposite).

CASINOS The **Casino de Maurice** (\ *602 1300;* ⊕ *21.00–04.00 Mon–Fri, 13.00–04.00 Sat/Sun*) is near the town hall in Curepipe. **Le Grand Casino** (\ *286 0405*) at Domaine les Pailles is open every evening. There is a **Ti Vegas** casino at St Jean Road, Quatre Bornes (\ *454 8800*).

SPA TREATMENTS **Spa Viva** at 102 St Jean Road, Quatre Bornes (\ *467 8907;* e *spaviva@intnet.mu*) offers massages and beauty treatments.

SHOPPING Quatre Bornes and Curepipe are known for their markets and bargain shops, Floréal for its knitwear and two of the island's largest, new shopping centres

are in the area, Bagatelle at Moka and Les Halles at Phoenix. For more information, see pages 70–3.

WHAT TO SEE IN CENTRAL MAURITIUS

MAURITIUS GLASS GALLERY (*Pont Fer, Phoenix;* \ *696 3360;* e *mgg@intnet.mu;* ⏰ *08.00–17.00 Mon–Sat; admission Rs50*) The workshop at Pont Fer produces handmade glass ornaments from recycled glass and aims to promote environmental awareness. Impressive glass-blowing demonstrations take place throughout the day except 12.00–13.00 and there is a shop selling the products, which are reasonably priced. You can have your hands, feet or other body parts cast in glass, but you need to wait three or so days for it to be ready then return to collect the finished product or have it delivered to your hotel for a small fee. Prices for the hand casting start at around Rs600 (child), Rs1,000 (adult). They will also produce custom-designed glassware. There is a museum containing items made since it opened in 1991. You can also buy the glassware at their shop at the Caudan Waterfront in Port Louis.

BOTANICAL GARDENS (*Curepipe;* ⏰ *06.00–18.00 daily; admission free*) The botanical gardens are a pleasant place in which to recover from the cacophony of Curepipe. There is a small lake where nandia palms can be seen.

DOMAINE DES AUBINEAUX (*Curepipe;* \ *676 3089;* e *sales@saintaubin.mu;* ⏰ *09.00–17.00 daily; admission adult/child Rs350/175*) An attractive colonial house built in 1872 as the home of the owners of the Bois Chéri Tea Estate. In 1881, it became the first house on the island to be provided with electricity. In 2001, it was converted into a museum. Visitors can take a guided tour of the interior, which contains antique furniture and photographs from the 19th and 20th centuries. The guide will explain the history of the family and the estate, as well as significant events in the island's past. The house is surrounded by a beautiful garden containing ancient trees. The visit is followed by a tea-tasting and lunch is also available. There is a small gift shop, selling locally made soap, rum and tea. Domaine des Aubineaux can be visited as part of the Route du Thé, which also includes a visit to the Bois Chéri Tea Factory and lunch at Le Saint Aubin (pages 167–8).

DOMAINE DE L'ETOILE (*Royal Rd, Moka;* m *5729 1050;* e *info@terrocean.mu; www.terrocean.mu;* ⏰ *09.30–16.30 daily*) This 1,200ha former sugar estate lies on the Grande Rivière Sud-est. The fields and forests, which are home to deer and many species of bird, can be explored on foot, horseback, quad bike, Segway or mountain bike. Archery is also available, using animal-shaped targets dotted around the forest. The estate has some beautiful scenery, including views of the coast from its hilltops. If you want to enjoy it at speed, there is a network of ziplines from 350m to 750m. The adventure playground for children (aged 3–12 years) is impressive and an unusual concept for Mauritius. There is a good restaurant serving Mauritian cuisine and some of the packages include lunch. Wear full-length trousers and bring mosquito repellent and suncream. Reservation recommended for all activities.

DOMAINE DE RAMBOUILLET (*La Nicolière;* m *5729 3737;* e *info@terrocean. mu; www.terrocean.mu*) Owned by the same group as Domaine de l'Etoile, this is another estate which provides experiences away from the beach, although it is smaller and less well known than most of its competitors. Deer, wild boar and

9

guinea fowl dwell in the forest, some of which is endemic. Mountain biking, hiking, quad biking and archery are all available.

EUREKA (*Moka;* \ *433 8477;* e *eurekamr@intnet.mu; www.maisoneureka.com;* ⊕ *09.00–17.00 Mon–Sat, 09.00–15.30 Sun; admission adult/child/under 12 Rs300/150/free (house & garden)*) This dainty Creole mansion, built in 1830, which is now open to the public, houses a restaurant and also offers accommodation in its grounds. It is set in pleasant gardens fronted by the Moka River, while the Moka mountain range towers behind the house. The house is decorated in colonial style with antique furniture, some of which was produced by the French East India Company. Every detail is designed to take you back to that era and it is certainly very evocative. Unfortunately, there is almost no information about the house's history on display, so you really need to ask for a guide to wander about with you. The staff seem to put more effort into the restaurant than the house but they are happy to show you around if you ask. The house is small and doesn't take long to visit, so if you are going to come to Eureka I would do so for lunch to make it worthwhile. The kitchen was built separate from the house to prevent fires and the meals served in the restaurant are still prepared there. A trail through the grounds leads down through woodland to a series of waterfalls, where you can swim if you are happy to brave the chilly water. The path is steep in parts so decent footwear is advisable. See also page 197.

MUSEUM OF INDIAN IMMIGRATION (*Le Réduit;* \ *433 1277;* ⊕ *09.00–16.00 Mon–Fri; admission free*) The museum holds records relating to the indentured labour scheme and Indian immigration. They can help visitors trace ancestors who came to Mauritius as indentured labourers.

MAURITIUS ONLINE

For additional online content, articles, photos and more on Mauritius, why not visit www.bradtguides.com/mauritius.

10

Island Dependencies

AGALEGA

Agaléga is situated between the Seychelles and Mauritius, west of the Mascarene Ridge, about 1,122km north of Mauritius. There are actually two islands (North and South), separated by a sandbank which can be forded at low tide. The north island is 12.5km long and 1.5km wide, while the south island is 7km long and 4.5km wide.

The islands were named by the Portuguese after the nationality of their discoverer in 1501, Juan de Nova, who was a Spanish Galician serving the King of Portugal. In 1808, the island received its first settlers, and in 1827 the French began to organise the production of coconut oil and copra, using slaves from Madagascar. Slave dungeons, a slave cemetery and a cemetery for whites dating from that period remain on the island.

There are nearly 300 people living on Agaléga, which is administered by the Outer Islands Development Corporation as an island plantation producing coconut oil. It is almost entirely covered with coconut palms and some casuarinas. North Island has the main coconut mill on it, as well as an airstrip and the main village, **Vingt Cinq**. Vingt Cinq (meaning 25) is thought to have been named after the number of lashes the slaves received as punishment for misdemeanours. The resident manager of the coconut plantation is responsible for a working population of 180 to 200. There is no running water on the island, drinking water is collected as run-off from roofs, and the roads are coral sand tracks. There is a police station and a primary school but to attend senior school children have to go to Mauritius. In 2002, Mauritius Post opened a post office on Agaléga but hit a problem when the local population popped in to buy stamps using coconuts and other objects. Agaléga had always used a barter system or paid for goods at the two local shops using government vouchers which debited their salary account. Nowadays, money is in circulation.

Agaléga has one attraction from a wildlife perspective: the Agaléga Island day gecko (*Phelsuma borbonica Agalégae*), endemic to the island.

The islands are not easy to reach. A ship visits twice a year to replenish supplies, and there are light aircraft flights, which are not for the faint-hearted.

ST BRANDON

The St Brandon Archipelago, also known as the Cargados Carajos Islands, is a grouping of sand banks and islets with a total land area of 1.3km². These lie 430km northwest of Mauritius, forming an arc from south to north, its convex side facing towards the east. There are 22 low-lying islands, parts of which are sometimes submerged, as well as numerous reefs and sandbanks. The larger of the islands are named **Cocos**, **Albatross** and **Raphael**, which is the administrative centre and home to a privately owned commercial fishing station.

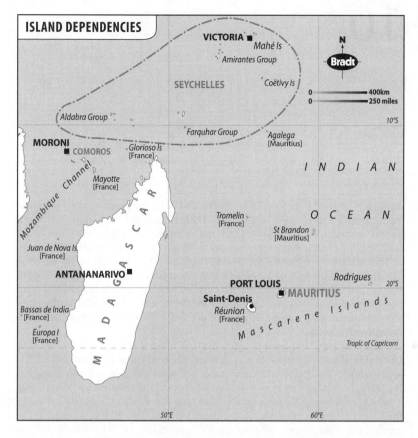

ISLAND DEPENDENCIES

VICTORIA
Mahé Is
Amirantes Group
SEYCHELLES
Coëtivy Is
Aldabra Group
Farquhar Group
Agalega
[Mauritius]
MORONI
COMOROS
Glorioso Is
[France]
Mayotte
[France]
Juan de Nova Is
[France]
ANTANANARIVO
Bassas de India
[France]
Europa I
[France]
MADAGASCAR
Mozambique Channel
Tromelin
[France]
St Brandon
[Mauritius]
PORT LOUIS
Saint-Denis
Réunion
[France]
MAURITIUS
Rodrigues
Mascarene Islands
Tropic of Capricorn
I N D I A N
O C E A N
N
Bradt
0 400km
0 250 miles
10°S
20°S
50°E
60°E

From 1546, the islands were shown on Portuguese charts as São Brandao, which is puzzling since St Brandon is an Irish saint. The Portuguese also called them Cargados Carajos, deriving the name from Coroa dos Garajãos, meaning 'reef of seabirds'.

Green sea turtles stop off at the archipelago for nesting and the islands abound with birds; in the past guano was the main export. In 1862, cotton was tried, without success. Cyclones, problems with fresh water, and the harsh conditions of life (no women) also affected the islands' development. Since the 1830s, the richness of the fishing grounds has been exploited and in 1910 there were 100 fishermen based in the islands.

Fish is salted and dried for export to Mauritius. Fishermen are engaged by the Outer Islands Development Corporation, which manages St Brandon, on a four to six months' contract. Their working day begins at dawn and by 07.00 they are at sea. After they have returned with their catch, the fish have to be gutted, cleaned and put in the salt beds.

The fishermen, several dozen of them from Mauritius, Rodrigues and the Seychelles, lodge in barracks. Raphael Island has a modest chapel, a house for the administrator and his staff, a hangar for the salt fish, a community hall and a shop.

In recent years, several companies have started offering catamaran cruises to St Brandon, primarily targeting fishing and diving fans. These include **Saint Brandon Cruises** (m 5728 3030; e info@saintbrandon.com; www.saintbrandon. com) and **Mauritius Catamaran** (269 1000; e info@mauritiuscatamaran.com;

www.mauritiuscatamaran.com). It takes around 30 hours to reach the islands by catamaran and the cruises typically last around ten days.

TROMELIN

Mauritius and the Seychelles claim sovereignty over Tromelin but France owns it and Madagascar wants it. It is a flat, sandy, barren place, less than 2km long and about 640m wide. It lies between the St Brandon Archipelago and Madagascar, actually closer to Madagascar than Port Louis, which is 564km away.

Mauritius's claim to ownership is based on the capitulation terms of 1810, as Tromelin was regarded then as a dependency of Mauritius. In 1954, the British allowed the French to build a meteorological station and landing strip on the island. France and Mauritius agreed a co-management treaty in 2010.

It was known in the 18th century as Ile des Sables or Sandy Island. In 1761, a French vessel named *L'Utile* carrying 160 slaves from Madagascar to Mauritius was shipwrecked on the reef which extends from its southern point. Of the 140 crew, 123 reached the island, but only between 60 and 80 of the slaves because most drowned in the hold where they were confined. The whites in the crew built a boat and reached Madagascar safely. They left the blacks on the island, promising to return. Although those who reached Madagascar asked the French authorities to send a ship to rescue the slaves left on the island, the request was refused on the grounds that France was at war and could not spare a vessel. It was 15 years before a French chevalier, M Tromelin, landed and found seven women living there and an eight-month-old child. They were the only survivors, having existed on shellfish, turtle and brackish water. He took them to Mauritius.

Tromelin is an important seabird nesting site, in particular for masked and red-footed boobies. It is also a nesting site for sea turtles and at night it swarms with hermit crabs. It is hard to reach because of the lack of a harbour and anchorages, and is not open to tourists.

THE CHAGOS ARCHIPELAGO

Officially, the Chagos Archipelago, together with Desroches, Farquhar and Aldabra, formerly part of the Seychelles group, now constitute the British Indian Ocean Territory (BIOT). However, Mauritius contests the sovereignty of the Chagos Archipelago, and the BIOT is not recognised by Mauritius. The archipelago lies 2,229km northeast of Mauritius, and the Chagos Islands are off-limits to visitors.

SIX ISLANDS Also known as the Egmont Islands, this group of six uninhabited coral atolls arranged in a horseshoe shape is 109km from Diego Garcia. When they were dependencies of Mauritius, they were harvested for coconuts as well as supplying pigs, poultry and fat-tailed land crabs. They are connected by shoals and access is difficult because of the reefs and breakers.

PEROS BANHOS A cluster of a score of small islands which form the largest group of the Chagos Archipelago, Peros Banhos forms a basin of 29km in length, north to south, and 19km in breadth from east to west. The main one, Ile du Coin, is about 3km long. They were also known as the Iles Bourdés after a M de Bourdé, who is credited with discovering them after the Portuguese had named them.

In the 18th and 19th centuries, the islands were home to up to 500 people employed in the coconut plantations and fishing station. In 1970, the British

10

Government removed the entire population to Mauritius. Part of Peros Banhos is now a nature reserve. Access to the islands is prohibited.

SALOMON ISLANDS Known as Les Onze Iles, being 11 in number, the Salomons were named after a ship called *Salomon*. They form a basin with a safe anchorage for vessels of small draught and are a popular anchoring spot for yachts, although permission is needed from the BIOT. Their soil is rich in coconut trees, which used to be harvested by resident Mauritians. The residents were removed by the British Government and the islands are now uninhabited. Remains of the island's buildings are now overgrown with vegetation. In the last century, these islands were noted for a rare tree called *faux gaiac*, which grew to a height of 40m, and was a deep chocolate colour, with sound wood when old. Fresh water could be obtained from wells. Turtles used to be found here but, owing to the presence of seals, not so many fish.

TROIS FRERES Actually four small islands, connected by shoals. Coconuts grow on all of them and fish, turtles and fresh water are all to be found. Nearby, between this group and Six Islands, are **Eagle** and **Danger** islands. All used to provide coconut oil for the Mauritius market.

DIEGO GARCIA

Diego Garcia is the largest of the islands of the Chagos Archipelago and undoubtedly the most famous due to the presence of a United States military base. It is in the form of a serpent bent double, its interior forming a broad, steep, coral wall standing in the ocean. This encompasses a lagoon which is a large natural harbour and safe anchorage. The island is 28.5km^2 in area with a steep coral reef all around, except at the entrance to the lagoon.

The French exiled leprous slaves to Diego Garcia from Mauritius claiming that the turtle, which would be their sole diet, would restore them to good health. In 1792, an English merchant ship sent two Indian crew members ashore for water and some of the leper residents – women as well as men – met them and showed them to a well. When the master of the ship learned of the encounter he made the seamen stay on the island and sailed away as fast as he could.

After the British takeover in 1810, the exiling of leprosy sufferers was discontinued and some 300 migrants, including Europeans, went voluntarily from Mauritius to set up a saltfish trading company and to plant and harvest coconuts. The settlement flourished peacefully for 150 years.

By 1965, the population of the entire Chagos Archipelago had grown to some 900 families, representing 2,000 inhabitants. The islands were dependencies of Mauritius and the *îlois* – the Creole term for the Chagos islanders – conducted trade with Mauritius through an irregular ferry link. They were content with their simple and presumably happy existence.

In the countdown to independence, Britain decided to detach Diego Garcia and the nearby islands from Mauritius, virtually taking them over a second time. The politicians in Mauritius were obliged to agree because, being a colony, they had little choice and gaining independence was their priority. Three million pounds in development aid was the reward while Mauritius stipulated two conditions for letting Britain keep Diego Garcia: it would be used for communication purposes only, and the atoll would be returned to Mauritius if Britain no longer needed it.

Having signed the agreement, Britain created a new colony: the British Indian Ocean Territory. The Chagos islanders were bemused, but the future soon became

clear. The ferry service linking them to Mauritius was stopped, the sole employer of labour was bought out by the British and the copra plantation was closed down. Work ceased, and so did food imports. Many of the *ilois* had to leave to survive.

Less than a year later, in 1966, Diego Garcia was leased to the United States of America for 'defence purposes'. The 2,000 *ilois*, 500 of whom lived on Diego Garcia, were removed to Mauritius and the Seychelles. Foreign Office documents reveal one British official wrote, 'unfortunately, along with the birds go some few Tarzans and Man Fridays whose origins are obscure and who are hopefully being wished on to Mauritius'. The lease to the US was for 50 years, with an option for a further 20 years, which both parties were scheduled to agree by December 2014. No agreement has been reached.

Today, Diego Garcia is the main US military base in the Indian Ocean, with superb port facilities, the latest in communications systems and a 3,600m runway capable of handling, and fuelling, B52 bombers. It is in an excellent strategic location and has been a key launch pad for aerial bombardments during the Iraq and Afghanistan campaigns. It is now the only inhabited island in the Chagos Archipelago, with a resident population of military personnel.

The removal of the Chagos islanders and the ongoing use of Diego Garcia as a US military base has caused an enduring cyclone of protest and controversy. After years of angry negotiations, Britain acknowledged that the Chagos islanders, who had been forcibly displaced from their homes, were entitled to better treatment than being abandoned in the backstreets of Port Louis. Compensation was paid in 1982, but mainly to the Mauritian Government, who had to accommodate the islanders.

In November 2000, the *ilois* won an historic victory in the English High Court, which upheld their right to return to their homeland. However, the British Government declared that this ruling had to be balanced with their treaty obligations to the US and affirmed that the right to return excluded Diego Garcia. Furthermore, the UK and US both said it was not their responsibility to arrange for the Chagos islanders to return.

In June 2002, the British Foreign and Commonwealth Office completed a feasibility study into resettlement of the islands and concluded that it would be difficult, precarious and costly. Harvard resettlement expert Jonathan Jenness commented that the study's conclusions were 'erroneous in every assertion'.

In June 2004, the British Government used the Royal Prerogative – effectively a decree by the government in the name of the Queen – to enforce the continued exile of the *ilois*. The Chagos islanders challenged the government's order and, in 2006, High Court judges ruled in their favour, granting them the right to return to the islands and describing the government's order as 'repugnant'.

The Court of Appeal upheld the decision in 2007, but, on 23 October 2008, the British Government won its appeal to Britain's highest court, the House of Lords, against the previous rulings allowing the Chagos islanders to return home. British Foreign Secretary David Miliband welcomed the ruling. On behalf of the government he expressed regret for the way the resettlement of the Chagos islanders was carried out, but noted: 'the courts have previously ruled that fair compensation has been paid and that the UK has no legal obligation to pay any further compensation'.

In April 2010, the British Government established a marine reserve around the Chagos Islands. While the marine environment around the islands certainly merits protection, the motivation behind the creation of the reserve was called into question when a cable released by Wikileaks revealed that a Foreign Office official

had told a US counterpart that 'establishing a marine park would, in effect, put paid to resettlement claims of the archipelago's former residents'.

In March 2015, the United Nations Permanent Court of Arbitration ruled that the Chagos Marine Protected Area was illegal under the United Nations Convention on the Law of the Sea because Mauritius had rights to fish the waters surrounding the archipelago, to the eventual return of the Chagos Archipelago and to the preservation of any minerals or oil discovered in or near the archipelago prior to its return. The judgement declared that the UK's undertaking to return the Chagos Archipelago to Mauritius once it was no longer needed for defence purposes meant Mauritius had an interest in significant decisions affecting the islands' future. This has given hope to Mauritius, which continues to claim the archipelago, and to its former inhabitants who continue to fight for repatriation and compensation. In June 2015, they went to the British Supreme Court to bring a challenge the 2008 ruling. Their legal team included human rights lawyer Amal Clooney, wife of Hollywood actor George Clooney, whose involvement is sure to shine a spotlight on their cause. However, with the US unlikely to give up its position on Diego Garcia, particularly while there is unrest in the Middle East, Diego Garcia is unlikely to be returned to Mauritius in the near future. Resettlement on one of the other islands is perhaps a more likely option.

UPDATES WEBSITE

You can post your comments and recommendations, and read the latest feedback and updates from other readers online at www.bradtupdates.com/mauritius.

Part Three

RODRIGUES

Country An integral part of Mauritius, with its own regional assembly

Location 560km east of Mauritius

Size Rodrigues has an area of 108km^2; it is 18km long (west–east) and 8km at its widest point (north–south). It is roughly equivalent in size to the British Channel Island of Jersey and is surrounded by 14 satellite islets.

History Discovered by Arabs, then Portuguese explorer Diego Rodriguez, in 1528. Some believe Diogo Fernandez de Pereira got there first in 1507. The first settlers were French Huguenots fleeing France, who arrived in 1691. The French colonised the island in 1725; the British took it in 1809. A dependency of Mauritius until 1968, when Mauritius gained independence, Rodrigues has remained part of Mauritius. Since 2002, it has had a degree of autonomy and has been governed by the Rodrigues Regional Assembly.

Nature Valleys and forest with rare wildlife, rugged coastline, beaches and coral reefs

Climate Generally warmer and drier than Mauritius. In summer (November to April), temperatures range from 29°C to 34°C, and in winter (May to October) from 15°C to 29°C. Subject to drought, winds from the southeast and prone to cyclones.

Capital Port Mathurin

Population Approximately 42,000 (2014); 98% of Creole origin

Economy Based on subsistence agriculture and fishing. Tourism and handicraft production are growing.

Language Creole is the everyday language; French is widely spoken and English much less so

Religion 97.5% of the population is Roman Catholic. Anglicans, Adventists, Hindus, Muslims and Rastafarians form a minority.

Currency Mauritian rupee (Rs), which is divided into 100 cents (cs).

International telephone code +230

Time GMT+4

Electricity 220V AC

For accommodation and restaurant price codes, see pages 64 and 66.

11

Background Information

OVERVIEW

Rodrigues is remote, a part of Mauritius but 622km further northeast. It is an incredibly special place.

There's something stark about the island and things are decidedly low key. It is not a tropical paradise but those in search of something offbeat will find it a fascinating, peaceful place to explore, with a people whose shy friendliness is genuine. Life here is slow and refreshingly uncomplicated. People are concerned with the essentials of human existence, like feeding their families and being part of a community, rather than office politics, global recession and conflict in the Middle East. Being such a small island, it has a delightful intimacy and sense of security, and no-one is ever too busy to stop for a chat.

As they are administratively linked, much of the information about Mauritius in *Chapters 1–3* is relevant to Rodrigues.

GEOGRAPHY

Like the other Mascarenes, Rodrigues is of volcanic origin. Its landscapes of steep hills, plunging valleys and scattered rocks create the impression that it is much larger than it is. The two highest points are Mont Limon, a mere 398m, and Mont Malartic at 386m.

There are no impressive mountains and no imposing rock formations; large rivers and lakes are also absent and there are only a few really attractive beaches. Where Rodrigues wins hands down is in the quality of its marine environment. The island is entirely surrounded by reefs, which offer some of the best underwater experiences available in the Indian Ocean. A vast lagoon (200km²) shelters some of the best beach and reef areas. Viewed from the island's hilltops, the lagoon is every shade of blue and dotted with tiny islets.

Much of the island features grass or scrub-covered slopes, some of which are rocky with black cliffs. At Plaine Corail, in the southwest, the landscape is especially harsh and barren. The remaining woodlands are severely degraded and cover only certain hillsides around the Solitude–Citronelle–Cascade Pigeon area. However, the Mauritian Wildlife Foundation is working hard to regenerate pockets of native vegetation (page 214). The higher reaches of the hilly interior are often covered by mist, at which time the surrounds take on a dreamy, sultry ambience.

Among the island's many coral caves is the often-visited, 795m-long Caverne Patate, near Plaine Corail, and those within the François Leguat Giant Tortoise and Cave Reserve. The tumbling Cascade Pigeon River offers some of the island's more attractive scenery. While much of the coast features rocky shores, there are also some white, sandy beaches on the east coast, like St François and Trou d'Argent.

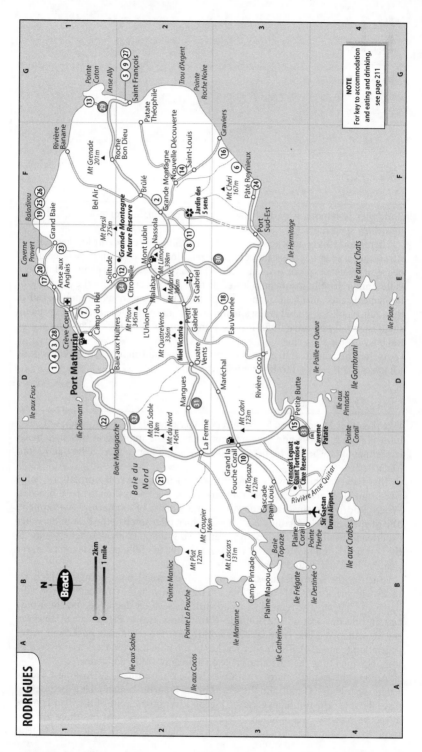

RODRIGUES

NOTE
For key to accommodation and eating and drinking, see page 211

The east coast tends to be windy but the beaches are incredibly beautiful and are invariably deserted bar the odd flock of sheep passing through.

Off the coast lies the stunning Ile aux Cocos, an uninhabited sand island and habitat for seabirds. It is one of the island's most popular excursions (pages 244–5).

NATURAL HISTORY AND CONSERVATION

FLORA AND FAUNA When the first settlers arrived on Rodrigues, they found an island largely swathed in woodland and populated by a bizarre ensemble of animals. These included two species of giant tortoises, fruit bats, herds of dugong in the lagoons and a variety of endemic birds.

Most conspicuous of these were the Rodrigues solitaire (*Pezophaps solitaria*), the island's answer to the Mauritian dodo. These extraordinary creatures shared their Mauritian cousins' fate and were soon exterminated. Trade in the two species of giant tortoise began in 1736. By the turn of the 19th century, they too were extinct.

Of 17 endemic species of vertebrate, just three remain: the Rodrigues warbler (*Acrocephalus rodericanus*), Rodrigues fody (*Foudia flavicans*) and the Rodrigues fruit bat (*Pteropus rodericensis*).

The two surviving endemic bird species are both threatened. The greyish Rodrigues warbler is classed 'near-threatened'. A survey in 1974 recorded just 32 warblers, by 1999 the number had climbed to 150, and in 2010 the population was at 4,000. Since 2010, an increase in the population has been observed but there has been no survey to confirm numbers. The increase is largely the result of habitat restoration by the Mauritanian Wildlife Foundation and has seen the population move from 'Endangered' to 'Near Threatened'.

The pretty yellow and orange Rodrigues fody has moved from 'Vulnerable' to 'Near Threatened' after a survey in 2010 revealed a population of around 8,000. This is a marked improvement on the numbers from 1974, when there were just 30 individuals.

To see the endemic birds, go to the Grand Montagne Nature Reserve, the areas along the island's central ridge, the woods around Cascade Pigeon River or Solitude, not too far from Port Mathurin. You should find both species within half an hour.

The endemic Rodrigues fruit bat is the last remaining indigenous mammal. As a result of conservation efforts, the population of Rodrigues fruit bats numbered

11

RODRIGUES
For listings, see pages 232–7

🏠 **Where to stay**

1	Auberge Anse aux Anglais	D1	9 Chez Claudine	G2	19 Le Ravenal	F1
2	Auberge de la Montagne	F2	10 Chez Clenya	C3	20 Le Récif	E1
3	Auberge le Lagon	D1	11 Chez Jeanette	F2	21 Le Refuge	C2
4	Auberge Les Filaos	D1	12 Coralie la Différence	E2	22 Les Cocotiers	E1
5	Auberge St Francois	F2	13 Cotton Bay	G1	23 Les Varangues	E1
6	Bakwa Lodge	F3	14 Domaine les Rosiers	F2	24 Mourouk Ebony	F3
7	Bellevue Guesthouse	E1	15 Gite la Caverne	D3	25 Petit Coin Villa	F1
8	Cases à Gardenias	F2	16 La Belle Rodriguaise	F3	26 Résidence Foulsafat	F1
			17 La Cabane d'Eté	D1	27 Tekoma	G2
			18 La Fantaisie	E3	28 Ti Pavillon	D1

✖️ **Where to eat and drink**

	Chez Claudine	(see 9)	La Belle Rodriguaise	(see 16)	Mourouk Ebony	(see 24)
	Chez Jeanette	(see 11)	32 Le Pandanus	D2	33 Resto La Caverne	D3
29	Chez Madame Larose	G1	Le Récife	(see 20)	34 Valerie's	E2
30	Domaine La Détente	E3	Le Refuge	(see 21)		
31	John's Resto	D2				

around 15,000 in 2015. Once, these famed 'blonde bats' were on the verge of oblivion. They were down to a population of fewer than 100 during the mid 1970s when the late Gerald Durrell and the Jersey Wildlife Preservation Trust (now the Durrell Wildlife Conservation Trust) undertook a collecting expedition to Rodrigues and Mauritius (see box below). Thanks to the intensive captive-breeding efforts which followed the JWPT expedition, along with habitat creation and restoration and sensitisation campaigns throughout Rodrigues by the Mauritian Wildlife Foundation, the bat population has increased substantially. Bats can be seen any time of the day, roosting in trees but they are easiest to spot from about 16.00 when they fly from their daytime rest sites. The best places to see them include Solitude, between Port Mathurin and Mount Lubin, or near Malabar.

Owing to continuous reforestation work, the outlook for the Rodrigues fody, Rodrigues warbler and Rodrigues fruit bat is bright, provided that their forest habitat is safeguarded.

THE DURRELL WILDLIFE CONSERVATION TRUST IN THE MASCARENES

When Gerald Durrell founded Jersey Zoo in 1959, he chose the dodo as the trust's symbol, vowing that its tragic story would never be repeated. He also had the conservation of species in the wild as his main goal, a concept that we now accept as normal, but something that was a radical departure for a zoo 50 years ago. Since that time, Jersey Zoo has become the Durrell Wildlife Conservation Trust. Building on Gerald's legacy, their mission is saving species from extinction. Conservation efforts are delivered through the three pillars of the Trust, the wildlife park in Jersey, the field programmes around the world and the training programmes that provide the conservationists of the future with the skills they need to save species.

When Gerald first visited Mauritius and Rodrigues in 1976, indigenous birds had been reduced to 13 species, including the world's rarest pigeon, falcon and parrot all teetering on the brink of extinction. Off the Mauritian coast, Round Island was the bleak, barren home of eight species of reptiles, including the world's two rarest snakes. Nearby Rodrigues had suffered drought and cyclones in addition to manmade indignities. The Rodrigues fruit bat was considered the world's rarest bat, and only two endemic species of native land birds remained. Small conservation efforts were under way but the international zoological community largely regarded the Mascarenes as paradise lost – it seemed that the legacy of the dodo would continue. With the encouragement of the Mauritian Government and the support of the International Council for Bird Preservation (now Birdlife International), Durrell mounted an intense conservation campaign to save some of these species. This effort led to the establishment of the Mauritian Wildlife Foundation (MWF) in 1984. Since that time MWF has become the leading non-government environmental organisation in Mauritius, championing the cause for biodiversity conservation and restoration in the islands. Durrell's commitment to encouraging and supporting local expertise continues.

With species such as the Mauritius kestrel and pink pigeon on the very edge of extinction, not only were drastic steps needed but the team had to develop new techniques and skills to ensure the last remaining individuals did not disappear. With only four kestrels and nine pigeons left, a combined response involving captive breeding and extensive field work was needed to start turning numbers around. Now there are over 300 kestrels and pink pigeons in the wild. As a result

ENDANGERED FLORA Most of the 49 endemic plant species are rare, with fewer than five wild plants widespread on the island. These include the madrinette (*Hibiscus liliiflorus*), a hibiscus endemic to Rodrigues, which has been saved from extinction. This was done after only two were found to remain on Rodrigues itself. One of the world's rarest plants, 'café marron' (*Ramosmania rodriguesii*), is Rodriguan. A lone specimen remains in the wild on the island, just off the road near Mont Plaisir, where it is carefully fenced in. In 1986, cuttings were sent to Kew Gardens, where one took root. Seeds were sent back from Kew to Rodrigues in 2007 and 2010 and in 2009 seedlings were planted close to the mother plant at Mont Plaisir. Between 2010 and 2012, more than 40 seedlings were planted in the nature reserve at Grande Montagne. Several cuttings have also been propagated in Rodrigues since the 1990s and there are now hundreds at Kew. Many of the island's indigenous plants are shared with the other Mascarenes, where they are usually more numerous.

of these joint achievements, the Mauritian Government have set up a national park in the last remaining natural forest, Black River Gorges. Similar successes were achieved for the echo parakeet which went from around 12 individuals to now more than 600 and the Rodrigues fruit bat which now numbers over 15,000 individuals. The skills developed with these species have been applied to conservation projects around the world and hundreds of students and researchers have studied the recovery of these populations, contributing greatly to our knowledge of threatened species recovery.

Developing from the restoration of these species was the concept of rebuilding Mauritius's highly threatened ecosystems, starting with some of the offshore islands and one in particular, Round Island. Round Island was used by sailors as a dumping ground for goats and rabbits and soon these animals grazed out the native vegetation, sending the native flora and fauna almost to extinction. After a major programme of eradication for the goats and rabbits it was possible to start working on the restoration of the plants and animals. Almost immediately the island's flora started to recover. Intensive work started on the endemic reptiles and together with management on the other offshore islands populations of Telfair's skink, Gunther's gecko and the Round Island boa have been shown to recover. Recently non-native tortoises have been introduced to the island to replicate the grazing functions carried out by now extinct native species and studies have shown how native plant species benefit from this, while introduced plants do not.

We have now extended this model to work on a number of the smaller islands off Mauritius. We are currently restoring the native reptiles to these islands and working with the National Parks and Conservation Service, a government agency, to restore vegetation and remove invasive species.

The world-renowned Durrell Wildlife Conservation Trust has enjoyed spectacular success with its Mascarene-related projects.

Donations may be made to the Mauritius Programme of Durrell Wildlife Conservation Trust, which works with the MWF, by sending a cheque in any currency to Durrell Wildlife Conservation Trust (*Les Augrès Manor, La Profonde Rue, Trinity, Jersey JE3 5BP, Channel Islands;* 01534 860000; e info@durrell.org; www. durrell.org). To find out more about the Durrells' fascinating work or to become a member, contact them at the same address or via their website.

11

The critically endangered shrub 'figue marron' (*Obetia ficifolia*), is extinct on Mauritius but is shared with Réunion, where it is known to be pollinated by a single, endangered species of butterfly. Another vulnerable shrub is the 'bois cabris' (*Clerodendron laciniatum*); growing to 3–4m high, it bears small clusters of white flowers. The hardwood tree 'bois d'olive' (*Cassine orientalis*), which attains a height of 20m, was once used to make furniture.

REFORESTATION The Mauritian Wildlife Foundation (MWF) has been doing marvellous work in Rodrigues, with help from the Rodrigues Regional Assembly. In 1996, a nursery was established at Solitude, where all the native Rodriguan plant species are being propagated.

Even the local pandanus, which are endemic and which appear plentiful, are threatened because of extensive rat damage. Like many of the threatened plant species, it has been used for centuries by Rodriguans in their daily lives. Whilst many of the plants have a medicinal purpose, the leaves of the pandanus are used for weaving. Some pandanus populations which are heavily harvested for woven handicrafts are at risk. The MWF has undertaken community projects to boost the numbers, with the help of villagers who take responsibility for the young plants. In the long term, both the plants and the villagers will benefit.

Very noticeable in the remaining Rodriguan woods is the high proportion (97%) of exotic vegetation. In particular, eucalyptus, aloes (*Furcraea foetida*) and lantana have taken over large tracts of land. However, the MWF is hard at work, weeding out the alien vegetation and replanting saplings of other fast-growing native trees.

Visiting a nursery like the one at Solitude or the nature reserves is certainly encouraging, and well worth the effort if you want to see the endemic and indigenous flora up close. When seeing the extent of the reforestation programmes and the commitment of the MWF staff and volunteers, one can't help but feel positive about the future of Rodriguan flora and fauna.

MARINE ENVIRONMENT Its glorious lagoon is one of Rodrigues's greatest assets and has benefited from a lack of industrial pollution. The coral reef is self-seeding and receives no coral zooplankton from elsewhere, which makes for a unique environment with limited biodiversity, including one species of coral, two species of fish and several crustaceans found nowhere else.

Being a small island with a growing population and developing tourism industry, the lagoon is prone to overfishing. Thankfully tourism is being developed carefully to minimise any negative impact. **Shoals Rodrigues** (page 218) does important work educating Rodriguans on marine environmental protection and promoting alternative livelihoods for fishermen and women. One of their key achievements has been the establishment of four marine reserves, where fishing is prohibited.

Traditionally ladies walk out into the lagoon and catch octopus, one of the staples of the Rodriguan diet. Recently, as a means of protecting the octopus and the reef, Rodrigues has introduced a closed season. Octopus can no longer be caught between August and October.

ABUNDANT SEABIRDS ON OFFSHORE ISLANDS The idyllic Ile aux Cocos is an island sanctuary, nature reserve and breeding ground for huge populations of seabirds. Common noddies (*Anous stolidus*) and lesser noddies (*A. tenuirostris*) are present in their thousands, nesting on casuarina ('filao') trees (*Casuarina equisetifolia*) wherever space permits. The sooty tern (*Onychoprion fuscatus*) and

the graceful fairy tern (*Gygis alba*) are also present. Part of Ile aux Cocos is fenced off to protect ground-nesting sites.

Nearby Ile aux Sables is a nature reserve and closed to the public. It is home to fairy terns, common noddies and lesser noddies. According to Ian Sinclair and Olivier Langrand, who co-authored the excellent field guide *Birds of the Indian Ocean Islands*, common tern (*Sterna hirundo*) and wedge-tailed shearwater (*Puffinus pacificus*) are also seen there.

For information on excursions to Ile aux Cocos, see page 245.

HISTORY AND POLITICS

Rodrigues shares its history with Mauritius although it was discovered later, in 1528, and retained the name of its Portuguese discoverer, Diego Rodriguez, throughout Dutch, French and British colonisation. Some historians maintain that it was discovered earlier, in 1507, by another Portuguese seafarer, Diogo Fernandez de Pereira.

The Dutch paid little attention to Rodrigues and the first known settlers were French, although they came during the Dutch period. These were nine French Protestants fleeing from France, led by François Leguat. They had actually been trying to reach Ile Bourbon (Réunion) but stumbled upon Rodrigues in 1691 and found the island covered in luxuriant vegetation, with an abundance of birds and tortoises. After two years, the settlers made it to Mauritius, where Leguat was arrested on the orders of the Dutch governor and charged with amber trafficking.

In 1725, France decided to colonise Rodrigues in the name of Louis XV and sent eight soldiers, 13 planters and 15 slaves. The colonisation was unsuccessful, although some of the slaves remained when the French left. The French noted that Rodrigues suffered from more cyclones and higher winds than Ile de France, and had a difficult approach through rocks and shoals to the harbour they called Port Mathurin.

The first permanent settler was a master mariner, Germain le Gros, who arrived in September 1792 to engage in fishing and trading. He was followed in 1793 by Michel Gorry and Philibert Marragon, who had visited previously in 1791. Marragon and his wife lived at L'Orangerie until both died on Rodrigues in 1826. They, and several slaves, are buried at L'Union, near a monument to the slaves (see also pages 231–2).

In the time-honoured manner of expatriates living on a small island, the three French settlers distrusted each other and soon fell out. Marragon was civil agent for the French Government, a position that did not deter him from entertaining and welcoming the crews of British ships when they put in for water and food, much to Le Gros's annoyance.

The fraternisation of the settlers on Rodrigues with the British made the new governor of Ile de France, General Decaen, keen to replace Marragon and the others with his own island's unwanted lepers. The plan failed. Marragon remained and the lepers went to Diego Garcia.

Marragon conducted a census in 1804 which shows the island's population as 22 whites (about half of them actually of mixed race) and 82 slaves. The majority of the slaves were from Mozambique, yet nearly a third (24) were born in Rodrigues.

In 1794, Britain decided to capture Ile de France, but their attempts were limited to foraging expeditions to Rodrigues. They wanted to take Rodrigues too, and concentrated on building up good relations with the settlers by paying for their supplies instead of looting. By August 1809, they had no qualms about making their intentions known and landed the first of their forces to capture Ile de France: 200 infantry and 200 sepoys (Indian soldiers trained by the British).

11

The occupation of Rodrigues began enthusiastically, with Colonel Keating, who was in command, writing home: 'These are some of the most delightful valleys I ever saw and the soil naturally rich in one of the finest climates in the world capable of producing every sort of vegetation and there is a sufficient quantity of land already cleared for cultivation and the feeding of cattle.' Keating imported cattle and slaves from Madagascar as more British troops assembled.

In July 1810, a force of 4,000 left Rodrigues and went on to capture Ile Bourbon (Réunion) from the French. Following their unexpected defeat at Vieux Grand Port in August, the British gathered a large force in Rodrigues for their successful assault on Ile de France in December 1810. After that, the British occupied Rodrigues until April 1812 when they withdrew, leaving behind most of the 300 slaves they had imported. British rule of Rodrigues was confirmed by the Treaty of Paris in May 1814.

The first British settler was a young man called Thomas Robert Pye, a lieutenant of the marines at a loose end, who was sent by Governor Farquhar in 1821. He stayed only two years. When slavery was abolished, those slaves who had not emancipated themselves already promptly left their owners and squatted on crown land. They finally settled in the mountains where their descendants still live today.

In the mid 19th century, several Europeans or near-Europeans settled in Rodrigues, mostly in the lowlands. They included shipwrecked sailors and minor British civil servants who liked the island. Some of the British married Rodriguan women while others had affairs with them and, as the saying goes in Rodrigues, 'left one or two portraits behind'.

The portraits and the mixed-blood population were centred on Port Mathurin, Baie aux Huîtres, Grand Baie and La Ferme. When the first steamer arrived in the 1890s, so did more settlers, including Indian and Chinese traders. By 1970, the Chinese owned 90% of all the shops on the island.

The growth of the population was rapid. As there were more men than women at first, most women had several partners, their children being raised as the children of the man of the moment. At the end of the 19th century, the population was 3,000. Twenty years later this had become 6,573. The population almost doubled in subsequent 20-year periods, becoming 11,385 in 1944, 18,587 in 1963 and 32,000 in 1981.

Rodrigues was administered as a dependency of Mauritius during the 158 years of British rule. Like a poor relation, it was mostly forgotten or neglected, with occasional official reports warning of the consequences of too large a population.

Since 1968, it has been an integral part of Mauritius. For many years it was run as a district of Mauritius, but Rodrigues sought greater autonomy over its affairs and on 12 October 2002 the newly created Rodrigues Regional Assembly met for the first time. The Assembly is made up of 18 members, plus an executive council headed by a Chief Commissioner. At present the Organisation du Peuple Rodriguais (OPR) has a majority of ten members. While the assembly may initiate legislation, this must pass through the Mauritian National Assembly to become law. For further information, visit the Assembly's website http://rra.govmu.org.

ECONOMY

Fishing and agriculture provide the livelihood of Rodriguans although the young hanker for employment either with government or in commerce. There is little vibrant private sector, in contrast to Mauritius.

Onions and garlic are grown for export to Mauritius and maize and chicken are produced for home consumption. Livestock (cattle, pigs, sheep) are also reared for the Mauritian and local markets. Octopus is dried and fish salted for export.

The traditional system of farmers growing maize and beans, helping each other with harvesting and existing on a barter basis has died out. People have become money and subsidy minded. As a district of Mauritius, social benefits filter through to the island from central government and international aid agencies.

A decline in agriculture over the last decade has resulted in a boom in small handicraft units, which is being encouraged by the growth of tourism. Handicrafts, in particular goods woven from pandanus leaves, are an important source of income, in particular for women.

The island's fishing industry is organised on a co-operative basis under the auspices of the Rodriguan Fishermen's Cooperative Federation. Fish is delivered to the area co-operative for distribution and sale on the island or for cold storage at the plant in Port Mathurin. Training in fishing methods, assistance with boat and equipment purchase, catch monitoring and marketing, and foreign aid funding are all provided under various schemes to sustain a viable fishing industry.

The tourism industry in Rodrigues is gradually being developed and has the potential to become one of the island's greatest income earners. The airport has been expanded and several mid-range hotels have been built, some of which are managed by groups with hotels in Mauritius. Rodriguans have, by and large, reacted positively to the establishment of tourism, with many families opening their homes to offer guesthouse-style accommodation. However, tourism in Rodrigues continues to struggle and the island has not received the number of visitors that had been expected.

It is vital that tourism in Rodrigues is developed gradually and thoughtfully. The Rodriguan way of life will be vulnerable to overdevelopment and the island's already stretched resources, water and waste disposal in particular, will be further tested. Rodrigues will never compete with Mauritius's beaches, luxury hotels and first-class service. Nor should it try to. It has a charm of its own, which will attract visitors who will relish the island as it is.

PEOPLE

Travellers coming to Rodrigues from Mauritius are often surprised by how different the population looks. Rodrigues has a predominantly Roman Catholic Creole population, descended from African and Malagasy slaves. Rodriguans sometimes feel closer to the Seychelles than to the Indo-Mauritian-dominated Mauritius. That's a contention visitors are often made aware of as Rodriguans speak freely about the neglect of their isolated backwater.

LANGUAGE AND EDUCATION

Creole is the everyday language but educated Rodriguans also speak French. Although English is the official language and is used in school and official communication, it is less spoken on Rodrigues than in Mauritius.

The secondary school in Port Mathurin is a joint venture between the Roman Catholic and the Anglican churches. There are five state secondary schools on the island, at Maréchal, Le Chou, Mont Lubin, Grande Montagne and Terre Rouge. Rodrigues College in Port Mathurin is partly private.

RELIGION

The Roman Catholic faith is very strong and is the religion of the majority. Other active religions are Anglicanism, Adventist, Islam and Hinduism.

Creoles and Chinese form the Roman Catholic community, although some Chinese are members of the Anglican Church. There are no Buddhists. The Muslim community is small, mostly traders, but supports a mosque in Port Mathurin. There are a few Rastafarians in the interior village communities.

SHOALS RODRIGUES

Shoals Rodrigues is a non-governmental organisation, which developed from the Shoals of Capricorn Programme, a three-year initiative led by the Royal Geographical Society.

The new organisation was established in September 2001 to continue the marine research, education and training activities on Rodrigues. With the combination of these three disciplines good progress is being made towards discovering more about the seas around Rodrigues and promoting sustainable resource use and marine conservation.

The Shoals Centre is based at Pointe Monier, on the outskirts of Port Mathurin, alongside the government agencies which have responsibility for the sea, such as the Coastguard, the Fisheries Protection Service and the Fisheries Research and Training Unit. Our work focuses on collecting information about the Rodrigues lagoon and seas, which can be used to improve the management of the important fishery resources and protect the biodiversity and health of the marine ecosystem. Our most recent project is the establishment of marine reserves around Rodrigues. We have just finalised a draft management plan for four northern marine reserves to aid the sustainability of the fisheries sector and the viability of alternative livelihoods for those who depend on fishing.

The Shoals Rodrigues Centre is run by a committed group of young Rodriguans with the help of a newly established board of trustees. Our work on the reef fisheries, zooplankton populations and the effect of land-based sediments has been developed in collaboration with foreign experts. We have been carrying out an extensive programme of coral reef surveys to monitor the health of the reef ecosystem and now have ten years' worth of data on the reefs of Rodrigues.

With training in the scientific collection and analysis techniques this local team is working towards building up important long-term data sets. Many new skills and techniques have been taught to a wide range of people on the island. These range from first aid, lifesaving and diving qualifications to marine tourist guide training. We also regularly visit fishing villages to give first aid and swimming training to fishermen and to discuss marine ecology and resource use.

Shoals Rodrigues is also a thriving centre for young people who come to learn more about the marine environment through 'Club Mer'.

The work of Shoals Rodrigues is supported by private donations, as well as a variety of organisations in Mauritius and abroad: the Decentralised Cooperation Programme, the Indian Ocean Commission, North of England Zoological Society, the United Nations Development Programme, GEF-SGP, the British and Australian high commissions, Barclays Bank, the US National Fish and Wildlife Foundation and the Sea Trust, as well as many others.

Visitors are welcome to come and see the work of the organisation at Pointe Monier. Contact Jovani Raffin (✆ 831 1225). If you would like to help or find out more visit www.shoals-rodrigues.net.

Witchcraft is also practised in the traditional Afro-Creole manner of believing in the efficacy of certain potions, charms, herbs, fortune telling and the warding off of evil.

CULTURE

Rodriguans pride themselves on their hospitality and refer to their remote haven as the 'anti-stress' island. It's certainly worth taking time to see some of the towns, villages and scenery and to get a feel for Rodriguan lifestyle.

Most of the people live either off the sea or the land. The crops cultivated – onions, garlic, chillies, potatoes and maize – are not the same as on Mauritius. As a result, the countryside bears no resemblance to that of Mauritius, but reminds many of the Transkei in southern Africa, with deep green valleys, cultivated lands, and herds of livestock (cattle, goats and pigs).

Maize cobs are left to dry on roofs, which is very reminiscent of Africa and something that is not seen in Mauritius. Sausages, left to cure in the sun, are also often seen on rooftops. The rather uninspiring but neatly built square houses one sees so much of in the countryside are government subsidised, built using coral bricks and designed to be cyclone-proof.

Water is very scarce in Rodrigues. Although there is a mains water supply, most houses have water tanks for collecting and storing water.

In late afternoon, fishermen can be seen sailing to shore in their pirogues and bringing in their nets, whilst at low tide groups of women wade out to the reefs to fish for octopus. This requires a great deal of skill as the octopus are well camouflaged.

One of the highlights of the week for most people is the market at Port Mathurin on Wednesday and Saturday, where much of the home produce is sold.

On weekend evenings the island vibrates to the sound of traditional music at nightclubs, hotels, community 'balls' and private celebrations. Dancing is a vital part of the Creole culture but the European influence is obvious: the *Scottish*, *polka*, *laval* (the waltz) and *quadrille* are still danced today, mainly by the older generation. The traditional *séga-tambour* has its roots in Africa and Madagascar. The *séga* of Rodrigues is said to be closer to its original form than that of Mauritius, thanks to its isolation from external influences. It is also known as the *séga coupé* because the only couple on the dance floor is continually separated by other male and female partners cutting in.

The European influence can also be seen in the musical instruments, namely the accordion, which gave rise to the *séga-kordion*. However, there is now concern amongst the older generation that the tradition of accordion playing is at risk, as few young people are learning to play the instrument. With the help of the European Union, a programme to teach the accordion to youngsters has been established. The Franco-Malagasy legacy to the Rodriguan folk group is a series of simple instruments, such as the drum, the *maravanne* (a small box filled with dry seeds), the triangle and the *bobre* (musical bow).

FESTIVALS One of the highlights of the Rodriguan calendar is **Fish Day** on 1 March, when celebrations throughout the island mark the first day of the dragnet fishing season. *Banané*, or New Year (from *Bonne Année*), is also a time for festivities, which typically last for a week. Families eat their fattened pigs and there is a drinking contest known as *Le Roi boire*.

On 12 October the island celebrates **Autonomy Day**, marking the day in 2002 when Rodrigues gained autonomy. Concerts and street fairs take place around the island.

The **Kreol Festival** at the beginning of December remembers the island's history and showcases its culture. Music, dancing and local food are, as usual, at the centre of the celebrations.

Accordion Day coincides with the Roman Catholic Assumption of the Virgin Mary on 15 August. The accordion has been central to the island's musical tradition since the 19th century and musicians from around the island gather to show-off their skills.

The **Sea Festival** takes place in September and includes a regatta. There is also a **kitesurfing festival** in June/July. For further information, see page 240.

UPDATES WEBSITE

You can post your comments and recommendations, and read the latest feedback and updates from other readers online at www.bradtupdates.com/mauritius.

12

Practical Information

HIGHLIGHTS

A visit to Rodrigues is about simplicity, nature and getting back to basics, and any stay here is inevitably enhanced by encounters with the supremely friendly and happy local residents. **Hiking** is an absolute pleasure thanks to the lack of traffic, abundance of tracks and glorious views of the ocean. A good option is a guided hike along **Sentier Pasner** with a villager who has been trained by the Mauritian Wildlife Foundation and can tell you about the local flora and fauna (see page 239). I would also recommend a walk along the east coast between Graviers and St François, stopping off at beautiful, isolated beaches such as **Trou d'Argent** and **Anse Bouteille** (page 243).

The vast, pristine lagoon is one of Rodrigues's greatest assets and offers excellent **diving and snorkelling** (pages 240–3). You can also explore the lagoon in a **transparent kayak** (page 239). The business is run by a co-operative of fishermen and women as part of a project to provide them with an alternative source of income and reduce the impact of fishing on the marine environment.

Ile aux Cocos, a sand islet and nature reserve off the west coast, is stunning (pages 244–5). It has been carefully protected, is an important nesting site for seabirds, and has staggeringly beautiful beaches.

Don't miss the **market** in Port Mathurin (Wednesday and Saturday). The fruit, vegetables, preserves and honey would win prizes at any British agricultural show, and the market is a great place to pick up locally made handicrafts, such as the ubiquitous bags made from pandanus leaves.

The **François Leguat Giant Tortoise and Cave Reserve** [210 C3] (page 244) is worth a visit and gives an insight into what the island would have looked like before humans arrived, when Rodrigues was the domain of giant tortoises and flightless solitaire birds. There are caves to explore here too, as well as at **Caverne Patate** [210 C4] (pages 243–4).

Many local people have opened their homes as guesthouses or little restaurants offering table d'hôte meals. **Sleeping and/or eating in a Rodriguan home** is an enriching way to experience local culture and home-cooked food. The sea provides much of the diet and fresh local fish and octopus are showcased in a variety of dishes.

The traditional **music and dancing** is slightly different from that in Mauritius, and includes variations like the *séga-tambour* (page 219). Many of the hotels organise a *séga* night and locals gather in homes and in restaurants on a Sunday to dance and catch up on gossip.

TOURIST INFORMATION

For information before you go, contact the Mauritius Tourism Promotion Authority (MTPA), either in your home country or in Mauritius (for contact details, see page 42).

The Rodrigues Tourism Office, which opened in 2006, is on Rue de la Solidarité, Port Mathurin (↘ *832 0866;* e *info.rodrigues@intnet.mu;* *www.tourism-rodrigues.mu;* ⏰ *08.00–16.00 Mon–Fri, 08.00–12.00 Sat, 08.00–10.00 Sun*). Its website contains plenty of useful information and it publishes some helpful brochures on the island.

EMERGENCY SERVICES

Police emergency ↘ 999
Police station Port Mathurin; ↘ 831 1536
Ambulance Queen Elizabeth Hospital; ↘ 831 1628
Coastguard ↘ 831 2182

At the same location is Discovery Rodrigues (↘ *832 1062;* e *discoveryrodrigues@intnet.mu*), a company owned by the Rodrigues Regional Assembly which runs the main tourist sites on the island. It is here you can buy permits to visit Ile aux Cocos (pages 244–5) and Caverne Patate (pages 243–4), although if you organise this through a tour operator they will usually take care of the permits for you.

TOUR OPERATORS

The sense of going somewhere 'off the beaten track' begins as soon as you try to get to Rodrigues. As yet, few tour operators feature the island. For tour operators running tours to Mauritius and Rodrigues, see pages 42–3.

RED TAPE

Entry requirements are as for Mauritius (see pages 43–4). Only Britain and France have honorary consulates in Rodrigues. For other countries, the relevant high commission, embassy or consulate in Mauritius has responsibility for Rodrigues (see pages 46–7).

UK
Mrs Suzanne Auguste CARE-Co Centre, Camp du Roi; ↘ 832 0120; e brhonconrod@intnet.mu

FRANCE
Mr Benoît Jolicoeur Jean Tac; ↘ 831 1760; e jolicoeur@yahoo.com

GETTING THERE AND AWAY

BY AIR Air Mauritius flies regularly between Mauritius and Rodrigues, with at least four flights per day in peak season and two per day in low season.

Demand for flights from Mauritius is high and reservations need to be made well in advance, and reconfirmed. The return airfare from Mauritius varies significantly depending on time of year and availability but it is generally expensive for non-citizens at around Rs7,000 return. However, it is possible to include Rodrigues on an Air Mauritius ticket from Europe to Mauritius at a reduced add-on rate, if it is bought prior to flying to Mauritius. Alternatively, tourists can soften the blow by buying the air ticket from a travel agent in Mauritius (instead of from Air Mauritius or overseas), as part of a package that includes accommodation.

Flights to Rodrigues have their own departure area at Sir Seewoosagur Ramgoolam Airport so you don't need to go into the main part of the airport building. The Rodrigues departure area is decidedly low key with a small snack bar and rows of seating. Passports must be shown even though this is a domestic flight and travellers do not have access to duty free. It is advisable to check in early, otherwise your seat may be given to someone on standby. The luggage allowance is

just 15kg, unless you are coming from overseas and have only transited Mauritius, in which case the allowance for your international flight applies.

Flying time between Mauritius and Rodrigues is 1 hour 30 minutes. The ATR42 has 48 seats and not much leg or arm space, so keep your hand baggage small.

Air Mauritius can be contacted at the airport (✆ 832 7700) or at their office in the ADS Building on Rue Max Lucchesi in Port Mathurin (✆ 831 1558; e mkrodrigues@ airmauritius.com).

BY SEA The sea crossing to Rodrigues from Mauritius takes around 36 hours but only 24 hours on the way back. It can be rough, particularly on the way to Rodrigues. The *Mauritius Trochetia* is a mixed cargo and passenger ship, and takes up to 108 passengers in cabins. It is worth knowing that much of the cargo is livestock, usually cattle and sheep being exported from Rodrigues to Mauritius. It makes two journeys per month between Mauritius and Rodrigues. The cabins are comfortable, particularly the deluxe ones. The tourist-class cabins don't have their own shower room and WC, but the first-class, semi-deluxe and deluxe cabins do. There are two restaurants, one much more upmarket than the other and it is certainly worth paying the extra, as the café-style one can get pretty hectic. Prices for second-class cabins start from Rs3,500 per person. The schedule for crossings is available online (*www.mauritiusshipping.net*) or you can contact the Mauritius Shipping Corporation in Mauritius (✆ 217 2284) or Rodrigues (✆ 831 0640).

ON ARRIVAL/DEPARTURE The first sight of Rodrigues, in the dry season, is of parched hillsides with cactus-like vegetation and box-type houses dotted all over an inhospitable landscape. Arriving by air, the views of the surrounding lagoon are spectacular.

The Sir Gaëtan Duval Airport [210 C4] (*www.airportofrodrigues.com*) is on the coast in the southwest of the island. When I first visited Rodrigues in 2002, the airport terminal was a tiny, one-storey building, with spectators waiting obediently behind the perimeter fence where jeeps and buses were parked. The person at the immigration desk had a hand-written list of the passengers due to arrive on each flight, and he checked the names off one by one. However, things have changed in the last few years. There is now a smart, new terminal building with a small duty-free shop, café, a couple of tiny souvenir shops and, in the arrivals area, a very short baggage carousel. The immigration and customs procedures have been formalised in line with those in Mauritius although the approach is still more relaxed here (see page 44). You don't have to be on Rodrigues long to notice that woven pandanus leaves are used to make almost anything, and it is great to see that this extends to the trays in which you put your belongings before they go through the X-ray machines.

Getting to your hotel Most hotels and guesthouses will provide airport transfers for a fee, usually around Rs500–800. It is a wise idea to pre-arrange transport, particularly if you are arriving after 16.30, because timetables and services can be a bit hit and miss in Rodrigues and things tend to close early. If you haven't pre-arranged transport you should be able to take a taxi, shuttle or bus during the day. There is a bus stop just outside the airport, opposite the police station, with buses to Port Mathurin from 06.00 to 16.30. The journey takes around 35 minutes and the bus can drop you off at the villages *en route*. It costs around Rs30.

Car parking is available at the airport for a flat fee of Rs20, or Rs40 for large vehicles. If you are planning to hire a car, **2000 Tours** (✆ *831 4703;* e *resa@rodrigues-2000tours.com; www.rodrigues-2000tours.com*) offers car hire from the airport and can also organise accommodation and excursions.

HEALTH AND SAFETY

There is no malaria on Rodrigues so you need not take prophylaxis. The advice on inoculations for Mauritius (see page 50) applies equally to Rodrigues.

Insect repellent is necessary as mosquitoes are abundant. Strong sunblock is essential. As in Mauritius, tap water can cause upsets, so it is advisable to drink bottled water.

There is one **hospital** on the island, the Queen Elizabeth Hospital [210 E1] (✆ *831 1628*) at Crève Cœur on the outskirts of Port Mathurin. In emergencies they will send an ambulance. Medical care is also available at the Mont Lubin Clinic (✆ *831 4403*) and La Ferme Clinic (✆ *831 7202*). There is a **pharmacy** (✆ *831 2279;* ⊕ *07.30–16.30 Mon–Sat, 07.30–11.30 Sun*) in Rue de la Solidarité, Port Mathurin, and one on Rue Mamzelle Julia.

A huge plus factor on Rodrigues is safety: crime, it would appear, is virtually absent. There are three prison cells, which are hardly ever occupied. Nevertheless, caution cannot be a bad thing and women should not walk alone at night or in dimly lit areas.

WHAT TO TAKE

Take light, casual cotton clothing. Bathing costumes and T-shirts are acceptable everywhere. Remember beach shoes to protect your feet against sea urchin spines whilst swimming. Comfortable trainers with a sturdy grip are sufficient for the hiking trails.

Paul Draper of CARE-Co gave me a handy tip for travellers to Rodrigues: take a second form of photo identification, other than your passport. If you lose your passport on Rodrigues, you will need a new one before you can board a flight back to Mauritius. Unfortunately, there are no embassies or consular officers on Rodrigues and the honorary consuls cannot issue passports, you need to go to Mauritius for that and to go to Mauritius you need a passport. So, you could well end up stranded in Rodrigues while your home country's authorities try to solve the conundrum.

In terms of what not to take, plastic bags are banned in Rodrigues so you should avoid taking them. It is a good excuse to buy and use some of the locally made woven pandanus bags.

MONEY AND BANKING

Hotels and most guesthouses and restaurants accept the major credit cards. Opening hours for banks are typically 09.15–15.15 Monday–Friday, and in some cases 09.15–11.15 Saturday. There are also **ATMs** in Mont Lubin and La Ferme.

$ **Barclays Bank** Rue de la Solidarité, Port Mathurin; ✆ 831 1553
$ **Mauritius Commercial Bank** Rue Max Lucchesi, Port Mathurin; ✆ 831 1833

$ **SBI Mauritius** Rue François Leguat, Port Mathurin; ✆ 831 1591
$ **State Bank** Rue Max Lucchesi, Port Mathurin; ✆ 831 1642

INBOUND TOUR OPERATORS The following agencies can provide transfers, excursions and activities, as well as car hire:

2000 Tours Rue Hajee Bhai Fatehmamode, Port Mathurin; ✆831 4703; e resa@rodrigues-2000tours.com; www.rodrigues-2000tours.com

Beraca Tours Baie aux Huîtres; ✆831 2198; e tropicalguy17@caramail.com

Ebony Tours Mourouk Ebony Hotel; ✆832 3351; e ebony@intnet.mu; www.mouroukebonyhotel.com

JP Excursions Port Mathurin; ✆832 1162; e jpexcursion@intnet.mu; www.jpexcursion-rodrigues.com

Rotourco Pl François Leguat, Port Mathurin; ✆831 0747; e contact@rotourco.com; www.rotourco.com

DRIVING Over the years the island's roads have improved enormously and there are now sealed roads to most corners of the island, with dirt tracks beyond those. Many more vehicles have been imported, although there are still relatively few cars on the island. Only a small percentage of the population owns a car but the number of scooters has increased noticeably in recent years. Regulations for drivers are as for Mauritius, except for the speed limit, which is 50km/h. Take care as there are many steep, windy, narrow roads which are not lit at night. 4x4 vehicles are common and are best suited to the conditions. There is no coastal road around the island; you have to keep climbing back up to the centre to get almost anywhere. There used to be only one petrol station on the island, but there are now three: Port Mathurin, Grand La Fouche Corail and Mont Lubin. Still, it is worth keeping an eye on the fuel gauge. Should you run out of fuel, most of the tiny village shops dotted around the island will sell you a couple of litres of petrol in a soft-drink bottle. The going rate for car hire is around Rs1,000 a day. In addition to the inbound tour operators listed above, **car hire** is available from Chez M et Mme Poupon (*Pointe Monier*; ✆877 4292).

Scooters, motorbikes and **bicycles** can also be hired, either from your hotel or one of the tour operators (see pages 42–3). You would need to be fit and determined to explore the island on a bicycle as the interior is deceptively hilly. Expect to pay around Rs650 per day for a scooter and Rs200 for a bicycle.

TAXIS There is just a handful of taxis on the island and they do not drive around looking for clients. Your best chance of finding one is at the bus station in Port Mathurin. Many of them are happy to be hired for the day to do a tour of the island, which should cost around Rs2,000. The tourist office can provide a list of taxi drivers and their contact details. Here is a selection:

Port Mathurin
🚗 **J D Payendee** ✆876 4144
🚗 **J S Edouard** ✆875 2215
🚗 **M J Limock** ✆875 2387

Baie aux Huîtres
🚗 **J B Meunier** ✆976 7086
🚗 **J P Meunier** ✆875 3583

Grand La Fouche Corail/airport
🚗 **J M Botte** ✆875 8509
🚗 **S Prudence** ✆875 4511

Mont Lubin/Grande Montagne
🚗 **J R Casimir** ✆875 6818

Pointe Coton
🚗 **M J Félicité** ✆875 2184

BY BUS The **bus station** is on the outskirts of Port Mathurin at the east end of Rue de la Solidarité. It's on the seafront beyond the Winston Churchill Bridge. On

one side are buildings housing snack bars and stalls selling an array of goods. The bus stops are on the other side, with the bus number and destination marked on each. The network is far-reaching as much of the population is without a car, but timetables are pretty 'flexible' and buses stop running at about 17.00. Travelling by bus is inexpensive: the maximum price for a ticket is usually around Rs30. Don't forget to raise your hand or clap in order to stop the bus.

HITCHHIKING Hitchhiking around Rodrigues is an absolute pleasure, because it's the 'done thing' to pick up anyone thumbing for a lift. You should, however, exercise due caution when accepting a lift from a stranger.

ACCOMMODATION

Although there are much-discussed plans to further develop tourism in Rodrigues, the industry is in its infancy. There are just a few small hotels and numerous guesthouses on the island and no tourism training school, so if you are hoping to find accommodation and service of mainland Mauritian standards, you will be disappointed.

However, visitors who are looking to experience a unique and simple island way of life will be delighted. Perhaps the best way to achieve this is to stay with a family or rent a house from a local, or at least eat a home-cooked meal at one of the many table d'hôte restaurants. Plenty of Rodriguans now offer this type of accommodation and dining, and a full list can be obtained from the tourist office. Details of many of the establishments are given in the following *Where to stay* and *Where to eat* sections in *Chapter 13*.

Lack of crime and limited accommodation means that camping is an option. Some of the best spots are around the beaches of the east coast.

Please note that as water is so scarce in Rodrigues, all of the hotels ask you to limit the amount that you use.

For accommodation price codes, see page 64.

RODRIGUAN RECIPE   *Translation by Alexandra Richards*

This recipe comes from *Les Délices de Rodrigues* by Françoise Baptiste, owner of Auberge de la Montagne and La Belle Rodriguaise (pages 233 and 234).

RODRIGUAN FISH CURRY
Ingredients (serves 6):

2kg of fish (firm, white fish is best)	sprig of thyme
5–6 tomatoes (diced)	sprig of parsley
2 onions (diced)	30g of saffron powder
3 cloves of garlic	salt and pepper to taste
crushed ginger	

Method: Cut the fish into slices. Add salt and pepper and leave to rest for 15 minutes. Heat the oil in a large frying pan, then fry the fish until golden. For the sauce, fry the garlic, ginger, onion, tomatoes and saffron, then add a pinch of salt and one teaspoon of lemon juice. Put the slices of fish into the sauce one at a time. Add the thyme and parsley and half a glass of hot water. Simmer for ten minutes. Serve with rice.

EATING AND DRINKING

Rodriguan food tastes fresh and healthy, perhaps because many of the ingredients are organically grown on the island. The chickens you see wandering free-range all over the island could well end up on your plate, usually in the form of a *cari poulet*. The *caris* are similar to those eaten in Mauritius, and are typically made from octopus, chicken or pork. Rodrigues is well known for its octopus, which is usually hand-fished by ladies walking through the lagoon at low tide and left to dry by the sea.

Maize is a staple part of the islanders' diet and is often eaten as maize soup. You will often see it, and pork sausages, drying on the roofs of houses. Other specialities include locally produced honey, kidney beans, chillies, papayas and limes.

If you choose to eat with a local family in one of the island's table d'hôte (see page 274), you may well find that the entire meal was prepared on a wood fire as this is how many Rodriguans cook.

As in Mauritius, rum is a popular drink, particularly after meals as a *digestif*.
For restaurant price codes, see page 66.

PHOTOGRAPHY

It is best to buy photography paraphernalia before you arrive in Rodrigues; choice on the island is limited.

COMMUNICATIONS

POST The main post office is at the eastern end of Rue de la Solidarité, Port Mathurin (❧ *831 2098*; ☉ *08.15–16.00 Mon–Fri, 08.15–11.45 Sat*). Internet access is available. There are small post offices in Grande Montagne, La Ferme, Rivière Coco and Mont Lubin.

TELEPHONE To call Rodrigues from overseas, after dialling the international access code dial 230 followed by the seven-digit number beginning with 831. From Mauritius, dial 095 followed by the seven digits.

There are a few coin-operated payphones in Rodrigues – at the airport, in Port Mathurin and also some villages, like La Ferme, Quatre Vents, Mont Lubin and Port Sud-est. Mobile-phone coverage is pretty good in Rodrigues, even beyond Port Mathurin. The Orange shop in Port Mathurin (*Rue Johnston;* ☉ *08.30–16.00 Mon–Fri, 08.30–12.00 Sat*) sells phonecards and local SIMs (you will need to produce your passport). It also has Wi-Fi.

INTERNET ACCESS/EMAIL There is a shortage of internet cafés on Rodrigues.

Internet access and Wi-Fi are available at the library in Port Mathurin, in the Alfred North-Coombs Building on the corner of Hajee Bhai Fatehmamode and François Leguat streets (☉ *09.00–16.30 Mon–Fri, 09.00–11.00 Sat*).

Internet access is also available at the post office in Port Mathurin. At the Orange shop in Port Mathurin (*Rue Johnston;* ☉ *08.30–16.00 Mon–Fri, 08.30–12.00 Sat*) you can get 30 minutes free Wi-Fi every 24 hours.

Wi-Fi is available at many of the guesthouses and hotels, and at some restaurants, such as Café la Gare at the bus station in Port Mathurin (m *5875 0965*; ☉ *08.00–17.00 Mon–Sat*).

12

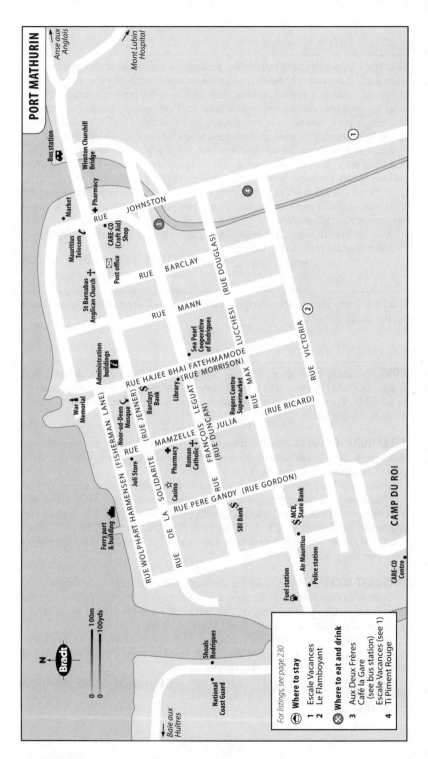

PORT MATHURIN

For listings, see page 230

Where to stay
1 Escale Vacances
2 Le Flamboyant

Where to eat and drink
3 Aux Deux Frères
   Café la Gare
   (see bus station)
   Escale Vacances (see 1)
4 Ti Piment Rouge

CAMP DU ROI

13

Exploring Rodrigues

PORT MATHURIN

The island's tiny capital is neatly laid out with a grid system of streets running parallel and perpendicular to the sea.

While it is small it is not as easy as you may think to find your way around. Few of the streets are signed and you will find even the locals don't know the street names, largely because they change with every change of administration. If asking directions, it is therefore advisable to use landmarks. The town is best explored on foot, partly because it allows you to avoid the puzzling one-way system.

Rue de la Solidarité runs the length of the town and emerges to cross over reclaimed land and on to the seaside village of **Anse aux Anglais** (English Bay).

A walk down Rue de la Solidarité leads past the colonial **house of the administrator** (built in 1873), with a cannon outside the gates. This is now the office of the island's executive council.

On the other side of the road is the **Rodrigues Tourism Office** (⬚ 832 0866; e info.rodrigues@intnet.mu; www.tourism-rodrigues.mu; ⊕ 08.00–16.00 Mon–Fri, 08.00–12.00 Sat, 08.00–10.00 Sun). They have information on the island and you can book excursions here.

Just near the tourist office, on the corner of Rue de la Solidarité and Rue Hajee Bhai Fatehmamode, is **Barclays Bank**. Behind the bank is the large, modern Alfred North-Coombs building, which houses the **library.** Here you can use computers and access Wi-Fi free of charge. In a courtyard in front of the library are kiosks, where members of the **Association Rodrigues Entreprendre au Féminin** (an association for local businesswomen) sell their wares, including delicious honey and pickles. Opposite Barclays Bank on Rue de la Solidarité, and almost hidden by one-storey houses, are the six miniature minarets of the **Noor-ud-Deen Mosque**, rebuilt in 1979–81.

Running parallel to Rue de la Solidarité, along the seafront, is Rue Wolphart Harmensen. This leads to the **port**, **customs office** and the offices of the **Rodrigues Regional Assembly**. At the port, opposite Rue Hajee Bhai Fatehmamode, is a **war memorial** with three rifles forming a tripod and two cannon shafts beside them. The inscription reads: '*Aux engagés volontaires Rodriguais 1914–18, 1939–45*' (For the Rodriguans who served 1914–18, 1939–45).

In 2012, a smart new **market** building was built at the eastern end of Rue de la Solidarité, just before Winston Churchill Bridge. The market is the highlight of the week in Rodrigues and it is worth timing your visit to make sure you can make it either the Wednesday or the Saturday one (see page 237).

On Rue Mamzelle Julia is the incredible **Joli Store**, a small bright blue store crammed with a staggering array of items from modern electronic goods to toys that seem to have been hanging in the shop since the 1970s.

On Rue Hajee Bhai Fatehmamode is an uncharacteristically modern and fashionable shop, which is the outlet for the **Sea Pearl Cooperative of Rodrigues** (m *5850 4323;* ⊕ *08.30–16.00 Mon–Fri, 07.30–14.00 Sat*). The co-operative farms oysters near Anse aux Anglais and uses the pearls and shells to make attractive and unusual jewellery. Knick-knacks made from recycled material are also on sale.

The **St Barnabas Anglican Church** and **Rodrigues College** school complex is at the eastern end of Rue de la Solidarité. The church is contemporary in style (built in 1977) with an interior tower. A simple, white **Roman Catholic church** is in Rue Mamzelle Julia. Mass is celebrated on Saturdays at 17.00 and Sundays at 07.00. There is a **pharmacy** just north of the church on Rue Mamzelle Julia and another one at the eastern (Anse aux Anglais) end of Rue de la Solidarité.

The **court house**, **police station**, **Air Mauritius office** and a **petrol station** are at the western (Baie aux Huîtres) end of Rue Max Lucchesi.

The **bus station** is over the **Winston Churchill Bridge** at the far eastern end of Rue de la Solidarité. Just beyond the bridge the road divides into two; one leads inland to Mont Lubin, whilst the coast road leads to Anse aux Anglais.

🏠 **WHERE TO STAY** *Map, page 228*

Mid range

🏠 **Escale Vacances** (23 rooms) Fond la Digue, Port Mathurin; m 5772 9303; e info@escale-vacances.com; www.escale-vacances.com. This one has been around for a while, having opened in Apr 1997. It lies in a quiet area on the outskirts of Port Mathurin. The en-suite rooms are clean & have AC, TV & minibar; some have a phone. It has a bar, pool & terrace. There is also a comfortable TV lounge with a small library. Free Wi-Fi is available in some areas of the hotel. The restaurant here is highly regarded (see below). **$$$**

Budget

🏠 **Le Flamboyant Hotel** (27 rooms) Rue Victoria, Port Mathurin; ☎ 832 0082; e resa@hotelflamboyant.com; www.hotelflamboyant.com. The building is uninspiring but central, & houses small, simple rooms with en suite, TV & minibar. There is a restaurant & a little pool. **$$**

✖ **WHERE TO EAT** *Map, page 228*

There is a small supermarket in the Rogers Centre on the corner of Rue Max Lucchesi and Rue Mamzelle Julia. Snack vendors are dotted all over town. There is a good one next to Safari Bar on the way to Anse aux Anglais. The market on Wednesdays and Saturdays is great for fruit and vegetables.

✖ **Aux Deux Frères** Patriko Bldg, Pl François Leguat; ☎ 831 0541; ⊕ from 08.30 daily, closed Thu evening & Sun lunch. Cuisine: French, pizza, Rodriguan. The menu consists largely of French dishes & pizza, with a few Creole dishes also on offer. Mains from Rs245, pizza from Rs215. Also take-away. **$$$**

✖ **Escale Vacances Hotel** Fond la Digue; ☎ 831 2555; ⊕ for lunch & dinner daily. Cuisine: Rodriguan, Chinese, European, seafood. Good standards of food & service. **$$$**

✖ **Ti Piment Rouge** Rue Johnston; ☎ 831 2840; ⊕ for lunch & dinner Tue–Sun. Cuisine: Rodriguan, Chinese, Mauritian, seafood. Small but extremely popular, especially for its seafood. Reservation recommended. **$$**

✖ **Café la Gare** Bus station; m 5875 0965; ⊕ 08.00–17.00 Mon–Sat. Cuisine: snacks, light meals, Rodriguan. A casual snack bar at the bus station serving sandwiches, pizza & light meals. Offers free Wi-Fi, which is handy. **$**

AROUND RODRIGUES

The island's fish shape has its head in the east and its forked tail in the west. The bay at **St François** is its mouth. The road from the airport at the western corner of

Rodrigues to Port Mathurin winds over the spine of mountains in the island's centre. These run north to south with deep ravines between them and offer breathtaking views down to the coast.

The Sir Gaëtan Duval Airport is at **Plaine Corail**. The quickest route to Port Mathurin and the east is via **Grand La Fouche Corail**, **Quatre Vents** and **Mont Lubin**. From Grand La Fouche Corail you can also head north or south to the coastal roads. The north coast road takes you through **Port Mathurin** as far as **Grand Baie**, whilst the southern equivalent ends at the Mourouk Ebony Hotel in **Pâté Reynieux**. Both offer picturesque drives through villages and smallholdings, where cattle and pigs can often be seen rummaging on the seashore. Mangroves have been replanted along both coasts and can be seen in various stages of development.

The road from Mont Lubin in the centre of the island down to **Anse Mourouk** is steep and winding, with 52 bends, giving you time to admire the spectacular view of the lagoon. The deep blue channel you can see snaking through the reef is known as La Grande Passe. Dotted through the lagoon you can also see a number of small islands, including Ile Hermitage, Ile Chat, Ile Plate and Ile Gombrani. There is a pleasant beach at Anse Mourouk, which is central to village life. Fish traps and fishing boats line the beach and children can often be seen playing football. Anse Mourouk can be windy and is popular with kitesurfers. Near the Mourouk Ebony Hotel you can **hire transparent kayaks** to explore the lagoon (see page 239). It is a wonderful initiative run by the local fishing community and certainly worth supporting.

Beyond Port Mathurin is **Crève Cœur**, where there is a **Hindu temple** dedicated to Shiva. Further along the coast is the pretty bay of **Anse aux Anglais**, which has a sandy beach and several places to stay. Scores of local ladies can often be seen walking out into the lagoon to catch octopus.

Almost all the island's roads lead to **Mont Lubin** before branching off in different directions. On the road from Port Mathurin to Mont Lubin, the **Queen Elizabeth Hospital** is on the right and the **meteorological station** is on the left. Opposite the meteorological station is a shrine to the Virgin Mary, **La Reine de Rodrigues**, built in 1954, with magnificent views over Port Mathurin and out to sea. Nearby is a cannon, placed there by the British to defend the island. On the same road around the area of **Solitude**, you're likely to see rare **Rodrigues fruit bats** in the late afternoon. It is worth taking the time to drop in at Valerie's at **Citronelle** to try some of her delicious cakes (page 237) and to support this wonderful local character.

In the centre of the island is **Mont Limon**, Rodrigues's highest point at 398m. From the road there is a short path leading to the summit, which offers far-reaching views around the island. Nearby, just south of the main road, is **St Gabriel**, which boasts the island's largest church. Recently renovated, it was originally built from limestone blocks from 1934 onwards by devoted parishioners who carried the coral, sand and cement on foot. The congregation is still devoted and there always seems to be someone at the church. On the road through St Gabriel is a **handicraft shop** (⊕ *09.00–15.00 Mon–Fri, 09.00–13.00 Sat*), run by the Rodrigues Women's Association, where ladies can often be seen weaving hats and bags. Their creations are also sold at the Port Mathurin market on Saturdays.

To the north of the main road is the tiny village of **L'Union**, where there is a low-key, pyramid-shaped **monument to the island's slaves**. According to its inscription, in 1736 the island's population was two whites and six black slaves. Nearby small stones mark the graves of unnamed slaves. This is also where you will find the **tomb of Philibert Marragon** and his wife – in contrast to the slaves' graves, rather elaborate. Marragon was one of the island's first permanent settlers,

arriving in 1793. He was a farmer and the island's first civil agent for the French Government (see also page 215).

There is no road along the east coast but this is where the island's best **beaches** are found, including the much-photographed **Trou d'Argent**. They can be reached on foot and are almost always deserted (page 243). A protected marine area stretches along the south of the island from Pointe Roche Noire in the east to Plaine Corail in the west.

Travelling west from Port Mathurin the road hugs the coast; octopus can often be seen hanging out to dry in the sun. At **Pointe la Guele** is the island's only (usually empty) **prison**, an incongruously cheerful building decorated with colourful murals and with fantastic sea views. In **Baie Malgache**, across the road from the sea, is a shop and restaurant (page 236) which opened in 2012 known as **Le Pandanus** (m *5440 2580; www.lepandanus.com;* ⏰ *08.30–16.00 Mon–Fri*). Local ladies can be seen putting the finishing touches to woven pandanus (*vacoas*) bags, hats, lunch boxes and more, which are on sale in the shop along with assorted souvenirs. The artisans are more than happy to chat and explain to you what they are doing. There is no better way to know you are buying local than to see the items being made and meet the person who created them.

At **La Ferme**, a school and church serve scattered dwellings. It was at this unassuming church that Pope John Paul II celebrated Mass on 15 August 1989.

The west is the driest part of the island and is sprinkled with small rural settlements. Beehives are a common site, as they are all over the island, producing the wonderful local honey. The lagoon is wide here and provides memorable views. At **Camp Pintade** is a small, new chapel in the shape of a boat, dedicated to St John. Before its construction in 2012, the residents of this part of the island had to travel to the church at La Ferme. The chapel was designed by Mauritian architect Jean Michel d'Unienville but the building work was carried out by Rodriguans. It is beautifully simple inside and out; there is no need for stained-glass windows here – the views of the hills and the sea through the plain glass are inspirational enough. The bell tower stands beside the church; like many in the Mascarenes it is external to minimise damage during cyclones. Mass is celebrated here on Saturdays at 15.30.

WHERE TO STAY

Upmarket

✳ 🏠 **Tekoma Hotel** [210 G2] (15 rooms) Anse Ally; ☎ 483 4970; e reservations@trimetys-hotels. com; www.tekoma-hotel.com. This new hotel has quickly become the pick of the hotels on the island. It sits on a hillside overlooking the sea in a quiet corner of the island. Rooms are in individual single-storey buildings & are cleverly staggered so they all have a view of the ocean. The rooms are the most modern on the island, spacious with AC, TV, safe, phone, minibar & outdoor seating. The bathrooms are particularly striking with double basins carved from rock & an enormous outdoor bath shielded from the wind. There is a pool down near the beach & a restaurant in the main building. The beaches here are beautiful & it is a pleasant walk along the coast to St François & Trou d'Argent.

There is a dive centre on site & a small wellness centre offering massage. The hotel's only real drawback is its windy location. **$$$$**

Mid range

🏠 **Bakwa Lodge** [210 F3] (6 rooms, 1 villa) Var Brulé Port Sud-est; ☎ 832 3307; e info@bakwalodge. com; www.bakwalodge.com. On the south coast, close to Mourouk, this new hotel lies in a windy spot & is popular with kitesurfers, especially Jun–Sep. The rooms are scattered through a garden, which leads down to the sea. The accommodation is clean, fresh & modern with polished concrete floors, wooden verandas, indoor & outdoor showers. The wooden louvred patio doors give it a nice, beachy feel but their practical purpose is to combat the gusty winds. All rooms have en suite, AC, safe, minibar, & tea/coffee

facilities. The villa can sleep up to 8 people. There is a good restaurant & excursions can be arranged. There is no pool. **$$$**

🏠 **Cases à Gardenias** [210 F2] (3 rooms, 3 villas) Mt Bois Noir; ☎ 832 5751; e casesagardenias@hotmail.com; www. casesagardenias.com. An unusual accommodation option for Rodrigues, with a sophisticated, European feel. This is probably because the owners, Mr & Mrs Verbeek Comarmond (a Belgian man married to a Mauritian) lived in France for many years. Marie-Line Comarmond is well known for her homemade jams & chutneys, which you will have the chance to taste at breakfast, and her homemade jewellery. The house & grounds are beautifully maintained & the European-style furnishings create an atmosphere of elegance. There are 3 en-suite rooms around the main house, which are ideal for couples. **$$$**

🏠 **Cotton Bay Hotel** [210 G1] (48 rooms) Pointe Coton; ☎ 831 8001; e reservation@cottonbay.intnet. mu; www.cottonbayhotel.biz. The en-suite rooms & 2 suites are housed in sea-facing 2-storey buildings. Rooms are spacious & have AC, TV, phone, minibar & small safe. The hotel has been around a while & despite several renovations is tired in parts. It has a pool, restaurant, games room, tennis court, kids' club & watersports, including free windsurfing & kayaking. The dive centre is one of the best on the island, but it is closed in winter (Jul/Aug). There are pleasant, albeit rocky, beaches in the area but it's an unattractive, windswept location & by Rodriguan standards is a long way from anywhere (30mins from Port Mathurin & 45mins from the airport). **$$$**

🏠 **Le Récif** [210 E1] (8 rooms) Caverne Provert; ☎ 831 1804; e ebony@intnet.mu; www.lerecifhotel. com. Overlooking the beach at Caverne Provert, not far from Port Mathurin. The 6 rooms & 2 apartments with kitchenette are clean, spacious, comfortable & have sea views. They are equipped with AC, TV & balcony. There is a restaurant serving Rodriguan meals & *séga* shows on weekends. A range of excursions & activities can be arranged. **$$$**

🏠 **Les Cocotiers** [210 E1] (32 rooms) Anse aux Anglais; ☎ 467 9700; e resa@otentik.mu; www. lescocotiersbeachresort.com. In a convenient location, on the beach just outside Port Mathurin. Simply furnished, colourful en-suite rooms with AC, TV, safe, minibar & phone. The open-air restaurant overlooks the sea & from the pool area

you can walk directly onto the beach. Reef shoes are advisable as it is stony. There is a small spa. The service is rather hit & miss. Wi-Fi available. **$$$**

🏠 **Mourouk Ebony Hotel** [210 F3] (30 rooms, 1 villa) Pâté Reynieux, Mourouk; ☎ 832 3351; e ebony@intnet.mu; www.mouroukebonyhotel. com. Perched on a hillside facing a vast lagoon & Ile aux Chats, this is a very popular hotel so book well in advance. The rooms are housed in neat, red-roofed, Creole-style chalets set in beautiful gardens. Rooms are simply furnished with en-suite facilities, AC, fridge & small terrace. There are no phones or TV. The villa is in a separate building with its own small pool; 2 bedrooms upstairs, kitchen & sitting room downstairs. There is a good restaurant (page 236) with a bar, & a small pool overlooking the ocean. There are mountain bikes for hire, a dive centre & a very well-equipped windsurfing, sailing & kitesurfing school. The hotel organises a range of excursions & evening entertainment. **$$$**

Budget

🏠 **Auberge de la Montagne** [210 F2] (3 rooms) Grande Montagne; ☎ 831 4607; e villa@ intnet.mu. This large house on a hill in this small village offers 3 self-catering studios with en suite & kitchenette. Owner, Françoise Baptiste, is a superb chef & author of the Rodriguan cookbook, *Les Délices de Rodrigues*. She can prepare delicious table d'hôte meals on request. **$$**

🏠 **Auberge le Lagon** [210 D1] (18 rooms) Jean Tac; m 5875 0707; e tipavillon@orange. mu; www.tipavillon.com. On the north coast, east of Port Mathurin, close to Grand Baie. Rooms are in 2-storey blocks in a pretty garden on a hillside overlooking the lagoon. The beach below the hotel is rather muddy & unappealing, but the beach at Grand Baie is within walking distance. The rooms are very plain & basic; they have en suite but few other amenities. There is no TV or fridge, & AC is at additional cost. On the plus side, they each have a balcony with sea view. The pool also has wonderful views of the sea. **$$**

🏠 **Auberge St François** [210 F2] (7 rooms, 3 studios, 2 villas) Batatrana, Nouvelle Découverte & St François; m 5254 8655; www. villa-rodrigues.com. Comfortable self-catering accommodation & en-suite rooms, in Creole-style houses within quiet grounds. Rooms are pleasantly furnished & have safe, mini-fridge &

Exploring Rodrigues   AROUND RODRIGUES

13

tea/coffee facilities. The island's best beaches are within walking distance & there is a restaurant. Excursions can be arranged. **$$**

🏠 **Coralie La Différence** [210 E2] (5 rooms) Solitude; ✆ 832 1072; e brigilou13@hotmail.fr. Opened in 2008 as Le Bois d'Olive. Accommodation at the top of the hill overlooking Port Mathurin, which is less than a 5min drive away. Rooms are en suite & have TV, phone & minibar. **$$**

🏠 **Domaine les Rosiers** [210 F2] (16 rooms) Coromandel; ✆ 831 4703; e 2000trs@intnet.mu; www.aubergelesrosiers.com. In a village location, inland. Comfortable, unpretentious en-suite rooms with AC, TV & balcony are huddled around a pleasant pool. There is a restaurant on site. The owners also have a tour operator, so excursions are easily arranged. **$$**

🏠 **Gîte la Caverne** [210 D3] (4 rooms) Corail Petite Butte; ✆ 831 7409; e felicitejeandavid41@gmail.com. A guesthouse opposite the entrance to Caverne Patate. The shady garden has sea views. The rooms are simple but comfortable & spacious: 2 have kitchen facilities. There is a restaurant next door. **$$**

✳ 🏠 **La Belle Rodriguaise** [210 F3] (12 rooms) Graviers; ✆ 832 4040; e villa@intnet.mu; www.labellerodriguaise.com. In 2009, Françoise & Laval Baptiste, owners of Auberge de la Montagne, opened their new small hotel on the coast at Graviers. It is in a fantastic location, completely off the beaten track (literally, the last couple of kilometres of the journey are on dirt track). The hotel is in well-maintained grounds on a hill overlooking the beach, with some wonderful coastal walks nearby, including the beaches of the east. It is an unspoilt location & in the mornings locals walk their cows & sheep along the beach to fresh pasture. The sea-facing, en-suite rooms are in 2-storey buildings. They are warmly decorated in tropical colours. There is a pool, an excellent little restaurant with wonderful, wide ocean views. Excursions & activities, such as a Creole cookery course with Françoise, can be arranged. **$$**

🏠 **La Cabane d'Eté** [210 D1] (2 apts) Baie Malgache; ✆ 831 0747; e phanuel@rotourco.com; www.lacabanedete.com. In a quiet location in the island's north. The 2-bedroom apartments have AC, TV & shared kitchen, & overlook the ocean. New, clean & comfortable. A lot of thought has gone into preparing the accommodation for visitors. **$$**

🏠 **La Fantaisie** [210 E3] (4 units) Eau Vannée; ✆ 832 6100; e fantaisie@intnet.mu; www.fantaisierodrigues.com. A variety of accommodation options overlooking the Mourouk lagoon. There is a rustic 3-bedroom house with pool, a house with 2 simple en-suite bedrooms, kitchenette & sitting/dining room, an apartment with en-suite room & kitchenette, & a charming Creole 'kaz' (rustic house) with a double en-suite room & sun deck. There is also a characterful cottage with a basic kitchenette & sitting area with fireplace, & a mezzanine sleeping area reached by a steep wooden ladder. **$$**

✳ 🏠 **Le Refuge** [210 C2] (9 rooms) Baie du Nord; ✆ 255 6459; e info@lerefuge.mu; www.lerefuge.mu. In a spectacular location with fabulous views of the lagoon & within a reasonable boat ride of Ile aux Cocos. It stands on the edge of a fishing community, where you can see the locals bringing ashore their catch. There are rooms in the impressive, family home & rooms & an apartment in a separate building in the grounds. Rooms are equipped with AC & have been carefully furnished. Meals are served at the main house & the food is excellent. Owner Marianna used to work at the Rodrigues Tourism Office & went to university in Australia, so not only can she share her top tips for exploring the island, she can do so in very fluent English. She is a very obliging & friendly host, & is more than happy to help arrange activities & excursions. Breakfast & dinner are included; lunch can be organised. **$$**

🏠 **Les Varangues** [210 E1] (1 villa, 3 apts) Grand Baie; ✆ 832 0022; e lesvarangues@intnet.mu; www.lesvarangues.com. Close to the pretty beach at Grand Baie. Offers a fully furnished 3-bedroom villa with AC, 2 studios & a 2-bedroom apartment. Accommodation is simply furnished but comfortable & clean. Paintings by local artists hang on the walls. There is a small pool. Can be booked on BB or HB basis. **$$**

🏠 **Petit Coin Villa** [210 F1] Caverne Provert (1 villa, 1 studio); e petitcoinvilla@btinternet.com; www.petitcoinvilla.com. Simple, fully equipped quality self-catering accommodation close to the beach. In a quiet spot but only 3 miles from Port Mathurin. **$$**

🏠 **Résidence Foulsafat** [210 F1] (2 rooms, 3 villas) Jean Tac; ✆ 831 1760; e benjos@intnet.mu; http://residencefoulsafat.com. In attractive gardens in the north of the island, close to Port

Mathurin. There are 2 en-suite rooms attached to the house, & 3 self-catering villas with 1, 2 or 3 bedrooms. The 1- & 2-bedroom villas are more rustic than the larger one, & the 1-bedroom villa has a kitchenette rather than full kitchen. Table d'hôte meals are served on the terrace, overlooking the pretty garden. **$$**

Shoestring

Auberge Anse aux Anglais [210 D1] (21 rooms) Anse aux Anglais; 831 2179; e aubergehung@yahoo.com; www.aubergehung. free.fr. Coming from Port Mathurin, turn right after Seth mini market & the hotel is on your left. The simply furnished rooms have en-suite facilities & phone, AC or fan, & 2 have a kitchenette. Rooms are spacious with whitewashed walls & a small balcony/terrace. Facilities include a restaurant, an open-air TV lounge & a pool. **$**

Auberge Les Filaos [210 D1] (14 rooms) Anse aux Anglais; 831 1644; e filaos@intnet. mu;. Opposite Auberge Anse aux Anglais, a 10min walk from Port Mathurin. The location is quiet & the gardens are a good place to relax; the beach is about 30m away. There are 10 en-suite rooms & 4 with shared bathroom. Rooms are stark but spacious with ceiling fan & balcony/terrace. There is a simple, clean restaurant & a pool. **$**

Bellevue Guesthouse [210 E1] (8 rooms) Crève Cœur; 831 1665; e gerard07@intnet. mu; www.gitebellevue-rodrigues.com. Set on a hill just east of Anse aux Anglais, overlooking Port Mathurin. M & Mme Edouard offer carefully decorated guesthouse accommodation in the grounds of their home. All rooms have en-suite facilities, kitchenette, & fan or AC. There is a TV in the dining room. The owners are incredibly enthusiastic & eager to please their guests, & Mme Edouard prepares delicious Rodriguan meals. **$**

Chez Claudine [210 G2] (4 rooms) St François; 831 8242; e cbmoneret@intnet.mu. In a tranquil spot on one of the island's best beaches. Fantastic views of the ocean & there are some great coastal walks in the area. Rustic rooms with

shared bathroom. There is a TV lounge & the table d'hôte meals are delicious. **$**

Chez Clenya [210 C3] (3 rooms) Grand La Fouche Corail; m 5875 2414; e priyaback@yahoo. com. Basic guesthouse accommodation with kitchenette. Owner Priya cooks tasty meals. **$**

✹ **Chez Jeanette (Le Tropical)** [210 F2] (9 rooms) Mt Bois Noir; m 5722 5665; e letropicalchezjeanette@yahoo.com; www. gite-letropical.com. Guests at Chez Jeanette are guaranteed a warm Rodriguan welcome & superb, authentic local cuisine cooked on a wood fire. The house is on a hill overlooking farmland &, in the distance, the ocean. Accommodation is in comfortable, clean en-suite rooms. There is a small disco here, popular with locals. This is also the site of the Jardin des 5 Sens garden (pages 245–6). A great option for those seeking a genuine experience of life in Rodrigues. **$**

Le Ravenal [210 F1] (5 rooms) Jean Tac; 831 0644; e ravenal@intnet.mu; www.ravenal. e-monsite.com. A great accommodation option & excellent value for money; a 5min walk from Caverne Provert Beach. A choice of en-suite rooms & 1- & 2-bedroom apartments, all with ocean view & veranda. All rooms are finished to a high standard, especially when compared with many of its competitors. Wi-Fi is free for guests. Home-cooked meals are provided on the terrace of the main house, & excursions can be organised. The pretty garden, panoramic ocean views & pool are an added bonus. **$**

Ti Pavillon [210 D1] (9 rooms, 2 studios, 1 apt) Anse aux Anglais; 875 0707; e tipavillon@ orange.mu; www. tipavillon.com. Just up from Auberge Anse aux Anglais, around 150m from the beach. Comfortable, colourful guesthouse accommodation. Most of the rooms feel reassuringly new. Accommodation is en suite & has AC (payable). The studios & apartment have a kitchenette & TV. Meals are taken on the terrace, which is decorated with colourful local art. Wi-Fi is free for guests. Within walking distance of shops, restaurants & the beach is handy. **$**

✕ **WHERE TO EAT** Most villages have a small general store, where you can buy essentials. Larger shops stocking food can be found in Anse aux Anglais, La Ferme and Port Mathurin. The best place for stocking up is the Port Mathurin market (page 237).

Bear in mind that some restaurants and tables d'hôte may only open for dinner if they have received half a dozen or more reservations.

In family homes

There is nothing like good old home cooking &, luckily for us, some Rodriguan families have opened up their homes for table d'hôte dinners. The following will serve up a traditional gastronomic delight if you reserve beforehand. Expect to pay around Rs400 pp for lunch or dinner.

✗ **Chez Claudine** [210 G2] St François; ☏ 831 8242

✳ ✗ **Chez Jeanette (Le Tropical)** [210 F2] Mt Bois Noir; ☏ 831 5860

✗ **Grand Lagon** Anse Quitor; ☏ 832 8101

✗ **Le Refuge** [210 C2] Baie du Nord; ☏ 255 6459

✗ **Niam Niam** Maréchal; ☏ 831 6560

Restaurants

✗ **Chez Madame Larose** [210 G1] Pointe Coton; ☏ 876 1350; ⌚ for lunch daily, dinner on reservation. Cuisine: Rodriguan, seafood. A charming, informal little restaurant just before the Cotton Bay Hotel. Dolly Larose prepares delicious, authentic Rodriguan dishes. $$

✗ **Domaine La Détente** [210 E3] Eau Claire; ☏ 831 2179; ⌚ for lunch daily, dinner on reservation. Cuisine: Rodriguan, Chinese, seafood. A large restaurant set on a hill with fantastic views of the lagoon & Ile Hermitage. $$

✗ **John's Resto** [210 D2] Mangues; ☏ 831 6306; ⌚ for lunch daily, dinner on reservation. Cuisine: Rodriguan, Chinese, seafood. This well-known restaurant has moved next door to where it used to be. It is nicely decorated & feels modern & clean. Good seafood & generous portions. The *bol renversé* (upside-down bowl) crammed with egg, rice & stir-fried meat, chicken or seafood is a hearty meal. Main courses from Rs180. $$

✳ ✗ **La Belle Rodriguaise** [210 F3] Graviers; ☏ 832 4040; www.labellerodriguaise.com. Cuisine: Rodriguan. The restaurant of this small hotel sits on a hill overlooking the ocean. Owner, Françoise Baptiste, is a well-known Rodriguan cook & author of cookery books. Table d'hôte meals are prepared using fresh, local ingredients & traditional recipes. Creole cookery courses with Françoise can be arranged. Reservation recommended. $$

✗ **La Marmite Resto** Crève Cœur; ☏ 831 1689; ⌚ for lunch & dinner daily. Cuisine: Rodriguan, Mauritian & Indian. The owner of this cheerfully decorated restaurant is a schoolteacher during the day & chef by night, cooking with his wife. Good

friendly service & great food – most people come back for more. $$

✗ **La Regalade** Anse aux Anglais; ☏ 713 8831; e laregalade.mailhos3@gmail.com; ⌚ for lunch & dinner daily. Cuisine: Rodriguan, French. A restaurant & bar across the road from the beach. There is musical entertainment every evening as the French owner, Bernard, is a musician. $$

✗ **Le Marlin Bleu** Anse aux Anglais; ☏ 832 0701; ⌚ for lunch & dinner Wed–Mon. Cuisine: Rodriguan, seafood, European. A friendly restaurant/bar across the road from the beach. It attracts a good local crowd, especially on weekend evenings. The menu is varied with something for everyone, from smoked marlin salad to pizza. $$

✗ **Le Pandanus** [210 D2] Baie Malgache; m 5440 2580; ⌚ 09.00–19.00 Mon–Sat, 11.00–18.00 Sun. Cuisine: Rodriguan. The restaurant attached to the handicraft shop serves tasty local dishes. The restaurant is on the 1st floor & there is a view across the road to the lagoon. $$

✗ **Le Récif** [210 E1] Caverne Provert; ☏ 831 1804; ⌚ for lunch & dinner Thu–Tue. Cuisine: Chinese, Rodriguan. Popular, smart place with evening entertainment on the weekends. $$

✗ **Les Trésors de la Buse** Anse aux Anglais; ☏ 876 3534; ⌚ 10.00–15.00 & 17.00–22.00 Tue–Sat, 09.00–12.30 Sun. Cuisine: French, pastries. Not far from Ti Pavillon guesthouse, around 250m from the seafront. In the grounds of a family home. Meals can be eaten on site or taken away. Main courses from Rs200. $$

✗ **Mourouk Ebony Hotel** [210 F3] Pâté Reynieux, Mourouk; ☏ 832 3351; ⌚ daily for lunch & dinner. Cuisine: Rodriguan, seafood. The restaurant at this hotel has a well-deserved reputation for excellent traditional food. Diners can enjoy the panoramic view of one of the prettiest parts of the coast & lagoon. If you are planning a dinner here, consider combining it with one of the hotel's Rodriguan entertainment evenings. $$

✳ ✗ **Restaurant Montagne Limon** Mt Limon; ☏ 832 4631; ⌚ 10.00–22.00 Mon–Sat. Cuisine: Rodriguan. This restaurant is run by a co-operative of Rodriguan women & by eating here you are supporting them & their families. The food is simple, authentic fare, like salted fish curry. The service, performed by members of the co-operative, is friendly but shy & charmingly diffident. $$

✗ **Resto La Caverne Corail** [210 D3] Petite Butte; ☏ 831 7407; ⌚ 10.00–20.00 daily. Cuisine:

Rodriguan. Opposite the entrance to Caverne Patate. This informal restaurant is on the 1st floor, with tables inside & on the balcony above the road. The octopus curry is very good. $$

✳ ✗ **Valerie's** [210 E2] Citronelle; ☏ 832 4350; ◷ 09.00–16.00 Mon–Sat. Valerie makes delicious homemade jams, chutneys, cakes, biscuits & bread. She also serves cakes & tea/coffee/hot chocolate on her patio overlooking the garden & the ocean. In the afternoon Rodrigues fruit bats fly around the area. I first met Valerie in 2011, not long after she opened her business & things were going well for this young entrepreneur. However, in 2012 she fell from the roof of her house while cleaning & very nearly didn't survive. The accident left her blind, but with a little help from friends & family this inspirational lady continues to bake wonderful goodies & always greets her customers with an enormous smile. $

NIGHTLIFE On weeknights Port Mathurin is transformed into what resembles a ghost town by about 20.30.

There is regular live entertainment (traditional music and dance) at most of the mid-range hotels. The *séga* nights at **Mourouk Ebony** on Wednesday and Saturday are a highlight of a visit to the island.

Safari Bar (☏ 832 1168; ◷ 16.00–22.00 Tue–Thu, 21.30–late Fri & Sat) just east of Port Mathurin is at the heart of the island's nightlife. During the week it is a pub, where people play pool, sing karaoke and catch up with friends. On the weekend the dance floor is the centre of the action. **Waves** nightclub, not far from the airport at Cascade Jean-Louis, is also popular with locals. Some restaurants have traditional music and dancing on a Sunday, such as **Le Pandanus** at Baie Malgache (m 5440 2580).

SHOPPING Rodrigues is not a souvenir hunter's paradise. That said, there has been a recent growth in the handicraft industry, which today provides employment for some 700 Rodriguans. They're involved in basketry, hat-making, textile-based crafts like embroidery, coconut crafts and jewellery. The Rodrigues branch of the national handicraft centre acts as co-ordinator and facilitates the development of the industry by hosting workshops, seminars and training sessions.

The hats you can buy in Rodrigues are made from fibre of vetyver, pandanus, coconut or latanier leaves. Basketry also utilises bamboo or sisal. Other items made from these materials include cradles, baskets, briefcases, tablemats, lampshades, letter holders and so on. In Port Mathurin, as well as the market, there are several roadside kiosks and curio shops which sell local handicrafts and food preserves, including hellishly hot chillies, mango and tamarind.

When doing your souvenir shopping, bear in mind that it is well worth supporting **CARE-Co** (see box *CARE-Co*, page 242).

WHAT TO DO IN RODRIGUES

PORT MATHURIN MARKET The market operates on Wednesdays and Saturdays and is crammed with stalls selling all manner of homemade and homegrown goodies: chutneys, drinks, woven baskets and hats, fruit and vegetables. For many locals this is the highlight of their week and a chance to catch up on the island's gossip. It's worth getting up early to see the market at its busiest, around 08.00. If you are going to buy souvenirs at the market it is worth seeking out those made in Rodrigues. When it comes to woven pandanus items, the ones made in Rodrigues tend to be the plain, non-coloured ones, while the brightly coloured bags, hats and drums are usually made overseas, mostly in Madagascar. On Saturday mornings watch out for a stall named **La Tourterie**, run by Marylou (m 5975 0031), who makes incredible pastries. The pies with intricately carved pastry toppings are truly impressive. **Mezon Rodrigues** sells delicious honey and spice bread.

CARE-CO WORKSHOP AND SHOP To arrange to visit the CARE-Co workshop at Camp du Roi in Port Mathurin contact Birgit Rudolph or Suzanne Auguste (✆ 831 1766). There are two CARE-Co shops where you can purchase jewellery and souvenirs, one adjoining the workshop (🕓 08.00–16.00 Mon–Fri) and one in Johnston Street (🕓 08.00–16.00 Mon–Fri, 08.00–12.00 Sat). For more details on CARE-Co see page 242.

SPORTING ACTIVITIES The companies listed in the *Inbound tour operators* section, page 225, can arrange activities such as hiking, fishing and bike rental.

Hiking Hiking in Rodrigues is a delight. There are virtually no fences, locals are used to getting around on foot and there are lots of regularly used tracks. Gorges, hills and deep valleys beckon keen hikers, and stunning views of the lagoon add interest. Along the way you are likely to encounter people tending crops, tethered cattle and young boys herding sheep. In most areas there is little tree cover and shade, so you will need to wear a hat and suncream. No special skills are required, as the hiking is mostly moderate or easy. You will need sturdy shoes for clambering over rocks.

The kiosk of the Entreprendre au Féminin and Eco Ballade outside the library in Port Mathurin has maps of the island (*carte verte*) with eight suggested hiking trails, titled *Sur les traces du chercheur d'or.*

AN INVITATION TO EXPLORE RODRIGUES ON FOOT

Marie Paule Sakoury of Eco Ballade – guided hikes and excursions

Eco Ballade is run by three women: Delphine, Anick and myself, Marie Paule. We started our business, mostly running hikes and nature tours, in early 2014. Our wish is to enable visitors to discover our lovely island naturally and respectfully. I wanted this venture to be a little one, with particular attention to nature, respecting every single tourist coming with us, and sharing much more than what we will see on our way. We like to share our personal life experiences and laughing is a great therapy on the way. I am passionate about nature, walking (never running – you don't need to do so here), taking time and meeting new people, and sharing my love of my island, having lived here since my childhood.

Each little track I will lead you along has its own story. It could be the track we used to take to school or to church. The one I am about to share with you is the one I would take with my sister, brothers and cousins to our grandparents' house every weekend. First we will climb Mont Limon to the island's highest point, from where we can see almost the whole island. I will then guide you down the hill, where we may pass an old man working in his garden or a woman with her child looking after her cattle. As we go, I will share with you what my grandparents and parents taught me about medicinal plants. We will come to a quiet green valley with stunning views of the lagoon, where pure white tropicbirds fly and sing freely above us. We can stop off at the zipline before dropping down to the coast to catch a fisherman's small boat. We can spend a few hours at sea, admiring the endless blue, then stopping off for a relaxing barbecue.

One important thing: I will ask you to help me collect some litter on our way. I need your help to keep my island clean.

I invite you to join me on a walk around Rodrigues and look forward to seeing you soon.

Mount Limon and Mount Malartic offer good opportunities for hiking. Walking along the eastern beaches is truly memorable and the pristine beach of Trou d'Argent is a fairly easy 30-minute walk from the coastal village of St François (page 243). Other good walks include Port Mathurin to Grand Baie and on to Pointe Coton and Port Mathurin to Baie du Nord.

Sentier Pasner✳ is an 8km hike which begins at Grand La Fouche Corail and takes you via Caverne Patate to a point just near the airport. The trail has been designed by the Mauritian Wildlife Foundation (MWF), who have trained local people to act as guides and explain the flora, fauna and landmarks along the way. It is a wonderful opportunity to spend some time with a local person and hear about life on Rodrigues as you walk through spectacular scenery. The path is not marked so a guide is essential. The route takes you through farmland, where flocks of sheep are curious onlookers. It takes you past a spring, where locals gather water and bring their livestock to drink. In parts there are panoramic views of the southwest coast, which provide an excellent photo opportunity. During the walk you pass several fenced areas where the MWF is working to regenerate native vegetation, including the nature reserve at Anse Quitor towards the end of the walk.

To arrange a guided hike along Sentier Pasner, contact the MWF (✆ 831 4558; e mwfrod@mauritian-wildlife.org; www.mauritian-wildlife.org).

Eco Ballade✳ (m 5787 6096; e eco.ballade@gmail.com; rodrigues-ecoballade. com) who offer guided hikes with a personal touch (see opposite). The three women share memories and knowledge of the island as you walk; they are also environmentally aware and make it their mission to pick up litter along the way.

Kayaking

Transparent kayak✳ (*Mourouk;* m *5443 1025;* ⊕ *09.00–16.00 daily; adult/child under 12 1hr Rs250/125, guided Rs400/200; 2hrs adult/child Rs450/225, guided Rs600/300*) is a great initiative designed to give fishermen and women an alternative source of income and at the same time relieve the pressure on the reef from overfishing. The project was established with help from the European Union. Near Mourouk are two shipping containers which have been converted to form the offices of this small enterprise, and which are staffed on a roster basis by members of a local association of fishermen and women. In 2015, there were three men and 11 women on the team.

The transparent kayaks are a wonderful way to explore the reef without getting wet, allowing you to see the coral and fish as you paddle. You can either hire a kayak and make your own way around the lagoon or pay a little extra and have one of the fishermen/women head out with you. Heading out with one of the team is a wonderful chance for a personal interaction with a local and to learn more about the role of the sea in the culture of this tiny island. As well as getting some exercise, you will be supporting sustainable employment in the area and giving the reef a break. You will need to know how to swim and wear a flotation device.

Mountain biking

Mount Limon and Mount Malartic offer good mountain biking. For bike hire, contact **Club Osmosis** (*Mourouk Ebony Hotel, Pâté Reynieux;* ✆ *832 3051;* e *osmosis@intnet.mu; www.osmosis-rodrigues.com*).

Ziplining

A series of ziplines span the ravines in the southeast of the island and offer spectacular views of the lagoon. The approach doesn't fill you with confidence, being through a field and with a meeting point under a pandanus tree but rest assured the course was created by an experienced Frenchman, who has installed similar ziplines in Mauritius. Tour operators and hotels can arrange ziplining or

you can call direct. You fly 100m above the gorges and the longest line is 400m, giving you a chance to see the island from a different perspective. The business, **Tyrodrig** (m *5499 6970; www.tyrodrig.com;* ⊕ *09.00–17.00 daily*) has become one of the island's top tourist activities and provides training and employment for young people from the village.

Windsurfing/kitesurfing
Reliable winds and a vast lagoon have made Rodrigues a world-class kitesurfing destination, particularly during the winter months (May–August). The **Rodrigues Kitesurfing Association** (*www.rodrigueskite. com*) is the best source of information and organises the annual Rodrigues International Kitesurf Festival, which takes place in June. The following offer kitesurfing lessons.

Cotton Kitesurf Cotton Bay Hotel; ✆831 8001; www.cottonbayhotel.biz
Osmowings Mourouk Ebony Hotel; ✆832 3051; www.kitesurf-rodrigues.com. Also offers surfing & stand-up paddle.

The Nest Kitesurfing Mourouk; ✆832 3180; www.thenestkitesurfing.com
Tryst Kitesurfing Safari (Andy Albert) ✆875 8457; e andyspirit7@yahoo.com; www.kiterodrigues.skyblog.com

Deep-sea fishing
Rodrigues offers excellent deep-sea fishing and has broken numerous records, including a 561.5kg Pacific blue marlin caught there in January 2007. October–June and December–April are the best times of year. Much of the information in the *Mauritius* section of the guide on the various species you can expect to catch is applicable to Rodrigues (see pages 85–6).

Blue Water Fishing Anse aux Anglais; ✆831 0919; e bluewater@intnet.mu
L'Oiseau des Iles Port Mathurin; ✆739 1865; e contact@defidailleurs.com; www.defidailleurs.com

Rod Fishing Club Johnston St, Port Mathurin; ✆875 0616; e contact@rodfishingclub.com; www.rodfishingclub.com

Glass-bottom boat
The establishment of marine reserves around the island meant the number of fishing grounds was reduced and a series of projects were implemented to provide alternative sources of income for those involved in fishing. **Shoals Rodrigues** (page 218) and a group of fishermen and women collaborated to set up a glass-bottom boat business at Rivière Banane (m *5825 9502*). Glass-bottom boat trips also depart from Anse Enfer (m *5768 8540*), near Mourouk and cost Rs1,100 including lunch.

Scuba diving and snorkelling
Having never been affected by industrial pollution, the reefs around Rodrigues offer rewarding scuba diving and snorkelling. Many people believe that the underwater experiences to be had there are superior even to those around the outer Seychelles or Maldives.

Snorkelling excursions can be arranged by many of the island's hotels and cost around Rs200 per person. This includes boat trips to and from the reefs.

The island's dive sites and dive centres are best suited to qualified divers with a reasonable amount of experience. Rodrigues lacks the shallow, clear, sandy-bottomed sites which beginners need and the instructors at the dive centres tend to focus on leading rather than teaching. However, some of the dive centres do offer resort courses for beginners.

Please note: Scorpionfish, lionfish (firefish) and stonefish are all common around Rodrigues and are highly venomous. Striped catfish and banded eels are

Tom Hooper

The corals on the reef slopes of Rodrigues are in very good condition, with around 140 different species of coral represented. Compared with places such as Indonesia or the Great Barrier Reef, this biodiversity is quite low. A coral reef is made up of countless individual animals called polyps. These invertebrate animals manufacture their skeleton from calcium in the seawater.

The following species are commonly found in Rodrigues:

ACROPORA This is the fastest-growing coral. With a very light and delicate skeleton the fingers of some branching shapes can grow 10cm a year. This group has a wide variety of shapes with forms which are branching, mounds, fingers and flat plates.

FAVIA This coral grows in huge mounds known as 'massive' formations. When alive it is a brown or green colour. Its polyps are translucent and come out at night to feed. They are very sensitive and can quickly retract back into the skeleton if they sense movement such as a fish about to take a nip of their tentacles.

FUNGIA These are called mushroom corals as they resemble field mushrooms with their disc shapes and radiating vanes. This coral has only one polyp with many bright green tentacles. Unlike other corals, this one does not stay cemented to the reef, but is free living and will be moved around by the waves.

GONIASTREA One of the toughest corals and is often found in places where other corals cannot survive. It can tolerate long exposure to the sun and muddy conditions. The skeleton looks a bit like honeycomb.

PAVONA Has a form which resembles leaves. The corallites are on both sides and have a very clear spider shape. They are brown in colour and are often found in muddy habitats such as around the channel at Port Mathurin, which is quite unusual for corals.

POCILLOPORA A coral with very fine branches. Sometimes these corals are a beautiful pink colour. Their bumpy corallites can look like popcorn!

PORITES This group are often large, rounded and dense balls. They are very slow growing, with a coral taking up to 50 years to reach the size of a football. Some huge colonies which reach the size of a car are thousands of years old and are sometimes cored to yield climatic information.

STYLOPHORA These corals live all around the tropics. Their larvae can travel for hundreds, if not thousands, of miles.

Exploring Rodrigues   WHAT TO DO IN RODRIGUES

13

present too. Wear gloves as protection from anemones on wrecks and watch out for black-spined sea urchins.

Dive centres The dive centres below offer a range of diving options and packages. The following is a rough guide to the prices you can expect to pay:

Single dive	Rs1,400 (qualified)
Beginner's resort course (pool lesson and sea dive)	Rs3,500
Night dives	Rs2,000
Five-dive package	Rs5,400
Ten-dive package	Rs10,000

These rates include equipment.

Bouba Diving Centre Mourouk Ebony Hotel, Pâté Reynieux; m 5875 0573 ; e boubadiving@intnet.mu; closed Aug. Run by NAUI instructor Benoît de Baize. **Cotton Dive Centre** Cotton Bay Hotel, Pointe Coton; m 5875 6800; e cottondivecentre@gmail. com; www.cottondive.com; closed Jul/Aug. Run by Jacques & Marie-Jose Degremont (CMAS 2-star instructor & CMAS-3 star diver, respectively); both are PADI dive masters. A well-run outfit with well-maintained equipment & good safety awareness.

CARE-CO (RODRIGUES) *

CARE-Co is a non-profit, non-government organisation with a centre for people with disabilities (blind, deaf and physically handicapped) founded in 1989 by Paul Draper MBE, one of two British expats living on the island.

The project's aim is to provide creative and remunerative employment, as well as education, for people with disabilities. There are no shareholders in the organisation, and profits are shared among the workforce. Surplus is reinvested.

Suzanne Auguste, originally from Scotland, is the second British expat living on the island and runs the educational aspect of the project, the Gonzague Pierre-Louis Centre. The school, which opened in 1994, is privately run for hearing and visually impaired children who, because of their disability, are unable to benefit from the formal education offered by their local primary school. The centre also provides the island's only hearing and sight tests. Suzanne is qualified to carry out hearing tests, but since there is no optician on the island specialists must come over from Mauritius. All the equipment, books and stationery are financed by private donation.

After completing their education, the youngsters are employed in the CARE-Co workshop and receive all the conditions of employment that anyone else would.

In the workshop, the team skilfully turns coconuts from Agaléga into necklaces, hair slides, bracelets, earrings, brooches, key rings and much more. The mobiles for babies are enchanting.

Care-Co also produces handmade soaps and delicious honey. The honey has already had huge success and won first prize at the international London Honey Show in 2009. With 45 employees, CARE-Co is one of the island's largest private-sector employers. Production activities are carefully chosen to fit in with the ability of the staff. The human benefits of CARE-Co both to individuals and Rodriguan society are evident but immeasurable.

To arrange to visit the CARE-Co workshop at Camp du Roi in Port Mathurin contact Birgit Rudolph or Suzanne Auguste (831 1766). There are two CARE-Co shops where you can purchase jewellery and souvenirs, one adjoining the workshop and one in Johnston Street. The shops and the workshop are both open 08.00–16.00 Monday–Friday, while the Johnston Street shop is also open 08.00–12.00 Saturday (closed Sunday and public holidays).

For further details of how you can help CARE-Co's vital work, see page 80.

Rodriguez Diving Anse aux Anglais; 831 0957; e rodiving@hotmail.com; www.rodriguez-diving.com

Tekoma Hotel Anse Ally; 483 4970; e info@tekoma-hotel.com; www.tekoma-hotel.com

Top dive sites

Grande Paté Near Port Mathurin, this site is outstanding for its coral gardens at depths of 8–28m.

Grand Bassin Beyond the waters of the pass, there are some superb sites at around 20–25m with large table corals. Occasional sightings of white-tipped reef sharks, large groupers and jacks are reported. The two islets of **Ile aux Sables** and **Ile aux Cocos** lie within an extensive fringing reef and can be visited at high tide. Both offer good diving and snorkelling, but go with skippers familiar with the area or else the chances of being shipwrecked are alarming here.

Pointe Coton At depths of 4–5m the diving is spectacular.

Off Port Sud-est People dive in the passage near the entrance to the barrier reef. Diving is best along the cliff, at 4–18m.

Gouzoupa Opposite Mourouk Ebony Hotel, this is an excellent site (depth 2–17m). There is a good chance of seeing large shoals of jacks, parrotfish and surgeonfish, and the area is rich in branching and other formations of coral. There are currents, so the site is best visited when there is little tide and conditions are calm.

Grand Baie Has excellent varieties of coral and fish (depth 2–20m).

Shipwrecks There are many wrecks around the reefs which ring Rodrigues. Those around the southern reefs include *Quatre Vingt Brisants*, *Clytemnestra* (1870) and *Nussur Sultan*. Northwest of Port Mathurin are the *White Jacket* (1871) and *Traveller*.

Beaches Aside from **Ile aux Cocos** and **Ile aux Chats**, the best beaches on Rodrigues itself are on the east coast at **Pointe Coton**, **Mourouk** and around **St François**.

The coastline between St François and **Graviers** is dotted with beaches, which are usually deserted. There are no roads in this part of the island and a walk along this coast is perfect for those in search of solitude, privacy and relaxation. To walk from St François to Graviers takes around 3 hours. You will need sturdy shoes: it is hilly in parts and involves some clambering over rocks.

You can get to the long, unspoilt beach of St François by bus or car, from where a 30-minute walk through the casuarina trees will take you to the small scallop-shaped cove of **Trou d'Argent** ('Silver hole'). This scallop-shaped beach sheltered on either side by black rock appears in just about all the island's tourism marketing material. The path continues south of Trou d'Argent to another beautiful cove, **Anse Bouteille**, which, as its name suggests, is in the shape of a bottle. This coast can be windy and the sea is often rough but the sheltered Trou d'Argent and Anse Bouteille are usually calm enough for swimming.

WHAT TO SEE IN RODRIGUES

CAVERNE PATATE [210 C4] There are many caves in the west of the island but Caverne Patate, near Corail Petite Butte, is the largest. The cave is 1,040m long

and 18m below sea level. When the cave was discovered many bones of the extinct Rodrigues solitaire were found. It takes around 45 minutes to do a guided walk through the maze of contorted stalactites and stalagmites. There is no boardwalk, handrail or lighting (torches are available) and the surface is uneven and, in parts, slippery, but on the plus side that makes it feel more adventurous and natural than it otherwise would.

You will be given a hard hat, but be sure to wear comfortable clothes and sturdy shoes. The cave is not suitable for those with limited mobility. Guided tours depart daily at 09.00, 11.00, 13.00 and 15.00. Tour operators can organise a visit, or tickets are available on site or from **Discovery Rodrigues** (*Rue de la Solidarité, Port Mathurin;* ✆ *832 1062;* e *discoveryrodrigues@intnet.mu; adult/child Rs100/75*).

It is worth bringing a little extra cash because on the approach to the caves are some modest stalls where ladies sell homemade jam and honey.

FRANCOIS LEGUAT GIANT TORTOISE AND CAVE RESERVE ✳ [210 C3] (*Anse Quitor;* ✆ *832 8141;* e *info@torti.intnet.mu; www.tortoisecavereserve-rodrigues.com;* ⊕ *09.00–17.00 daily; admission adult/child Rs200/100 (reserve), Rs320/160 (cave & reserve)*) Guided tours depart at 09.30, 10.30, 12.30 and 14.30. A popular attraction for Rodrigues, established by the owners of La Vanille Réserve des Mascareignes in Mauritius. The tour begins with a visit to the tortoise nursery, where giant Aldabra tortoises (*Dipsochelys elephantina*), and radiated tortoises (*Astrochelys radiata*) from Madagascar (*Dipsochelys radiata*) are bred. In September 2015, 2,160 baby tortoises had been born at the reserve since January 2008, making a total of around 2,660 tortoises at the reserve. Visitors can sponsor a baby tortoise and receive regular updates on its progress. The tour then takes you down into a natural amphitheatre, formed by a collapsed cave, where you can walk among adult tortoises. There is also an enclosure of Rodrigues fruit bats. The reserve is planting native and endemic plants in the area, with the help of the Mauritian Wildlife Foundation, gradually returning the landscape to the way it would have been when tortoises covered the island.

You can add a tour of the **caves** to your tortoise visit. The tours through the cave are informative (although can be rather too long). There is a boardwalk, handrail and lighting, but you'll have to negotiate some very narrow gaps during the walk and climb some steep steps. The reserve plans to open another cave more suited to those with limited mobility. There is an excellent **museum** here, which tells the story of Rodrigues, as well as that of the various extinct species of the Mascarenes. There is a small souvenir **shop** and a **café**. You will need to allow around 2½ hours for the reserve and cave visit.

ILE AUX COCOS ✳ [210 A2] This shallow sand island, around 4km off the west coast, is unquestionably the most popular day trip available, and rightly so.

Ile aux Cocos is an incredible place. A nesting site for brown noddies (*Anous stolidus*), lesser noddies (*Anous tenuirostris*) and fairy terns (*Gygis alba*), it was made into a nature reserve in 1986 and has been carefully protected. A few simple measures have helped to keep it pristine: no fires are allowed, watchmen take it in turn to stay on the island and guard it, and all visitors must leave by 15.00 and take their rubbish with them. Until 1955 a family lived on the island for extended periods and even grew crops. Today it is uninhabited except for the watchmen and there is only one building on the island, where visitors gather to begin a guided tour.

The birds on Ile aux Cocos have almost no fear of humans and no predators so you can get unusually close to them. The adorable pure white fairy terns lay their eggs directly on the branches of trees, where they must balance them carefully.

The lesser noddies also nest in the trees, while the brown noddies nest on the ground. Rows of them can be seen lining the beach either sitting on eggs or tending to newly hatched chicks. One end of the island is fenced off to protect the birdlife, in particular the migratory birds which visit, such as sooty terns.

The beach here has to be one of the most beautiful on earth. The lack of hotels, bars and crowds makes it all the more special. The best spot to swim is found by walking as far as you can along the beach to the right of the building (as you face it). Stop just before you reach the fence which marks the protected area. The water is shallow here and all you can see as you sit on the water's edge is sand, the sea, waves breaking on the reef in the distance and the birds flitting across the sky. The boat trip is usually on a small fishing boat from Pointe Diable and can take up to an hour. On the return journey the boats head into the wind and the crossing can be long, wet and cold.

Most hotels and tour operators organise full-day trips, which include lunch. A full-day excursion costs around Rs2,000 (including the permit fee for the island and lunch).

Discovery Rodrigues (*Rue de la Solidarité, Port Mathurin;* \ *832 1062;* e *discoveryrodrigues@intnet.mu*) sells the permit required to visit the island (adult/child Rs125/75) and they can provide a list of boatmen who will take you there. You need to book directly with the boat driver or a tour operator, and most of them will organise the permit for you.

An operator who is regularly recommended as being very flexible and accommodating is **Andy Albert** (\ *875 8457;* e *andyspirit7@yahoo.com; www.kiterodrigues.skyblog.com*). **JP Excursion** (\ *832 1162;* e *jpexcursion@intnet.mu; www.jpexcursion-rodrigues.com*) also has a good reputation.

ILE AUX CHATS [210 E4] (Cat Island) is an uninhabited islet in the vast lagoon fronting the Mourouk Ebony Hotel. Like Ile aux Cocos it is home to colonies of noddies. A full-day excursion there organised by a hotel or a tour operator costs around Rs1,000 and includes a beach barbecue. It is more lively than Ile aux Cocos and has not been protected to the same degree, but it does offer tranquil waters for swimming and snorkelling. You can also stop off for diving/snorkelling at Gouzoupa *en route* (page 243), and some excursions include a visit to **Ile Hermitage** as well. Expect to pay around Rs1,950 for the full-day excursion visiting both islands with lunch.

GRANDE MONTAGNE NATURE RESERVE [210 E2] (*MWF, Forestry quarters, Solitude, Rodrigues;* \ *831 4558;* e *mwfrod@mauritian-wildlife.org; www.mauritian-wildlife.org;* ⊕ *08.00–15.00 Mon–Fri, 08.00–12.00 Sat; guided tour adult/child Rs200/100*) Since 1996, the MWF has been working to restore the Grande Montagne Nature Reserve, removing non-native species and planting endemic and indigenous species grown at its facility at Solitude. There is a visitor centre at Grande Montagne with displays on the island's flora and fauna, including the extinct solitaire bird. Enthusiastic and knowledgeable staff will take you around and explain the conservation project. Guided tours take place at 09.30 and last for up to 2 hours. To arrange to visit the reserve or the Solitude endemic nursery contact the MWF directly. Mosquito repellent is highly recommended.

JARDIN DES 5 SENS [210 F2] (*Mt Bois Noir;* \ *831 5860;* e *jardincinqsensrodrigues@yahoo.com;* ⊕ *daily; guided visits 10.00, 11.00, 13.00, 14.00, 15.00; adult/child Rs250/150*) Located just behind Le Tropical guesthouse, this garden was planted

by the owners in 2011 and it is incredible how quickly it has grown. It is very low-key, like everything in Rodrigues, but a guide will take you on a tour of the garden explaining the various plants, including their traditional medicinal and culinary uses, and pointing out indigenous and endemic species. The garden is arranged into areas designed to appeal to each of the five senses. It begins with smell and touch, then moves on to the taste section, which includes a tasting of a herbal tea and cake made from some of the plants you have seen, and you are invited to guess which ones. You then move on to sight, where colourful flowers are the centrepiece, and finally the sound section where you are invited to read and guess the meaning of Creole phrases painted on a wall. The whole tour takes no more than an hour and is just interactive enough to keep children interested, although the entry fee seems a little steep.

MIEL VICTORIA (*Bigarade;* m *5939 3634; www.miel-victoria.e-monsite.com;* ⊕ *08.00–15.00 Mon–Fri; free admission*) Almost every second home in Rodrigues seems to keep bees and produce honey. The island's honey is excellent, thanks to the pristine environment and lack of air pollution. In addition, eucalyptus and endemic plants add flavour. At Miel Victoria you can learn about beekeeping and honey production via a guided tour of the hives, followed by a tasting of honey products. Honey, sweets made with honey and cosmetics incorporating honey are on sale.

UPDATES WEBSITE

You can post your comments and recommendations, and read the latest feedback and updates from other readers online at www.bradtupdates.com/mauritius.

Part Four

REUNION

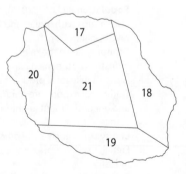

Country An overseas department of France

Location Island in the western Indian Ocean, south of the Equator and north of the Tropic of Capricorn

Size 2,512km²

History Discovered by Arab and Malay sea traders around the 10th century, then by the Portuguese. In 1642, it was annexed for France but remained uninhabited. The first settlers were exiled from Madagascar in 1646. After Napoleon Bonaparte surrendered to Britain in 1810, Britain received Réunion but showed no interest in the island and never assigned a governor to it. The island was handed back to France after the Treaty of Paris in 1814. In 1848, the island's name was changed from Ile Bonaparte to Réunion. On 19 March 1946, Réunion was declared a Département d'Outre-Mer (overseas department) and it remains one of France's last colonies.

Climate The island features some 200 microclimates. Broadly speaking, the climate around the coast is tropical while in the mountainous uplands it is temperate. The hot and rainy summer lasts from November to April, while the remaining months are cooler and drier. Cyclones may occur from January to March.

Nature Réunion has the highest mountains in the Indian Ocean, one of the world's most active volcanoes, more remaining natural forests than on the other Mascarenes, black volcanic beaches in the south and east, white sandy beaches on the west coast, coral reefs, rare birds and waterfalls in abundance.

Visitors 406,000 tourists in 2014, 78% from France. Visitors come all year round; busiest times coincide with French school holidays.

Capital St-Denis

Government The island is administered by a *préfet* (prefect), who is delegated by the French Government

Population 843,617 (2015), mostly Creole (blend of Franco-Africans, but also groups with Indian and Chinese origins). Substantial community of metropolitan French.

Economy Since the mid 1990s tourism has taken over from traditional industries as the main currency earner. Most goods are imported from France, while local products are exported to France by agreement. Traditional exports are geranium and vetyver oils, sugar and vanilla. Inflation and unemployment are high, with rates exceeding those of mainland France.

Language French is the official language. Creole spoken in daily life but French used in more formal situations. English barely spoken outside tourist industry.

Religion Christianity, Hinduism, Islam, Buddhism. Some islanders adhere to tribal lore.

Currency The euro (€)

Rate of exchange £1=€1.28, US$1=€0.89, Rs40=€1 (March 2016)

International telephone code +262

Time GMT+4

Electricity 220V AC

Weights and measures Metric system

14

Background Information

GEOGRAPHY

Réunion is situated in the western Indian Ocean, 700km east of Madagascar. Mauritius, the nearest of the Mascarenes, lies 227km to its northeast.

Réunion's volcanic birth is estimated to have started some 2½ million years ago. First to rise up from the Indian Ocean floor was its oldest and highest peak, the formidable Piton-des-Neiges (Snow Peak – 3,069m), said to have become extinct about 500,000 years ago. It is the highest mountain in the western Indian Ocean but, despite its name, snow is very rarely seen on its peak. More recently (about 380,000 years ago), the aptly named Piton-de-la-Fournaise (Furnace Peak) evolved. It stands at 2,631m and is one of the world's most active volcanoes. Since 1998, the volcano has erupted almost every year. The lava tends to flow down the eastern slope of the volcano, spilling into the sea and modifying the coastline with every eruption. The 2007 eruption, one of the largest recorded, added some 200ha to the island's area.

The two mountain ranges and three vast natural amphitheatres known as 'cirques' (Cilaos, Mafate and Salazie) account for much of the island's rugged interior. Converging at the 2,991m summit of Le Gros Morne, the amphitheatres give Réunion its wildly dramatic appearance, as well as breathtaking hiking trails, waterfalls, forests and gorges. Its landscapes are remarkable and over 40% of the island has been designated a UNESCO Natural World Heritage Site.

Réunion retains more original forest than do the other Mascarenes. Where there are accessible tracts of arable land, fields of geranium, vetyver and sugarcane are cultivated. Tucked away between the ravines, on small patches of level ground called *ilets*, are vineyards and lentil fields.

The inhospitable interior means that the majority of the population is concentrated in towns along the narrow coastal plains. Réunion does not have the abundance of wide sandy beaches that Mauritius enjoys but there are both black- and white-sand beaches along the west and south coasts. Coral reefs and lagoons are also dotted along the west and south of the island.

CLIMATE

The island lies in the path of moist tropical weather pattern circulations, rainfall being highest in the eastern region. In fact, a world record for rainfall of over 12m in a year was claimed in the 1980s for Takamaka, a gorge in Réunion's interior uplands.

Waterfalls are numerous and a prominent feature of the scenery, especially in the many steep ravines. In the amphitheatre of Salazie, for example, there are around 100 waterfalls, plunging like silvery ribbons down sheer, green cliffs.

The weather along the coast is pleasant almost all year round, although in winter the southeasterly trade winds can make the south coast unbearably

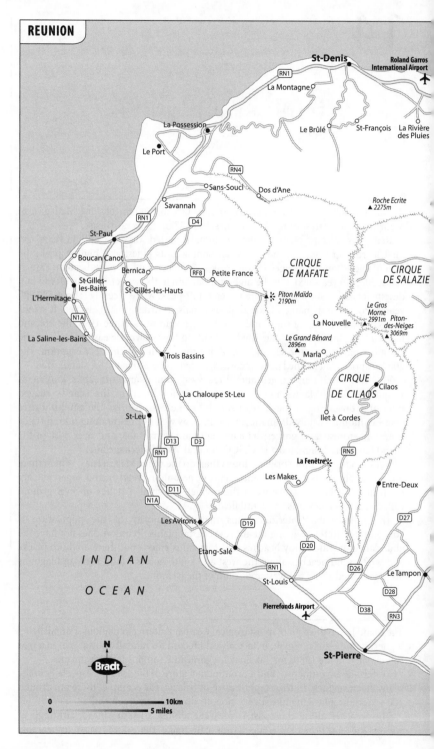

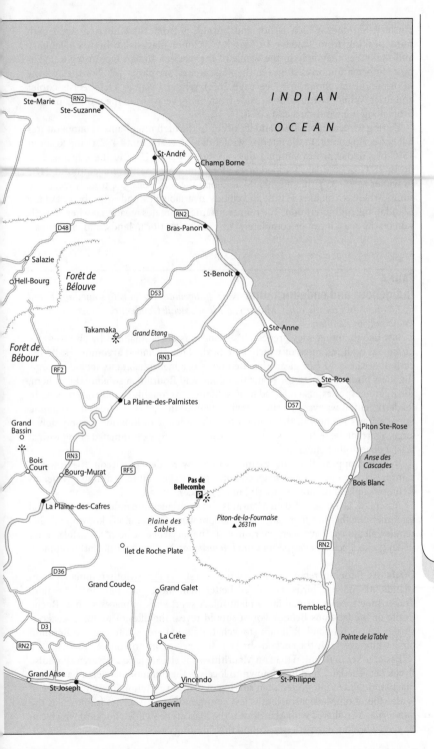

blustery. Summer, which is hot and humid, is from November to April with rains peaking from January to March. Cyclones may strike between January and March, as they may in the whole of the western Indian Ocean region. (For more information on cyclones in the Mascarenes, see pages 4–5. For the cyclone information telephone line, see page 265.) Winter (May to October) is cooler and drier. Winter temperatures, aside from being very low in the mountains, also drop along the windward east coast.

During winter nights, frost and ice occur in the high mountains as temperatures fall to freezing point. In the interior, winter days start at around 4°C, rising to about 15°C by midday, whilst summer days are fairly warm, 15°C in the morning and up to 25°C by midday. Temperatures along the west coast average around 21°C in winter to 31–35°C in summer. Skies along the west coast are usually clear and sunny, whereas a blanket of mist and clouds invariably descends over the rest of the island in the mid-afternoon. The numerous microclimates mean that when there is rain on the coast it can be completely clear in the interior uplands, and vice versa.

NATURAL HISTORY AND CONSERVATION

FAUNA
Indigenous and endemic fauna *Note 'indigenous' pertains to something found in Réunion and on the other Mascarene Islands, whilst 'endemic' means something found only in Réunion.*

Just like the other Mascarenes, this island was once inhabited by an ensemble of animal oddities, most of which were birds. From detailed accounts left by the earliest settlers, we can glean that Réunion's original inhabitants included large, flightless birds similar to the Mauritian dodo and Rodriguan solitaire. Like them, the Réunion species, also referred to as 'solitaire', was roughly the size of a turkey. To its detriment, it was very trusting, having evolved in a predator-free environment. Some experts are now of the opinion that the solitaire of Réunion was possibly a large, aberrant, terrestrial ibis. In any case, it was swiftly exterminated along with at least a dozen other endemic birds.

It would appear that the extinct species were dependent on the lowland rainforests, because these were felled long ago for agriculture and timber, whereas Réunion's upland rainforests are still in magnificent shape.

Absent (as is the case also on Mauritius and Rodrigues) are indigenous, terrestrial mammals; neither are there any native amphibians. Of Réunion's known endemic reptiles, all but two have been exterminated. The survivors are both colourful species of day gecko: *Phelsuma inexpectata* and *P. bourbonas*. Neither is particularly common.

Birds As Réunion retains more natural forest than most other Indian Ocean islands, its endemic birds have fared better than those elsewhere in the region. Today, nine species are still fairly plentiful. A short walk in places such as Roche Ecrite or the fabulous Bébour Forest should reveal the likes of Réunion cuckoo-shrike, Réunion bulbul, Réunion stonechat, Réunion grey white-eye and Réunion olive white-eye. Only the cuckoo-shrike is somewhat uncommon and furtive.

Easier to see in Réunion than on Mauritius is the elegant little Mascarene paradise flycatcher. The land bird best known to locals is the Réunion harrier, a handsome black-and-white raptor often seen soaring over lush vegetation in search of prey. It is also found on Madagascar but is less common there. Locally, it is known as the *papangue*. Also shared with Mauritius is the Mascarene swiftlet, flocks of which can be seen wheeling energetically around their nesting caves.

A USEFUL PEST: GOYAVIER

Considering the large number of invasive exotic plants which have run rampant in Réunion, it is refreshing to note that one of these pests, the goyavier (*Psidium cattleyanum*), is actually extremely useful.

Introduced from eastern Brazil, the goyavier is a fairly nondescript shrub which grows to a height of 8m. Its deep red fruit somewhat resembles a miniature guava. It is an excellent source of vitamin C.

After being picked, the fruit tastes quite acidic, but innovative Réunionnais have found many uses for it.

For starters, goyavier cocktails are hallucinatory! Alternatively, try the exceedingly potent rum punch flavoured with it. Goyavier jam, too, is really tasty. So significant has this fruit become in Réunion, that there is even a two-day Goyavier festival, held every June in La Plaine-des-Palmistes.

Two small, threatened seabirds are high on the lists of visiting birders: the Réunion black petrel (*Pterodroma atterima*) and the Barau's petrel (*Pterodroma baraui*). Both are virtually confined to Réunion and breed in the inhospitable heights of Piton-des-Neiges, which they leave just before dusk for nocturnal foraging jaunts far out at sea.

Sometimes, however, fledgling petrels which are not familiar with artificial lights in coastal buildings fly into the buildings. Many are killed in this way and a campaign is under way to foster an awareness of the petrels' plight. People are requested, if they find injured petrels, to bring them to local experts who then treat and release the birds back into the wild. Owing to their rarity, the precise nesting locations of these petrels are kept secret, known only to a few dedicated ornithologists.

A third highly localised, small seabird is the Mascarene shearwater (*Puffinus atrodorsalis*), thought to inhabit only the Mascarenes and Comoros.

The national bird is the white-tailed tropic-bird, or *paille en queue*, often seen flying gracefully in the vicinity of its sheer nesting cliffs.

FLORA Nobody who visits the lush montane forests in places such as Bébour-Bélouve, La Roche Ecrite, Cilaos (Plateau du Matrum), Salazie and Maïdo can fail to leave impressed. The same applies to the heathlands higher up, such as those of Brûlé de St-Paul, Maïdo and Grand Bénard, at about 1,600–2,400m.

Thanks to the inaccessibility of most of the interior uplands, large tracts of Réunion's original forest still remain intact. The habitat types which have suffered most at the hands of man are lowland evergreen rainforests (everywhere, but especially in the eastern half) and the much drier scrub and woodlands of the west. Some 98,972ha of forest are under the care of the Office National des Forêts (ONF), which controls about 39% of Réunion. The French state presides over the coastal environment. The island's only nature reserve is Mare Longue.

Réunion has some 848 indigenous plant species, of which 237 are endemic. There are several impressive botanical gardens around the island, where endemic and indigenous plants can be seen. At the Mascarin Jardin Botanique de la Réunion, above St-Leu, visitors can enjoy guided walks around the gardens with experienced botanists or ecologists (pages 344–5).

Commonly seen on the forest floor in humid places is the fern *Marattia fraxinea*. It is shared with Mauritius, Madagascar and the Comoros. Much more impressive is the tree fern *Cyathea borbonica*, which dominates the 5,146ha Bébour-Bélouve forest

14

area. It attains a height of 10m and is also found in Mauritius. One bamboo, *Nastus borbonicas*, is endemic and easily identifiable by its papyrus-like clusters of leaves.

In dry western Réunion are two endemic succulents, although they aren't common. The one you're most likely to see is the aloe, *Lomatophylum locrum*, which bears yellow and dull-orange flowers.

There are many orchids endemic to the western Indian Ocean islands and, of these, some seven species are unique to Réunion. Most are now very rare. Indigenous orchids tend to have white blooms, with many flowering from December to March. *Angraecum mauritanium* is also found in Mauritius and, like other 'comet' orchids, it features a very long spur. Presumably, it is pollinated by hawk moths as other 'comet' (angrecoid) orchids are. *Aeranthes arachnites* is less showy and is shared with the other Mascarenes. The diminutive *Bonniera appendiculata* is extremely rare and endemic, with blooms shaped like a very thin starfish.

Some of the palms local to the Mascarenes are on the verge of extinction. An exception is the attractive *Hyophorbe indica*, endemic to Réunion. Today, it's still quite plentiful. The same applies to the large, endemic 'latanier rouge' (*Latania lontaroides*), which has fan-shaped leaves with a distinct reddish hue. However, the 'white palm' (*Dictosperma album*, also found in Mauritius) is virtually extinct in the wild, because it is often used for heart of palm salad. That said, it has been cultivated very successfully.

Hibiscus are well represented in the Indian Ocean islands. Two rare species are unique to Réunion and Mauritius. Both are now protected. *Hibiscus boryanus* has scarlet or orange-red flowers, while those of *H. columnarus* are a bright yellow.

The shrub *Ruizia cordata* is possibly Réunion's best-known endemic, because it is used as a 'flagship' species, to educate the public about the plight of endangered life forms. It is highly endangered and its silvery leaves are used in certain Tamil rituals. Unfortunately, researchers have not yet determined what the shrub's pollinators are.

Foetidia mauritanium is an endemic hardwood used for construction. Its pungent wood is apparently not attacked by termites, hence its popularity, and as a consequence, its rarity. The silvery endemic tamarind, *Acacia heterophylla*, is abundant and it is the preferred wood for furniture production.

Two endangered shrubs – *Pouzolia laevigata*, used for treatment of fever, and *Obetia ficifolia*, which is shared with Rodrigues – are known to have their own, specific pollinator butterfly species. The extreme rarity of these shrubs means that their pollinator butterflies are also endangered.

HISTORY

From about the 10th century, Arab and Malay traders occasionally stopped by on Réunion. They never settled because the island lacked a large harbour and protected lagoons, which featured so prominently on Mauritius.

The Portuguese were the next to arrive. First was explorer Tristan da Cunha, who accidentally landed in the area in 1507 and named the island Santa Apollonia. In 1512, Pedro Mascarenhas renamed it Mascareigne, the name still applied to the island group as a whole. The Portuguese did not settle.

The first French arrival was in 1642, when a French East Indiaman landed, planted the French flag and departed. The French, meanwhile, had claimed nearby Madagascar, where they established several ill-fated settlements, notably in the giant island's southeast at Fort Dauphin.

It was from Fort Dauphin that Réunion's first settlers came, in 1646. The then governor of Madagascar, Sieur Pronis, exiled a dozen-odd troublesome Frenchmen

to Réunion. They were left there to fend for themselves and lived in caves around what is now St-Paul.

A fleet of five French ships brought more settlers in December 1649. The island's name was then changed to Ile Bourbon, after Colbert Bourbon, who had founded the French East India Company. Twenty French volunteers and 42 Malagasy slaves, under Etienne de Regnault, established the island's first permanent settlement.

By the late 1600s, Réunion had become a prominent pirate base, as international seafaring riff-raff realised the island was conveniently removed from the French military machine. Well-known pirate captains (including the likes of Captain William Kidd) ruled that no weapons were to be brought ashore and that no treasure was to be buried on the island. In 1713, the French East India Company arrived in full force, sinking many of the pirate vessels. Aiming to make the island profitable, they set up a garrison and brought in hundreds of African and Malagasy slaves from 1715 to 1730, despite contravening their own regulations by doing so. The slaves were put to work on coffee, cotton and spice plantations.

In 1735, Bertrand Mahé de Labourdonnais arrived in the Mascarenes to administer Ile Bourbon and Ile de France (Mauritius) simultaneously, on behalf of the French East India Company. He was responsible for a mini industrial revolution in Réunion, building schools, roads, clinics and a successful export infrastructure. Labourdonnais held his position until 1746, when he left for India. In June 1764, the French East India Company collapsed and the French crown assumed control of its assets. Ile Bourbon was virtually forgotten during the French Revolution. It then fell under the jurisdiction of the Colonial Assembly and, in 1794, was finally

THE ABOLITION OF SLAVERY: A UNIQUE CASE

Abolition of slavery on this particular French colony proved to be a convoluted process. Initially, slavery had been banned outright in 1794 by the First French Republic. But slave owners baulked, maintaining that one stroke of a pen could not simply eliminate all their investments involved in labour purchases (at least not without compensation). Napoleon therefore reinstated slavery.

When the French monarchy was abolished in 1848 and the Second Republic came into being, the question of banning slavery arose once again in the light of the French motto – 'Liberty, Equality, Fraternity'.

So on 27 April 1848, slavery was abolished for a second time, but with the necessary compensation to slave owners. When the French commissioner arrived on 13 October to announce the new law, he was refused permission to set foot on the island. The following day, he declared that although slavery had been abolished according to the law passed in April, slaves would have to return to work and finish harvesting the crops; only after that was their freedom to be discussed.

This situation was strikingly different from those in Martinique and Guadeloupe, where slaves heard about the new law on 22 May and immediately demanded instant freedom, announcing that they would never again work as slaves. To drive the point home, they promptly set about burning down some of their (former) owners' houses and business premises.

Eventually, on 20 December 1848, slavery on Réunion was abolished in practice. Former slaves were not only granted liberty, but France also gave them equality, as citizens with full civil rights.

14

renamed Ile de la Réunion. Slavers who had not been ousted from their feudal landlord positions insisted on referring to it as Ile Bonaparte, after Napoleon.

In 1806, Réunion's agriculture was devastated by a cyclone and the island was rendered wholly dependent on France. Four years later, after Napoleon surrendered to British forces, Réunion was ceded to Britain. On 9 July 1810, the British navy arrived and set about establishing a Royal Marine garrison. They did not assign a governor to Réunion, preferring to invest effort and resources in Mauritius and the Seychelles. Following the signing of the Treaty of Paris (1814) by the British and the French, Réunion, then known as Ile Bonaparte once again, was handed back to France.

France invested heavily in the island: towns were established, the sugar industry was developed and immigration was actively encouraged. With the birth of the Second French Republic in 1848, the name 'Réunion' was reinstated. Slavery was abolished in 1848, spelling the liberation of some 63,000 slaves (see box, page 255). The subsequent lack of labour meant that the Colonial Assembly indentured Indians, Chinese and Arabs between 1848 and 1855.

From 1850 to 1870, the island flourished and the economy boomed, thanks to the sugar industry and the island's location on the trade routes between Europe, India and the Far East. This period of prosperity was followed by a dramatic decline, attributable to two main causes. Firstly, the opening of the Suez Canal in 1869 removed the need for ships to circumnavigate Africa in order to reach the Far East. Secondly, the use of sugarbeet in Europe, in lieu of expensive imported sugar, dealt a severe blow to the sugar industry. An exodus to Europe ensued.

The two world wars drained Réunion significantly. In World War I, about 15,000 Réunionnais left to fight in Europe. During World War II, Nazi Germany blockaded the French island colonies. Consequently, nothing left or arrived in Réunion for two years and the island declined into a state of famine. By the end of 1942, that abominable blockade was broken. On 9 March 1946, the French Government officially declared Réunion a Département d'Outre-Mer. Today Réunion remains a department of France and thereby a member of the European Union.

GOVERNMENT AND POLITICS

Réunion, together with Martinique, Guadeloupe, French Guiana and Mayotte, is a French Département d'Outre-Mer (DOM), or overseas department. It is administered by a *préfet* (prefect), who is appointed by the French Government. The island elects seven deputies to the National Assembly and four representatives to the Senate. General and Regional councils for Réunion are elected every six years.

As in Mauritius, the white and Indian communities are substantially better off than the Creole population, which causes underlying socio-economic tensions. The economic well-being of Réunion and containment of these tensions depends heavily on continued financial assistance from France. Although there are groups who would like to see independence for Réunion, the majority of the population is aware that this would mean forfeiting the significant financial benefits of their association with France, something which they are not prepared to do.

ECONOMY

Réunion derives huge economic benefit from its status as a department of France, which is apparent in its excellent roads, modern buildings, health care facilities and smart shops. Although unemployment is typically over 40%, Réunionnais are entitled to the same unemployment benefit as a resident of mainland France

(see page 258). The GDP per capita in 2013 was US$26,369, which means that if Réunion were a country in its own right, it would rank 35th in the world.

In many ways Réunion is similar to Hawaii in terms of its economic history, although unlike Réunion, Hawaii had a native population when it was discovered by Westerners. Réunion was first settled by a small group of Europeans, who subsequently brought in large numbers of slaves to work plantations of coffee and spices. Attention was then turned to sugar.

Following the abolition of slavery in 1848, Tamil labourers were recruited. In the late 19th century, Chinese and Muslim (Gujarati) immigrants came. Like Hawaii, Réunion began exporting sugar and fruit, particularly pineapples. Floriculture (notably of anthuriums) was developed, as were fisheries and tourism. Today, the fishing and tourism industries are still growing, not yet having been developed to their full potential.

FISHERIES Réunion's fishing industry has benefited greatly from the fact that stocks in the Indian Ocean are in better condition than in other waters. Tuna and swordfish are filleted and exported by airfreight to France, Italy and the UK. Red tuna is exported to Japan, a new market for the island. Réunion also has some barren islets around which Patagonian toothfish and lobsters are caught and frozen for export.

SUGAR The only agricultural industry in Réunion which has been developed to its full potential (in terms of land usage and technology) is the sugar industry. It accounts for around 25% of the island's agricultural production and provides income for some 5,000 small-scale farmers. It employs some 18,000 people. The island's mountainous interior means that only a narrow strip of land between the coastline and interior is suitable for agriculture – around 20% of the island's land area. The sugarcane grown on these slopes plays an important part in reducing erosion. Réunion sells its sugar above world market prices, which is possible because the industry is heavily subsidised.

TOURISM The target that Réunion hoped to achieve by the year 2000 was only 500,000 tourists per annum. They fell slightly short with 430,000 arrivals and the number was down to 380,500 in 2007. The fall was largely attributed to the follow-on effect of the chikungunya virus outbreak of 2006 (see box, page 51). In 2014, 406,000 tourists landed in Réunion, down from 471,268 in 2011. Of the total number of visitors, almost half stayed with friends or family. Despite efforts to encourage more English-speaking and German tourists, the vast majority (78%) are from metropolitan France.

At present, tourism is the industry which holds the largest potential for growth. The limited amount of English spoken on the island is a stumbling block, although attempts are being made to increase English teaching in Réunion and to expose Réunionnais students to anglophone countries by sending them on exchange visits. And I have to say, in the 17 years that I have been visiting Réunion the amount of English spoken by those working in tourism has noticeably increased.

Also standing in the way of tourism development is the limited number of airlines flying to Réunion. Almost all long-haul flights are via France or Mauritius. Réunion is very under-marketed in the anglophone world. Until 2015 few people outside France had heard of Réunion Island. When wreckage of Malaysian Airlines flight MH370, which had gone missing on 8 March 2014 on its way from Kuala Lumpur to Beijing, washed up on Réunion Island in July 2015 it attracted worldwide attention. Bizarrely, it generated a wave of tourism publicity for the island.

14

A large number of well-publicised shark attacks in recent years has not helped the tourism industry. Since 2011, there have been 17 shark attacks around the island, seven of them fatal. That said, the effect is possibly partially offset by the regular volcanic eruptions, which do attract visitors.

FOOD Foodstuffs exported are largely tropical fruits, spices and rum. Business is booming for the local gift parcel courier service, Colipays, which delivers parcels of fruit, sweets and flowers around the world. Most are sent to France, either by Réunionnais who have relatives there or by expatriate French.

Concerns like Coca-Cola arrived in the 1950s, to be followed later by other soft drinks, alcoholic beverages and a range of dairy products. Many are now manufactured locally under French patents.

UNEMPLOYMENT There is a very high rate of unemployment in Réunion, currently around 30% but as high as 60% in the 15–25 age bracket. According to the French Catholic dictum, the lowest economic strata in society must not be left in the lurch. So even if people don't have jobs, they are still provided with homes and are accorded a set minimum revenue (the Revenue Minimum d'Insertion), which enables them to survive. This leads to many people not really needing or wanting to work and increasingly those who do go out and find jobs do so for the sake of dignity, not finances. That said, almost half the population lives below the poverty line. One sees fewer people living on the streets in Réunion than is the case in Europe, not simply thanks to the RMI but also because there is still a strong sense of family solidarity in Réunion. People will take in the homeless.

In February 2012 riots broke out across the island, protesting unemployment, high fuel prices and the high cost of living. Buildings were damaged, cars set on fire and police injured; riot police were flown in from mainland France.

PEOPLE

The faces of today's Réunionnais attest to the racial diversity of their ancestors. About 40% of the population is Creole (of mixed African/European origin), while Europeans make up around 35%, Indians 20% and Chinese 3%.

It is often hard to pinpoint the ethnic origin of Réunionnais, but colloquial terms are freely used by the locals to describe themselves: a *Cafre/Cafrine* is a black man/woman of African origin, a *Malbar/Malbaraise* is an Indian man/woman, a *Yab* is a white Creole, usually from the interior, and *Zarab* refers to a Muslim. The locals refer to the white French who live on and visit the island as *Zoreilles*, which literally means 'ears' in Creole. The word is thought to originate from the French slavers straining to understand the Creole spoken by their slaves. Some believe in a less palatable explanation – that the French used to cut off the ears of their slaves, who therefore referred to the whites as *Zoreilles*.

LANGUAGE

As in Mauritius, the Creole language is a powerful unifying force amongst Réunionnais of every ethnic origin. French is the island's official language and is spoken by the majority in formal situations, but between friends and family Creole is favoured. It is not identical to the Creole of neighbouring Mauritius but there are similarities as both derive largely from French with some African, Malagasy and local terms thrown in. There is no grammar and the language is written phonetically.

Réunionnais have been battling for some time to have Creole recognised as a language and taught in schools. When I taught in Réunion it was very clear that the pupils confused Creole and French without realising it, thereby dragging down their examinations marks. Many people campaigned for Creole to be taught in schools so that children would grow up treating it as a separate language from French. Thankfully, in 2002, the first trainee teacher of Creole qualified at the University of St-Denis and Creole is now an optional subject on the school curriculum.

Although it is taught in schools, very little English is spoken in Réunion. Anglophone visitors are still a novelty, so locals are generally patient and make an effort to help and to understand those who struggle to communicate in French.

For some handy Creole phrases see pages 362–3.

RELIGION

The majority of the population (about 86%) is Roman Catholic. Many of the island's towns are named after saints, and roadside shrines line every route. However, many Réunionnais follow more than one religion. For this reason, Tamil festivals, such as Cavadee, and Hindu festivals, like Dipavali, are celebrated with great enthusiasm. Chinese New Year is also welcomed with a great deal of noise and festivities.

Some descendants of the Malagasy still practise ancient rites, like summoning the spirits via a living family member, particularly on All Saints' Day. You may meet people who have been baptised into the Roman Catholic Church and who go to Mass, but seek help from a Malagasy spirit or Hindu god in times of trouble.

Sorcery (*gris gris*) is also practised on the island. In St-Pierre, the grave of the famous sorcerer and murderer, Sitarane, continues to be visited by those seeking his assistance (see box, page 282).

Roadside shrines where the colour red dominates are a familiar sight in Réunion. They are dedicated to Réunion's national saint, Saint Expédit, who is usually depicted as a Roman legionnaire. The saint is revered by Réunionnais of all faiths, who generally turn to Saint Expédit when they want revenge or to put a curse on someone. It is fascinating how an originally Christian concept has been distorted to incorporate beliefs in sorcery and superstition (see box, page 359).

EDUCATION

The education system is on the French model, with primary schools, *collèges* (10–15 years) and *lycées* (15–18 years). State-run schools in Réunion suffer from the same problems as those in mainland France (*la Métropole*), such as overcrowded classes, underfunding and poor morale amongst teachers. Both teachers and pupils follow French counterparts by striking at regular intervals.

The University of St-Denis offers a good range of courses, including modules in Creole studies, Creole-language classes and tropical environment studies. Around 12,000 students are admitted per year. It is possible for foreign students to study at the University of St-Denis on an exchange programme, although competition for places can be fierce. The ERASMUS programme allows students already at university in the European Union to study for a year in another European university, which of course includes St-Denis. Speak to your university or contact the University of St-Denis (❋ *0262 938322;* e *contact@univ-reunion. fr; www.univ-reunion.fr*). The International Student Exchange Programme provides similar opportunities for students in the US. For more information visit www.isep.org.

While Réunionnais are quite happy to refer to themselves using terms linked to their ethnicity (see page 258), ethnic and cultural distinctions are more blurred here than in Mauritius, largely because mixed marriages have long been practised. Ubiquitous alongside the African and Indian cultures are elements of French culture. However, while Réunionnais may support France in sporting events, there is a degree of resentment towards '*les métropolitains*' or '*zoreilles*' (French mainlanders). Music and food are important elements of Creole culture, and loyalty to family and friends is highly valued.

MUSIC Music is an important part of life in Réunion and enjoys considerable government funding aimed at keeping Creole culture alive. The main traditional styles are *séga* and *maloya*, which stem from the island's African roots. These are often blended with modern European styles. *Séga* is shared with Mauritius, although each island has its own variations.

Séga blends tropical rhythms with European instruments like violin, accordion and the banjo. The songs usually deal with slavery, island life and romance. *Maloya* was born in the slave communities of the 18th century, and the lyrics traditionally express misery and anger. The rhythm is African and the instruments are percussion. Vocals tend to be plaintive and repetitive, and the style is often compared to the blues. For many years it was forbidden to sing *maloya* in public but those days are gone and recently *maloya* has enjoyed a surge in popularity. The best-known *maloya* artists include the late Gramoun Lele and Daniel Waro. Leading popular bands who combine *maloya* with other (Western) styles are Ti Fock (jazz *maloya*), Baster and Ousa Nousava (electric *maloya*), and Natty Dread (local reggae).

Séga and *maloya* are combined with reggae to produce *séggae* and *maloggae* respectively. Popular Mauritian musician Kaya was a pioneer of *séggae* until his controversial death in 1998 (see box, page 185). *Zouk*, from the Caribbean islands, is also popular and frequently played in nightclubs. It has a slower rhythm than *séga* and *maloya* and romance is usually the theme.

Réunion regularly hosts music festivals combining performances by foreign and local artists. Best known of these is KabaRéunion, held each October over ten days to celebrate the World Music Movement. Visitors may also have the opportunity to attend one of the numerous concerts simply entitled '*Kabar*', which are organised by associations, clubs, neighbourhoods or private individuals. These are normally free and feature mostly unknown musicians from Réunion. The atmosphere is decidedly 'underground'.

ARCHITECTURE European settlers brought with them European styles of architecture, which can now be seen side by side with traditional Creole buildings. In some cases, the two styles are blended in the one building. Both Mauritian and Réunionnais Creole architecture utilise the *lambrequin*, a carved wooden or metal fringe adorning the roof.

Thanks to energetic conservation efforts on the part of the French Government, Creole architecture tends to be better preserved in Réunion than it is in Mauritius. Particular efforts have been made to restore and maintain Réunion's many delightful *'ti cases*, the humble dwellings of ordinary Creole families. These are typically small, single-storey, wooden homes painted in bright colours, featuring shuttered windows, a corrugated-iron roof and decorative *lambrequin*. The best examples of these are found in Hell-Bourg, Entre-Deux, Cilaos and Rivière St-Louis.

15

Practical Information

WHEN TO VISIT

Cyclone season, January to March, is best avoided. Even if a cyclone does not strike, rains are plentiful at this time. If hiking is on your itinerary, you may prefer to visit in winter (April to October) as trails can become impassable after the heavy rains of summer. Accommodation for hikers becomes very booked up during the winter, so try to book well in advance.

The other factor to consider is the French school holidays. Flights and hotels tend to be very full at any time which coincides with school holidays in mainland France (*la Métropole*): Christmas, Easter and from July to September.

HIGHLIGHTS

Unlike most island destinations, it is Réunion's interior, not its coastline, which draws visitors back year after year.

HIKING For many, hiking is *the* reason for visiting Réunion, which boasts over 1,000km of well-maintained trails. The island's three **cirques**, formed by the collapse of ancient volcanic craters, are a hiker's dream, with spectacular mountainous scenery punctuated by thundering waterfalls. **Mafate** is the most remote of the cirques and only accessible on foot or by helicopter. It can, however, be seen from the spectacular viewpoint at **Piton Maïdo**. For non-hikers the cirques are still a 'must-see', not least for their spectacular scenery and cool, clean mountain air. The cirques of **Cilaos** and **Salazie** can be reached by road. The pretty town of Cilaos is set in a basin surrounded by mountains and is known for its thermal springs. Salazie is the wettest and greenest of the cirques, with numerous waterfalls and pretty Creole villages, such as **Hell-Bourg**, rated one of the most beautiful in France.

High on your list of things to do in Réunion should be hiking around **Piton-de-la-Fournaise**, one of the world's most active volcanoes – provided it's not erupting, of course. Keen hikers will also enjoy the two-day climb of **Piton-des-Neiges**, which can be timed so you arrive at the summit to watch the sun rise over the Indian Ocean.

If hiking doesn't appeal or you are short of time, you needn't miss out on seeing the interior – **helicopter rides** over the island are becoming increasingly popular.

ADVENTURE SPORTS Réunion offers all manner of adventure sports and **activities** – climbing, canyoning, mountain biking, horseriding and paragliding to name but a few. For water-based activities try **scuba diving** at St-Gilles-les-Bains.

CULTURE Those seeking culture will be spoilt for choice. The **Creole people** are incredibly friendly and only too happy to share aspects of their culture with visitors.

Music and dance are central to Creole life. Head to a nightclub in St-Pierre, or a live show, and locals will be glad to teach you to dance the *séga*, *zouk* or *maloya*. You can't leave Réunion without sampling the delicious **Creole cuisine** – try *cari ti-jacques* or *rougail saucisses*, and follow your meal with a *rhum arrangé* (fruit-infused rum). There are festivals all year round: highlights include **Tamil fire-walking** ceremonies and the **Abolition of Slavery** celebrations on 20 December.

SUGGESTED ITINERARIES

Thanks to the well-maintained coastal road, you can drive around the island in one day but there is plenty to see along the way so allow more time if you can. A one-week stay will suffice for most visitors, especially those combining Réunion with another destination, such as Mauritius or Madagascar. However, if you are planning to spend several days hiking, or a few days relaxing on the beach at the end of your visit, you will need to allow two weeks.

ONE WEEK Most visitors will arrive at the airport in **St-Denis**, where you can pick up a hire car and begin exploring. If you are willing to brave the traffic, have a quick look around the capital, which offers a European café culture in a tropical setting and some good examples of colonial and Creole **architecture**. Continue on to the beach resort of **St-Gilles-les-Bains** for two nights, making sure you get the chance to snorkel in the lagoon at L'Hermitage. Get up early on the first morning and drive up to **Piton Maïdo** for spectacular views of the **Cirque de Mafate**. A picnic in the forest on the way down is always very pleasant.

Head to **Cilaos** – the long, hair-raising drive means you will need to spend at least one night. The following morning, hike one of the shorter trails, such as Bras Rouge, which takes you to a waterfall. If you have longer than one week on the island, hikes up the extinct **Piton-des-Neiges** start here and you can spend a night at the *gîte* at the base of the summit before getting up early to climb to the top in time for sunrise.

From Cilaos head back down to the coast and spend the night at **St Pierre**, the hub of the south coast. It has a lively nightlife, some great **restaurants** and the daily **markets** are one of the best places on the island to pick up souvenirs. If you can time your visit to include the large Saturday morning street market, all the better.

From St Pierre head up towards the volcano **Piton-de-la-Fournaise** and spend the night at one of the nearby hotels ready for an early start and a climb to the rim of the crater.

Return to St Pierre and head eastwards, through **St Joseph** and along the east coast. Between **St-Philippe** and **Ste-Rose** is where you will see the remnants of past **lava flows** and the path they took down the eastern face of Piton-de-la-Fournaise to the sea. The coast in this area is rugged – lava cliffs constantly pounded by the ocean. Don't miss **Piton Ste Rose**, where lava has skirted around the church.

Spend two nights in the **Cirque de Salazie**, at the delightful village of **Hell-Bourg**. Take in the fresh mountain air, explore the cirque and perhaps have a go at canyoning.

Returning to the coast, continue north back to St-Denis, stopping off at **St-André** to learn about **vanilla** production.

TOURIST INFORMATION

Marketing the island as a tourist destination is the responsibility of Ile de la Réunion Tourisme, based in St-Denis at Place du 20 Décembre 1848 (✆ *0810 160000;* e *resa@ reunion.fr; www.reunion.fr*). Ile de la Réunion Tourisme works in conjunction with

French tourist offices abroad, which should be able to give you information and advice on Réunion prior to departure. It publishes numerous useful information booklets on the island, including the invaluable *Run Guide*, which contains contact details of hotels, restaurants, tourist attractions, activity operators, etc. Its website (*www.reunion.fr*) is also packed with information. They also run a booking centre, including an excellent reservations website, where you can download a very comprehensive brochure and book accommodation, tours and activities (*www. resa.reunion.fr*). (For other useful websites, see page 366.)

Practical and tourist information is also available at www.guide-reunion.com. The website www.batcarre.com has current information about events, and they produce a free magazine, which is widely available on the island.

Everyday enquiries during your stay on the island should be directed to the regional tourist offices, located in each of the major towns (see *Tourist information* in the relevant town description). Information about French tourist offices abroad can be found on www.france.fr.

TOUR OPERATORS

Tour operators specialising in the Indian Ocean islands are able to secure special low-cost airfares to Réunion, as well as competitive rates on accommodation. Many offer a stay in Réunion combined with a visit to Mauritius, the Seychelles or Mayotte. Unfortunately, there are few tour operators outside France that offer package holidays to Réunion. A list of tour operators running tours to Mauritius as well as tours to Réunion can be found on pages 42–3. South African tour operator **Animal Tracks & Island Ventures** (*17 David Pl, Glendower, Edenvale 1610;* +27 11 454 0543; info@ animaltracks.co.za; www.animaltracks.co.za) only runs tours to Réunion.

RED TAPE

ENTRY REQUIREMENTS Holders of European Union or Swiss passports do not need a visa for a stay of up to three months but do need to carry a valid passport or identity card. The same applies for nationals of certain other countries, including Australia, the US, Canada, New Zealand, South Africa and Mauritius. Chinese and Indian nationals do not require a visa for a stay of up to 15 days, but to qualify for this exemption need to book their travel as part of a package or through a licensed tour operator in Réunion. For nationalities that do require a visa, note that as Réunion is not part of the Schengen area, a visa for France that does not specify Réunion is not valid. Before you travel, ensure your passport is valid for at least three months after the scheduled date of departure from Réunion. The French Embassy or Consulate in your home country will be able to provide up-to-date information and handle visa applications. All visitors must be in possession of a return ticket.

STAYING ON European Union passport holders have little difficulty staying or working in Réunion. Those on non-European Union passports who wish to stay longer than three months will need to apply for a *carte de séjour* (residence permit). French bureaucracy makes this far harder than it should be and applications are usually only accepted if you have been offered a job on the island or cannot leave for medical reasons. You will need to go to the *Préfecture* in St-Denis armed with copious documents, including certified translations of your birth certificate, a letter from your potential employer, passport photos, etc. The requirements change regularly so it is best to check with the Service d'Etat Civile et des Etrangers at the *Préfecture* (0262

15

407777; www.reunion.pref.gouv.fr; ⊕ *08.00–13.00 Mon–Fri)* or visit www.service-public.fr. Non-European Union passport holders wishing to work in Réunion need a work permit as well as a residence permit. Information on working, investing or setting up a business in Réunion is available at www.adreunion.com.

IMMIGRATION There are two channels – one for European Union passport holders and one for all other nationalities. Staff are generally efficient.

CUSTOMS There is no limit on the amount of alcohol, tobacco or currency that can be brought in from European Union countries. Visitors arriving from non-European Union countries are permitted to import free of duty the following:

Cigarettes	200 or 100 cigarillos or 50 cigars or 250g of tobacco
Wine	4 litres
Beer	16 litres
Alcohol over 22% proof	1 litre
Alcohol under 22% proof	2 litres
Medicines	Quantities corresponding to the duration of stay
Personal items	Up to a value of €430, or up to a value of €150 if under 15 years of age
Currency	Amounts over €10,000 must be declared

Plants and animals The importation of plant material, dairy and meat products is prohibited. For enquiries, contact the Direction des Services Vétérinaires (\ *0262 486132*); they also handle requests for the importation of pets. Cats and dogs must be microchipped, have a valid anti-rabies certificate and health certificate. Other requirements vary depending on the country of origin.

CONSULAR HELP As Réunion is not an independent country, few countries have diplomatic representation on the island. Below is a list of honorary consulates. In the event of a serious problem, British and American visitors should contact their respective embassies in Paris. The country code for telephoning France is +33.

In Réunion

E China 50 Rue Général de Gaulle, 97400 St-Denis; \0262 989698; e chinaconsul_re_fr@mfa.gov.cn

E Germany 64 Av Eudoxie Nonge, 97490 Ste-Clotilde; \0692 736898; e st-denis@hk-diplo.de

E India 266 Rue Maréchal Leclerc, 97400 St-Denis; \0262 417547; e congendia@wanadoo.fr

E Madagascar 29 Rue St Joseph Ouvrier, 97400 St-Denis; \0262 720730

E Mauritius 377 Rue Maréchal Leclerc, 97400 St-Denis; \0262 904028; e consulat.maurice.reunion@orange.fr

E Switzerland 107 Chemin Crève-Cœur, 97460 St-Paul; \0262 455574; e poldestpol@wanadoo.fr

In France

E UK 35 Rue du Faubourg, St-Honoré, 75383 Paris; \01 44 51 31 00; e france.enquiries@fco.gov.uk

E USA 4 Av Gabriel, 75008 Paris; \01 43 12 22 22; www.france.usembassy.gov

USEFUL CONTACTS

EMERGENCY SERVICES

Police \17 (emergency); \0262 907474 (non-emergency)
Ambulance \15

Fire service \18
Coastguard \0262 434343
Mountain rescue \0262 930930

Directory enquiries ☎12
Weather forecast ☎3250 (from a land line);
☎0892 680808 (from a mobile phone)
Cyclone information ☎0897 650101

Volcano information ☎0262 275292; ☎0262
275461 (recorded message)
Hiking trail information ☎0262 373839
Traffic information ☎0262 972727

GETTING THERE AND AWAY

BY AIR The majority of visitors arrive by air, from Africa, Europe or other Indian Ocean islands. The main airport is Roland Garros International Airport, which is 11km east of the main town, St-Denis (pages 292–300). The airport at Pierrefonds, in the south of the island, used to handle only flights within the Indian Ocean, but now receives some flights from Paris. For more information, see page 266.

The only direct flights from Europe to Réunion are from France and take 11 hours from Paris. A number of airlines have introduced flights from regional airports in France. These flights are considerably dearer during high season, ie: French school holidays. If you are travelling from any other part of Europe you will need to fly to France to connect with an onward flight. However, most airlines offer special fares for the flight to Paris if you are carrying on to Réunion. Alternatively, fly to Mauritius and on to Réunion from there. For airline offices in Réunion, go to www.reunion.fr.

From Europe
✈ **Air France** 12 flights per week from Paris to St-Denis.
✈ **Air Austral** 11 flights per week from Paris to St-Denis, 2 flights per week from Lyon, Bordeaux, Nantes & Marseille. 7 flights per week from Paris to Pierrefonds.
✈ **Corsairfly** Daily flights from Paris to St-Denis.

From the US
To Paris by any airline & then as above. Air Mauritius can arrange visits of 2–3 days to Réunion as extensions to holidays in Mauritius. For Air Mauritius details, see pages 48–9.

From Australia
✈ **Air Mauritius** Weekly flights to Mauritius from Perth, then on to Réunion.

From Africa
✈ **Air Austral** Up to 2 flights weekly from Johannesburg. Also flights from Madagascar (Antananarivo, Nosy Be & Tamatave).
✈ **Air Madagascar** Several flights per week from various destinations in Madagascar, including Antananarivo, Nosy Be & Tamatave.

From the Indian Ocean islands
✈ **Air Austral** Several flights daily between Mauritius & St-Denis. Daily flights from Mauritius to Pierrefonds. 2 flights per week between Pierrefonds & Rodrigues. 10 flights per week from Mayotte & 2 from the Comoros (Moroni) to St-Denis; up to 2 flights per week from the Seychelles.
✈ **Air Mauritius** Several flights daily between Mauritius & St-Denis. Daily flights from Mauritius to Pierrefonds.

BY SEA Few cruise ships stop off at Réunion, although the number is rising. Lots of glamorous French yacht owners keep their vessels in St-Gilles-les-Bains and may be looking for crew if you're lucky. Try asking at the local tourist office or around the port, where everyone seems to know each other.

At the time of writing the passenger ferry service between Mauritius and Réunion had ceased and there were no plans to re-establish it.

ON ARRIVAL/DEPARTURE

ROLAND GARROS INTERNATIONAL AIRPORT The airport, which is named after a French aviator born in Réunion (1888–1915), is 11km east of St-Denis (☎ *0262*

488068; *www.reunion.aeroport.fr. For flight information,* `0262 281616`.). Although relatively small, this is a well-organised airport. There are souvenir shops, a post office, a bank and ATMs in the entrance hall of the terminal building. The bank and post office are open on weekdays and Saturday mornings, but close for lunch. There is also a very helpful tourist information desk with lots of leaflets. Next to the desk is a touch-screen information point – follow the instructions on the screen and it gives you details of hotels (which you can then telephone free), transport, entertainment, etc. The restaurants and bars are upstairs, and there is rather pricey internet access and free Wi-Fi. The departure lounge has a duty-free shop and snack bars. The main car-hire companies, including Budget, Avis, Hertz and Europcar, are represented at the airport, with offices in a separate building on the right-hand side of the car park as you exit the terminal building. (For details, see pages 270–1.)

Parking at the airport is free for the first 15 minutes, then €1 per hour and €35 per day.

Luggage Baggage reclaim is located just beyond immigration. For a trolley you will need a €1 coin, which you will get back when you return it.

Getting to your hotel There is a shuttle-bus service (*navette*) between Roland Garros International Airport and St-Denis city centre, which makes around 13 return trips daily between 07.00 and 19.45. The journey takes around 20 minutes and costs from €4.

A taxi to the centre of St-Denis costs from €20. Fares are higher after 20.00. If you can't find a taxi, which may be the case on a public holiday or at night, `0262 488383`.

PIERREFONDS AIRPORT The south of the island is now conveniently linked to neighbouring Indian Ocean islands by flights to and from Pierrefonds Airport, 7km west of St-Pierre (`0262 968000`; e *info@pierrefonds.aeroport.fr; www.pierrefonds. aeroport.fr. For flight information,* `0262 967766`.).

A bus service (Line T) connects St-Pierre bus station and the airport to all the main towns on the west coast with its final stop Roland Garros Airport in St-Denis. It operates from the airport from 05.25 to 18.00 daily. The Noctambus is an on-demand shuttle bus, which operates from 20.00 to 04.00 on Friday, Saturday and the eve of public holidays. You need to sign up for membership via www.civis.re or at Alternéo offices, and you need to call to book it (`0262 554060`). Taxis between the airport and St-Pierre cost around €15.50 (`0262 385484`). Car rental can also be arranged in the terminal building. Parking at the airport is free.

HEALTH *with Dr Felicity Nicholson*

Although there are mosquitoes on Réunion, they are not malarial so you don't need prophylaxis. However, watch out for malarial symptoms developing if you've just arrived from a malarial area such as Madagascar.

No inoculations are compulsory but medical practitioners usually recommend those for hepatitis A, hepatitis B, tetanus, diphtheria and polio.

Medical care is excellent, conforming to French standards throughout the island. You can usually turn up at a doctor's surgery and be seen fairly promptly without an appointment. Medical care is expensive and European visitors should carry a European Health Insurance Card in order to take advantage of reciprocal agreements and to claim refunds of fees. The form can be obtained from post offices in your home country or online (*www.hse.ie*).

Water is officially said to be safe to drink throughout the island but it can cause occasional minor upsets. It's best to stick to drinking mineral water, which costs around €1.20 per 2-litre bottle, and to avoid having ice in drinks. You should be particularly careful to avoid tap water after heavy rains or cyclones, as the supply can be contaminated. As with any tropical country, always try to peel or wash fruit before eating it.

As in Mauritius, there is an uncomplicated attitude to sex, and AIDS has arrived on the island.

SAFETY

Violent crime is rare, but you should take sensible precautions. Pick-pocketing and burglary do occur but are not widespread. There are some nasty tales of hikers disappearing in the cirques, particularly Mafate. If you plan to hike it is best to go in a group and make sure that you tell someone which route you are taking and how long you expect to be away.

Be wary in bars and nightclubs as a large number of both locals and visitors tend to drink excessively, which can lead to tension and drink-driving. As in Mauritius, stray dogs can be a problem, particularly as they tend to hang around in packs. As well as being a potential danger to pedestrians, they can cause traffic accidents, so be wary whether on foot or in a vehicle.

There are usually one or two shark attacks off the coast of Réunion each year and the number is on the rise, so avoid swimming outside lagoons and netted areas. When a 13-year-old boy was killed by a shark in April 2015, he was the seventh fatal shark-attack victim since 2011 (see box, page 291).

WOMEN TRAVELLERS

Women attract a lot of unwanted attention in Réunion. A pair of sunglasses can be very helpful as it enables you to avoid eye contact. Women should not walk alone at night. Knowledge of French or Creole helps in such situations and a few firm but polite words are usually sufficient. There have been incidences of women being attacked on quiet stretches of beach (even during the day), so try to remain within sight of other people.

TRAVELLERS WITH DISABILITY

Réunion is better equipped than neighbouring Mauritius for disabled travellers. By law, all hotels of a certain size and classified three star or above must have some rooms equipped for the disabled. However, some hotels with fewer than three stars also have rooms for the disabled.

GAY/LESBIAN TRAVELLERS

In recent years the island's tourism board has instigated a big push for Réunion to become more gay friendly. Many tourism companies, in particular hotels, have signed Réunion's Gay Friendly Charter and carry a gay-friendly certification, which can assist gay and lesbian travellers in choosing their accommodation. There are plenty of gay-friendly bars and nightclubs, particularly in St-Denis, St-Pierre and St-Gilles-les-Bains. In the broader community, however, homophobia exists and travellers should avoid public displays of affection.

TRAVELLING WITH KIDS

Unlike Mauritius, only a handful of hotels have kids' clubs but most of the hotels are child friendly and some offer a baby-sitting service. Accommodation designed for hikers is less likely to be kitted out for children. Being part of France, the infrastructure is good, and there are large supermarkets stocking baby paraphernalia. The main car-hire companies can supply car seats at additional cost.

WHAT TO TAKE

Don't forget that Réunion is part of France so visitors from EU countries should carry a European Health Insurance Card (page 266).

Credit cards are widely accepted and cash easily changed at the many banks. You should be able to buy everything that you need in Réunion, although it is likely to be more expensive than in your home country. Mosquito repellent and suncream are essential. Sockets take two-pin continental plugs, so carry an adaptor if necessary.

Take light, comfortable clothing, with a smart-casual outfit for dinner in hotels. Include beachwear, not forgetting beach/swimming shoes to protect your feet from sea-urchin spikes and sharp coral. Warm clothing will come in handy for the evenings, particularly in the interior. The mountains can get very cold so you'll need rain gear and really warm clothing; and good hiking boots if you plan to explore the trails.

As ever, travel insurance is essential. If you plan to partake in any of Réunion's many activities, such as canyoning or paragliding (see pages 286–9), make sure your travel insurance covers this.

MAPS Tourist maps of the island are available at tourist offices; many hotels also have a supply. A road map, which shows real-time traffic congestion, is available online (*www.infotrafic.re*).

Hikers will need detailed maps, which are widely available. Maps produced by the Institut National de l'Information Géographique et Forestière (*90 Av de Flandre, 75019 Paris, France; www.ign.fr*), known as IGN maps, are the equivalent of the UK's Ordnance Survey maps. Réunion is covered by six IGN maps. Those of most use to hikers are 4402 RT, which covers St-Denis and the cirques of Mafate and Salazie, plus the northern part of the Cirque de Cilaos, and 4406 RT, which covers the volcano area. Map 4405 RT covers St-Pierre and the Cirque de Cilaos. For more information, see page 284.

MONEY

The main French banks, such as Crédit Agricole and BNP Paribas, have branches in all the main towns. Banks are generally open 08.00–16.00 Monday–Friday. ATMs are widespread on the coast and you can withdraw money using Visa, MasterCard, Cirrus and Eurochèques. Credit cards are widely accepted. If you're travelling to the interior, take sufficient cash with you as there are very limited banking facilities.

The currency exchange rates in March 2016 were as follows: £1=€1.28, US$1=€0.89, Rs40=€1.

BUDGETING

Réunion is an expensive destination because so many goods are imported but with careful planning travelling costs can be kept down. Markets and roadside stalls sell

fruit, vegetables and handicrafts at very reasonable prices. Eating out in restaurants is not cheap but *camions bars* (mobile snack bars) are a good option for those on a budget, serving everything from *samoussas* to pizzas.

You can keep accommodation costs low by staying in *meublés de tourisme* (self-catering holiday rentals, referred to in Réunion as 'furnished flats'), *chambres d'hôtes* and *gîtes* (see page 274). There is an excellent, inexpensive bus service. *Taxis collectifs*, which take passengers until the car is full, are far cheaper than ordinary taxis as you pay a proportion of the fare.

If you are staying in one of the island's more upmarket hotels, expect meals and drinks to be pricey. Bars and nightclubs are also expensive: most clubs charge around €12–15 for entry and drinks are often around €8.

Finally, you are bound to be tempted to try some of the many outdoor activities on offer in Réunion, so allow for some extra expenses.

GETTING AROUND

INBOUND TOUR OPERATORS Inbound tour operators meet visitors on behalf of hotels and overseas tour operators. They can arrange transport, accommodation, excursions and activities with multi-lingual guides. Here is a selection.

Bourbon Tourisme 14 Rue Rontaunay, 97463 St-Denis; ℡0262 330870; e contact@bourbontourisme.com; www.bourbontourisme.com

Comptoir Corail 12 Pl des Coquillages, Boucan-Canot, 97434 St-Gilles-les-Bains; ℡0262 338838; e comptoircorail@orange.fr; www.comptoircorail.com

Connections Réunion 53 Route de Domenjod, 97490 Ste-Clotilde; ℡0262 931398; e resa@connections-reunion.com; www.connections-reunion.com

Horizon Réunion 6 Ligne d'Equerre, 97432 Ravine des Cabris, St-Pierre; ℡0262 024000; e contact@horizon-reunion.com; www.horizon-reunion.com

Mille Tours 9 bis Rue Sarda Garriga, 97460 St-Paul; ℡0262 225500; e milletours.individuel@wanadoo.fr; www.milletours.com

Réunitours 27 Av de Bourbon, 97434 St-Gilles-les-Bains; ℡0262 331111; e contact@reunitours.com; www.reunitours.com

COACH TOURS

Groupe Transports Mooland ZI Bel-Air, BP24, 97899 St-Louis; ℡0262 913939; e s.fontaine@transports-mooland.fr; www.groupetransportsmooland.com. Offers a good range of tours.

Moutoussamy et Fils 77 Rue André Lardy, Za la Mare, 97438 Ste-Marie; ℡0970 359198; e moutoussamyetfils@wanadoo.fr; www.moutoussamyetfils.fr. Also offers a good range in modern AC vehicles.

Transports Souprayenmestry 2 Chemin Souprayen, Ravine à Marquet, 97419 La Possession; ℡0262 448169; e transports-souprayenmestry@wanadoo.fr. Offers guided tours in comfortable, AC coaches. They leave early in the morning, picking up passengers from all the main towns along the west coast, from St-Pierre to St-Denis. There are various tours offered each week, such as Salazie, Piton-de-la-Fournaise, Cilaos & the island tour. Ask at the nearest tourist office or contact them directly.

DRIVING Réunion's roads are overcrowded. Driving through towns such as St-Denis and St-Pierre during peak hours can be exasperating. The coastal road between St-Leu and St-Gilles-les-Bains is prone to very heavy traffic and there are invariably long queues around L'Hermitage. A road map, which shows real-time traffic congestion, is available online (*www.infotrafic.re*). In 2009, a new road, known as La Route des Tamarins, was constructed between St-Paul and

L'Etang-Salé-les-Bains, designed to bypass the towns of the west coast and alleviate the traffic pressure on the area. It has achieved that to a certain extent, but this area still sees a lot of traffic. A planned new coastal road from St-Denis to Le Port is set to be France's most expensive piece of road. It will be built on pylons in the ocean, is scheduled to be completed in 2018 and is expected to cost €1.66 billion.

Driving is on the right and road markings are as in France. The roads are well maintained but the standard of driving is frighteningly bad at times. Every year over 100 people are killed on the island's roads and the situation is not improving. For many young Réunionnais a car is a status symbol and they seem to believe that the faster they drive, the more their image benefits. The speed limit on the dual carriageway that runs along much of the west coast is 110km/h, although you wouldn't know it. Drink-driving is a real problem and some people even smoke *zamal* (locally grown marijuana) whilst at the wheel. Stray dogs also cause their fair share of accidents, so keep your eyes peeled. Don't be put off hiring a car! It is one of the best ways to see the island and gives you valuable independence. Just be vigilant.

Car and motorbike hire Most visitors will hire cars for at least one day whilst on the island. Car hire can be arranged either through your hotel, tour operator or directly. The main car-hire companies have desks at Roland Garros Airport. Cars can be hired on a daily basis plus mileage or for longer periods with unlimited mileage. Air conditioning may cost extra but is a real blessing in the summer.

The requirements vary but the minimum age for car hire is usually 21 years and you must have held a driving licence for two years. You will be asked to pay in advance and provide a deposit. Do check that the insurance cover that comes with the car is fully comprehensive (*tous risques*). Some car-hire companies may try to tell you that no firm offers fully comprehensive insurance – not true. Make sure you know what 'excess' you will have to pay if you cause an accident; some companies keep costs down by scrimping on insurance.

Expect to pay around €50–55 per day (1–3 days) for a Peugeot 206 or about €100–110 per day for a 4x4. As noted above, air conditioning may be extra.

Take extra care on the roads on a **motorbike** or **moped**, as drivers are not courteous. Hire is by the day and usually includes unlimited mileage, with reduced rates for seven days or more. You will need to leave a deposit and, as with cars, check that you are happy with the insurance cover provided.

Expect to pay around €35 per day for a 125cc moped (1–7 days) and €65–70 per day for a 600cc motorbike (1–7 days).

Car-hire companies

🚗 **ADA Location** 3 Rue de la Croix Rouge, ZAE La Mare, 97438 Ste-Marie; ☎ 0262 215901; airport, ☎ 0262 488183; e info@ada-reunion.com; www.ada-reunion.com

🚗 **Avis Réunion** 83 Rue Jules Verne, BP 8, 97821 Le Port; ☎ 0262 421599; airport, ☎ 0262 488185; 82 Rue Marius et Ary Leblond, 97410 St-Pierre; ☎ 0262 350090; e resa@avis-reunion.com; www.avisreunion.com

🚗 **Budget** 1 Rue Edouard Manes, ZI du Chaudron, 97490 Ste-Clotilde; ☎ 0262 488626; airport, ☎ 0262 280195; 2 Chemin des Anglais, Zac des Mascareignes, 97420 Le Port; ☎ 0262 448716; e budget.run@caille.com; www.budget-reunion.com

🚗 **Europcar** 123 Av Leconte de Lisle, 97434 St-Gilles-les-Bains; ☎ 0262 931415; airport, ☎ 0262 282758; e europcar-reunion@wandoo.fr; www.europcar-reunion.com

🚗 **Hertz** 7 Rue de la Pépinière, ZAE La Mare, 97438 Ste-Marie; ☎ 0262 532255; 29 Av de Bourbon, 97434 St-Gilles-les-Bains; ☎ 0262 245375; 100 Av Luc Donat, 97410 S-Pierre; ☎ 0262 456996; airport, ☎ 0262 280593; e reservations@hertzreunion.com; www.hertzreunion.com

If you rent a car you feel you should use it each day – such a pity in a lovely island like Réunion, where the hiking is superb and the bus service excellent. In the two weeks that we were there we travelled by bus, hitchhiking and on foot, and saw everything we wanted to see.

The yellow buses, or *cars jaunes*, are great. Each bus stop displays the timetable (so it is easy to plan your day), buses arrive on time, their destination is clearly displayed on the front, and the driver will make an unauthorised stop if you are caught out between official bus stops.

The only problem with buses is that they are infrequent on some routes (about every 2 hours around St-Philippe, for instance) so hitchhiking is a useful alternative. We (two women) found it easy and fun – and very good for our French, even if the Creole accent put a strain on our understanding.

🚕 **ITC Tropicar** 27 Av de Bourbon, 97434 St-Gilles-les-Bains; ☎0262 240101; e contact@ itctropicar.com; www.itctropicar.re
🚕 **National Citer** 65 Bd du Chaudron, 97490 Ste-Clotilde; ☎0262 974974; airport, ☎0262 488377; e contact@citer.re; www.citer.re

Motorbike/moped-hire companies
🏍 **Harley Davidson Flying Twin** 205–7 Rue du Général de Gaulle, 97434 St-Gilles-les-Bains;

☎0262 458883; e manager@flying-twin.com; www.hdreunion.com. Harley Davidson rentals.
🏍 **Moto Loc OI** 8 Chemin Recherchant, Ravine des Cabris, 97432 St-Pierre; ☎0692 285555; www. motoloc-oi.fr
🏍 **974 Motoloc** 3 bis Rue Georges Pompidou, 97436 St-Leu; ☎0692 694842; e reservation@ 974motoloc.com; www.974motoloc.com
🏍 **Scootloc974** 22 Lot les Charmilles, 97434 La-Saline-les-Bains; ☎0692 505054; www. scootloc974.com

TAXIS Taxis are generally expensive and not easy to find outside the main towns. Stands are usually situated in town centres, often near the bus station or market, and there are stands at the two airports. They don't tend to hang around looking for passengers in the evening, so you'll probably need to order one and there is a surcharge for night-time rides. Most taxis have meters but it's not a bad idea to negotiate a fare beforehand, otherwise you may be charged 'tourist rates'. A cheaper option is a *taxi collectif* (shared taxi). The driver waits until the car is full before leaving, then each passenger pays a proportion of the fare. They usually depart from bus stations. The only disadvantage is that you could be waiting a while in quieter areas for the taxi to fill up, and they only run during the day. You can usually pick up a *taxi collectif* from the bus station in either St-Pierre or St-Denis, which runs the full length of the west coast between the two towns.

Taxi firms
In and around St-Denis
🚕 **Allo Taxi** m 0692 854134
🚕 **Roland Garros Airport Taxis** ☎0262 488383
🚕 **Taxi by Henrico Lauret** 110 Chemin de la Source, 97400 St-Denis; ☎0692 314314; www. taxi-la-reunion.fr
🚕 **Taxis Paille-en-Queue** ☎0262 292029
🚕 **Taxis Plus** ☎0262 283774

St-André
🚕 **Taxis Léopards** ☎0262 460028

St-Benoît
🚕 **Taxis les Marsouins** ☎0262 505558

St Philippe
🚕 **Taxi Hoareau** m 0693 319394

St-Pierre
🚕 **Taxi Idmont**   m 0692 006565
🚕 **Taxis du Sud**   ☎0262 599293
🚕 **Taxis Saint-Pierrois**   ☎0262 385484

Le Tampon
🚕 **Boyer Taxi**   m 0692 319380
🚕 **Taxi rank**   ☎0262 271169

St-Louis
🚕 **RUN Taxis**   m 0692 663061

St-Leu
🚕 **Taxi rank**   ☎0262 348385

St-Paul
🚕 **Taxis de la Buse**   ☎0262 456434
🚕 **Taxis de St-Paul**   ☎0262 455828
🚕 **Taxis St-Paulois**   ☎0262 240883

Cilaos
🚕 **Taxi Figuin**   ☎0262 391945

BY BUS Travel between towns is provided by the excellent bus service (*cars jaunes*). Buses are a reliable, easy and cost-effective way to get around the island. *Cars jaunes* are easily distinguished from the buses which operate within towns because, as the name indicates, they are bright yellow.

Cars jaunes tickets cost €2 for a single ticket (excluding express *Z'éclair* buses), €8 for a book of five tickets, €6 for a day ticket (unlimited journeys) and €10 for a day ticket for a family (two adults, three children). A weekly ticket is €15, a monthly ticket is €38 and a quarterly ticket €100. The express (*Z'éclair*) single tickets cost €5 (€10 on board the bus), €20 for a book of five tickets and €15 for a day ticket. A weekly express ticket is €38, monthly €150, quarterly €360 and yearly €1,300.

You can buy the single tickets on the bus or at *cars jaunes* sales and information points around the island, but the multiple tickets have to be bought at the sales and information points. Local bus etiquette dictates that you should get on at the front and off at the back. Don't forget to validate your ticket by putting it in the machine as you get on, and keep hold of it as on-the-spot checks are frequent. Stops are mostly on request, so you will need to clap your hands to signal that you want to get off.

Listed below are bus routes with the duration of each journey. On the main routes buses are regular (every 1–2 hours) and service is from around 05.00 to 18.30. On quieter routes (like the east coast) buses are less frequent and operate from around 07.00 to 17.30. Fewer buses run on Sundays and public holidays. Each bus stop displays a timetable so planning is easy. The French for bus station is *gare routière*.

Line E1 St-Benoît to/from St-Denis (express, via Le Chaudron)
Line E2 St-Benoît to/from St-Denis
Line E3 St-André to/from St-Denis (via Ste-Marie)
Line E4 St-André to/from St-Denis (via St-Suzanne)
Line 01 St-Denis to/from St-Pierre (express via La Route des Tamarins)
Line 02 St-Denis to/from St-Pierre (express via the coast road)
Line 03 St-Paul to/from St-Denis (express)
Line 04 St-Paul to/from St-Denis
Line S1 St-Benoît to/from St-Pierre (via Le Grand Brulé)

Line S2 St-Benoît to/from St-Pierre (via the Plaines)
Line S3 St-Joseph to/from St-Paul (via the coast road)
Line S4 St-Pierre to/from St-Paul
Line S5 Entre-Deux to/from St-Pierre
Line T St-Pierre to/from Ste-Marie (via the beaches, Pierrefonds Airport & Roland Garros Airport)
Line ZE St-Benoît to/from St-Denis (via Roland Garros Airport)
Line ZO St-Pierre to/from St-Denis (via La Route des Tamarins, non-stop, Mon–Sat): 1hr 10mins

If you need more information, current fares, schedule updates or timetables, contact *Cars Jaunes* (☎ 0810 123974; www.cg974.fr).

HITCHHIKING Hitchhiking in Réunion is relatively easy but women should not attempt it alone. Plenty of drivers won't stop, and you may end up doing a fair amount of walking but on such a beautiful island this is no hardship.

ACCOMMODATION

As there are only a limited number of hotels on Réunion, accommodation should preferably be booked well in advance, particularly if you are travelling during peak season (November–January, March and April, July–October). Try to book at least six weeks prior to departure.

Accommodation in Réunion is divided into 'classified' and 'unclassified', with a star rating system applied to the classified hotels. It is this star system, devised by the French Government, which is reflected in this guide. Star ratings are allocated by the *préfet*.

Price brackets have been supplied as a guide only – rates do change regularly, according to season and demand. It is therefore better to judge a hotel by its description than by the price. In any case, if the hotel is booked as part of a package holiday including flights, the public rate is never what you, the guest, actually pay. Even for those who make their own hotel bookings direct, there could be significant discounts on the public rates at luxury, upmarket and mid-range properties. The vast majority of hotels offer considerable discounts for children and infants are often accommodated free of charge. It is worth visiting the websites of hotels as many, particularly the larger ones, publish special offers on the internet.

The price brackets are based on the hotels' public rates for a standard double room, per room per night during high season on half board, based on two people sharing. However, budget and shoestring properties are likely to be sold on a bed and breakfast or self-catering (room only) basis.

A tax (*taxe de séjour*), calculated on the room rate and the duration of your stay, is payable when you settle your account. As in Mauritius, the board basis is indicated, either all-inclusive (AI), full board (FB), half board (HB), bed and breakfast (BB) or room only (RO). (For definitions of these terms, see page 64.)

There are very few upmarket hotels in Réunion and the service does not compare to that in Mauritius, but accommodation with plenty of character is easy to find. As well as hotels there are guesthouses (*gîtes de France*), self-catering holiday rentals (*meublés de tourisme*, also known as furnished flats), rural farm inns (*fermes auberges*), mountain huts/lodges (*gîtes de montagne*), guesthouses/huts on hiking trails (*gîtes d'étape*), 'VVF' holiday villages and youth hostels (*auberges de jeunesse*).

All types of accommodation can be booked online at www.resa.reunion.fr and www.allonslareunion.com. Bookings can also be made at tourist offices around the island.

15

ACCOMMODATION PRICE CODES		
Double room per night on half board (HB):		
Luxury	$$$$$	€622+
Upmarket	$$$$	€277–622
Mid range	$$$	€138–277
Budget	$$	€69–138
Shoestring	$	€69

CHAMBRES D'HOTE Bed-and-breakfast-style accommodation. These are not self-catering and the owner lives in the house; some also offer table d'hôte meals. Staying in such accommodation can be a marvellous experience as the owner and guests usually all dine together. Double rooms cost from €25 per night on BB. Table d'hôte meals start at around €18 (very worthwhile). Can be booked as per *gîtes ruraux* (see below).

GITES DE FRANCE Classified guesthouses of reasonable standard, found throughout Réunion. Can be booked as per *gîtes ruraux* (see below).

GITES RURAUX Self-catering accommodation, with owners living on the property but not in the house itself. They carry the 'Gîtes de France' label. Prices are typically between €230 and €1,200 per *gîte* per week for between two and 14 people. For bookings, contact Gîtes de France (◊ *0262 729781; www.gites-de-france-reunion. com*) or www.resa.reunion.fr.

MEUBLES DE TOURISME Furnished flats and villas, classified from one to four stars. Guides to these self-catering holiday rentals, published annually, are available at tourist offices. Those that are categorised *Clé Vacances* are regularly inspected and have been awarded an additional mark of quality. Information on those properties, including availability, is online at www.clevacances.com.

You can book directly with the owners, at tourist offices or via the Réunion Island tourism reservation website (*www.resa.reunion.fr*). Most owners insist on a minimum stay of at least two nights. Rates often depend on length of stay. No meals are provided.

GITES DE MONTAGNE AND REFUGES DE RANDONNEE Basic mountain huts, mostly on hiking trails. Expect to pay from €14.50 per person per night.

GITES D'ETAPE Often in small villages; those with the Gîtes de France label are usually better in quality. Dinners and breakfasts prepared by hosts. No self-catering. Can be booked as per *gîtes de montagne* (see above).

REFUGES (rest huts) Basic. No self-catering, as meals (dinners, breakfasts) are prepared by host.

CAMPSITES There used to be very few options for camping in Réunion but in recent years more and more campsites have opened up, particularly in the centre of the island. They are often simple campsites on a private farm, and a good way to enjoy the natural environment and get to know some local people. Some also have self-catering cabins or basic dormitory-style accommodation. There is a new campsite close to the beach at L'Hermitage, which has on-site safari tents as well as pitches for your own tent. Some people pitch a tent or string up a hammock by the beach, but it is worth bearing in mind there is no security. Camping for one night in forests is acceptable but any longer is frowned upon. For a tent site, expect to pay from €15. You can book campsites directly or via www.resa.reunion.fr.

YOUTH HOSTELS There are several youth hostels on the island, including in Hell-Bourg (◊ *0262 474131*), Entre-Deux (◊ *0262 395920*) and St-Denis (◊ *0262 411534*). Expect to pay around €15 for a dormitory bed.

Eating in Réunion is a pleasure. There is such variety, with Creole, Chinese and French restaurants in almost every town. Surprisingly, Indian cuisine is harder to find.

Traditional Creole food is slightly spicy and includes elements from French and Indian culinary styles. The mainstay of Creole cuisine is the *cari* – fish, meat or poultry in a tasty sauce packed with spices. It is eaten with rice and *grains* (beans or lentils) and accompanied by *rougail*, a kind of spicy chutney often made with tomatoes, onions and chillies. Tuna, shark and swordfish make delicious *cari*, as do *camarons* (large freshwater prawns). *Cari poulet* (chicken *cari*) and *rougail saucisses* (a spicy pork sausage in a tomato-based stew) are a good inexpensive option. *Cari ti-jacques* (curried young jackfruits) is very traditional, as are duck with vanilla and *cabri massalé* (masala spiced goat stew). If you're feeling adventurous, look out for *cari tang* (curried tenrec – similar to a hedgehog), although this is rarely seen on menus nowadays.

For traditional food in a family atmosphere, try a table d'hôte. If you're on a tight budget, there is a very healthy population of *camion bars* (mobile snack bars) on the island, serving inexpensive filled baguettes, *samoussas* and other light meals.

Most towns have fish sellers on the seafront. If you have access to a kitchen, there is nothing better than cooking freshly caught tuna or shark. Try to buy it in the morning though, because the stalls are not refrigerated and fish that has sunbathed for 8 hours is more than a little risky.

Whilst there are plenty of tasty options for seafood lovers, vegetarians are not well catered for on the island. Restaurants with a French flavour usually serve a variety of salads, whilst vegetarian Creole fare includes *achards* (spicy, pickled vegetables) and *brèdes* (a mixture of greens). If you would like a vegetarian meal, you may well have to ask for a dish to be prepared specially, and then politely decline when the waiter offers to add some ham to make it more interesting! The French for vegetarian is *végétarien*, vegan is *végétalien*.

On Sundays Réunion goes for a picnic. We're not talking a wicker hamper filled with a few Scotch eggs and some cheese sandwiches. This is picnicking on the grandest scale, a real family affair. Réunion is equipped with excellent picnic facilities, not merely tables but also barbecue areas. From the beaches to the forests, people can be seen picnicking, some arriving as early as 10.00 to claim their favourite spot and prepare their *cari*. If you are ever invited to join in, don't miss the opportunity.

As in Mauritius, rum – as a by-product of the sugar industry – is big business. *Rhum arrangé* is made by adding fruit and spices to white rum and allowing it to ferment for several months. You are likely to be offered a *rhum arrangé* at the end of your meal in most restaurants or alternatively a *punch* (pronounced 'ponsh'), which also has rum as the main ingredient but is more fruity and less powerful.

Réunion: Practical Information   EATING AND DRINKING

15

RESTAURANT PRICE CODES

Average price of a main course:

Expensive	$$$$$	€36
Above average	$$$$	€24–36
Mid range	$$$	€12–24
Cheap & cheerful	$$	€6–12
Rock bottom	$	up to €6

Here are two of the most popular examples of Creole cuisine, as prepared by culinary wizard Mamie Javel, author of Creole cookbook, *La Réunion des Mille et une Saveurs*. Mamie Javel used to run one of the island's top restaurants, Relais des Cîmes in Hell-Bourg (page 359), where meals are still prepared according to her famous recipes.

COCONUT CHICKEN

Cooking time = 30 minutes
Ingredients (serves 4):

1 chicken (1.5kg)	100g grated coconut
6 ripe tomatoes	½ teaspoon turmeric
3 large onions	20 peppercorns
5 cloves of garlic	3 cloves
1 sprig of thyme	4 tablespoons of oil
25cl fresh or tinned coconut milk	salt to taste

Method: Cut chicken into pieces. Finely chop the onions and tomatoes. Crush the garlic, peppercorns and cloves. Heat the oil in a large pan and lightly brown the chicken pieces. Add the onions, garlic, peppercorns and cloves. When the onions have softened, add the tomatoes. Cook until the mixture has reduced, then add the turmeric. Stir continuously and add a glass of water. Cover and allow to simmer for 20 minutes. Finally, add the coconut milk. Serve sprinkled with grated coconut.

VANILLA TROUT

A speciality in Hell-Bourg, Cirque de Salazie, where you can also catch your own trout which will then be prepared for you.

Cooking time = 20 minutes
Ingredients (serves 4):

4 trout, each weighing 200g	butter to taste
50cl crème fraîche	soya sauce
½ vanilla pod	salt and pepper to taste
2 cloves of garlic	

Method: Clean trout, salting the insides. Grill fish for five minutes on each side. Just before they are cooked, sprinkle a few drops of soya sauce over each fish, turn and heat again for two minutes. Meanwhile, prepare the vanilla cream.

Crush the garlic cloves. Cook in butter on low heat. Add cream, making sure that it doesn't stick to the pan. Slice the vanilla pod lengthways, using the knife to scrape the vanilla seeds from the pod into the sauce. Then add the rest of the pod to the mixture. Stir continuously. Season with salt and pepper.

Presentation: Pour the vanilla cream on to the plates and place the trout on top. Pour a tablespoon of heated rum over each trout and light. Serve with mixed vegetables.

When in a bar you may hear people ordering '*une Dodo*'. This is not as ridiculous as it sounds – the local brand of beer is called 'Dodo'. Throughout the island you will see advertising depicting a cheeky, smiling dodo with the Creole slogan '*la dodo lé la*' (the dodo is here). It is usually the cheapest beer on offer and is very popular. Just take care not to order '*un dodo*'; not even the most skilled of barmen can produce one of those.

Réunion produces some excellent agricultural products, including honey, vanilla, coffee, sugar, turmeric, bananas, pineapples, coconuts and lychees. Information on agricultural tours is available at www.agrotours-reunion.com.

To assist you in choosing a restaurant, we have provided a rough indication of the price using codes to represent the average price of a main course.

WORKING HOURS

Offices are typically open 08.00–12.00 and 14.00–18.00 Monday–Friday. Shops open 08.30–12.00 and 14.30–18.00 Monday–Saturday. Some food shops are open on Sunday mornings. State administrative offices are a law unto themselves, many opening for very limited hours.

PUBLIC HOLIDAYS

New Year's Day	1 January
Easter Monday	variable (March/April)
Labour Day	1 May
1945 Victory	8 May
Ascension Day	variable (May)
Whit Sunday	variable (May)
Bastille Day	14 July
Assumption	15 August
All Saints' Day	1 November
1918 Armistice	11 November
Abolition of Slavery	20 December
Christmas Day	25 December

FESTIVALS

Réunion has many festivals and new ones pop up regularly. A full list is available at www.cg974.fr.

JANUARY/FEBRUARY/MARCH

Fête du Miel (honey), La Plaine-des-Cafres, January (duration: seven days)
Thaipoosam Cavadee (Tamil festival), January/February (variable)
Chinese New Year, January/February (variable)
Tamil fire-walking ceremonies, throughout the island, January/February
Fête de St Vincent (patron saint of vineyards), Cilaos
Fête de la Tradition et de la Nature (Fête Tangue), La-Chaloupe-St-Leu: tasting of civet de tangue (tenrec stew)

APRIL/MAY/JUNE

Varusha Pirappu (Tamil New Year), April
Fête de l'eau (watersports), St-Benoît, April
Fête de la Vanille, Bras-Panon, May (duration: ten days)

Festi'Salaz, Hell-Bourg, Cirque de Salazie, May
Fête des Goyaviers, Plaine-des-Palmistes, June (duration: two days)
Festival of Music, main towns, June
Comedy festival, main towns, June

JULY/AUGUST/SEPTEMBER
Bastille Day, throughout the island, 14 July
Fête du vacoa, St-Philippe, August
Tamil fire-walking ceremonies, August
La Salette (Roman Catholic pilgrimage), St-Leu, 9–19 September

OCTOBER/NOVEMBER/DECEMBER
Florilèges (flower show), Le Tampon, October (duration: two weeks)
Dipavali (Hindu Festival of Light), November
Fête du Curcuma (turmeric), St-Joseph, November
Fête des Lentilles (lentils), Cilaos, November

SHOPPING

Réunion is not a bargain-hunter's paradise. Clothing here tends to be imported from France and is therefore expensive. Parts of St-Denis and St-Gilles and, to a lesser extent, St-Pierre are reminiscent of fashionable Parisian streets with their chic boutiques and effervescent French sales assistants.

The only bargains to be had are in the wonderful local markets. St-Paul claims to have the biggest and best weekly market, which takes place on Fridays and Saturdays. The markets in St-Pierre are also worth a visit. The covered markets are open daily, selling mostly handicrafts, but the Saturday morning market on the seafront is hugely popular for fresh produce, as well as souvenirs. The markets in St-Denis, particularly the Grand Marché, are rather touristy. Sadly, few of the handicrafts on sale at the island's markets and in shops are made in Réunion. The majority come from Madagascar and even Indonesia. A lot of work has recently been put into promoting Réunionnais handicrafts and they are gradually becoming more readily available, both in small souvenir shops and the markets. The French for handicrafts is *artisanat*.

Worthwhile souvenirs include geranium oil, rum, vanilla and products made from woven pandanus (*vacoas*) leaves. Vanilla grown on the island can be bought direct from producers or tourist offices. The vanilla sold in the markets is often from Madagascar and is cheaper.

MARKETS
St-Denis	Grand Marché daily except Sunday, Petit Marché daily
Ste-Marie	05.00–12.00 Saturday
Ste-Suzanne	05.00–12.00 Tuesday
St-André	04.00–12.00 Friday
Bras-Panon	07.00–12.00 Thursday
St-Benoît	05.00–12.00 Saturday
St-Joseph	08.00–14.00 Friday
St-Pierre (covered)	07.00–18.00 Monday–Saturday
St-Pierre (seafront)	06.00–13.00 Saturday
St-Louis	daily
St-Leu	07.00–12.00 Saturday
St-Gilles-les-Bains	05.00–12.00 Wednesday

L'Hermitage	07.00–12.00 Sunday
St-Paul (seafront)	04.00–20.00 Friday, 04.00–13.00 Saturday
St-Paul (covered)	08.00–16.00 Monday–Saturday
Cilaos	07.00–13.00 Sunday

ARTS AND ENTERTAINMENT

Local tourist offices should be able to tell you what's going on while you're in Réunion. Also useful is *L'Azenda* (www.azenda.re), a monthly free magazine and website containing details of concerts, theatre productions, cinema, art and exhibitions. You can buy tickets through the website. A similar website, www.kwelafe.re, covers live music, shows, cinema, exhibitions, etc. The website www.cine974.com has details of what is showing at the island's cinemas.

THEATRE AND DANCE The arts in Réunion have benefited greatly from financial grants from France. Cultural events happen throughout the year – plays, music, dance, and even stand-up comedy. Several theatre troupes are well established on the island: Théatre Vollard (*www.vollard.com*), Théatre Talipot and Compagnie Act 3 (*www.cieacte3.com*) are the best known. Théatre Talipot has participated in the Edinburgh Festival and in South Africa's Grahamstown Arts Festival.

There are numerous theatres, including the open-air theatre in St-Gilles-les-Bains, a wonderful setting (✆ *0262 419324; www.theatreunion.re*). The Théâtre les Bambous (*www.lesbambous.com*) specialises in contemporary productions. Le Palaxa (*www.palaxa*.re) is a live music venue in Ste-Clotilde, on the outskirts of St-Denis, with plenty going on. Most publish a programme for the coming season, which you can get from the tourist offices.

ART GALLERIES The best of Réunion's many galleries is the Musée Léon Dierx, at 28 Rue de Paris in St-Denis (✆ *0262 202482*) (page 302). The focus of the permanent exhibition is modern and contemporary art, including works by the likes of Gauguin, Picasso, Bernard, Maufra, Erro and Chen Zen.

There are numerous commercial art galleries selling art, particularly in St-Denis, such as Galerie Cadre Noir at 11 Rue de Paris in St-Denis (✆ *0262 214488*).

LITERATURE Despite the work of organisations such as ADER (Association for Réunionnais Authors), Réunion's literature is little known beyond the Mascarene Islands.

The first novel written by a Réunion-born author and set on the island was *Les Marrons* by Louis-Timagène Houat, published in Paris in 1844. Houat was an abolitionist and *Les Marrons* provides a detailed portrait of Réunion society in 1833, condemning slavery and racism. As do many later Réunionnais novels, *Les Marrons* explores the themes of runaway slaves and romance between a black slave and a white woman.

'Colonial novels' thrived at the height of colonial expansion (1920–30), when authors such as Marius-Ary Leblond attempted to exalt the virtues of the colony. Marius-Ary Leblond was the pseudonym used by two cousins, George Athenas and Aimé Merlo, who published 20 novels and over 250 articles under that name. *Ulysse Cafre* (1924) tells the story of a slave who goes in search of his son, revealing the clash between black magic and Christianity.

The 1970s saw the birth of what is known as the 'Réunionnais novel', dealing with Creole issues throughout the island's history. Well-known authors publishing

15

from the 1970s to the present include Anne Cheynet, Axel Gauvin, Agnès Gueneau and Jean-François Sam-Long. Sam-Long's novel *Madame Desbassyns* draws on the life story of the plantation owner of the same name, who is said to have been a particularly cruel woman. The true story of Madame Desbassyns is told at the Musée de Villèle at her former estate near St-Gilles-les-Hauts (see page 345).

The poet Leconte de Lisle is undoubtedly the best known of Réunion's literary figures. He was born in St-Paul in 1818 and went on to be admitted to the prestigious Académie Française. He is buried in the seafront cemetery in St-Paul. Poet Léon Dierx (1838–1912), who was born in St-Denis and later moved to France, was a disciple of Leconte de Lisle. If you are able to read French, you can find works by Leconte de Lisle and Léon Dierx in the island's bookshops.

NIGHTLIFE St-Denis, St-Gilles-les-Bains and St-Pierre are the three towns where people head for a night out. St-Pierre wins hands down as far as I'm concerned – it is the only town with lots of bars and clubs that still offer a genuine local, tropical flavour. If French Riviera is more your style, then St-Gilles-les-Bains has exactly what you want. The numerous nightclubs there cater almost exclusively for French holidaymakers. St-Denis has a real mixture and you're likely to bump into English-speaking students from the university. Wherever you go out, prepare to dance to an eclectic mixture of musical styles, likely to include *séga*, *zouk*, reggae and *maloya*, as well as French, British and American chart music. (For more information on local music, see page 260.) Throughout the island there are bars offering regular live music.

Casinos are popular with locals and are found in the main towns, including St-Denis, St-Gilles-les-Bains and St-Pierre. Going out in Réunion is not cheap. Entry to nightclubs is expensive, typically around €12, and drinks are costly too.

PHOTOGRAPHY

Réunion offers superb opportunities for the amateur photographer, in particular its stunning landscapes. It is courteous to ask people before taking their photo and it is particularly important to do so when you visit the island's interior, where people are less accustomed to the eccentricities of tourists. Film, digital memory cards and developing are readily available but tend to cost more than in Europe.

MEDIA AND COMMUNICATIONS

MEDIA Local newspapers and magazines are in French. You may be able to find international newspapers on sale in St-Denis's larger bookshops. The island's main newspapers are *Le Quotidien* (*www.lequotidien.re*) and *Le Journal de l'Ile de la Réunion* (*www.clicanoo.re*). For visitors, the most useful magazines are *Azenda* (*www.azenda. re*) for information on events, concerts, etc; *Bat'Carré* (*www.batcarre.com*) for news, events and culture; and *Buz Buz* (*www.buzbuz.re*) for what's currently trendy on the island. *Océan Indien* is a glossy, quarterly, French-language magazine crammed with beautiful photographs and articles showcasing the western Indian Ocean region.

The island's state-run television channel is Réunion Première, which includes programmes from mainland France. Popular independent channels include Antenne Réunion and Kanal Austral. Almost all programmes are in French.

The local state radio station is Réunion Première, and various Radio France stations are also available. There are numerous commercial radio stations, many of which play a good proportion of local music, such as Kreol FM, Radio Free Dom, Exo FM and Radio Arc-en-Ciel.

POST All towns of any size have a post office which is open 08.00–12.00 and 14.00–17.00 Monday to Friday, and until midday on Saturday. Details of post offices are available at www.laposte.fr. The postal codes for the main towns are as follows:

St-Denis	97400	St-Gilles-les-Bains	97434
St-Benoît	97470	St-Paul	97460
St-Philippe	97442	La-Plaine-des-Cafres	97418
St-Joseph	97480	La-Plaine-des-Palmistes	97431
St-Pierre	97410	Cilaos	97413
Le Tampon	97430	Salazie	97433
St-Leu	97436		

TELEPHONE Telecommunications are straightforward. To call Réunion from abroad, use the IDD code 262 followed by the local number minus the initial zero. All land-line numbers begin with 0262 and mobile numbers begin 0692/3. There are public payphones and most take phonecards (*télécartes*), which are sold in post offices, newsagents and shops displaying the sign.

By far the cheapest way to make international calls is to buy an international phonecard, available at newsagents. You can make calls from any touchtone phone by first dialling a freephone number, then the code on the back of the card. Mobile reception is generally good in Réunion, unless you are in the mountainous centre where it is patchy. The main service providers are Orange and SFR Réunion. You should confirm with your service provider before travelling that your phone will work. If you have an unlocked phone, you can buy a pre-paid local SIM, which is the most cost-effective solution. Top-ups are widely available at supermarkets, newsagents, etc.

INTERNET ACCESS/EMAIL Using local Wi-Fi is the easiest way to access the internet. A growing number of cafés offer free Wi-Fi. The Wi-Fi Zotspot network offers up to 2 hours of free access per day at its hotspots, which include the tourist offices. There are still some internet cafés in the main towns. Prices vary but you can expect to pay €7–12 per hour.

If you are resident on the island, your local *médiathèque* should provide free internet access but you'll need to prove that you live in the surrounding area. You will see throughout the island a number of *Cyber Bases*. These were created by local government to increase internet usage by Réunionnais. They offer computer and internet classes, and free internet access. However, the *Cyber Bases* encourage tourists not to use their facilities, but rather to go to an internet café, leaving the *Cyber Bases* facilities for locals.

BUSINESS

While not being a viable alternative for labour-intensive concerns because of the high cost of labour, Réunion is suitable for capital-intensive businesses. A range of tax incentives and grants are available to investors and it is worth noting that anything manufactured in Réunion gets the prestigious 'made in France' label. The island also benefits from European standards of infrastructure and excellent connectivity through its two airports and its port.

The Agence de Développement de la Réunion (\ *0262 922492; www.adreunion. com*) can provide advice on investing in or setting up a business in Réunion, as well as long-term assistance for businesses. There are incentives for such investors, who are assisted by tax elimination schemes and direct subsidies.

Those who wish to learn more about investment opportunities in Réunion and other Indian Ocean islands might want to obtain copies of *L'Eco Austral* (*www. ecoaustral.com*), a bimonthly economic newspaper, or visit the website of the Agence de Développement de la Réunion (*www.adreunion.com*).

BUYING PROPERTY

The regulations around buying property in Réunion are as for buying property in France. There is an abundance of information available online, including at www. globalpropertyguide.com.

CULTURAL ETIQUETTE

Although beachwear is fine for a resort, it may be frowned upon away from the beach and for women, it will attract unwanted attention. If visiting temples or mosques, dress conservatively and remove your shoes before entering. Women should carry a long-sleeved top and sarong, just in case. You may be asked to remove leather items when visiting Hindu temples and cover your head at certain mosques.

The large number of young, single mothers in Réunion is likely to shock most visitors. Domestic violence is also a problem and frequently goes undetected.

If you see strange objects on the side of the road, such as red pieces of material, coconut, or parts of chickens, resist the temptation to interfere with them. They are often left by people practising black magic as part of a spell. Keep your eyes on the road as many drivers will swerve to avoid such objects, for fear of being cursed.

It is perhaps also useful to know that, for some superstitious Réunionnais, various actions must be avoided in order to prevent attracting bad spirits. These include burning hair, burning a shoe or putting wood in a cross shape on the fire.

LE SITARANE

The place of Le Sitarane in Réunion's history and folklore has been assured by people's unshakable fascination with his story. It is said that he was actually quite a pleasant man until he was led into crime and black magic by one St-Ange Calendrin. They formed a gang, which began in 1907 to commit the horrific acts, forcing their way into their victims' homes, burgling them, murdering them and using their bodies in black-magic rituals. Fear seized the population around St-Pierre and Le Tampon for two years, as the gang repeatedly evaded capture. Eventually, ten arrests were made. The ringleaders, St-Ange Calendrin, Sitarane and Fontaine, were condemned to death. However, shortly before the execution, Calendrin's punishment was mysteriously toned down and he was deported to French Guiana. Sitarane and Fontaine were publicly guillotined in St-Pierre in 1909.

Sitarane's tomb still holds both fear and fascination for the local population. Those who dabble in gris gris (black magic) visit his grave to ask for assistance in their practices, whilst those who fear black magic ask for his protection. His grave, which is red and black, is almost always strewn with offerings of rum, cigarettes, red material and candles. From the main entrance to the cemetery, the grave is on the far left near the wall, under a tree. Locals would advise you not to take photos of it, for fear of upsetting the occupant. It is also considered bad luck to mention Sitarane by name.

16

Activities

Réunion's beaches may not be world class but its list of sporting activities certainly is. Activities have become big business in Réunion, so there are usually several operators to choose from, and it is good to know that reputable operators must adhere to French safety standards.

Most activities can be booked through www.resa.reunion.fr, the tourist information offices around the island (pages 262–3) or local tour operators (see below).

MULTI-ACTIVITY COMPANIES

Below are the contact details of a few multi-activity operators and an indication of the kinds of activities that they can arrange.

Alpanes 153 Av Daniel Ramin, Grand Bois; m 0692 777530; e contact@alpanes.com; www. alpanes.com. Hiking, kayaking & canyoning.

Austral Aventure 42 Rue Amiral Lacaze, Hell-Bourg, 97433 Salazie; ✆ 0262 324029; m 0692 875550; e canyon@australaventure.fr; www:australaventure.fr. Hiking, canyoning, white-water rafting, climbing, paragliding & mountain biking.

Evasion Kréol 6 Rue des Becs Roses 97412, Bras-Panon; ✆ 0692 613455; e contact@ evasionkreol.com; www.evasionkreol.com. Hiking, canyoning.

Jean-Yves Hervet 26 Av des Moutardiers, Plateau Caillou, 97460, St-Paul; ✆ 0262 324568; m 0692 766643; e jyhervet@wanadoo.fr. Hiking, white-water rafting & mountain biking.

Ric à Ric 15 Chemin Clément Fossy, S-Leu; m 0692 865485; e ricaric@canyonreunion.com; www.canyonreunion.com. Canyoning, white-water rafting & climbing.

Run Evasion 23 Rue du Père Boiteau, 97413 Cilaos; ✆ 0262 318357; 69 Rue Marius & Ary Leblond, 97410 St-Pierre; ✆ 0262 964684; www. run.evasion.voici.org. Hiking, canyoning, climbing & mountain biking.

HIKING

Réunion's rugged interior makes it the best hiking destination in the western Indian Ocean. More than 1,000km of trails criss-cross the island's mountains.

Hiking accommodation can be booked via www.resa.reunion.fr or at the tourist offices on the island. The tourist offices can also provide information on hiking trails, accommodation along the routes, grading of routes and other activities on offer in rural areas. The website of **Office Nationale des Forêts** (*www.onf.fr*) provides maps of hiking trails and information on access and recent closures. The website www. randopitons.re (in French only) has useful information to help with planning your next hike. The trails are well managed and marked according to the official French system. The two **Grande Randonnées hiking trails** (GR R1 and GR R2) are marked with red and white paint. Other footpaths are indicated in red and yellow. The **GR R1**

trail, known as Le Tour du Piton-des-Neiges, is a complete circle, which covers the north of Cirque de Cilaos, passes through Hell-Bourg and around Cirque de Salazie, then into Mafate and back to Cilaos via the Col du Taïbit. **GR R2**, or La Grande Traversée de l'Ile, cuts across the island from St-Denis to the coast near St-Philippe, via the cirques, Entre-Deux, the Plaines and Piton-de-la-Fournaise. The trails classified as Sentiers Marmailles are easy walks of less than 3 hours, designed to be suitable for children. There are 42 listed in a book, *Sentiers Marmailles*, published by the Office Nationale des Forêts (for details of other publications on hiking, see page 365).

Even for organised hikes, you must bring along your own backpack, sleeping bag, torch, Swiss army knife, crockery, cutlery, toiletries (including loo paper), warm clothing, appropriate footwear (sturdy hiking boots), rain gear, sun protection and any personal medication.

A good **map** is essential: 4402 RT is ideal for most hikes as it covers Cirque de Mafate, Cirque de Salazie and the northern part of Cirque de Cilaos, including the whole of the GR R1 trail. It is widely available from the tourist offices. To obtain maps prior to travel, contact the Institut Géographique National, 107 Rue de la Boétie, 75008 Paris. (See also the map of the cirques on page 351.)

Always let someone know where you are going and how long you plan to be away. Avoid hiking alone. Do check the weather forecasts and make sure that you are well prepared and equipped. If the worst does happen, the following are the official **distress signals** (helicopters do fly across the island regularly):

- Arms raised above your head in a 'V' shape
- Red flare
- Red square and a white circle

The *gendarmerie nationale* has a 24-hour emergency line (✆ *0262 930930*). (See also box, page 356. For literature on hiking see page 365.)

GUIDED HIKES There are a number of state-certified guides and organisations operating in the mountains.

Expect to pay around €50–65 per person per day for a guided hike with the following companies or the multi-activity companies listed on page 283.

Kokapat Rando 109 Chemin Farjeau, Trois Mares, Le Tampon; ✆ 0262 333014; e contact@ kokapatrando-reunion.com; www.kokapatrando-reunion.com
Rando Run Trekking 2 Impasse des Acacias, 97427 Etang-Salé-les-Bains; ✆ 0262 263131;
m 0692 852256; e gilbert.aureche@gmail.com; www.randorun-trekking.com
Rando Trek Réunion 139 Bd de l'Océan, Manapany les Bains; ✆ 0692 015956; e randotrekreunion@gmail.com; www.randotrek-reunion.com

ACCOMMODATION FOR HIKERS There are numerous options open to hikers but remember to book well in advance. Most can be booked through the local tourist offices on the island or through www.resa.reunion.fr. The following types of accommodation are available in rural areas: *gîtes de montagne*, *gîtes d'étape*, *gîtes ruraux*, *chambres d'hôte*, *fermes auberges* and *refuges* (rest huts). For further details, see page 274.

Gîtes de montagne/gîtes d'étape These mountain houses/huts are the most plentiful type of accommodation on hiking routes and are often the only option in remote outposts.

Reservations must be made well in advance to avoid disappointment (they prefer it if people book six months before travelling, particularly for high-season months), with payment preferably two weeks before arrival. Late reservations may be accepted, as there are often last-minute cancellations. Meals can be arranged through the caretakers, at least a day in advance, by phone. Pay for your meals directly, in cash.

Note that *gîtes de montagne* and *gîtes d'étape* are basic, dormitory-type accommodation. Some visitors have arrived to find that other guests have hogged all the blankets and pillows for themselves, but this is rare. Most do not have hot water and a few don't have showers, so they really are only suitable as overnight stops.

All *gîtes* provide two blankets, a pillow and two sheets per person. Some kitchen utensils and a gas cooker are provided as well (speak to caretakers). Lighting in *gîtes* is usually by means of solar power.

Below is a selection of mountain *gîtes*. Expect to pay around adult/child €18/14, breakfast €8, dinner €20.

Piton-de-la-Fournaise
🏠 **Volcan** (57 beds) Mr Picard; ☎ 0692 852091

Roche Ecrite
🏠 **Plaine des Chicots** (36 beds) Mr Bonald; ☎ 0262 439984

Basse Vallée
🏠 **Basse Vallée** (16 beds) Mr Bénard; ☎ 0262 373625

Piton-des-Neiges
🏠 **Bélouve** (34 beds, 2 dbl rooms) Mrs Rosset; ☎ 0262 412123; e gite.belouve@wanadoo.fr
🏠 **Caverne Dufour** (48 beds) Mr Dijoux; ☎ 0262 511526

Rivière des Remparts
🏠 **Roche Plate** (31 beds) Mrs Morel; ☎ 0262 591394

Cilaos
🏠 **Gîte du Pavillon** (13 beds, 1 dbl room) Mr Ethève; ☎ 0262 450816; e etheve.eric@sfr.fr. Between St-Louis & Cilaos.
🏠 **La Roche Merveilleuse** (27 beds, 4 dbl rooms) Mr Payet; ☎ 0262 318242

Mafate
🏠 **Gîte Le Poinsettia** (30 beds, 2 dbl, 1 trpl rooms) Mr Boyer; ☎ 0262 550233
🏠 **Gîte Oreo** (12 beds) The Oreo Family; ☎ 0262 435857
🏠 **Grand Place Cayenne** (16 beds, 2 dbl rooms) Mr C Thomas; ☎ 0262 438542
🏠 **Ilet à Bourse** (16 beds, 2 dbl rooms) Mr C Thomas; ☎ 0262 434393
🏠 **La Nouvelle 1** (12 beds, 5 dbl rooms, 10 4-person bungalows) Mr A Begue; ☎ 0262 436177
🏠 **La Nouvelle 2** (12 beds, 1 dbl room) Mrs Oréo; ☎ 0262 435857
🏠 **Marla** (16 beds, 4 dbl rooms) Mrs Hoareau; ☎ 0262 437831
🏠 **Roche Plate** (24 beds) Mrs Thiburce; ☎ 0262 436001

GRAND RAID DE LA REUNION – THE MADMAN'S DIAGONAL

Grand Raid de la Réunion, also known as La Diagonale des Fous (the madman's diagonal) is an ultramarathon which takes place on the island each October. The 162km route crosses the island diagonally and climbs five peaks. Runners climb just over 9,000m during the race. The volcano, Cilaos and Mafate all feature on the route. Of the 2,500 or so starters, only around 70% finish the race, and the winning time is usually around 22 hours. If that sounds like your sort of thing, further information is available at www.raid-reunion.com.

16

Salazie

⌂ **La Mandoze** (24 beds, 3 dbl rooms) Mr Manoro; ✆ 0262 478965

⌂ **Relais des Gouverneurs** (20 beds, 1 dbl room) ✆ 0262 477621;

CANYONING

Canyoning, or abseiling down waterfalls, is becoming increasingly popular amongst thrill-seekers in Réunion. The island, with its innumerable waterfalls and spectacular gorges, boasts the ideal landscape. Canyoning starts at around €45 per half day, €55 per full day. For details of multi-activity operators that organise canyoning, see page 283.

MOUNTAIN BIKING

Mountain bikes are all the rage in Réunion and are available for hire in most activity centres. The island has over 1,400km of marked trails, which meet French Cycling Federation standards. Popular trails are around Maïdo, Entre-Deux, Cilaos, Salazie, Piton-de-la-Fournaise and the coast around Ste-Rose.

The French for mountain bike is *VTT* (*vélo tous terrains*) (pronounced 'vay-tay-tay'). You will also see suggested routes marked on large boards in many tourist areas.

Once a year, usually in November, Réunion plays host to one round of the Mega Avalanche international series of downhill mountain-bike races. The races in this series are unusual for the downhill discipline as they are mass-start races of up to 25km. Packages which include flights, accommodation and bike transport are available from mainland France. For more information, visit www.ucc-sportevent.com.

The going rate for hire is around €5 per hour, €10–12 per half day, €20 per day. Helmets and gloves are extra. Some companies organise group rides, which cost around €40 per half day and include instructor, gear and insurance.

Descente VTT Télénavette 3 Rue Ste-Alexis, 97434 St-Gilles-les-Bains; ✆ 0262 245026; m 0692 211111; e telenavette@oceanes.fr; www.telenavette.com

Rando Réunion Passion 3 Rue du Général de Gaulle, 97434 St-Gilles-les-Bains; ✆ 0262 242619; e randoreunion@wanadoo.fr; www.vttreunion.com

Services Cycles 17 Rue Amirale Lacaze, 97410 St-Pierre; ✆ 0262 702193; e iougy@live.fr

VTT Réunion 04 Chemin de la Ravine Sèche, 97427 Etang-Salé; ✆ 0262 380197; e vttreunion@gmail.com; www.vtt-reunion.com

HORSERIDING

On horseback is the ideal way to explore Réunion's rugged interior. Rides can be arranged for just an hour, a half day, a full day or several days. Some of the establishments around La Plaine-des-Cafres offer rides to the volcano Piton-de-la-Fournaise.

Riding schools vary considerably in standard, although instructors are usually qualified. Although most establishments are affiliated to the French Equestrian Federation, many are reluctant to loan hats, even if they have them. If you insist, you will usually get one, which is important as the terrain in the interior is invariably rocky and uneven. An hour's ride will usually cost around €25–35, a half day €50–60, a full day €90–115.

Alti Merens 120 Rue Maurice Kraft, 97418 La Plaine-des-Cafres; m 0692 314792; e centreequestre.alti-merens@orange.fr; www.alti-merens.re. A very picturesque place to ride & the Merens horses from the Pyrenees are ideally suited to the rough ground.

Centre Equestre de la Fenêtre 31 Route de Mont Plaisir, 97421 Les Makes; ℄ 0262 378874; e cef97421@hotmail.fr. Riding lessons as well as trekking through the pretty, mountainous surrounds.

Centre Equestre de la Montagne 50 Chemin Couilloux, St-Bernard, 97417 La Montagne; ℄ 0262 236251. Long-established & well run. Closed Mon.

Centre Equestre du Cap 124 Route Hubert Delisle, 97416 Chaloupe St-Leu; m 0692 823576; e club@ceducap.fr; www.ceducap.fr. Has beautiful views of the coast. Offers lessons as well as hacking.

Club Hippique de L'Hermitage Zac Hermitage, Chemin Ceinture, 97434 St-Gilles-les-Bains; ℄ 0262 244773; www.chh974.ffe.com. Close to the beach. Lots of very chic French regulars, so it feels a bit cliquey. The focus is on lessons & competing.

Ecurie du Relais 75 Chemin Léopold Lebon, Manapany-les-Hauts, 97429 Petit-Ile; ℄ 0262 567867; www.ecuriedurelais.com. Located in the south, not far from St-Joseph. Treks from 1hr to several days. Closed Mon, except during school holidays.

Ecuries d'Eldorado 22 Chemin Band'colons, 97427 Etang-Salé-les-Hauts; m 0692 877448; e ecuries.eldorado@gmail.com; www.eldorado.re. Forest & beach rides, from 1hr to several days. Closed Mon.

Ecuries de Notre Dame de la Paix 37 Chemin de la Chapelle Notre Dame de la Paix, 97418 La Plaine-des-Cafres; ℄ 0262 593449; m 0692 614679; e antoine-patrick.lauret@wanadoo.fr. Offers treks from 1hr to several days, including to the volcano.

Ecuries du Volcan 9 bis Domaine de Bellevue, 97418 La Plaine-des-Cafres; ℄ 0262 351056; m 0692 666290. Accessible to people with limited mobility.

Equirun 37 Allée Montignac, 97427 Etang-Salé; ℄ 0262 265252; e equirun.reunion@orange.fr; www.equirun-centre-equestre-reunion.com. More of a riding school than a trekking centre, but it does offer rides through Etang-Salé Forest & to the beach.

Ferme Equestre Auberge du Pont-Neuf 59 ter, CD 11 Pont Neuf, 97425 Les Avirons; m 0692 445178; e ferme.pontneuf@caramail.com. An attractive farm, which offers accommodation as well as horseriding.

Ferme Equestre du Grand Etang RN3, Pont Payet, 97470 St-Benoît; ℄ 0262 509003; m 0692 868825; e riconourry@wanadoo.fr. A wide range of rides offered, including treks of up to 8 days.

Ile aux Poneys Chemin Carosse D 100, Voie Cannière, 97435 St-Gilles-les-Hauts; ℄ 0692 022367; e ileauxponeys974@gmail.com; http://l-ile-aux-poneys.eklablog.com. The focus here is on providing children from the age of 2 years with the experience of contact with a pony.

La Porte des Cascades Rue des Arums, 97431 La Plaine-des-Palmistes; ℄ 0692 665496. Offers treks throughout the island.

Les Chevaux du Maïdo Route Forestière des Cryptomérias, 97423 Le Guillaume; m 0692 926270; www.leschevauxdumaido.jimdo.com. In the pretty, cool forested area on the way to Piton du Maïdo. Offers treks through this beautiful area, as well as lessons.

Shai Ena 38 Chemin de la Vanille, 97434 St-Gilles-les-Bains; ℄ 0692 887000; e shaiena@me.com; www.shaiena.com. Western-style riding on quarter horses. Specialises in 2hr sunset rides on the west coast.

GOLF

Although not a popular sport amongst locals, Réunion boasts a few beautiful courses. All the clubs offer trolley and club hire, as well as lessons. In all cases, the green fees shown for weekends also apply on public holidays. Lessons cost in the region of €20 for 30 minutes.

Bassin Bleu Country Club 75 Rue Mahatma Gandhi, Villèle, 97435 St-Gilles-les-Hauts; ℄ 0262 700300; e golf@bassinbleu.fr; www.bassinbleu.fr; ⊕ daily. 18-hole par-72 course. Has a restaurant serving lunch, bar & pool. Green fees €60 (18 holes), €35 (9 holes).

Golf Club Colorado 52 Chemin du Colorado, 97417 La Montagne; ☎0262 237950; e gcc4@wanadoo. fr; www.golfclubcolorado.fr; ⊕ daily except Mon morning. 9-hole par-68 course. Snack bar. Green fees for 18 holes €30 weekdays, €40 weekends.

Golf Club de Bourbon 140 Les Sables, 97427 Etang-Salé; ☎0262 263339; e contact@golf-bourbon.com; www.golf-bourbon.com; ⊕ daily except Mon morning. Beautiful 18-hole

par-72 course with hordes of tropical plants. Attractive clubhouse with a restaurant (closed Mon) & swimming pool. Green fees €48 for 18 holes weekdays, €60 weekends; €27 for 9 holes weekdays, €35 weekends.

Golf Vert Lagon La Saline-les-Bains; ☎0692 740607; www.bassinbleu.fr; ⊕ winter 12.00–19.00 Wed–Fri, 09.00–19.00 Sat/Sun. A pitch & putt course with 5 holes between 55m & 75m. €10 (5 holes).

4X4 EXCURSIONS

The going rate for excursions in 4x4 vehicles is around €90–95 per person per day (usually including lunch).

Kréolie 4x4 4 Impasse des Avocats, 97414 Entre-Deux; m 0692 865226; e kreolie4x4@hotmail.fr; www.kreolie4x4.com

MICROLIGHTING

Microlighting offers a bird's-eye view of some of the island's greatest assets. The French for microlight is *ULM* (*Ultra Léger Motorisé*) (pronounced 'oo-el-em').

Felix ULM 63 rue Marthe Bacquet Cambaie, 97460 St-Paul; ☎0262 430259; m 0692 873232; e felixulm@wanadoo.fr; www.felixulm.com. Lagoon €65, Cirque de Mafate €65, Mafate/Salazie/ Cilaos €145.

Mascareignes Airlines Chemin de l'Aerodrome, 97410 St-Pierre; ☎0262 325325; m 0692 725160; e mascareignes@gmail.com. Volcano €90, Mafate/ Salazie/Cilaos/Trou de Fer/lagoon €130.

Papangue ULM 10 Allée Belynted, Chemin Segret 97419 La Possession; ☎0692 088586; www. papangue-ulm.fr. Cirque de Salazie from €80.

Les Passagers du Vent Base ULM ZI de Cambaie, 97460 St-Paul; ☎0262 429595; m 0692 687055; e contact@ulm-reunion.com; www.ulm-reunion.com. Introductory flight €45, Cirque de Mafate €67, Mafate/lagoon €110, Mafate/Salazie/ Cilaos/Trou de Fer €145.

PARAGLIDING

Paragliding is very popular, particularly in the hills above St-Leu. Beginners glide in tandem with an instructor. The French for paragliding is *parapente*. Expect to pay around €75 for an introductory flight over the lagoon (a descent of about 800m).

Air Lagon Parapente 67 Rue Jean-Baptiste de Villèle, Les Colimaçons, 97436 St-Leu; m 0692 875287; e airlagon@wanadoo.fr; www.airlagon-parapente.fr

Azurtech 3 Impasse des Plongeurs, La Pointe des Châteaux, 97436 St-Leu; ☎0262 349189; m 0692 850400; e contact@azurtech.com; www. azurtech.com

Bourbon Parapente 4 Rue Haute, BP 12 97898 St-Leu; m 0692 875874; e master@bourbonparapente. com; www.bourbonparapente.com

Chris Rutter (paragliding instructor); ☎0692 529629; e sky-chris@hotmail.fr

Modul'Air Aventure 26 Ruelle des Bougainvilliers, 97434 St-Gilles-les-Bains; m 0692 040404; e nicodid@orange.fr; www.modulair-parapente.com

Parapente Réunion 103 Rue Georges Pompidou, 97436 St-Leu; ☎0262 248784; m 0692 829292; e info@parapente-reunion.fr; www. parapente-reunion.fr

BUNGEE JUMPING

Bungee jumpers leap from the Pont d'Anglais Suspension Bridge between Ste-Anne and Ste-Rose. The organisers (*www.elasticjump.com*) need to have a group of people jumping on each occasion, so you may not be able to jump until several days, or even weeks, after your initial enquiry. Jumps take place on weekends and cost around €70.

HELICOPTER RIDES

If your time on Réunion is limited, a helicopter ride is a great way to see the island. The most popular flights cover the island's main attractions: the volcano, the cirques, the coast, Trou de Fer, etc. Prices are in the range €85–300 per person, depending on the itinerary. A short, 15-minute flight will start from around €95, while a 45-minute flight is around €260.

Corail Helicoptères Aéroport de Pierrefonds, 97410 St-Pierre; 0262 222266; m 0692 006666; e info@corail-helicopteres.com; www.corail-helicopteres.com

Helilagon Itiport de l'Eperon, 97467 St-Paul; 0262 555555; e heliglagon@helilagon.com; www.helilagon.com

WATERSPORTS

Surfing used to be very popular in Réunion, particularly around St-Leu, which drew surfers from around the world. However, a shocking number of shark attacks in recent years led to a 2013 ban on surfing and swimming off Réunion (see box, page 291). **Stand-up paddle** is the latest craze to hit Réunion and you will see plenty of people giving it a go in the lagoons. Expect to pay around €30 for a one-hour individual surfing lesson or €20 for a group lesson.

Réunion offers a wide variety of dive sites with the best **diving** being on the west coast, around St-Leu and St-Gilles-les-Bains. There is something for every diver in Réunion, from coral reefs inside the lagoon to large flats and steep walls beyond the reef. There are a number of shipwrecks to explore, but they are best left for the experienced diver as some can be as deep as 55m (181ft).

All dive centres cater for all levels. Expect to pay around €65 for an introductory dive of about 20–30 minutes. Dives for those with experience cost around €50 or €260 for six dives. **Snorkelling trips**, with equipment supplied, can usually be arranged by dive centres for around €20. If you don't speak French, check before you book that the dive centre can provide an English-speaking instructor as it's essential that you understand the safety instructions.

SURFING AND STAND-UP PADDLE
The following surf schools cater for all levels, from children to competition training.

Ecole de Stand-Up Paddle du Lagon et de Surf des Roches-Noires La Saline-les-Bains; m 0692 860059; e bertrand.surf@wanadoo.fr; www.ecole-surf-reunion.com
Ecole de Surf Bourbon Réunion 25 Rue Amirale Lacaze, St-Pierre; 0692 661673;

e ecolesurfbourbonreunion@gmail.com; www.ecolesurfbourbonreunion.com
Ecole de Surf de St-Leu 22 Chemin des Tourterelles, St-Leu; 0692 654492; www.surf-reunion.com

WATERSKIING
Ski Club de St-Paul 1 Rue de la Croix, 97460 St-Paul; 0692 851496; www.skiclubdelareunion.com; 10.30–18.00 Mon,

Wed & Thu, 09.00–18.00 Sat/Sun. Caters for all levels of ability.

SAILING

The majority of private yachts are kept in the marinas at St-Gilles-les-Bains & St-Pierre, where you may be able to organise sailing trips on an ad hoc basis. Alternatively, contact one of the following companies:

Bataloc Port de Plaisance, 97434 St-Gilles-les-Bains; ☎0262 334867; e www.batalocs@wanadoo.fr; www.rj73.com/batoloc. Boat hire, fishing.

Bleu Indien 7 Rue Andromède, Le Mont Roquefeuille, 97434 St-Gilles-les-Bains; m 0692 853753; e bleu_indien@hotmail.com; www.bleuindien.com. Boat hire, plus fishing, wake-boarding & scuba-diving gear.

Compagnie des Pirates 4 Rue Général de Gaulle, 97434 St-Gilles-les-Bains; ☎0692 700277; e oceandream@live.fr; www.lacompagniedespirates.re. Sailing, cruises.

Croisieres & Decouvertes Ilot du port de Saint-Gilles-les-Bains; ☎0262 332832; e info@grandbleu.re; www.grandbleu.re. Sailing & cruises.

SCUBA DIVING

Abyss Plongée 17 Bd Bonnier, 97436 St-Leu; ☎0262 347979; e abyss-plongee@wanadoo.fr; www.abyss-plongee.com

Bleu Marine Réunion Port de Plaisance, 97434 St-Gilles-les-Bains; ☎0262 242200; e contact@bleu-marine-reunion.com; www.bleu-marine-reunion.com

Bleu Océan 25 RN1, 97436 St-Leu; ☎0262 349749; e bleuocean2@wanadoo.fr; www.bleuocean.fr

Corail Plongée Port de Plaisance, 97434 St-Gilles-les-Bains; ☎0262 243725; e info@corail-plongee.com; www.corail-plongee.com

O Sea Bleu Enceinte Portuaire, 97434 St-Gilles-les-Bains; ☎0262 242330; e oseableu@reunion-plongee.com; www.reunion-plongee.com

Réunion Plongée 13 Av des Artisans, 97436 St-Leu; ☎0262 347777; e contact@reunionplongee.com; www.reunionplongee.com

Sub Excelsus 1 Impasse des Plongeurs, ZA Pointe des Châteaux, 97436 St-Leu; ☎0262 347365; e contact@excelsus-plongee.com; www.excelsus-plongee.com

OTHER WATERSPORTS

Oasis Eaux Vives 38 Ilet Coco, St-Benoît; ☎0692 001623; e rvpiaut@wanadoo.fr; www.oasisev.com. White-water rafting.

Planch'Alizé 25 Rue des Mouettes, 97434 La Saline-les-Bains; ☎0262 246261; www.planchalize.net. Hire of windsurfers, kayaks, pedaloes & snorkelling equipment.

Stade en Eau Vives Intercommunal 2 Rue du Stade, 97441 Ste-Suzanne; ☎0262 566612; e contact@sevi.re; www.sevi.re; ⊕ Tue–Sun. White-water centre on an artificial river, offering kayaking & rafting for all levels of experience. From €4/hr.

THIM Nautique 165 bis Rue du Général de Gaulle, 97434 St-Gilles-les-Bains; ☎0262 242324; e thim.loc@wanadoo.fr. Boat & jet-ski hire, waterskiing.

DEEP-SEA FISHING

In 2003, a female fishing world record was achieved in the waters off Réunion, when Catherine Lavit caught a blue marlin weighing 551kg. Other fish caught off Réunion include bonito, tuna, wahoo, dorado, shark and swordfish.

The French for deep-sea fishing is *la pêche au gros*. Expect to pay around €80–90 per person per half day and €50 for those who don't want to fish but just go along for the ride. Drinks and light refreshments are often included.

Albacore Port de Plaisance, St-Gilles-les-Bains; ☎0262 330441

Blue Marlin Port de Plaisance, St-Gilles-les-Bains; m 0692 652235; www.bluemarlin.fr

Bourbon Fishing Club Port de Plaisance, St-Gilles-les-Bains; ☎0693 912976; e bourbonfishingclub@hotmail.fr; www.bourbonfishingclub.com

Maevasion Port de Plaisance, St-Gilles-les-Bains; ☎0262 333804; e maevasion974@gmail.com; www.maevasioncom

WHEN WILL IT BE SAFE TO GO BACK IN THE WATER?

At the end of 2015, there had been a staggering 20 shark attacks and seven fatalities off the coast of Réunion since 2011. In 2013, two people died in shark attacks and the government took the controversial step of banning surfing and swimming in the waters off the island. In April 2015, 13-year-old Elio Canestri, one of the island's most talented young surfers, defied the ban, as many had done, and took his board into the water. He was killed by a 2.5m bull shark. Bull sharks and tiger sharks are the most common species around the island.

People pointed to various factors as contributing to the rise in attacks: overfishing, the 1999 ban on shark meat for human consumption and offshore fish farms. The island's residents, particularly the surfing fraternity, were furious and called for a shark cull.

The government has endeavoured to find an alternative solution to a cull. Shark nets have been installed on several popular beaches, including Boucan Canot and Roches Noires. In 2015, they also began trialling smart drum lines, which use cameras and sensors to send mobile-phone alerts to marine teams who then catch, tag and release the shark. How successful this will be remains to be seen.

A solution does need to be found. The shark problem is believed to have cost Réunion millions of euros in lost tourism revenue.

Réunion Fishing Club 10 Enceinte Portuaire, 97434 St-Gilles-les-Bains; 0262 243610; m 0692 761728; e contact@reunionfishingclub.com; www.reunionfishingclub.com

Reunion Pêche Au Gros St-Gilles-les-Bains; 0262 333399; e j.c.lavit@wanadoo.fr; www.runevasion.com/pecheaugros

GLASS-BOTTOM BOATS

These are a good way for non-divers to see the marine environment and are suitable for children of any age.

Grand Bleu Port de Plaisance, 97434 St-Gilles-les-Bains; 0262 332832; e info@grandbleu.re; www.grandbleu.re. The Corail Safari boats allow for a submarine-like underwater viewing experience on the coral reef. Trips last 40mins & depart at least 5 times daily. Dolphins are often seen in the early morning. Adults from €12.

BOAT CRUISES AND DOLPHIN WATCHING

Grand Bleu Port de Plaisance, 97434 St-Gilles-les-Bains; 0262 332832; e info@grandbleu.re; www.grandbleu.re. Offers a range of boat cruises, including one incorporating kayaking and snorkelling (adult/child €30/20), a sunset cruise (adult/child €30/20), & catamaran cruises (half-day adult/child €60/30, full-day adult/child €90/50). Also 2hr morning cruises (08.00 & 10.15) in search of dolphins, whales & other marine life. Adult/child €30/18.

17

Northern Réunion

As the Roland Garros International Airport and the department's main city, St-Denis, are located on the north coast, it is the start (and end) point of most Réunion holidays. The far north of Réunion is generally defined as the area around St-Denis, extending inland to St-François, Plaine d'Affouches and the wonderful hiking area of Roche Ecrite, on the northern edge of the Cirque de Salazie.

ST-DENIS

Founded in 1669, this attractive coastal city in northern Réunion is home to around 146,000 inhabitants. St-Denis took over as capital from St-Paul in 1738, after being declared as such by the then governor Mahé de Labourdonnais. Understandably, people refer to St-Denis (pronounced 'san de-nee') as the capital, and it is the administrative capital of the island, but Réunion's status as a *Département d'Outre-Mer* means that Paris is the true capital.

St-Denis is bordered by the sea to the north and backed by high, green mountains to the south, so its setting is very appealing. It is also blessed with a heavy concentration of attractive, historic buildings. Although it sits on a tropical island, its trendy cafés, delightful-smelling *boulangeries*, smart boutiques and frequent traffic jams give it a distinctly French flavour.

The simple grid system makes it an easy place to explore, and it is possible to see the town's main attractions in a day's walkabout. The seafront promenade known as **Le Barachois** [294 B1], once a port, is a good place to start. A park containing tall palms runs along the top of the seawall, where cannons left over from the days of war with the British face defiantly out to sea. The bars and restaurants in the area really come to life in the evenings, and on Sundays Le Barachois is the place to go for a walk. Le Barachois is at the centre of the town's social life and hosts regular events, such as the night markets on the first Saturday of the month. At **Place Sarda Garriga** [294 B1] (named after the governor who published the decree abolishing slavery) you'll see the statue of Roland Garros, a famed St-Denis-born aviator after whom the international airport is named.

St-Denis is perfect for lovers of history and architecture, with its wealth of old buildings. The ***Préfecture***, [294 A2] the island's administrative offices near Le Barachois, is in an attractive, colonnaded former French East India Company building, constructed in 1735. **Palais de Rontaunay** [294 B3] (*5 Rue Rontaunay*) is a dainty, wooden, Creole building constructed around 1850 by a businessman and then acquired by the island's administration in 1863 as its headquarters. On Avenue de la Victoire is the Tuscan-style **Cathédrale de St-Denis** [294 B3], which was built in 1829, destroyed by lightning and rebuilt in 1844. Further along is the impressive **old town hall** [294 B4], completed in 1860, lighting up the street with its sunflower-

yellow exterior. In front of it is the **Monument aux Morts** [294 B4], erected in 1923 in honour of the Réunionnais casualties of World War I.

In terms of sites of interest per square metre, **Rue de Paris** is one of the most worthwhile streets to wander. It is lined with wonderful **colonial buildings**, many of which are 19th-century Creole mansions built for those made wealthy by the sugar industry. Most of the buildings display plaques explaining their history, but if you would like to hear about them in more detail, the tourist office provides guided tours of the street. Unfortunately, the majority of the buildings are closed to the public but they can be appreciated from the outside. The beautiful **Maison Carrère** [294 B5], at 14 Rue de Paris, dates from 1820 and now houses the **tourist office** [294 B5], so can be visited. **Maison Déramond** [294 B4], at number 15, is classed as an historic monument both for its fine 18th- and 19th-century architecture and its past famous residents. Poet Léon Dierx was born here in 1838 and former French prime minister Raymond Barre was born here in 1924. Today it is occupied by the Ministry of Culture and Communication and easily recognised thanks to its gorgeous pale sage-coloured walls. At number 18, on the corner of Rue Félix Guyon, is the much-photographed **La Maison Mas** [294 B5], also known as **La Villa du Département**. It was built in the 1790s by the first mayor of the town, and is now the office of the regional administration. Another attractive Creole building is at number 49, the **Villa de la Région** [294 B5], formerly the **Villa du Général**, which was built in the 1840s and restored in 2005.

At the far southern end of Rue de Paris is the **Jardin de l'Etat** [294 C7] (pages 301–2), established by French botanists after the property was bought in 1767 by an Officer Cremont. This is also where you will find the **Musée d'Histoire Naturelle** [294 C2] (Natural History Museum; page 302).

The main **market** (*grand marché*) [294 B5] and its smaller counterpart (*petit marché*) [295 F5] are both on Rue Maréchal Leclerc, although almost at opposite ends (page 299). Also on Rue Maréchal Leclerc, not far from the *petit marché*, is the town's colourful **Tamil temple** [295 F5]. Further west along the same street is the **Noor E Islam Mosque**, also known as **La Grande Mosquée** [294 D4], which was the first Islamic religious building to be constructed in France. Construction began in 1898, driven by a small group of Gujarati traders, and was completed in 1905. Its minaret was finished in 1975 and at 32m tall dominates the streetscape, making its presence felt even more sharply during the call to prayer every evening at sunset. Inside the mosque is a peaceful courtyard, which contains the ablutions area for pre-prayer washing. The mosque attracts a steady stream of worshippers, but is open to visitors (*09.00–12.00 & 14.00–16.00*). The prayer room can only be visited with a guide, and you will need to dress appropriately and remove your shoes.

GETTING THERE AND AWAY During peak hours traffic in St-Denis can be pretty intimidating for the uninitiated, especially with its intricate one-way system. The town is small enough to explore on foot and Le Barachois is a good place to leave your car.

The *cars jaunes* **bus station** [295 F3] is on the seafront and can be reached from Boulevard Lancastel. This is where you will arrive if you get the shuttle bus from Roland Garros International Airport (pages 265–6). The bus routes are displayed here and there are regular buses to St-Pierre, via the towns of the west coast, and to St-Benoît on the east coast. St-Denis city buses are a good way of getting around, except during rush hour. Timetables are available from the bus station or the tourist office.

Taxis are easy to find at the bus station but are expensive. Shared taxis (*taxis collectifs*) also depart from the bus station.

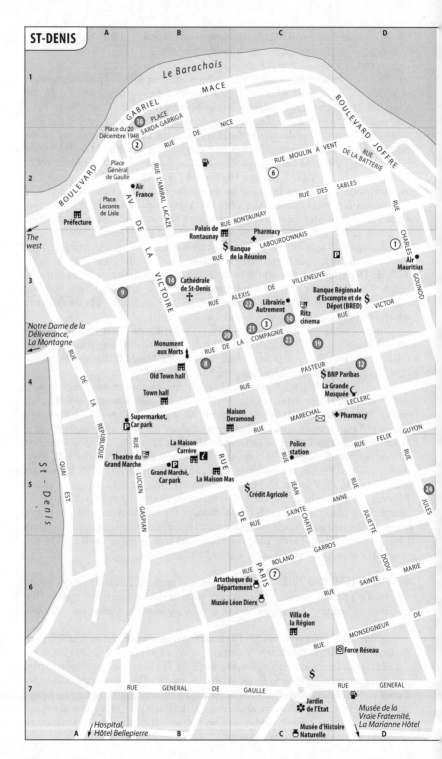

ST-DENIS

Le Barachois

MACE

GABRIEL
PLACE
SARDA GARRIGA
Place du 20
Décembre 1948
②
RUE
DE
NICE
BOULEVARD JOFFRE

RUE MOULIN A VENT
⑥
DE LA BATTERIE
RUE

BOULEVARD
Place
Général
de Gaulle
RUE DES SABLES
RUE
Place
Leconte
de Lisle
● Air
France
AV.
RUE L'AMIRAL LACAZE
DE
Préfecture
The
west
RUE RONTAUNAY
Palais de
Rontaunay
Pharmacy ✚
LABOURDONNAIS
P
① Air
Mauritius
CHARLES
GOUNOD
$ Banque
de la Réunion
RUE
VILLENEUVE
LA
Cathédrale
de St-Denis
⑭
Banque Régionale
d'Escompte et de
Dépot (BRED) $
⑨
VICTOIRE
RUE
ALEXIS
DE
Librairie ●
Autrement
⑳②
Ritz
cinema
⑩
VICTOR
RUE
Notre Dame de la
Délivrance,
La Montagne
⑳
②③①
RUE DE LA
COMPAGNIE
②③
⑲
Monument
aux Morts
RUE
DE
PASTEUR
$ BNP Paribas
⑫
⑧
Old Town hall
La Grande
Mosquée ℓ
LECLERC
Town hall
RUE
MARECHAL
✉
✚ Pharmacy
RUE
DE
LA
Supermarket,
Car park
P
Maison
Deramond
RUE
FELIX
GUYON
RUE
REPUBLIQUE
GASPIAN
LUCIEN
Theatre du
Grand Marche
La Maison
Carrère
ℹ
P
Grand Marché,
Car park
La Maison Mas
Police
station ●
RUE
JEAN
RUE
RUE
St - Denis
QUAI
EST
$ Crédit Agricole
DE
RUE
SAINTE
ANNE
CHATEL
JULIETTE
⑳
JULES
GARROS
DODU
MARIE
ROLAND
RUE
PARIS
⑦
Artothèque du
Département
SAINTE
DE
Musée Léon Dierx
Villa de
la Région
MONSEIGNEUR
RUE
ⓔ Force Réseau
$
RUE
GENERAL
DE
GAULLE
RUE
GENERAL
P
Hospital,
Hôtel Bellepierre
Jardin
de l'Etat
Musée d'Histoire
Naturelle
Musée de la
Vraie Fraternité,
La Marianne Hôtel

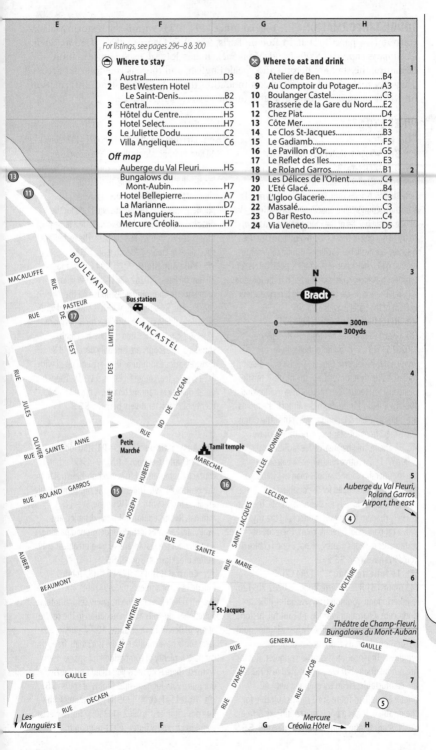

For listings, see pages 296–8 & 300

Where to stay

1	Austral	D3
2	Best Western Hotel Le Saint-Denis	B2
3	Central	C3
4	Hôtel du Centre	H5
5	Hotel Select	H7
6	Le Juliette Dodu	C2
7	Villa Angelique	C6

Off map

Auberge du Val Fleuri	H5
Bungalows du Mont-Aubin	H7
Hotel Bellepierre	A7
La Marianne	D7
Les Manguiers	E7
Mercure Créolia	H7

Where to eat and drink

8	Atelier de Ben	B4
9	Au Comptoir du Potager	A3
10	Boulanger Castel	C3
11	Brasserie de la Gare du Nord	E2
12	Chez Piat	D4
13	Côte Mer	E2
14	Le Clos St-Jacques	B3
15	Le Gadiamb	F5
16	Le Pavillon d'Or	G5
17	Le Reflet des Iles	E3
18	Le Roland Garros	B1
19	Les Délices de l'Orient	C4
20	L'Eté Glacé	B4
21	L'Igloo Glacerie	C3
22	Massalé	C3
23	O Bar Resto	C4
24	Via Veneto	D5

N

Bradt

| 0 | | 300m |
| 0 | | 300yds |

Bus station

Auberge du Val Fleuri,
Roland Garros
Airport, the east

Petit Marché

Tamil temple

Théâtre de Champ-Fleuri,
Bungalows du Mont-Auban

St-Jacques

Les Manguiers E

Mercure
Créolia Hôtel

Northern Réunion ST-DENIS

17

295

TOURIST INFORMATION The **tourist office** [294 B5] is within the historic Maison Carrère (see page 302) at 14 Rue de Paris, 97400 St-Denis (✆ *0262 418300; www. lebeaupays.com;* ⊕ *09.00–18.00 Mon–Sat*). It has lots of useful information and literature, the staff are helpful and speak English, and there is free internet access. They can make bookings for accommodation throughout the island. Information on what's on in St-Denis is available online at www.saintdenis.re.

WHERE TO STAY

Mid range

⌂ **Best Western Hotel Le Saint-Denis***
[294 B2] (122 rooms) 2 Rue Doret; ✆0262 218020;
e reception@hotel-le-saint-denis.com; www.
hotel-le-saint-denis.com. Centrally located, near Le
Barachois. Comfortable, spacious rooms with AC, TV,
phone & minibar. 54 of the rooms have a sea view,
so try to get one of those. Rooms equipped for the
disabled are available. Facilities include conference
rooms, Wi-Fi, snack bar, restaurant & pool. Caters for
business travellers & lacks character, but the location
is good. There is no car park; parking is on the street
in front of the hotel (payable). **$$$**

⌂ **Hôtel Bellepierre****** [294 A7]
(85 rooms) 91 bis Allée des Topazes, Bellepierre;
✆0262 515151; e info@hotel-bellepierre.com;
www.hotel-bellepierre.com. St-Denis's only 4-star
option is slightly removed from the hustle & bustle,
being in a residential/commercial area overlooking
the city, around 15mins from the airport. The rooms
are unremarkable & lacking some of the little extras
you expect from a 4-star property. They do have
AC, TV, phone, minibar, tea/coffee facilities, safe
& free Wi-Fi. Executive rooms have a balcony &
are considerably more spacious than the standard
rooms. Rooms equipped for the disabled are
available. Caters largely for business guests. There
is a very modern restaurant overlooking the city,
plus a car park, pool & tennis court. There are no
restaurants or shops nearby, so not a good choice if
you don't have a car. **$$$**

⌂ **Le Juliette Dodu*** [294 C2]
(43 rooms) 31 Rue Juliette Dodu; ✆0262 209120;
e juliettedodu@orange.fr; www.hotel-juliette-
dodu.com. Charming hotel in a beautiful, historic
Creole building with fabulously fussy lambrequin
decoration along its roofline & around the
windows. The location is central yet quiet. Rooms
are not luxurious but were renovated in 2012 &
are comfortable, clean & equipped with AC, TV,
phone & minibar. There are 2 rooms suitable for
the disabled. It has a pool, jacuzzi, library & free
Wi-Fi. A big selling point is the free parking. **$$$**

⌂ **Mercure Créolia*** [295 H7] (107 rooms)
14 Rue du Stade, Montgaillard; ✆0262 942626;
e H1674@accor.com; www.accorhotels.com. Large,
modern hotel 3km from the centre with impressive
views of the city & ocean. Rooms have AC, TV,
phone, minibar & safe. Rooms equipped for the
disabled are available. Facilities include a large pool,
fitness centre, free Wi-Fi & car park. The restaurant
specialises in Creole & French food. **$$$**

⌂ **Villa Angelique***** [294 C6] (7 rooms)
39 Rue de Paris; ✆0262 484148; www.villa-
angelique.fr. Charming guesthouse on the
characterful Rue de Paris, which is crammed with
historic buildings. The house was built between
1894 & 1906, & renovated in 2009 to a high
standard. The rooms are carefully decorated &
feature antique furniture. They are equipped with
AC, TV, safe, tea/coffee facilities & Wi-Fi. There is a
good-quality restaurant on site. A great location,
plenty of character & very homely. **$$$**

Budget

⌂ **Austral Hotel*** [294 D3] (50 rooms)
20 Rue Charles Gounod; ✆0262 944567; e hotel-
contact@hotel-austral.fr; www.hotel-austral.fr. In
the centre of town. Unremarkable but comfortable
en-suite rooms with AC, TV, phone, Wi-Fi &
minibar. Rooms equipped for the disabled are
available. Facilities include underground parking,
a small pool & a restaurant serving breakfast only.
Buffet breakfasts are good. **$$**

⌂ **Central Hotel*** [294 C3] (57 rooms) 37
Rue de la Compagnie; ✆0262 941808;
e central.hotel@wanadoo.fr; www.centralhotel.re.
Functional, no-frills accommodation in the centre
of town. Rooms have en suite, AC, TV, phone, &
safe; some have minibar. There is a small, free
car park & plenty of competition for spaces. Be
warned, there is no lift & you could find yourself
dragging your luggage up 3 flights of stairs. **$$**

⌂ **Hotel Select** [295 H7] (55 rooms) 1 bis
Rue des Lataniers; ✆0262 411350; e hotelselect@
wanadoo.fr; www.hotel-select-reunion.fr.

A 10min walk from centre of town. Comfortable, refurbished en-suite rooms with AC, TV, safe & phone. It has a small pool but it is surrounded by tall buildings so isn't terribly inviting. Parking & Wi-Fi (payable) available. **$$**

⌂ **La Marianne**** [294 D7] (24 rooms) 5 Ruelle Boulot; \0262 218080; e hotel-la-marianne@wanadoo.fr; www.hotel-la-marianne-reunion.fr. Close to the Jardin de l'Etat, a few mins' walk from the centre of town. Rooms are basic & very plain with en suite, AC, & TV. There is a safe at reception but not in the rooms. 3 of the rooms are equipped with kitchenette & are more expensive. There is a car park. Rooms are over 4 floors but there is no lift. There are better options. **$$**

Shoestring

⌂ **Hôtel du Centre** [295 H5] (35 rooms) 272 Rue Maréchal Leclerc; \0262 417302; e hotelducentrerun@wanadoo.fr; www.hotelducentre-reunion.fr. Very basic

accommodation in a less than pleasant area. The small rooms have AC & TV; some have en suite. There is a small car park. Breakfast is taken on a pleasant patio, but there are better options. **$**

⌂ **Les Manguiers** [295 E7] (20 apts) 9 Rue des Manguiers; \0692 919292; e manguiers@wanadoo.fr; www.lesmanguiers.re. Simple self-catering apartments in a 3-storey building, including 2 equipped for the disabled. All have 1 double room, bathroom, sitting area, kitchenette, AC, TV, phone & balcony. Wi-Fi is payable. **$**

Self-catering holiday rentals

⌂ **Bungalows du Mont-Auban**** [295 H7] (3 bungalows) 27 bis Chemin Montauban, La Bretagne, Ste-Clotilde; \0262 525008; e loc.974@wanadoo.fr. Set in a pleasant garden about 30mins' drive from the centre of St-Denis. Each bungalow has 2 bedrooms, bathroom, sitting area, kitchenette & terrace. Bungalow from €560 (4 people).

✖ **WHERE TO EAT** For self-caterers, there is a **Continent hypermarket** between St-Denis and Roland Garros Airport, as well as several smaller supermarkets in town. For eating out, there are numerous restaurants, street vendors, snack bars, bistros, brasseries and cafés, which are part and parcel of St-Denis's café society. There is a good concentration of *camions-bars* (food vans) around Le Barachois, where you can pick up a cheap lunch or dinner. However, finding a restaurant that's open Sunday lunchtime can be a challenge. Below is a cross-section of St-Denis's eateries:

✖ **Atelier de Ben** [294 B4] 12 Rue de la Compagnie; \0262 418573; www.atelier-de-ben.com; ⊕ for lunch Tue–Fri & dinner Tue–Sat. Cuisine: French. An upmarket, thoroughly modern restaurant serving creative cuisine & widely acknowledged as one of the best restaurants in town. It's small & very popular, so a reservation is highly recommended. **$$$$**

✖ **Au Comptoir du Potager** [294 A3] 8 bis Rue Labourdonnais; \0692 855931; ⊕ 08.00–16.00 Mon–Fri, for dinner Fri/Sat. Cuisine: French. Cosy restaurant serving creative dishes made using fresh, seasonal produce. **$$$**

✖ **Brasserie de la Gare du Nord** [295 E3] 1 Bd Joffre; \0262 415487; ⊕ 08.30–23.00 daily. Cuisine: French, ice cream. The building which houses this restaurant/bar dates from the late 18th century & was originally a train station then a bus station. It now boasts a very modern interior. It attracts a good local crowd, especially as a bar on weekend evenings. **$$$**

✖ **Chez Piat** [294 D4] 60 Rue Pasteur; \0262 214576; ⊕ for lunch Mon–Sat, dinner Tue–Sat. Cuisine: French. It may not look like much from the outside but within lies a stylish restaurant with a romantic atmosphere. The restaurant has been going since the 1970s & has a healthy number of regulars. European dishes with a Creole twist. **$$$**

✖ **Côte Mer** [295 E2] 4 Pl Etienne Regnault; \0692 534480; www.cotemer.re; ⊕ 10.00–00.30 Tue–Sun. Cuisine: French, ice cream. A modern restaurant, lounge bar & ice-cream parlour overlooking the ocean. Seating is either in the colourful, trendy interior or on the veranda with sea views. Popular & gets busy, especially in the evenings. **$$$**

✖ **Le Clos St-Jacques** [294 B3] 5 Ruelle Edouard; \0262 215909; ⊕ for lunch Mon–Fri, dinner Tue–Sat. Cuisine: French. A long-established restaurant in an attractive Creole house next to the cathedral & close to the university. Specialises in Mediterranean cuisine. **$$$**

✗ **Le Gadiamb** [295 E5] 104 Rue Roland Garros; 📞0262 201079; 🕐 for lunch & dinner Mon–Sat. Cuisine: Creole. Excellent, simple Creole dishes prepared on a wood fire, followed by some nicely presented desserts. Between the old Creole house & the shady patio area, it has plenty of atmosphere. $$$

✗ **Le Reflet des Iles** [295 E3] 114 Rue Pasteur; 📞0262 217382; www.lerefletdesiles.com; 🕐 lunch & dinner Mon–Sat. Cuisine: Creole. Popular restaurant serving good-quality, authentic Creole food, grilled meat & fish, & salads. $$$

✗ **Le Roland Garros** [294 B1] 2 Pl du 20 décembre 1848; 📞0262 414437; 🕐 07.00–midnight daily. Cuisine: French, Creole. A French *bistrôt*-style eatery in a handy location at Le Barachois. It gets pretty busy, especially at lunchtime. The menu is in English, as well as French. Free Wi-Fi. $$$

✗ **O Bar Resto** [294 C4] 32 Rue de la Compagnie; 📞0262 525788; 🕐 08.00–02.00 Mon–Sat. Cuisine: French. A trendy, modern bar/restaurant in the centre of town, opposite Hotel Central. There is a tempting cocktail menu & regular live music. $$$

✗ **Via Veneto** [294 D5] 151 Rue Jules Auber; 📞0262 219271; 🕐 for lunch Mon, for dinner Tue–Sat. Cuisine: Italian, French. Casual, centrally located restaurant serving Italian classics, like pizza, as well as simple French dishes such as steak with pepper sauce. $$$

✗ **Le Pavillon d'Or** [295 G5] 224 Rue Maréchal Leclerc; 📞0262 214986; 🕐 for lunch & dinner Mon–Sat. Cuisine: Chinese. Relaxed atmosphere. Hosts regular dancing lunches & dinners. $$

✗ **Les Délices de l'Orient** [294 C4] 59 Rue Juliette Dodu; 📞0262 414420; 🕐 for lunch & dinner Tue–Sat. Cuisine: Chinese. Large, popular restaurant with a relaxed atmosphere. $$

✗ **L'Eté Glacé** [294 B4] 19 Rue de la Compagnie; 📞0262 201401; 🕐 10.30–14.30 Mon, 10.30–18.00 Tue–Sat. Very French tea rooms offering a wide variety of teas & coffees, plus homemade pastries & ice cream. Art is exhibited & on sale. $$

✗ **L'Igloo Glacerie** [294 C3] Cnr Rues Jean Chatel & Compagnie; 📞0262 213469; 🕐 11.00–midnight Mon–Sat, 15.00–midnight Sun. Cuisine: light meals, ice cream. 2 separate shops on either side of the road offering a huge range of ice creams, sorbets & crêpes, plus light meals. $$

✗ **Boulanger Castel** [294 C3] 43 Rue de la Compagnie; 📞0262 212766; 🕐 06.00–14.00 & 15.30–19.00 Tue–Sat, 07.00–12.00 Sun. Cuisine: French, bakery, tea rooms. A large, traditional bakery with a well-deserved reputation for fine breads & patisserie. Eat in or take-away. $

✳ ✗ **Massalé** [294 C3] 30 Rue Alexis de Villeneuve; 📞0262 217506; 🕐 10.00–20.00 Mon–Thu & Sat, 14.00–20.00 Fri & 11.00–20.30 Sun. Cuisine: Indian snacks. Eat-in or take-away. Tiny family-owned establishment, which has been operating since 1977. On offer is a tempting variety of delicious *samoussas*, *bonbons piments* & other tasty bites, which cost from around 80c. You can easily make a full meal of the treats on offer. $

NIGHTLIFE The European theme continues into the night in St-Denis, with lots of bars and ice-cream parlours open until late, particularly around the cathedral. Behind the cathedral and evidently named in its honour is **K-T Dral** (*5 Ruelle St-Paul;* 📞 *0692 959200*), which is a restaurant as well as a bar in a characterful old building and has regular live music. Other popular restaurant/bars include the **Brasserie de la Gare du Nord**, and **Côté Mer** and **O Bar** (see above). **Le Bar à Cas** (*19 Rue Pasteur;* 📞 *0262 201768;* 🕐 *06.30–late daily*) is a tapas bar, restaurant and pub, which has regular live music and karaoke nights. **Le Zanzibar** (*41 Rue Pasteur;* 📞 *0262 200118*) is another restaurant/bar, where customers hit the dance floor later in the evening. For true nightclubs most people head to St-Gilles-les-Bains, but St-Denis does have the gay-friendly **Le Prince** (*108 Rue Pasteur;* 📱 *0692 382828;* 🕐 *Fri/Sat nights*). The **Casino de Saint-Denis** is in Le Barachois (📞 *0262 413333;* 🕐 *24/7*), hosts regular poker tournaments and is very popular with locals.

ENTERTAINMENT For details of what is happening in St-Denis, www.saintdenis.re is a useful resource.

Cinema

There are 2 cinemas in St-Denis, usually showing international films dubbed into French:

🎬 **Ritz** [294 C3] 53 Rue Juliette Dodu; 🎬 0262 210862

🎬 **Ciné Lacaze** cnr Rues Amiral Lacaze & Rontaunay; 🎬 0262 412000. Schedules are available at www.cine974.com.

Theatre

The tourist office can provide information on forthcoming productions, or have a look online either at the theatre's own website or www.azenda.re.

🎭 **Théâtre du Grand Marché** [294 B5] Centre dramatique de l'Océan Indien, 2 Rue Maréchal Leclerc; 🎭 0262 203399; www.cdoi.re

🎭 **Théâtre de Champ-Fleuri** [295 H7] 2 Rue du Théâtre; 🎭 0262 419315; www.theatreunion.com

Live music

Le Palaxa 23 Rue Léopold Rambaud, Ste-Clotilde; www.palaxa.re. Live music venue, which has regular concerts & supports local artists.

SHOPPING In St-Denis, both **grand marché** (main market) [294 B5] and **petit marché** (small market) [295 F5] are on Rue Maréchal Leclerc. The main market (⊕ *08.30–17.30 Mon–Sat*) sells mostly handicrafts, largely from Madagascar. The small market (⊕ *06.00–18.00 Mon–Sat, 06.00–12.00 Sun*) has mostly fruit, vegetable, flower and spice stalls. A **night market** takes place at Le Barachois on the first Saturday of the month (⊕ *19.00–midnight*). With handicrafts, food and entertainment, it makes for a fun evening out. There are markets in **Le Chaudron** on Wednesday and Sunday mornings, **Le Moufia** on Saturday morning, **La Source** on Thursday morning and **Les Camélias** on Friday morning. You'll find a range of handicrafts at the markets, as well as in the **Galerie Artisanale** at 75 Rue du Karting in the suburb of Ste-Clotilde (🎬 *0262 295666; www.lagalerieartisanale.re*; ⊕ *12.30–20.30 Mon, 08.30–20.30 Tue–Sat, 09.00–12.30 Sun*), but prices around St-Denis may be higher than in smaller towns.

Librairie Autrement (*82 Rue Juliette Dodu;* 🎬 *0262 909060; www.sa-autrement. com*) is an excellent bookshop, and stocks a host of books on the Mascarene Islands.

Chic French clothing shops are popping up all over St-Denis. They are not cheap but stock some very appealing, good-quality clothes.

OTHER PRACTICALITIES

Money and banking Many French banks are represented in St-Denis and most have ATMs. Here is a selection:

$ **Banque de la Réunion** 27 Rue Jean Chatel; 🎬 0262 400123

$ **Banque Nationale de Paris Paribas (BNPP)** 67 Rue Juliette Dodu; 🎬 0820 840830

$ **Banque Régionale d'Escompte et de Dêpot (BRED)** 33 Rue Victor MacAuliffe; 🎬 0820 336491

$ **Caisse d'Epargne de la Réunion** 49 Rue du Général de Gaulle; 🎬 0821 010032

$ **Crédit Agricole** 14 Rue Félix Guyon; 🎬 0262 722934

Communications There are a number of **post offices** in the capital. The main post office [294 C4] (🎬 *0262 979505;* ⊕ *07.30–18.00 Mon–Fri, 08.00–12.00 Sat*) is at 60 Rue Maréchal Leclerc, on the corner of Rue Juliette Dodu.

Public **telephones** are widespread and, as throughout the island, the majority take phonecards (*télécartes*). These can be bought at post offices, newsagents and shops displaying the sign.

Medical care The main **hospital** [294 A7] is on Allée des Topazes, Bellepierre (🎬 *0262 905050*) and there are numerous medical practitioners. There are plenty

of **pharmacies** – a good starting point is Rue Maréchal Leclerc, where there are several, including one opposite the main post office.

AROUND ST-DENIS

East of St-Denis is the booming district of **Ste-Clotilde**, where the University of Réunion campus is found. **St-François** is a residential area in the mountains overlooking St-Denis, with a mild climate and lush vegetation. Higher up, at 800m, is **Le Brûlé**, a starting point for hikes on the **Plaine-des-Chicots**, which rises to the **Roche Ecrite** (2,275m). This overlooks the Cirque de Salazie. **La Montagne** is another residential area west of St-Denis, praised for its pleasant climate. The winding road lined with flamboyant trees features some excellent viewpoints. At La Montagne is **Parc du Colorado**, a well-used open space where on weekends you will find people from St-Denis picnicking, walking, horseriding or playing golf at the Golf Club du Colorado (page 288).

About 12km east of St-Denis city centre is the village of **Ste-Marie**. There is little to see in the village itself but nearby **Rivière des Pluies** is known for its statue of the **Black Virgin (La Vierge Noire)**. The statue stands in a tall white shrine to the left of the village church, surrounded by an explosion of flower arrangements and row upon row of candles. People arrive in droves to pray to her for good health, prosperity and protection. The story goes that a runaway slave fled to the place where the shrine now stands. There, the Black Virgin appeared to him, instructing him to hide under a flimsy bush. The slave complied, although the bush was much too small to conceal him properly. Just before the slave hunters reached the spot, the Black Virgin instantly increased the size of the bush, thereby completely covering the runaway. To honour her, the slave then carved the statue and, subsequently, the shrine was erected.

 WHERE TO STAY

Mid range

⌂ **La Villa des Cannes★★★★** (3 rooms) 17 lot Lisa, Chiendent, Route du Paradis, Ste-Marie; ☏0262 373213; www.lavilladescannes.com. In a residential area above Ste-Marie with views down to the coast. Beautifully appointed guesthouse accommodation with an elegant feel. The 3 individually decorated rooms are very spacious & have en suite, AC, coffee machine, daily maid service & free Wi-Fi. The 2 ground-floor rooms have direct access to the garden. The tropical garden is a pleasant place to relax & there is a generously sized pool. **$$$**

⌂ **Tulip Inn★★★** (65 rooms) 31 Av Leconte de Lisle, Ste-Clotilde; ☏0262 977777; e info@tulipinnsainteclotilde.com; www.tulipinnsainteclotildedelareunion.com. A new hotel which opened in 2014. The architecture is not to everyone's taste, being extremely modern & colourful. The rooms have en suite, AC, TV, safe, minibar & free Wi-Fi. There is a decent pool. Although breakfast is served, there is no restaurant for lunch & dinner & few options in the area. You will need to have a car if staying here. **$$$**

Budget

⌂ **Auberge du Val Fleuri★★** [295 H5] (8 villas) 91 Route de la Roche Ecrite, St-Denis; ☏0262 230107; e aubergevalfleuri@orange.fr; www.aubergevalfleuri.fr. In a park setting around 30mins by car from St-Denis, near Roche Ecrite & good hiking country. The wooden chalets are well equipped. There is a restaurant overlooking the countryside. A sauna/hammam, jacuzzi & bikes are available at no extra charge. **$$**

⌂ **La Case d'Aymline** (3 rooms) 45 Rue des Deux Canons, Ste-Clotilde; ☏0692 717803; e lacasedaymline974@hotmail.fr; www.lacasedaymline.com. An en-suite double room plus 2 self-catering studios around a pretty courtyard. All accommodation is nicely decorated & has Wi-Fi. A quiet location & friendly welcome. **$$**

ORGANISED TOURS The **tourist office** (*14 Rue de Paris, 97400 St-Denis;* ✆ *0262 418300*) offers organised tours of St-Denis, Ste-Marie and Ste-Suzanne. Details of guided tours offered by Guid'A Nou are available at www.explorerlareunion. com. They include a guided tour of La Rue de Paris in St-Denis, with its numerous historic houses (*tours depart 09.00, 14.00, 16.00; adult/child €20/10*), and a tour of St-Denis's religious buildings (*tours depart 09.00, 12.00; adult/child €25/10*) and last 3 hours.

HIKING On the outskirts of St-Denis and beyond you'll find picturesque hamlets in breathtaking surroundings. There are plenty of options in terms of hiking trails.

Inland from Roland Garros Airport, southeast of St-Denis, is the waterfall of **Le Chaudron**. Its name comes from the cauldron-like formation into which it plunges. Getting there entails an 8km hike, which takes around 2 to 3 hours (grading: moderate).

Hiking trails around **Roche Ecrite** ('written rock') are some of the island's best. The Roche Ecrite forest road is also where you can see most of the island's endemic birds. A 10km, 4-hour hike (grading: difficult) takes you to the remote **Bassin du Diable** (Devil's Pond). Alternatively, you could try the 9km, 4-hour walk (grading: easy) to **Piton Laverdure**, an extinct volcanic peak, which features a mass of flowers in October and November. A popular and easily reached picnic spot is **Cascade Maniquet** (30 minutes' walk).

The Roche Ecrite walk itself is wonderful, though quite challenging, and can be done in a day. It is, however, recommended that you stay overnight at the Plaine-des-Chicots *gîte*. If you have a car, you can leave it at the Mamode Camp forest road car park but there have been reports of cars being stolen or damaged here. The first leg, which is the part covered by birding tour groups, involves the 3-hour walk to the *gîte* on the **Plaine-des-Chicots** path (5km), through tamarind and bamboo forest. The second leg is on the Roche Ecrite path (4km, 1½ hours). Do this early in the morning for the best weather. From a rocky spur covered with inscriptions (the 'written rock'), you can see the magnificent amphitheatres of Salazie and Mafate. On the way back, stop off at the **Soldiers' Cave (Caverne des Soldats)**, overlooking Rivière des Pluies. Another path leads to **Mare aux Cerfs (Stags' Pond)**.

The energetic (and fairly fit) can continue from Roche Ecrite, west to **Plaine d'Affouches**, which means a 3-hour hike past a disused prison, Ilet à Guillaume. You can continue even further, to **Dos d'Ane** village, by taking the path branching off after Ilet à Guillaume. Ardent hikers can confront the steep trail into the Cirque de Salazie. Bring warm clothing since night temperatures are often around freezing point.

GOLF There is a nine-hole course at La Montagne, called **Golf Club du Colorado**. For more information, see page 288.

HORSERIDING The **Centre Equestre de la Montagne** is at La Montagne. For more information, see page 287.

JARDIN DE L'ETAT [294 C7] (*Pl de Metz, St-Denis;* ⊕ *06.00–18.00 daily; admission free*) At the southern end of Rue de Paris is this botanical garden, which features plant species from around the world. It was originally created in 1773 by the French

Northern Réunion **WHAT TO SEE IN NORTHERN REUNION**

17

East India Company. New plants introduced to the colony were grown here before being distributed to the landowners. French botanist Pierre Poivre also had a big influence and there is a bust of him in the garden. The ponds are attractive and there is a quintessentially French Wallace fountain designed to help passers-by quench their thirst. It is a beautiful, tranquil place in which to spend a few hours and on the weekends is a popular picnic spot for locals. Guided visits start at 09.30, 11.00, 13.00, 14.45 and 16.30 Monday to Friday. Mosquito repellent is recommended. The garden is closed during high winds. Within the garden is the Natural History Museum (see below).

MUSEE D'HISTOIRE NATURELLE [294 C7] (*1 Rue Poivre, St-Denis;* \ *0262 200219;* e *museum@cg974.fr; www.cg974.fr;* ⊕ *09.30–17.30 Tue–Sun; admission adult/child €2/1*) The Natural History Museum is within the Jardin de l'Etat, in an elegant building constructed in 1837 for the colony's administrator. The museum was created here in 1855 and is the oldest on the island. The stark white building with its impressive first-floor gallery makes a fine setting for the collection. The permanent exhibition features extinct and rare species of the western Indian Ocean, including the solitaire, Réunion's dodo-like bird. Exchanges with museums in France, Australia and elsewhere have allowed it to create impressive exhibitions.

MUSEE LEON DIERX [294 C6] (*28 Rue de Paris, St-Denis;* \ *0262 202482;* e *musee.dierx@cg974.fr; www.cg974.fr;* ⊕ *09.30–12.00 & 13.00–17.30 Tue–Sun; admission €2*) Housed in a former bishop's residence built in 1845, this modern and contemporary art museum was created in 1911 by Réunionnais writers George Athénas and Aimé Merlo, who published under the pseudonyms Marius and Ary Leblond. They dedicated the museum to poet Léon Dierx (page 280) and soon amassed an impressive collection, largely through donations. Well worth a visit, it houses original works by the likes of Gauguin, Renoir, Maufra, Erro, Chen Zen and even Picasso, as well as work by local artists. There is wheelchair access in Rue Ste-Marie.

MUSEE DE LA VRAIE FRATERNITE [294 D7] (*28 Bd de la Providence, St-Denis;* \ *0262 210671;* ⊕ *09.00–17.00 Wed & Sat; admission adult/child €2/1*) A small museum run by Roman Catholic nuns. The exhibits are designed to represent the island's different communities and cultures throughout their history.

LA MAISON CARRERE [294 B5] (*14 Rue de Paris, St-Denis;* \ *0262 418300;* e *maisoncarrere@lebeaupays.com; www.lebeaupays.com;* ⊕ *09.00–18.00 Mon–Sat; admission adult/child €3/1.50, €4 with audio-guide*) Self-guided or guided tours (guided tours every hour) of the attractive Creole mansion which now houses the tourist office. The house was originally built in 1820 as a simple, single-storey wooden building. In 1905, Raphaël Carrère, who had made his fortune in the sugar industry, moved into the house with his wife and five children. They extended the house and added the upper floor. The house has been carefully restored and is decorated as it would have been during the days of the Carrère family.

JARDIN DE CENDRILLON (*48 Route des Palmiers, 97417 La Montagne;* m *0692 863288;* e *lejardindecendrillon@wanadoo.fr; tours last 1½hrs & cost adult/child €20/10*) Pleasant private garden in the hills above St-Denis, created in 1935. The orchids are a particular feature. Guided tours must be booked in advance.

JARDIN DES AFFOUCHES (*250 Route Antide Boyer, 97417 La Montagne;* ↳ *0692 704036;* e *bernard.courtis@gmail.com;* ⊕ *09.00–12.00 Wed & Sun; adult/child €8/3.50*) Guided visits of a private garden of over 1ha, which contains a wide range of plants, including coffee, spices and medicinal plants.

JARDIN DE LA VALLEE HEUREUSE (*Allée Félicien Vincent, Le Brûlé, 97400 St-Denis;* ↳ *0692 878187;* ⊕ *09.00 2nd Sun each month; adult/child €8/4*) Guided visits of a Creole garden, which dates from the 19th century and became an historic monument in 2012. There is plenty to see in this shady garden, which is well stocked with endemic and native species and home to abundant local birdlife. Reservation essential.

ARTOTHEQUE DU DEPARTEMENT [294 C6] (*26 Rue de Paris, 97400 St-Denis;* ↳ *0262 417550;* ⊕ *09.30–17.30 Tue–Sun; admission free*) This contemporary art gallery exhibits work from regional artists.

FOLLOW BRADT

For the latest news, special offers and competitions, subscribe to the Bradt newsletter via the website www.bradtguides.com and follow Bradt on:

17

🅕 www.facebook.com/BradtTravelGuides
🐦 @BradtGuides
📷 @bradtguides
🅟 www.pinterest.com/bradtguides

18

Eastern Réunion

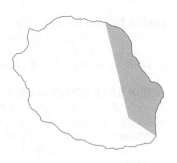

The sparsely inhabited eastern region stretches from Ste-Suzanne in the north through St-André and Bras-Panon to St-Benoît, continuing southwards to La Pointe de la Table. It is a lush area of sugarcane, lychee fields and vanilla. In fact, a visit to one of the vanilla estates is one of the highlights of the east. The region includes the awe-inspiring active volcano, Piton-de-la-Fournaise.

Although it is the south which has earned the adjective *sauvage* (wild), it could equally be applied to the unspoilt east coast. This is the region which receives the most rain and it is the one into which violent cyclones tear when they rage in the western Indian Ocean between January and March. Most of the east coast consists of black volcanic rock or cliffs, against which rough seas lash continuously. The regular activity of Piton-de-la-Fournaise constantly adds to Réunion's surface area, as lava flows out of the crater towards the eastern coast, solidifying as it hits the ocean.

STE-SUZANNE TO BRAS-PANON

The colonial houses and flowery gardens of **Ste-Suzanne** render the atmosphere somewhat more pleasant than is the case in bustling St-André. It is one of the island's oldest settlements, dating from 1667, and is best known for its **lighthouse**, at the western end of town. The lighthouse, which was built in 1845 and is the only one on the island, can be visited on certain days each month via the tourist office (see opposite). On the outskirts of Ste-Suzanne is **La Vanilleraie**, where you can learn about vanilla production (page 315). Ste-Suzanne also boasts the only artificial river in the Indian Ocean at its whitewater sports centre (for more information, see page 314).

Ste-Suzanne lies on the river of the same name, and the town is within easy reach of several waterfalls which punctuate the river. The first, **Cascade Niagara**, is signposted from the southern end of town, just beyond the church. The short drive takes you through cane fields and you can park right at the foot of the falls. Although far less impressive than its Canadian namesake, it is a pretty waterfall, 30m high. Further inland, **Bassin Boeuf** is a series of beautiful, natural rock pools in the river, which are ideal for swimming and picnicking. Take the D51 towards Bagatelle and follow the signs for Bassin Boeuf. From the parking area it is about a 5-minute walk to the river. Further south, in the area known as Quartier Français, is **Cascade Délice**. The waterfall here is small, only around 4m high, but the area is well wooded and the shady picnic area is popular with locals on the weekends. To reach it take the D46, then follow Rue Ste-Vivienne to the end, where there is a parking area.

St-André is a large industrial town with factories galore, and is surrounded by agricultural land. It is the centre of Réunion's Tamil community, the descendants of the indentured labourers brought to the area to work in the sugarcane plantations and factories. As you walk through St-André you will no doubt notice it has a

very Indian feel, in stark contrast to the west coast with its heavy concentration of French expats. There are some vibrantly coloured Tamil temples, decorated with statues and carvings, such as the **Temple du Petit Bazaar** (*Av Ile de France*). Tamil temples are beautiful from the outside but, for a closer look, the tourist office can arrange a visit of the **Temple du Colosse** (page 314) just outside the town. St-André is the best place to see awe-inspiring **Tamil ceremonies and festivals** such as fire-walking and Cavadee (see page 69).

The **tourist office** is within **Maison Valliamé**, an attractive Creole house of 1925. Guided tours are available (page 315) and exhibitions and events are held here.

On the coast, a few kilometres from the centre of St-André among sugarcane fields, is **Parc Nautique du Colosse** (*www.saint-andre.re;* ⊕ *08.30–23.00 daily*). The park features boutiques, eateries, picnic areas and a children's playground, you can also hire bikes and go-karts here. Watersports, such as sailing, take place on the lake and on the second Sunday of the month the park hosts a produce market.

It was in the area of St-André that debris from missing Malaysia Airlines flight MH370 was found washed up on the coast in July 2015. The flight had disappeared on 8 March 2014 while flying between Kuala Lumpur and Beijing.

About 2km south of St-André is the turning to **Salazie** and **Hell-Bourg** (see pages 357–60).

Continuing south along Route Nationale 2 (RN2), you come to **Bras-Panon**, the centre of the vanilla industry. Worth a visit is **Pro Vanille**, which explains the production of vanilla (see page 315). The nearby village of **Rivière des Roches** is where much of the island's *bichiques* are fished, a small sprat-like fish usually served in *cari*. In the village is a turning to two beautiful natural pools beneath wooded waterfalls: **Bassin La Paix** and **Bassin La Mer**. About 3km from the RN2, you come to a track that leads to Bassin La Paix, where you can leave your car. It is a short walk through lush woods to the *bassin*. A sizeable waterfall plunges into the deep pool, where a quick dip offers welcome respite from the tropical sun. If you continue uphill for another 30 minutes, you'll arrive at the second pool, Bassin La Mer, arguably even more attractive than the lower one. It's in this area (the tumbling river between the two pools) that people come to do 'water hiking', in other words hiking upstream in the river itself.

Beyond Bras-Panon, on the RN2 to St-Benoît, is a turning to the viewpoint at **Takamaka**. The road winds gradually upwards for about 15km before reaching Takamaka. From the car park, there is a wonderful view of a semicircle of mountains painted with the thin strips of waterfalls. It is the starting point for a walk of 6.5km to the Electricité de France platform at Bébour.

TOURIST INFORMATION The **tourist office** in Ste-Suzanne is at 18 Rue du Phare (✆ *0262 521354;* ⊕ *09.00–12.30 & 13.30–17.00 Mon–Sat*). There is also a tourist office in **St-André**, at Maison Valliamé, 1590 Chemin du Centre (✆ *0262 461616;* ⊕ *09.00–12.30 & 13.30–17.00 Mon–Fri*).

WHERE TO STAY

Budget

⌂ **Le Pharest*** (1 room, 5 bungalows) 22 Rue Blanchet, Ste-Suzanne; ✆ 0262 989110; e pharest-reunion@wanadoo.fr; www.pharest-reunion.com. Basic accommodation in 1 double room & wooden cabins of various sizes in a shady garden. The cabins sleep between 2 & 8 people, are colourfully decorated & each has its own bathroom & free Wi-Fi. However, only 1 of the cabins (La Papangue) has a kitchen. 2 of the cabins are suitable for those with limited mobility. There is a pool & a casual restaurant serving breakfast & dinner. AC is at additional cost (€4.50 per day). **$$**

Shoestring

🏠 **Ferme Auberge Lucinda** (2 rooms) 87 Chemin Bruna, 97412 Bras-Panon; ✆0692 062963; e nazelucinda@gmail.com. Guesthouse accommodation on an attractive smallholding, where goats, rabbits, wild boar & poultry are reared & fruit, vegetables & spices are grown. The 2 rooms are well maintained & have a double bed, bunk beds & en suite. Lucinda also runs an excellent table d'hôte (see below) & breakfast here features some delicious homemade jams. Good value for money. **$**

🏠 **L'Auberge du Désert** (8 rooms) 2606 Chemin Bras des Chevrettes, 97440 St-André; ✆0262 466443; e aubergedudesert974@ gmail.com; www.portail-ile-reunion.com/ aubergedudesert. In a peaceful, countryside location 10mins from St-André. Simply furnished en-suite rooms for either 2 or 4 people. There is a good-sized pool & meals are available. **$**

🏠 **Residence du Niagara** (5 bungalows) 1 Chemin de la Renaissance, 97441 Ste-Suzanne; ✆0262 523892; e residenceduniagara@gmail. com; http://residence-du-niagara.pagesperso-orange.fr. Self-catering accommodation in spacious, well-maintained grounds on the Ste-Suzanne River. Each cabin can accommodate 2 adults & 1 child, & 1 is suitable for those with reduced mobility. They are simply furnished & have their own bathroom, TV, AC & a pleasant outdoor area with table & chairs. Linen is provided & there is a maid service twice a week. There are sunloungers & barbecues in the garden for guests to use. **$**

Self-catering holiday rentals

🏠 **Les Gîtes Ango** (3 houses) 140 Commune Ango, Ste-Suzanne; ✆0262 521900; e gitesango@ wanadoo.fr; www.gites-ango.com. The 3 gîtes are grouped around a pool, 2 sleep 4 people & the 3rd sleeps 8. The houses are Creole style with modern, comfortable interiors. They are nicely furnished & well maintained, each with their own garden. Only the largest house has AC. All 3 gîtes have access to the sauna, hammam & jacuzzi on site. A great self-catering option. 2-bedroom gîte from €525 per week, 4-bedroom gîte from €920 per week.

✕ WHERE TO EAT

✕ **Le Beau Rivage** Rue de la Vielle-Eglise, Champ-Borne; ✆0262 460866; ⏱ 10.00–23.00 Tue–Sat, for lunch Sun. Cuisine: Creole, French, Chinese. In a pleasant location on the seafront, beside the ruined church. Fairly smart & very popular. **$$$**

✕ **Le Beauvallon** Route du Stade, Rivière des Roches; ✆0262 504292; ⏱ 09.00–15.00 daily, dinner Fri/Sat on reservation. Cuisine: Creole, Indian. A large, airy restaurant in the Bras-Panon area, overlooking the mouth of Rivière des Roches. A great place to try the local speciality, *cari bichiques*. Reservation recommended. Main courses from €12. **$$$**

✕**Restaurant Velli** 336 Route de Champ Borne, 97440 St-André; ✆0262 460338; www.restaurant-velli.com; ⏱ 10.00–16.00 Sun–Fri. Cuisine: Creole, French, Indian. Good food in pleasant surroundings, either inside with the benefit of AC or in a shady garden. **$$$**

✕ **Ti Piment** 1 bis Rue Roberto, 97412 Bras-Panon; ✆0262 234679; ⏱ Tue–Sun. Cuisine: Creole, French. Relatively new restaurant with a fairly modern feel. Offers carefully prepared Creole dishes, French classics & decent pizzas. Hosts theme nights on weekends, such as paella night, mussels night or karaoke. **$$$**

✕ **Ferme Auberge Eva Annibal** 6 Chemin Rivière du Mât, 97412 Bras-Panon; ✆0262 515376; ⏱ for lunch & dinner Mon–Sat, lunch Sun. This family-run table d'hôte has been operating since 1986. It is very popular & guests eat at long tables, meaning you can swap stories throughout the meal. This place is famous for its duck with vanilla. Reservation essential. 3-course meal €25/12.50 (adult/child). **$$**

✕ **Ferme Auberge Lucinda** 87 Chemin Bruna, 97412 Bras-Panon; ✆0692 062963; ⏱ on reservation. Cuisine: Creole. An excellent table d'hôte on a smallholding with good views. The produce from the farm is used to great effect in creating delicious dishes, such as goat curry, guinea fowl with lychees & smoked pork with papaya. Reservation essential. 3-course meals from €25/15 (adult/child). **$$**

✕ **La Cuisine de Clémencia** 18 Chemin des Glaïeuls, Bras Pistolet, Ste-Suzanne; ✆0262 475278; ⏱ on reservation. Cuisine: Creole. Good-quality table d'hôte serving traditional Creole meals cooked over a wood fire. €25/12.50 (adult/child). **$$**

Edmond Albius was born a slave in Ste-Suzanne in 1829. His mother died during his birth and his master, Féréol Bellier Beaumont, adopted Edmond. At the age of 12, Albius invented a technique for pollinating the vanilla orchid by hand, launching the vanilla industry.

The vanilla plant is an orchid native to Mexico, but its pollination is a tricky business. Buds form on the plant after three years, blooming for just a few hours on one day per year. Vanilla has one natural pollinator, the Melipona bee (*Apis melipona*), which is native to Mexico.

French colonists brought vanilla plants to Réunion and Mauritius in the 1820s, planning to cultivate vanilla, which had become a valuable commodity by that stage. However, there was no insect to pollinate the orchid outside Mexico and the plants could not reproduce. Great botanists of the day worked on the problem, and in 1837 a Belgian botanist discovered that pollination was required to set the fruit from which the vanilla pod is formed. However, his method of artificial pollination was slow, complicated and not commercially viable.

Beaumont, a Réunion Island landowner, had received some vanilla plants from the government in France. Only one of the plants survived for any length of time but it didn't fruit. Young Edmond Albius, who had already learned how to artificially pollinate the watermelon plant, tried his luck with the vanilla plant. He was successful and developed a method of pollinating the plants quickly and easily using a thin stick and his thumb. Beaumont sent Albius to other plantations to teach other slaves how to pollinate vanilla. The Indian Ocean's vanilla industry was born and by 1898 Réunion had overtaken Mexico as the world's largest producer of vanilla beans.

Albius's technique is still used today, as you will see if you do a tour of one of the island's vanilla plantations. In 1848, following the abolition of slavery, Albius moved to St-Denis, where he worked as a kitchenhand. He was convicted of stealing jewellery and sentenced to ten years in prison, but after five years the governor granted him clemency in light of his significant contribution to the vanilla industry. Albius died a poor man in Ste-Suzanne in 1880.

ST-BENOÎT TO STE-ANNE

Originally built almost entirely of wood, St-Benoît was flattened by a fire in the 1950s and then rebuilt in brick and cement. Although it is referred to as the capital of the east, the town itself is not particularly inspiring; most tourists simply pass through *en route* to the attractions inland. At peak times, the traffic can be horrendous.

The **banks** (**Crédit Agricole** and **Banque de la Réunion**) are found on Rue Georges Pompidou and there is a **tourist information point** in the town centre, near the covered market (⊕ *13.00–18.00 Wed, 09.00–12.00 Fri*). The main **tourist office** for the area is in Ste-Anne (page 308). **Rivière des Marsouins** (Porpoise River) runs through St-Benoît, and *bichiques* are caught at the mouth of the river. **Ilet Bethléem** is a beautiful spot on the river, where people come to frolic in the water and picnic. In 1855, the wife of Governor Hubert Delisle, concerned by the poverty in the area, created a workhouse here run by nuns and built a

chapel, which remains. The chapel, dedicated to Madame de Fatima, is a site of pilgrimage and a mass is held here at Christmas. To reach Ilet Bethléem take the exit marked Bethléem from the RN2; at the end of the road is a car park, from where it is around a 15-minute walk.

About 10km southwest of St-Benoît on the RN3 (towards La Plaine-des-Palmistes) is the turning to **Grand Etang**, a lake once considered sacred by slaves, who would conduct rituals on its shores. There are some pleasant walks here and it is a very popular picnic spot, particularly on weekends. On the same road is the pretty village of **La Confiance**, about 6km from St-Benoît.

About 5km south of St-Benoît on the RN2 lies Ste-Anne, a charming village that has proudly preserved many of its Creole houses. As a result, it has a great deal more character than St-Benoît and is worth a stop. Just off the main road is the village's highly unusual **church**. The original building, dating from 1857, was rebuilt by Father Daubenberger and his parishioners from 1892. The result is an extravagant building embellished with intricate stone carvings, mostly of flowers and fruit. Prior to a renovation between 2010 and 2012 it was a rather grubby pink colour, but now sports a range of pastel hues and is far more beautiful as a result. The tourist office can organise guided tours of the church. Near the church is the **tourist office** and a small shop called Ilôt Savons (\ *0262 729592*), which sells locally made soap.

Just north of Ste-Anne on the RN2 is **La Grotte de Lourdes**, a shrine to the Virgin Mary. It is said that in 1862 a tidal wave hit the area, but the locals hid in a cave and were saved. They built the shrine, which still attracts many pilgrims, as a symbol of their gratitude to the Virgin.

GETTING THERE AND AWAY Getting to St-Benoît is not difficult: *cars jaunes* (buses) run regularly to and from St-Denis (Lines E1 and E2) and there are buses to and from St-Pierre, either along the coast road (Line S1) or inland via La Plaine-des-Palmistes (Line S2).

TOURIST INFORMATION The **tourist office** (\ *0262 470509*; ⊕ *09.00–12.00, 13.00–17.30 Mon–Sat*) is at Place de l'Eglise in Ste-Anne. The staff are very helpful and speak some English. They can book accommodation, activities and tickets for events.

 WHERE TO STAY

Upmarket

✳ ⌂ **Diana Dea Lodge****** (30 rooms) 94 Chemin Helvetia Cambourg, 97470 Ste-Anne; \0262 303357; e resa@diana-dea-lodge.re; www.diana-dea-lodge.re. This new addition on a 150ha estate in the hills above Ste-Anne has brought some much-needed luxury to the east-coast accommodation scene. The en-suite rooms are modern but have a rustic, hunting-lodge feel thanks to the abundance of wood & stone. They are equipped with AC, TV, phone, safe, minibar & balcony/terrace. One of the standout features of each room is a bath with a view of the coast. There is a good restaurant, a pleasant pool area with expansive views & a spa. Excellent service by Réunion's standards. **$$$$**

Shoestring

⌂ **L'Orangeraie** (2 rooms, 1 bungalow) Pont Payet, 97470, St-Benoît; \0262 509760; e orangeraie@hotmail.fr; http://monsite. orange.fr/orangeraie. A friendly guesthouse set in beautiful gardens. Tasty homemade cuisine using produce grown on site. Comfortable, clean accommodation in a peaceful location. **$**

Self-catering holiday rentals

⌂ **Le Saint Alexandre****** (7 cabins) 14 Chemin Pont Payet, 97470 St-Benoît; \0262 509045; e saint.alexandre@hotmail.fr; www. saintalexandre974.com. Cute, well-equipped Creole cabins in a peaceful garden. They sleep up to 5 people & have a TV & Wi-Fi. €380 per week.

Camping

Å Le Bois Joli Coeur (5 tent pitches, 3 cabins) 120 Chemin Ceinture, 97437 Ste-Anne; `0692 615602; e edvin97437@yahoo.fr; www. campingleboisjolicoeur.re. A well-maintained campsite with 5 tent sites & 3 wooden cabins for 2 people. There is a communal kitchen, meals area & games area. You can visit the owner's smallholding & Creole meals can be arranged. Cabins from €40 per night, tent pitches from €15/10 (adult/child). **$**

✗ WHERE TO EAT There are large **Cora** and **Champion** supermarkets, both signed from the RN2.

✗ Les Letchis 42 Ilet Coco, 97470 St-Benoît; ` 0262 503977; www.lesletchis.re; ⊕ for lunch & dinner Tue–Sat, lunch Sun. Cuisine: French, Creole, seafood. In a pleasant garden setting on the banks of the Rivière des Marsouins. Elegant surroundings & sophisticated dishes. Seafood is the speciality. **$$$**

✗ Le Vieux Domaine 204 Route Nationale 2, 97470 St-Benoît; `0262 509050; ⊕ for lunch Sun–Fri, for dinner Tue–Sun. Cuisine: Creole, European. Good food in a peaceful setting. **$$$**

✗ Kiosque des Mandarines 747 Route de Takamaka, 97470 St-Benoît; `0692 849192; ⊕ for lunch daily, dinner on reservation. Cuisine: Creole. Friendly, family-run restaurant serving authentic Creole cuisine prepared on a wood fire. There are only a few dishes on the menu each day, but they are usually happy to assist with any special requests. Located on the D53 between St-Benoît & Takamaka. **$$**

OTHER PRACTICALITIES
Communications The **post office** in St-Benoît is at 12 Rue Georges Pompidou. There is also one on the RN2 in Ste-Anne.

STE-ROSE AND SURROUNDS

On the way from Ste-Anne to Ste-Rose, you pass a large suspension bridge, **Le Pont d'Anglais**, which was built in 1894. Adrenalin junkies now practise bungee jumping from the bridge over the **Rivière de l'Est**.

Surrounded by endless sugarcane fields, **Ste-Rose** is on the shoulder of the Piton-de-la-Fournaise volcano. There's something savage about the coastline here, with its black, rocky cliffs and wild, wild seas. Swimming is not on, but I am told by those in the know that the scuba diving offshore is excellent. (If you do this, make sure you go with very experienced people as the sea is potentially murderous.) In terms of sporting activities, the area is possibly best known for its **mountain-biking** trails (see page 313).

Ste-Rose is essentially a fishing village which has grown up around the harbour. At the harbour is a monument in honour of the defeated British naval commander, Corbett, who died in a battle with the French in 1809. The **post office** is at 184 Route Nationale 2. **Pharmacie Boyer** is at 447 RN2 in Piton-Ste-Rose.

Ste-Rose's big claim to fame is the church of **Notre Dame des Laves**, which is actually at **Piton-Ste-Rose**. On 12 April 1977, Piton-de-la-Fournaise blew its top once again, spewing out a wall of molten lava that rushed directly towards Piton-Ste-Rose. Everything in its path was destroyed: houses, trees and crops. The lava began crossing the road in front of the church. And then the unbelievable happened. The lava separated exactly at the church's front door and forked around it, flowing on either side until the two halves met on the other side of the church and continued towards the sea. Locals thought it was a miracle. Going inside the church and examining the framed photographs and newspaper clippings depicting that incredible event, you can see why. You'll also see a painting of Christ halting the lava. Some strange things have happened on this island.

Heading south of Ste-Rose, you'll arrive at **Pointe des Cascades**, Réunion's easternmost point. Just below it is **Anse des Cascades**, a beautiful quiet bay, backed on three sides by very high, very steep cliffs. The 'cascades' referred to plummet down the green cliffs into a pool. This is a popular area for local fishermen and colourful fishing boats lie in neat rows along the shore. There's a dense palm grove with several picnic spots and a small restaurant. The bay has a magical feel and people come here from all over the island to enjoy the natural beauty and remote surrounds. Needless to say, it becomes packed on weekends. Once again, swimming is not safe and mosquito repellent is advisable.

GETTING THERE AND AWAY Ste-Rose lies on the St-Pierre–St-Benoît coastal bus route (Line S1) and there is a stop almost directly outside Notre Dame des Laves.

WHERE TO STAY

Budget

⌂ **Ferme Auberge La Cayenne** (6 rooms) 317 Ravine Glissante, 97439 Ste-Rose; 📞0262 472346; www.ferme-auberge-lacayenne.fr. Comfortable, light & airy en-suite rooms with TV, balcony/terrace & sea view. There is a good family-run restaurant on site. **$$**

⌂ **Hotel La Fournaise** (23 rooms) 154 RN2, Ste-Rose; 📞0262 270340; e hotellafournaise2@ wanadoo.fr; www.hotellafournaise.fr. Fresh, clean, unfussy en-suite rooms with AC, TV & phone, & wooden, Creole-style furniture. Some rooms have a view of the sea. There is a good restaurant & a pool. **$$**

Shoestring

⌂ **Le Joyau des Laves** (4 rooms) Piton Cascades, RN2, Piton-Ste-Rose; 📞0262 473400; e ljdl@joyaudeslaves.com; www.joyaudeslaves. com. This guesthouse is in a wonderful setting on a hillside overlooking the sea, south of Ste-Rose. The rooms are simply furnished & have en-suite facilities; 1 is designed to be accessible to the disabled. There is a restaurant on site. **$**

WHERE TO EAT

✗ **Gingembre Combava** Hotel La Fournaise, 154 RN2, Ste-Rose; 📞0262 470340; ⌚ for lunch & dinner daily. Cuisine: Creole, French, seafood. A clean, fairly smart restaurant where local produce & seafood take centre stage. Reservation recommended. **$$$**

✗ **Anse des Cascades Restaurant** Anse des Cascades, Piton-Ste-Rose; 📞0262 472042; ⌚ 11.00–16.00 Sat–Thu. Cuisine: French, Creole, seafood. Popular, informal restaurant in an idyllic setting within this bay where waterfalls tumble down the cliffs & rows of fishing boats bob about on the ocean. It gets very busy on weekends. Dinner on reservation. Dish of the day from €10. **$$**

✗ **Auberge du Poisson Rouge** 503 RN2, Piton-Ste-Rose; 📞0262 473251; ⌚ for lunch Tue–Sun, for dinner Tue–Sat. Cuisine: Creole, French, Chinese, seafood. Casual atmosphere. The menu changes each day but usually only has a limited number of options. Good reputation for fish dishes. Main courses from €10. **$$**

✗ **Ferme Auberge de la Cayenne** 317 Ravine Glissante, 97439 Ste-Rose; 📞0262 472346; www. ferme-auberge-lacayenne.fr; ⌚ on reservation. Cuisine: Creole. Traditional Creole food prepared using local, seasonal produce, much of which is grown on the farm. Specialities include duck with lychees & goat curry. 3 courses from €28. **$$**

✗ **Joyau des Laves** Piton Cascade, RN2, Piton-Ste-Rose; 📞0262 473400; ⌚ for lunch Wed–Mon, for dinner daily. Cuisine: Creole. Reservation only. Table d'hôte meals from €16. **$$**

✗ **La Roz-i-dor** 7 Chemin des Anglais, 97439 Ste-Rose; 📞0262 471352; ⌚ for lunch & dinner daily. Cuisine: Creole. A relaxed atmosphere, tasty Creole dishes & very reasonable prices make this a good option. Take-away available. **$**

NIGHTLIFE On Saturday nights, the energetic might want to try the disco **Roz d'Zil** (*317 RN2, Ravine Glissante;* 📞*0262 473606*), which has been popular with the local crowd for many years.

From the road between Ste-Rose and St-Philippe (RN2) you can see the **lava flows** which attest to the fact that Piton-de-la-Fournaise is one of the world's most active volcanoes. Each flow is marked with the date of the eruption from which it originated. For obvious reasons, there are very few houses on this part of the island.

One of the first lava flows you come to as you drive south from Ste-Rose is that of the April 2007 eruption, one of the biggest ever recorded, and which added an incredible 45ha to the island's surface. A viewing platform has been built just off the main RN2 road. Walking on the solidified lava gives you a chance to admire the coiled patterns of rope lava and appreciate the beauty and drama of this extraordinary place. Do take care, though, as lava is very uneven, sometimes fragile and can be very sharp.

The lava flows from the 1970s and 1980s have been colonised by pioneer plants such as sword ferns, lichens, mosses and a few small herbaceous plants.

About 4km north of St-Philippe is the turning to the **Puits Arabe** (well of the Arabs), where there is car parking and a picnic area. The well and the nearby staircase carved into the lava were not built by the Arabs but by Europeans in around 1830, using techniques that had been used by the Arabs for centuries.

A circular path of approximately 2km takes you along the coast and through a volcanic wonderland known as the **Jardin Volcanique**, where signs give explanations of the various lava flows, including one dating from 1776. The path takes you to the lava cliffs around **Pointe de la Table**, which are a perfect illustration of how the volcano has added tens of hectares to the island's surface area. These particular cliffs were the result of the 1986 eruption, which added 30ha to the island. The views are breathtaking and the furious sea appears to be locked in a constant battle against the intruding lava.

At **Pointe du Tremblet** is a rugged (usually deserted) beach trapped between steep lava cliffs blanketed with rich, green vegetation and furious seas. The beach was formed following the 2007 eruption and the sand here is of the dark, volcanic variety. The beach is a 500m walk from the parking area. Back on the RN2, around the village of Le Tremblet, you will find houses and stalls selling local produce, including flowers and vanilla. **Escale Bleue** sells vanilla and offers guided tours of their family-run vanilla plantation (page 316).

South of **Bois Blanc** is **La Vierge au Parasol** (the Virgin with the Umbrella). She is easily recognisable, dressed in blue and carrying a blue umbrella, designed to help her in her struggle to protect the local families and crops from the fury of the volcano. The local mayor had the Virgin removed just prior to the January 2002 eruption, for fear that she would be destroyed. Local residents were furious and still claim that had she been left there, she would have diverted the lava and they would have had a miracle to rival that of Piton-Ste-Rose. After the 2002 eruption she was re-positioned next to Notre Dame des Laves Church at Piton St-Rose but in 2010 was moved back to her current position, beside the lava flows near Bois Blanc. She is invariably surrounded by a range of offerings from locals of all religions who seek her protection.

✗ WHERE TO EAT

✗ Chez Moustache 9 RN2, Le Tremblet; m 0692 332703; ⊕ for lunch Wed–Mon. Cuisine: Creole, Chinese. On the main road through Le Tremblet.

A small, casual restaurant serving simple, tasty, traditional dishes cooked on a wood fire. $$

18

Most people consider this to be Réunion's single most striking attraction. **Piton-de-la-Fournaise** (Furnace Peak) is one of the world's largest and most impressive shield volcanoes, reaching 2,631m. It is also one of the world's most active, erupting on average every year. As activity can last for several weeks or more, as was the case during the most recent eruptions in 2015, the erupting volcano draws crowds of spectators. In-depth information on the volcano can be found at the **Cité du Volcan** in La Plaine-des-Cafres (see pages 349–50) and online at www.fournaise.info.

When Piton-des-Neiges was still active, some 300,000 years ago, Piton-de-la-Fournaise rose up to its southeast and the successive layers of lava from both the volcanoes created the eerily lunar Plaine des Sables.

The drive to the volcano is an adventure in its own right. From La Plaine-des-Cafres you climb through an Alpine landscape dotted with cows sporting cowbells, which look as if they should be advertising Swiss chocolate. There are several spectacular viewpoints, including the panorama of Piton-des-Neiges looming over La Plaine-des-Cafres, and perhaps most striking of all, the view of La Vallée de la Rivière des Remparts at **Nez de Boeuf**. This valley, which stretches for 23km, is lined by cliffs rising up to 1,000m and looks almost tunnel-like as you peer down into it. And then you catch sight of a lone village on the valley floor, **Roche Plate**, and are left wondering how people manage to live in such isolation. Certainly, according to the information board at the viewpoint, life is not easy for those villagers, who battle cyclones and landslides on a regular basis.

The landscape becomes gradually stranger until you begin your descent to the barren moonscape that is **La Plaine des Sables**, preceding the volcano crater. Then it's an uphill stretch to **Pas de Bellecombe** (2,311m), which offers a fantastic view of the volcano and outer crater. There is a kiosk (⊕ *07.30–16.00 daily*) displaying information on the volcano and the **walks**, which is worth reading before you set off as it indicates the routes and their level of difficulty. The building also contains toilets and sells drinks. You can leave your car in the car park whilst you walk. It is best to set off as early as possible in the morning when the skies are clear because in the afternoon the clouds roll in like a thick fog and it can become dangerous. It is also best to complete the walk before it gets too hot, as the dried lava absorbs and radiates heat. You will walk across solidified lava, so take care and make sure you have suitable footwear. Water, some food, suncream and a sunhat are essential, as is some warm clothing. For safety reasons, it is important that you stick to the marked paths.

From Pas de Bellecombe the walk starts with a descent via steep steps to the floor of the outer crater. Various routes are marked with paint, some shorter and easier than others. The most popular takes you straight across the outer crater towards the classically cone-shaped volcano directly in front of you. Since the recent eruptions, the walk is rather more arduous than it was and to reach the crater takes around 7 hours return. Don't be surprised, or too demoralised, if you are passed by eager Frenchmen in Lycra running the path, just for fun. On the way to the crater you will come across some distinctive formations, such as **Formica Leo**, a scoria cone formed in 1753, and a natural cavern in the lava known as **Chapelle de Rosemont**.

The fit and energetic can try one of the many hiking trails that lead up to the volcano from various other parts of the island. Grading on all of them is difficult. Alternatively, you could see it from the air, as part of an unforgettable helicopter ride over the island. Whichever you choose, don't miss out on seeing the volcano: it is a mind-boggling, primal experience. There is a *gîte* at Pas de Bellecombe known

as Gîte du Volcan, where visitors can stay overnight (below). It is also a handy place to have lunch after walking to the crater.

You can explore the volcanic landscape in more creative ways too, either on horseback or by hiring a mountain bike (for more information, see below). If you want to get particularly close and personal with the volcano, you can even take a tour of the lava tunnels (page 314).

GETTING THERE AND AWAY There is one road to the volcano from Bourg-Murat (the RF5). If you hire a car, check that the agreement does not exclude you from taking it to the volcano. There are no buses but you could get a taxi from Bourg-Mourat. Alternatively, if you have the time and the energy, you can walk.

WHERE TO STAY
Shoestring

⌂ **Gîte du Volcan** (dorms) Pas de Bellecombe, 97439 Ste-Rose; m 0692 853091. On the road to Piton-de-la-Fournaise, just 600m from the volcano car park & the starting point of the walk to the summit. This is one of the island's better mountain houses. There are dormitories for 4–12 people & shared bathrooms, plus some small rooms for 2. Linen is provided. Don't plan

on a long hot shower; hot water is in short supply & is payable. There is a good restaurant with superb views (below). The sunsets & sunrises here are incredible. Being the only option for miles around, it gets very booked up & during busy periods you will need to reserve your accommodation well in advance. Expect to pay around €18 RO pp.

WHERE TO EAT

✳ ✗ **Gîte du Volcan** Pas de Bellecombe, 97439 Ste-Rose; m 0692 853091; ⏲ Thu–Tue. Cuisine: Creole. Good-quality food in a stunning setting with magnificent views of the rugged landscape leading up to the volcano. A meal here is well

deserved after you have walked the volcano & it is a lovely way to prolong your time in the crisp mountain air. You pay a slight premium for the location. Reservation recommended. $$$

WHAT TO DO IN EASTERN REUNION

CREOLE COOKERY COURSE – FAR FAR KREOL (*tourist office, 18 Rue du Phare, Ste-Suzanne;* ℡ *0262 521354;* e *info@lebeaupays.com; www.lebeaupays.com;* ⏲ *Tue, Thu, Sat & Sun; adult from €39*) Through the tourist office you can organise to spend a day learning about Creole cookery in Bagatelle, near Ste-Suzanne. The course teaches the basics of cooking a Creole meal on a wood fire and culminates in a tasting of a range of local dishes, such as *samoussas*, fish stew and pork curry.

MOUNTAIN BIKING There are eight mountain-bike trails around Ste-Rose, which vary from 5km to 44km and are graded according to difficulty. The trails are marked on a large signboard at the Marina Snack Bar, which you'll find at a conspicuous viewpoint near groves of pandanus trees. Most of the trails start at the four grey reservoirs you'll see up on the slopes above Ste-Rose. A mountain bike can be a good way to explore the area around Piton-de-la-Fournaise.

HORSERIDING There are several horseriding centres in the east, many of which offer treks to the volcano.

HIKING The highlight of hiking in the east is Piton-de-la-Fournaise, and there are numerous trails of varying difficulty which will take you there (for more

18

information, see pages 312–13). The most popular and straightforward is to walk to the summit of the volcano from the Pas-de-Bellecombe car park, but even that is a challenging hike.

WHITEWATER SPORTS (*Stade en Eau Vives Intercommunal, 2 Rue du Stade, 97441 Ste-Suzanne;* \ *0262 566612;* e *contact@sevi.re; www.sevi.re*) The whitewater centre at Ste-Suzanne offers kayaking and rafting.

EXPLORE THE LAVA TUNNELS (*Envergure Réunion;* \ *0693 432352;* e *envergure. reunion@gmail.com; www.canyon-speleo.re; adult/child from €50/35*) Reassuringly qualified in caving and canyoning, Julien and Simon lead tours of lava tunnels created by Piton-de-la-Fournaise. An extraordinary experience exploring the bizarre and rather eerie lava formations, including stalactites, stalagmites and huge caverns. There are tours of varying difficulty, the easiest of which is open to children from the age of six years. If you suffer from even the mildest claustrophobia, this probably isn't for you. The tours last 3, 5 or 6 hours. They recommend you bring sturdy shoes, long trousers, wet-weather gear, a change of clothes, water and a snack. Hard hats and lights are provided. The meeting point is the parking area near the Vierge au Parasol (page 311).

ENTERTAINMENT
Theatre
🎭 **Théatre Conflore** Chemin Champ Borne, St-André; \ 0262 582875; www.theatreconflore.fr
🎭 **Théâtre Les Bambous** 29 Av Jean Jaurès, St-Benoît; \ 0262 503863; www.lesbambous.com

Cinema
🎬 **Salle Multimédia Guy Alphonsine** 270 Rue de la Gare, St André; \ 0262 466315

SHOPPING There are **markets** in **Ste-Suzanne** on Tuesday morning, **St-André** on Friday morning, **Bras-Panon** on Thursday morning and **St-Benoît** on Saturday morning. Roadside stalls selling delicious, locally made honey, jam and vanilla are a common sight in the east.

WHAT TO SEE IN EASTERN REUNION

BEL-AIR LIGHTHOUSE (*tourist office, 18 Rue du Phare, Ste-Suzanne;* \ *0262 521354;* e *info@lebeaupays.com; www.lebeaupays.com;* ⊕ *2nd Sat & last Tue each month 10.00–12.30 & 13.30–16.30; admission €2; guided tour €5*) The only lighthouse on the island was built in 1845 and has been classed as an historic monument since 2012. When the tower is open you can climb the bright red spiral staircase of 88 steps for beautiful views along the coast. Access to the tower is restricted to children over six years of age and 1.2m tall. Artists hold exhibitions at the lighthouse (details available at www.lebeaupays.com), and there is a pleasant picnic area adjacent to it.

TAMIL TEMPLES There are some impressive, ornate and colourful Tamil temples around St-André. The tourist office can organise a guided tour (*€8.50*) of the large Temple du Colosse at Champ-Borne, about 4km from St-André.

BOIS ROUGE SUGAR FACTORY/SAVANNA RUM DISTILLERY (*2 Chemin Bois-Rouge, St-André;* \ *0262 585974;* e *tafia_galabe@rhum-savanna.com; www. distilleriesavanna.com;* ⊕ *Jul–Dec 09.00–20.00 Mon–Fri, 09.00–18.00 Sat; combined*

tour: admission adult/child €10/7; Jan–Jun 10.00–18.00 Mon–Sat; distillery only: adult/child €5/3.50; children under 7 are not allowed at the sugar factory; reservation a day in advance essential) Just north of St-André, the Bois Rouge sugar factory offers guided tours during its operational season, from July to mid-December. Tours of the Savanna Distillery, exploring rum production and ending with a tasting, are available all year. Both tours can be provided in English, but you will need to book in advance. Combined tours of the sugar factory and the distillery are possible from July to December and last around 2 hours. You will need to wear closed-toe shoes and trousers or shorts, rather than a skirt, are advisable. The visit is not suitable for those with a fear of heights. There is a good shop on site selling a tempting range of rum and sugar.

MUSEE DAN TAN LONTAN (*2208 Chemin du Centre, St-André;* \ *0262 584789;* ⊕ *09.00–17.00 Tue–Sun; admission adult/child €4/2*) Dan tan lontan is Creole for 'in times past'. This small, grandpa's shed-style collection of local antique objects provides an insight into daily life on the island years ago. Watch out for the rather dubious-looking mannequins. The passionate owner provides guided tours on reservation.

MAISON VALLIAME (*1590 Chemin du Centre, St-André;* \ *0262 469163; guided visits 09.30, 10.45, 13.45 & 15.00 Mon–Sat; admission adult/child €9.50/4.50*) Guided visits of the impressive three-storey, wooden Creole mansion which houses the St-André Tourist Office. Built in 1925 for a Doctor Martin, it was sold in 1954 to an Indian family named Valliamé. Guided visits last around 45 minutes.

DIORE FOREST This 250ha forest is rich in bird and plant life, including endemic orchids, and offers some very pleasant walking country. There is a picnic area and a walk of around 3km leads to a viewpoint over the Cirque de Salazie. From St-André take the road towards Salazie, then follow the signs.

PRO VANILLE (*21 RN2 Bras-Panon;* \ *0262 517102;* e *provanille.reunion@orange. fr; www.provanille.fr;* ⊕ *09.00–12.00 & 13.30–17.00 Mon–Sat; admission €5*) This vanilla co-operative was created in 1968 and is now made up of almost 140 producers. A very professional guided tour of the facility and a film tell the story of vanilla and the various stages involved in its production. The fascinating tours last about 45 minutes and include a tasty vanilla-flavoured coffee. There is a well-stocked, delicious-smelling shop selling vanilla products and nicely packaged vanilla-related souvenirs. They even have an online shop so you can order vanilla from Réunion wherever you are in the world.

LA VANILLERAIE (*Domaine du Grand Hazier, Allée Chassagne, Ste-Suzanne;* \ *0262 230726; www.lavanilleraie.com;* ⊕ *09.00–12.00 & 13.30–17.00 Mon–Sat; guided tours 09.00, 10.00, 11.00, 14.00, 15.00 & 16.00; admission adult/child €5/3*) Vanilla from 40 growers is gathered together and used to make a range of products, including *rhum arrangé*. You can take a guided tour of the facility (45 minutes) and learn about the history of vanilla production. Carefully created products, like rum jelly with vanilla, are sold at the shop. The location sets La Vanilleraie apart from its competitors as it is on the historic **Domaine du Grand Hazier**, a sugar plantation since the early 20th century. It is possible to book a guided tour of the 18th-century planter's house, which is surrounded by a large garden of fruit trees and endemic species (\ *0692 685019; admission adult/child under 12 €5/free*).

18

LA PLANTATION DE VANILLE ROULOF (*470 Rue Deschanets, St-André;* \ *0692 108715;* e *plantationvanille@orange.fr; www.lavanilledelareunion.com;* ☺ *guided tours 11.00, 14.00, 15,00, 16.00 Mon–Sat; tours €4*) The Roulof family has been growing vanilla in the St-André area for over 100 years, and today the plantation is in the hands of the fourth generation of the family to grow vanilla. Guided tours of this working vanilla plantation last around 1 hour and, having marvelled at the process, you can buy the Roulof vanilla on site. Being a small, family-owned plantation, it has a lovely intimate feel. A genuine family business rather than just a tourist attraction.

LE DOMAINE DE COCO (*Chemin du Cap, Ste-Anne;* \ *0692 277519;* e *contact@ domainedecoco.com; www.domainedecoco.com;* ☺ *tours 10.30, 14.30 daily, reservation essential on weekends; tours adult/child €7/4*) Agriculture-themed guided tours of this 11ha farm explain sugar production and the cultivation of tropical fruit trees, spices and medicinal plants. The land here has been in the hands of the Bébeau family for three generations.

MAISON DU LETCHI (*353 RN2, Les Orangers, Ste-Anne;* \ *0692 606388; www. maison-letchi.re; guided tours on reservation 10.30 & 14.30 Tue–Sun; tours €6*) Lychees are symbolic of the Christmas season in Réunion, when they are eaten all over the island with great enthusiasm. You will see them for sale in markets and at roadside stalls. The owner of this lychee plantation offers guided tours on reservation.

VANILLA BOURBON (*Le Petit-Brûlé;* \ *0692 157637; guided tours 09.00 & 13.00 Mon–Sat; admission adult/child €7/4; reservation essential*) Just north of Ste-Rose, this vanilla plantation tour is interesting as much for its setting in an unspoilt forest rich in endemic trees and birds as it is for the insight it provides into vanilla production. The tours, which last around 2 hours, are usually led by dedicated owner Maryse Mounier, who created the plantation in 2006.

ESCALE BLEUE (*RN2, Le Tremblet;* \ *0262 370399;* e *contact@escale-bleue.fr; www. escale-bleue.fr;* ☺ *09.30–12.00 & 13.30–17.00 Mon–Sat; guided tours adult/child €5/3*) About 8km north of St-Philippe, this family-run business has been producing vanilla since 1986. They sell vanilla and vanilla products on site. You can drop in just to buy their produce or take a guided tour of the plantation and workshop. The guided tours are intimate and relaxed, and certainly don't have that mass tourism feel. The owner usually takes the tours himself, and they last around 30–45 minutes. Tours are conducted in French, but you can book one in English in advance.

19

Southern Réunion

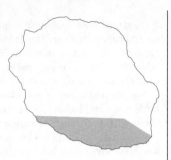

The southern part of the island stretches from the town of St-Philippe in the southeast up to Le Tampon and from there down to Etang-Salé-les-Bains in the southwest.

The bustling coastal town of St-Pierre has deservedly earned the unofficial title of 'capital of the south' and is the gateway to the *sud sauvage* (the wild south), the name given to the rugged southeast coast. This is an area which lies in the shadow of Piton-de-la-Fournaise, with a coastline of black volcanic cliffs, the remains of lava flows stopped in their tracks by the sea. By contrast, there are some good white-sand beaches further west around St-Pierre and a large, black-sand beach at Etang-Salé-les-Bains.

The southern towns have plenty of charm and character, generally featuring small, neat Creole-style homes surrounded by colourful gardens. Creole gardens characteristically serve more than just a decorative purpose, containing flowers, medicinal plants, tropical fruit and vegetables intentionally bunched together in each flowerbed. There is a flourishing cottage industry in this region, including Creole furniture, lacework, honey, pâté and cheeses.

ST-PHILIPPE AND SURROUNDS

St-Philippe is small, peaceful and few tourists spend any time here. This makes it worth staying for a night or two. The town has a backdrop of sugarcane and forested mountains and sits in the shadow of Piton-de-la-Fournaise. The residents largely make their living from vanilla, fishing and handicrafts woven from pandanus leaves. The pandanus tree, known locally as *vacoa(s)*, thrives in this part of the island. In the past its leaves were used in the construction of houses. The fruit is eaten in a variety of local dishes, as a salad, gratin or curry. In August St-Philippe hosts the **Fête de Vacoa** to celebrate the plant.

St-Philippe has the basic necessities: a few restaurants, a **pharmacy**, a **post office**, a **petrol station** and an ATM near the town hall. There is a small **supermarket** but the prices tend to be exaggerated, so locals recommend shopping in St-Joseph.

A few kilometres west of St-Philippe is **Le Baril**, where you will find a pandanus-lined coast and two adjacent swimming pools, one fresh water and one which is a corralled area of sea. The best rock-pooling area is to the east of the swimming pool, where colourful fish are often trapped in pools in the volcanic rocks. This is the place to watch rock-skippers (or mud-skippers), an amphibious species of goby. This fish has evolved large, powerful pectoral fins to enable it to escape potential predators by leaping from the sea to the safety of rocks.

The charm of St-Philippe and Le Baril is not the designated sights, of which there are few, but the lava flows and coastal and forest walks. Between St-Philippe and Le Baril is the **Réserve Naturelle de Mare Longue**. Incorporated into this forest area

is the *sentier botanique*, a path through a beautiful section of primary forest where the indigenous trees are labelled. A clearly marked Grande Randonnée hiking trail runs straight up the mountainside but you can also take the longer forest road which is easier on the legs and excellent for birdwatching. Bring a picnic and enjoy the flora, fauna and views of this lush region.

For the best views of pounding waves, craggy headlands and graceful tropical birds visit **Cap Méchant**, about 2km west of Le Baril. From here you can walk along the headland, through casuarina trees and vanilla plantations. This is also where you will find **Les Puits des Français** (the wells of the French), the southernmost of a series of mysterious holes in the lava coastline. Similar holes are at Le Baril (**Puits des Anglais**) and Le Tremblet (**Puits du Tremblet**).

GETTING THERE AND AWAY St-Philippe is easily reached by bus as it lies on the St-Pierre–St-Benoît coastal route (Line S1).

TOURIST INFORMATION There is a small **tourist office** (*41a Rue Leconte Delisle*; ✆*0262 977584;* ◷ *09.00–12.00 & 13.00–17.00 Mon–Fri, 10.00–12.00 & 13.00–17.00 Sat*) on the main coastal road.

⌂ WHERE TO STAY
Budget
⌂ **Hotel Le Baril**** (13 rooms) 62 RN2, Le Baril; ✆0262 370104. A small hotel perched on a typically wild stretch of coast. With limited accommodation in the area, this hotel gets busy so try to book well in advance. The en-suite rooms (1 with disabled facilities) are fairly simple & a little dark, but some have spectacular views of the pounding sea. At the time of writing, the hotel was partway through a much-needed renovation.

There is also a small pool & a good restaurant overlooking the sea (below). **$$**

Shoestring
⌂ **Domaine du Vacoa** (2 rooms) 12 Chemin Vacoa, St-Philippe; ✆0262 370312; e bigot. anna@live.fr; www.domaineduvacoa.fr. Simply furnished, clean rooms with AC, TV & Wi-Fi. Both have direct access to the garden, where there is a pool. Table d'hôte meals are available. **$$**

✕ WHERE TO EAT
✕ **Marmite du Pêcheur** RN2, Ravine Ango, St-Philippe; ✆0262 370101; ◷ for lunch Thu–Tue. Cuisine: Creole, French, seafood. Tucked away among houses, signed from the main road through St-Philippe. It may not look very special from the outside but this restaurant is smart & clean on the inside & has a reputation for superb seafood dishes. **$$$**
✕ **Etoile de Mer** Cap Méchant, Basse Vallée; ✆0262 370460; ◷ 11.30–22.00 daily. Cuisine: seafood, Creole, Chinese. Large, unpretentious restaurant known for its excellent seafood & traditional Creole meals cooked on a wood fire. **$$**

✕ **Hotel Le Baril** RN2, Le Baril; ✆0262 370104; ◷ for lunch & dinner daily. Cuisine: Creole, Chinese. Informal with friendly service & a sea view. **$$**
✕ **La Bicyclette Gourmande** 43 Rue Leconte Delisle; ✆0262 977863. Cuisine: Creole, French, Chinese. A cosy, relaxed restaurant near the tourist office. The menu features local specialities, such as the fruit of the pandanus (vacoas) tree, known as *pin pin.* **$$**
✕ **Le Cap Méchant** Basse-Vallée; ✆0262 370061; ◷ for lunch Tue–Sun. Cuisine: Creole, Chinese. Large & popular seafront restaurant serving good food in generous portions. Reservation recommended. **$$**

ST-JOSEPH AND SURROUNDS

The area around St-Joseph is known for its production of turmeric, an important ingredient in *cari*, and, like St-Philippe, for the weaving of pandanus fronds to

produce baskets, hats and bags. Between St-Philippe and St-Joseph is the village of **Vincendo**. There is usually a black-sand beach at La Marine de Vincendo, although its presence depends on the tide.

Further west on the RN2, before you reach St-Joseph, is the turning to **Rivière Langevin**. This is a magical spot. The drive takes you through the village of Langevin, with its colourful Creole houses facing the river. Female residents can often be seen doing their washing on the rocks, whilst the men play dominoes in little huts on the riverbank. The road is lined with picnic tables and there are several restaurants serving Creole food.

You pass a hydro-electric station, then small banana and pineapple plantations. On the left is an adorable little chapel built around a cave, with a shrine to Saint Expédit, typically painted red.

It is a picture-perfect river shrouded by trees, with water bubbling around boulders, pausing in pools and then setting off again towards the sea. You can park and walk a short distance to **Le Trou Noir**, a pool beneath a waterfall, ideal for a refreshing dip. Further along the road, after a steep and winding climb, you can get a close-up view of some more beautiful falls, **La Cascade de Grand-Galet**. The road ends in the pretty village of **Grand-Galet**, above the falls.

St-Joseph is an attractive little town astride the **Rivière des Remparts**. However, it doesn't hold much interest for tourists, other than being an occasional stopover point for people heading eastwards. The **banks**, a **post office**, numerous restaurants, a **pharmacy** and a **medical centre** are on Rue Raphael Babet. To the east of St-Joseph is **Manapany-les-Bains**, a seaside village with a protected natural swimming pool and a beach.

The pretty village of **La-Plaine-des-Gregues** lies around 11km inland from St-Joseph and is the centre of turmeric and ginger cultivation. Turmeric has been found to have a multitude of health benefits so if you would like to stock up on it, or other spices, you can do so at **Maison du Curcuma** (*14 Chemin du Rond, La-Plaine-des-Gregues*; ✆ *0262 375466; www.maisonducurcuma*; ⊕ *09.00–12.00 & 13.30–17.00 daily*). Between the Rivière des Remparts Bridge and La-Plaine-des-Gregues is **Le Piton Entonnoir**, a grassy hilltop with fantastic views down towards St-Joseph and the coast. It is easy to see why this is a popular jumping-off point for paragliders.

Inland from St-Joseph on the D33 is the village of **Grand Coude**, sheltered between vivid green mountains. Tea bushes grow here, the remnants of a time when tea production was the main activity, which is explained at the **Labyrinthe en Champ Thé** (page 331). If this doesn't sound like… well… your cup of tea, there is the **Maison du Laurina**, which tells the story of the local **Bourbon Coffee** (page 331).

TOURIST INFORMATION There is a **tourist office** at Manapany-les-Bains (*15 Allée du Four à Chaux*; ✆ *0262 373711*; ⊕ *09.00–17.00 Mon–Fri, 10.00–17.00 Sat*). You can book accommodation here or gather information on activities in the area.

WHERE TO STAY There are no hotels in St-Joseph but there are plenty of furnished flats and houses in the area, some of which are listed below.

Budget

La Plantation (4 rooms) 124 Chemin de Jean Petit, St-Joseph; ✆ 0262 456328; e contact@ la-plantation.re; www.la-plantation.re. A spacious, modern house on the hillside overlooking the coast. Beautifully decorated en-suite rooms with AC & TV. The room in the garden, known as 'La Case', has a sitting area & kitchenette. There is an attractive, infinity pool overlooking St-Joseph & the ocean, & a jacuzzi. Free Wi-Fi. A very comfortable & surprisingly affordable option, but you will need a car if staying here. **$$**

⌂ **Rougail Mangue** (5 rooms) 12 Rue Marcel Pagnol, Plateau Vincendo, St-Joseph; ✆ 0262 315509; e contact@rougailmangue.com; www. rougailmangue.com. Better than average guesthouse accommodation in a large, tropical garden north of St-Joseph, at Vincendo. There is plenty of space to relax here, with 2 communal sitting areas, a barbecue, outdoor kitchen & pool. The 4 en-suite rooms are particularly spacious & carefully decorated with modern bathrooms. Some of them have bunk beds as well as a double. There is also a cute wooden bungalow away from the main house with TV, mini fridge & kettle. Free Wi-Fi. AC & use of the jacuzzi are at additional cost, nevertheless this is good value for money. **$$**

Self-catering holiday rentals

⌂ **La Case**** (6 apts, 3 rooms) 2 Rue Jean Bart, St-Joseph; ✆ 0262 560750; e contact@

case.fr; www.case.fr. Comfortable studios & apartments with AC, TV, shared pool & sea views. The rooms are en suite & simply but nicely furnished. Room from €37 per night (2 people) RO, studio from €50 (2 people), apartment from €300 (5 people).

⌂ **La Villa du Barrage**** 21 Route de Grand-Galet, Langevin, St-Joseph; ✆ 0262 314268; e Maillot.Franck@wanadoo.fr. The owner rents out the ground floor of his home in a very pleasant, peaceful location overlooking Rivière Langevin, a 15min walk from the Cascade de Grand-Galet. It's a steep climb to the village & you'll need a car to get there. From €330 per week (4 people).

⌂ **L'Eau Forte**** 137 bis, Bd de l'Océan, Manapany-les-Bains; ✆ 0262 563284; e eau-forte@wanadoo.fr; www.eau-forte.fr. An apartment for 2 people overlooking the bay. From €300 per week (2 people).

✗ **WHERE TO EAT** St-Joseph has the usual well-stocked **supermarkets** (in this case, **Score** and **Champion**), which are just west of the town on either side of the RN2. There is also a Leader Price supermarket in the centre of town.

✱ ✗ **Le Bel Air** 39 Rue Lesquelin, Les Lianes, St-Joseph; m 0692 691247; ☉ for lunch & dinner daily, on reservation 48hrs in advance. Cuisine: Creole. A farmhouse in the hills above St-Joseph, with sea views. Meals are prepared using fresh ingredients from the farm. **$$$**

✗ **Chez Jo** 143 Bd de l'Océan, Manapany-les-Bains; ✆ 0262 314883; ☉ winter 09.00–18.00 Fri–Wed, summer 09.00–20.00 Fri–Wed. Cuisine: Creole, French, Chinese, snacks. Casual eatery with tables on a covered terrace. **$$**

✗ **Pizzeria la Gondole** 36 bis Rue Raphael Babet, St-Joseph; ✆ 0262 561612; ☉ for lunch & dinner Mon–Sat, dinner Sun. Cuisine: Italian. On the main road, just to the west of town. Cosy restaurant serving excellent pizzas & other Italian fare. Good value for money. **$$**

✗ **Chez Jim** 194 Route de la Passerelle, Langevin; ✆ 0262 565601; ☉ for lunch daily. Cuisine: Creole, snacks. Also take-away. Informal & friendly, across the road from the river. Serves hearty Creole *caris*. A good stopping off point after a visit to the waterfall. **$**

ST-PIERRE AND SURROUNDS

On the RN2 between St-Joseph and St-Pierre is the turning to **Grande Anse**. This is a stunning bay surrounded by densely wooded slopes, with a wonderful white-sand beach. Swimming, however, is only safe in the purpose-built pool. It's a perfect place for a picnic, with barbecue areas scattered amongst the palm trees. Unfortunately, this means it can be unpleasantly crowded on weekends. There is a cave in the cliffs around which clouds of Mascarene swiftlets wheel and scream excitedly. From the hillside you can see Réunion's only outlying island, **Petit Ile**, a nesting site for birds.

St-Pierre is the largest town in the south, home to some 80,000 people representing all of the island's various ethnicities. To call this town bustling is putting it mildly. St-Pierre is especially popular with Réunionnais holidaymakers, who prefer to come here while the French head for glitzy St-Gilles.

The focal point of the town is **Boulevard Hubert Delisle**, the road along the seafront. It is strewn with restaurants, ice-cream parlours and bars, as well as a

casino. Across the road from the casino is a stretch of white, sandy **beach** – nothing to write home about, but adequate nevertheless. The park in front of the beach has undergone a makeover and it is now a very pleasant place to sit, although it still attracts the odd drunk in the evenings. During winter the strong winds around St-Pierre can make the beach a no-go zone. Snorkelling in the lagoon just off the beach is very rewarding and you'll invariably see many people doing just that.

The **harbour** [322 C4], which is to the east of the beach, has also been expanded and smartened up, with a little help from the European Union. It now boasts a wide promenade, marina and brand-new shops. Nearby is the **Bassin de Radout**, a dry dock preserved since the 19th century.

The area around the seafront is gradually acquiring a European feel, with designer clothing shops creeping in, but as you climb the hill into the centre of town that fades. The town centre, with its numerous (particularly Chinese and Indian) clothing stores, boutiques, bars and restaurants, brings to mind images of urban southeast Asia or Mauritius, rather than Europe. Despite the recent 'smartening up', this remains a Réunionnais town and the people are genuinely welcoming and helpful.

As you head up Rue François de Mahy, away from the seafront, you'll pass an ornate **mosque** [322 C3]. Provided you dress respectfully, you are welcome to visit between 09.00 and midday and from 14.00 to 16.00 (material is provided to cover your legs). The **town hall** [322 D4] at the southern end of Rue Archambaud is worth a look for its colonial architecture. It was formerly a coffee warehouse owned by the French East India Company, built between 1751 and 1773.

There is a **covered market** (*marché couvert*) [322 C4] on Rue Victor le Vigoureux, selling a good range of handicrafts (mostly from Madagascar), as well as fruit, vegetables and spices. On Saturdays, a **street market** operates at the far western end of Boulevard Hubert Delisle (which is blocked off to cars), selling more of the same and is well worth a visit. Although the market now sells many touristy souvenirs, it is a great place to see locals doing their weekly shop, stocking up on fruit and vegetables, buying live chickens, and – equally important – catching up on the week's gossip. Watch out for the stall that sells delicious, freshly squeezed sugarcane juice. Try to get to the Saturday market early – it's all finished by noon. Talking of shopping, **Cazal** [322 D4] (✆ 0262 353535), at 39 Rue Désiré Barquisseau, is a very good **bookshop**.

Also at the western end of Boulevard Hubert Delisle is the **cemetery** [322 B5], where Hindu, Chinese and Christian graves lie side by side. The most-visited grave of all is that of the African sorcerer and murderer, Simicoundza Simicourba, better known as **Le Sitarane** (see box, page 282).

The seafront at the western end of town has been redeveloped in recent years and now has a children's playground, funfair and snack bars. Out on the water you are likely to see kitesurfers, particularly on one of St-Pierre's windy days. The Centre Commercial du Grand Large has a large **supermarket**, as well as other smaller shops.

About 10km north of St-Pierre on the RN3 is **Le Tampon**. Many of those who work on the south coast choose to live in or around Le Tampon, which enjoys a cooler climate. The town itself is of little interest, except that it is *en route* to La Plaine-des-Cafres, and therefore the volcano. Le Tampon is best known for the flower festival (Florilège) held there annually in October.

GETTING THERE AND AWAY The main **bus station** [322 C4] is at 1 Rue du Presbytère (✆ 0262 356728). There are regular buses between St-Denis and St-Pierre (Lines O1, O2 and the express ZO), and between St-Benoît and St-Pierre via the coast (Line S1) and via Les Plaines (Line S2). There are also buses to Entre-Deux (Line S5). To reach Cilaos you need to get a bus to St-Louis and change.

The Altérneo bus line (✆ *0800 355354*) operates within St-Pierre and to the outlying villages, such as **Ravine des Cabris**, **Grand Bois** and **St-Louis**. The station for these buses is next to the covered market, on Rue François Isautier. **Taxis** are found at both bus stations.

On the coast 7km west of St-Pierre is **Pierrefonds Airport**, with flights to/from neighbouring Indian Ocean islands. (For details, see page 266.)

TOURIST INFORMATION The **tourist office** [322 D3] (*Capitainerie du Port de Plaisance Lislet Geoffroy, Place Napoléon Hoareau;* ✆ *0820 203220; www.sud.reunion.*

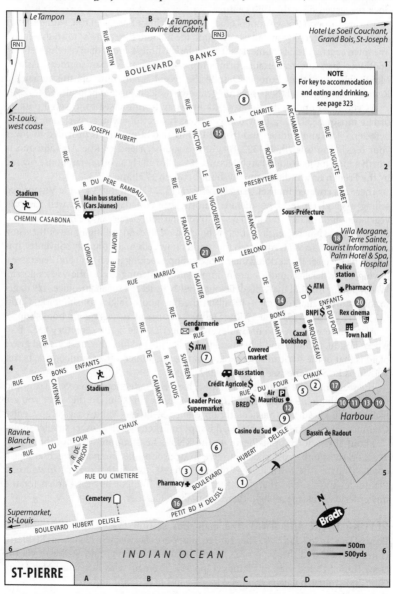

fr; ⏰ 08.00–18.00 Mon–Sat, 08.00–12.00 Sun) is near the marina. This is one of the island's larger tourist offices and the staff are happy to assist with the booking of accommodation and local guided tours. There is no guarantee that there will be English-speaking staff, but several of them can 'get by' in English.

🏠 WHERE TO STAY
Upmarket

🏠 **Palm Hotel & Spa***** [322 D3]
(48 rooms, 8 suites, 3 cabins) Rue des Mascarins, Grande Anse; 📞0262 563030; e hotel@palm.re; www.palm.re. The only 5-star option in the south. The hotel opened in 2007, in a quiet location perched on the cliffs above Grande Anse. The beach at Grande Anse can be reached via a forest path; it takes about 5mins from the hotel & there is a shuttle bus to bring you back up. The rooms are in buildings dotted around a 3.5ha tropical garden. Rooms are finished to a high standard (comparable with those seen in Mauritius), with en suite, AC, TV, phone, safe, minibar & Wi-Fi. The 3 cabins are designed for couples & are built on stilts on the hillside overlooking the ocean. There are 3 good restaurants, 2 pools & a fitness centre. The hotel's trump card is an elegant spa. The beach at Grande Anse is not suitable for swimming & there are no

shops or restaurants nearby – for these you can head into St-Pierre which is about 7mins away by car. The hotel also has regular entertainment & can organise excursions. **$$$$**

🏠 **Villa Delisle**** [322 C5] (41 rooms)
42 Bd Hubert Delisle; 📞0262 707708; e info@hotel-villadelisle.com; www.hotel-villadelisle.com. A boutique hotel located right in the centre of town, adjacent to the casino & across the road from the seafront & beach. The rooms are extravagantly decorated with feature wallpaper above the bed & stylish bathrooms. The standard rooms are a bit on the small side but there is a choice of stylish restaurants & a spa. Very central, good-quality accommodation. **$$$$**

Mid range

✳ 🏠 **Alizé Plage** [322 C5] (15 rooms)
17 bis Bd Hubert Delisle; 📞0262 352221; e alizeplage@ilereunion.com; www.hotel-restaurant-alize-plage.re. The best location in town, right on the beach. Clever use has been made of little space to create simple, comfortable rooms. Each is equipped with en-suite facilities, AC, TV, phone & Wi-Fi. Facilities include a good restaurant (page 326), a bar with regular live music & some free watersports, such as kayaks & pedaloes. The central location, live music & lively restaurant mean this is not a relaxing retreat but it is a convenient place to lay your head after enjoying the town's famous nightlife. **$$$**

🏠 **Domaine des Pierres*** (41 rooms)
60, CD26, Route de l'Entre-Deux; 📞0262 554385; e domainedespierres@wanadoo.fr; www.domainedespierres.com. Near Pierrefonds Airport, within easy reach of the hustle & bustle of St-Pierre, if you have a car. The en-suite rooms are in bungalows scattered in a garden. They are tastefully decorated, clean & have AC, TV, phone, safe, Wi-Fi & terrace. Rooms equipped for the disabled are available. Facilities include a restaurant, bar & pool. **$$$**

🏠 **La Plantation** (5 rooms) 79 Rue Amiral Lacaze, Terre Sainte; 📞0262 456328; e contact@

la-plantation.re; www.la-plantation.re. A fully renovated guesthouse in a great location in Terre Sainte, across the street from a small beach but only a 15min walk to the centre of St-Pierre. The 5 rooms have been carefully decorated with a shabby chic seaside theme. They are all en suite & have AC. There is an inviting pool within the walled garden. Breakfast is served on the balcony overlooking the lagoon. Double from €115 BB. **$$$**

⌂ **Le Victoria***** (30 rooms) 8–10 Allée des Lataniers, Grand-Bois; 📞 0262 509567; e reservation@levictoria.re; www.levictoria. re. This small hotel, around a 5min drive from St-Pierre, has undergone numerous changes of management. It has always had potential, being located on the seafront (no beach here, just rugged black rock), but has finally had the renovation it needed. The rooms are in bungalows around a small pool, & are equipped with AC, TV, phone & free Wi-Fi. **$$$**

⌂ **Lindsey Hotel***** [322 C4] (17 rooms) 21b Rue François Isautier; 📞 0262 246011; e lindseyhotel@yahoo.fr; www.lindsey-hotel-reunion.fr. A modern 3-storey wooden, blue building houses the 17 comfortable en-suite rooms with AC, TV, phone & Wi-Fi. There is a rather stark pool area (no trees for shade) & a fitness room. **$$$**

⌂ **Villa Belle** [322 C1] (6 rooms) 45 Rue Rodier; m 0692 658999; e villabelle@wanadoo. fr; www.villabelle.e-monsite.com. A guesthouse of a high standard in a renovated Creole house towards the top of town. The Creole rooms in the main house are decorated with antiques & have a sophisticated feel. They are spacious & have AC, TV & small kitchenette. The 2 colonial rooms are gorgeous, built over a pool stocked with koi carp. Rooms are huge & have luxurious touches like an outdoor shower & private terrace. The spa suite is even bigger at 90m² & has its own *hammam* & jacuzzi. General facilities include a pool, plus a *hammam* & jacuzzi (payable). The restaurant serves breakfast & dinner on reservation. Meals are taken on the elegant veranda overlooking the garden. Considering it is in a busy part of town, this guesthouse is very peaceful. If you walk down to the seafront, bear in mind it is a steep walk back up the hill, which takes around 20min. Importantly, there is secure parking. Gay-friendly. **$$$**

⌂ **Villa Morgane** [322 D3] (9 rooms) 334 Rue Amiral Lacaze, Terre Sainte; 📞 0262

258277; www.hotel-villamorgane-reunion.com. Upmarket guesthouse accommodation in a large house in the residential area of Terre Sainte, a 15min walk from St-Pierre & a 5min walk from a small beach. The rooms are each lavishly decorated with a different theme, some Asian, some Italian. Suite Alexandra is my favourite, not just for the name but because it's a little more understated than those with floor-to-ceiling frescoes. There is a pretty garden, pool & jacuzzi but no secure parking. **$$$**

Budget

⌂ **Hotel Cap Sud**** [322 B5] (16 rooms) 6 Rue Caumont; 📞 0262 257564; e hotel-capsud@ orange.fr; www.hotel-capsud-reunion.com. About 300m from the beach & town centre in a plain 3-storey building. En-suite rooms with AC, TV & phone. They're spartan but clean. A modern 2-bedroom self-catering apartment is also available. **$$**

⌂ **Hotel Le Soeil Couchant**** [322 D1] (8 rooms) 2 Chemin de l'Araucaria, Mont Vert les Bas; 📞 0262 311010; e hotel.hda@orange.fr; www.hotelhda.com. A small hotel in an inland village around 20mins from St-Pierre, with views to the coast. Simple en-suite rooms with TV, phone, Wi-Fi, some have balcony. There is a pleasant pool area. **$$**

⌂ **Le Jardin Mandaline** [322 C5] (4 rooms) 1 Rue Ibrahim Vally; 📞 0692 688610; www.le-jardin-mandaline.re. A great guesthouse option 50m from the seafront & close to all the main attractions, like the covered market & nightlife. The rooms are nicely decorated, feel modern & have AC & TV. There is a very good restaurant here (page 325) & rooms can be booked on HB. **$$**

⌂ **Le Suffren** [322 C5] (17 studios) 14 Rue Suffren; 📞 0692 855902; e lesuffren@orange.fr; www.hotelsuffren.com. A few mins' walk from the beach & main attractions. Large but rather soulless studios equipped with AC, TV & phone; most have a minibar & all but 1 have a balcony. **$$**

Shoestring

✳ ⌂ **Chez Papa Daya** [322 D4] (17 rooms) 27 Rue du Four à Chaux; 📞 0262 256487; e chez.papa. daya@orange.fr; www.chezpapadaya.com. An old favourite in an excellent central location, not far from the beach. Cheerful, spotless rooms, with AC & fridge, some with en-suite facilities.

All rooms have AC, mini fridge & Wi-Fi. There's a well-equipped shared kitchen, as well as a TV lounge & a small garden. Security is good & there are 5 parking spots (not secure) for residents. Popular choice for those on a budget & the best of its kind in town. En-suite dbl from €40. **$**

⌂ **Le Nathania** [322 D4] (14 rooms) 12 Rue François de Mahy; ☎ 0262 250457; e info@ hotelnathania.fr; www.hotelnathania.com. Centrally located about 150m from the seafront & the main bar & restaurant strip. Rooms are rather plain & have a TV & fan, some have en-suite facilities & most have AC. Facilities include parking & use of a shared kitchen & laundry. Wi-Fi is available. A good location for those on a budget. **$**

Self-catering holiday rentals

⌂ **Case Paradis**** 194 bis Impasse Poudroux, Route Ligne Paradis, St-Pierre; ☎ 0262 254928; e contact@caseparadis.com; www.caseparadis.com. A studio & 2 apartments for up to 6 people, a 10min drive from St-Pierre. There is a pleasant garden, parking & Wi-Fi. From €196 per week (2 people).

⌂ **Oasis Terre Rouge****** 41 Chemin Mézino, Terre Rouge; ☎ 0692 312880; e contact@ oasisdeterrerouge.com; www.oasisdeterrerouge. com. Fully furnished accommodation with pool, to the east of St-Pierre. There are 1-bedroom apartments & 3-bedroom villas with AC & everything you need for a self-catering stay. There is a pleasant garden, barbecue & secure parking. From €1,185 per week (6 people).

✗ **WHERE TO EAT** There is a well-stocked **Score Jumbo hypermarket** on the way out of town, at the Centre Commercial du Grand Large, at the far western end of Boulevard Hubert Delisle. There are smaller supermarkets in the town centre. St-Pierre is packed with restaurants to suit all budgets. Just opposite the main beach, on the corner of Boulevard Hubert Delisle and Rue Victor le Vigoureux is a collection of *camions bars* (snack bars). They serve a great range of inexpensive, tasty food, such as *samoussas*, filled baguettes and *bombons piments*.

I suppose I should also add that just at the entrance to St-Pierre from St-Louis is a branch of McDonald's (they really are everywhere, aren't they?).

Here is a selection of restaurants including a cross-section of culinary styles:

✗ **La Baie des Anges** 28 Av François Mitterand, Terre Sainte; m 0692 397965; ⊕ for lunch & dinner Mon–Sat, closed Thu dinner & Sat lunch. Cuisine: French, seafood. In a charming Creole house, nicely decorated inside. On the menu are traditional French dishes & plenty of seafood. Local ingredients are used wherever possible, although the beef comes from France. **$$$$**

✗ **La Pierre de Lune** 60, CD26, Route de l'Entre-Deux; ☎ 0262 554385; www.domainedespierres. com; ⊕ for lunch & dinner daily, closed Mon lunch. The restaurant at the Domaine des Pierres hotel is of a good standard. Meals are taken either inside or on a terrace overlooking the garden. **$$$$**

✳ ✗ **Le Flagrant Délice** [322 C2] 115 Rue François de Mahy; ☎ 0692 872803; ⊕ for lunch Tue–Fri, dinner Tue–Sat. Cuisine: French. A smart restaurant in a Creole house at the top of town, where meals are taken around a pool. The menu is creative & dishes are beautifully presented. **$$$$**

✗ **Le Jardin Réunionnais** [322 B5] 9 Petit Bd Hubert Delisle; ☎ 0262 911528; ⊕ for lunch & dinner Tue–Sun. Cuisine: French, Creole. A neat little place at the eastern end of Petit Bd Hubert Delisle. Dining is either in the walled garden or inside in the cosy, colourful restaurant. There is also a trendy little bar. The dishes are of high quality & very professionally presented. **$$$$**

✗ **Le Saint Hilaire** [322 C5] 1 Rue Ibrahim Vally; tel: 0692 688610; ⊕ for dinner Tue–Sat. Cuisine: French, European. Small & intimate restaurant at Le Jardin Mandaline guesthouse. It is within a pleasant tropical garden, not far from the seafront. Serves sophisticated dishes. **$$$$**

✗ **Les Cinq Sens** [322 D3] 32 Rue Auguste Babet; ☎ 0262 108984; ⊕ for lunch & dinner Mon–Sat. Cuisine: French. Fine French food with a romantic atmosphere to match. **$$$$**

✗ **Les 3 Brasseurs** Chemin de la Zone (Cité Canabady); ☎ 0262 963060; www.les3brasseurs.re; ⊕ 08.30–late daily. Cuisine: French, German. Out of town, in an industrial estate. One for beer lovers – a micro-brewery, beer retailer & restaurant. Has that chain-restaurant feel. Regular evening entertainment. Free Wi-Fi. **$$$$**

✗ **Alizé Plage** [322 C5] 17 bis Bd Hubert Delisle; 0262 352221; ⊕ for lunch & dinner 10.00– 22.00 daily. Cuisine: French, Creole, seafood. St-Pierre's best location – on the seafront. Good food overlooking the beach. The bar has regular live music & is a great place to relax & to people-watch. $$$

✗ **Belo Horizonte** [322 D4] 10 Rue François de Mahy; 0262 223195; ⊕ for lunch Mon–Sat, for dinner Thu–Sat. Cuisine: European, Creole. Unpretentious restaurant with a pleasant courtyard area. A broad menu, including pizza, seafood, paella & even kangaroo. $$$

✗ **DCP** [322 D4] 38 Bd Hubert Delisle; 0262 322171; ⊕ for lunch & dinner daily. Cuisine: French, seafood. Comfortable restaurant with contemporary décor. Serves fresh fish straight from local boats. $$$

✗ **Le Cabanon** [322 D4] 28 Bd Hubert Delisle; 0262 257146; ⊕ for lunch & dinner Tue–Sun. Cuisine: Italian, French, grills. This one has been around for many years. It is fairly large & serves simple fare like pizza, salads & burgers. $$$

✗ **Le Cap Méchant d'Abord** Bd Hubert Delisle; 0262 917199; ⊕ for lunch & dinner Tue–Sat, for lunch Sun. Cuisine: Creole, Chinese. Popular, large, buffet restaurant at the far eastern (Terre Sainte) end of Bd Hubert Delisle. One of very few restaurants on the seafront side of the road, overlooking the harbour. Excellent *caris*, especially prawn (*camarons*), served with the traditional accompaniments. Reservation recommended, especially on weekends. $$$

✗ **Le Castel Glacier** [322 C3] 38 Rue François de Mahy; 0262 229656; ⊕ 11.00–18.00 Mon/ Tue, 11.00–23.00 Wed/Thu, 14.00–23.00 Fri/Sat,

14.00–23.00 Sun. Cuisine: ice cream, light meals. Offers a wide range of ice cream, salads & crêpes. Free Wi-Fi. Modern & comfortable. $$$

✗ **Le Marin Bleu** 45 Rue Amirale Lacaze, Terre Sainte; 0262 356165; ⊕ for lunch & dinner Mon–Sat. Cuisine: Creole, French, seafood. Quiet location opposite the seafront in Terre Sainte. Well known for its seafood. $$$

✗ **Le Moana** [322 D4] 25 Bd Hubert Delisle; 0262 327338; ⊕ for lunch & dinner daily, but occasionally closes on a Sun for no obvious reason. Cuisine: French, Creole, Italian. Pleasant restaurant with an airy, tropical feel. Menu offers plenty of choice. $$$

✗ **O Baya** [322 D3] 7 Rue Auguste Babet; 0262 596694; ⊕ 12.00–22.30 Tue–Sat. Cuisine: French, Creole. Has a trendy décor with comfy chairs & a well-stocked bar. Traditional French dishes, seafood & salads take centre stage. $$$

✗ **Utopia** [322 C3] 68 Rue M et A Leblond; 0262 351583; ⊕ for lunch & dinner Mon–Sat. Cuisine: European. In an old, atmospheric Creole house, with tables inside & in the garden. Upmarket food, a creative menu & vast portions. $$$

✗ **La Jonque** [322 C4] 2 Rue François de Mahy; 0262 255778; ⊕ for lunch daily, for dinner Wed–Mon. Cuisine: Chinese. Remains popular, although the apparent lack of cleanliness is off-putting. $$

✗ **L'Eté Indien** [322 D4] 46 Bd Hubert Delisle; 0262 255752; ⊕ 11.30–22.00 Wed–Mon. Cuisine: European, ice cream, snacks. This one has been around for at least 15 years & is still as popular as ever. Simple dishes, which aren't outstanding. $$

NIGHTLIFE From my point of view, St-Pierre's nightlife is by far the best on the island. It has an abundance of bars and nightclubs open until the early hours of the morning, but perhaps the best thing about going out in St-Pierre is that it retains its Réunionnais feel and has not been transformed into a mini St-Tropez or Ibiza, as is the case in St-Gilles-les-Bains and parts of St-Denis.

There is a string of bars along Boulevard Hubert Delisle, most of which have live music several times a week.

Alizé Plage (0262 352221; ⊕ 18.00–02.00 daily), on the main beach, has a relaxed open-air bar with regular live bands. **Five** (8 Rue Francois de Mahy; 0692 970222; www.five.re) opposite the seafront is a bar, restaurant and nightclub and draws a very trendy crowd. It targets a slightly older crowd than some and plays plenty of cheesy 1980s music. **The Factory** (40 Bd Hubert Delisle; 0262 593178) is a decent restaurant but also a popular bar. **Long Board Café** (18 Petit Bd Hubert Delisle; 0262 391799) is in an adorable Creole house on the seafront and has

regular live music, theme nights and karaoke. Nightclubs don't really get going until after about 23.30 and are open until the early hours, usually Friday and Saturday and on the eve of public holidays. Some open from Wednesday to Saturday. Expect to pay in the region of €12 for entry, which usually includes one drink. The favourite club of the moment is **Le Duplex** (✆ *0262 389674*) on Boulevard Hubert Delisle. It plays a good mix of European chart music and local *séga*, *maloya* and *zouk*. From the first-floor balcony there is a good view of the harbour. Cherwaine's, a local favourite, was replaced by **Paradize Club** in 2015 (*6 Rue Auguste Babet*).

Also out of the town centre are **Le Chapiteau** (✆ *0262 310081*) at Montvert-les-Bas and **Apollo Night** (✆ *0262 495891;* ⊕ *Sat night & Sun afternoon*) in Ravine des Cabris. The very popular **Casino du Sud** is at 47 Boulevard Hubert Delisle (✆ *0262 252696;* ⊕ *until 02.00 Sun–Thu, until 03.00 Fri/Sat; slot machines* ⊕ *from 10.00 daily; tables* ⊕ *from 21.15 Mon–Sat, from 16.00 Sun*), and has a very modern bar.

For **cinemas** in St-Pierre, see page 330.

OTHER PRACTICALITIES
Money and banking There are plenty of banks in town, including **Banque Nationale de Paris** [322 D3] on Rue des Bons Enfants. **Crédit Agricole** and **BRED** are both on the corner of Rues du Four à Chaux and Victor le Vigoureux. They all have ATMs. There is also an ATM conveniently located outside the casino.

Medical Pharmacies are dotted around town, and include a particularly well-stocked and helpful one at the far western end of Boulevard Hubert Delisle, near the cemetery.

Communications The main **post office** [322 D4] is on Rue des Bons Enfants. There are several payphones on Boulevard Hubert Delisle, including two near the beach, outside the Alizé Plage.

Several of the cafés in St-Pierre have Wi-Fi access. **Cyber One Café** (*44 Rue des Indes;* ✆ *0262 549744*) is an internet café.

ST-LOUIS TO L'ETANG-SALE

St-Louis is essentially a residential and industrial town. Despite all the new buildings there, it has retained much of its Creole character and it is one of the few places where you may see bullock carts used, particularly during the sugarcane harvest.

The **Chapelle du Rosaire** here was built in 1732 by Barbe Payet and is the oldest religious building on the island. The chapel is signed from the south of the town and reached via Rue de la Chapelle.

St-Louis is the gateway to the **Cirque de Cilaos**, with buses leaving from the station at the southern end of town. Inland from St-Louis, **Entre-Deux** ('between two') is so named because it lies between two rivers, which join and become Rivière Ste-Etienne. It is a pretty village and is one of the best places to see colourful Creole houses and gardens. There is some good hiking here, including up **Le Dimitile** (1,837m) for views over the Cirque de Cilaos (pages 350–6). Tours by 4x4 also climb Le Dimitile.

About an hour's drive inland from St-Louis, nestled in alpine scenery, is the village of **Les Makes**. It stands at 1,200m and is home to the Indian Ocean's only **Observatory** (page 332). Around 10km beyond Les Makes is **La Fenêtre** (The Window), a spectacular viewpoint over the Cirque de Cilaos and a lovely spot for a picnic.

St-Louis is surrounded by fields of sugarcane. The **Gol Sugar Refinery (Sucrerie du Gol)**, which can be seen from the main road to Etang-Salé, was one of the

19

island's first, built in 1816. It is still operational and guided tours are available during harvest season (see page 332).

Opposite the sugar refinery is one of the island's few identified slave cemeteries, **Le Cimetière du Père Lafosse**. Père Lafosse was a priest, an abolitionist and Mayor of St-Louis. He is buried in the cemetery, along with some of the island's earliest slaves. His tomb has become a place of pilgrimage, particularly on 20 December, the anniversary of the abolition of slavery.

L'Etang-Salé is the name given to the area encompassing the coastal village of **L'Etang-Salé-les-Bains** and, slightly inland, **L'Etang-Salé-les-Hauts**. The two are separated by the large Etang-Salé Forest.

Etang-Salé-les-Bains is largely a residential area, branching outwards from the main street. It has all the essentials: restaurants, shops, a **post office** and **ATM** facilities. The vast 5km, black-sand beach is popular with locals and tourists alike, although it is noticeably quieter than the beaches around St-Gilles-les-Bains. There are designated swimming areas but the waves can be pretty powerful.

TOURIST INFORMATION The **tourist office** in Entre-Deux (*13 Rue Fortuné Hoareau;* \ *0262 396980; www.ot-entredeux.com;* ⊕ *08.00–12.00 & 13.30–17.00 Mon–Sat*) organises guided tours of the village and can provide information on hiking in the area.

The **tourist office** in L'Etang-Salé-les-Bains (\ *0820 203220;* e *accueil. oteetangsale@gmail.com; www.sud.reunion.fr;* ⊕ *09.00–12.00 & 13.00–16.30 Mon–Thu, Sat*) is in a former railway station at 74 Rue Octave Bénard, the main road through town. They have plenty of literature, including lists of guesthouses and houses to let. Handicrafts are on sale and the staff are helpful.

 WHERE TO STAY

Mid range

🏠 **Floralys*** (52 rooms) 2 Av de l'Océan, L'Etang-Salé-les-Bains; \0262 917979; e reservation@floralys.re; www.floralys.re. In the centre of the village, across the road from the beach. The rooms are in bungalows dotted around a pleasant garden. Some are suitable for families & a few have a kitchenette. Rooms are unremarkable, equipped with AC, TV, phone, minibar & terrace. It has a large pool, 2 tennis courts, a restaurant & bar. Family fun is the aim here, & there is a water fun-park on site (page 330). **$$$**

🏠 **Le Dimitile**** (18 rooms) 30 Rue Bras Long, Entre-Deux; \0262 392000; e direction@ dimitile.eu; www.dimitile.eu. This delightful little hotel is built around a 17th-century Creole house (*case*). It is set in pretty, tropical gardens & has an impressive mountain backdrop. The rooms around a pleasant pool are large, well maintained & equipped with en suite, fan, TV, phone, safe & fridge. There is a restaurant & tennis court. **$$$**

Budget

🏠 **Boabab et Palmiers** (5 bungalows) 36 Chemin du Cap, Etang-Salé; \0692 133679; e infos@baobabetpalmiers.com; www. baobabetpalmiers.com. Inland but only a few mins from the beach by car. 5 bungalows for 2 people, 1 for 4 people. Comfortable, nicely decorated self-catering accommodation in wood cabins in a garden with pool. From €400 per week (2 people). **$$**

Self-catering holiday rentals

🏠 **Chez Florelle*** & *** 26 Rue Hubert Delisle; \0262 265194; e rivireflorelle@wanadoo. fr; http://perso.wanadoo.fr/casepei. A 2-bedroom villa & a 2-bedroom apartment. Villa from €320 per week, apartment from €500 per week (5 people).

🏠 **Le Fangourin** 7 Chemin Petit Bon Dieu, La Rivière St-Louis; \0262 391572; e elise.baret@ wanadoo.fr; www.lefangourin.com. 2 self-catering apartments in a house, which sleep 2 to 6 people. From €244 per week (2 people).

🏠 **Zot case en natte*** 5 Impasse Alamandas, Etang Salé; \0262 265773; e waro-lauret@wanadoo.fr. A typical wooden Creole house

with 2 bedrooms, sitting room, dining room & kitchen. From €441 per week (4 people).

Camping

⋏ Camping Entre 2 Songes (6 pitches, dormitory) 9 Chemin Macaire, Entre-Deux; ☎0692 825775. Good facilities for a small campsite, including 2 communal kitchens & bathrooms. As well as the tent pitches, there are 6 beds in a house on site. Free Wi-Fi. **$**

⋏ Camping Municipal Rue Guy Hoarau, L'Etang-Salé-les-Bains; ☎0262 917586. A large campsite near the beach with amenities blocks & barbecue areas. **$**

✖ WHERE TO EAT

✖ Délices et Douceur 15 Av de Bretagne, L'Etang-Salé-les-Bains; ☎0692 318831; ⊕ 09.30–19.00 daily. Cuisine: French, seafood, international. A cosy, informal eatery serving simple, good-quality food & delicious ice cream. **$$$**

✖ La Langue d'Oc 137 bis Av Raymond Barre, L'Etang-Salé-les-Bains; ☎0692 172315; ⊕ for lunch Mon–Fri, dinner Thu–Sat. Cuisine: French. A little inland, towards L'Etang-Salé-les-Hauts. This restaurant produces excellent dishes, which are carefully presented. The ingredients are clearly fresh. Reasonable value for money. **$$$**

✖ L'Arbre à Palabres 29 Rue Césaire, Entre-Deux; ☎0262 444723; ⊕ for lunch Thu–Sun, for dinner Tue, Fri, Sat. Cuisine: Creole, African, Chinese. In an adorable Creole building. Consistently good food in characterful surroundings with an African feel. **$$$**

✖ Le Bambou 56 Rue Octave Bénard, L'Etang-Salé-les-Bains; ☎0262 917028; ⊕ for lunch & dinner Thu–Tue. Cuisine: Italian, seafood. A popular restaurant with a menu offering plenty of choice. Family friendly. Decent pizzas. **$$$**

✖ Le Play Off Golf Club de Bourbon, 140 Les Sables, L'Etang-Salé-les-Bains; ☎0262 264349; ⊕ for lunch Tue–Sun. Cuisine: Creole, European. Beautiful setting in stunning gardens, near the pool. Friendly service. **$$$**

✳ ✖ Nomeolvides 20 Rue de la Poudrière, St-Louis; ☎0262 160959; www.nomeolvides.fr; ⊕ for lunch & dinner Tue–Sat. Cuisine: French. A secret worth sharing. This place is tucked away in a garden in a side street. It is super trendy, with comfy outdoor chairs & extensive cocktail & wine menus. The dishes are innovative, modern twists on French classics. **$$$**

✖ La Carangue 1 Rue Roger Payet, L'Etang-Salé-les-Bains; ☎0262 917087; ⊕ for lunch Fri–Wed, for dinner Fri–Tue. Cuisine: Italian, Chinese. Informal, small restaurant opposite the Floralys Caro Beach Hotel. Unpretentious food. **$$**

✖ Luna Rossa Av de l'Océan, L'Etang-Salé-les-Bains; ☎0262 265554; ⊕ for lunch & dinner daily. Cuisine: Italian. Mostly outdoor plastic seating, with an informal, 'snack bar' atmosphere. **$$**

WHAT TO DO IN SOUTHERN REUNION

HIKING Experienced, fit hikers may want to tackle the route from St-Joseph to Piton-de-la-Fournaise. It'll take two days, camping overnight or staying at the *gîte* in Roche Plate. From there, another day's hiking (grading: difficult) eastwards will have you at the Plaine des Sables, then the volcano. Along the Rivière des Remparts route you can still see some of the original wilderness (lowland forests, secluded natural pools, heathland) which once dominated southeast Réunion.

From Entre-Deux you can walk to the top of Le Dimitile (grading: difficult). It is an arduous climb and you will need a full day, or you can stay overnight at one of the *gîtes* near the summit.

GOLF Golf Club de Bourbon (*140 Les Sables, L'Etang-Salé;* ☎ *0262 263339;* e *contact@golf-bourbon.com; www.golf-bourbon.com*) is situated between St-Louis and L'Etang-Salé-les-Bains, easily reached from the RN1 using the Les Sables exit. Arguably the island's best golf course. A well-maintained 18-hole course with fantastic tropical vegetation. The club covers 75ha and there is an attractive clubhouse, swimming pool and restaurant. For more information, see page 288.

HORSERIDING There are equestrian centres in Petit-Ile, Les Makes, and L'Etang-Salé. For more information, see page 287.

ENTERTAINMENT
Cinema
◼ **Rex** Rue Auguste Babet in St-Pierre; ☎ 0262 250101. Fairly smart cinema, showing international films dubbed in French & occasionally shows foreign-language films (Spanish, Italian, etc). ◼ **Cinéma Royal** 8 Rue Amiral Lacaze, St-Joseph; ☎ 0262 565559.

Theatre
As well as the 2 listed here, Etang Salé has a theatre on Place Fourcade (☎ 0262 265097; www.theatredessables.re).

🎭 **Théâtre Luc Donat** 20 Rue Victor le Vigoureux, Le Tampon; ☎ 0262 272436; e direction@theatrelucdonat.re; www.theatrelucdonat.re. Regular plays, dance shows, jazz concerts & classical music recitals. During the first 2 weeks of June it hosts an annual comedy festival. 🎭 **Sham's Theatre** ☎ 0692 704704. In the old sugar factory at Pierrefonds. Also puts on productions.

THEME PARK AkOatys at the Floralys Hotel in Etang-Salé-les-Bains (2 *Av de l'Océan;* ☎ *0262 914914;* e *contact@akoatys.com; www.akoatys.com;* ⊕ *10.00–18.00 daily; admission €15 for those under 1.4m tall, €20 for others*) has a series of waterslides and a café.

SHOPPING The **covered market** (⊕ *09.00–17.00 daily*) is on Rue Victor le Vigoureux in St-Pierre and is ideal for souvenir shopping, as is St-Pierre's busy Saturday-morning **street market** (page 321). The markets in St-Louis are open daily.

CAHEB (*83 Rue Kervéguen, Le Tampon;* ☎ *0262 270227;* e *caheb@geranium-bourbon.com; www.geranium-bourbon.com*) sells essential oils and custom-made perfumes created from local geranium and vetyver.

The village of La Rivière St-Louis is known for its **woodworking** artisans. Their creations can be viewed and purchased at St-Louis Artisanat Bois (*1 RN5 Bois de Nèfles Coco, La Rivière St-Louis;* ☎ *0262 261375*).

You can buy turmeric, ginger and other spices at **Maison du Curcuma** (*14 Chemin du Rond, La-Plaine-des-Gregues;* ☎ *0262 375466; www.maisonducurcuma;* ⊕ *09.00–12.00 & 13.30–17.00 daily*), which also has some displays on how they are cultivated in this area.

WHAT TO SEE IN SOUTHERN REUNION

ECO-MUSEE AU BON ROI LOUIS (*1 Rue de la Marine, St-Philippe;* ☎ *0262 371298;* ⊕ *09.00–12.00 & 14.00–16.30 Mon–Sat; admission adult/child €5/2; visits last 1½hrs*) Guided visits to a Creole house built around 1850, containing an assortment of antique tools, weapons, furniture, coins, documents and agricultural equipment.

LE JARDIN DES PARFUMS ET DES EPICES (*7 Chemin Forestier, Mare Longue, St-Philippe;* ☎ *0262 370636;* m *0692 660901;* e *fontaine.patrick.e@orange.fr; www.jardin-parfums-epices.com; admission €5.50, tours €6.10; tours daily at 10.30 & 14.30, reservation recommended*) A private garden between Le Baril and St-Philippe, which is more like a chunk of forest, where 1,500 endemic and exotic species grow side by side. You can visit independently, or guided tours (about 90 minutes) explain the origin and use of the plants, be it medicinal, culinary or furniture making. At present tours are offered in French only. There is a shop selling

products derived from the plants here, such as spices, jams and soaps. Mosquito repellent is advisable.

LE JARDIN D'ORCHIDEES (*16 Rue Léon de Heaulme, St-Joseph;* ☎ *0692 077495; www.jardin-orchidees.com;* ⊕ *09.00–12.00 & 14.00–17.00 Wed–Sat; admission adult/child under 15 €5/free*) Also known as Le Jardin de Vandas, this garden is made for orchid lovers and displays thousands of colourful varieties.

LABYRINTHE EN CHAMP THÉ (*Rue Emile Mussard, Grand Coude;* ☎ *0262 546140;* e *info@enchampthe.com; www.enchampthe.com;* ⊕ *09.00–12.00 & 13.00–16.00 daily; guided tours 10.00 & 14.00 on reservation; admission €5.50, tours €8*) Inland from St-Joseph on the D33 is the pretty village of Grand Coude with its stunning mountainous backdrop. Until the 1970s tea was grown here in abundance but the industry was not viable and the plants were abandoned. They now have new life in them, thanks to a couple of passionate tea lovers. As well as the usual agro-tour describing how tea, geranium oil and other local products are created, there is a large maze for visitors to tackle. Locally grown tea and essential oils are sold.

LA MAISON DU LAURINA (*15 Chemin de la Croizure, Grand Coude;* ☎ *0262 563948;* e *lamaisondulaurina@gmail.com; www.lamaisondulaurina.fr; guided tours on reservation only on weekends; tours €11*) Laurina is the scientific name of the local Bourbon Pointu variety of coffee, a dwarf cultivar with a low caffeine content. You can visit the coffee plants, have a picnic and, of course, taste the coffee.

LA MAISON DE L'ABEILLE (*68 Chemin Laguerre, Petit-Ile; tel; 0262 569503;* ⊕ *09.30–12.00 & 13.30–17.00 Wed–Sat, 09.30–12.00 Sun; guided tour on reservation adult/child €3/2.50*) An adorable, little beekeeping agro-museum, which offers guided tours explaining the ins and outs of beekeeping and honey production. Réunion produces excellent honey, thanks to the clean air and abundance of tropical plants. Speciality honeys, such as lychee, are on sale in the shop here.

DOMAINE DU CAFE GRILLE (*10 Allée des Cèdres, St-Pierre;* ☎ *0262 241540; www.domaine-cafe-grille-st-pierre.com;* ⊕ *09.30–17.00 Tue–Sun; guided tours 10.30 & 14.30 Tue–Sat, 10.30 & 15.00 Sun*) This is a relatively new attraction and a great deal of care has been put into getting it just right. It provides an excellent way to learn about the plant species, both exotic and native, that have created Réunion's landscape as you see it today. The 4ha garden is crammed with tropical plants, divided into various zones. Guided tours explain the many species, including their uses in cooking, medicine and construction. The displays are not limited to plants, there is also a still used for making essential oils and a traditional *case en paille* (a house made of pandanus fronds). The tours last around 90 minutes and are very informative. At the café you can sample coffee grown on the island.

LA SAGA DU RHUM (*Chemin Frédeline, St-Pierre;* ☎ *0262 358190;* e *sagadurhum@sagadurhum.fr; www.sagadurhum.fr;* ⊕ *10.00–18.00 daily, guided tours 10.00, 11.00, 14.00, 15.00, 16.00; admission adult/child €10/7*) A family-owned rum distillery, which dates back to 1845 and is still operational today. The distillery is in full flow during the sugarcane harvest (July–December) and the visits are more interesting during that period, although the museum can be visited at any time of year. One-hour tours of the distillery include a film on rum production and rum tasting. The museum is modern and well run with information, including audioguides,

19

available in English. One of the key exhibits is a steam-powered sugar mill, which dates from the 1940s. The museum is wheelchair accessible and there is, of course, a shop on site selling rum-inspired souvenirs.

SUCRERIE DU GOL (*Le Camp du Gol, St-Louis;* ☎ *0262 910547; 1½hr guided tours Jul–Dec 09.00–19.00 Tue–Sat; admission adult/child €5/3; on reservation only; children aged under 7 are not allowed*) If you find yourself passing innumerable lorries laden with sugarcane on the roads then it is harvest season and the Sucrerie du Gol is open to visitors. This sugar refinery claims to be the largest in the European Union. Originally built in 1817, it processes a million tonnes of sugarcane each year and produces around 100,000 tonnes of sugar. Guided tours explain the process in French or English, and there are audioguides. Atmospheric night tours are also available (Thursday to Saturday). Sugar products are on sale in the shop. Flat, enclosed shoes must be worn and be prepared for plenty of noise and dust.

MUSEE DES ARTS DECORATIFS DE L'OCEAN INDIEN (*17a Chemin Maison Rouge, St-Louis;* ☎ *0262 912430; www.museesreunion.re;* ⊕ *13.00–17.00 Mon, 09.00–17.00 Tue–Sun; admission adult/child €4/2*) On the historic Maison Rouge estate, which from 1725 to 1827 belonged to the Desforges Boucher family who were pioneers in the growing of coffee on Réunion. When the estate passed into new hands, sugar was planted and in 1830 a sugar refinery was built, which operated until 1896 and was destroyed in 1920. The museum is housed in the old stables and displays a changing collection of furniture, textiles, porcelain, art and more. There is still a coffee plantation here of the local Bourbon pointu variety, which can be visited, and you can sample the finished product at the museum shop.

OBSERVATOIRE ASTRONOMIQUE LES MAKES (*18 Rue Georges Bizet, Plaine des Makes;* ☎ *0262 378683;* e *accueilobs.astronomique@orange.fr; www.ilereunion.com/ observatoire-des-makes;* ⊕ *09.00–12.00 & 14.00–17.00 Mon–Fri, 09.00–12.00 Sat; guided tours 09.30, adult/child €4/2.50; night observation adult/child €7.50/4.50; on reservation only*) Observatory about an hour's drive inland from St-Louis, at an altitude of 1,000m. Observation sessions are led by passionate and knowledgeable people. On a clear day, you can study the surface of the sun. The viewings of the night skies are particularly interesting, but it can be chilly so wear warm clothes.

CROC PARC (*1 Route Forestière, L'Etang-Salé-les-Hauts;* ☎ *0262 914041;* e *orizon. reunion@wanadoo.fr; www.crocparc.re;* ⊕ *10.00–17.30 daily; admission adult/child €9/7*) About 2km from the RN1, between l'Etang-Salé-les-Bains and l'Etang-Salé-les-Hauts. The park is home to over 165 Nile crocodiles (*Crocodylus niloticus*), which are not bred for their skin or meat, but are simply there for the benefit of the public. They can grow up to around 6m in length and weigh nearly a tonne, and some of the residents here are getting pretty big. Seeing large numbers of crocodiles crammed into a small space can be a bit confronting. The gardens are pleasant (many of the plants are labelled), there are copious birds (wild and caged), as well as a small collection of farm animals, a snack bar, minigolf, children's playground and a souvenir shop. On weekends, locals will spend the whole day here, enjoy a picnic with family and make use of the playground. Crocodiles don't tend to do very much so a good time to visit is Wednesday or Sunday at 16.00 when they are fed.

20

Western Réunion

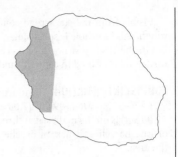

The western region stretches from Les Avirons in the southwest, all the way up to La Possession. Inland, the scenic Route Hubert Delisle links several small settlements along the western 'heights' from Les Avirons to Bois de Nèfles in the north.

The west coast is Réunion's sea, sun and sand holiday mecca, featuring 27km of beaches. It is the driest part of the island, so more often than not the weather is hot and sunny. Water temperatures generally average 20–26°C.

The coast around the historic town of St-Leu is known for its black-sand beaches. There are also black-sand beaches at St-Paul but it is the clean, white-sand beaches at Boucan Canot, Roches Noires and L'Hermitage that draw the crowds. In 2013, following a series of shark attacks, the government banned swimming and surfing in the waters around Réunion (see box, page 291). In early 2016 shark nets had been installed at several beaches in the west, including Boucan Canot and Roches Noires, and the netted beaches were re-opened to swimmers.

Offshore, particularly around St-Gilles-les-Bains and St-Leu, there are colourful coral reefs, perfect for diving and snorkelling. St-Gilles-les-Bains is Réunion's main tourist resort; it has been developed with tourists in mind and while visitors may enjoy the idea of a French seaside resort in a tropical setting, those seeking an authentic Réunionnais experience will not find it here. As you head north, the coast becomes more rugged and the area around Le Port is primarily industrial.

While the west of the island is best known for its coastal resorts, those who head inland are rewarded with attractive villages, incredible viewpoints and excellent hiking. In particular, Piton Maïdo provides unforgettable views of the Cirque de Mafate.

ST-LEU

The settlement of St-Leu was created in 1776 and soon became an important beef-rearing and coffee-growing region. By 1806, the population of this prosperous town consisted of 463 free people and 5,352 slaves. A few buildings remain from this era: the **town hall**, formerly a coffee warehouse, and the church, which was begun in 1788. The **Chapelle de Notre Dame de la Salette**, behind the church, was begun during the cholera epidemic of 1859 as a plea for St-Leu to be spared. It was, although thousands died in neighbouring towns.

The big waves to the north of St-Leu used to draw surfers from around the world, but the spike in shark attacks in recent years has almost completely put paid to that. It is still a popular area for diving and there is a beach with lifeguards in the centre of town. You will often see paragliders floating above the town and the beach, having leapt off from the hills behind St-Leu.

St-Leu has a noticeably more relaxed air about it than St-Gilles and, although it has some good hotels, it has not been totally colonised by tourists.

Visible from the coast road south of St-Leu, is **Le Souffleur**. When the sea is rough, this blowhole is spectacular.

On the RN1, just north of St-Leu is **Kélonia**, a former turtle farm, where sea turtles are now bred in captivity and studied. It is well worth a visit (see page 344).

TOURIST INFORMATION The tourist office (✆ *0262 346330;* e *ot.stleu@wanadoo.fr;* ⊕ *13.30–17.30 Mon, 09.00–12.00 & 13.30–17.30 Tue–Fri, 09.00–12.00 & 14.00– 17.00 Sat*) is on the main street through town, Rue Général Lambert, on the corner of Rue Barrelier. It has an excellent stock of leaflets and offers guided tours of the area.

WHERE TO STAY

Upmarket

✳ 🏠 **Le Blue Margouillat****** (14 rooms) Impasse Jean Albany, Zac du Four à Chaux, St-Leu; ✆ 0262 346400; e info@blue-margouillat. com; www.blue-margouillat.com. A spacious, elegant Creole-style mansion on the hillside above St-Leu with wonderful sea views. The 12 rooms & 2 suites are beautifully decorated, all with AC, TV, phone, free Wi-Fi, & balcony/terrace with sea view. Little touches, like local toiletries, make you feel spoilt. The suites are very private & spacious, ideal for a romantic retreat or for families. They have gorgeous baths, as well as an outdoor shower & spa. There is 1 room equipped for the disabled. Meals are served around the pool or on the veranda (see opposite). The service is good & many of the staff speak good English. HB packages available. **$$$$**

Mid range

🏠 **Iloha Seaview Hotel***** (80 rooms) 44 Rue Georges Pompidou, St-Leu; ✆ 0262 348989; e hotel@iloha.fr; www.iloha.fr. Set on a hill overlooking St-Leu. There are 14 double rooms in the main building, 2 with disabled facilities. Bungalows in the garden house 40 rooms (20 with kitchenette) & 10 family bungalows for up to 4 adults & 2 children (with kitchenette). As part of a renovation in 2011, 16 new 'Guetali' rooms were built to accommodate 2 adults & 2 children; they overlook a separate pool & kitchenette. All accommodation has AC, TV, phone & safe. There is a restaurant by the main pool, a second (Italian) restaurant & a small spa offering massage & beauty treatments. Not by the beach, but St-Leu is nearby & the grounds are a pleasant place to relax. A car is helpful if you want to explore from here. Reasonable value, especially for families. **$$$**

Budget

🏠 **Kaz Ti Piment***** (3 rooms) 20 Rue Edouard Carpy, Piton St-Leu; ✆ 0262 252952; e contact@ tipiment.re; www.tipiment.re. In a residential area in the hills about St-Leu, which does feel very suburban, but there are views of the coast from the pool. The rooms are pleasant but not exceptional. A car would be handy if staying here. **$$**

🏠 **Villa Mascarine***** (2 rooms, 3 s/c apts) 396 Rue Georges Pompidou, Les Colimaçons, St-Leu; m 0692 934649; e contact@villamascarine.fr; www.villamascarine.fr. On the hillside overlooking the coast, this attractive Creole-style guesthouse has 2 B&B rooms plus 3 self-catering studios. The rooms are spacious, clean & nicely furnished, equipped with en suite, TV, safe & fridge. The studios have a kitchenette & terrace; 1 has a sitting room. The pool & jacuzzi have far-reaching views of the coast. You will need a car if staying here. Breakfast is provided; from Sep to Jun table d'hôte meals are served Mon & Tue. A HB option is available with dinner on the other nights at Le Mascarin restaurant. Min stay 2 nights BB, 1 week self-catering. **$$**

Self-catering holiday rentals

🏠 **Les Azalées***** 5 Chemin des Azalées, La Chaloupe, St-Leu; ✆ 0262 548714. A 3-bedroom apartment with living area, kitchen, TV & veranda. From €450 per week (2–4 people).

🏠 **Bungalows Murat**** 273 Chemin Dubuisson, St-Leu; ✆ 0262 348504; e bungalows. murat@orange.fr; www.bungalows-murat.re. 5 simple but comfortable bungalows for 2–4 people, on the hillside above St-Leu. From €250 per week (2 people).

🏠 **Résidence les Pêcheurs** (6 villas) 27 Av des Alizés, St-Leu; ✆ 0262 349125; e residence. les.pecheurs@wanadoo.fr; http://les.pecheurs. pagesperso-orange.fr. 6 self-catering villas in a

pleasant garden with pool, close to the beach. They are simply furnished but the kitchens should have everything you need. There is a communal laundry, which is payable. From €322 per week (2 people).

✗ WHERE TO EAT There is a **Super U supermarket** in the centre of town.

✗ **Le Bleu Margouillat** Impasse Jean Albany, Zac du Four à Chaux, St-Leu; 📞0262 346400; ⏱ for lunch & dinner daily. Cuisine: French, Creole. Fine food in an elegant setting around the pool & overlooking the coast. Good service. Reservation essential. $$$$

✻ ✗ **Il Etait Une Fois** 1 Ruelle Rivière, St-Leu; 📱0692 689619; ⏱ for lunch Tue–Fri, dinner Sat. Cuisine: French. On a small street not far from the seafront. This place has a relaxed atmosphere with rustic tables snuggled in corners on the terrace, but the menu is sophisticated. Deserves its reputation for outstanding food. Reservation recommended. $$$

✗ **Iloha Seaview Hotel** Pointe des Châteaux, St-Leu; 📞0262 348989; www.iloha.fr; ⏱ for lunch & dinner daily. Cuisine: European, Creole. The main restaurant of the hotel is by the pool, with views of the ocean. A very pleasant setting for a meal & the food is good. Reservation recommended. $$$

✗ **Lagon** 2 bis Rue du Lagon, St-Leu; 📞0262 347913; ⏱ for lunch & dinner Wed–Mon. Cuisine: French, Creole, seafood, snacks. Tables are on a large, wooden deck which leads directly on to the beach. $$$

✗ **La Varangue** 52 Rue du Lagon, St-Leu; 📞0262 347926; ⏱ for lunch Tue–Sun, for dinner Tue–Sat. Cuisine: French, grills. The best location in town, right on the beach. Tasty grilled meat & seafood is central to the menu. Free Wi-Fi. $$$

✗ **Villa Vanille** 69 Rue du Lagon; 📞0262 340315; ⏱ for lunch & dinner daily, closed Tue in winter. Cuisine: French, Creole, seafood. Close to the beach at the southern end of town. Tables are on a pleasant, shady deck. The seafood dishes are particularly impressive. $$$

✗ **Auberge du Relais** 211 Rue du Général Lambert; 📞0262 348185; open for lunch & dinner Mon–Fri, dinner Sat. Cuisine: Creole. On the main road in the centre of town. This unassuming little place punches above its weight with its delicious, authentic, Creole food. Friendly, personal service. $$

OTHER PRACTICALITIES

Money and banking There are banks on the main street through town, including **Banque de la Réunion** at 52 Rue Général Lambert.

Communications The **post office** is near the harbour on Rue de la Compagnie des Indes and has **ATM** facilities.

Medical Care can be obtained at the **Pharmacie de la Salette**, near which there are doctors' surgeries.

ST-GILLES-LES-BAINS AND SURROUNDS

The area around St-Gilles-les-Bains is Réunion's premier beach holiday hangout. The island's best beaches and seaside hotels are here. However, it must be said that even these beaches do not compare to those of Mauritius.

As you head north from St-Leu along the coast, you come to the largely residential area of **La-Saline-les-Bains**. There are decent beaches, popular for snorkelling and windsurfing, and they tend to be less crowded than those in St-Gilles-les-Bains.

Continuing north, before you hit St-Gilles itself, you pass the turning to L'Hermitage – arguably the island's prettiest beach. The beach is protected by a long lagoon; the water is clear, shallow and good for swimming. It is one of the few places considered safe for swimming following the increase in shark attacks in recent years.

The bustling town of St-Gilles is packed with restaurants, bars, pubs and trendy nightclubs. It is a playground for hip, young, French holidaymakers, who come

to enjoy the sunshine, the sea and the busy nightlife. Many travellers find it too 'commercialised' and crowded; for others it is the ideal way to unwind after hiking in the mountains. You will not get an authentic taste of Réunion in St-Gilles. It is a town built by Europeans for Europeans, a fact captured by one of my Réunionnais friends in his description of it as a *ghetto zoreilles* (white people's ghetto). Certainly, it does feel like a mini St-Tropez and traffic congestion is a real problem along this section of coast.

The **harbour** [337 B2] (Port de Plaisance) is also a lively place, where all manner of watersports can be arranged. This is where you'll find the excellent **Aquarium de la Réunion** [337 B2] (see page 345).

About 3km inland from St-Gilles-les-Bains, on the road to St-Gilles-les-Hauts, is the starting point for the walk to three waterfalls plunging into pools (*bassins*): **Bassin du Cormoran**, **Bassin des Aigrettes** and **Bassin Bleu**. It takes about 2 hours and Bassins des Aigrettes and Bleu are ideal for a quick dip. You will have to take your shoes off and get your feet wet on parts of the walk, and you will need mosquito repellent.

Also on the road to St-Gilles-les-Hauts is the **Village Artisanal de l'Eperon**, where handicrafts and art produced by local artisans are on sale. The products include miniature Creole houses, leather goods and clothes; there are restaurants on site.

GETTING THERE AND AWAY All the towns along the west coast, including St-Gilles-les-Bains, are easily reached on the non-express St-Denis–St-Pierre buses (Line O2).

TOURIST INFORMATION There is a well-stocked **tourist office** [337 B2] (\ *0810 797797; e accueil@ouest-lareunion.com; www.ouest-lareunion.com; ⊕ 10.00–13.00 & 14.00–18.00 daily, including public holidays*) at 1 Place Paul Julius Bénard, St-Gilles-les-Bains. They can also make bookings for accommodation and activities.

 WHERE TO STAY
Upmarket

🏠 **Hotel le Récif*** [337 B3] (132 rooms) 50 Av de Bourbon, L'Hermitage; \0262 700100; e reservation@luxresorts.com; www.hotellerecif. com. The rooms & suites, including 4 rooms for the disabled, are housed in 2-storey Creole-style buildings scattered in a large garden. Rooms are colourfully decorated & have AC, TV, phone, safe, minibar & balcony/terrace. Facilities include a restaurant, bar, snack bar, 2 pools, tennis & kids' club. A family-friendly hotel with an emphasis on activities. In a great location, opposite L'Hermitage Beach. **$$$$**

🏠 **Le Boucan Canot**** [337 B1] (50 rooms) 32 Rue Boucan Canot, Boucan Canot; \0262 334444; e hotel@boucancanot.com; www. boucancanot.com. An attractive Creole-style building in a good location with direct access to Boucan Canot Beach. The rooms & suites are modern & decorated in cool, natural tones. They are equipped with AC, TV, phone, Wi-Fi, minibar, safe & balcony. 2 rooms are equipped for the disabled. Almost all the rooms have a sea view so try to make sure yours does. The suites are particularly comfortable & able to accommodate families. Facilities include a restaurant overlooking the sea (page 340), pool & regular evening entertainment. **$$$$**

🏠 **Le Saint Alexis**** [337 B1] (58 rooms) 44 Route de Boucan Canot, St-Gilles-Les-Bains; \0262 244204; e reception@hotelsaintalexis.com; www. hotelsaintalexis.com. This hotel is on the beach at Boucan Canot. The hotel has been around for years but has been kept fresh with refurbishments. All rooms & suites have AC, TV, phone, safe, spa bath, minibar & balcony/terrace. The suites are very spacious. There are 2 pools, a spa, a gym & a restaurant overlooking the ocean. **$$$$**

🏠 **Lux Ile de la Réunion***** [337 B7] (174 rooms) 28 Rue du Lagon, L'Hermitage, St-Gilles-les-Bains; \0262 700000; e reservation@ luxresorts.com; www.luxislandresorts.com. A resort-style hotel set in gardens that run along the island's best beach. The 23 bungalows house

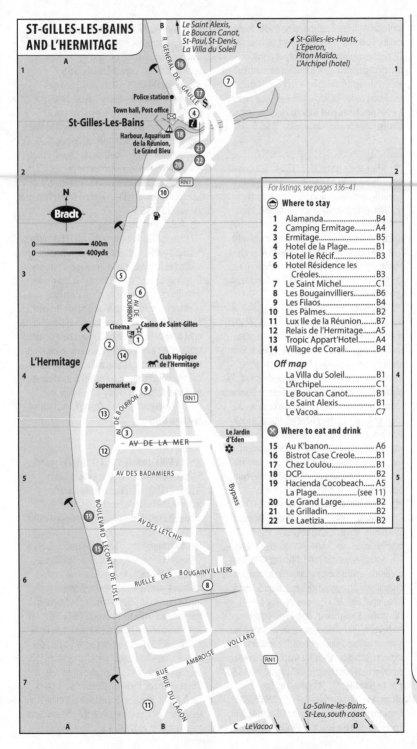

ST-GILLES-LES-BAINS AND L'HERMITAGE

Le Saint Alexis,
Le Boucan Canot,
St-Paul, St-Denis,
La Villa du Soleil

St-Gilles-les-Hauts,
L'Eperon,
Piton Maïdo,
L'Archipel (hotel)

Police station
Town hall, Post office
St-Gilles-Les-Bains
Harbour, Aquarium
de la Réunion,
Le Grand Bleu

Bradt

0 — 400m
0 — 400yds

AV DE BOURBON

Cinema   Casino de Saint-Gilles

L'Hermitage

Club Hippique
de l'Hermitage

Supermarket

AV DE BOURBON

Le Jardin
d'Eden

AV DE LA MER

AV DES BADAMIERS

Bypass

BOULEVARD LECONTE DE LISLE

AV DES LETCHIS

RUELLE DES BOUGAINVILLIERS

AMBROISE VOLLARD

RUE DES BOUGAINVILLIERS

RUE DU LAGON

La-Saline-les-Bains,
St-Leu, south coast

Le Vacoa

For listings, see pages 336–41

Where to stay

1   Alamanda.....................B4
2   Camping Ermitage......A4
3   Ermitage......................B5
4   Hotel de la Plage.........B1
5   Hotel le Récif...............B3
6   Hotel Résidence les
      Créoles........................B3
7   Le Saint Michel............C1
8   Les Bougainvilliers......B6
9   Les Filaos....................B4
10   Les Palmes..................B2
11   Lux Ile de la Réunion...B7
12   Relais de l'Hermitage...A5
13   Tropic Appart'Hotel.....A4
14   Village de Corail..........B4

Off map

     La Villa du Soleil...........B1
     L'Archipel....................C1
     Le Boucan Canot..........B1
     Le Saint Alexis.............B1
     Le Vacoa.....................C7

Where to eat and drink

15   Au K'banon.................. A6
16   Bistrot Case Creole......B1
17   Chez Loulou.................B1
18   DCP............................B2
19   Hacienda Cocobeach......A5
     La Plage...................(see 11)
20   Le Grand Large............B2
21   Le Grilladin.................B2
22   Le Laetizia..................B2

well-maintained rooms, including 4 with disabled facilities & 8 suites. As you'd expect, all have AC, TV, phone, minibar & safe. Plenty of activities: tennis, badminton, gym & some watersports. There are 3 restaurants, including a very good Creole restaurant on the beach, where they cook over a wood fire. Also a pool & a kids' club. The large gardens provide a feeling of space. **$$$$**

Mid range

⌂ **Alamanda Hotel**★★ [337 B4] (70 rooms) 81 Av de Bourbon, L'Hermitage; ☎0262 331010; e reservation@alamanda.re; www.alamanda. re. After a much-needed refurbishment, this 2-star option is now pretty good value. The hotel is close to the casino & nightlife, & 5mins' walk from the beach. En-suite rooms with AC, TV, phone, Wi-Fi & balcony/terrace overlook either the pool or small garden. It has 2 restaurants, bar, gym & pool. **$$$**

⌂ **Ermitage**★★★ [337 B5] (44 rooms) 40 Av de la Mer, Les Filaos, L'Hermitage; ☎0262 245025; e reservation@ermitage.re; www.ermitage.re. Family-friendly hotel 150m from the beach. Rooms are in a 2-storey building & overlook the pool, garden or car park. They are equipped with AC, TV, phone, Wi-Fi, minibar & balcony/terrace. Standard rooms are on the small side but junior suites are ideal for families as they have a living area with sofa bed, a kitchenette & 2 bathrooms. The hotel was renovated recently & has a clean, modern feel. Facilities include a restaurant, bar, car park & pool, which feels rather overlooked by the rooms bunched around it. **$$$**

⌂ **Hotel Résidence les Créoles**★★★ [337 B3] (10 rooms, 22 studios, 10 apts) 43 Av de Bourbon, St-Gilles-les-Bains; ☎0262 265265; e resa@ hotellescreoles.com; www.hotel-les-creoles.com. This recently renovated hotel is around 150m from the beach, amidst the bars, clubs & restaurants of L'Hermitage. Accommodation feels fresh & new & is equipped with AC, TV, phone, minibar & Wi-Fi. The studios & apartments have a well-equipped kitchenette. The buildings exude Creole style & are grouped around a pleasant pool. The restaurant only serves breakfast but there is a snack bar & there are plenty of restaurants within walking distance. **$$$**

⌂ **Le Nautile**★★★ (43 rooms) 60 Rue Lacaussade, La-Saline-les-Bains; ☎0262 338888; e nautile@runnet.com; www.hotel-nautile.com. Pretty hotel on the beach. The rooms are fairly plain, with AC, TV, phone, Wi-Fi, minibar, safe & balcony/terrace. Facilities include a restaurant, bar, library & pool. Regular evening entertainment. Several of the staff speak English. **$$$**

⌂ **Le Swalibo**★★★ (30 rooms) 9 Rue des Salines, La-Saline-les-Bains; ☎0262 241097; e info@swalibo.com; www.swalibo.com. A charming small hotel, 5mins' walk from the beach. Rooms are bright, colourful & spacious with AC, TV, phone, minibar, safe & balcony. Not much privacy – the balconies & small garden are overlooked by other rooms. Facilities include a restaurant, pool & jacuzzi. Beach umbrellas, kayaks & snorkelling gear are available. **$$$**

⌂ **Relais de l'Hermitage**★★★ [337 A5] (173 rooms) 123 Av Leconte de Lisle, L'Hermitage; ☎0262 244444; e reservation@relais-hermitage-saintgilles.fr; www.relais-hermitage-saintgilles. fr. Sprawling hotel spread through a 3ha garden with direct access to the beach. Rooms have views of either the mountains (& car park) or the pool. All have AC, TV, phone, safe, free Wi-Fi & minibar, & most have balcony/terrace. 5 rooms have disabled facilities. It's a busy hotel, where everyone seems to take advantage of the activities – pool, tennis courts, minigolf, kayaks, pedaloes & snorkelling equipment. There's a family atmosphere, but the kids' club operates only during French school holidays. **$$$**

Budget

⌂ **La Villa du Soleil**★★ [337 B1] (13 rooms) 54 Route Nationale, Plage de Boucan Canot; ☎0262 243869; e lavilladusoleil@wanadoo. fr; www.lavilladusoleil.com. A small hotel with simple, colourful en-suite rooms equipped with AC, TV & Wi-Fi. **$$**

⌂ **L'Archipel**★★★ [337 C1] (64 studios & apts) 9 Rue de la Cheminée, Grand Fond, St-Gilles-les-Bains; ☎0262 240534; e reservation@archipel-residence.com; www.archipel-residence.com. On the road to St-Gilles-les-Hauts, but there is a free shuttle service to the beaches & St-Gilles-les-Bains town centre. There are 52 studios for up to 3 people & 12 apartments for up to 3 adults & 2 children, including 2 with disabled facilities. They are equipped with AC, TV, phone, kitchenette & balcony/terrace. There is a pleasant pool, snack bar & tennis. Breakfast is available but there is no restaurant for evening meals & the free shuttle to the coast stops at 17.00. **$$**

🏠 **Le Saint Michel**** [337 C1] (15 rooms) 196 Chemin Summer, St-Gilles-les-Bains; ☎0262 931393; e contact@anthurium.com; www. anthurium.com. A small, hotel 5mins from the beach. En-suite rooms with AC, TV, phone, free Wi-Fi & balcony/terrace. There is a restaurant & a pool. **$$**

🏠 **Les Bougainvilliers**** [337 B6] (15 rooms) 27 Ruelle des Bougainvilliers, L'Hermitage; ☎0262 338248; e bougainvilliers@ wanadoo.fr; www.hotel-bougainvillier.com. Around 300m from L'Hermitage Beach. Rooms are comfortable & fresh, with en suite, AC, TV & fridge. A room with a balcony costs around an extra €10 per night. There is a pool in the garden & a communal kitchen but no restaurant. Free Wi-Fi. Reasonable value for money. **$$**

🏠 **Les Filaos**** [337 B4] (44 rooms) 101 Av de Bourbon, St-Gilles-les-Bains; ☎0262 245009; e les-filaos@orange.fr; www.hotelfilaos. com. Unfortunately next to a busy road with a nightclub & supermarket in front of it but only a 200m walk from the beach. Small, simply furnished en-suite rooms with AC, TV, phone, & balcony/terrace; the 7 apartments have a kitchenette. Rooms with disabled facilities are available. It has a bar & pool. **$$**

🏠 **Les Palmes**** [337 B2] (21 apts) 205 Rue du Général de Gaulle, St-Gilles-les-Bains; ☎0262 244712; e soresum@wanadoo.fr; www. hoteldespalmes.fr. The accommodation is in bungalows in a tropical garden, 200m from the beach. Rooms are basic & a little tired, equipped with en suite, AC, TV & phone. There is a pool. **$$**

🏠 **Marina**** (10 apts) 6 Allée des Pailles en Queues, Lot Champagne, Boucan-Canot; ☎0262 330707; e hotelmarina@wanadoo.fr; www. hotelmarinareunion.com. Rather plain self-catering AC studios in pretty gardens 200m from Boucan Canot Beach. They are equipped with TV, phone & Wi-Fi & sleep either 2 or 4 people. There is a small pool & tiny gym. Close to shops & public transport. **$$**

🏠 **Tropic Appart'Hotel***** [337 A4] (40 studios & apts) 102 Av de Bourbon, L'Hermitage; ☎0262 225353; e info@ residencetropic.com; www.tropicapparthotel. com. Comfortable self-catering accommodation 5mins' walk from L'Hermitage Beach. The studios & apartments feel clean & modern, & have AC, TV, phone, safe & Wi-Fi. The apartments accommodate up to 4 people & have 2 bathrooms. There is a pool

& car park. Can be booked on HB with meals at local restaurants. **$$**

Shoestring

🏠 **Hotel de la Plage** [337 B1] (9 rooms) 20 Rue de la Poste, St-Gilles-les-Bains; ☎0262 240637; e hoteldelaplagereunion@hotmail.fr; www.hoteldelaplage.re. Budget accommodation 100m from Roches Noires Beach. Brightly coloured: walls, tables, chairs & more. Small, basic rooms, most with AC. En-suite double with TV from €50 BB. **$**

🏠 **Le Vacoa** [337 C7] (16 rooms) 54 Rue Antoine de Bertin, L'Hermitage; ☎0262 241248; e levacoa@levacoa.com; www.levacoa.com. Simple, family-run guesthouse 300m from the beach. Rooms are comfortable & clean with en suite, AC, TV & fridge. There is a communal kitchen for guest use & a pool. Wi-Fi is free. **$**

Self-catering holiday rentals

This area has plenty of apartments & villas to let to holidaymakers, many of which represent excellent value for money. Here is a selection:

🏠 **Les Gîtes de Boucan Canot****** 255 Chemin de la Vanille, Boucan Canot; ☎0692 651391; e lesgitesdeboucancanot@orange.fr; www. lesgitesdeboucancanot.com. 8 spacious 2-bedroom & 1-bedroom wooden cabins with everything you need for a self-catering stay, including dishwasher, washing machine, Wi-Fi & satellite TV. Each has a decent-sized terrace & garden. The cabins are well spread throughout the gardens, so you have some privacy. 2 are suitable for people with limited mobility. There are 2 pools on site & the beach is around 1km away. You will need a car here. Excellent self-catering option. From €500 per week (2 people), €900 per week (4 people).

🏠 **L'Ilot Vert**** (5 apts, 3 bungalows) 1 Rue des Salines, La-Saline-les-Bains; ☎0262 339211; e jean-pierre.fouque@wanadoo.fr; www.ilotvert. re. A few mins' walk from the beach. Well-maintained, simply furnished apartments (2–6 people) around a small pool, all equipped with AC, TV & phone. Wi-Fi available. There is a car park. Apartment from €65 per night (2 people).

🏠 **Résidence les Boucaniers**** (9 studios, 6 apts) 29 Rue du Boucan Canot, Boucan Canot; ☎0262 242389; e les-boucaniers@wanadoo.fr; www.les-boucaniers.com. Across the road from

Boucan Canot Beach, with AC, TV, & balcony/terrace. The accommodation is sea facing & rooms on the 1st floor have a good view of the coast. 1 room with disabled facilities is available. Well situated but feels rather tired & the kitchenettes are basic. Studio/4-person apartment from €70/100.

🏠 **Senteur Vanille***** (9 units) Route du Théatre, St-Gilles-les-Bains; ☏0262 240488; e senteurvanille@wanadoo.fr; www.senteurvanille.com. Slightly inland amidst a wealth of tropical plants, not far from Boucan Canot Beach. Accommodation is in Creole bungalows in the garden or elegant, elevated wooden chalets with a view of the ocean. All accommodation is beautifully furnished & invites relaxation. Good value for money. Studio from €85 per night for 2 people RO.

Camping

⛰ **Camping Ermitage***** [337 A4] (86 pitches, 20 safari tents) 60 Av de Bourbon, L'Hermitage; ☏0262 963670; e contact@campingermitage.re; www.campingermitage.re. A large campsite in a great location on L'Hermitage Beach. As well as tent pitches, there are 20 huge safari tents with 2 bedrooms & kitchen. There is no pool but there are play areas, Wi-Fi & a kids' club. **$$**

Villages Vacances Famille (VVF): family holiday villages

You must be a member of VVF to stay here. For more information, see page 273.

🏠 **Village de Corail** [337 B4] (129 s/c studios) 80 Av de Bourbon, 97434 St-Gilles-les-Bains; ☏0262 242939; e contact@villages-des-australes.com; www.villages-des-australes.com. Each studio has a kitchenette, dining area & terrace. Up to 2 extra beds can be added per studio. **$$**

✖ WHERE TO EAT

Scores of restaurants are crammed into St-Gilles-les-Bains and the surrounding area. In addition, you'll see numerous snack bars and, for those who are self-catering, well-stocked supermarkets in the centre of town (**Score, Champion**). There is also a **Score supermarket** in L'Hermitage and a large **Champion supermarket** in La-Saline-les-Bains.

Here is a cross-section of restaurants:

✖ **La Plage** [337 B7] Lux Ile de la Réunion, 28 Rue du Lagon, L'Hermitage, St-Gilles-les-Bains; ☏0262 700000; ⏲ for dinner Wed–Sat, for lunch Sun. Cuisine: Creole. Very good Creole restaurant facing the beach. Traditional dishes, like *rougail saucisses*, are cooked on a wood fire. **$$$$**

✖ **Le Cap** 32 Rue Boucan Canot, Boucan Canot; ☏0262 334444; ⏲ for lunch & dinner daily. Cuisine: French, Creole, seafood, grills. Upmarket restaurant at Hotel Boucan Canot, overlooking the water. Specialities include heart of palm salad & grilled lobster. **$$$$**

✖ **Au K'banon** [337 A6] Plage de L'Hermitage; ☏0262 338494; ⏲ for lunch daily, for dinner Thu–Sat. Cuisine: European, Creole, snacks, ice cream. In a fabulous location right on the edge of the water. There is a restaurant section, as well as a snack bar. The desserts are particularly good. **$$$**

✖ **Bistrot Case Creole** [337 B1] 57 Rue du Général de Gaulle, St-Gilles-les-Bains; ☏0262 242884; ⏲ for lunch Tue–Fri, dinner Tue–Sat.

Cuisine: French, Creole. French *bistrot* & Creole meals. Popular Creole buffet dinners. Good value for money. **$$$**

✖ **DCP** [337 B2] Pl du Marché, St-Gilles-les-Bains; ☏0262 330296. Cuisine: European, seafood. It may look pretty casual but this place prides itself on preparing the freshest seafood caught in the waters around the island. **$$$**

✖ **Hacienda Cocobeach** [337 A5] Plage de L'Hermitage; ☏0262 338143; ⏲ from 09.00–late daily. Cuisine: Creole, European. Trendy restaurant/bar on the beach & the place to be seen. Tables are gathered in a garden & palms give it a tropical atmosphere. A lively & popular bar but you can have a quiet meal during the day; there are actually 2 restaurants within, 1 more upmarket than the other. **$$$**

✖ **Le Grand Large** [337 B2] 42 Port de Plaisance, St-Gilles-les-Bains; ☏0262 278635; ⏲ for lunch daily, dinner Thu–Sun. Cuisine: European. Casual restaurant near the aquarium, overlooking the marina. Serves simple fare such as steak & chips, pizzas & crêpes. Wi-Fi available. **$$$**

✗ **Le Grilladin** [337 B2] 121 Rue de St-Laurent, St-Gilles-les-Bains; 0262 244582. Cuisine: Creole, French. Casual restaurant near the tourist office. $$$

✗ **Chez Loulou** [337 B1] 84 Rue Général de Gaulle, St-Gilles-les-Bains; ✆0262 244636; ⏲ 07.00–13.00 & 15.00–19.00 daily, closed Sun evening. Cuisine: snacks, Creole, French. In a colourful Creole building in the centre of town, opposite Le Forum shopping centre. Excellent bakery which also serves a small range of meals (these vary – just look at the blackboard outside). Internet access available on site. Good value for money. $$

✗ **Le Laetizia** [337 B2] 21 Rue du St Laurent, St-Gilles-les-Bains; ✆0262 244964; ⏲ for lunch & dinner daily. Cuisine: Italian, crêpes, snacks. Light meals, such as pizza, in a relaxed atmosphere. $$

NIGHTLIFE The harbour in St-Gilles and the town itself are full of bars, whilst most of the nightclubs and the casino are in L'Hermitage. The downside of nightclubbing in Réunion is that it will dent your wallet severely. In the St-Gilles-les-Bains area you can expect to pay in the region of €12–14 for entry and, on top of that, drinks are expensive. Some clubs are open only on weekends, some only on a Saturday night, but many also have a themed night on Wednesday. They tend to get going at around midnight and are open until about 05.00. Most play a mixture of music, but being St-Gilles there is less local music (*séga*, *zouk*, etc) than in St-Pierre, for example. Most clubs won't let you in wearing trainers or flip-flops.

There are various free publications, available in tourist offices, which will tell you what is going on, where and when in terms of nightlife (page 280), as will the website www.azenda.re.

Bars are easily found on the main streets of St-Gilles and around the marina. **Cubana Club** (*122 Rue du Général de Gaulle;* ✆ *0262 332491*) is usually packed. There is a well-stocked bar, a brasserie, a cigar lounge and regular events. Wednesday night is jazz night, while Thursday is salsa night. Other popular spots on Rue du Général de Gaulle include **Jungle Village** (✆*0693 017963*) and **Chez Nous** (✆*0262 240808*). At L'Hermitage, the gay-friendly **Hacienda Cocobeach** (✆ *0262 338143*) draws a crowd day and night.

O'Chicaya (*205 Rue du Général de Gaulle;* ✆ *0692 460656*) is a nightclub with a tropical atmosphere and attracts a lively crowd of young, French partygoers. The ever-popular **Moulin du Tango** in L'Hermitage (*9 Av des Mascareignes;* ✆ *0262 245390;* ⏲ *Wed & Fri/Sat nights*) is a large club, with open-air dance floors and several bars.

There is also the **Casino de Saint-Gilles** [337 B4] at L'Hermitage (✆ *0262 244700;* ⏲ *10.00–02.00 Mon–Thu, 10.00–04.00 Fri/Sat; slot machines ⏲ from 10.00, the tables from 21.00*).

OTHER PRACTICALITIES
Money and banking The main banks have branches, with ATMs, on Rue du Général de Gaulle. There are also ATMs outside the post office, at the Score supermarket and at the casino in L'Hermitage.

Communications The **post office** [337 B1] is on Rue de la Poste, near Roches Noires Beach. Wi-Fi is available at **Le Forum** shopping centre on the main street, as well as many of the cafés.

ST-PAUL TO LA POSSESSION

St-Paul, the original Réunionnais capital and the site where the first settlers were abandoned, is a favoured weekend escape for residents of St-Denis, as it has the nearest beach to the capital. It's also the centre of Réunion's yachting fraternity, and international yachting events are regularly hosted here.

Western Réunion ST-PAUL TO LA POSSESSION

20

Of note is the seaside **cemetery**, or **Cimetière Marin**, which has become an unlikely tourist attraction. Signposts guide visitors around the tombs of the famous and infamous occupants. One of these is the notorious pirate Olivier Levasseur, or **La Buse**, who was hanged in 1730. His tomb features a skull and crossbones. People delving into witchcraft still leave bottles of rum and cigarettes on his grave at night. Some apparently do this in order to communicate with his spirit and find out where he hid his treasure. The late and legendary treasure-hunter Bibique, who was an expert on pirate history, was positive that Levasseur's treasure is buried in Réunion somewhere. St-Paul-born poet **Leconte de Lisle** (1818–94) is also buried here. Across the road from the cemetery and to the south of town is the **Grotte des Premiers Français**, the cave in which the island's first settlers lived. They were 12 French rebels exiled from Madagascar in 1646.

There are some lovely old **colonial mansions** (now government offices) along the coastal road, Quai Gilbert. Look out for the small **park** with its old French cannons, set up to protect St-Paul but never utilised. There's also a **war memorial** for the Réunionnais soldiers who were killed in both world wars.

The most important attraction St-Paul holds for visitors is the vibrant street **market**, which residents proudly claim is the island's best. It operates on Friday and Saturday mornings. As well as souvenirs, there is plenty in the way of exotic food and the market is surrounded on three sides by snack bars.

St-Paul is also the gateway to the picturesque **Maïdo** area in the so-called 'Western Heights', overlooking the west coast. Piton Maïdo (2,190m) affords breathtaking views of the **Cirque de Mafate**. From the coast, you take winding rural roads through cane fields and vegetable plots, after which you pass by the famed **geranium fields** and finally, much higher up, forests. There are several distilleries along this road, where you can buy **essential oils**.

The forests signal a change in climate, as you enter the cool, green, high-lying area on the lip of the Cirque de Mafate. The serene **Forêt de Tévelave** makes a great spot for a picnic. On the winding RF8 road, halfway between **Le Guillaume** and Piton Maïdo, is **Petite-France**, an area where fields of geraniums (actually a pelargonium plant native to South Africa) are cultivated for their essential oil. Réunion's geranium oil is of the highest quality and so is much sought after in the pharmaceutical/essential oils industry.

It's a slow drive of 30km, but worth it. It's best to reach the viewpoint in the early morning before the clouds roll in. The peaks that you see are **Le Gros Morne** (2,991m) and **Piton-des-Nieges** (3,069m). The villages below are **Roche Plate**, **La Nouvelle** and **Ilet des Orangers**, whose combined inhabitants number some 600. It is a mind-boggling sight – a miniature world of isolated communities cupped in a deep crater, untainted by electricity pylons, roads and large buildings. The development of Réunion has passed them by, except for an unreliable water supply that was laid on in 1982. Many of the residents have never seen a car – incredible when you think that just 12km away as the crow flies, people are sitting in a traffic jam on their way to the office.

Further north on the west coast is **Le Port**, Réunion's main harbour, an uninspiring industrial town outside of which is the Nelson Mandela Stadium, where international sporting events are held. Tourists tend to pass through Le Port and **La Possession** on the way to St-Paul or St-Gilles. However, the coast road is impressive, wedged between sheer cliffs and the sea.

TOURIST INFORMATION There is a tourist office in Le Port (0810 797797; e accueil@ouestlareunion.com; www.ouest-lareunion.com; 09.00–12.30 & 13.30–17.00 Mon–Fri) at 22 Rue Léon de Lépervanche.

WHERE TO STAY

Upmarket

Roche Tamarin Lodge & Spa**
(20 rooms) 142 Chemin Bœuf Mort, La Possession;
0262 446688; e infos@villagenature.com; www.
lodgetamarin.com. Superb wooden chalets on
stilts on the forested hillside above La Possession.
Chalets sleep up to 3 people & are rustic yet
elegant, with mosquito nets, en suite, TV, phone,
kitchenette, Wi-Fi & veranda. The 2 romantic suites
have a jacuzzi on the balcony. Facilities include a
pool, small but very relaxing spa, barbecue area,
restaurant, shop & conference room. A relaxing
hideaway. **$$$$**

Self-catering holiday rentals

36 La Baie** 36 Rue de la Baie, St-Paul;
0262 225702; e volk-hug@wanadoo.fr; www.
bungalow36labaie.com. Simple 1-bedroom
bungalow on the seafront. Apartment from €420
per week (2 people).

Marie Cascade** 46 Rue Frédéric Chopin,
La Palmeraie 2, La Possession; 0262 322041;
e m.cascade@soleil974.com; www.creole.org/
cascade. Well-equipped apartment in owner's
house with 1 bedroom & sofa-bed. Washing
machine, TV, phone & small private garden.
Apartment from €290 (2 people).

WHERE TO EAT There are plenty of snack bars along the seafront in St-Paul,
particularly around Quai Gilbert.

Le Jardin 456 Rue St-Louis, St-Paul; 0262
450582; for lunch Mon–Sat. Cuisine: French,
seafood. One of the more elegant restaurants in
the area, serving sophisticated dishes such as
duck with prawns. Good, professional service.
$$$$

Chez Doudou 394 Route du Maïdo, Petite-
France; 0262 325587; 08.00–16.00 Tue, Thu–

Sun. Cuisine: Creole. Traditional Creole dishes cooked
over a wood fire. Reservation recommended. **$$$**

Au Petit Gourmet 430 Route du Maïdo;
0692 924634; 09.30–16.00 Thu–Tue. Cuisine:
Creole. Unassuming little restaurant serving
authentic Creole cuisine with all the trimmings. On
the road to Piton Maïdo. **$$**

WHAT TO DO IN WESTERN REUNION

HIKING Piton Maïdo not only provides magnificent views down into the Cirque de
Mafate; you can also hike into the cirque from here. It is a steep path and involves
some difficult clambering over rocks. Less challenging is a walk through Maïdo's
beautiful tamarin forest, where you can take advantage of the tremendously clear
and fresh air.

WATERSPORTS All manner of watersports can be organised along the west coast.
St-Leu and St-Gilles-les-Bains are the two main areas for scuba diving.

GLASS-BOTTOM BOATS Glass-bottom boat trips depart from St-Gilles-les-Bains.

CATAMARAN AND DOLPHIN-WATCHING CRUISES Cruises depart from St-Gilles-
les-Bains.

HORSERIDING There are riding centres in St-Leu, Les Avirons, L'Etang-Salé,
St-Gilles-les-Bains and Le Guillaume.

GOLF Golf du Bassin Bleu at St-Gilles-les-Hauts and Golf Club du Bourbon at
Etang-Salé are popular courses.

PARAGLIDING The hills above St-Leu are the most popular area on the island for
paragliding.

20

ACTIVITY CENTRE

Forêt de l'Aventure Route Forestière des Cryptomérias, Petite France, Maïdo; ☎0692 300154; e foretaventuremaido@yahoo.fr; ⊕ 09.00–17.30 daily except Tue & Thu; last entry at 15.30; admission adult/child under 16 years €20/15; reservation recommended. An activity centre in the forest with flying-fox slides & rope bridges. Minimum height of 140cm is required.

ENTERTAINMENT

☞ **Le Théâtre de Plein Air** Route du Théâtre, St-Gilles-les-Bains; ☎0262 244771; e tpa.technique@odcreunion.com. The open-air theatre takes 1,000 spectators & has regular performances, particularly of local music.

🎬 **Grand Ecran** L'Hermitage; ☎0262 244666. Rather smart cinema.

BUYING ESSENTIAL OILS There are several distilleries on the road to Piton Maïdo where you can buy geranium and other essential oils. At **Maison du Géranium** (☎ 0692 821500; http://maisondugeranium.pagesperso-orange.fr; ⊕ 08.00–16.00 daily) you can see their simple wood-fired still. They also offer guided tours through the forest, on reservation, and there is a shop on site.

MARKETS There are markets in **St-Leu** on Saturday morning, **St-Gilles-les-Bains** on Wednesday morning and the island's largest market takes place in **St-Paul** all day Friday and Saturday morning.

WHAT TO SEE IN WESTERN REUNION

KELONIA ✳ (*Pointe des Châteaux, St-Leu;* ☎ *0262 348110;* e *contact@kelonia.org; www.kelonia.org;* ⊕ *09.00–18.00 daily; guided visits at 10.00, 11.30, 14.00, 15.15 & 16.30; admission adult/child €7/5*) Formerly Ferme Corail, this conservation project used to be a farm, breeding turtles for their meat and shells, which were used to make jewellery and ornaments. Thankfully, since the international ban on this activity, the farm has become a centre for captive-breeding and release programmes and the study of the sea turtles of the Indian Ocean. There are seven species of sea turtle in the world and five are found around Réunion.

Most of the turtles here are green sea turtles (*Chelonia mydas*). Once abundant on the island, they are rare now, having been eaten almost to extinction by the early colonisers. The displays are interesting and informative; most are only in French. You may be shocked to see trinkets made from turtle shells on sale in the shop, but the shells apparently came from the remaining stock, obtained before the ban.

MUSEE DU SEL (*Pointe au Sel les Bas, St-Leu;* ☎ *0262 346700;* ⊕ *09.00–12.00 & 13.30–17.00 Tue–Sun; admission free*) St-Leu is the only place on the island where salt is produced. Just south of St-Leu, this small but modern museum tells the story of salt production (in French only). There is an informative film, which lasts about 15 minutes and a few exhibits. Unfortunately, when last visited the museum was looking in need of a make-over. On the plus side, stopping here allows you to get a close look at the salt pans.

MASCARIN JARDIN BOTANIQUE DE LA REUNION (*2 Rue du Père Georges, Domaine des Colimaçons, St-Leu;* ☎ *0262 249227;* ⊕ *09.00–17.00 Tue–Sun; guided tours 11.00, 14.00, 15.00; admission adult/child €6/3*) Signed from the main road just north of St-Leu. A guided walk around this botanical garden allows you to see and learn

about the island's native flora, as well as spices and plants used for their fruit, seeds or essential oils. Unfortunately, the gardens have not been cared for as well as they might have been and as a tourist attraction it needs some attention before it really draws a crowd. There is a souvenir shop and a snack bar.

STELLA MATUTINA AGRICULTURAL AND INDUSTRIAL MUSEUM (*6 Allée des Flamboyants, Piton St-Leu;* \ *0262 345960;* ⊕ *13.00–17.30 Mon, 09.30–17.30 Tue–Sun; last entry 16.45; admission adult/child €9/6*) Housed in a former sugar factory, this museum tells the story of Réunion's agricultural and industrial development, covering the production of coffee, sugar, rum, spices and perfume. The turning to the museum is on the coast road south of St-Leu. There is an excellent restaurant, 4D cinema and a shop. Audioguides, available in English, French or German, cost €2.

AQUARIUM DE LA REUNION ✳ [337 B2] (*Port de Plaisance, St-Gilles-les-Bains;* \ *0262 334400;* e *aquarium.reunion@wanadoo.fr; www.aquariumdelareunion.com;* ⊕ *10.00–18.00 Tue–Sun; last entry 17.30; admission adult/child €9.50/6.50*) Interactive displays and carefully planned tanks make this a fascinating aquarium, particularly good for children. Coral, seahorses, barracudas and all the snorkeller's favourites are to be seen in an environment that is intended to be as close as possible to their natural one. It takes at least an hour to have a good look around.

MUSEE DE VILLELE (*Domaine Panon-Desbassyns, St-Gilles-les-Hauts;* \ *0262 556410;* e *musee.villele@cg974.fr;* ⊕ *09.30–17.30 Tue–Sun*) A colonial estate, formerly owned by Madame Desbassyns, who is said to have been a particularly cruel plantation owner who mistreated her 300 slaves. Her story inspired Jean-François Sam-Long's novel *Madame Desbassyns* (page 280). The Chapelle Pointue (Pointy Chapel), where she is buried, the former slaves' hospital and the garden can be visited free of charge. Guided tours of the Chapelle Pointue and the ground floor of the house (built 1787) can be arranged and cost €2.

LE JARDIN D'EDEN [337 C5] (*155 RN1, L'Hermitage;* \ *0262 338316;* e *jardin. eden0328@orange.fr; www.jardineden.re;* ⊕ *10.00–18.00 daily; admission adult/child 8/4*) Exploring this 2.5ha garden, which focuses on ethnobotany, takes around 1½ hours. There are over 600 species of plant and plenty of birds. This is also possibly your best chance of seeing a chameleon on the island. The garden is divided into themed areas, such as spices, cacti, zen and a water garden. One of Réunion's best known, and possibly most widely grown plants, *zamal* (marijuana) makes an appearance in a cauldron once used to serve food to slaves, with a plaque explaining '*car la drogue est un terrible esclavage*' ('because drugs are a terrible form of slavery'). Information booklets are available in English, French and German.

LE CIMETIERE MARIN (*St-Paul;* \ *0692 863288;* e *contact@guid-a-nou.com; www. guid-a-nou.com; guided tour 09.00 Fri*) While you can wander around the cemetery under your own steam, this 1-hour guided tour recounts the stories behind some of the more interesting occupants, such as La Buse, the pirate, and Leconte Delisle, the poet.

MAISON DE LA MANGUE (*50 Chemin de la Vanille, Grand Fond, St-Paul;* m *0692 574839; www.;maison-mangue.re; guided tours Tue–Sun on reservation; tours €6*) Mangoes are grown all over Réunion and make an appearance in all sorts of traditional dishes. This mango plantation provides guided tours with an expert who explains their cultivation. Tours are followed by a tasting.

20

21

The Interior

No visit to Réunion is complete without at least a few days spent exploring the magnificent, mountainous interior. Visitors cannot fail to be impressed by the island's three natural amphitheatres (the Cirques of Salazie, Cilaos and Mafate), with their imposing green mountains, punctuated by waterfalls plunging down steep gorges. The island's interior also boasts the highest mountain in the Indian Ocean (Piton-des-Neiges, 3,069m) and one of our planet's most active volcanoes, the monstrous 2,631m Piton-de-la-Fournaise (see pages 312–13).

There are also the two upland plains: Plaine-des-Palmistes is adjacent to spectacular and vast primary forests, while the much higher Plaine-des-Cafres is surrounded by dairy farms, evoking images of the Swiss Alps in summer. This noticeable resemblance to the Alps is enhanced by quaint mountain villages with charming architecture, a backdrop of imposing slopes and a reputation for producing excellent cheeses.

The best way to explore the interior, particularly the cirques, is on foot. Over 1,000km of hiking trails criss-cross the island, attracting enthusiasts from around the globe (see pages 283–6).

LA PLAINE-DES-PALMISTES

The floriferous village of Plaine-des-Palmistes, in the permanently humid uplands high above St-Benoît, is divided into Premier Village, Deuxième Village and Petite-Plaine.

The magnificent waterfall of **Cascade Biberon**, which tumbles 240m down a sheer mountainside, is easily reached from Premier Village on the RN3. It is signed from Plaine-des-Palmistes. Getting there involves an uncomplicated walk of 3km from the parking area. Most of the goyavier which grows wild in Réunion now comes from this area and, in season, you're bound to see groups of people clambering about in the forests, harvesting the small, red fruit.

The **town hall** and **post office** are on Rue de la République. There's also a **war memorial**, in honour of the soldiers who died in World War I.

South of Plaine-des-Palmistes, just beyond **Col de Bellevue** on the RN3, is a large shrine to **Saint Expédit**, with a statue of the man himself in a Roman legionnaire's outfit. A plaque tells how he was whipped and beheaded on 19 April AD303 for not renouncing Christ (see box, page 359).

Plaine-des-Palmistes is the gateway to the fabulous primeval rainforests of **Bébour-Bélouve**. These luxuriant forests constitute the single most important stop in Réunion for naturalists.

Leaving the town for the Bébour-Bélouve forest area, you drive out along Route de la Petite Plaine, towards steep, misty slopes and ridges. *En route*, you pass dairy and vegetable farms, again very reminiscent of Switzerland, Italy or France. The

road winds its way steadily uphill; turn right following the arrow pointing to Bébour-Bélouve and you'll see the first slopes swathed in evergreen montane forest.

Dominating these forests are hundreds of thousands of tree ferns, from which the name 'Plaine-des-Palmistes' was (erroneously) derived. For a short distance you then drive along a dirt road, to the sign 'Forêt de la Petite Plaine', where there is a comprehensive information board about the forests of Bébour (5,800ha of primary forest) and Bélouve (889ha of primary forest).

While no wood may be removed from Bébour, tamarind wood can be taken from Bélouve, within reason and under strict supervision. There is also a zone called Canton de Duvernay, where Cryptomeria wood may be extracted. Signs advise the following rules for all the forests: *No litter, no fires, no radios and no removing of indigenous flora.*

Continue past **Canton de Duvernay**, after which you pass the **Col de Bébour** and **Rivière des Marsouins** area to your right, and you'll arrive at another large roadside information board, where a wonderful trail commences into Bébour.

This trail, which can be walked in an hour, involves a level stretch along the mountainside (roughly 1,030m above sea level), so can be managed by almost anyone. Mosses, lichens and other epiphytes festoon the trees, clotting on the branches, like enormous, outrageous wigs. Often, these epiphytes have a yellowish or sometimes reddish hue, so the forest is really unusual in that everything appears almost golden, not green. If you search carefully among the epiphytes, you might find some of the indigenous orchids, but they're uncommon.

Also present are most of the birds unique to Réunion: Mascarene paradise flycatchers, Réunion bulbuls, Réunion stonechats, Réunion olive white-eyes and Réunion grey white-eyes. In the sky watch out for Mascarene cave swiftlets, Mascarene martins and Réunion harriers.

Along the road from here to Bélouve Forest are miles and miles of primary forest swathing steep, mist-enshrouded slopes and valleys.

When you see increasing numbers of the silvery tamarind trees, you'll know you're approaching Bélouve Forest. There is a point signposted and cordoned off, beyond which vehicles are not allowed. It's a short walk along a road flanked by impressive tamarind forest, to the Gîte de Bélouve. There's a breathtaking viewpoint at the back of the *gîte* over a wide, deep valley and a disused cable-car station.

GETTING THERE AND AWAY Plaine-des-Palmistes lies on the RN3, which links St-Pierre and St-Benoît. Buses travel the whole route about three times a day (Line S2), whilst others just run between Plaine-des-Palmistes and St-Benoît (*www.cirest.fr*).

 WHERE TO STAY There are several *gîtes* in the area and a *ferme auberge* (farm inn). For further details, see pages 273–4.

Budget
 Ferme du Pommeau** (19 rooms) 10 Allée des Pois de Senteur, Plaine-des-Palmistes; \0262 514070; e la-ferme-du-pommeau@ wanadoo.fr; www.pommeau.fr. Accommodation on a small farm. Comfortable, unfussy Creole-style en-suite rooms with AC, TV & phone. Rooms equipped for the disabled are available. There is an excellent restaurant & bar, & tours of the farm can be arranged. **$$**

Self-catering holiday rentals
 Massilia** 9 Rue Louis Parny, Plaine-des-Palmistes; \0262 460799; e marlene.poiny-toplan@wanadoo.fr. An 8-bedroom house with large kitchen & 3 bathrooms, able to sleep up to 18 people. From €470 per weekend (8 people).

 Poiny-Toplan** 4 Rue Delmas Hoareau, Plaine-des-Palmistes; \0262 460799; e marlene. poiny-toplan@wanadoo.fr. Pretty Creole-style

villa with 6 bedrooms, 2 bathrooms, living room, kitchen & large veranda. Garden & parking. From €250 per weekend (2 people).

Camping

⚑ Camping des Capucines 2 Impasse des Pâquerettes, Plaine-des-Palmistes; ☎0262 475948. As well as tent pitches, this picturesque campsite offers self-catering cabins for up to 4 people. **$**

✕ **WHERE TO EAT** Supplies can be bought at the **Chez Alexis supermarket**, near the Shell petrol station in Plaine-des-Palmistes. Most of Plaine-des-Palmistes's restaurants are on Rue de la République, so finding a meal isn't difficult. Here is a selection:

✳ ✕ **Ferme du Pommeau** 10 Allée des Pois de Senteur, Plaine-des-Palmistes; ☎0262 514070; ⊕ for lunch & dinner daily, closed Sun evening. Cuisine: Creole, French. Excellent home-cooked food at the farm inn. Reservation recommended. **$$$**

✕ **Les Plantanes** 167 Rue de la République, Plaine-des-Palmistes; ☎0262 513169; ⊕ for lunch

Tue–Sun, dinner on reservation. Cuisine: Creole, Chinese. Traditional dishes prepared with local ingredients. **$$$**

✕ **Café des Arts** 325 Rue de la République, Plaine-des-Palmistes; m 0692 655741; ⊕ 09.00–19.00 Wed–Mon. Cuisine: snacks. Informal café opposite the post office. Serves salads & sandwiches. **$$**

LA PLAINE-DES-CAFRES

As you drive away from Plaine-des-Palmistes in a southwesterly direction, the road takes you higher and higher, away from the forests and into a rather desolate-looking expanse featuring harsh, scrubby vegetation and grassland. You'll also see fields of dairy cattle. This is Plaine-des-Cafres, much of which is around 2,000m above sea level.

In the village of **Bourg-Murat**, just north of Plaine-des-Cafres town, is the turning which takes you onto the road to the volcano (RF5, La Route du Volcan), Piton-de-la-Fournaise. This is also where you'll find the **Cité du Volcan** (pages 349–50).

Many of the towns that line the RN3 between here and **Le Tampon** are named according to their distance from the sea, hence Le Dixneuvième and Le Quatorzième, etc. As well as producing cheese, the area is known for its geranium oil and honey.

The town of Plaine-des-Cafres is the starting point for some arduous trekking routes to places like Piton-des-Neiges, of which there are excellent views from here on clear mornings. On the main road you'll find a **post office** and **banks**. The area has a very laid-back atmosphere and, despite nearby attractions like the volcano, does not swarm with tourists. The climate can be pretty chilly, especially when the afternoon clouds smother the area in a cool fog.

If you take the turning towards **Bois Court** at the crossroads in Vingt-troisième, the road will take you to the viewpoint over the gorges of **Rivière des Citrons**. You'll see majestic waterfalls and, way down below, the isolated hamlet of **Grand Bassin**. The energetic can hike the 2km down to Grand Bassin, where there are several *gîtes*.

TOURIST INFORMATION The **tourist office** (☎ 0262 274000; ⊕ 09.00–12.30 & 13.30–17.00 Mon–Sat) is at 160 Rue Maurice et Katia Kraft off the RN3.

⌂ WHERE TO STAY
Budget

⌂ **Auberge du Volcan**** (15 rooms) PK27-RN3 Bourg-Murat, La Plaine-des-Cafres; ☎0262 275091; e aubvolcan@wanadoo.fr. Basic en-suite rooms with TV & heater. There is a restaurant (see opposite). **$$**

⌂ **L'Ecrin**** (21 rooms) PK27-RN3, Bourg-Murat, La Plaine-des-Cafres; ☎0262 590202; e reception@hotel-ecrin.re; http://hotel.ecrin. pagesperso-orange.fr. Conveniently located

about 150m from Cité du Volcan & the road to the volcano. Rooms have TV, phone & heater, & most have mountain views. Family units have kitchenette. Rooms equipped for the disabled are available. It has a restaurant, sauna & minigolf. **$$**

✳ ⌂ **Les Géraniums**** (25 rooms) RN3, 24ème km, La Plaine-des-Cafres; \0262 591106; e hotelgeranium@wanadoo.fr; www.hotellesgeraniums.com. Commands panoramic views of Piton-des-Neiges, Bois Court & Dimitile Mountain. Comfortable, spacious en-suite rooms with TV, phone & heater. The atmosphere is peaceful & the staff are friendly. Try to get a room with a mountain view. There is a good restaurant (see below). **$$**

⌂ **Les Grevilleas***** (5 rooms, 1 villa) 7 Ter, RN3, PK20, La Plaine-des-Cafres; \0262 591797; www.grevilaire.com. Mrs Vilcourt offers guesthouse & *gîte* accommodation. The guesthouse is on the small family farm. The rooms are en suite & simply furnished. The Creole-style 3-bedroom *gîte* sleeps up 6 people & has wonderful views to the coast. **$$**

✖ WHERE TO EAT

✖ **Le Vieux Bardeau** 24ème km, La Plaine-des-Cafres; \0262 590944; ⊕ for lunch & dinner Fri–Wed. Cuisine: Creole. Elegant restaurant in a charming Creole house, set back from the main road. Superb Creole dishes with a creative twist. **$$$$**

✖ **Auberge du Volcan** Bourg-Murat, La Plaine-des-Cafres; \0262 275091; ⊕ 06.30–22.00, closed Sun evening & Mon. Cuisine: Creole, French. Quaint, French provincial décor & tasty food. **$$$**

✖ **La Ferme du Pêcheur Gourmand** RN3, 25ème km, La Plaine-des-Cafres; \0262 592979. Cuisine: French, Creole. This small farm has a charming table d'hôte restaurant with a reputation for excellent, home-cooked French food. Duck is the speciality here. Many of the ingredients (including the ducks) are produced on the farm. Lunch & dinner on reservation only. **$$$**

✖ **Les Géraniums** 24ème km, La Plaine-des-Cafres; \0262 591106; ⊕ for lunch & dinner daily. Cuisine: Creole, French. Excellent food & wonderful views. The speciality is a sauce made from geranium mushrooms. Reservation recommended. **$$$**

WHAT TO SEE AND DO IN LA PLAINE-DES-PALMISTES AND LA PLAINE-DES-CAFRES

Cheese tasting/buying There are several places where you can sample and buy cheeses in the Plaines. One of the best is **Palais du Fromage** (\ *0262 592715;* ⊕ *10.00–17.00 Thu–Sun*) on the Route du Volcan in Bourg-Murat.

Horseriding There is some fantastic riding country around the Plaines. The equestrian centres around La Plaine-des-Cafres offer treks to the volcano (usually two days). For more information, see page 287.

Domaine des Tourelles (*Rue de la République, Plaine-des-Palmistes;* \ *0262 514759;* e *contact@tourelles.re; www.tourelles.re;* ⊕ *09.00–17.30 Mon & Wed–Fri, 09.00–17.00 Tue, 10.00–17.00 Sat/Sun; admission free*) A wonderful Creole house, built in the 1920s, where all manner of Réunion-made handicrafts and ornaments are on sale. During the week, artisans can be seen crafting their products in the workshops on site. Visitors can also organise to do educational botanical walking tours of the area, which cost (adult/child) around €4/2.

Cité du Volcan ✳ (*RN3 Bourg-Murat, La Plaine-des-Cafres;* \ *0262 590026;* e *secretariat@maisonduvolcan.fr; www.museesreunion.re;* ⊕ *13.00–17.00 Mon, 09.30–17.00 Tue–Sun; admission adult/child €9/6; 4D cinema €2*) Formerly La Maison du Volcan, this museum has been completely revamped and reopened to the public in August 2014. A lot of money has been spent and it is now packed with high-tech interactive displays and even has a 4D cinema (€2 supplement).

If you haven't been to a 4D cinema, it is worth it and this one is full of surprises. The entrance to the museum bodes well, as you pass through a multi-sensory lava tunnel, and the rest of it doesn't disappoint. There are excellent exhibitions on the island's geological origins, Piton-de-la-Fournaise and volcanoes in general. It is well worth a visit before seeing the real thing, not least because there is a webcam showing what is happening around Piton-de-la-Fournaise.

THE CIRQUES

A substantial portion of Réunion's interior is taken up by three 'cirques' or gigantic natural amphitheatres, which were formed when ancient volcanic craters collapsed. Subsequent erosion by the elements completed the job. The cirques, which differ considerably from each other in scenery and climate, converge at Piton-des-Neiges.

The first inhabitants of the cirques were runaway slaves or *marrons* of Malagasy origin, who fled to the mountains to escape slave hunters. Hence many villages in the cirques have Malagasy names.

CIRQUE DE CILAOS The name 'Cilaos' is derived from a Malagasy word meaning 'the place you never leave'. This is the southernmost and driest of Réunion's cirques, covering roughly 100km². It lies between the island's two highest peaks: **Piton-des-Neiges** (3,069m) and **Grand Bénard** (2,896m). Where remote mountain hamlets now nestle on small, flat plots called *ilets*, runaway slaves once sought shelter.

About 10,000 people live in this cirque, where the climate is conducive to cultivation of lentils (for the nationally popular *cari* dishes), vineyards (for local wine production) and tobacco. The climate is widely renowned as the healthiest of all Réunion's microclimates and the thermal springs are said to have healing properties (see pages 354–5). Note that evenings, even in summer, can be very cold, whilst the days are normally pleasant, with sunny mornings. Ordinarily, a cloak of mist descends on the town by about 15.00, adding to the dreamy ambience.

Getting to the town of Cilaos, the largest settlement in the cirques and an absolutely charming place, entails the infamous uphill drive from St-Louis on the coast. I say 'infamous' because this 34km road features 200 sharp hairpin bends and you won't forget negotiating it in a hurry. The trip will take you at least 2 hours, with stops at awesome viewpoints. Sadly, the road has seen many fatalities, as is evident from the presence of numerous roadside shrines.

Many visitors remark on the similarity of Cilaos's scenery to that of the western European Alps in summertime. This is mostly true of the region around the town of Cilaos itself, which is at 1,200m, but there are also some lush tropical forests.

Cilaos is known for the **embroidery** which is produced here and numerous shops sell locally made examples.

You used to be able to visit **thermal springs** in the forest just outside the town, which were discovered in 1819. Unfortunately a rock slide during a cyclone covered the springs and they can no longer be reached. Visitors can still experience the thermal waters at the Irénée Accot Thermal Centre (see pages 354–5).

Above the town of Cilaos is the small settlement of **Ilet à Cordes**, said to be named for the ropes that the runaway slaves used to reach the small plateau on which it sits. It is cradled within steep slopes and arriving there you feel as if you are the first to discover it. The 430 or so inhabitants are predominantly farmers; **lentils** have been grown here since 1835 and are the main crop, harvested around September and left to dry in the sun.

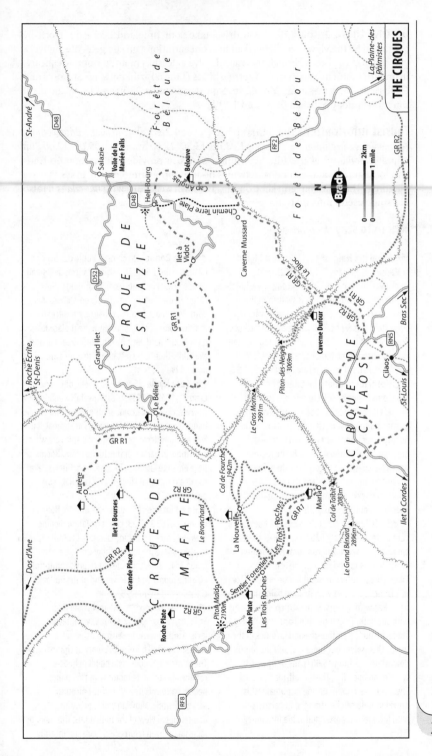

Getting there and away If you drive, take your time and take care. Don't be distracted by the view – you'll need all the concentration you can get! Alternatively, you can take the bus, although this may involve at least as many, if not more, heart-in-mouth moments as driving. Alternéo buses (Line 60) run between St-Louis and Cilaos about 12 times a day Monday to Saturday between 05.30 and 18.30 and eight times on Sunday between 05.30 and 17.30.

Tourist information The tourist office (0820 203220; e accueil.cilaos@gmail. com; www.sud.reunion.fr; 08.30–12.30 & 13.30–17.00 Mon–Sat, 09.00–12.00 Sun & public holidays) is at 2 Rue MacAuliffe. Staff can provide information on trails and local guides, and can book activities or accommodation for any hikes you are planning. There is a souvenir shop on site. The town website (www.ville-cilaos.fr) also has some useful information.

Where to stay Map, opposite

Mid range

Hotel des Neiges* (31 rooms) 1 Rue de la Mare à Joncs, Cilaos; 0262 317233; e reservation@hotel-des-neiges.com; www.hotel-des-neiges.com. About 15mins' walk from the town centre. Plain but spotless rooms of varying sizes, standards & prices all with en-suite facilities & phone. Additional 2 pools, jacuzzi & sauna. There is a computer with internet access available for guest use. Parts of the hotel are a little dark. **$$$**

Hotel les Chenêts-Le Cilaos**** (46 rooms & suites) 40E Chemin des Trois Mares, Cilaos; 0262 318585; e reservation@leschenets.fr; www.leschenets-lecilaos.re. Good-quality accommodation within a Creole-style building. TV, phone & minibar in the rooms, which are spacious & nicely furnished. There is a restaurant but meals are also cooked the traditional way on a wood fire in the garden. There is a pool & a spa. **$$$**

Tsilaosa**** (15 rooms) 21 Rue du Père Boiteau, Cilaos; 0262 373939; e accueil@tsilaosa.com; www.tsilaosa.com. A supremely pretty hotel situated right in the centre of Cilaos. The architecture wouldn't be out of place in a French ski resort with its long balconies bedecked with flowers. Romantic en-suite rooms with spa bath, TV, phone, minibar & free Wi-Fi. There are no tea-/coffee-making facilities in the rooms themselves but there is a cosy tea room downstairs, from 15.00 (page 354) with a welcoming open fire. There is off-road parking. There is no restaurant on site but breakfast is provided & HB can be arranged in partnership with local restaurants. Good value for money. **$$$**

Budget

Bois Rouge (5 rooms) 2 Route des Sources, Cilaos; m 0692 699430; e giteleboisrouge@gmail. com; www.leboisrouge.com. Charming yellow Creole house with 5 comfortable en-suite rooms with TV, minibar, heating & balcony/terrace. There is a cosy lounge with fireplace, a great place to relax after a hard day's hiking. Wi-Fi & car parking available. There is no restaurant so rooms are sold on a BB basis. **$$**

Case Nyala (5 rooms) 8 Ruelle des Lianes, Cilaos; 0262 318957; e case-nyala@wanadoo. fr; www.case-nyala.com. Another charming Creole house on a quiet street. The rooms are immaculate & beautifully decorated. The public areas are warm & inviting, in particular the dining room. Rooms have en-suite facilities, TV & heating. Guests have use of a communal kitchen. Wi-Fi available in public areas. **$$**

Le Platane (4 rooms) Rue du Père Boiteau, Cilaos; 0262 317723; e rest.leplatane@orange. fr; www.hotel-restaurant-cilaos.re. Centrally located, above the restaurant of the same name (page 354). Unremarkable but clean & comfortable en-suite rooms. At the lower end of the budget category price-wise. **$$**

Le Vieux Cep* (45 rooms) 44 Rue St-Louis, Cilaos; 0262 317189; e contact@levieuxcep.re; www.levieuxcep.re. Popular, centrally located hotel with plenty of charm. The attractive, Creole-style building houses comfortable en-suite rooms with TV, phone, heater, balcony & free Wi-Fi. The balconies are worthwhile, allowing you to enjoy an uninterrupted view of the mountains. The superior rooms have been refurbished & are significantly

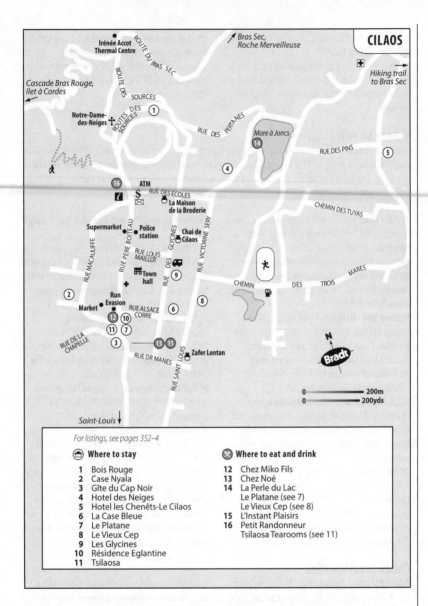

CILAOS

Bras Sec,
Roche Merveilleuse

Hiking trail
to Bras Sec

Irénée Accot
Thermal Centre

Cascade Bras Rouge,
Ilet à Cordes

ROUTE DU BRAS SEC

ROUTE DES SOURCES

ROUTE DES SOURCES

Notre-Dame-
des-Neiges

RUE DES PERTANES

Mare à Joncs
(14)

RUE DES PINS (5)

(4)

(16)
ATM
RUE DES ECOLES

CHEMIN DES TUYAS

La Maison
de la Broderie

Supermarket
Police
station
Chai de
Cilaos

RUE MACAULIFFE
RUE PÈRE BOITEAU
RUE DES GLYCINES
RUE VICTORINE SERY

RUE LOUIS
MAILLOT

Town
hall
(9)

CHEMIN
DES
TROIS
MARES

(2)
Run
Evasion
Market
(12)(10)
(11)(7)
RUE ALSACE
CORRE

RUE DE LA
CHAPELLE

(3)

RUE DR MANES

RUE SAINT LOUIS

Zafer Lontan

(6)
(8)

N

Bradt

0   200m
0   200yds

Saint-Louis

For listings, see pages 352–4

🏠 **Where to stay**

1 Bois Rouge
2 Case Nyala
3 Gîte du Cap Noir
4 Hotel des Neiges
5 Hotel les Chenêts-Le Cilaos
6 La Case Bleue
7 Le Platane
8 Le Vieux Cep
9 Les Glycines
10 Résidence Eglantine
11 Tsilaosa

❌ **Where to eat and drink**

12 Chez Miko Fils
13 Chez Noé
14 La Perle du Lac
     Le Platane (see 7)
     Le Vieux Cep (see 8)
15 L'Instant Plaisirs
16 Petit Randonneur
     Tsilaosa Tearooms (see 11)

smarter than the standard rooms. Rooms for the disabled available. Facilities include an excellent restaurant (page 354), pool, sauna & jacuzzi. Good value for money. **$$**

🏠 **Résidence Eglantine***** (7 studios) 2–4 Rue Alsace Corre, Cilaos; m 0692 826464; e residence.eglantine@wanadoo.fr; www. residence-eglantine.fr. Self-catering accommodation close to the main street, in a large Creole building. Simple but adequate studios with

kitchenette, TV & heating. There are communal barbecues, parking & Wi-Fi. **$$**

Shoestring

🏠 **La Case Bleue** (1 dbl room, dormitory – 11 beds) 15 Rue Alsace Corré, Cilaos; \ 0692 657496; e etheve.valerie@gmail.com; www. gitecasebleue.e-monsite.com. Backpacker-style accommodation in a Creole house. Breakfast €6. Dormitory bed from €16, dbl €40 RO. **$**

Self-catering holiday rentals

⌂ **Gîte du Cap Noir*** 19 C RN, Cilaos;
☏0262 317547; e j-f.grondin@wanadoo.fr. A few
mins from the town centre. Has 3 double rooms & a
mezzanine with 4 further double beds. From €500
per week.

⌂ **Les Glycines**** (2 studios & 1 1-bed apt) 20
Rue des Glycines, Cilaos; ☏0262 317033;
e lesgylcinescilaos@gmail.com. In the centre of
town. Each has TV, kitchenette & parking. From
€245 per week (2 people).

✗ Where to eat *Map, page 353*

There is a **supermarket** on Rue du Père Boiteau, as well as bakeries, greengroceries
and butcher's shops. The covered market (*marché couvert*) on the main street (Rue
du Père Boiteau) sells fruit and vegetables, meat, a variety of local jams (goyavier,
papaya, etc) and sweet Cilaos wine.

✗ **Chez Miko Fils** 25 Rue du Père Boiteau, Cilaos;
☏0262 317052; ⏱ for lunch & dinner Fri–Wed,
closed Sun dinner. Cuisine: Creole. Indoor & terrace
dining on the main street. A selection of Creole
dishes & grilled meat & fish; vegetarians may
struggle. More reasonably priced than many of its
competitors. $$$

✗ **Chez Noé** 40 Rue du Père Boiteau, Cilaos;
☏0262 317993; ⏱ 10.00–15.00 & 18.00–21.00
Tue–Sun. Cuisine: Creole. Popular restaurant
in a pink Creole house in the centre of Cilaos.
Traditional homemade food in an atmospheric
setting, complete with log fire. $$$

✗ **La Perle du Lac** 9 Rue de la Mare à Joncs,
Cilaos; ☏0262 310640; ⏱ Wed–Mon, closed Thu
dinner. Cuisine: Creole. This restaurant overlooks
Mare à Joncs Lake & serves good-quality Creole
buffet food. $$$

✗ **Le Vieux Cep** 2 Rue des Trois Mares, Cilaos;
☏0262 317189; ⏱ for lunch & dinner daily.
Cuisine: Creole, French. Wide range of dishes with
specialities including duck *cari* with corn & the
delicious home-smoked pork with Cilaos lentils.
The restaurant's excellent reputation is well

deserved. Reservation recommended, particularly
for dinner. $$$

✗ **L'Instant Plaisirs** 28 Rue du Père Boiteau;
☏0692 457199; ⏱ 11.30–21.30 Fri–Sun. Cuisine:
French, *crêperie*. A bright, modern restaurant with
indoor seating & a pleasant outdoor area. Serves
tasty crêpes with all manner of fillings. $$$

✗ **Le Platane** 46 Rue du Père Boiteau;
☏0262 317723; ⏱ for lunch & dinner, closed
Wed. Cuisine: Creole, French, Italian. Neat little
restaurant in a yellow & green Creole house in the
centre of town. Wi-Fi available. $$

✗ **Petit Randonneur** 60 Rue du Père Boiteau;
☏0262 317955; ⏱ 09.00–18.00, closed Tue
afternoon & Wed. Cuisine: Creole. Simple,
reasonably priced food. $$

✗ **Tsilaosa Tearooms** 21 Rue du Père Boiteau,
Cilaos; ☏0262 373939; ⏱ 15.00–17.00 daily.
Cuisine: tearooms. The Tsilaosa Hotel serves a range
of exotic teas, pancakes & homemade cakes as
afternoon tea, in comfortable surroundings. The
fireplace near reception is a real feature – a copper
still salvaged from a sugar factory that was being
demolished. $$

Other practicalities

Money and banking There is no bank
but there is an **ATM** outside the **post office**. Bring
sufficient cash with you as this is the only ATM in
Cilaos and it cannot always be relied upon.

Communications The **post office** is in the main street through the village (Rue du
Père Boiteau), not far from the church. **Internet access** is available at **the tourist office**.

Medical The **hospital** (☏ *0262 317050*) is at Les Mares and there are two
pharmacies on the main street, Rue du Père Boiteau.

What to see and do in Cirque de Cilaos

Spa treatments Irénée Accot Thermal Centre (*Route de Bras-Sec, Cilaos;*
☏ *0262 317227;* e *thermes-cilaos@cg974.fr; www.cg974.fr;* ⏱ *08.00–12.30 & 14.00–*

18.00 Mon–Sat, 09.00–17.00 Sun & public holidays, closed Wed afternoon) Just above the town of Cilaos, the Irénée Accot Thermal Centre was opened in July 1988, its proprietors having capitalised on the combination of thermal springs and beautiful, tranquil surrounds.

Certain elements in the water, like sodium, magnesium and calcium, are apparently effective in the treatment of complications varying from rheumatism to digestive ailments.

A range of treatments is offered from spa baths and hammam to health packages lasting several days. A 30-minute massage is around €45. The combination options are good value and typically include two or more of the following: sauna, mineral spa bath, shiatsu, algae or Dead Sea salt treatment and electro-belt massage.

Hiking Needless to say, Cilaos has numerous possibilities for those into walking, hiking or lengthy treks. Even if you do only one of the short walks to nearby villages, you can still enjoy some breathtaking views. Two simple options which come to mind here are the roads to **Bras Sec** village and to the **Roche Merveilleuse**, a superb mountain viewpoint overlooking the whole cirque.

You can also drive to the base of Roche Merveilleuse from where a short climb up some steps takes you to the viewpoint. From the village you can walk to the impressive waterfall known as **Cascade Bras Rouge** (grading: moderate). It involves walking down a steep path and, of course, back up it and takes approximately 2½ hours. You descend along a steep, wooded path into the bottom of a gorge, where the river runs. The huge boulders alongside the river make good, de facto sunloungers and you can dip your toes in the chilly water before braving the walk back up.

For the adventurous, Cilaos is the starting point for the arduous 2-day trek to **Piton-des-Neiges** (for more details, see page 261).

Mountain biking Cilaos is an excellent area for mountain biking. There are two particularly popular routes: the first starts in town, then crosses **Plateau des Chênes** and ends at **Roche Merveilleuse** (grading: moderate). The other starts in **Bras Sec** village, then takes you to **Bras de Benjoin** village and on to Cilaos. **Run Evasion** at 23 Rue du Père Boiteau has mountain bikes and helmets for hire (for more information, see page 286).

Other outdoor activities Cilaos is a popular area for numerous other pursuits, especially **canyoning** and **river hiking**. Run Evasion has an outlet on the main road in Cilaos, which sells outdoor equipment and can arrange activities. For details of activities and operators, see pages 283–91.

Cilaosa Parc Aventure (*Route de Bras Sec;* m *0692 032627;* e *contact@cilaosparc. com; www.cilaosparc.com;* ① *09.00–17.00 daily during school holidays, Wed, Sat/ Sun at other times; adult/child 8–12 years, child 3–7 years €20/15/12 for 3hrs*) Five minutes from the town centre, this adventure park has high ropes courses strung between trees in a stunning setting.

La Maison de la Broderie (*4 Rue des Ecoles, Cilaos;* \ *0262 317748;* ① *09.30– 12.00 & 14.00–17.00 Mon–Sat; 09.30–12.00 Sun; admission €2*) An insight into the traditional **embroidery** for which Cilaos is known. As well as displays of completed embroidery, you will see ladies at work and have the opportunity to marvel at them producing intricate pieces. Items are on sale.

Chai de Cilaos (*34 Rue des Glycines, Cilaos;* \ *0262 317969;* e *contact@ lechaidecilaos.com; www.chaidecilaos.reunion.fr;* ☉ *09.00–12.00 & 14.00–17.30 Mon–Sat; wine tasting €5*) Grapes were introduced by the French in 1771 and a co-operative of growers around Cilaos continues to produce wine. Chai de Cilaos is the only wine producer on the island. There are guided tours and a short film (in French) exploring the history of wine production in the Cilaos area. Visitors can taste and buy some of the Vin de Pays de Cilaos wine.

Zafer Lontan (*30 Rue de St Louis;* \ *0262 319421;* ☉ *10.00–12.00 & 13.30–17.30 Mon, Wed–Sat; admission to the art gallery is free; guided museum visit adult/child €5/4*) Within lies an interesting display of artefacts from the area, charting the history of Cilaos up to 200 years ago. Of particular interest are the recreation of a Creole kitchen and living area, slave chains and a gun used to hunt runaway slaves. There is also a projection room where you can watch 1950s cartoons, on reservation.

CIRQUE DE SALAZIE The largest of the cirques, Salazie measures about 12km by 9km and has a population of about 8,000. Its name comes from a Malagasy word meaning 'good place to stay'.

DAY HIKES AROUND HELL-BOURG

Hell-Bourg is *the* centre for hiking in Réunion. Apart from its superb mountain scenery and numerous trails, it's such a pretty village that it invites a stay of a few days even for casual walkers. Be warned, however: it rains a lot in Hell-Bourg and the most popular trails are consequently very muddy. Good rain gear and waterproof hiking boots are a prerequisite.

An information sheet on the walks ('Liste des Balades dans le Cirque de Salazie') is available from the tourist office in Hell-Bourg (for contact details, see page 358). They are also marked on map 4402 RT (St-Denis) in the IGN 1:25,000 series of six maps covering Réunion. It is useful to know that the official French trail system, the Grandes Randonnées, is marked by red and white paint. Other footpaths are indicated in red and yellow.

As a warm-up try **Les Trois Cascades** (1 hour there and back) where you'll find a series of waterfalls in a lovely mountain setting, or the 4-hour walk (there and back) to **Source Manouilh**. More challenging is the climb up to the top of the escarpment and Bélouve Forest. Beginning at the town hall, this is a 2-hour slog up a well-constructed path to the **Gîte de Bélouve** where, disconcertingly, you'll find some parked cars (it is connected by forest road to Plaine-des-Palmistes). The altitude gain from Hell-Bourg to the *gîte* is about 500m, so it's hard work but the views and vegetation on the way up are magnificent. The return takes only about an hour.

Once here, you can walk to the famous **Trou de Fer**, a deep pool fed by waterfalls hurtling down the sheer mountainsides that surround it. However, you should allow at least 4 hours for this walk (there and back). The latter part of the trail can be very muddy and difficult, and although it looks level on the map it is steeply up and down the whole way. So if you are an average hiker you need to leave Hell-Bourg early in the morning to be sure to be back before dark, and be fit enough for a 7-hour walk. It's much better, therefore, to stay in the comfortable dormitories in the *gîte*. Book as far in advance as possible (\ *0262 412123;* e *gite.belouve@wanadoo.fr*).

The cirque was only settled by European farmers during the mid 19th century, after a hot spring was found at **Hell-Bourg**. A military hospital was established in 1860 to treat soldiers wounded during unrest in Madagascar. Thanks to its pleasant climate, Hell-Bourg became a popular place for coastal inhabitants to visit during the hot months. In 1948, a severe cyclone somehow destroyed the hot spring and Hell-Bourg was all but deserted until 1980, when the government realised its potential value for culture and nature-oriented tourism.

Cirque de Salazie is the greenest of the cirques and has no fewer than 100 waterfalls, which drop down incredibly high, steep gorges. Réunion's best-known waterfall, the exquisite **Voile de la Mariée**, or 'Bridal Veil', is in this cirque. Salazie is the most accessible of the cirques, a picturesque 20-minute drive from St-André.

Salazie and Hell-Bourg The drive inland from St-André takes you into increasingly lush and verdant surroundings, along the Rivière du Mât (you also pass through a village of the same name). Then, looming up ahead, are the high gorges, usually shrouded in a mist mantle. You'll know you're approaching the mouth of the cirque when you see several narrow waterfalls, one of which continually showers on to the tarred road, giving you a free carwash. A signpost announces it as '*Pisse en l'air*' (I don't think that one needs translating!).

Salazie is the area where Réunion's most famed vegetable, the *chouchou* (*Sechium edule*), known in English as the chayote or choko, is cultivated. You will see many small homes surrounded by frames engulfed by this fast-growing climbing plant. The uses for it are many and menus in the area's eateries typically feature everything from *chouchou* stuffed with prawns and melted cheese to *chouchou* cake as a dessert.

The first town you'll come to in the cirque is Salazie itself, but most visitors continue to the smaller town of Hell-Bourg, quite a distance higher up. Few tourists spend any time in Salazie but it does have a **petrol station**, small **supermarket** and a **post office** complete with **ATM** and **payphone**. Both Salazie and Hell-Bourg have **pharmacies**.

As you continue on the winding road from Salazie to Hell-Bourg, it is worth stopping at the **Point du Jour** viewpoint for fantastic views of the cirque. There is a map indicating which peak is which.

Nearby is the sign to the lake of **Mare à Poule d'Eau**, which can be reached on foot or mountain bike. This is where the local inhabitants used to come to collect their water. The village of the same name is just a little further on, shortly beyond which are the famous **Voile de la Mariée Falls** (Bridal Veil Falls). The falls are signed and there is space to pull in and admire them from the road as they tumble into the gorge below.

As you travel between Salazie and Hell-Bourg it is worth making the 15km detour to **Grand Ilet**. It is a pretty, unspoilt village cupped by the cirque's commanding mountains. The village's **Church of St Martin** is a beautiful example of Creole architecture, with its *lambrequin* (filigree-style decoration), its light blue shutters and its tamarind shingle walls. A sign next to the bell tower, which is now in the grounds of the church, tells the building's tortured history – detailing the numerous times it has been destroyed, moved and rebuilt. In the centre of Grand Ilet is a mountain-biking station with a signboard detailing the local trails. **Grand Ilet** is the starting point for hikes to St-Denis via **La Roche Ecrite**, while nearby **Le Bélier** allows access to the hiking trails which connect Cirque de Salazie and Cirque de Mafate. The viewpoint at **Mare à Martin** provides good views of the cirque and its villages.

In contrast to Salazie, which has little charm, **Hell-Bourg** is picture-postcard-perfect. Residents will proudly tell you that Hell-Bourg was awarded the prestigious title of 'Most Beautiful Village in France' in 2000 (I know, 'in France' still seems odd, doesn't it?). It features small Creole houses with tiled roofs, intricate railings and

21

explosions of colourful flowers in the small gardens and ubiquitous flower boxes. EU money has been made available to restore many of the **Creole houses** to their former glory. The wrought-iron *lambrequins* on the front of the eaves are typical, as are the bright colours.

Hell-Bourg is popular with tourists – there are many **souvenir shops** and numerous good Creole restaurants.

Getting there and away Salazie is easily reached by car or local bus service from St-André along a twisty but well-maintained road. Buses travel regularly between Salazie and Hell-Bourg, except on Sunday.

Tourist information Information about the area, hiking and bookings at *gîtes de montagne* are available from the **tourist office** in Hell-Bourg (*47 Rue Général de Gaulle, Hell-Bourg;* ☎ *0262 478989;* e *info@oti-est.re;* ⊕ *08.30–12.00 & 13.00–17.30 Mon–Sat*).

🏠 *Where to stay*

Budget

🏠 **Le Relais des Gouverneurs***** (5 rooms) 2 bis Rue Amiral Lacaze, Hell-Bourg; ☎ 0262 477621. In a large colonial-style house. The rooms are simply but comfortably furnished & have en suite, TV & heating. Free Wi-Fi. **$$**

✳ 🏠 **Les Jardins d'Héva**** (10 rooms) 16 Rue Auguste Lacaussade, Hell-Bourg; ☎ 0262 478787; e lesjardinsdheva@orange.fr. Opened in 2006 by one of the island's leading mountain guides, Alice Deligey, this cosy hotel is sure to be a hit with visitors to the cirque. The hotel is perched above the main part of Hell-Bourg, with views of the cirque from the restaurant & the grounds. The charming en-suite rooms (with terrace & phone) are housed in 5 colourful chalets with a Creole flavour. Guests can use the mini spa (sauna, hammam, jacuzzi), which is welcome relief for tired hikers. The restaurant serves Creole food prepared with local ingredients. If you feel inspired, Creole cooking lessons are also available. **$$**

🏠 **L'Orchidée Rose** (6 rooms) 26 Rue Olivier Manès, Hell-Bourg; ☎ 0262 478722; e reservation@orchideerose.net; www. orchideerose.net. On a quiet backstreet. Rooms have en-suite facilities, TV & Wi-Fi, are clean & well furnished. There is a restaurant for evening meals. **$$**

🏠 **Relais des Cîmes**** (29 rooms) 67 Rue du Général de Gaulle, Hell-Bourg, Salazie; ☎ 0262 478158; e info@relaisdescimes.com; www. relaisdescimes.com. A very popular hotel in the centre of Hell-Bourg, so book well in advance. The rooms are comfortable with en suite, TV, phone & heater; many have superb views. The new rooms are particularly appealing. The restaurant here is legendary (see opposite). **$$**

Self-catering holiday rentals

🏠 **Chez Festin**** 3 Impasse Plateaux Sisayhes, Hell-Bourg; ☎ 0262 465461. Simply furnished 3-bedroom house with terrace & parking. From €280 per week (6 people).

Camping

🏕 **Camping Le Relax** (25 tent pitches) 21 Chemin Bras-Sec; m 0692 665889; www. campinglerelax.e-monsite.com. Tent pitches at this campground are in a beautiful setting with many fruit trees. There is an equipped kitchen & amenities block. Adult/child €11/6. **$**

✖ *Where to eat* There are small **general shops** in both Salazie and Hell-Bourg, where you can stock up on food for hiking. The **supermarket** in Hell-Bourg on the corner of Rues Général de Gaulle and Cayenne is probably your best bet.

✖ **La Cascade Blanche** 3 Pl de l'Escalier, Salazie; ☎ 0262 583997; ⊕ 10.00–17.00 Mon–Fri, 10.00–18.30 Sat/Sun. Cuisine: Creole, French.

Quirky, colourful restaurant serving traditional dishes cooked over a wood fire. **$$$**

✳ ✗ Relais des Cîmes 67 Rue Général de Gaulle, Hell-Bourg; ☎0262 478158; ⊕ for lunch & dinner daily. Cuisine: Creole, French. Arguably the island's best Creole cuisine. This well-known restaurant was founded by Mamie Javel, author of a superb Creole cookbook titled *La Réunion des Milles et Une Saveurs*. In 2006, Mamie Javel, aged 85, finally retired to St-Denis, but her cuisine lives on at this restaurant. Meals are prepared using local products & according to Mamie Javel's famous recipes. Copies of her Creole cookbook are on sale in the restaurant. The décor is unmistakably French, with red & white checked tablecloths & curtains. The *cabri massalé* (goat curry) & the *poulet coco* (coconut chicken) are superb. 3-course menus are good value. **$$$**

✗ Chez Alice 1 Rue des Sangliers, Hell-Bourg; ☎0262 478624; ⊕ for lunch & dinner Tue–Sat, dinner Sun. Cuisine: Creole, French, Chinese. Unpretentious restaurant set back on a side street. Creole dishes served with an array of side dishes. 3-course menus from €19. **$$**

✗ Crêperie Le Gall 55 Rue du Général de Gaulle, Hell-Bourg; ☎ 0262 478748; ⊕ 11.00–19.00 Sat–Thu. Cuisine: French, crêpes, snacks. A cosy, informal place on the main street. Serves a large range of crêpes, including the house speciality – 'La Créole', which comes with banana flambéed in local rum. Savoury snacks, salads & ice cream are also available. **$$**

SAINT EXPEDIT

As well as the roadside shrines to Christ and the Virgin Mary, there are many dedicated to Saint Expédit, which are typically red. Regarded as the national saint of Réunion, he is revered by Réunionnais of all religions.

Saint Expédit has taken on something of a sinister nature in the island's folklore. He is considered particularly effective and prompt (expeditious) at carrying out requests for revenge by placing curses on people. However, in return he demands payment, otherwise he will punish the person who requested his assistance. For this reason the red shrines are typically smothered by offerings, such as candles, flowers and red material, as well as messages of thanks.

Don't be surprised if you see decapitated statues of Saint Expédit in roadside shrines. The damage is either punishment for an unfulfilled request or has been done in order to break a curse that someone feels has been put on them by the saint.

The story of Saint Expédit is very confused. He is believed by many to have been a Roman legionnaire, named Expeditus, who was beheaded on 19 April AD303 in Malatya (Turkey) for not renouncing Christ.

However, some maintain that this story is a fabrication and that the saint's popularity in Réunion is the result of a misunderstanding. The story goes that at the time of the early colonists, the religious community was having difficulty impressing the importance of its values on the population, so wrote to the Vatican to request some religious relics to help them drive their message home.

Finally, at the end of the 19th century a small wooden box arrived bearing the word *expédit* (despatched). Inside were a few scattered bones. The religious community rejoiced – the relics that they had requested had at last arrived. After some discussion, they concluded that the remains must belong to Saint Expédit, as that was the inscription on the box.

Whichever version you believe, the Church's position is clear. In 1905, Pope Pius X demanded that Saint Expédit's name be struck off the list of martyrs and all images of him removed from churches. By this stage Saint Expédit was already adored throughout Réunion and his popularity has never wavered.

✗ **Ti-Chouchou** 42 Rue du Général de Gaulle, Hell-Bourg; ✆ 0262 478093; ⊕ for lunch & dinner Sat–Thu. Cuisine: Creole, French. Eat-in or take-away. As the name suggests, specialises in *chouchou*. Popular, so try to book in advance. $$

Other practicalities

Money and banking Neither Salazie nor Hell-Bourg has a bank but there is an **ATM** outside the post office in Salazie.

Communications There are **post offices** in Salazie, Hell-Bourg and Grand Ilet.

Medical There is a **pharmacy** at Mare à Vielle Place in Hell-Bourg, and one in Salazie.

What to do in Cirque de Salazie

Hiking Most of Salazie's visitors come here, at least in part, for the hiking. The tourist office can provide information on hiking trails in the area, as well as give advice on adventure sports such as **canyoning**. For more information, see pages 283–6.

Mountain biking Numerous trails snake around Salazie, Hell-Bourg and Grand Ilet. For more information, see page 286.

What to see in Cirque de Salazie

Maison Folio (*20 Rue Amiral Lacaze, Hell-Bourg;* ✆ *0262 478098;* e *m.folio@ wanadoo.fr;* ⊕ *09.00–11.30 & 14.00–17.00 daily; admission adult/child under 10 €5/free*) This much-photographed Creole home, lived in by the same family for generations, has preserved the style of the 19th century. Built in 1870 and renovated in the late 1970s, the house, garden and furniture all accurately reproduce the era. Note that the kitchen and dining room are in a separate building at the back, which was the norm in Creole homes. In the garden, ornamental, medicinal and edible plants are typically bunched together in each flower bed. Members of the Folio family provide a very personal guided tour, full of anecdotes.

Creole houses (Cases Créoles) (*Guided tours are arranged via the tourist office; 11.00, 15.30 Tue & on reservation; tour €8*) A leaflet on Hell-Bourg's Creole houses and the route you can follow to see them is available at the tourist office and costs €5. Alternatively, you can join a guided walking tour of Hell-Bourg, with a local guide providing information on the architecture, history and residents of the village's Creole homes.

CIRQUE DE MAFATE Spanning 72km², Mafate is the smallest and most tropical of the cirques. On its northern rim is the **Plaine d'Affouches**, which overlooks St-Denis and the north coast. On its western rim is **Piton Maïdo** (2,190m), which overlooks the dry west coast. To its south lies the Cirque de Cilaos.

Mafate is a wild, sparsely inhabited, mystifying place. Its name has suitably intriguing origins: it is said that a Malagasy sorcerer and runaway slave, named Mafaty (meaning 'dangerous one'), lived at the foot of **Le Bronchard** (1,261m). He was eventually caught in 1751 by François Mussard, a bounty hunter.

The cirque's first inhabitants were indeed runaway slaves after the agricultural colonisation of the island in the 1730s, then the *Créoles Blancs* (White Creoles) arrived following the abolition of slavery in 1848. Today, approximately 650 people reside in remote mountain hamlets, such as **Marla**, **La Nouvelle** and **Aurère**.

MAFATE – A TOUGH GIG FOR A POSTMAN

Until his retirement in 2003, Angelo Thiburce performed what must surely be the toughest postal delivery round in the world. For 37 years he delivered the post, plus lottery tickets, medication and essentials, on foot to Mafate. His postal round was 120km long and took him four days each week. During his career he walked and ran 180,000km in the line of duty with his backpack full of post, the equivalent of 4½ times around the world.

In 1999, he was awarded the French *Ordre Nationale du Mérite* (National Order of Merit). In the final years of his work as a postman he featured in several documentaries and became increasingly well known.

When Angelo retired in 2003, he was replaced by a helicopter which delivers the post to the cirque and two postal workers who distribute the letters to the approximately 300 families scattered around Mafate. Even after his retirement to Le Port, Angelo made a hobby of long-distance walking and running.

They live off the land, in virtual isolation from the outside world. There are no roads, just 100km of walking trails. Supplies such as medication are brought in by helicopter, yet many of the Mafatais have never seen a car.

Ideally, visitors should spend at least two days in Mafate to get a feel for the cirque. Access is on foot from Cilaos, via the **Col du Taïbit**, from Hell-Bourg via the **Col des Bœufs**, and from **Maïdo**, **Sans-Souci**, or **Dos d'Ane**. The easiest option is from Hell-Bourg; even easier is flying in by helicopter. There is rustic accommodation for hikers in many of the villages, including **Marla**, **La Nouvelle** and **Roche-Plate**. There are walks that can be done in a day; for instance, the walks from the car park at Col des Bœufs to either La Nouvelle or Marla take around 4 or 5 hours return. From Cilaos to Marla return takes around 6 hours. When it comes to planning your hike, www.reunion-mafate.com is a useful resource, complete with suggested hikes.

If your time is limited, **Piton Maïdo**, which is accessible by car from St-Paul, provides superb views of the cirque.

🏠 **Where to stay** Many independent hikers choose to camp in this remote area. It can be a wonderful experience with fabulous starry skies. However, it does get very cold so bring along suitable clothing. If you do camp, be sure to clear up completely when you leave.

The alternatives to camping are *gîtes de montagne* and *gîtes d'étapes*. For details of these, see pages 273–4.

🍴 **Where to eat** If you're staying in a gîte, you can order breakfast and dinner in advance. You'll need to bring any other food with you, to fuel all that walking. If you run out of snacks, don't despair – there are small food shops in most of Mafate's villages, including La Nouvelle, Marla, Roche Plate, Grande Place les Hauts, Ilet à Malheur, Aurère and Ilet aux Orangers. They are usually closed on Sunday afternoon and Monday morning.

Réunion: The Interior **THE CIRQUES**

21

Appendix 1

LANGUAGE

To speak Creole, the slightest knowledge of French will be useful for the formalities: for instance, 'Good morning' is '*Bon-zoor*'. Here are some useful phrases that differ from the French. They have been written phonetically (as they should be pronounced).

USEFUL PHRASES

	Mauritian Creole	Réunionnais Creole
How are you?	*Ki man yeah?*	*Komon ee lay?*
Very well, and you?	*Mwa bee-an, eh oo?*	*Lay la eh oo?*
I'm not well	*Mwa pa bee-an*	*Mi lay pa bee-an*
What is your name?	*Ki oo non?*	*Komon oo apel?*
How old are you?	*Ki arj too on?*	*Kay laz oo nayna?*
What are you doing?	*Ki toe pay fare?*	*Ko sa oo fay?*
I don't understand	*Mwa pa kompran*	*Mi kompran pa*
Speak slowly	*Pa koz tro veet*	*Koz doosmon*
I don't speak Creole	*Mwa pa koz Kreol*	*Mi koz pa Kreol*
I don't know	*Mwa pa konnay*	*Mi konnay pa*
How much is it?	*Koomian sa?*	*Koomian i koot?*
It's too expensive	*Li tro ser*	*Lay tro ser*
Good/That's fine	*Li bon*	*Lay bon*
Where are you going?	*Kot oo pay allay?*	*Oo sa oo sa va?*
I want to go to …	*Mwa oo-lay al …*	*Mi vay allay a …*
Take me to the hotel	*Amen mwa lotel*	*Amen a mwa a lotel*
I want to stay	*Mwa pay restay*	*Mi vay restay*
Would you like a drink?	*Oo poo bwah keek soz?*	*Oo vay bwah keek soz?*
I'd like wine	*Mwa oo-lay do van*	*Mi voodray do van*
What's this?	*Ki etay sa?*	*Ko sa ee lay?*
I love you	*Mwa kontan twa*	*Mi em a-oo*
Goodbye	*Sallaam*	*Na wa/nooa troov*

PRONOUNCING PLACE NAMES Stressed syllables are shown in bold.

Baie du Tombeau	Beige-tom-**bo**
Beau Bassin	Bo Bas**sa**
Belle Mare	Bel-mar
Case Noyale	Kaz noy-**al**
Curepipe	Kewr-**peep**
Grand Bassin	Gron Bas**sa**
Gris Gris	Gree-gree

Ile aux Aigrettes	Eel-oh-say**gret**
Ile aux Cerfs	Eel-oh-**sair**
Mahébourg	Mayberg *or* Mah-ay-bour
Morne Brabant	Morn Bra**bon**
Port Louis	Por(t) Loo-**ee**
Port Mathurin	Por(t) Ma-to-**ra**
Quatre Bornes	Katr born
Réduit	**Ray**dwee
Rodrigues	Rod**reegs**
Rose Hill	Roh**zill**
Souillac	**Soo**-ee-yak
Triolet	**Tree**-oh-lay
Trou aux Biches	Troo-oh-**beesh**
Trou d'Eau Douce	Troodoh-**doo**
Vacoas	**Va**-kwa

In Réunion (Ray-oo-nee-on), standard French pronunciation applies.

Appendix 2

FURTHER INFORMATION

GENERAL
Books

Adams, Douglas and Carwardine, Mark *Last Chance to See* William Heinemann, London, 1990. Beautifully written and illustrated, including a section on the endangered Mascarene wildlife (especially Mauritian birds).

Ellis, Dr Matthew and Wilson-Howarth, Dr Jane *Your Child Abroad: A Travel Health Guide* Bradt, 2014 (3rd edition). An invaluable guide for those travelling or resident overseas with babies and children of all ages. Available as an eBook.

Ventor, A J *Where to Dive in Southern Africa and off the Islands* Ashanti Publishing, 1991. Excellent for divers and non-divers alike. Well-written general reviews of all the Mascarenes, plus all the necessary information for divers and snorkelling enthusiasts.

Websites

www.fco.gov.uk/travel Foreign and Commonwealth Office website with up-to-date country-specific advice. Should be consulted prior to travel.

www.nhs.uk/healthcareabroad National Health Service website giving general travel health advice and country-specific inoculation recommendations. Also, everything you need to know about obtaining, completing and using an EHIC form.

www.smartraveller.gov.au Australian Government website with up-to-date country-specific advice. Should be consulted prior to travel.

www.travel.state.gov US State Department website with up-to-date country-specific advice. Should be consulted prior to travel.

MAURITIUS AND RODRIGUES
Books
History

Vaughn, Megan *Creating the Creole Island, Slavery in 18th-century Mauritius* Duke University Press, 2005. Excellent insight into Mauritius as a land of slaves and their masters.

Natural history

Durrell, Gerald *Golden Bats and Pink Pigeons* Fountain, 1979.

Michel, Claude and Owadally, A W *Our Environment, Mauritius* Mauritius, 1975.

Sinclair, Ian, and Langrand, Olivier *Birds of the Indian Ocean Islands* Struik/New Holland, 2004. The definitive field guide for birdwatchers visiting the western Indian Ocean. Includes many interesting discoveries made during the 1990s.

Language

Lee, Jacques K *Mauritius: Its Creole Language* Green Print, 2008.

Activities

Mountain, A and Halbwachs, Y *The Dive Sites of Mauritius* Struik, 1996.

Travel guides/tourist booklets

MTPA *Mauritius Info Guide* Mauritius Tourism Promotion Authority. General information plus lists of restaurants, hotels and activity operators. Maps of Mauritius and Port Louis. Brief section on Rodrigues. Free.

MTPA *Rodrigues: Your Guide* Mauritius Tourism Promotion Authority. Background and practical information, including hotels and restaurants. Map of the island. Free.

General

Baptiste, Françoise *Les Délices de Rodrigues* Payenké, 2008. Excellent Rodriguan recipe book.

Newspapers

Mauritius News, 'The first Mauritian Newspaper Overseas' published monthly; 583 Wandsworth Road, London SW8 3JD; ✎ 020 7498 3066; e editor@mauritiusnews.info; www.mauritius-news.info

Websites

www.gov.org Mauritian Government website with extensive information, including the latest economic news and links to all departments and government bodies.

http://statsmauritius.gov.org Up-to-date statistics on Mauritius.

www.tourism-mauritius.mu Mauritius Tourist Promotion Authority website. Contains background and practical information, including visa requirements. Provides details of hotels, restaurants and things to see in Mauritius.

www.maurinet.com Designed for tourists and business visitors. Hotel and restaurant contact details can be easily found, as well as the usual background information. The business guide contains listings of company contact details for a multitude of sectors.

www.tourism-rodrigues.mu MTPA website on Rodrigues. General tourist information. Very comprehensive.

http://metservice.intnet.mu Weather and cyclone information.

www.airmauritius.com Website of the airline. Includes schedule and route details, as well as online booking.

REUNION
Books
Natural history

Moyne-Picard, Marylène and Dutrieux, Eric *Fonds sous-marins de L'Ile de la Réunion* Ouest France, 1997. Guide to the marine environment around Réunion, plus information on the best dive sites. In French only.

Activities

Fédération Française de la Randonnée Pédestre *Topoguide: L'Ile de la Réunion*. Comprehensive guide to the GR R1 and GR R2 trails, including maps. In French only.

Office Nationale des Forêts *Itinéraires Réunionnais* Bat' Karé. Information on hiking and suggested trails. In French only.

Office Nationale des Forêts *Sentiers Marmailles* Bat' Karé. 42 easy walks of less than 3 hours, designed with children in mind. In French only.

Reynaud, Luc *52 Balades et Randonnées Faciless à La Réunion* Orphie, 2003. 52 easy and moderate hikes. In French only.

Travel guides/tourist booklets

Comité du Tourisme de la Réunion *Guide des 24 Communes*. Focuses on the places of interest in each of the island's 24 communes. In French only.

Comité du Tourisme de la Réunion *Le Guide Run*. Published annually. Invaluable information on what to see in each region, plus hotel and restaurant contact details. In French and English.

General

Gélabert, Serge *La Réunion Fruit d'une Passion* Serge Gélabert, 1998. Largely photos with some text on the island. In French only.

Gélabert, Serge and Javel, Mamy *La Réunion des Mille et Une Saveurs* Serge Gélabert, 1998. Excellent Creole recipe book. In French only.

Grenson, Jan. *La Cuisine de la Réunion* Editions Orphie, 2004. Réunionnais recipes, from *punch* to *cari*. In French only.

Websites

www.reunion.fr Website of the Ile de la Réunion Tourisme. A must for anyone planning a trip. Packed with information available in English and numerous other languages about every aspect of the country. Includes information on accommodation, restaurants and activities.

www.resa.reunion.fr Booking service for Ile de la Réunion Tourisme, where you can make reservations for accommodation, activities, excursions and more.

www.allonslareunion.com Information on accommodation, restaurants, car hire, excursions and activities in French and English.

www.guide-reunion.com Background, practical and tourist information in French.

www.ilereunion.com General website in French only, with hotel, restaurant and activities information. Useful descriptions of each region and major towns with things to see. Also, weather and traffic information and useful phone numbers.

www.creole.org Aims to give a feel of what Réunion is actually like, with an emphasis on culture. Contains photographs, Creole recipes, accommodation and restaurant information. Mostly in French, although parts are in English.

www.batcarre.com Information about events and culture on the island.

www.buzbuz.re Information about the latest trends on the island.

www.meteo-reunion.com Weather information for the island, including satellite pictures and cyclone news.

Index

INDEX OF ADVERTISERS

above The traditional *séga* dance has its roots in slavery (DC/DT) page 38

left Mauritius's many cultures and religions mean an abundance of vibrant festivals (RJS/DT) pages 68–70

below Vital to *séga* music is the drum beat provided by the *ravane*, a goatskin tambourine (AR) page 38

above **La Cascade de Grand-Galet at Langevin is one of Réunion's many striking waterfalls** (AR) page 319

right **Fishermen in Rodrigues use traditional lobster pots made from *vacoas* leaves** (NS) pages 32–3

below **Regular lava flows from Piton-de-la-Fournaise have created a bizarre lunar landscape** (AR) pages 312–13

above   **Cilaos is the most accessible of Réunion's three natural amphitheatres, created by the collapse of ancient volcanic craters** (SB/S) pages 350–6

left   **A peaceful morning at Tamarin on Mauritius's west coast** (AR) pages 173–7

below   **A typical Rodriguan smallholding provides food for the family as well as produce to sell at the Port Mathurin market** (AR) pages 216–17

Colonial architecture
Carefully restored, Château de Labourdonnais in the north of Mauritius is a fine colonial sugar planter's mansion
(AR) page 137

Local traditions and culture
Grand Bassin comes into its own during Hindu festivals such as Ganesh Chaturthi, honouring the elephant-nosed god
(AR) page 69

Stunning beaches and bays
Rodrigues's unspoilt eastern beaches, such as Anse Bouteille, are typically deserted
(AR) page 243

Mascarene
Islands
Don't
miss...

Colourful markets
Markets like the one
in Port Louis provide a
snapshot of everyday life
(AR) page 102

Rugged landscapes
The stunning Piton-de-la-Fournaise
on Réunion is one of the world's
most active volcanoes
(AR) pages 312–13

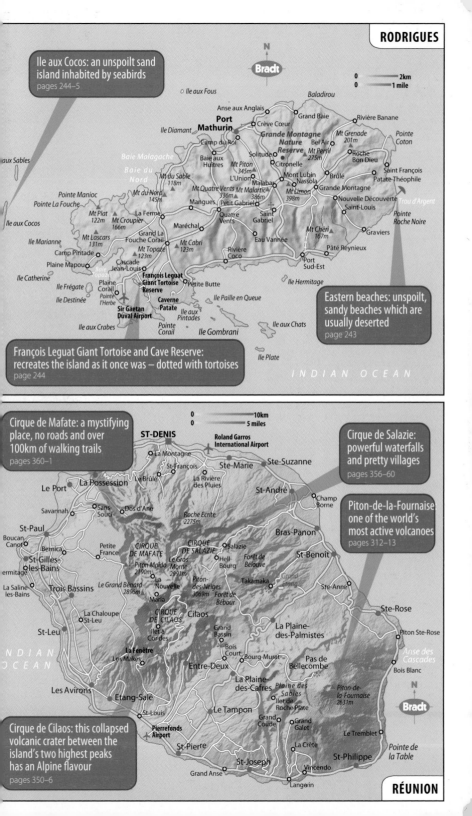

RODRIGUES

Bradt

N

| 0 | 2km |
| 0 | 1 mile |

Ile aux Cocos: an unspoilt sand island inhabited by seabirds
pages 244–5

o Ile aux Fous

Baladirou

Anse aux Anglais

Ile Diamant

Port Mathurin

Crève Cœur

Grand Baie

Rivière Banane

Mt Grenade 201m

Pointe Coton

Camp du Roi

Baie Malagache

Baie aux Huîtres

Grande Montagne Nature Reserve

Bel Air Mt Persil 275m

Solitude

Citronelle

Roche Bon Dieu

Saint François

aux Sables

Baie du Nord

Mt Piton 345m

L'Union

Mont Lubin Nassola

Brûlé

Patate-Théophile

Pointe Manioc

Mt du Sable 118m

Malabar

Grande Montagne

Pointe La Fouche

Mt du Nord 145m

Mt Quatre Vents 336m Mt Malartic 386m

Mt Limon 398m

Nouvelle Découverte

Trou d'Argent

Ile aux Cocos

Mangues

Petit Gabriel

Saint-Louis

La Ferme

Quatre Vents

Saint Gabriel

Pointe Roche Noire

Ile Marianne

Mt Plat 122m

Mt Croupier 166m

Maréchal

Mt Lascars 131m

Grand La Fouche Corail

Mt Cabri 123m

Eau Vannée

Mt Chéri 167m

Graviers

Camp Pintade

Mt Topaze 123m

Rivière Coco

Pâté Réynieux

Plaine Mapou

Cascade Jean-Louis

Baie Topaze

Port Sud-Est

Ile Catherine

Plaine Corail

François Leguat Giant Tortoise Reserve

Petite Butte

Ile Hermitage

Ile Frégate

Pointe l'Herbe

Caverne Patate

Ile Paille en Queue

Ile Destinée

Sir Gaëtan Duval Airport

Ile aux Pintades

Ile aux Chats

Ile aux Crabes

Pointe Corail

Ile Gombrani

Ile Plate

INDIAN OCEAN

Eastern beaches: unspoilt, sandy beaches which are usually deserted
page 243

François Leguat Giant Tortoise and Cave Reserve: recreates the island as it once was – dotted with tortoises
page 244

Cirque de Mafate: a mystifying place, no roads and over 100km of walking trails
pages 360–1

| 0 | 10km |
| 0 | 5 miles |

ST-DENIS

Roland Garros International Airport

Cirque de Salazie: powerful waterfalls and pretty villages
pages 356–60

La Montagne

Ste-Marie

Ste-Suzanne

Le Port

St-François

La Possession

Le Brûlé

La Rivière des Pluies

St-André

Champ Borne

Savannah

Sans-Souci

Dos d'Ane

Roche Ecrite 2275m

Piton-de-la-Fournaise: one of the world's most active volcanoes
pages 312–13

St-Paul

Boucan Canot

Bernica

Petite France

CIRQUE DE MAFATE

CIRQUE DE SALAZIE

Salazie

Bras-Panon

St-Gilles-les-Bains

Piton Maïdo 2190m

Le Gros Morne 2991m

Hell Bourg

Forêt de Béloue

St-Benoît

ermitage

La Saline-les-Bains

Le Grand Bénard 2896m

La Nouvelle

Piton-des-Neiges 3069m

Forêt de Bébour

Takamaka

Grand Etang

Ste-Anne

Trois Bassins

Marla

Ste-Rose

La Chaloupe St-Leu

CIRQUE DE CILAOS

Cilaos

Piton Ste-Rose

St-Leu

Ilet à Cordes

Grand Bassin

La Plaine-des-Palmistes

Anse des Cascades

INDIAN OCEAN

La Fenêtre

Les Makes

Bois Court

Bourg-Murat

Pas de Bellecombe

Bois Blanc

Les Avirons

Entre-Deux

N

Etang-Salé

La Plaine-des-Cafres

Plaine des Sables

Piton-de-la-Fournaise 2631m

Bradt

St-Louis

Ilet de Roche-Plate

Cirque de Cilaos: this collapsed volcanic crater between the island's two highest peaks has an Alpine flavour
pages 350–6

Pierrefonds Airport

Le Tampon

Grand Coude

Grand Galet

Le Tremblet

Pointe de la Table

St-Pierre

La Crête

St-Joseph

St-Philippe

Grand Anse

Vincendo

Langevin

RÉUNION

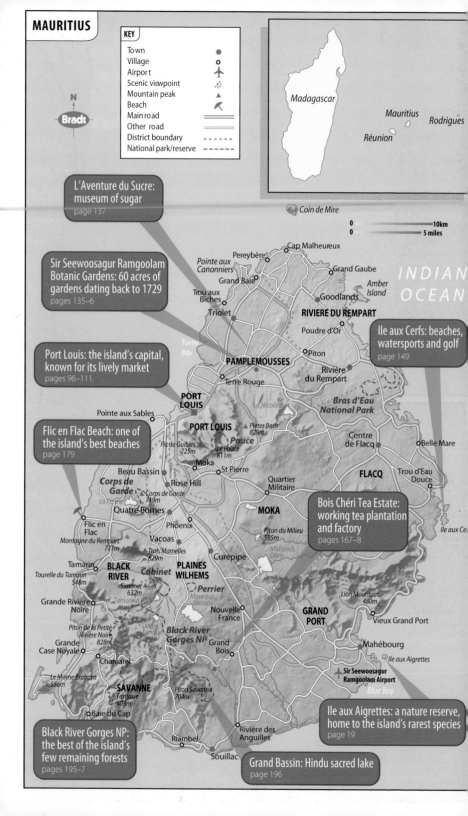

MAURITIUS

KEY
Town	●
Village	○
Airport	✈
Scenic viewpoint	⚜
Mountain peak	▲
Beach	⚓
Main road	═══
Other road	───
District boundary	‑‑‑‑
National park/reserve	‑ ‑ ‑

N
Bradt

Madagascar

Mauritius   *Rodrigues*

Réunion

L'Aventure du Sucre: museum of sugar
page 137

Sir Seewoosagur Ramgoolam Botanic Gardens: 60 acres of gardens dating back to 1729
pages 135–6

Port Louis: the island's capital, known for its lively market
pages 96–111

Flic en Flac Beach: one of the island's best beaches
page 179

Ile aux Cerfs: beaches, watersports and golf
page 149

Bois Chéri Tea Estate: working tea plantation and factory
pages 167–8

Ile aux Aigrettes: a nature reserve, home to the island's rarest species
page 19

Black River Gorges NP: the best of the island's few remaining forests
pages 195–7

Grand Bassin: Hindu sacred lake
page 196

Coin de Mire

INDIAN OCEAN

0 _____ 10km
0 _____ 5 miles

Cap Malheureux
Pereybère
Pointe aux Canonniers
Grand Gaube
Grand Baie
Amber Island
Trou aux Biches
Goodlands
Triolet

RIVIERE DU REMPART

Poudre d'Or
Piton
Rivière du Rempart

Turtle Bay

PAMPLEMOUSSES
Terre Rouge

La Nicolière

PORT LOUIS

PORT LOUIS
Pointe aux Sables
Pieter Both 820m
Pouce
Pic de Guibies 725m
Le Pouce 811m
Moka
St Pierre
Quartier Militaire

Bras d'Eau National Park

Centre de Flacq
Belle Mare

FLACQ
Trou d'Eau Douce

Beau Bassin
Rose Hill

Corps de Garde
La Ferme
Corps de Garde 719m
Quatre-Bornes
Phoenix
Vacoas
Trois-Mamelles 629m

MOKA

Piton du Milieu 585m

Ile aux Ce...

Curepipe

Midlands Dam

Tamarin
Tourelle du Tamarin 548m

BLACK RIVER

Cabinet
Simonet 632m
Tamarind Falls
Montagne du Rempart 777m
Flic en Flac

Mare aux Vacoas

PLAINES WILHEMS
Perrier

Lion Mountain 480m

Grande Rivière Noire
Piton de la Petite Rivière Noire 828m
Mare Longue
Nouvelle France

GRAND PORT

Vieux Grand Port

Grande Case Noyale

Black River Gorges NP
Grand Bois

Mahébourg
Ile aux Aigrettes

Chamarel

Le Morne Brabant 556m

SAVANNE
Fantaisie 403m

Piton Savanne 704m

Sir Seewoosagur Ramgoolam Airport

Blue Bay

Baie du Cap
Rivière des Anguilles
Riambel
Souillac

Mauritius
Rodrigues • Réunion

the Bradt Travel Guide

Alexandra Richards

edition
9

www.bradtguides.com

Bradt Travel Guides Ltd, UK
The Globe Pequot Press Inc, USA

CALGARY PUBLIC LIBRARY

NOV   2016